P9-DMX-651

AMERICAN WOMEN'S HISTORY

A Student Companion

WOMAN FOREVER
LIBERTY
EQUALITY
MARCH
"RESPECTFULLY INSCRIBED TO
WOMANHOOD OF THE UNIVERSE
WOMAN FOREVER
JUSTICE
LIBERTY
LIBERTY
VICTORY
EQUALITY
EQUALITY
JUSTICE
JUSTICE
VICTORY
BY E.T. PAULL
PUBLISHED BY E.T. PAULL MUSIC Co 243 WEST 42nd ST.
NEW YORK
PRICE
50¢
PHILADELPHIA, PA.
JOS. MORRIS CO.
SPRINGFIELD. MASS.
A. H. GOETTING.
BERLIN, GERMANY,
C. M. ROEHR.
NEW YORK
CROWN MUSIC CO.
NEW YORK
ENTERPRISE MUSIC CO.
LONDON, ENG.
B. FELDMAN.
CHICAGO, ILL.
F. J. A. FORSTER CO.
NEW YORK.
PLAZA MUSIC CO.
TORONTO, CANADA.
W. R. DRAPER.
J. A. ALBERT & SON, SYDNEY, AUSTRALIA.
Copyright
MCMXVI.
By E.T. PAULL.
LITH. BY A. HOEN & CO. RICHMOND, VA.
COPYRIGHT FOR ALL COUNTRIES.

Student Companions to American History
WILLIAM H. CHAFE, GENERAL EDITOR

AMERICAN WOMEN'S HISTORY

A Student Companion

Glenna Matthews

Oxford University Press
New York

For my mentor, Carl Degler, pioneering student of women's past
For my granddaughters, Monica and Margaret, representatives of women's future

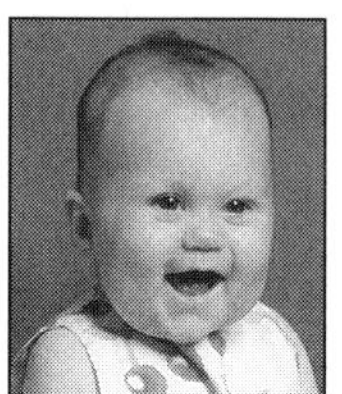

OXFORD
UNIVERSITY PRESS

Oxford New York
Athens Auckland Bangkok Bogotá Buenos Aires Calcutta
Cape Town Chennai Dar es Salaam Delhi Florence Hong Kong Istanbul
Karachi Kuala Lumpur Madrid Melbourne Mexico City Mumbai
Nairobi Paris São Paulo Singapore Taipei Tokyo Toronto Warsaw
and associated companies in
Berlin Ibadan

Published by Oxford University Press, Inc.
198 Madison Avenue, New York, New York 10016
www.oup.com

Matthews, Glenna.
American women's history: a student companion / Glenna Matthews.
p. cm. -- (Oxford student companions to American history)
Includes biographical references and index.
Summary: Alphabetical articles on major events, documents, persons, social
movements, and political and social concepts connected with the history of women in America.
ISBN 0-19-511317-9
1. Women--United States--History--Encyclopedias, Juvenile.
[1. Women--History--Encyclopedias.] I. Title. II. Series.
HQ1410.M378 2000
305.4'0973'03--dc21 99-087245

9 8 7 6 5 4 3 2 1

Printed in the United States of America
on acid-free paper

On the cover: (top left) spinning wheel; (top right) Elizabeth Cady Stanton with her daughter Harriot; (bottom) panel from *California Agriculture* mural by Maxine Albro, 1934, in Coit Tower, San Francisco

Frontispiece: Sheet music from 1916 of a march commemorating women's struggle for justice and equality

CONTENTS

PREFACE

When I was growing up, the field of women's history didn't exist. If you read the typical history textbook, you learned about Betsy Ross and the American flag—but precious little else about the female half of the population. I didn't rebel against this state of affairs, because I didn't know any better.

And yet, looking back, I did rebel in my own way. My rebellion consisted in reading biographies of great women, thus providing myself with information I couldn't get in the classroom. At first I read books for young people, and then I graduated to adult biographies in my hometown library. Before I'd finished high school, I'd exhausted the stacks of the Laguna Beach Public Library and had learned about an impressive range of European-American women, including Elizabeth Blackwell, the first woman doctor in the United States; Joan the Mad Queen of Spain; Elizabeth I of England; and Eleanor of Aquitaine. It was Elizabeth I who specially captured my imagination. In fact, my best friend—a partisan of Mary, Queen of Scots—and I used to have long arguments at slumber parties about whether Elizabeth was justified in executing Mary, her cousin.

I didn't understand then that I was preparing myself for a career as a women's historian, but in retrospect it would have been difficult for a young girl to equip herself any better in the 1950s. I fell in love with the study of the past. I also learned a lot about female power and female courage. I'm proud to have studied with Carl Degler, who published his first article on women's history just about the time I was graduating from high school. He has been, quite literally, one of the creators of the field.

Things are better now, and this book is a demonstration of that proposition: young women and men of today can benefit from a whole new world of research about women's history. Before, you could learn about queens and a tiny handful of other women. Now, students can learn about women from a vast array of backgrounds. And if they fall in love with the subject, they know they can devote the rest of their lives to studying it, something that never would have occurred to me when I was growing up.

In preparing the list of entries for this volume, I began by combing my own brain, and then I went to the indexes of books I respect. After completing that process, I submitted my preliminary list to a number of experts such as the young people's librarian at the Berkeley Public Library. It was she, for example, who suggested the entry on coming of age rituals, based on her observations of what young people actually look up when they go to the library.

Because the choice of entries was so challenging, I decided to lean toward "firsts"—the first woman to achieve an important goal, the first organization to take a particular stand, and so on. I worked very hard to make the book as balanced as possible in terms of region as well as race and religion. Friends and acquaintances lobbied for me to include their favorites, a process from which I learned a great deal.

I'm delighted to have two granddaughters who are growing up at a time when they can learn about someone besides Betsy Ross. May they build glowing futures on a foundation of knowledge about the female past.

HOW TO USE THIS BOOK

The articles in this *Companion* are arranged alphabetically, so you can look up words, concepts, or names as you come across them in other readings. You can then use the SEE ALSO listings at the end of an article to find entries about related subjects. Sometimes you may find that the *Companion* deals with information under a different article name than what you looked up. The book will then refer you to the proper article. For example, if you look up Journalism, you will find the notation "SEE Media." If you cannot find an article on a particular subject, look in the index to guide you to the relevant articles. All people are listed alphabetically by last name; for example, the entry for Eleanor Roosevelt is listed under R as Roosevelt, Eleanor. In the case of individuals who are known by more than one name, the entry will be found under their legal name rather than the one they assumed later in life. So if you look up Nellie Bly, you will find the notation "SEE Seaman, Elizabeth Cochrane."

You can also use this *Companion* topically, by reading all the articles about a particular aspect of women's history. Below are several groupings of topics around common themes.

Notable individuals: Many more women appear in the book as significant actors than merely those to whom an individual entry is devoted. For example, I decided not to write a whole entry on the California architect Julia Morgan, but rather to discuss her career at length in the essay on architecture. What this means is that the reader should consult the index for proper names—as well as the list of entries—in order to learn about a particular woman.

Information about historically important books can be found under the author's name; for example, you would look under Stowe, Harriet Beecher, to read about *Uncle Tom's Cabin.*

Concepts: An important concept, such as privacy, will be the subject of its own entry but will also show up in other entries. For example, privacy is also discussed in the entry on the legal decision *Griswold* v. *Connecticut.* I have used the SEE ALSO suggestions to provide cross-referencing in these instances.

Historic events: Important events, such as the American Revolution and western movement, are discussed both for their general relevance to American history and for the particular role that women have played in them. Information on events that do not have a separate entry, such as the Vietnam War, can be found in other entries, such as Peace movements; use the index to find these terms.

Groups and organizations: Many articles are devoted to groups in which women have organized to work for social or political change. Some are specifically devoted to women's causes, such as the National Women's Party, and others, such as the United Farm Workers, have united men and women for a common goal. There are also articles on cultural and ethnic groups to which women belong, such as Protestants and Asian Americans.

Professions: A brief history is provided for each of the major professions traditionally occupied by women, such as teaching and nursing. In an article about a field traditionally restricted to men, such as technology, you will find information about pioneering women, such as engineer Emily Roebling, who made important contributions, and information about recent developments in employment patterns.

Further reading: To help you find out more about a specific topic or subject, important recent books are listed at the conclusion of most entries. More general sources and broad overviews appear in the FURTHER READING guide at the end of the book.

Museums and historic sites: A partial list of museums and historic sites is included at the end of the book in Appendix 2. Some of them, such as the Tenement Museum in New York, are not limited to women's history, but all bear importantly on women's experience. Some museums and sites may not provide a great deal of information, but they often give impressions or provide a sense of time and place that cannot be found elsewhere.

Websites: There are a growing number of internet sites devoted to aspects of women's history. The FURTHER READING section in the back of this book provides links to internet addresses and resources. Web pages for the museums and historic sites listed in Appendix 2 have been included when available.

Abolitionism

When the antislavery movement, also known as abolitionism, first began to gather steam in the 1830s, it was considered scandalous for women to speak in public—and there was no organized women's movement. By the time the Civil War broke out in 1861, however, abolitionist women were routinely giving public lectures, and many of them were pioneering women's rights activism, too. In fact, in defending their right to speak out against slavery, these women also challenged the unfair traditions that assigned women to domestic, rather than public, roles.

As early as the 1790s, black and white women had begun to organize into volunteer groups for social betterment through their churches. At first these groups were not political. When the time came for action against slavery, however, many women around the country already had the habit of getting together with other women. Thus they could more easily organize to take a stand.

During the years when the abolitionist movement was growing in strength, women—who could not then vote or run for office—made many contributions. They circulated antislavery petitions and gave lectures, for example. Even someone who was too shy to give a talk could make a quilt to raise money for the cause. Other women took risks to help escaped slaves find their way to freedom by offering them food and shelter. Women also authored some of the most powerful writing about slavery, including the 1852 novel *Uncle Tom's Cabin* by Harriet Beecher Stowe.

The high-profile role played by women was controversial not only in society at large but also within the movement itself. Antislavery reformers, who tended to be the most progressive people in the country, were deeply divided about whether it was right for women to give talks. This is an indication of how much courage it took for women to participate. On one occasion a mob in Philadelphia even burned down a lecture hall shortly after a woman had given an antislavery talk there.

In working to free the slaves, both black and white women such as Sojourner Truth, Lucy Stone, and Lucretia Mott were also working to free themselves, as the abolitionist movement became linked with women's rights efforts. The southern-born sisters Angelina and Sarah Grimké, for example, began speaking out for women's rights after their antislavery activism met with stern opposition from organizations such as the General Association of Congregational Ministers of Massachusetts.

SEE ALSO

Grimké, Angelina and Sarah; Mott, Lucretia Coffin; Stone, Lucy; Stowe, Harriet Beecher; Truth, Sojourner

FURTHER READING

Goldberg, Michael. *Breaking New Ground: American Women 1800–1848.* New York: Oxford University Press, 1994.

Matthews, Glenna. "'Little Women' Who Helped Make This Big War." In *Why the Civil War Came,* edited by Gabor Boritt. New York: Oxford University Press, 1996.

Yee, Shirley. *Black Women Abolitionists.* Knoxville: University of Tennessee Press, 1992.

Abortion

Throughout American history millions of girls and women have chosen to terminate their pregnancies. Abortion,

Anti-abortion demonstrators use engaging images and other emotional appeals—as well as child demonstrators—in support of their cause.

whether by surgical means or by various home preparations, is as old as history. Over the generations, though, there have been enormous variations in a woman's access to an abortion. Was it or was it not legal—and at what stage of the pregnancy? Was it or was it not affordable? Was it morally acceptable?

Until the mid-19th century most states did not have laws regulating abortion. Scholars believe that the first state laws aimed at criminalizing abortion were the result of the medical profession's attempt to consolidate its hold on obstetrics, the medical management of pregnancy and childbirth. The American Medical Association, the professional association of physicians, was founded in 1847; in order to enhance their own control over medical procedures, its leaders led a campaign that resulted in antiabortion statutes in every

New York women march for abortion rights in 1972. This is a cause that has mobilized activists as few others have—though it stirs passions among opponents as well.

state in the country by the end of the 19th century. Not only was abortion illegal but so was the distribution of devices for or information about the prevention of pregnancy.

In the early 20th century, women began to campaign for birth control—but not yet for abortion. Nonetheless millions of illegal abortions were performed by midwives, doctors, and lay practitioners—some of whom were not very skilled. Scholars have calculated that, between the time the procedure was outlawed and the *Roe v. Wade* Supreme Court decision that legalized abortion in 1973, thousands of women died as the result of poorly performed illegal abortions.

Attitudes toward abortion began to change in the 1960s. The possibilities for women expanded in many areas in those years: they had better access to education, to athletic participation, and to job opportunities. Women wanted not merely to limit the size of their families, as they could with existing birth-control methods, but to control their fertility completely by avoiding any unwanted pregnancies so as to take advantage of the new opportunities.

At first, as the demand for abortions increased, certain states eased access to abortion, because liberal doctors began to redefine and broaden the medical justifications for terminating a pregnancy. Then in 1973 the U.S. Supreme Court, ruling in the case of *Roe* v. *Wade,* legalized abortion across the country, although the opinion limited it to first trimester, and let states impose laws against later abortions. Those who found abortion to be morally objectionable were outraged.

Today the issue of abortion remains hotly contested, with the very definition of abortion under dispute owing to the introduction of drugs that can induce the body to shed an embryo "the morning after" sexual intercourse. For certain religious groups, such as Catholics, abortion has always been seen as immoral, because in their eyes it involves the taking of life. Feminists and organizations such as Planned Parenthood are just as avid in their support of a woman's right to choose abortion. These issues and feelings are further complicated concerning pregnancies resulting from rape.

The U.S. Supreme Court seems committed to keeping the procedure legal—though circumscribed in some ways, based on how far along a woman is in her pregnancy. Even so, poor women often have difficulty in obtaining an abortion because of the Hyde Amendment, which denies Medicaid funding for it. This measure, introduced in 1976 by Republican Representative Henry Hyde, has played an important part in the split between Republicans and Democrats over abortion policy. Many scholars believe that the Democrats' much more favorable position on reproductive rights has played a large role in the growing strength of Democratic affiliation among women.

SEE ALSO

Birth control; *Roe* v. *Wade* (1973)

FURTHER READING

Mohr, James. *Abortion in America.* New York: Oxford University Press, 1978.

Reibstein, Larry. "Arguing at Fever Pitch." *Newsweek,* Jan. 26, 1998.

Reagan, Leslie J. *When Abortion Was a Crime: Women, Medicine, and Law in the United States, 1867–1973.* Berkeley: University of California Press, 1997.

Abzug, Bella Savitsky

- *Born: July 24, 1920, New York, N.Y.*
- *Education: Hunter College, B.A., 1942; Columbia University, LL.B., 1947*
- *Accomplishments: Founder (1961) and chair (1961–70), Women Strike for*

Peace; U.S. Representative (Democrat–N.Y.) (1971–77); cofounder, National Women's Political Caucus (1971); inducted into the National Women's Hall of Fame (1994)
- *Died: Mar. 31, 1998, New York, N.Y.*

Elected to the U.S. House of Representatives in 1971, Bella Abzug became one of the best-known feminist spokeswomen of her day. Courageous, assertive, and sometimes even combative, she always let people know her opinions about the issues that mattered to her.

She was born Bella Savitsky to Russian-Jewish immigrant parents. In 1944 she wed stockbroker and novelist Martin Abzug, and they later had two daughters. In 1947 the talented young woman graduated from Columbia Law School and immediately threw herself into civil rights and civil liberties work. During the 1950s, at a time when unfair charges about people's so-called radical past were being made in a very irresponsible way, she defended those accused of being communists. This was a time when Republican Senator Joseph McCarthy had been flinging charges about communists in the government and in the entertainment world, and had helped create a climate of fear about being so identified.

Bella Abzug's campaign poster from the 1970s puts a feminist spin on the traditional idea of separate spheres for men and women, in which women belong in the home and only men can act in the public sphere.

Arriving in Congress at the height of the Vietnam War, Abzug outspokenly denounced U.S. involvement there. In addition to the energy she put into legislation on behalf of all women, such as their having equal access to financial credit, she also introduced the first lesbian/gay civil rights bill in 1975.

After she became nationally known, she was never seen in public without a hat. She explained that, early in her legal career, she had adopted the habit of wearing a hat so that she would not look like a secretary: in those days, the women lawyers were few and far between.

SEE ALSO

Congress, U.S.; Politics

FURTHER READING

Abzug, Bella. *Bella! Ms. Abzug Goes to Washington.* Edited by Mel Ziegler. New York: Saturday Review Press, 1972.

Abzug, Bella, and Mim Kelber. *Gender Gap: Bella Abzug's Guide to Political Power for American Women.* Boston: Houghton Mifflin, 1984.

Mansnerus, Laura. "Bella Abzug, 77, Congresswoman and a Founding Feminist, Is Dead." *New York Times,* April 1, 1998.

Adams, Abigail Smith

- *Born: Nov. 11, 1744, Weymouth, Mass.*
- *Education: No formal education*
- *Accomplishments: Prolific correspondence (letters published in 1840, 1876, 1947, 1963) provides a vivid record of her era; First Lady, 1797–1801*
- *Died: Oct. 28, 1818, Quincy, Mass.*

The wife of the second President of the United States (John Adams) and the mother of the sixth (John Quincy Adams), Abigail Adams was a remarkable figure in her own right. In the first place, her lively personality attracted friends who included many of the most accomplished men and women of her day. Moreover, she was extraordinarily outspoken in her opinions. Above all, she was one of the great letter writers of 18th-century America.

Adams's marriage was unusual in that her husband, deeply involved in the events leading up to the outbreak of the American Revolution in 1776, traveled incessantly for many years on behalf of the revolutionary cause (thus providing all the more opportunities for correspondence). Required to rear their children with little help from him, Adams was sustained by their shared belief in the future of the American experiment.

Today she is especially well known for a letter she wrote to her husband when he was attending the Continental Congress in 1776. Urging him to "Remember the Ladies," in drawing up plans for a new government, she said that he and his fellow Patriots—as those who supported the American Revolution were called—should take action to restrain the tyranny of husbands as well as that of King George III and his ministers. In those days husbands had all the financial control in families, and Abigail Adams thought this was unfair. As she explained to her husband on June 17, 1782,

> Patriotism in the female sex is the most disinterested of all virtues. Excluded from honours and from offices, we cannot attach ourselves to the State or Government from having held a place of eminence. Even in the freest country our property is subject to the controls and disposal of our partners, to whom the Laws have given a sovereign authority. Deprived of a voice in Legislation, obliged to submit to those Laws which are imposed upon us, is it not sufficient to make us indifferent to the publick Welfare? Yet all History and every age exhibit Instances of patriotical virtue in the female sex, which considering our situation equals the most Heroick of yours.

FURTHER READING

Adams, Abigail Smith. *The Book of Abigail and John: Selected Letters of the Adams Family.* Edited by L. H. Butterfield, Marc Friedlander, and Mary-Jo Kline. Cambridge: Harvard University Press, 1975.

Bober, Natalie S. *Abigail Adams: Witness to a Revolution.* New York: Simon & Schuster, 1995.

Gelles, Edith. *Portia: The World of Abigail Adams.* Bloomington: Indiana University Press, 1992.

Withey, Lynn. *Dearest Friend: A Life of Abigail Adams.* New York: Free Press, 1981.

Addams, Jane

- *Born: Sept. 6, 1860, Cedarville, Ill.*
- *Education: Rockford College, B.A., 1882*
- *Accomplishments: Founder, Hull House settlement (1889); first woman president of the National Conference of Social Work (1910); chairman, International Congress of Women, the Hague (1915); Nobel Peace Prize for her work on behalf of international peace (1931)*
- *Died: May 21, 1935, Chicago, Ill.*

Jane Addams of Chicago was a pioneer in working on behalf of poor immigrants. The daughter of businessman John Addams and his wife Sarah (Weber) Addams, Jane was only two years old when her mother died. Despite this tragedy, Jane went on to obtain a college education at Rockford Female Seminary in Illinois, a rare achievement for a woman then. After receiving her degree in 1882, she faced a difficult decision about what to do with her life.

The choices available to an educated woman at that time were quite limited: many of the professions we now think of as "female," such as nursing and librarianship, were in the infancy of their development. Moreover, Addams suffered from health problems. A trip to

The founder of Hull House as a young woman. Jane Addams was an intellectual as well as an activist, bringing to the settlement house some of the leading thinkers of her day.

Europe in 1883, however, gave her an interest in the plight of the urban poor, whose housing and living conditions she saw were often filthy and unsafe. The terrible situation of many city dwellers, there and closer to home, in Chicago, combined with her personal need for something meaningful to do, led Addams to found the first American settlement house, Hull House. There, middle-class people could put their skills to use directly to help poor people.

In 1889 Addams and her close friend Ellen Starr moved into a decaying mansion in an immigrant neighborhood in Chicago. With financial support from other well-to-do women, they began to offer classes on such subjects as hygiene and child care to their neighbors. Before long, Hull House attracted brilliant men and women concerned about social problems who went to live there for periods ranging from short stays to many years. Over time, Hull House and its roster of distinguished residents, such as Florence Kelley and Frances Perkins, provided leadership for dealing with many urban problems—such as poor sanitation—caused by industrialization and by the mass immigration into the United States during the late 19th and early 20th centuries.

Programs at Hull House and its sister settlement houses in other parts of the country provided the energy for conducting studies in what we now call urban sociology—the study of people and institutions in a city—in addition to spurring political activism and providing practical training. Jane Addams, having witnessed the slaughter during World War I, 1914–18, was an important leader of an international women's peace movement. For this, she won the Nobel Peace Prize in 1931.

Interestingly, Addams believed in approaching the needy with the attitude that each side had something to learn from the other, as when the poor shared the customs and culture of their homelands with their benefactors. Nonetheless, historians still debate the extent to which the reformers could truly relate to poor people as fellow human beings as well as the ultimate usefulness of the settlement houses. In other words, to what extent were the settlement house workers just good-natured busybodies?

SEE ALSO

Settlement-house movement

FURTHER READING

Addams, Jane. *Twenty Years at Hull-House: with Autobiographical Notes.* New York: Penguin, 1998.

Carson, Mina. *Settlement Folk: Social Thought and the American Settlement Movement.* Chicago: University of Chicago Press, 1990.

Crocker, Ruth. *Social Work and Social Order.* Urbana: University of Illinois Press, 1992.

Diliberto, Gioia. *A Useful Woman: The Early Life of Jane Addams.* New York: Scribner, 1999.

Kittredge, Mary. *Jane Addams.* New York: Chelsea House, 1988.

Wise, Winifred Esther. *Jane Addams of Hull-House.* New York: Harcourt, 1963.

Adolescence

People who live long enough to grow to maturity will pass through the developmental stage called adolescence, a transitional phase between childhood and adulthood. Many cultures herald the arrival of puberty, or sexual maturity, with coming-of-age rituals, a sign that adolescence is worthy of recognition. The 20th century, however, has seen vast changes in the way young people handle adolescence.

The changes have happened for many reasons. In the first place, the development of a widespread consumer culture after World War II has placed more goods in the hands of young people than ever before in human history. Earlier generations did not have access to cars, musical equipment, records and CDs, televisions, and computers of their own—and they probably did not have rooms of their own either, because families were much larger then.

With the availability of such goods, and with more mothers employed outside the home than ever before, late-20th-century American young people, especially young women who earlier would have been chaperoned, have a level of independence and access to sophisticated information that would have been unimaginable to the generations before the 1960s. They are also living in the midst of a revolution in sexual attitudes, accompanied by a similar one in access to the means of preventing pregnancy, that has been transforming the culture since the 1960s. Finally, late-20th-century young women have access to a range of choices about what to do with their lives, given almost unlimited career possibilities for women that were unavailable to earlier generations.

Sociologists are still trying to figure out what all of this change means for the stability of the American home. How much is positive in that it increases human freedom? How much is negative because young people are at risk to drop out of school, become pregnant out of wedlock, or abuse drugs or fall short of their potential in new ways? These questions are still being asked. What we do know is that teen peer culture is now extremely powerful and that a whole industry has grown up to cater to teen tastes in movies, music, video games, and clothing.

SEE ALSO

Coming-of-age rituals; Consumer culture

FURTHER READING

Brumberg, Joan Jacobs. *The Body Project: An Intimate History of American Girls.* New York: Random House, 1997.

Peiss, Kathy Lee. *Hope in a Jar: The Making of America's Beauty Culture.* New York: Metropolitan Books, 1998.

Affirmative action

Affirmative action means that employers and admissions offices take the extra step to choose a person who belongs to a group that has been discriminated against in a case where several possible candidates are roughly equal. In 1964 Congress passed the Civil Rights Act, a law that opened up a whole new world of legal remedies for women and people of color. But there was concern that the law did not go far enough in remedying the effects of past discrimination. As a result, in September 1965 President Lyndon B. Johnson issued Executive Order 11246 calling on employers with federal contracts to take additional, active steps in order to integrate their workforces in terms of color—"affirmative action," in other words.

Pressure from the Women's Bureau, a branch of the Department of Labor created to "promote the welfare of wage earning women," and from women's groups convinced Johnson to add gender to the executive order in 1967. After the passage in 1972 of Title IX of the Education Act amendments governing higher education, the Department of Health, Education, and Welfare began to look for evidence of affirmative action on behalf of women in admissions and hiring practices when it evaluated whether colleges and universities were complying with Title IX's affirmative action requirements. Soon states were drawing up their own affirmative action programs.

Sometimes there has been confusion over what affirmative action is. It is not a quota system or a rigid requirement that people of color or women *must* be hired. Rather, it is a program to encourage recruitment of those from historically excluded groups. Also, if two candidates are roughly equal, taking affirmative action means hiring the person from the previously discriminated-against group. It does *not* mean hiring or admitting an unqualified person.

Nonetheless, affirmative action has proved to be quite controversial. For example, the very means of determining when people competing for precious jobs or admissions slots are roughly equal is far from clear-cut. White men have often feared that they are losing out to less-qualified women and people of color. Using affirmative action guidelines in college admissions has stirred much resentment among those who fail to get into a desirable institution and are therefore convinced that less-qualified applicants have stolen "their" places.

The future of affirmative action is unclear. In 1996, for example, California voters passed Proposition 209, a broadly written initiative aimed at repealing the practice across the board in public entities. What *is* clear is that during the years when the program has been in place, affirmative action has created new opportunities for women as in the transformation of law school and medical school admissions such that women are around 50 percent of those admitted.

SEE ALSO

Civil Rights Act (1964); Education Act Amendments (1972)

AFL-CIO

The American Federation of Labor (AFL) was founded in 1886 and soon became the mainstream labor union organization. In the mid-1930s its dominance was challenged by a new group, the Congress of Industrial Organizations (CIO). For years the two groups contended for members, and then in the mid-1950s they merged to form the AFL-CIO.

The AFL took as its guiding principle that a union should be composed of workers in a skilled craft. With this philosophy it was disproportionately composed of white men, because they were the ones who had access to craft employment.

The philosophy of the CIO was to organize all the workers in a particular industry, irrespective of skill level. With this approach, the group brought far

Women on a picket line around 1949, backed by the CIO. It is noteworthy that these black women were staunch union members, because the labor movement had resisted organizing both women and African Americans.

more women into organized labor than had the AFL.

The AFL, for example, would have gone into a factory and tried to organize only the engineers and machinists—all men. The CIO would have gone into the plant and tried to organize the men and women on the assembly line, too.

Though the CIO brought hundreds of thousands more women workers into its ranks than had the AFL, neither group had women in top leadership positions for many years. In fact, not until two decades after the merger, in the 1970s, did a woman sit on the executive board of the AFL-CIO.

SEE ALSO
Labor movement

African Americans

The history of African-American women begins in the 1600s with the terrible pain of being wrenched from their homeland, sold into slavery, and transported in chains across the Atlantic. Once on American shores, the newly arriving Africans were thrust into unfamiliar work, treated like property, and forbidden from forming legally binding marriages. Over the decades a small number managed to achieve freedom, but even as freed people they faced poorly paid work and few opportunities compared to what was available to the white population.

Despite this history of struggle and pain, African-American women have repeatedly been leaders and innovators, defying the odds against their achievements. The first American-born woman to give a public political speech, for example, was the African American Maria Stewart, who spoke about the rights of free African Americans in Boston in 1832. The first woman to be admitted to practice law before the bar of Washington, D.C., was the African American Charlotte Ray in 1872. Free African-American women began organizing clubs as early as the 1790s, and a black woman, Phillis Wheatley, began publishing poetry even earlier. Harriet Tubman, an escaped slave, was the best-known "conductor" on the Underground Railroad, leading other escaping slaves to freedom in the late 1800s.

Such accomplished women, as well as those who remained slaves and fought for smaller triumphs on a daily basis, were able to achieve what they did, in part, because the family traditions that Africans brought with them to this country proved valuable in helping people cope. Less reliant than the Europeans on the marriage bond and more on the extended family of aunts, uncles, and other kin, Africans could draw strength from these ties, even if a marriage were disrupted by the sale of a spouse. In addition, the African spiritual heritage, combined with the profound Christian beliefs often adopted in America, gave downtrodden people a power of resistance that they might not have otherwise had. Moreover, the Protestant emphasis on literacy, enabling a person to read the Bible, gave free blacks an incentive to learn.

Usually denied access to public education in the early 1800s, African-American women would often find ways to learn anyway. As a result of their achieving an education and thus the ability to participate in society, many leading abolitionists in the period leading up to the Civil War of 1861–65 were African-American women.

After the Union victory in the war, and the resulting abolition of slavery,

These young workers in the Urban League office enjoyed a type of employment that was not available to African-American women on a widespread basis until after World War II.

the 14th and 15th Amendments belatedly granted African-American men voting citizenship (with a watered-down version for women that didn't include the vote) in 1868 and 1870 respectively. Most blacks still had less access to education than did the white population, however, and discrimination confined them to the least desirable jobs. Because so many men were poorly paid, many African-American women were forced to take jobs to help support their families, most often as maids. Not until World War II (1941–45) and then later in the 1960s, after the victories of the civil rights movement, could African-American women aspire to the same range of employment as white women.

Over the years since emancipation, many black women have been active on behalf of woman suffrage and women's rights. Journalist and anti-lynching crusader Ida B. Wells-Barnett founded a suffrage club for black women in Chicago, for example. Women played major roles in the civil rights movement, with Rosa Parks, who refused to surrender her seat on a bus in Montgomery, Alabama in 1955, acting as a significant catalyst. But there have been tensions between white and black activists, often the result of racism among white women, going back to the time of suffrage leaders Elizabeth Cady Stanton and Susan B. Anthony (who referred to black men as "Sambo" when arguing that if black men could vote, so should women) right after the Civil War in the late 1860s.

The history of African-American women in the 1990s shows increasing professional achievement by many as certain discriminatory barriers are eliminated by civil rights laws and increased access to education: indeed, women such as television talk show host Oprah Winfrey and writers Maya Angelou and Toni Morrison are central to American culture. It also, however, reveals that many thousands of women are trapped in poverty because they live in inner cities where there are few opportunities for education and advancement. African-American men have suffered from a high unemployment rate, and this has placed a terrible strain on families, and a burden on women.

In the late 1990s, there were a number of black women in Congress and in other positions of authority, but neither they nor anyone else has been able to figure out what to do about the plight of the impoverished in the face of an evident lack of political will in the country to spend the money on jobs programs, on better housing, or on higher-quality education for all students.

SEE ALSO

Citizenship; Civil rights movement; 14th Amendment; Ray, Charlotte E.; Slavery; Stewart, Maria W. Miller; Terrell, Mary Eliza Chruch; Wells-Barnett, Ida B.; Wheatley, Phillis

FURTHER READING

Hine, Darlene Clark, and Kathleen Thompson. *A Shining Thread of Hope.* New York: Broadway Books, 1998.

Hine, Darlene Clark, Elsa Barkley Brown, and Rosalyn Terborg, eds. *Black Women in America.* New York: Carlson, 1993.

Kelley, Robin D. G., and Earl Lewis, eds. *The Young Oxford History of African Americans.* 11 vols. New York: Oxford University Press, 1997.

Agriculture

On the farm, women generally have had one of two roles: As farm wives, they have worked hard but also enjoyed some benefits from their labor. As farm workers, they have toiled as slaves or as paid workers who often have been unfairly treated by employers. A small number of unmarried women have run their own farms, but with great difficulty. For that matter, unmarried men have historically had a hard time making a go of it on a farm, too.

Farm wives constitute a particularly good example of the way in which women's unpaid work is both essential and yet relatively invisible, both to the men in their lives and to economists computing a statistic such as the sum of American productivity. By taking care of the many tasks necessary to keep the farmstead operating, farm wives make it possible for their husbands to spend more time working the farm, and thus contribute indirectly to overall farm productivity. On occasion farm wives have worked in the fields side by side with their men. Often they have raised garden crops for the family table or tended chickens and dairy cows for "butter and egg" money, yet most discussion of "farmers" ignore the activities of women.

Farm women often state in interviews that they find themselves doing several things simultaneously. Scholars are documenting the extent to which women have contributed to farm incomes by their willingness to pitch in wherever they are most needed.

Invariably women's housework—such as sewing for themselves and the children, cooking for a crew of men during harvest season, or canning and freezing the garden crops—has preserved the family's precious cash resources for other purposes. Evidence shows that a woman's power in the family is based on her economic contribution. Because farm wives' contributions are often not directly monetary, these wives have rarely influenced family decisions in a way that reflects their true importance.

Women who have worked in the fields have had lives filled with even greater difficulty. During the time of slavery, for example, a woman field worker might well have had to keep going throughout most or all of a pregnancy. In many parts of the country in the 1990s, poorly paid migrant workers harvested crops under grueling conditions; they might, for example, stoop to pick strawberries for hours at a time in the hot sun.

Women in both categories, farm wives and farm workers, have organized to improve their lives. Starting in the late 19th century, women have been very active in the Grange, a farmer advocacy group that they could join on the same basis as men and that has promoted causes such as farm and rural cooperatives, preservation of farmland, and the elimination of government farm programs. In the 1890s they were also active in the farm-based political movement known as Populism that advocated radical changes in the economy to benefit farmers. In the 20th century, women have provided a bedrock of support for the most successful trade union for farm workers, the United Farm Workers, founded in California in the 1960s.

SEE ALSO

Populism; United Farm Workers (UFW)

FURTHER READING

Jellison, Katherine. *Entitled to Power: Farm Women and Technology, 1913–1963.* Chapel Hill: University of North Carolina Press, 1993.

Jensen, Joan. *With These Hands: Women Working on the Land.* New Haven: Yale University Press, 1986.

Sigerman, Harriet. *Land of Many Hands: Women in the American West.* New York: Oxford University Press, 1997.

Albright, Madeleine Korbel

- *Born: May 15, 1937, Prague, Czechoslovakia*
- *Education: Wellesley College, B.A., 1959; Columbia University, M.A., 1968, Ph.D., 1976*
- *Accomplishments: Professor of international affairs, Georgetown University, 1982–93; president, Center for National Policy, 1989–93; U.S. ambassador to the United Nations, 1993–96; U.S. secretary of state, 1996–*

The first woman to be appointed as secretary of state, Madeleine Albright has had a career in which she has defied the odds against women as high-level diplomats to reach her current position.

Albright was born in eastern Europe shortly before the Nazis began to invade

Before being appointed secretary of state, Madeleine Albright gained public attention as U.S. ambassador to the United Nations and Security Council president. Here she briefs reporters on the work of the Council at a 1993 U.N. press conference.

parts of that region. Her parents saw what was coming and managed to flee to London just before the outbreak of World War II (1941–45). They returned to Prague after the war, but left again, this time for the United States, when they realized that the communists would soon be in control there. They raised their daughter to be a Roman Catholic, and she did not learn until 1997 that the family was, in fact, Jewish and that three of her four grandparents were killed in the Nazi Holocaust.

After arriving in the United States at the age of 11, young Madeleine Korbel attended private school in Denver and then went off to Wellesley College in Massachusetts, from which she graduated with a degree in political science in 1959. Soon thereafter, she married the media heir Joseph Medill Patterson Albright, and the couple had three children. Albright did what was then unusual for a wife and mother and continued her education, obtaining a master's degree and a doctorate in international relations from Columbia University. While at Columbia, she studied with Zbigniew Brzezinski, who would become President Jimmy Carter's national security adviser in the 1970s.

Doctorate in hand, she went to work for Maine Democratic senator Edmund Muskie and then for her mentor Brzezinski during the Carter administration. After Carter's defeat in 1980, Albright taught at Georgetown University in Washington, D.C. Her marriage had ended, and she set herself up as the hostess of a Georgetown salon devoted to discussing foreign relations; Bill Clinton, among others, took notice.

When Clinton became President in 1993, he appointed Albright to be his ambassador to the United Nations. There her toughness won her the esteem of a broad range of those in the foreign policy establishment. When Clinton nominated her as secretary of state, the vote in the Senate was 99 to 0 in her favor. She was sworn in on December 6, 1996. This was an immensely significant development for all American women, proving that women can wield power at the top government level; only the President himself has more authority over the conduct of foreign policy.

FURTHER READING

Blackman, Ann. *Seasons of Her Life.* New York: Scribner, 1998.

Freedman, Susan. *Madeleine Albright: She Speaks for America.* New York: Watts, 1998.

Gibbs, Nancy. "The Many Lives of Madeleine." *Time,* January 17, 1997.

Alcott, Louisa May

- *Born: Nov. 29, 1832, Germantown, Pa.*
- *Education: Tutored at home by father until age of 16; later studied under Henry David Thoreau, Ralph Waldo Emerson, and Theodore Parker*
- *Accomplishments: Editor,* Merry's Museum *(children's magazine, 1867–68); first woman to register to vote in Concord, Massachusetts, 1879; author,* Flower Fables *(1855);* Hospital Sketches *(1863);* Little Women *(1868–69);* An Old-Fashioned Girl *(1870);* Aunt Jo's Scrap Bag *(1872–82);* Little Men *(1871);* Eight Cousins *(1875);* Rose in Bloom *(1876);* A Modern Mephistopheles *(1877);* Work: A Story of Experience *(1873);* Jo's Boys *(1886);* Behind a Mask *(1975);* Plots and Counterplots *(1976)*
- *Died: Mar. 6, 1888, Boston, Mass.*

Louisa May Alcott was the author of *Little Women,* written for an audience of younger readers and one of the best-loved books of all time. She was the second of four daughters born to the brilliant but improvident educator Bronson Alcott, who thought more about philosophy than about supporting his family, and his more practical

The March family as illustrated in an 1893 edition of Alcott's Little Women. *The book has been a favorite of young girls since it was published in the late 1860s, and has been adapted for the screen several times.*

wife, Abby May, who contrived ways to make ends meet under very difficult circumstances. Alcott grew up in a home in Concord, Massachusetts, that was full of high-minded idealism—if short on material comfort. Her parents' circle included the writer Ralph Waldo Emerson and other eminent American intellectuals and reformers of the day.

As the girls grew up, they accepted the need to contribute to the chronically tight household finances. Along the way, Alcott worked as a seamstress, a domestic servant, and a teacher, among other occupations.

In 1861, when Alcott was 28 years old, the Civil War broke out. Her life—along with lives of millions of other Americans—was permanently transformed. She volunteered as a nurse, going to Washington, D.C., to carry out her duties. Although health problems cut short her service, she published a memoir about her nursing experiences, *Hospital Sketches,* thereby launching her true career as a writer. *Little Women* came out in 1868.

Though she wrote many other books, some for an adult audience, none would match the enduring popularity of her masterpiece about the four March sisters, Meg, Jo, Beth, and Amy—a family that was closely based on her own. Generations of young women, from many backgrounds, have loved reading the story of their lives which Alcott continued to tell in three sequels: *Litle Men, Aunt Jo's Scrap Bag,* and *Jo's Boys.* Before the publication of the books about the March family, Alcott had published various, often sensational, short stories pseudonymously in New England periodicals. After the *Little Women* books, her works were mostly literature for young people, sometimes with feminist angles on their characters' lives.

FURTHER READING

Burke, Kathleen. *Louisa May Alcott.* New York: Chelsea House, 1988.

Elbert, Sarah. *A Hunger for Home.* Philadelphia: Temple University Press, 1984.

American Association of University Women

In the late 1800s, as the first sizable generation of American women to have attended college took its place in society, many had the desire to help others and to keep alive the spirit of high aspirations for women. College alumnae, as a result, founded the American Association of University Women in 1882. Today the group has a broad-ranging set of programs to support graduate education for women as well as women's community leadership. For example, in 1992 the group published a widely publicized report on gender bias in the schools, and the harm it does to girls and women.

The AAUW is made up of three groups: the Association itself, which lobbies for education and equity; the AAUW Educational Foundation, which provides funding for research by and on girls and education, community projects, and fellowships for women throughout the world; and the AAUW Legal Advocacy fund, which funds and supports women involved in legal suits protesting sex discrimination in higher education.

During World War I, the American Red Cross put enormous effort into raising money from women to support the men on the battlefields of Europe.

American Red Cross

The American Red Cross is a private, voluntary organization that plays so useful a role during times of war and disaster that people tend to forget that it is not an arm of the government.

During the late 19th century, a group of European men began a reform effort aimed at making war more humane by setting up rules for civilized behavior during conflicts and by establishing a trusted provider of medical relief during hostilities. Their first meeting took place in Geneva, Switzerland, in 1863. Out of this effort came the Geneva Convention, governing the conduct of nations engaged in war, and the establishment of the International Red Cross.

The United States signed the Geneva Convention and joined the Red Cross as the result of the leadership of Clara Barton. Coming out of the Civil War (1861–65) as one of the country's most esteemed women owing to her valiant wartime nursing, Barton learned about the new European initiatives to make war more humane. Knowing only too well about the brutality that war encourages, Barton devoted herself for many years to building support for the Red Cross in the United States.

Barton's efforts were successful in 1882 when the United States ratified the Geneva Convention treaty; the American Red Cross was founded that same year. Appointed as the first U.S. representative to the international group, Barton talked Red Cross leaders into adding disaster relief to the list of their wartime activities.

In the late 20th century, the Red Cross is available to provide relief for any natural disaster that occurs. Another important service is the collection of blood donations. The American Red Cross also assists the government in meeting its obligations under various humanitarian treaties such as the Geneva and Hague conventions. The organization has had more than one distinguished woman leader since Barton, such as Elizabeth Dole, director from 1990 to 1999.

SEE ALSO

Barton, Clara

FURTHER READING

Gilbo, Patrick F. *The American Red Cross: The First Century.* New York: Harper & Row, 1981.

Pryor, Elizabeth Brown. *Clara Barton: Professional Angel.* Philadelphia: University of Pennsylvania Press, 1987.

American Revolution

One of the most exciting "finds" made by historians has been the substantial role women played in the American Revolution. Though only a few women actually fought in the war—Deborah Sampson, who in 1782 disguised herself as "Robert Shurtliff," joined Washington's army, and later tended to her own wounds in order to keep her identity hidden, was the best known—women showed their patriotism in many other ways.

After the end of the French and Indian War in 1763, the British decided that the American colonists had to start paying for their own defense, and Parliament began trying out a number of new taxes, each of which proved extremely unpopular with much of the American population. Until the fighting between the Americans and British actually broke out, the most successful means of protesting taxes proved to be the consumer boycott. If the British taxed tea, for example, then American Patriots switched to coffee or chocolate. If Americans did not buy tea, they would not have to pay the tax.

A boycott cannot be successful, however, unless women cooperate. If a man wants his household to quit buying British-made cloth, his wife will be responsible for supplying the homespun substitutes—and she has to have some idea of why she is taking this step. For this reason, historians now believe, more women entered into discussions about politics in the years between 1763 and the Declaration of Independence on July 4, 1776, than perhaps at any prior time in human history.

Not all colonists defied the British; some stayed loyal to the mother country, in some cases fleeing to Canada or abroad. Historians are trying to uncover how much say a woman might have had in deciding whether to be a Loyalist or a Patriot. At that time the legal system considered a married woman to be "covered" by her husband's identity and not in possession of an independent will—but the reality might have been different from the legal theory. We do know, for example, that groups of women collected contributions for the Patriot cause, and Abigail Adams expressed the will of many women when she wrote her famous letter to her

This wartime woodcut, from "A New Touch on the Times . . . By a Daughter of Liberty," published in Massachusetts in 1779, reveals the determination of women to support the Patriot cause. Some rejected traditional female roles and took on men's jobs.

husband, John Adams, as he attended the Continental Congress in 1776, asking him to "Remember the Ladies." Intense devotion to the new nation inspired the Patriot poet and writer Mercy Otis Warren to write a three-volume history of the American Revolution in 1805—the first work of history written by an American woman.

Yet when the fighting stopped in 1783, followed by the founding of a new nation in 1787, women received little for the devotion so many had displayed. Women's rights had not been mentioned in the Declaration of Independence nor in the Constitution. Only in New Jersey were property-owning women (which meant single women, since married women could not own property in their own names) granted the right to vote, in 1776. In 1807, however, the New Jersey state legislature revoked the law as part of a general effort to disfranchise the politically marginal, including blacks and immigrants as well as women.

Women did benefit from the Revolution, however. The Declaration of Independence had announced important principles of human rights, even if women's rights were not singled out. When she drafted a statement of women's rights at Seneca Falls in 1848, for example, Elizabeth Cady Stanton modeled it on the Declaration of Independence. And many men, eager to train upstanding citizens for the new republic, were willing to invest unprecedented sums of money in establishing female educational institutions so that girls could grow up to be mothers capable of instilling patriotic values in their children.

The notion of Republican Motherhood, which developed in the 1780s and 1790s, provided a somewhat paradoxical step forward for women of Revolutionary times. This idea held that the Republican Mother, by raising her children to be good Republican citizens and by influencing her husband's opinions, could play an important role in politics. This role, however, required that she stay within the domestic sphere. Despite this limitation, the idea of Republican Motherhood became important in many early women's movements.

SEE ALSO

Adams, Abigail Smith; Citizenship; Constitution, U.S.; Declaration of Independence; Sampson, Deborah; Warren, Mercy Otis

FURTHER READING

Berkin, Carol. *First Generations: Women in Colonial America.* New York: Hill and Wang, 1996.

Kerber, Linda. *Women of the Republic.* Chapel Hill: University of North Carolina Press, 1980.

Norton, Mary Beth. *Liberty's Daughters.* Boston: Little, Brown, 1980.

Salmon, Marylynn. *The Limits of Independence: American Women, 1760-1800.* New York: Oxford University Press, 1994.

Anarchism

A very influential strand in the American radical tradition has been anarchism, a philosophy calling for free association among equally empowered men and women and for a society based on voluntary cooperation rather than government authority. Anarchists want to liberate people from the coercive power of government institutions. Anarchists were especially visible and important in the United States in the late 19th and early 20th centuries. They wrote and spoke about their beliefs, and occasionally they also used direct action, including acts of violence, to advance their cause.

Probably the best-known American anarchist was the writer, lecturer, and agitator Emma Goldman. She and her colleagues spoke tirelessly on behalf of such causes of concern to women as reproductive and sexual freedom. When the women's movement of the 1960s and 1970s adopted the slogan "The personal is political," they were echoing the earlier anarchist call for personal liberation.

SEE ALSO

Goldman, Emma

FURTHER READING

Falk, Candace. *Love, Anarchy, and Emma Goldman.* New York: Holt, Rinehart & Winston, 1984.

Wexler, Alice. *Emma Goldman in America.* Boston: Beacon, 1989.

Anderson, Marian

- *Born: Feb. 27, 1897, Philadelphia, Pa.*
- *Education: Philadelphia High School for Girls, graduated 1921*
- *Accomplishments: NAACP Spingarn Medal (1939); Swedish Litteris et Artibus medal (1952); first African-American soloist to sing with the New York Metropolitan Opera (1955); author,* My Lord, What a Morning *(autobiography, 1957); Presidential Medal of Freedom (1963); UN Peace Prize (1977); U.S. National Medal of Arts (1986); Grammy Award for Lifetime Achievement (1991)*
- *Died: Apr. 8, 1993, Portland, Oreg.*

One of the great concert singers of her generation, Marian Anderson was also the first African American to perform in a starring role at the Metropolitan Opera House in New York. That historic debut did not occur, though, until she was almost 53 years old.

Anderson began singing at her Baptist church in Philadelphia when she was very young, and her beautiful voice gained attention from the start. But as the daughter of a poor family, she could not easily afford the type of lessons that would prepare her for a professional career. Then when she was a senior in high school, her church helped her to raise money to study with a well-known Italian vocal coach. Singing in concerts along the East Coast, she came to the attention of the Rosenwald Fund, which gave her a fellowship to study in Europe for an extended period of time.

Marian Anderson performs for African-American troops (the military was then segregated) during World War II. Anderson forged an outstanding career as a classical recitalist despite discrimination that kept her from making her Metropolitan Opera deubt until late in her career.

Anderson's third recital in Paris in 1934 resulted in a contract with Sol Hurok, a leading theatrical impresario. This was an important breakthrough, but racial barriers still stood in the way of her career in the United States. The most dramatic example occurred in 1939 when the Daughters of the American Revolution denied Anderson permission to sing at Constitution Hall in Washington, D.C. In response, First Lady Eleanor Roosevelt arranged for her to give a concert to 75,000 people at the Lincoln Memorial.

The following years brought many triumphs, such as worldwide tours in which the programs included African-American spirituals, but no Metropolitan Opera performance until the civil rights movement was well underway. In the 1950s President Dwight Eisenhower further recognized Anderson by appointing her to the U.S. delegation to the United Nations.

As for her personal life, in 1943 she married the architect Orpheus Fisher, a marriage that lasted until his death in 1985.

SEE ALSO

Music

FURTHER READING

Anderson, Marian. *My Lord, What a Morning: An Autobiography.* 1955. Reprint, Madison: University of Wisconsin Press, 1992.

Ferris, Jeri. *What I Had Was Singing: The Story of Marian Anderson.* Minneapolis: Carolrhoda, 1994.

Patterson, Charles. *Marian Anderson.* New York: Watts, 1988.

Angelou, Maya

- *Born: Apr. 4, 1928, St. Louis, Mo.*
- *Education: High school*
- *Accomplishments: Northern Coordinator, Southern Christian Leadership Conference (1959-60); honorary doctorates from many colleges and universities; Reynolds Professor of American Studies, Wake Forest University (1981–); NAACP Spingarn Medal (1994); author,* I Know Why the Caged Bird Sings *(1969);* Just Give Me a Cool Drink of Water 'fore I Diiie *(1971);* Gather Together in My Name *(1974);* Singin' and Swingin' and Gettin' Merry Like Christmas *(1976);* And Still I Rise *(1978);* The Heart of a Woman *(1981);* Shaker, Why Don't You Sing? *(1983);* All God's Children Need Traveling Shoes *(1986);* Now Sheba Sings the Song *(1987);* I Shall Not Be Moved *(1990);* Life Doesn't Frighten Me *(1993);* Wouldn't Take Nothing for My Journey Now *(1993);* My Painted House, My Friendly Chicken and Me *(1994)*

Maya Angelou (born Marguerite Johnson) is an American writer known especially for her autobiographical book *I Know Why the Caged Bird Sings* (1969) and for her poem "On the Pulse of Morning," which she read at President Bill Clinton's first inauguration, in 1993.

An African American, Angelou spent her childhood in a small town in Arkansas under the care of her grandmother. There she encountered both tender care and, from the white community, discriminatory treatment. As she entered her teens, she moved to San Francisco to join her mother. She eventually became a dancer and actress, and then a writer.

Her books celebrate the survival of the human spirit under horrifying circumstances—which Angelou herself has known only too well. When she was eight years old she was raped by one of her mother's boyfriends (who was subsequently killed by her uncles), and for several years afterwards would not speak. After moving to San Francisco she worked at various times as a cocktail waitress, a prostitute and madam, a cook, and a dancer. Neither that early trauma nor anything else she has encountered since in the way of discrimination has silenced her voice of hope for a better future for all people.

FURTHER READING

Angelou, Maya. *I Know Why the Caged Bird Sings.* New York: Random House, 1969.

Shapiro, Miles. *Maya Angelou.* New York: Chelsea House, 1998.

Anthony, Susan Brownell

- *Born: Feb. 15, 1820, Adams, Mass.*
- *Education: High school (private Quaker boarding school near Philadelphia)*
- *Accomplishments: American Anti-Slavery Society agent (1856–61); publisher (with Elizabeth Cady Stanton),* The Revolution *(1868–70); co-founder, National Woman Suffrage Association (1869); president, National American Woman Suffrage Association (1892–1900)*
- *Died: Mar. 13, 1906, Rochester, N.Y.*

American women owe their ability to vote to Susan B. Anthony—and to her

Susan B. Anthony (standing) consults with her long-time collaborator, Elizabeth Cady Stanton. Though the picture is obviously posed, it captures something of their mutual trust and respect over many decades.

friend and colleague Elizabeth Cady Stanton. For many decades Anthony and Stanton spoke, wrote, organized, demanded, and cajoled the American public with one aim in view—woman suffrage. Though neither of them lived to see the ratification of the 19th Amendment, granting women the right to vote, in 1920, their lives did encompass many positive changes for women, such as improvements in the laws governing married women's ability to hold property in their own names. No doubt encouraged by this, Anthony pronounced, "Failure is impossible."

Susan was the second of eight children born to Daniel and Lucy (Read) Anthony. Her father, who ran a school, came from a Quaker background, which ensured that young Susan would be exposed to unconventional views about women; the Quakers, for example, were unusual enough to permit women to be preachers. In addition, prominent reformers, including many devoted to the abolition of slavery, visited the Anthony household. Coming to maturity, Anthony, who never married, taught school for a number of years before becoming a lecturer on the evils of drinking.

In 1850, shortly after the first women's rights convention at Seneca Falls, New York, Anthony met Elizabeth Cady Stanton, who had helped organize the event. Partly as a result of a rebuffed attempt to speak at a male-dominated temperance meeting in 1852, Anthony was converted to the cause of women's rights, although she maintained an interest in abolition and in the crusade against drinking, too. Her first step toward women's rights advocacy was to organize the Woman's New York State Temperance Society. Until the end of her long life, she worked and traveled unceasingly for her causes.

In 1872 Anthony tested what she considered to be an unjust state law barring women from voting by attempting to vote in the Presidential election as part of a concerted attempt by suffragists to break new constitutional ground. Arrested, tried, and convicted for her act of defiance, Anthony was never forced to pay the fine that was her penalty. Thus she could not fight the case all the way to the Supreme Court as she had hoped.

Toward the end of her life, Anthony became president of the National American Woman Suffrage Association, an organization she and Stanton had helped found. Once sneered at for her "outlandish" views, Anthony ended her life as a revered figure in American life. Only the racism to which she occasionally resorted in arguing for the importance of securing votes for women—she and Stanton argued that if "Sambo" (black men) could vote, why not women—sullies the memory of her place in American history.

SEE ALSO

National American Woman Suffrage Association (NAWSA); Seneca Falls Convention; Stanton, Elizabeth Cady

FURTHER READING

Anthony, Katharine. *Susan B. Anthony: Her Personal History and Her Era.* Garden City, N.Y.: Doubleday, 1954.

Flexner, Eleanor, with Ellen Fitzpatrick. *Century of Struggle.* Cambridge: Harvard University Press, 1996.

Lutz, Alma. *Susan B. Anthony: Rebel, Crusader, Humanitarian.* Boston: Beacon, 1959.
Weisberg, Barbara. *Susan B. Anthony.* New York: Chelsea House, 1988.

Anti-suffrage organizations

The first public call for votes for women took place at Seneca Falls, New York, in 1848, but the young suffrage movement was then too weak and, seemingly, too marginal to provoke more than ridicule. As the movement grew, however, it began to attract organized opposition. Beginning in the 1870s, committees of women (often the wives of prominent conservative men) worked to block suffrage by writing to newspapers and by testifying in front of legislative hearings. Anti-suffragists claimed that if women could vote they would lose special protections and influence that came to them through their roles as wives and mothers.

By 1911 there were enough local groups to warrant the founding of a national umbrella organization, the National Association Opposed to Woman Suffrage (NAOWS). At its height, NAOWS claimed a membership of some 350,000. In addition to this grassroots opposition by some women, the cause of woman suffrage always attracted hostile attention from liquor interests, because most suffragists also called for the prohibition of alcoholic beverages—many of the suffragist organizations had grown out of temperance groups. These anti-suffrage efforts notwithstanding, the 19th Amendment, granting women the vote, became a part of the U.S. Constitution in 1920.

"HOME!": The title of this drawing voices the outrage of those defenders of the home who believed that women were abandoning their duties as wives and mothers in pursuit of suffrage. The note tacked to the wall reads "Back some time this evening"; the weary father is left to comfort the children.

Architecture

For most of U.S. history, architecture has been a virtually all-male profession. Until the 19th century, a man entered the field by studying in the office of a practicing architect. In the aftermath of the Civil War of 1861–65, schools of architecture were founded within universities to offer more formal training, but they admitted only men until the Massachusetts Institute of Technology began admitting women in the 1880s.

One of the pioneering women architects—who refused to let these barriers get in her way—was California's Julia Morgan. Morgan was the first

The magnificent 137-foot-high Mediterranean Revival mansion Casa Grande, often called Hearst Castle, was designed by architect Julia Morgan for newspaper magnate William Randolph Hearst. With 130 rooms, it combined a variety of historic European design styles with modern materials and building techniques.

woman to study in the College of Engineering at the University of California at Berkeley, from which she graduated in 1894. Encouraged to pursue a career in architecture by the accomplished Bernard Maybeck, she went to Paris to study, where she became the first woman to enter the Ecole des Beaux Arts. Completing her study in France, she returned home to become the first woman licensed to practice architecture in California.

What made Morgan's career was her encounter with the powerful philanthropist Phoebe Hearst. Hearst, the first woman regent for the University of California, believed in Morgan's gift and became her patron. With this sponsorship, Morgan went on to design some 800 structures in northern California and to leave her imprint on the region. She also designed the flamboyant home of Phoebe Hearst's son, media baron William Randolph Hearst, in San Simeon, California.

During the course of the 20th century, women gradually assumed respected roles as interior designers and decorators, so they were beginning to be taken seriously as professionals in a related field. With the birth of feminism in the late 1960s, schools of architecture began to change their admissions policies and even to recruit women students. In the 1990s there are a few women deans of such schools and a few very well known women architects such as M. Rosaria Piomelli, Denise Scott Brown, and Rebecca Binder. Nonetheless, in 1998, fewer than 10 percent of the members of the American Institute of Architecture were female.

Although women have had difficulty becoming professional architects, there is a long history of creative design by women in the area of domestic architecture and interior design. Because the home has traditionally been the woman's workplace, many women have pondered how to make it more comfortable and more efficient. For example, in 1869 Catherine Beecher and Harriet Beecher Stowe published the pioneering *The American Woman's Home.*

FURTHER READING

Berkeley, Ellen Perry, ed. *Architecture: A Place for Women.* Washington, D.C.: Smithsonian Institution Press, 1989.

Boxer, Sarah. "So That's Why Walls Conceal Heating Vents." *New York Times,* June 5, 1999.

Goldfrank, Janice, ed. *Making Ourselves at Home: Women Builders and Designers.* Watsonville, Calif.: Papier-Mache Press, 1995.

Hayden, Dolores. *The Grand Domestic Revolution.* Cambridge: MIT Press, 1981.

That Exceptional One: Women in American Architecture, 1888–1988. Washington, D.C.: American Architectural Foundation, 1988. (exhibition catalog)

Wharton, Edith, and Ogden Codman, Jr. *The Decoration of Houses.* Rev. ed. New York: Norton, 1997.

Asian Americans

Asian Americans have had a history unlike immigrants from any other continent. In the 19th century, Asian immigration to the United States was overwhelmingly male because U.S. immigration policy was specifically designed to keep out women from China, Japan, Korea, the Philippines, and India: the men were desirable as laborers, but policy makers tried to prevent families from being formed. Those few women who did come over in this period were exceptionally vulnerable because they usually arrived as single women and were sometimes subjected to enforced captivity in a house of prostitution run by immigrant gangsters. Only in the 20th century have Asian women immigrants been treated the same as male immigrants by federal policy.

The first Asians to arrive in substantial numbers were Chinese men who came to work as laborers for the railroads. They were unable to become naturalized citizens, because a law passed in 1790 had said that citizenship was only for "free white persons." Anti-Chinese attitudes soon appeared, fueled by resentment from white male workers who feared competition from these poorly paid immigrants. In response to this sentiment, Congress in 1882 passed the Chinese Exclusion Act, a law that banned Chinese immigration completely except for merchants and was not repealed until 1943. In 1952 they gained the right to become naturalized citizens.

When Japanese immigrants, largely male, began to enter the United States in the late 19th century, they, too, faced prejudicial treatment. Forbidden by state law from owning land in California, where most had arrived, they were unable to become naturalized citizens until 1952 owing to federal law. Moreover, as enough women began to arrive so that families could be formed, western states segregated Asian-American children in their school systems. During World War II, the internment of more than 100,000 Japanese Americans, many of whom had been born in the United States and were therefore citizens, was a further indignity suffered because Americans were terrified of all those of Japanese ancestry after the Japanese attack on Pearl Harbor in 1941.

Documentary photographer Dorothea Lange recorded this sad image of Japanese Americans—evicted from their homes in San Francisco after a Presidental order in 1942—awaiting the next stage of their journey to a detention center.

As grim as this history is, both scholars and writers such as the Chinese Americans Maxine Hong Kingston and Amy Tan are beginning to provide a picture of how communities and the women in them survived—and even flourished—in these harsh conditions, which included being consigned to Chinatowns or Japantowns from which they ventured out only at their peril in the early years. Chinese-American women in San Francisco, for example, began to form voluntary mutual aid associations in the first half of the 20th century, thereby challenging their traditional roles in the culture. A few women even succeeded in becoming professionals. Japanese-American women were active in voluntary associations in their Buddhist or Christian churches. During the 1930s Chinese-American textile workers organized a somewhat successful strike for better wages and working. And during World War II, Chinese-American women faced the largest range of employment opportunities in their history; with male workers gone to war, women moved quickly to take advantage of job possibilities outside of Chinatown.

At the end of the 20th century, there is great cultural vitality among the Asian component of U.S. society, fostered by the growth in the numbers of Asian Americans after immigration laws were liberalized in 1965. Women from Southeast Asia, especially Vietnam, have come in much greater numbers, as have women from Korea, India, and the Philippines. There is a split in their experiences, with many immigrant women from Asia working as low-paid operatives in high-tech industries, and others—who come from wealthier families or who were otherwise able to achieve a good education—moving into business and professional jobs offering a bright future.

In addition to Kingston and Tan, there are many other Asian American women who are significant figures in American life, such as ice skaters Kristi Yamaguchi and Michelle Kwan, broadcaster Connie Chung, actress Joan Chen, congresswoman Patsy Takemoto Mink, designer Vera Wang, and comedian Margaret Cho. Chinese American Maya Lin designed the Vietnam War Memorial in Washington, D.C., and other women make documentary films, sculpt, and paint. Their work is widely recognized throughout the country as well as in their own communities.

SEE ALSO

Immigration; Kingston, Maxine Hong; Tan, Amy

FURTHER READING

Lee, Mary Paik. *Quiet Odyssey.* Seattle: University of Washington Press, 1990.

Matsumoto, Valerie. *Farming the Home Place.* Ithaca: Cornell University Press, 1993.

Wong, Jade Snow. *Fifth Chinese Daughter.* Seattle: University of Washington Press, 1989.

Yung, Judy. *Unbound Feet.* Berkeley: University of California Press, 1995.

Baker, Ella

- *Born: Dec. 13, 1903, Norfolk, Va.*
- *Education: Shaw University, B.A., 1927*
- *Accomplishments: Helped form the Southern Christian Leadership Conference (1957); organizer, Student Nonviolent Coordinating Committee (1960)*
- *Died: Dec. 13, 1986, New York, N.Y.*

Not as well known to the American public as some of the other leaders—mostly male—of the civil rights movement, Ella Baker is a significant figure who helped bring change to the African-American community.

Born in the segregated South, Baker graduated from all-black Shaw University in North Carolina as the class valedictorian. In 1927 she moved to New York City and threw herself into politics in Harlem, the large black community there. During the 1930s she helped to organize the Young Negroes Cooperative League, which formed black cooperatives to pool community resources and provide various services to their members. During the

Ella Baker (left), one of the most important architects of the civil rights movement, with NAACP colleagues at a conference in York, Pennsylvania, in 1945. Because she often worked behind the scenes, she is not as well known as some of her male colleagues.

1940s she worked for the National Association for the Advancement of Colored People (NAACP), the main organization challenging segregation. A seasoned activist, she became in the 1950s the interim director of the Southern Christian Leadership Conference (SCLC). This group, dedicated to a campaign of nonviolent protest to end segregation and discrimination, was born out of the bus boycott led by Martin Luther King, Jr., in Montgomery, Alabama.

But Baker was not happy with SCLC because she felt that the group of male ministers in the leadership did not take women seriously, and she left the organization in 1960. When students began holding "sit-ins" to desegregate drugstore lunch counters early in 1960, she called for a conference of student leaders to be held at her alma mater, Shaw University. Out of that meeting in April 1960 came the Student Nonviolent Coordinating Committee, or SNCC (pronounced "snick"), one of the most important civil rights groups of the 1960s because it mobilized people in rural communities in the South. Baker then worked to register black voters in Mississippi, a drive that in 1964 led to the founding of the Mississippi Freedom Democratic Party, a group that tried (unsuccessfully) to replace the racist mainstream Mississippi Democratic Party at the Democratic presidential convention that year.

A bridge figure connecting the generations, Baker inspired with the power of her moral vision as much as she led.

SEE ALSO

Civil rights movement

FURTHER READING

Payne, Charles. "Ella Baker and Models of Social Change." *Signs* 14, no. 4 (Summer 1989): 885-89.

Ball, Lucille

- *Born: Aug. 6, 1911, Jamestown, N.Y.*
- *Education: High school*
- *Accomplishments: Roles in many movies (1933–74); created and starred in comedy series* I Love Lucy *(1951–57) and* The Lucy Show *and* Here's Lucy *(1962–74); president, Desilu Productions (1962–67) and Lucille Ball Productions (1967–89)*
- *Died: Apr. 26, 1989, Los Angeles, Calif.*

Lucille Ball was not only the star of *I Love Lucy,* one of the most popular television comedies of all time, but she was also a pioneer businesswoman in the male-dominated Hollywood of the 1950s and 1960s. Her popularity on the small screen led directly to her power as an executive.

During her early years, Ball was briefly a chorus girl on Broadway and a model before committing herself to a movie career. In 1951 she was enjoying some success as a movie star—she had leading roles but was not one of the really big stars of her day—when she and Desi Arnaz, the Cuban bandleader she had married in 1941, got the chance to costar in a comedy for the then-new medium of television.

Television executives worried that the audience might not accept a man who spoke with a pronounced accent, but they need not have: viewers loved the relationship between the two, married both on and off the set. "Lucy" was always trying to wheedle her way into her husband's nightclub act, and "Ricky" always found a way to prevent that from happening. *I Love Lucy* ran from 1951 to 1957, followed by other less successful "Lucy" shows featuring both actors together or Ball as a single woman. In fact, Ball and Arnaz divorced in 1960—they had had two children—and in 1961 Ball married actor Gary Morton.

Ball and Arnaz had founded Desilu Productions in 1951, and when they divorced, Ball bought out Arnaz, becoming president of the firm herself, which then had annual gross revenues of $25 million. In 1967 she sold Desilu and formed her own company, Lucille Ball Productions. It has been said that there is always someplace in the world where *I Love Lucy* is playing at any given time.

SEE ALSO

Television

FURTHER READING

Brady, Kathleen. *Lucille.* New York: Hyperion, 1994.

Harris, Warren G. *Lucy & Desi: The Legendary Love Story of Television's Most Famous Couple.* New York: Simon & Schuster, 1991.

Sanders, Coyne Steven, and Tom Gilbert. *Desilu: The Story of Lucille Ball and Desi Arnaz.* New York: Morrow, 1993.

Barton, Clara

- *Born: Dec. 25, 1821, North Oxford, Mass.*
- *Education: Liberal Institute (advanced school for women teachers), Clinton, N.Y., attended 1850–51*
- *Accomplishments: Founder (1881) and president (1881–1904), American Red Cross; author,* History of the Red Cross *(1882) and* The Red Cross in Peace and War *(1899)*
- *Died: Apr. 12, 1912, Glen Echo, Md.*

Known to most people primarily as the founder of the American Red Cross—created to serve as a neutral dispenser of humanitarian aid during war—Clara Barton was that and much more. Throughout her long life she had the courage to break down barriers to women's achievements in many different areas.

Through the weary years of the war Clara Barton stayed at her post.

Clara Barton gives a wounded soldier a drink from a canteen. She founded the American Red Cross during the Civil War and achieved a national reputation for heroism.

The youngest of five children, Clara was an eager student. At 18 she began to teach school herself. From that time on she would enjoy a remarkably public career. In 1852, for example, at a time when women were not supposed to speak before mixed audiences, she testified before a school board in Bordentown, New Jersey, on behalf of free public schools. In the years just before the Civil War (1861–65), she obtained employment in the U.S. Patent Office, becoming one of only four women clerks there. By the time the war came, she had already proved she was willing to behave unconventionally.

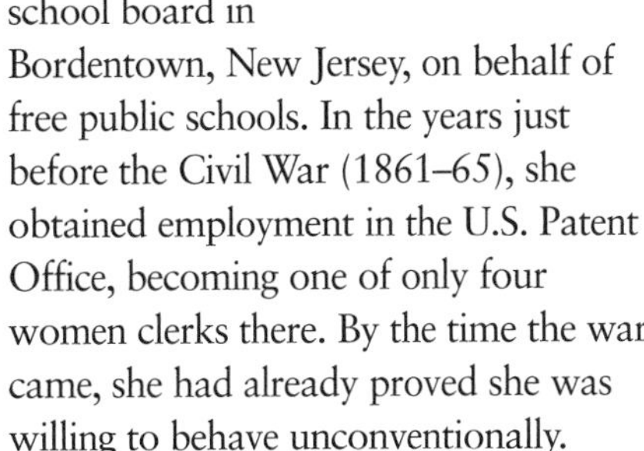

When the war started—a war that would eventually cost more than 600,000 lives—no one realized how long it would last or how much sacrifice it would entail. The U.S. Army had only 26 doctors in its ranks. Soon military leaders were overwhelmed by the need for medical personnel. At this point, they were willing to work with women, both formally through established programs and informally when women such as Barton began to show up near a battlefield to nurse, bringing with them much-needed supplies.

Hundreds of women nursed soldiers on both sides of the conflict, but none was better known than the Northern Barton. Her courage and resourcefulness in getting supplies to the battlefield led to national fame that, after the war, she employed on behalf of causes she believed in—such as the movement to make war more humane. After lobbying successfully for the United States to sign the Geneva Convention (which set up rules for fighting wars), Barton became the first American woman to hold a diplomatic appointment when she represented her country at an International Red Cross conference in 1884 (in 1881 she had established the American Association of the Red Cross, which later became the American Red Cross). She also led the Red Cross in broadening its activities to include relief after natural disasters.

SEE ALSO

American Red Cross; Civil War; Nursing

FURTHER READING

Burton, David Henry. *Clara Barton: In the Service of Humanity.* Westport, Conn.: Greenwood Press, 1995.

Oates, Stephen B. *A Woman of Valor: Clara Barton and the Civil War.* New York: Free Press, 1994.

Pryor, Elizabeth Brown. *Clara Barton.* Philadelphia: University of Pennsylvania Press, 1987.

Beauty pageants

The Miss America pageant, founded in 1921, was the first national beauty contest in the United States. That the founding took place in the 1920s—the same decade when the celebrity culture of movie stars and movie magazines fully blossomed—was no coincidence. Beauty pageants and new standards of female beauty were intimately related to one another.

Caring about how she looked was *not* new for a woman in the 20th century. But before 1900, respectable women used no cosmetics—or if they "painted," they did it so skillfully that it was unobtrusive. Beginning in the late 19th century, this began to change, and a whole structure of small and large companies making perfumes and other beauty preparations appeared. By 1920 the growing cosmetics industry was promoting rouge, powder, lipstick, and eye makeup—and "respectable" women were buying. This happened just as the cult of the movie star was taking shape. Movies had become an important part of American culture in the years between 1910 and 1920, and the allure of wanting to look like their favorite stars helped convince women that they should use makeup to maximize their own beauty.

The Miss America contest symbolized all of these changes, and during the years of its greatest cultural significance—between its founding and the birth of the modern women's movement around 1970—the winner of the Miss America pageant defined what an American beauty should look like. She must be long-legged, slender, and, if not necessarily blonde, very Anglo in appearance. In the 1990s the winners of the Miss America pageant and the

The Atlantic City Pageant of 1925 featured a swimsuit competition. So did the Miss America pageant, which had been founded in Atlantic City four years earlier.

many other pageants patterned after it have exhibited a broader range of racial and ethnic characteristics.

Women's movement activists have objected to beauty contests not only because they generally promote a narrow definition of beauty, but also because, in the opinion of most feminists, they call too much attention to looks, at the expense of other traits.

FURTHER READING

Banner, Lois. *American Beauty.* Chicago: University of Chicago Press, 1983.

Beecher, Catharine Esther

- *Born: Sept. 6, 1800, East Hampton, N.Y.*
- *Education: No formal education*
- *Accomplishments: Co-founder, Hartford Female Seminary (1823); founder, Western Female Institute, Cincinnati (1832); organizer, American Woman's Educational Association (1852); author,* A Treatise on Domestic Economy *(1841);* The Duty of American Women to Their Country *(1845);* Common Sense Applied to Religion *(1857);* The American Woman's Home *(with Harriet Beecher Stowe, 1869)*
- *Died: May 12, 1878, Elmira, N.Y.*

Born to a remarkable family, Catharine Beecher was the first child of the prominent clergyman Lyman Beecher; 10 others followed in the course of his three marriages. Catharine's mother, Roxana Foote Beecher, died when the girl was 16, and as the oldest child she had to accept substantial responsibility for her brothers and sisters.

As a young woman teaching at a boarding school for girls, Beecher suffered the loss of her fiancé, Alexander Fisher, who died at sea. This tragedy changed her life, and she became a pioneer "career woman" rather than marry someone else. Her father's stern version of Protestantism suggested that Fisher might have died without being saved—he had attended church, but there had been no moment at which he had accepted Christ as his personal savior—and Beecher could not accept that her dead lover was condemned to damnation. As a result, she also became very independent in her religious outlook.

During the course of her life, Beecher taught, founded schools, lectured, and organized groups of women to teach in frontier communities. In 1841 she wrote a best-selling book of domestic advice, *A Treatise on Domestic Economy,* in which she argued that woman's role was in the home, where she could have strong influence on American society. Indeed, she felt that women's position in the home gave them greater influence in some areas:

> In matters pertaining to the education of their children, in the selection and support of a clergyman, in all benevolent enterprises, and in all questions relating to morals and manners, they have a superior influence. In all such concerns, it would be impossible to carry a point contrary to their judgment and feelings; while an enterprise sustained by them, will seldom fail of success.

Her religious ideas, more liberal about salvation than those of her father, were original enough to inspire research by 20th-century students of theology. She formed several women's educational institutions, through which she urged the training of young women in domestic sciences and teaching. She was also an early advocate of calisthenics (free-body exercises involving bending, twisting, stretching, kicking, and jumping).

So famous was Beecher in her own day that her renown came close to matching that of her sister Harriet

Beecher Stowe, the author of *Uncle Tom's Cabin,* and that of her brother Henry Ward Beecher, the country's best-known clergyman.

SEE ALSO

Stowe, Harriet Beecher

FURTHER READING

Beecher, Catharine Esther, and Harriet Beecher Stowe. *The American Woman's Home: or, Principles of Domestic Science.* New York: Arno, 1971.

Sklar, Kathryn. *Catharine Beecher: A Study in American Domesticity.* New York: Norton, 1973.

Bethune, Mary McLeod

- *Born: July 10, 1875, Mayesville, S.C.*
- *Education: Scotia Seminary, Concord, N.C., graduated 1893; Moody Bible Institute, Chicago, graduated 1895*
- *Accomplishments: Founder, Daytona Normal and Industrial Institute for Negro Girls (1904); president, Bethune-Cookman College (1923–42, 1946–47); founder, National Council of Negro Women (1935); special adviser to President F. D. Roosevelt on minority affairs (1935–44); director, Division of Negro Affairs of the National Youth Administration (1936–44)*
- *Died: May 18, 1955, Washington, D.C.*

A woman of boundless energy, Mary McLeod Bethune served in the administration of President Franklin Delano Roosevelt in the 1930s, where she became the highest-ranking African-American woman in the federal government. But that was only one of her many achievements.

Mary McLeod was born to a life of rural poverty as the 15th of 17 children. Nonetheless she acquired an education from Scotia Seminary, a missionary-run school in Concord, North Carolina.

Mary McLeod Bethune, the president of Bethune-Cookman College, was the most prominent member of the "Black Cabinet" during President Franklin Roosevelt's administration. At this meeting of the National Youth Administration, Bethune was joined by First Lady Eleanor Roosevelt, her colleague in many a fight for social justice.

After marrying Albertus Bethune and giving birth to one child, Mary McLeod Bethune went on to become an outstanding educator.

In 1904, Bethune founded the Daytona Normal and Industrial Institute for Negro Girls in Daytona Beach, Florida. The small school was built on land that had been a city dump, and for furniture and materials, its founder had to scrounge through dumps and trash piles. In 1923, the school merged with Cookman College to become Bethune-Cookman College, of which she was president for many years, and which is still in existence.

She was also important because of her work with African-American women's clubs. This was at a time when black voting in the South was limited both by legal means and by terrorist tactics directed against would-be voters. African Americans necessarily relied on nongovernmental means of protecting their interests. Under these circumstances, the National Association of Colored Women, founded in 1896, was a potent force for social change and collective action. Thus to be a clubwoman active in the NACW, as was Bethune, was to be at the heart of the action, and she went on to form the National Council of Negro Women in 1935.

Bethune's outstanding work in organizing clubs that developed programs for delinquent girls, for example, brought her to the attention of First Lady Eleanor Roosevelt, who advocated Bethune's appointment to a governmental post. And in 1936 Franklin Roosevelt did appoint her to head the Division of Negro Affairs of the National Youth Administration. Bethune was the only woman in the informal Black Cabinet, a group of high-ranking African Americans who advised Roosevelt on matters of concern to their community. Bethune also served as an adviser to the U.S. delegation to the founding of the United Nations in San Francisco in 1945.

SEE ALSO

African Americans; Clubs, women's; New Deal

FURTHER READING

Halasa, Malu. *Mary McLeod Bethune.* New York: Chelsea House, 1989.

Birth control

Throughout much of human history, people have found ways to limit family size. Methods have included abortion (which was not illegal in the United States until the mid-19th century), late marriage, infanticide, and male withdrawal during sex. What is new in the 20th century is that methods have become more reliable and birth-control devices are widely available.

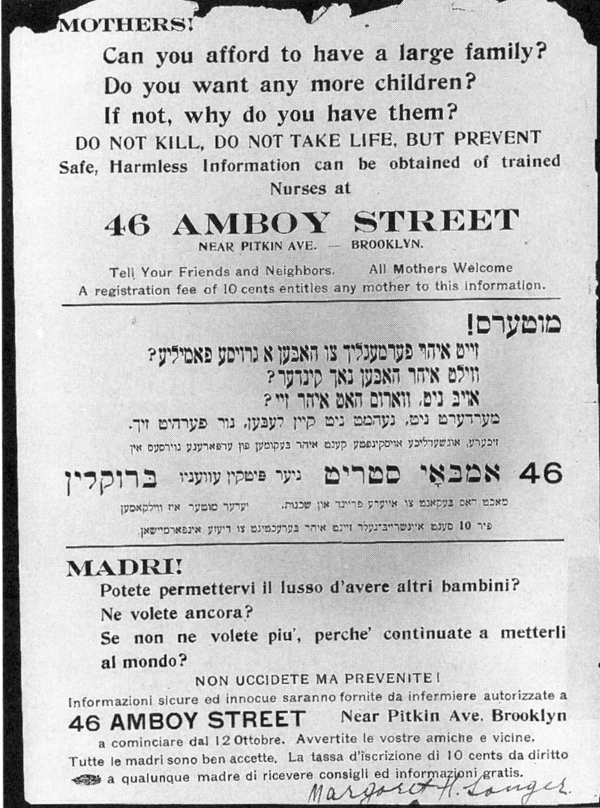

This flyer advertises the services of Margaret Sanger's birth control clinic in Brooklyn, New York, in three languages: English, Yiddish, and Italian. Founded in 1916, it was the first such clinic in the nation.

The size of the American family began to decline as early as 1800: that year the average white woman had 7.04 children, in 1900 she had 3.56 children, and by 1997 the average was about 2.06 children.

Fearing that this decline might undermine the strength of the family, in 1873 Congress passed the Comstock Law, which defined information about contraception as pornography, and made it illegal to distribute this "obscene" material through the mail. When coupled with laws forbidding abortion that had been passed shortly before, women's ability to limit family size suffered.

In the early 1900s women's rights crusaders such as Emma Goldman and Margaret Sanger began to speak out on the need for better birth control—Sanger coined the term itself—and for better access to it. Doctors began to work on improving the devices that were then available and creating new ones.

In the 1930s the Comstock Law was overturned by a court decision. In the 1960s and 1970s the U.S. Supreme Court issued a number of key decisions that improved women's access both to birth control and to abortion. In *Griswold* v. *Connecticut* (1965), the Court asserted a constitutional right to marital privacy that ensured access to birth-control information and devices for married women, and its decision in the 1973 case *Roe* v. *Wade* legalized abortion.

In 1960 the birth-control pill, which prevents conception by using hormones to stop women from ovulating (producing eggs), was placed on the market. This new form of contraception, which put women entirely in control of their reproductive capacities, was heartily embraced by many. The sense of freedom the pill gave to women led to what is referred to as the sexual revolution of the 1960s, when it became more common and accepted for people to engage in sexual activity outside marriage and with many partners. In 1976, for example, among unmarried girls who were sexually active, 27 percent of white girls and 45 percent of black girls had become pregnant by the age of 18. This constituted a problem for school authorities who were torn between wanting to provide birth control information to cut down on teenage pregnancy, and yet afraid that they would be accused of encouraging teenage sexuality. This is still an issue today.

At the end of the 20th century, Americans still do not have completely satisfactory solutions to the problem of controlling fertility. Pre-pill devices such as condoms, which many people still use, partly because they offer some protection from venereal diseases and AIDS, are not always reliable. The pill and various other medical interventions such as the intrauterine device (IUD) have been found to have potentially serious side effects, such as the increased risk of blood clots with pill use. In addition, access to birth control has often been difficult for poor women, because it is too expensive.

Imbalances also remain in place after the sexual revolution: health insurance companies have been much quicker to pay for drugs to treat male impotence than to pay for contraception for women. Given the limited nature of social support and other resources—and therefore the need to control unwanted population growth—safe, inexpensive, and effective ways of preventing pregnancy remain a top research priority.

SEE ALSO

Goldman, Emma; *Griswold* v. *Connecticut* (1965); *Roe* v. *Wade* (1973); Sanger, Margaret Higgins

FURTHER READING

Holmes, Helen B., Betty B. Hoskins, and Michael Gross, eds. *Birth Control and Controlling Birth: Women-Centered Perspectives.* Clifton, N.J.: Humana Press, 1980.

Nourse, Alan E. *Birth Control.* New York: Watts, 1988.

Swisher, Karen L., ed. *Teenage Sexuality: Opposing Viewpoints.* San Diego: Greenhaven, 1994.

Birthrate

The birthrate is the number of children born, on the average, in a given population. It will fluctuate greatly over time, depending on whether people are using artificial means of preventing pregnancy, whether women have access to abortion, and how healthy, economically and physically, the population is. Hard times, for example, can mean that people postpone marriage until they can afford to take care of a family; the later that marriage takes place, on the average, the lower the birthrate, because women begin to lose their fertility in middle age.

Since 1800 the birthrate in the United States has declined more or less steadily, except for the baby boom generation born after World War II (1941–45). The baby boom happened because many people had postponed marriage and children during the Great Depression of the 1930s; then the United States fought a war in which millions of men served overseas in the armed forces. When the fighting ended—and with improved economic conditions for most Americans since the 1930s—the birthrate climbed for some years, with some 25 babies born for every thousand people in the population in 1955, compared to 19 in 1940—before going down to about 18 per thousand again in the 1960s. In the 1990s the birthrate hovered around 15 births per thousand.

Black Panther Party

Two college students, Huey Newton and Bobby Seale, founded the Black Panther Party for Self-Defense in Oakland, California, in 1966 to provide social-welfare programs for poor blacks and advocate self-defense against police brutality. The Panthers would eventually be led by a woman, Elaine Brown, starting in 1974. Born not only out of idealism but also out of despair about the inner city, the group seemed to embody the slogan so much heard in the 1960s: Black Power, the call adopted by militant blacks who rejected the nonviolent civil rights tactics of Martin Luther King, Jr. During the

The Black Panther party and the North East Women's Liberation organization distributed this 1969 poster to promote the release of six of its members from a Connecticut prison.

late 1960s the group spread to many other big cities.

The Panthers announced that they believed in armed struggle against oppression, but they also said they would not fight unless attacked first. They were frequently photographed with guns. Nonetheless, they invested a great deal of effort in organizing free meals for black schoolchildren in Oakland, an activity that was relatively unpublicized. It was their militant statements about the need for armed struggle that attracted attention from the local police and FBI. As a result, many Panthers, both in California and in other states as the organization grew, were harassed by law enforcement officials. (Some of them may have engaged in criminal activity.)

By the early 1970s the Panthers were losing strength because some had been murdered (by their enemies or during law enforcement raids) and some were in prison. When Elaine Brown became their leader, she had to contend with a tradition of ultra-macho discipline in the group as well as with the hostility of the authorities. Brown turned the party's focus to more conventional politics and social service.

Despite all of the Panthers' problems, their achievements include the establishment of the free meal program and their pioneering and successful pressure to found the country's first African-American Studies program at Merrit Community College in Oakland.

FURTHER READING

Brown, Elaine. *A Taste of Power: A Black Woman's Story.* New York: Pantheon, 1992.

Foner, Philip S., ed. *The Black Panther Speaks.* Philadelphia: Lippincott, 1970.

Newton, Huey, with J. Herman Blake. *Revolutionary Suicide.* New York: Harcourt Brace Jovanovich, 1973.

Black, Shirley Temple

- *Born: Apr. 23, 1928, Santa Monica, Calif.*
- *Education: High school*
- *Accomplishments: Special juvenile Academy Award for "outstanding contribution to screen entertainment during the year 1934" (1935); U.S. Ambassador to Ghana (1974–76); U.S. Chief of Protocol (1976–77); U.S. Ambassador to Czechoslovakia (1989–92); National Board of Review Career Achievement Award (1992); Kennedy Center honoree (1998)*

For much of the 1930s, the second most famous female in the United States (after First Lady Eleanor Roosevelt) was a little girl—movie star Shirley Temple. Her charm, dimples, curls, and good cheer were just what the country needed at a time when the Great Depression had thrown many people out of work. Many Americans were scared and worried about the future, and seeing a plucky little girl in action may have given them courage—as President Roosevelt said, "as long as our country has Shirley Temple, we will be alright."

Young Shirley began taking dance classes at the age of three and was chosen to appear in short films before her fourth birthday. By the time she was six, she was a big star. She appeared in one hit film after another during the 1930s, playing in comedies and musicals, and for several years she was Hollywood's biggest box-office draw, starring in some 40 movies before she was twelve. Her better known films include *Stand Up and Cheer* (1934), *Bright Eyes* (1934), *The Little Colonel* (1935), *Curly Top* (1935), *Poor Little Rich Girl* (1936), *Wee Willie Winkie* (1937), and *Rebecca of Sunnybrook Farm* (1938). Then she grew up, and the magic faded.

After a brief early marriage to fellow actor John Agar, she married TV executive Charles Black in 1950. As an adult she has been active in public life, serving as a delegate to the General Assembly of the United Nations in the late 1960s and early 70s. She was the U.S. ambassador first to Ghana, 1974–76, and then to Czechoslovakia, 1989–92.

SEE ALSO

Movies

FURTHER READING

Black, Shirley Temple. *Child Star.* New York: Warner Books, 1989.

Hammontree, Patsy Guy. *Shirley Temple Black.* Westport, Conn.: Greenwood Publishing Group, 1998.

Blackwell, Alice Stone

- *Born: Sept. 14, 1857, Orange, N.J.*
- *Education: Boston University, B.A., 1881*
- *Accomplishments: Editor,* Woman's Journal *(1881–1917); secretary, National American Woman Suffrage Association (1890–1918)*
- *Died: Mar. 15, 1950, Cambridge, Mass.*

Alice Stone Blackwell was the only child of two of the 19th century's best-known activists for women's rights—Lucy Stone and Henry Blackwell. Indeed, her mother's name became a synonym for a woman who chose to keep her own name after marriage—a "Lucy Stoner."

A Phi Beta Kappa graduate of Boston University, Blackwell edited the nation's leading women's rights publication, the *Woman's Journal* (founded by her mother) for 35 years. Though she had resented having to compete with her mother's causes as a child, as an adult she devoted herself to woman suffrage as well as to many other humanitarian efforts such as the peace movement and equal treatment for African Americans. In 1930 Blackwell published a biography of her mother on which she had worked for some 40 years.

Suffragist Alice Stone Blackwell followed in her parents' footsteps as editor of the Woman's Journal. *Her parents, Lucy Stone and Henry Blackwell, had one of the 19th century's most famous—and most egalitarian—marriages.*

SEE ALSO

Stone, Lucy; Suffrage, woman

FURTHER READING

Blackwell, Alice Stone. *Growing up in Boston's Gilded Age: The Journal of Alice Stone Blackwell, 1872–1874.* Edited by Marlene Deahl Merrill. New Haven: Yale University Press, 1990.

Blackwell, Antoinette Brown

- *Born: May 20, 1825, Henrietta, N.Y.*
- *Education: Oberlin College, literary (non-degree) course completed 1847, theological course completed in 1850, but official graduation and license denied because she was a woman*
- *Accomplishments: Minister, Congregational church in South Butler, N.Y. (1853–54); minister, Unitarian church in Elizabeth, N.J. (1854–1921); author,* Shadows of Our Social System *(1855);* Studies in General Science *(1869);* The Sexes Throughout Nature *(1875);* The Physical Basis of Immortality *(1876);* The Philosophy of Individuality *(1893);* The Making of the Universe *(1914);* The Social Side of Mind and Action *(1915)*
- *Died: Nov. 5, 1921, Elizabeth, N.J.*

A suffragist and abolitionist before the Civil War (1861–65), Antoinette Brown Blackwell lived long enough to vote in 1920, after the 19th Amendment made that act possible for all American women. In addition to lecturing on behalf of her many reform causes, Blackwell was a writer and the first woman to be ordained a minister in a mainstream Protestant denomination.

The seventh of 10 children born to Joseph and Abby (Morse) Brown, the young Antoinette had an unusual thirst for education as she was growing up. Working as a teacher for a short while, she put away money for higher education. With financial support from her father, too, she entered Oberlin College in Ohio in 1846, a few years after the college had become the first in the country to admit women. There she met a woman who would be her lifelong friend and comrade, the suffragist Lucy Stone.

Though officially enrolled at Oberlin, the young women did not have the same experience as the male students:

the women were, for example, expected to do mending for their male colleagues. Antoinette Brown rebelled. But when she announced that she wanted to study theology, she *really* upset the college authorities.

Persevering, the young woman was ordained as a Congregationalist minister in 1853, after having graduated from Oberlin. But she gave up her pastorate in Savannah, New York, after only one year, because her religious views were evolving toward Unitarianism, a more liberal creed. In later years she occupied many pulpits as a guest minister. In addition, she wrote a searching response to Charles Darwin's *The Descent of Man.* Called *The Sexes Throughout Nature,* it appeared in 1875 and argued that women could not be deemed biologically inferior to men unless and until men were to share domestic duties. Remarkably, she and Lucy Stone—who had worried that they would never find supportive men—married brothers, Samuel and Henry Blackwell, who were fellow reformers and supported their wives' activism.

SEE ALSO

Religion; Science; Stone, Lucy; Suffrage, woman

FURTHER READING

Cazden, Elizabeth. *Antoinette Brown Blackwell.* Old Westbury, N.Y.: Feminist Press, 1983.

Blackwell, Elizabeth

- *Born: Feb. 3, 1821, Counterslip, England*
- *Education: Geneva Medical College (now Hobart College), Geneva, N.Y., M.D., 1849*
- *Accomplishments: First woman doctor of medicine in modern times; founder, New York Infirmary (1857); organizer, Woman's Central Association of Relief, and U.S. Sanitary Commission (1861); founder, Woman's Medical College, New York (1868); co-organizer, England National Health Society (1871); professor of gynecology, London School of Medicine for Women (1875–1907)*
- *Died: May 31, 1910, Hastings, England*

Elizabeth Blackwell was the first woman in modern times in either the U.S. or Europe to earn a medical degree. Born to a family of reformers and innovators—her younger sister Emily also became a doctor, and her brothers Samuel and Henry married the suffragists Antoinette Brown and Lucy Stone, respectively—Blackwell moved with her parents and siblings from England to the United States at the age of 11. Once in this country the Blackwells made contact with like-minded reformers who envisioned a more just relationship between men and women.

The first woman in the United States to practice medicine, Dr. Elizabeth Blackwell came from a remarkable family, many of whose members (both men and women) were advocates for women's rights.

In order to satisfy her personal dream of becoming a physician, Elizabeth Blackwell had to persist in the face of enormous odds. Turned down by 29 medical schools, she eventually won admittance to Geneva College in New York. There she was treated as an "oddball" by the townspeople and her fellow students alike. But in 1849 she received her degree.

Facing further discouragement and harassment after graduating, in 1857 Blackwell founded the New York Infirmary for Women and Children, staffed entirely by women, where she could practice medicine with fewer difficulties. Having played a leading role in pioneering medical education for women in this country—she actively recruited women to nurse during the Civil War, for example—she returned to England in 1868. She then lived in the British Isles for the rest of her life.

SEE ALSO

Medicine

FURTHER READING

Blackwell, Elizabeth. *Pioneer Work in Opening the Medical Profession to Women: Autobiographical Sketches.* New York: Schocken Books, 1977.

Brown, Jordan. *Elizabeth Blackwell.* New York: Chelsea House, 1989.

Kline, Nancy. *Elizabeth Blackwell: A Doctor's Triumph.* Berkeley, Calif.: Conari Press, 1997.

Morantz-Sanchez, Regina. *Sympathy and Science: Women Physicians in American Medicine.* New York: Oxford University Press, 1985.

Blatch, Harriot Stanton

- *Born: Jan. 20, 1865, Seneca Falls, N.Y.*
- *Education: Vassar College, B.A., 1878, M.A. 1894; Boston School of Oratory, one-year course*
- *Accomplishments: Founder, Equality League of Self-Supporting Women (1907); organizer, first suffrage parades in the United States (1910); director, Speaker's Bureau, U.S. Food Administration (1917); author,* Mobilizing Woman-Power *(1918);* A Woman's Point of View, Some Roads to Peace *(1920);* Elizabeth Cady Stanton, as Revealed in Her Letters, Diary and Reminiscences *(with Theodore Stanton, 1922);* Challenging Years *(autobiography, with Alma Lutz, 1940)*
- *Died: Nov. 20, 1940, Greenwich, Conn.*

Harriot Stanton Blatch was the sixth of seven children born to suffragist and women's rights leader Elizabeth Cady Stanton and her husband, Henry Stanton. An honors graduate of Vassar College in 1878, Harriot Stanton had also received a liberal education in her parents' household. Because she married an English businessman in 1882—she met William Henry Blatch on board a ship—Blatch developed ties to the women's movements on both sides of the Atlantic. Indeed, she and her husband lived for twenty years in Basingstoke, England, before they and their daughter moved back to the United States to live in New York. When they returned, Harriot Stanton Blatch was ready to assume a leadership position in the American suffrage movement.

Blatch's contribution lay particularly in calling attention to the plight of working-class women: in 1907 she founded a new suffrage organization, the Equality League of Self-Supporting Women, whose purpose was to rally working-class women to push for the vote, which had been a relatively elitist cause until then. With this as her base, Blatch became an effective lobbyist on behalf of women's causes at the New York state capitol in Albany. She was also a primary organizer of the first of many mass parades for suffrage, which injected new vigor into the women's movement and gave it a more publicity-oriented flavor.

SEE ALSO

Stanton, Elizabeth Cady

FURTHER READING

DuBois, Ellen Carol. *Harriot Stanton Blatch and the Winning of Suffrage.* New Haven: Yale University Press, 1997.

Bloomer, Amelia Jenks

- *Born: May 27, 1818, Homer, N.Y.*
- *Education: High school*
- *Accomplishments: Founder and editor,* The Lily: A Ladies Journal Devoted to Temperance and Literature *(1849–55)*
- *Died: Dec. 30, 1894, Council Bluffs, Iowa*

The name of Amelia Bloomer will always be associated with the innovation in dress for women she tried to popularize: Turkish pantaloons, or "bloomers," worn with a short skirt. Bloomer believed these would give women more freedom of movement than the long, voluminous skirts then fashionable.

Amelia Jenks was a school teacher and private tutor for several years before she married Dexter C. Bloomer, a Quaker newspaper editor, in 1840. The couple settled in Seneca Falls, New York, shortly before the historic women's rights convention took place there in 1848. Attending the convention, she became a convert to the cause. As the editor of a newspaper for women called the *Lily* (probably the first paper edited entirely by a woman) she publicized a new style of attire—that is, the pantaloons—first worn by Elizabeth Smith Miller, the daughter of a well-known abolitionist, Gerrit Smith. Bloomer's articles attracted national attention, and it was *her* name that was attached to the costume, one that she herself wore for six or eight years before deciding that it was drawing attention away from more substantive issues.

Amelia Bloomer wearing the garment—pants under a skirt—that made her name into a common noun. Though people laughed at her when she appeared in bloomers, she was a woman ahead of her time.

In the early 1850s, Bloomer made many speaking appearances in New York and elsewhere, and after she sold the *Lily* in 1855, she continued to be active in reform through writing and lectures.

SEE ALSO

Fashion; Seneca Falls Convention

FURTHER READING

Bloomer, Dexter C. *Life and Writings of Amelia Bloomer.* New York: Schocken, 1975.

Blumberg, Rhoda. *Bloomers!* New York: Bradbury, 1993.

Bly, Nellie

SEE Seaman, Elizabeth Cochrane (Nellie Bly)

Boston marriage

The term *Boston marriage* was used in the 19th century to describe two women who lived together for many years, almost like a married couple. There was little public discussion of sexuality in those years—let alone lesbian and gay sexuality—but it seems to have been generally assumed that a Boston marriage was sexless. Now modern scholars are not so sure. In any case, many women of high achievement, such as those who pioneered university teaching, lived in Boston marriages, apparently with great satisfaction. Writer Sarah Orne Jewett and Annie Adams Fields, a publishing magnate's widow, for example, developed a romantic friendship which became a long-term union when their father and husband (respectively) died.

SEE ALSO
Sexuality

Bourke-White, Margaret

- *Born: June 14, 1904, New York, N.Y.*
- *Education: Columbia University, 1922–23; University of Michigan, 1923–25; Cornell University, A.B., 1927*
- *Accomplishments: Staff photographer,* Fortune *magazine (1929–36); staff photographer,* Life *magazine (1936–69)*
- *Died: Aug. 27, 1971, Stamford, Conn.*

Photographer Margaret Bourke-White took some of the images that have been indelibly identified with the 20th century. Among these, for example, are her pictures of a Nazi death camp at Buchenwald after World War II.

Margaret Bourke-White attended several universities before graduating from Cornell in 1927. While a student there, she demonstrated her promise by memorably photographing the campus and the surrounding landscape. In 1929 she became one of the first photographers for the new *Fortune* magazine, with a studio in the Chrysler building in New York City. In 1936 she joined the staff of the photo-news magazine *Life,* for which she took many of her best-known pictures.

During World War II Margaret Bourke-White had an official assignment to photograph military maneuvers and even battles, though she had to overcome obstacles along the way. Early in the war, she traveled to North Africa by ship when she was not allowed to fly with the men she was covering.

Although she subscribed to a machine-age aesthetic that saw beauty in factories, Bourke-White also photographed the rural poor during the Great Depression. During World War II she covered the fighting as an official Army Air Force photographer , despite the many barriers she faced as a woman among mostly male soldiers and officials.

A brief early marriage to Everett Chapman, an engineering graduate student at Cornell, ended in a year. In the 1930s Bourke-White had a relationship with the writer Erskine Caldwell, to whom she was married from 1939 to 1942. In 1937 they published a book about the victims of the Great Depression, *You Have Seen Their Faces.*

FURTHER READING

Bourke-White, Margaret. *Portrait of Myself.* New York: Simon & Schuster, 1963.

———. *The Photographs of Margaret Bourke-White.* Edited by Sean Callahan. Greenwich, Conn.: New York Graphic Society, 1972.

Callahan, Sean. *Margaret Bourke-White: Photographer.* Boston: Little, Brown, 1998.

Daffron, Carolyn. *Margaret Bourke-White.* New York: Chelsea House, 1988.

Bradstreet, Anne

- *Born: Around 1612, probably Northampton, England*
- *Education: No formal education*
- *Accomplishments: Wrote poetry published as* The Tenth Muse Lately Sprung up in America *(1650) and* Several Poems *(1678)*
- *Died: Sept. 16, 1672, North Andover, Mass.*

Anne Bradstreet was the first English-language poet to publish while resident in the American colonies. Her Puritan father, Thomas Dudley, was the steward of the earl of Lincoln, and the young girl therefore had access to a fine library while growing up. She married fellow Puritan Simon Bradstreet in 1628, and she and her husband sailed to the New World on board the *Arbella* in 1630, the voyage that led to the founding of Massachusetts.

At first Bradstreet suffered from shock at finding herself so removed from the comforts of home. But in 1632 she began to write poetry. In 1650 her brother-in-law, apparently unbeknownst to her, oversaw the publication of her first book of poetry in London, *The Tenth Muse Lately Sprung up in America.* Drawn from the poetry she had privately circulated among her friends and family, it enjoyed a considerable success.

In addition to her role as a pioneering literary woman, Anne Bradstreet was the mother of eight children. Modern critics now believe that the love poems she wrote to her husband are her strongest work. One of the best known of these is titled "To My Dear and Loving Husband":

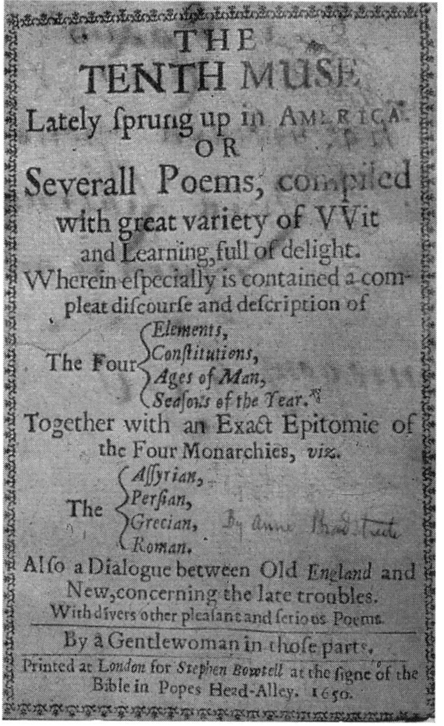

THE
TENTH MUSE
Lately ſprung up in AMERICA.
OR
Severall Poems, compiled
with great variety of VVit
and Learning, full of delight.
Wherein eſpecially is contained a compleat diſcourſe and deſcription of
The Four: *Elements, Conſtitutions, Ages of Man, Seaſons of the Year.*
Together with an Exact Epitomie of
the Four Monarchies, *viz.*
The: *Aſſyrian, Perſian, Grecian, Roman.*
Alſo a Dialogue between Old *England* and
New, concerning the late troubles.
With divers other pleaſant and ſerious Poems.
By a Gentlewoman in thoſe parts.
Printed at *London* for *Stephen Bowtell* at the ſigne of the
Bible in Popes Head-Alley. 1650.

The title page of Anne Bradstreet's The Tenth Muse Lately Sprung up in America, *a collection of poems published in England in 1650. Bradstreet was the New World's first English-language poet.*

If ever two were one, then surely we.
If ever man were lov'd by wife, then thee;
If ever wife was happy in a man,
Compare with me, ye women, if you can.
I prize thy love more than whole
Mines of gold
Or all the riches that the East doth hold.
My love is such that Rivers cannot quench,
Nor ought but love from thee give recompense.
Thy love is such I can no way repay,
The heavens reward thee manifold, I pray.
Then while we live, in love let's so persever
That when we live no more, we may live ever.

FURTHER READING

Martin, Wendy. *An American Tryptich: Anne Bradstreet, Emily Dickinson, and Adrienne Rich.* Chapel Hill: University of North Carolina Press, 1984.

White, Elizabeth Wade. *Anne Bradstreet, "The Tenth Muse."* New York: Oxford University Press, 1971.

Bradwell v. *Illinois* (1873)

In a pioneering lawsuit, Myra Bradwell's lawyer contended in his brief before the U.S. Supreme Court in 1873 that the 14th Amendment to the U.S. Constitution should have overridden an Illinois court decision forbidding her, as a married woman, from practicing law. This was a historic suit—although unsuccessful—because it was the first attempt to use the amendment to extend women's rights.

From an abolitionist family, Bradwell studied law under the tutelage of her lawyer husband. During the Civil War (1861–65) she was active in the Chicago branch of the U.S. Sanitary Commission, which raised money and gathered supplies for hospitals. She then edited *The Chicago Legal News,* a journal respected throughout the Midwest for its summaries of legal developments. In 1869 she passed the Illinois state bar exam, but the state supreme court denied her admission to the bar on the grounds that, as a married woman, she could not enter into legally binding contracts with clients. Her lawyer at that time argued that, on the basis of the 14th Amendment's "privileges and immunities" clause, she, as a citizen, should enjoy the privilege of admission to the bar.

Although the U.S. Supreme Court ruled against her, Myra Bradwell did practice law, at first as an honorary member of the Illinois Bar Association and as a regular member beginning in 1890, when the state bar reversed its decision on her original motion of 1869, in spite of the fact that the Supreme Court ruling had not been overturned. By the time of her death at the age of 62, she was known as the most distinguished woman lawyer in the country.

SEE ALSO

14th Amendment; Law

Brent, Margaret

- *Born: Around 1601, Gloucestershire, England*
- *Education: Some basic schooling*
- *Accomplishments: First woman landholder in Maryland; executor of estate of early Maryland governer, Leonard Calvert (1646)*
- *Died: Around 1671, Westmoreland County, Va.*

The American Bar Association gives an award every year to an outstanding woman lawyer—the Margaret Brent Award. The prize honors this 17th-century colonist considered to be the first American woman attorney.

Not much is known about Brent's life in England. In 1638 she moved to Maryland with several members of her family. She and her sister Mary soon acquired more than 70 acres of farmland, and she later obtained much more land from her brother Giles, so much that she became one of the large landowners in the colony. Her business dealings so impressed the governor that he made her the executor of his will. This responsibility, plus the need to protect her own holdings, led Brent to make a number of appearances in court, where she ably and vigorously held her own in what were normally all-male proceedings. In 1651 she moved to Virginia, along with other members of her family.

SEE ALSO
Law

Buck, Pearl Sydenstricker

- *Born: June 26, 1892, Hillsboro, W. Va.*
- *Education: Randolph-Macon Woman's College, B.A., 1914*
- *Accomplishments: Pulitzer Prize for* The Good Earth, *1932; Nobel Prize for literature, 1938; co-founder, East and West Association (1942); founder, Welcome House (interracial adoption agency, 1949); founder, Pearl S. Buck Foundation (1964); author,* East Wind, West Wind *(1930);* The Good Earth *(1931);* Sons *(1932);* A House Divided *(1935);* Fighting Angel *(1936);* The Exile *(1936);* Dragon Steel *(1942);* Imperial Woman *(1956);* The Child Who Never Grew *(1950);* The Townsman *(under the name John Sedges, 1945);* My Several Worlds *(autobiography, 1954)*
- *Died: Mar. 6, 1973, Danby, Vt.*

Pearl Buck was the first American woman to win the Nobel Prize for literature, an award bestowed primarily for her novel *The Good Earth,* published in 1931. As a famous author, she devoted much of her later life to a variety of humanitarian causes, especially those involved with disadvantaged children.

Pearl Sydenstricker was born in West Virginia to missionary parents, who took her to China with them when she was an infant. She returned to the United States to attend college and graduated from Randolph-Macon Woman's College in Virginia in 1914. Degree in hand, she went back to China, where she taught and married the missionary John Buck. While teaching in Nanking for 10 years, she published one novel, *East Wind, West Wind* (1930) before *The Good Earth* brought her international acclaim.

In 1992 the U.S. Postal Service honored Pearl Buck, winner of both Nobel and Pulitzer Prizes, on the 100th anniversary of her birth.

The Good Earth tells the story of a Chinese peasant woman and her family and is filled with deep sympathy for the lives Buck had witnessed from childhood on. It was subsequently made into a successful movie.

Moving back to the United States for good in 1934, Buck obtained a divorce and married her publisher, Richard Walsh. She continued to write, including the book *Of Men and Women,* which came out in 1941. In it Buck analyzed the plight of the American housewife in terms that anticipated much of what Betty Friedan would say in *The Feminine Mystique* in 1963. Buck said that American housewives were "starving at the sources" of their self-esteem because their lives were so undervalued.

FURTHER READING

Conn, Peter. *Pearl S. Buck: A Cultural Biography.* New York: Cambridge University Press, 1996.

La Farge, Ann. *Pearl Buck.* New York: Chelsea House, 1988.

Business

Even before women could vote, before married women could get credit in their own name, and before women had access to higher education, a small number of American women were involved in running businesses, sometimes quite successfully. Often women cooperated with their husbands in operating a tavern or a printing company, to name two types of businesses in which women were substantially involved. If the husband died, his widow might well have continued to run the business on her own. In the colonial period there was even a legal category known as *feme sole,* which meant a married woman (one who technically did not control property in her own name) who received permission from a court to operate as a single woman for business purposes.

A few women became *very* successful businesspeople in the 19th century. There was, for example, a Quaker woman named Rebecca Lukens who inherited and operated a profitable iron foundry in Pennsylvania in the years before the Civil War. When the war broke out, she received orders for iron from munitions companies. True to her pacifist Quaker principles, she refused to sell her product for the manufacture of weapons.

One of the most remarkable businesswomen in U.S. history was Madame C. J. Walker, who sold her hair-straightening preparations to African Americans throughout the country. The first black woman to become a millionaire, Walker invented her formula in 1905 and then launched a very aggressive campaign to market it. By the time of her death in 1919, she had built a town house in New York City and a villa on the Hudson River. She also engaged in very substantial giving and provided scholarships for black students and support for the National Association for the Advancement of Colored People.

Muriel Siebert was the first woman to become a member of the New York Stock Exchange, in 1967. Ten years later Ms. Siebert became New York State's first woman Superintendent of Banks, with responsibility for the soundness of all banks in the state. This was the highest position in banking supervision or regulation ever held by a woman.

For all the success of women like Lukens and Walker, the world of business did not represent opportunity for most women until the 1970s. Typically before this period, the woman employed in a business setting was a secretary. Although her job might have involved a great deal of responsibility, it was underpaid, and it was not a position from which one could be promoted to management level. A few women, such as Elizabeth Arden and Estee Lauder in cosmetics, launched successful businesses of their own.

Since the birth of the modern women's movement in the late 1960s, many things have improved for women in the business world. In the first place, the law has given married women access to credit in their own name so that they can more easily launch their own businesses. Legal change such as Title IX of the Education Act amendments of 1972, mandating affirmative action in university admissions, has given women much better access to business education than they ever had in the past.

Today a young woman who aspires to a business career can expect to attend a high-powered graduate school of business rather than secretarial school, as in the past. In 1992 women were 41.5 percent of all those employed in managerial, executive, and administrative positions, up from only 26.5 percent in 1978. Moreover, women-owned businesses currently employ 1 in 5 of American workers.

Yet scholars still speak of a "glass ceiling" for women in business that prevents women from rising to the very top. For all their progress, women are still infrequently found among the heads of major corporations and banking houses. People still tend to associate "male" traits such as drive and aggressiveness with business success, and that has held many women back, because if they are aggressive they are seen as unfeminine, and if they are not, they are seen as incompetent.

As of 1998 women still earned, on the average, only 76 percent of the average male wage. Yet this discouraging news is not the final word. In 1999, Carly Fiorina took charge of the Hewlett-Packard Corporation, a Silicon Valley, California, high-tech firm, thus becoming the first woman to head a Fortune 30 firm (one of the 30 biggest companies in the country). Her top subordinate in the firm is Ann Livermore, who heads the Enterprise computing division. In short, these women and the widespread admiration they enjoy may be signs that the glass ceiling is finally beginning to crack.

FURTHER READING

Kwolek-Folland, Angel. *Incorporating Women: A History of Women and Business in the United States.* New York: Twayne, 1998.

Cable Act (1922)

The Cable Act changed the basis for married women's citizenship. Prior to the passage of this law, a female U.S. citizen who married a foreign national forfeited her U.S. citizenship. (A man, however, could marry a noncitizen and still retain his U.S. nationality.) Moreover, the Cable Act required female noncitizens who married U.S. citizens to go through a naturalization process if they wanted to become U.S. citizens themselves. In short, the law went a long way toward allowing women to approach the issue of citizenship as independent individuals, the same as men.

SEE ALSO

Citizenship

Cabrini, Saint Frances Xavier

- *Born: July 15, 1850, Sant'Angelo Lodigiano, Italy*
- *Education: Teaching certificate, 1870*
- *Accomplishments: Founder, Missionary Sisters of the Sacred Heart (1880); founder of many schools, hospitals, and orphanages throughout the Americas; canonized Catholic saint (1946)*
- *Died: Dec. 22, 1917, Chicago, Ill.*

Mother Frances Cabrini was the first U.S. citizen to be canonized as a Roman Catholic saint. Born in Italy, she became a teacher and then a nun. In 1889 she came to the United States, concerned about the religious circumstances of the increasing number of Italian immigrants to these shores, where they worshipped at Catholic churches dominated by earlier-arriving Irish. Traveling back and forth between the United States and Italy, she brought over many other nuns and began establishing orphanages. She founded the order known as the Missionary Sisters of the Sacred Heart to further this purpose.

For many years Mother Cabrini traveled extensively, opening orphanages in several countries in Latin America and Europe as well as in U.S. cities. In 1909 she became a U.S. citizen. Eleven years after her death in 1917, the Catholic Church began considering her for possible sainthood. She was canonized in 1946.

FURTHER READING

Di Donato, Pietro. *Immigrant Saint: The Life of Mother Cabrini.* New York: St. Martin's, 1990.

Lorit, Sergio C. *Frances Cabrini: A Saint for America.* New York: New City Press, 1988.

Sullivan, Mary Louise. *Mother Cabrini, "Italian Immigrant of the Century."* New York: Center for Migration Studies, 1992.

Calamity Jane

SEE Cannary Burke, Martha Jane (Calamity Jane)

Cannary Burke, Martha Jane (Calamity Jane)

- *Born: May 1, 1852 (?), Princeton, Mo.*
- *Education: No formal education*
- *Accomplishments: Toured with Wild West shows (1895–1901)*
- *Died: Aug. 1, 1903, Terry, S.D.*

There were two Calamity Janes, one a legend and one a real woman. Sometimes their lives resembled one another, but not often.

Calamity Jane always claimed she had been secretly married to Wild Bill Hickok, legendary frontier marshal, and asked to be buried next to him (as she was). Here, dressed typically in men's clothes, she looks every bit the fiery renegade of myth.

The real woman, born Martha Jane Cannary, lived a rough life, working as a cook, dance-hall girl, and prostitute in various frontier areas in the 1860s and 1870s, where she was known to drink heavily and to shoot off her guns when she needed to blow off steam. She eventually settled in Deadwood, South Dakota. Her fondness for wearing male clothes gave her access to bars usually closed to women, and, unlike most of the frontier prostitutes, she frequently lived with one man for an extended period of time. She may have worked as a bull-whacker, whipping along teams of oxen as they crossed the plains. In 1891 she married hack driver Clinton Burke, but he soon left her.

But most of the other roles of the legendary Calamity Jane—Indian fighter, stagecoach driver, Pony Express rider—were probably inventions. In the years following the Civil War (1861–65), the American public was hungry for romance about the West. Magazine writers who were covering the colorful frontier life in Deadwood took some known facts about a real woman and embroidered them to come up with the character of Calamity Jane, a creature of dazzling exploits. Cannary Burke herself contributed to this mythical character with a pamphlet titled "Calamity Jane, Written by Herself" that she hawked in the last, poverty-ridden years of her life.

FURTHER READING

Casey, Robert J. *The Black Hills and Their Incredible Characters.* Indianapolis: Bobbs-Merrill, 1949.

Mumey, Nolie. *Calamity Jane, 1852–1903: A History of Her Life and Adventures in the West.* Denver: Range Press, 1950.

Carson, Rachel

- *Born: May 27, 1907, Springdale, Pa.*
- *Education: Pennsylvania College for Women, B.A., 1929; Johns Hopkins University, M.A., 1932*
- *Accomplishments: National Book Award for* The Sea Around Us *(1952); author,* Under the Sea Wind *(1941);* The Sea Around Us *(1951);* The Edge of the Sea *(1955);* Silent Spring *(1962)*
- *Died: Apr. 14, 1964, Silver Spring, Md.*

In 1962 Rachel Carson published *Silent Spring,* which alerted the American public to the environmental dangers posed by pesticides.

After graduating from Pennsylvania College for Women in 1929, Carson obtained a master's degree in biology from Johns Hopkins University and did postgraduate work at the Woods Hole Oceanographic Institution, a research center for marine biology in Massachusetts. In 1936 she obtained a job as an aquatic biologist with the U.S. Bureau of Fisheries, and in 1947 she became the editor in chief of publications at the U.S. Fish and Wildlife Service. Combining scientific training with literary skill, Carson published several books before *Silent Spring,* most notably *The Sea Around Us* about marine biology for a popular audience in 1951.

Rachel Carson did much of her biological research at Woods Hole, Massachusetts. In 1962 she would publish Silent Spring, *a book that helped launch the modern environmental movement.*

When Carson sounded the environmental alarm in 1962, many dismissed her as unduly worried, a silly, hysterical woman. She died before learning how fully she would be vindicated by subsequent research that proved that pesticides *are* harmful, and by the birth of an environmental movement that called for close monitoring of pesticides and took her as a prophet.

SEE ALSO

Environmental movement

FURTHER READING

Lear, Linda. *Rachel Carson: Witness for Nature.* New York: Holt, 1997.

Cassatt, Mary

- *Born: May 22, 1844, Allegheny City, Pa.*
- *Education: Pennsylvania Academy of Fine Arts, 1861–65*
- *Accomplishments: Showed paintings in many Paris Salon exhibits (1870s and 1880s); French Legion of Honor (1904)*
- *Died: June 14, 1926, Mesnil-Theribus, France*

Mary Cassatt was an American painter at a time when not many women were able to achieve careers in the visual arts.

When Cassatt was growing up, her well-to-do father took the family on a four-year-long trip to Europe. Having seen so much thrilling art in museums there, young Mary returned to the United States determined to become a painter. She studied briefly and unsatisfactorily—to her—in Pennsylvania and then received her family's reluctant permission to go to Paris for training in artists' studios. While in Europe, she also spent intensive periods of study in Italy and Spain. In 1872 one of her paintings was accepted for exhibition at the Paris Salon, her first major achievement and the mark that she was now a true professional.

Cassatt set herself up in Paris as a professional painter at a time when enormous changes in the French art world were taking place: a dazzling new group of artists, known as Impressionists, was experimenting with the effects of light and trying to paint their "impressions" of scenes using dots or small strokes of paint. Cassatt became friends with many Impressionists, especially with Edgar Degas, and exhibited in some of their shows, although her style diverged from theirs. In 1877 her parents and sister Lydia moved to Paris to join her.

Except for a few brief trips back to the United States, Cassatt spent the rest of her life in France. In addition to the European influences on her work, she also learned a great deal from Japanese prints she saw in Paris. In addition to her early mastery of impressionistic colors and pastels, she later explored various techniques of printmaking. Cassatt's most frequent subjects in her later, most mature work were mothers and children.

SEE ALSO

Painting

FURTHER READING

Barter, Judith F., ed. *Mary Cassatt, Modern Woman.* New York: Art Institute of Chicago/Abrams, 1998.

Pollock, Griselda. *Mary Cassatt: Painter of Modern Women.* New York: Thames and Hudson, 1998.

Cather, Willa Sibert

- *Born: Dec. 7, 1873, Back Creek Valley, Va.*
- *Education: University of Nebraska, B.A., 1895*
- *Accomplishments: Pulitzer Prize for* One of Ours, *1922; author,* Alexander's Bridge *(1912);* O Pioneers! *(1913);* The Song of the Lark *(1915);* My Antonia *(1918);* One of Ours *(1922);* A Lost Lady *(1923);* Death Comes for the Archbishop *(1927);* Lucy Gayheart *(1935);* Sapphira and the Slave Girl *(1940)*
- *Died: Apr. 24, 1947, New York, N.Y.*

As memorably as any American novelist, Willa Cather evoked the spirit of place, especially the Nebraska where she grew up, and the Southwest, with which she became acquainted and fell in love as an adult. Such books as *My Antonia, O Pioneers!, Death Comes to the Archbishop, A Lost Lady,* and *The Song of the Lark* are enduring classics.

Born in the backcountry of Virginia, young Willa moved to Nebraska

This 1936 portrait of Willa Cather is one of a series of celebrity portraits by photographer Carl Van Vechten. The photo, with Cather posed in front of a wall of books, seems to support her claim to be one of the outstanding literary figures of her generation.

with her family when she was nine. There she witnessed the struggles to survive in a harsh climate undertaken not only by her own family but also by neighboring immigrants from Bohemia, Germany, and Poland. Later, she would translate her memories into books.

Cather graduated from the University of Nebraska in 1895 and soon thereafter became a journalist, moving to New York in 1906. Between 1908 and 1912 she was managing editor of *McClure's* magazine, and in 1912 she published her first novel, *Alexander's Bridge*. From that time on, she supported herself with her fiction. In 1916 she went to New Mexico for the first time, returning in the 1920s. She won the Pulitzer Prize in 1922 for *One of Ours*.

Cather is especially interesting to modern scholars, because she played with her gender identity as a young woman, calling herself, for example, "Willie," and dressing in male clothes on some occasions. Today many lesbians claim her as a foremother, although her sexual orientation is not definitively known.

SEE ALSO
Literature

FURTHER READING

Ambrose, Jamie. *Willa Cather.* New York: St. Martin's, 1988.
Keene, Ann T. *Willa Cather.* New York: Messner, 1994.
O'Brien, Sharon. *Willa Cather: The Emerging Voice.* New York: Oxford University Press, 1987.

Catholics

With nearly 54 million members, the Roman Catholic Church is the largest single denomination in the United States today. The Church's positions on what women should believe, as well as on what role they should play in the Church, is no small matter.

Many of the early Church fathers took a dim view of women and of sexuality: Mary, the Virgin Mother of Christ could be exalted, but all other women, particularly non-virgins, were seen as a source of corruption because Eve tempted Adam and because of the widespread lack of understanding of sexuality and the workings of the female body. During succeeding centuries, the women who were canonized as saints were either unmarried or widowed. Nuns were required to hold themselves aloof from sexuality and to live in all-female convents. Priests—necessarily male—and monks were also required to be unmarried. Despite much change in church ritual over the centuries, residues of these attitudes still remain. Women are still excluded from the priesthood, and marriage remains forbidden for those who take religious orders.

During the height of the Church's power and influence in Western Europe, however, there *were* opportunities for women, although not on the same scale as for men. Women in convents may not have been able to marry, but they

Nuns in traditional habits and wimples preside over an outdoor meal at a California mission in the late 19th century. By 1900, Catholic sisters were teaching in almost 4,000 parochial schools and 700 academies for young women across the country.

could pursue learning to a remarkable extent. Some of the great learned doctors of the Church—Saint Teresa of Avila, who is known for her deeply pious writing, for example—have been female. A few of the female saints, such as Italy's Saint Catherine of Siena, enjoyed astonishing influence; in the 1300s she prevailed on the pope to return to Rome from France, where the papacy had then relocated. Catherine achieved her influence in part because of her extreme revulsion to the body and to sexuality, which made the Church feel that she was more spiritual.

By the time the American colonies were founded, the Catholic Church no longer enjoyed complete sway over Europe. Martin Luther had launched the Protestant Reformation in Germany, where in 1517 the established Church became Lutheran rather than Catholic, and England had become a Protestant power in the 1530s. As a result, the colonists who traveled to America were primarily Protestant, and the population would remain so until the large-scale immigration from Catholic Ireland and southern Europe from the mid-19th century onward. In the 20th century, large-scale immigration from Mexico and Central America has contributed to the Catholic population in the United States. About one-quarter of the U.S. population today is Catholic.

Despite the predominance of Protestantism in the early U.S., there was some growth of Catholicism from within the country rather than just from immigration. An important example is New York–born Elizabeth Ann Seton, who converted to Catholicism after travels in Italy, and founded the Sisters of Charity religious community in Baltimore in the early 1800s. When Catholics began to immigrate to the United States in large numbers in the 1840s, certain orders of nuns who immigrated too played an immensely valuable role in building schools and colleges, in teaching, and in providing social services to their fellow Catholics.

In the 1990s the Catholic Church is the largest institution opposing a woman's right to use birth control devices or to choose an abortion. Further, many other denominations now allow women to become clergywomen or rabbis, but the Catholics do not. There is now an important feminist Catholic critique of some Church stances, such as the opposition to women clergy, by women who are devout but who want their Church to respond more quickly to societal changes in the status of women.

SEE ALSO

Religion

Carrie Chapman Catt, the president of the National American Woman Suffrage Association, urged Congress to recognize the enormous contribution that women had made to the U.S. effort in World War I by giving them the right to vote. In the illustration on the cover, a soldier appeals to Uncle Sam on behalf of American women.

Catt, Carrie Chapman

- *Born: Jan. 9, 1859, Ripon, Wis.*
- *Education: Iowa State College (now University), B.A., 1880*
- *Accomplishments: First woman superintendent of schools (Mason City, Iowa, 1883); organizer, Iowa Woman Suffrage Association (1887–90); president, National American Woman Suffrage Association (1900–04, 1915–21); founder, National League of Women Voters (1921); founder (1925) and chair (1925–32), National Committee on the Cause and Cure of War*
- *Died: Mar. 9, 1947, New Rochelle, N.Y.*

Carrie Chapman Catt, a superb organizer, led the National American Woman Suffrage Association (NAWSA) at the moment of victory in 1920 when the 19th Amendment granted all American women the right to vote.

Young Carrie Lane grew up in Iowa, graduated from Iowa State College in 1880, became a teacher, and quickly rose to be superintendent of schools in Mason City. In 1885 she married newspaperman Leo Chapman, who died of typhoid fever in 1886. As a young widow, she began to support herself as a newspaper writer and a lecturer on women's issues and also became active in the Iowa woman suffrage movement. Her second marriage to George Catt in 1890 provided her with a supportive mate who was a fellow believer in woman suffrage—in fact, they had a prenuptial contract (unusual in those times) that provided her with four months every year of free time to work for woman suffrage.

Before too long Catt's many talents as a speaker and as a fund-raiser brought her to the attention of the aging suffragist leader Susan B. Anthony. In 1900 Anthony chose Catt to become her successor as the leader of NAWSA. Catt later resigned the position in 1904 because of her husband's poor health. George Catt died in 1905, leaving his widow comfortably well-off, and Carrie Chapman Catt henceforth devoted herself full-time to women's issues.

Catt returned to the national leadership of NAWSA in 1915. By this time the group had a new, militant rival in the struggle: the Congressional Union (it would become the National Woman's Party). While NAWSA worked behind the scenes, the members of the new group picketed the White House on behalf of suffrage. Catt had to make many tough political choices as well as handle internal strife within suffrage circles. When the United States entered World War I in April 1917, for example, she had to decide whether to support the war effort—which she did—or to support the pacifist convictions of many prominent women.

After the ratification of the 19th Amendment, Catt threw her energy into the newly formed League of Women Voters aimed at training women for citizenship.

SEE ALSO

League of Women Voters; National American Woman Suffrage Association (NAWSA); 19th Amendment

FURTHER READING

Fowler, Robert Booth. *Carrie Catt: Feminist Politician.* Boston: Northeastern University Press, 1986.

Van Voris, Jacqueline. *Carrie Chapman Catt: A Public Life.* New York: Feminist, 1987.

Chesnut, Mary Boykin Miller

- *Born: Mar. 31, 1823, Camden, S.C.*
- *Education: High school*
- *Accomplishments: Personal diary (excerpts published 1905, 1949; entire diary, 1981) provides vivid record of her era*
- *Died: Nov. 22, 1886, Camden, S.C.*

During the Civil War (1861–65), Confederate supporter Mary Boykin Chesnut kept a diary, and today it is one of our best sources of knowledge about the South during the Civil War in general and about the life of a well-to-do woman in particular.

The daughter of Stephen Decatur Miller, who was first the governor of South Carolina and then a U.S. senator from that state, Mary Boykin Miller married James Chesnut in 1840. He, too, was a successful politician, serving as a senator from South Carolina just before it seceded from the Union. During the Civil War, he was active politically in the Confederacy, too. Thus, all her life Mary Chesnut had a front-row seat for observing her society.

An ardent states' rights advocate—that is, one who believed that a state government had final authority over the federal government—and a Confederate loyalist, Chesnut was nonetheless critical of slavery, mostly from the point of view of the South's white women. As she wrote in her diary, "God forgive us, but ours is a monstrous system, a wrong and iniquity. Like the patriarchs of old, our men live all in one house with their wives and concubines; and the mulattoes one sees in every family partly resemble the white children." Moreover, in the diary she was unsparingly candid in her opinions about the prominent men around her. For all these reasons, her diary has fascinated several generations of readers.

FURTHER READING

Woodward, C. Vann, ed. *Mary Chesnut's Civil War.* New Haven: Yale University Press, 1981. [Annotated edition of her diary with a biographical essay]

Childbirth

For much of human history—that is until the 20th century—childbirth has been one of the riskiest of undertakings, dangerous for both the mother and the child. By modern standards there was an appalling loss of life so that, for example, a woman might bury half of her children in infancy. Moreover, women were able to control their fertility only haphazardly at best, so this painful and sometimes deadly experience was one that the average woman could expect to face many times in the course of her life. We know from the diaries of colonial American women, for example, that they feared childbirth for themselves and their daughters and prayed steadily for favorable results.

But if childbirth was frightening and dangerous in colonial America, it was also an experience of female solidarity: older women, usually including a midwife, a woman who specialized in attending at births, would gather to shepherd the new baby into the world. Many midwives were undoubtedly highly competent practitioners, and thus many women who had large families went on to enjoy long lives.

By the late 18th century, as the profession of medicine was growing and developing (and becoming an exclusively male occupation, which it remained until the mid-19th century), doctors began to take over more of the deliveries from midwives. This was a mixed blessing for their patients, because the doctors were all too often germ carriers themselves. Because the precise details of disease transmission were then unknown, a doctor would go from the bed of a person with a highly infectious disease straight to a woman giving birth—without necessarily washing his hands carefully in between. Many women succumbed to what was called childbed fever as a result.

In the mid-19th century, women began to experience profound changes in the nature of childbirth. In the first place, doctors began to use a variety of anesthetics to alleviate pain. Secondly, medical science began to develop a

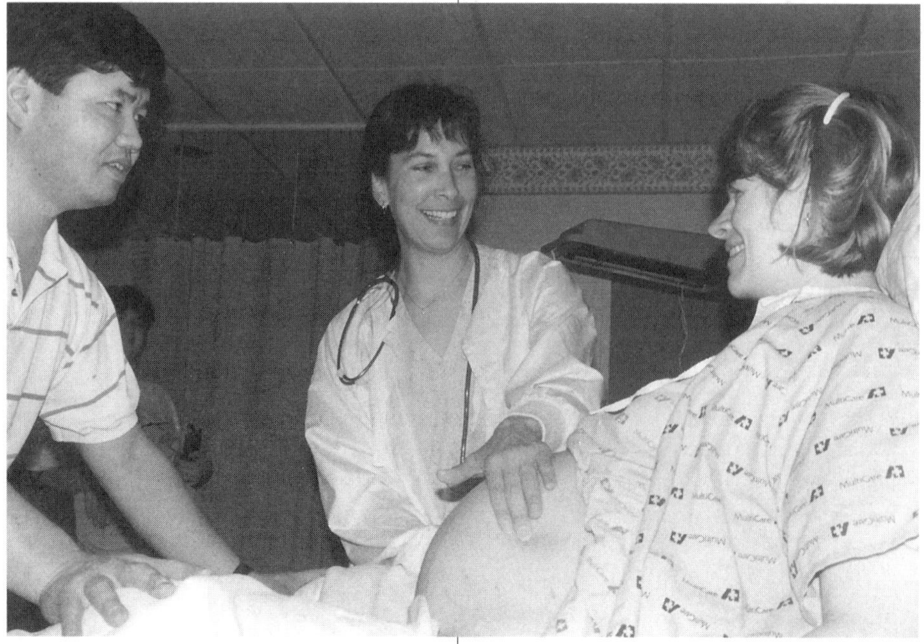

There has been a steady rise in the number of midwives delivering babies, from 3.7 percent of all births in 1989 to 7 percent in 1997. Midwifery focuses on the woman as a future mother, not just as a patient, and husbands are present as coaches.

sounder understanding of the origins of disease and the techniques to control its transmission. By the first decades of the 20th century, more and more babies were being born in hospitals—and the hospitals themselves were safer than earlier ones had been—and more and more babies and mothers were surviving their joint ordeal. Mortality rates declined markedly in the early 20th century.

Giving birth in a hospital had its problems, however: by the mid-20th century, childbirth had become an alienating experience for many women. Although the delivery was much safer than in the past, often the doctor and his expertise seemed to be the focus of attention rather than the mother and her feelings. One of the most successful reforms launched in the name of the modern women's movement has been to humanize the experience for mother, child, and other family members. Now the hospital staff is aware that a mother and baby need to bond and that the mother needs her friends and family around for support. Many hospitals allow friends and family in the delivery room and arrange for a baby to share a room with the new mother. In a sense, for many mothers childbirth has returned to being a community event.

Despite the greater sensitivity to the needs of the mother, modern American childbirth still involves more technology than in any other country in the world. Women in labor, for example, are routinely hooked up to electronic equipment that monitors the baby's heartbeat—a practice that reassures some women but disturbs others because it restricts their mobility during labor.

Not everyone in the United States, however, has access to good prenatal care and to medical care during the birth itself because it is costly. Poor women have much worse care than in other advanced industrial democracies, and as a consequence, the United States ranks only 21st in the world in its newborn survival rate.

SEE ALSO

Medicine; Midwifery

FURTHER READING

Leavitt, Judith Walzer. *Brought to Bed: Childbearing in America, 1750–1950.* New York: Oxford University Press, 1986.

Susie, Debra Anne. *In the Way of Our Grandmothers: A Cultural View of Twentieth-Century Midwifery in Florida.* Athens: University of Georgia Press, 1988.

Ulrich, Laurel Thatcher. *A Midwife's Tale.* New York: Knopf, 1990.

Child care

When both parents are employed outside the home, someone else must care for their young children. The governments of most advanced industrial countries in the world subsidize nonparental child care programs, because citizens in these countries believe that the whole society has a stake in seeing that children are well treated.

In the United States, on the other hand, there have been only a few brief experiments with federally supported child care, such as during World War II (1941–45). Even during this national emergency, when Congress passed the Lanham Act setting up 3,100 nurseries, only a small fraction of the children of those performing war work were in such a nursery. Later, during the 1960s as part of President Lyndon Johnson's War on Poverty, Congress established the Head Start program for poor children, a worthy effort but nothing like the scale of public support for child care

The availability of quality child care is a necessity for mothers who work outside the home. Typically, such child care centers are run by other women.

in most highly industrialized countries. In the final two decades of the 20th century, some corporations have launched programs to provide child care within the company for parents who work there, as a way of increasing employee productivity by decreasing stress about child care and other needs.

The United States has been so resistant to publicly supported child care partly because of the influence of religious conservatives, who believe that mothers should stay home with their children and therefore do not want to encourage women to take jobs outside of the home. Another factor, no doubt, has been the powerful strain of individualism in American culture, which places a high value on solving one's own problems, rather than looking to the government for solutions.

Whatever the reason for the lack of public support for child care in the United States, there is widespread agreement that the current situation—in which millions of families scramble to provide adequate child care on their own—does not work well.

FURTHER READING

Rose, Elizabeth R. *A Mother's Job: The History of Day Care, 1890–1960.* New York: Oxford University Press, 1999.

Childhood

The experience of being a child in the United States has changed dramatically over the generations. In the colonial period the family was much less democratic than it would later become, and children were subject to the possibly stern authority of their parents, especially their fathers. Families were large, though the high infant mortality rate made it likely that even a mother who had given birth to many children would not be surrounded by a large number of them.

Households were productive units in which even quite young children had roles to play in the work going on around them: for example, a girl might have helped with child care or with churning butter. In this deeply religious world, children could also expect to spend a great deal of time in church, where, if it had not already occurred to them to worry, they would be reminded about how likely it was that they would die an early death. In colonial times, childhood was neither sentimentalized nor protected as it would later be.

Beginning in the late 1700s, both childhood and motherhood started to enjoy more value owing to changes in Protestantism, and the quintessential democratic American family began to emerge to mirror the new republic. Family size began to decrease, and as a result the emotional bonds within the family became ever more intense, and middle-class children began to be treated more like the family jewels than the family workhorses.

In the 19th century, communities and states passed laws creating the first systems of public education. For children outside the middle class—slave children, for example, or working-class children of immigrant parents—childhood continued to be a time of hard, sometimes dangerous, labor.

In the 20th century child labor was abolished, owing to tremendous struggles by reformers over many decades. The Supreme Court having struck down earlier legislation, Congress passed the Fair Labor Standards Act in 1938, which contained provisions forbidding child labor. Further, women activists pressured for the formation of a federal Children's Bureau, established in 1912, to oversee and promote the welfare of children through programs addressing issues such as child labor exploitation, child abuse, and foster homes and adoption.

The century has also seen the continuing shrinkage of family size together with high rates of divorce, with the consequence that many children are now being raised in, by older standards, startlingly small households, perhaps by single mothers.

Though child labor has disappeared and the infant mortality rate has gone down, there are still threats to the well-being of children. Most serious is the plight of those born to poor families who cannot afford good nutrition, good health care, and decent housing. Government agencies have calculated that some 23 percent of American children under age six live below the poverty line. Another serious problem is the lack of adequate child care for children whose parents work. The United States lags behind most of the industrialized world in providing publicly supported child care, and parents must come up with their own solutions.

SEE ALSO

Child care; Children's Bureau, U.S.; Industrialization

FURTHER READING

Reinier, Jacqueline. *From Virtue to Character: American Childhood, 1775-1850.* New York: Twayne, 1996.

Schmitt, Eric. "Day-Care Quandary: A Nation at War With Itself." *New York Times,* January 11, 1998.

Child, Julia McWilliams

- *Born: Aug. 15, 1912, Pasadena, Calif.*
- *Education: Smith College, B.A., 1934*
- *Accomplishments: Co-founder, L'Ecole des Trois Gourmandes (1951); creator of various T.V. cooking shows:* The French Chef *(premiered 1962),* Julia Child and Company *(premiered 1978),* Dinner at Julia's *(premiered 1983),* Baking with Julia *(premiered 1996); author,* Mastering the Art of French Cooking *(1961);* From Julia Child's Kitchen *(1975);* Julia Child & Company *(1978);* Julia Child and More Company *(1979);* The Way to Cook *(1989);* Julia Child's Menu Cookbook *(1991);* Cooking with Master Chefs *(1993);* Julia's Menus for Special Occasions *(1998);* The

French Chef Cookbook *(1998);* Julia's Delicious Little Dinners *(1998);* Julia and Jacques Cooking at Home *(1999);* Julia's Breakfasts, Lunches, and Suppers *(1999);* Julia's Beautiful Informal Meals *(1999)*

A woman who led a revolution in how Americans cook by popularizing French cuisine, Julia Child also wrote and talked knowledgeably about elaborate cookery, staking out her claim to turf that had been male-dominated for centuries.

Born and raised in California, young Julia McWilliams went east to college, graduating from Smith College in 1934. After the United States entered World War II in 1941, she joined the Office of Strategic Services, hoping to become a spy. Instead, she became a file clerk—but one who was sent to exotic locations abroad. Posted to Ceylon (now Sri Lanka), she met the love of her life, Paul Child. He was older than she, sophisticated—and he loved good food. The daughter of a well-to-do family, Julia McWilliams had never paid much attention to what went on in the kitchen. She suddenly had a very strong incentive to learn.

The war ended in 1945, and the couple returned to the United States, where they married in 1946. Paul Child then joined the U.S. Foreign Service and was sent to France for six years. Accompanying her husband, Julia Child took the opportunity to become an even more proficient cook by attending Le Cordon Bleu cooking school in Paris. As it happened, she took to her studies with great aptitude and enthusiasm. Before too much longer she had started a cooking school of her own with two French women, Simone Beck and Louise Bertholle. In 1961 the three published a book aimed at an American audience, *Mastering the Art of French Cooking.* Reviewers acclaimed it as the best and most authoritative treatment of its subject for its time.

With television programs and cookbooks, Julia Child introduced Americans to the principles of classic French cooking, a field that had traditionally been dominated by male chefs. In this 1971 cooking show, she instructs her television audience in preparing a curry dinner.

As well-received as the cookbook was, Julia Child owes her celebrity not to it but to the television show that followed. Having returned to the U.S., the Childs settled in Cambridge, Massachusetts. Impressed by the success of the cookbook, WGBH in Boston asked Child to appear on a new cooking program, "The French Chef." Quite simply, the new star captivated TV audiences with her offbeat charm as she reassured people that they could be French chefs, too. Once, for example, she spent considerable time and effort on the air wrestling with a lobster that didn't want to be boiled.

Since then, Child has published many more cookbooks and appeared on many more television programs. Her husband died in 1994, but she has continued with her work, not only popularizing good food but also lending her name and energy to efforts to preserve the history of cuisine.

SEE ALSO
Cooking

FURTHER READING

Fitch, Noel Riley. *Appetite for Life: The Biography of Julia Child.* New York: Doubleday, 1997.

Child, Lydia Maria

- *Born: Feb. 11, 1802, Medford, Mass.*
- *Education: Little formal education*
- *Accomplishments: Founder,* Juvenile Miscellany *(periodical for children, 1826); editor,* National Anti-Slavery Standard *(1841–43); author,* Hobomok *(1824);* The Frugal Housewife *(1829);* An Appeal in Favor of That Class of Americans Called Africans *(1833);* Fact and Fiction *(1846);* The Freedmen's Book *(1865);* An Appeal for Indians *(1868)*
- *Died: Oct. 20, 1880, Wayland, Mass.*

One of the leading lights of a remarkable generation of reformers in 19th-century New England, Lydia Maria Child was a domestic advice writer, an ardent antislavery advocate, and a journalist.

Lacking the opportunity to obtain a college education—none was available for women in her day—Lydia Maria Francis was able to educate herself because she loved to read. She published her first novel, *Hobomok,* when she was in her early 20s. This tale of the love between a white woman and a noble Indian established her as a writer. In 1828 she married fellow writer David Child, and in 1829 she published a very successful book of advice, *The Frugal Housewife,* which offered suggestions such as "Look frequently to the pails, to see that nothing is thrown to the pigs which should have been in the grease-pot. Look to the grease-pot and see that nothing is there which might have served to nourish your family, or a poorer one."

Child's life might have proceeded along a somewhat predictable path for a married woman writer except for two things. In the first place, her husband was always impractical, so she had to be the main breadwinner. In the second place, she had fiery beliefs about the evils of slavery, beliefs that led her to publish an early exposé called *An Appeal in Favor of That Class of Americans Called Africans.* With this trumpet blast, she created a furor even in Boston (which would later become more friendly to antislavery views).

Lydia Maria Child had a literary career that spanned many decades. Early in her career, she wrote a best-selling book of domestic advice, but she also wrote impassioned denunciations of the evils of slavery.

Unlike some of the other women abolitionists, Child never took to the lecture platform, but hers was always one of the most powerful literary voices calling out for human freedom. In the 1850s, as the slavery crisis between North and South deepened, she wrote pieces for the *New York Tribune* that reached tens of thousands of readers and helped shape public opinion.

SEE ALSO

Abolitionism

FURTHER READING

Karcher, Carolyn L. *The First Woman in the Republic: A Cultural Biography of Lydia Maria Child.* Durham, N.C.: Duke University Press, 1994.

Matthews, Glenna. "'Little Women' Who Helped Make This Big War." In *Why the Civil War Came.* Edited by Gabor Boritt. New York: Oxford University Press, 1996.

Osborne, William S. *Lydia Maria Child.* Boston: Twayne, 1980.

Children's Bureau, U.S.

When Congress established the Children's Bureau within the Department of Commerce and Labor in 1912, it was a significant victory for women reformers. Indeed, this was the first time in American history that women had "a bureau of their own" within the federal government, one for which they had lobbied and that they would largely staff themselves. The former settlement-house worker Julia Lathrop was appointed by the President to be the first head of the Children's Bureau.

The Children's Bureau's purposes of promoting child and maternal health and welfare came about because, beginning in the 1880s, middle-class women had been going into slum neighborhoods where they would observe the need for greater government involvement in this area. From these settlement-house women and their networking activities came the vision of publicly supported programs for child protection focusing on improved health for mothers and babies and on the abolition of child labor. The founding of the bureau showed that male politicians were listening to women's call for a national program.

Historians now debate how much real good the elite women in these networks did; because they were so convinced that they knew what was best for working-class families, whose members might, for example, have been eager to hold onto the wages of their children. Probably the Bureau's greatest success came with the crusade to bring down the maternal and infant mortality rate by improving hygiene, nutrition, and medical practice for pregnant women and then for women and their babies after the delivery. In the years before 1946, when it was shut down, the Bureau gathered scientific knowledge about such issues and then published pamphlets that spread the knowledge throughout the country.

SEE ALSO

Settlement-house movement

FURTHER READING

Lindenmeyer, Kriste. *A Right to Childhood: The U.S. Children's Bureau and Child Welfare, 1912–46.* Urbana: University of Illinois Press, 1997.

Muncy, Robyn. *Creating a Female Dominion.* New York: Oxford University Press, 1991.

Chisholm, Shirley

- *Born: Nov. 30, 1924, Brooklyn, N.Y.*
- *Education: Brooklyn College, B.A., 1946; Columbia University, M.A., 1952*
- *Accomplishments: Representative (Democrat–Brooklyn), N.Y. state legislature (1964–68); U.S. Representative (Democrat–N.Y., 1969–83); Purington Professor, Mount Holyoke College (1983–87)*

The first African-American woman to serve in Congress, Shirley Chisholm has played a ground-breaking role throughout her life.

Born in Brooklyn, Chisholm graduated from Brooklyn College and then obtained a master's degree from Columbia University. She taught and served as the director of a day-care center before deciding to run for the New York state

In 1972 Shirley Chisholm, a congresswoman from Brooklyn, ran unsuccessfully for President in a race that mobilized many African-American women to become involved in politics. Originally elected in 1968, Chisholm was the first black woman to serve in Congress.

legislature in 1964. After two terms there, she decided to try for the U.S. House of Representatives.

Chisholm's run for Congress in 1968 was historic for more than one reason. Not only would she be the first black woman in the House, but she was also a pioneer in targeting women voters as a constituency. Earlier, women running for public office had frequently downplayed their gender, afraid to turn off male voters. According to her autobiography, Chisholm's Republican opponent that year was suggesting that she was a "bossy female," and one of her campaign workers realized that this strategy could be made to backfire, because far more women than men were registered to vote in her district.

Chisholm won the election and served with distinction for several terms. While in Congress, she became known for her opposition to weapons development and to the Vietman War, and for her support of full-employment proposals. In 1972 she ran for the Democratic nomination for the Presidency. Although she did not win the nomination—indeed never had a chance of so doing—her decision to run played a big role in mobilizing black women around the country to get involved in politics.

SEE ALSO

Congress, U.S.; Politics

FURTHER READING

Chisholm, Shirley. *Unbought and Unbossed.* Boston: Houghton Mifflin, 1970.

Chopin, Kate O'Flaherty

- *Born: Feb. 8, 1851, St. Louis, Mo.*
- *Education: St. Louis Academy of the Sacred Heart, graduated 1868*
- *Accomplishments: Author,* At Fault: A Novel *(1890);* Bayou Folk *(1894);* A Night in Acadie *(1897);* The Awakening *(1899);* A Vocation and a Voice *(1991)*
- *Died: Aug. 22, 1904, St. Louis, Mo.*

The daughter of an Irish immigrant father and a French Creole mother, Kate O'Flaherty Chopin wrote fiction set in late 19th-century Louisiana in a voice unlike anyone else's. Her vivid, sensual prose brings the region alive. Her favored theme of the relationship between love and personal fulfillment for a woman makes her writing seem startlingly modern.

After marrying the New Orleans merchant Oscar Chopin in 1870, Kate Chopin quickly gave birth to six children. She also read widely and was especially drawn to the French literature of her day, which she could read in the original, because her mother had spoken French. Her husband died in 1882, and she returned to her mother's St. Louis home. A few years after her mother died in 1885, Chopin began to publish.

The author of many fine short stories, Chopin is best known today for her novel *The Awakening,* published in 1899. A daring story of an unhappily married woman and her search for happiness, the work attracted much criticism at the time because the heroine had an adulterous affair. Her editors subsequently suspended publication of her last collection of short stories, *A Vocation and a Voice,* which was not published until 1991. Chopin died of a brain hemorrhage in 1904.

FURTHER READING

Toth, Emily. *Kate Chopin.* New York: Morrow, 1990.

Cities

When the United States was founded, the overwhelming majority of Americans lived on farms. Now the reverse is true: most people live in towns, suburbs, or cities. The national census of 1920 was the first time that researchers found more people in towns than on farms, the result of a long-term trend toward urbanization that has progressed steadily since 1800.

As more Americans moved into towns and cities, the lives of women changed dramatically. The many women's clubs and reform societies that began to be founded in the early 19th century, for example—out of which came the woman suffrage movement—could only have happened when clusters of women lived in town, where they were close enough to meet regularly. And town-dwelling women had the time to devote to churches and voluntary societies, because they could purchase such items as soap rather than making most things by hand as farm women did.

The pace of urbanization quickened in the years after the Civil War (1861–65) as millions of immigrants began arriving in U.S. cities. The newcomers encountered such problems as overcrowded and unsanitary apartments known as tenements, where women had to keep house for their families under difficult conditions. If they worked outside the home, they often had poorly paid jobs in factories—or maybe they did sewing piecework at home, which was even more poorly paid. In some city neighborhoods, people lived near the filthy waste of the stockyards or garbage dumps. Seeing—and deploring—the hardships endured by immigrant families in big cities, some middle-class women, such as Jane Addams in Chicago and Lillian Wald in New York, founded settlement houses in immigrant neighborhoods where they could work to improve the newcomers' lives.

Increasingly in the years since World War II, middle-class Americans have fled to the suburbs, leaving crowded inner cities that have often become the site of poverty and hopelessness for those left behind.

Beginning in the 1960s and 70s, however, this trend began to be counteracted by grassroots and government-level efforts mounted to improve the quality of life in major cities. By the end of the 20th century, parks had been built and land set aside for community gardens; city revitalization projects had fostered the creation of public plazas and other spaces set aside, indoors and out, for public events such as free concerts, theater productions, and community sports team use. In many cases these improvements crossed class lines, making the lives of women with children easier by giving children safe places to play, and programs to participate in after school. But it is difficult in spaces with such vast populations with widely varying needs to help everyone all the time. Most cities have a wide gap between the wealthy consumers of luxury goods on the grand avenues and shopping streets and the third-shift workers struggling to support their families.

The second half of the 20th century also saw the construction of housing projects that marginalized lower-income families in overpopulated neighborhoods with insufficient support services and little new development, giving rise to pockets of crime.

In spite of improvements in the quality of life in American cities, there are constant new arrivals, success and failure in business and government, and rises and falls in the economy that promote incessant change. As in the late 19th century, big cities challenge society to find compassionate and imaginative ways of dealing with urban problems created by poverty, joblessness, and despair.

SEE ALSO

Addams, Jane; Settlement-house movement; Wald, Lillian

FURTHER READING

Chudacoff, Howard P. *The Evolution of American Urban Society.* Englewood Cliffs, N.J.: Prentice Hall, 1988.

Goldfield, David R. *Urban America: A History.* Boston: Houghton Mifflin, 1990.

Citizenship

Most Americans take it for granted that women are citizens the same as men. Women's path to full citizenship, however, has been long and winding and has involved far more than winning the right to vote with the 19th Amendment in 1920.

When the new nation came into being under the Constitution in 1789, according to the tradition of English common law—the basis for the legal system in the colonies—a husband controlled the body of his wife, to which he wanted unrestricted physical access. She could not be held responsible in the same way as a man, because if she were, her husband might forfeit his right to her body—that is, if she were jailed for debt, he would lose her domestic and sexual services. Since this assumption was so powerful, a married woman's citizenship was filtered through her husband's. He could probably vote and serve on juries, but she could not. Nor did she have any right to control her own property or to determine where the couple might live. Together, these restrictions are known as the doctrine of coverture.

There is only one woman student in this 1921 class preparing for U.S. citizenship. It was not until 1922 that the Cable Act gave each woman a nationality of her own; before then, the citizenship of a woman was determined by that of her husband.

Beginning in the late 1830s, some states began to pass reforms that allowed married women to own their own property. Then came the woman suffrage movement, which took many decades to achieve victory. Ratification in 1868 of the 14th Amendment, which granted citizenship to ex-slaves, offered the promise of helping women also achieve full citizenship because it spelled out the access to and privileges of citizenship more fully than ever before. But that promise would not be fully realized for 100 years.

Even after women received the right to vote in 1920, many more reforms would need to be made before all women were equal citizens. The Cable Act of 1922, for example, made it possible for an American woman to marry a foreign national without forfeiting her own citizenship (a right men already had). In 1952 women and men from Asia gained the right to become naturalized citizens for the first time.

In 1971 in the *Reed* v. *Reed* decision, which dealt with the laws of executorship, the U.S. Supreme Court applied the 14th Amendment, with its citizenship provisions, to gender discrimination for the first time, overturning a case in which a father had automatically been made the executor of a son's estate. Both parents, who were separated, had applied for the right.

It was not until 1975 that the Supreme Court unequivocally gave women in every state the same right to serve on juries as men.

Since long before the settling of America, there had been two main routes to citizenship (for men): through the bearing of arms or through the ownership of property. That is, men who fought for their country or who were landowners were seen as having the necessary independence of will to enjoy the privileges of voting and other aspects of citizenship. Women, however, had neither of these options available to them when they began their drive for the vote, so they had to wage a prolonged campaign of protest instead. Due in part to these protests, laws and judicial decisions now have given married women the right to control their own property, and women can even join the military—although still not on quite the same basis as men due to differences in combat status.

SEE ALSO

Cable Act (1922); 14th Amendment; Married Women's Property Acts; 19th Amendment; *Reed* v. *Reed* (1971); Suffrage, woman

FURTHER READING

Bredbenner, Candice Lewis. *A Nationality of Her Own.* Berkeley: University of California Press, 1998.

Kerber, Linda. *No Constitutional Right to Be Ladies: Women and the Obligations of Citizenship.* New York: Hill & Wang, 1998.

Civil Rights Act (1964)

Though designed as a remedy for discrimination against African Americans, the Civil Rights Act of 1964 has also proven to be of immense value to women. This is because Title VII of the act, the employment provision, bars discrimination on the basis of sex as well as of race. The law made it illegal to put women at a disadvantage in hiring, benefits, or promotion practices.

It was Howard Smith, a southern Congressman, who introduced the word *sex* into Title VII, apparently because he wanted to see the whole effort go down to defeat and thought he could make it look ridiculous by adding language about discrimination against women to the bill. Very quickly a group of women led by Democratic Congresswoman Martha Griffiths of Michigan seized the opportunity to push for the inclusion of sex as a serious part of what the bill encompassed. The legislation passed. The new act set up an Equal Employment Opportunity Commission (EEOC) to monitor enforcement and to hear complaints.

It soon became clear that the EEOC initially had far less interest in discrimination against women than against people of color. As a result, a group of feminists founded the National Organization for Women in 1966 to press for enforcement of the new law. Women also took Title VII claims to court, winning cases having to do with gender discrimination in the workplace, for example, that brought major reforms to the American legal system.

SEE ALSO
Law; National Organization for Women (NOW)

Civil rights movement

The civil rights movement refers to the struggle for African-American rights and equality in the 1950s and 1960s. Women played a role in that struggle that is still underappreciated, because certain male leaders—above all, Martin Luther King, Jr.—received so much attention and because women's contributions were so often "invisible."

Beginning in the late 19th century, southern and border states passed laws requiring the segregation of schools, public accommodations, and transportation. So thoroughgoing was the system in its heyday that, in the most profoundly segregated states, blacks and whites even swore on different Bibles in court. The U.S. Supreme Court had stated in the *Plessy* v. *Ferguson* decision of 1896 that segregation was permissible as long as the facilities for African Americans were "separate but equal."

Another problem for black people in the South was the fact that they had been effectively disenfranchised by a combination of terror and legal means such as poll taxes to make voting difficult. Discouraged from voting, blacks were more vulnerable to poor treatment by those who were prepared to take advantage of their weak position: in a democracy, those without a vote lack the most basic means of exercising their citizenship and can't, for example, have a voice in choosing a local sheriff.

From the early 20th century and the founding of the National Association for the Advancement of Colored People (NAACP), civil rights crusaders began taking legal steps to challenge segregation. Early court victories for the NAACP include a 1917 decision that declared unconstitutional a Louisville ordinance that required blacks to live in certain parts of the city, and a 1923 decision stating that blacks could not be excluded from juries. World War II (1941–45) accelerated a change in racial attitudes, because it created so much economic opportunity for African Americans. This economic opportunity for blacks led to changed attitudes on the part of whites because they were all forced to work side by side for the same cause.

When the war ended in 1945, a new mood emerged among blacks: they were determined to demolish segregation in the South. The NAACP brought many lawsuits to change the status quo, the best known of which was *Brown* v. *Board of Education of Topeka, Kansas* (1954), in which the U.S. Supreme Court struck down the earlier *Plessy* v. *Ferguson* doctrine and declared that the racial segregation of schools was unconstitutional.

Women were on the front lines of the civil rights movement from its earliest days. These demonstrators, jailed in Raleigh, North Carolina, in 1963, clap hands together in their cell.

Women stood shoulder to shoulder with men in taking the risks required to end Jim Crow, as the system of segregation was called. In 1955 seamstress Rosa Parks boarded a bus in Montgomery, Alabama, and refused to surrender her seat to a white person. This incident triggered the Montgomery bus boycott, during which black riders walked or joined car pools instead of riding the city buses. Other women helped create and sustain the boycott by disseminating notices about it and by walking to work and avoiding the bus system. Ella Baker, less well known than some of the men, launched the Student Nonviolent Coordinating Committee, which mobilized rural communities as did no other organization.

Many a female student walked through a crowd of taunting, spitting whites so as to desegregate a school. At the grassroots, local level, women registered voters—frequently a hazardous undertaking because of threats from whites—fed northern civil rights activists, and kept hope alive with their courage and religious faith in troubled times. A white woman named Viola Liuzzo paid with her life for her activism. She had gone south from Detroit to work for social justice and was driving in a car with an African American when she was shot and killed by Ku Klux Klansmen who had followed them.

By the time that the movement slowed down after the assassinations of Martin Luther King, Malcolm X, and the two Kennedy brothers in the 1960s, there had been immense change in the law, in judicial decisions, and in attitudes. Moreover, many female civil rights activists—black and white alike—had discovered a power to force change that they had never known they had.

SEE ALSO

Baker, Ella; Parks, Rosa McCauley

FURTHER READING

Crawford, Vicki, Jacqueline Rouse, and Barbara Woods, eds. *Women in the Civil Rights Movement.* Bloomington: Indiana University Press, 1993.

Dunn, John M. *The Civil Rights Movement.* San Diego, Calif.: Lucent Books, 1998.

Civil War

During the Civil War—which raged from 1861 to 1865 and took the lives of more than 600,000 men (thus making it the most deadly war the United States has ever fought)—more women were more involved in public activities than at any previous time in American history. This is a story that is still unknown to most Americans.

When the war came, both black and white northern women had a well-established network of clubs, and many also had a growing habit of activism, including antislavery activism. Therefore, it is not surprising that Union women quickly organized to raise funds and gather supplies for wounded and sick soldiers. In the South, the tradition of female activism was less developed, because it was a far more conservative region, but there, too, women organized for humanitarian and patriotic purposes. On both sides women had to keep farms and businesses running without their husbands' help.

The heroic nurse Clara Barton has found a well-deserved place in most history books as the founder of the American Red Cross. There were, however, many other still-unknown heroines, women who devoted themselves tirelessly to activities that had previously been completely outside of their experiences. One such woman was Chicago's Mary Livermore. She and her colleague

This bronze and granite monument in Washington, D.C., honors the nuns who served as nurses during the Civil War. Each of the 12 figures represents a religious order that sent nuns to the soldiers' aid.

Jane Hoge ran the local office of the U.S. Sanitary Commission (an organization which owed its very existence to female prompting), which had been established in 1861 to inspect and improve the general conditions (from clothing and food to ventilation and sewage treatment) under which soldiers lived in their camps. In this position they coordinated a vast midwestern web of women's groups that were sewing for the men recovering in hospitals.

Because money was always in short supply, Livermore and Hoge conceived the idea of a Sanitary Fair—a giant craft show—to raise funds for their work, an idea copied in other parts of the country. All in all they shipped nearly 80,000 packets of pajamas and other supplies for invalids to hospitals, with a cash value estimated at more than $1 million. When the war ended, Livermore became a dedicated women's rights activist.

Other women worked as nurses—at a time when there was no formal training for nurses—they foraged for food for the wounded, they agitated for President Abraham Lincoln to free the slaves, they raised money on an enormous scale, and a few even put on male clothes and fought. A few also spied for the cause they believed in, whether North or South—Confederate sympathizers Belle Boyd and Rose O'Neal Greenhow and abolitionist Elizabeth ("Crazy Betsy") Van Lew were some of the better known. After the war, many who had been active revised their earlier ambitions, becoming better educated or more activist than what they might originally have planned for their lives.

SEE ALSO

Barton, Clara; Confederate women

FURTHER READING

Clinton, Catherine. *Civil War Stories.* Athens: University of Georgia Press, 1998.

———. *The Other Civil War: American Women in the Nineteenth Century.* New York: Hill & Wang, 1984.

———. *Tara Revisited: Women, War, and the Plantation Legend.* New York: Abbeville, 1995.

Clinton, Catherine, and Nina Silber, eds. *Divided Houses: Gender and the Civil War.* New York: Oxford University Press, 1992.

Faust, Drew Gilpin. *Mothers of Invention: Women of the Slaveholding South in the American Civil War.* Chapel Hill: University of North Carolina Press, 1996.

Matthews, Glenna. *The Rise of Public Woman.* New York: Oxford University Press, 1992.

Clinton, Hillary Rodham

- *Born: Oct. 26, 1947, Chicago, Ill.*
- *Education: Wellesley College, B.A., 1969; Yale Law School, J.D., 1973*
- *Accomplishments: Director, Arkansas School of Law legal-aid clinic (1974–77); twice named one of the nation's most influential lawyers by* National Law Journal *(1988, 1991); First Lady, 1992–*

In 1998 Hillary Rodham Clinton attended a conference on Women of the 21st Century in Sofia, Bulgaria. As First Lady she traveled widely promoting issues of particular concern to women and children.

As First Lady, Hillary Rodham Clinton has been the most activist—and the most controversial—Presidential wife since Eleanor Roosevelt in the 1930s and 1940s. Moreover, Clinton has been the first to have a full-fledged career.

As a young girl, Hillary Rodham followed the Republican allegiance of her parents—she was a Goldwater girl in 1964. But by the time she reached Wellesley College, from which she graduated in 1969, the student movement of the 1960s was well underway, and she had become a Democrat. Like many other idealistic young people of her generation, such as her husband-to-be Bill Clinton, she became deeply engaged with the country's social problems, paying particular attention to the plight of poor children. After Wellesley, she attended Yale Law School—from which she graduated in 1973—and there she met fellow student Bill Clinton.

Hillary Rodham was for a brief time in the mid-1970s an attorney for the Watergate committee investigating the misdeeds of President Richard Nixon. Then she worked for the Children's Defense Fund, an advocacy group that works for the rights of children. But in 1975 she married Bill Clinton and moved with him to his home state of Arkansas, where he quickly threw himself into politics. He became governor of Arkansas in 1978, and from that moment on, his wife alternated her official duties with work for the Rose Law Firm. During these years, she developed a reputation as having one of the best legal minds in the country.

Even during her husband's first run for the Presidency in 1992, Clinton found herself with more than one outbreak of bad press. At one point she said offhandedly to a reporter that she had not wanted to stay home and "bake cookies." That comment drew widespread criticism, because it seemed to demean stay-at-home mothers. She also had to decide how to deal with her husband's infidelities, presenting a steely dignity to the public eye.

As First Lady, Clinton has had fierce critics and equally fierce defenders. Her critics point to her failure in trying to get Congress to pass health-care reform legislation and accuse her of meddling—because she was not the one who had been elected to office. Her defenders say that it would be a shame to waste her talents and point to the usefulness of her trips abroad, which have raised the visibility for such causes as female literacy in Third World countries. In the wake of the Monica Lewinsky scandal, she has become a much more popular figure: many speculate that she will go on to have an illustrious political career of her own. What is clear is that she has had a major impact on the role of the First Lady. It is unlikely that any of her successors will be as low-profile as most of her predecessors.

FURTHER READING

Clinton, Hilary Rodham. *It Takes a Village: And Other Lessons Children Teach Us*. New York: Simon & Schuster, 1996.

Clothing

SEE Bloomer, Amelia Jenks; Sewing

Clubs, women's

From very early in American history, people have organized into clubs. European travelers have often, in fact, commented on Americans' fondness for joining organizations. Men and women, people from many different racial, class, or ethnic backgrounds—all have formed their own religious, social, educational, political, professional, and charitable organizations. Such clubs have been especially important for women, because they were forbidden—both legally and informally—access to so many other public activities. Joining a club has often been a woman's first step into a lifetime of activism.

President Calvin Coolidge welcomed members of the New York Women's Republican Club to the White House in 1924. After gaining the vote in 1920, women gained increasing influence in national politics.

Women's clubs were first formed in the 1790s when groups of black and white women each organized for religious purposes, for poor relief, or for helping orphans. When a group of women gathered together, however, they often used the opportunity to talk about what was wrong with American society and what they could do to change it. Many northern women, for example, gained their commitment to abolishing slavery from meeting and talking in such groups.

Women's clubs were also important because they allowed women to assume leadership roles. In a society in which there was no tradition of female leadership in public, the simple act of chairing a meeting required courage and led to personal growth. As club members, women also had to go into society and raise money from businessmen and meet with government officials, becoming part of the public sphere.

Over the decades, women's clubs have crusaded to abolish slavery, to prevent the abuse of alcohol, to improve schools, and to advance the cause of suffrage and other women's rights. Other women's clubs have crusaded against suffrage and changes in women's roles. It is clear in examining the history of all the legislation that benefited women in the 1970s that women's clubs played a very significant role in their lobbying efforts; for example, they besieged Congress with telephone calls when the Equal Rights Amendment was under consideration in the early 1970s.

SEE ALSO

Abolitionism; General Federation of Women's Clubs (GFWC); Religion

FURTHER READING

Blair, Karen. *The Clubwoman as Feminist.* New York: Holmes & Meier, 1980.

Scott, Anne Firor. *Natural Allies.* Urbana: University of Illinois Press, 1991.

Coalition of Labor Union Women (CLUW)

One of the truly significant organizations to be formed after the birth of modern feminism in the late 1960s was the Coalition of Labor Union Women (CLUW), founded in 1974. The goal of CLUW has been to build bridges between the women's movement and organized labor. Indeed, a woman must be a union member to join. CLUW works both to get women to join unions and to get unions to be more responsive to the needs of their female members. Equal pay, family leave, and occupational health and safety are especially important issues for the organization, and it has helped transform the consciousness of the traditionally male-led labor movement.

SEE ALSO

Labor movement

Cold war

When World War II ended in 1945, Americans thought they could look forward to a bright future. They had won the war, they possessed a monopoly on the knowledge of how to build atomic weapons (or so they thought), and most other countries in the world were so war-torn that they posed no threat and, in fact, needed U.S. help. It came as a bitter and unhappy shock when the Soviet Union, led by Joseph Stalin, began to behave in an antagonistic way soon after the war—and then Americans learned that the Soviets possessed atomic secrets, too. Suddenly, the postwar world looked very dangerous.

The cold war was the period of tension that existed between the United States and its allies, on one hand, and the Soviet Union and its allies, on the other, for more than 40 years. Scholars still argue about which nation was ultimately responsible for the cold war. Did President Harry Truman push Stalin into being especially aggressive with his own feistiness? How much of the Soviet domination of Eastern European countries such as Poland, Hungary, and Czechoslovakia could have been prevented by more adroit U.S. diplomacy? We may never have full answers to these questions.

The first stage of the cold war in the 1950s was particularly scary, because Americans were fearful about a nuclear attack. Some people built bomb shelters in their backyards. American schoolchildren were taught to get under their desks in the event of an attack—a position that would have done very little good had an attack actually happened.

Historians now believe that the conservatism of the decade, including beliefs about a woman's place being in the home, may have owed much to the sheer level of public anxiety unleashed by the cold war. People wanted reassurance and comfort, rather than social change, especially where women and family were concerned. Those few figures who represented cultural rebellion, such as James Dean, Marlon Brando, or Elvis Presley, were invariably male.

The cold war was "cold" because it did not involve bloodshed and the heat of actual battle, but it was a "war" because most Americans felt that their way of life was under attack. The cold war ended in 1989 with the breakup of the Soviet Union.

FURTHER READING

May, Elaine Tyler. *Homeward Bound.* New York: Basic, 1988.

———. *Pushing the Limits: American Women, 1940 to 1961.* New York: Oxford University Press, 1994.

Coming-of-age rituals

Many of the ethnic cultures and religious denominations that are part of the United States celebrate a young woman's transition from childhood to adulthood. Such celebrations can focus on her new capacity to make informed moral and religious choices, on her new fertility, or on her "coming out" to society and taking on new social roles.

A young Apache woman covered in golden pollen as part of the Apache Girls' Puberty Ceremony at Fort Apache Indian Reservation in Arizona. Rituals to mark the onset of sexual maturity are celebrated in many different cultures.

According to anthropologists, many preindustrial cultures recognized female puberty—a girl coming to sexual maturity—as worthy of celebrating. Among people whose food supply was a matter of ongoing concern—who lived in areas where a crop failure could decimate the population—the ability to create new life was so important that it almost seemed magical. Hence it was something to note in a special way. More than one Native American group in America has adhered to such a custom of celebrating a young woman's fertility. Apaches, for example, celebrate the Sunrise Ceremony, in which Apache girls spend four days performing various ceremonies, dances, and songs to become imbued with the physical and spiritual power of Changing Woman, the mythical mother of the Apache people.

Other groups have not focused on the biological aspects of puberty but, rather, on the social aspects. Among people in the upper class, for example, many observe the tradition of the debutante, whereby a girl in her late teens is introduced to society at a lavish ball, either by herself or with other girls making their social debut.

Countless young girls have also enjoyed "sweet 16" parties that recognize the significance of this milestone but without the lavish expense of a debutante ball.

In the Mexican-American community, there is the tradition of the quinceañera. This is a gala event celebrating a young woman's 15th birthday. It can include prayers at church, a formal dinner, a reception, and a dance.

Many religions, too, have noted the transition to adulthood with special rituals. In a number of Christian denominations, a young person undergoes a "confirmation" to formally accept the beliefs of the faith. Within Judaism, the bar mitzvah, for boys only, has long been a central part of growing up. In this ceremony a boy of 13 is called to the Torah, meaning that he is allowed to read the first five books of the Bible in temple. Since the late 1960s there has been a parallel bat mitzvah for girls among Reform and Conservative Jews. As with the quinceañera, the bar and bat mitzvahs combine both the religious and the social, because the parties to celebrate this moment can be quite elaborate.

FURTHER READING

Liptak, Karen. *Coming-of-Age: Traditions and Rituals Around the World.* Brookfield, Conn.: Millbrook Press, 1994.

Sita, Lisa. *Coming of Age.* Woodbridge, Conn.: Blackbirch Press, 1999.

Commission on the Status of Women

When President John F. Kennedy took office in 1961, he immediately faced a dilemma with respect to the long-simmering controversy over the proposed Equal Rights Amendment (ERA). Some of his supporters were for it, and some—those close to the labor movement, which had long opposed the ERA—were against it. The U.S. Women's Bureau persuaded Kennedy that it would be a good idea to appoint a high-level commission to study issues related to women, so that he could come up with an informed policy about the ERA, among other reasons.

To Kennedy's delight, former First Lady Eleanor Roosevelt agreed to chair the commission. Cooperation from the most respected woman in the country ensured that other high-profile women, and men, would get involved, too. The 26-member commission issued a report in 1963 that addressed many issues of concern to women, such as the cost of sex discrimination on the job. The report recommended against passage of the ERA, suggesting instead that women's equality could best be pursued in the courts on the basis of the 14th Amendment, which said that no citizen could be denied the "equal protection of the laws."

What was undoubtedly most important about the commission was its role as a catalyst for the modern feminist movement. Following the example of the federal-level commission, each state established a similar commission studying discrimination against women. Out of these networks came much energy for reform. More particularly,

President John F. Kennedy greets the members of the Presidential Commission on the Status of Women, including Eleanor Roosevelt, the second woman to the left of JFK. He was the first President to appoint such a commission.

the National Organization for Women was founded at a national gathering of state commissions in 1966.

SEE ALSO

Equal Rights Amendment (ERA); National Organization for Women (NOW); Women's Bureau, U.S.

FURTHER READING

Harrison, Cynthia. *On Account of Sex.* Berkeley: University of California Press, 1988.

Communications

SEE Media

Communism

During the 19th century—when many people worked long hours at backbreaking labor in factories, often in dangerous conditions—there was an abundance of new theories about how to achieve a better world. Many of these theories were based on the idea of socialism, a system of public ownership of large industrial enterprises.

German social thinker Karl Marx, author of the *Communist Manifesto,* published in 1848, and his disciple Friedrich Engels developed what was probably the most influential theory, which called for the end of private property and the overthrow of the ruling capitalist class in industrialized societies. These ideas led to the founding of the international communist movement in the late 19th century, to the Russian Revolution in 1917, and to the launching of the American Communist party in the aftermath of the Russian Revolution. The term *communism* refers to the idea of people joining together and holding property in common.

In the 1930s, at the height of communism's attraction for Americans who wanted to build a more just world—and before the cruelties launched in its name in the Soviet Union, Eastern Europe, and China were widely known—certain women believed that the Communist party might be a vehicle for gender justice, too. The party always subordinated this issue to more strictly economic matters centering on class, but the fact that the American Communist party had many well-known and powerful women leaders, such as leading orator Elizabeth Gurley Flynn, lent it credibility—at least for a time.

Starting in the 1950s, revelations about the terrible suffering inflicted by various communist regimes around the world prompted a loss of American membership. Also in the 1950s, efforts spearheaded by Senator Joseph McCarthy to rid government and other institutions of communist influences created an atmosphere of persecution that led more people to drop any ties they might have had with the American Communist party. With the crumbling of the communist regimes in the Soviet Union and in Eastern Europe in the early 1990s, the Communist party has become a marginal force in American life.

FURTHER READING

Kaplan, Judy, and Linn Shapiro, eds. *Red Diapers: Growing Up in the Communist Left.* Urbana: University of Illinois Press, 1998.

Klehr, Harvey. *The Soviet World of American Communism.* New Haven: Yale University Press, 1998.

Comparable worth

For those hoping to equalize the wage gap between men and women, the call for comparable worth is the demand for equal pay for jobs requiring comparable backgrounds or training. In 1999 a woman earned, on the average, only about three quarters of the salary a man earned. In 1963 Congress had passed the Equal Pay Act, mandating equal pay for the same jobs for men and women. Though only the jobs covered by the Fair Labor Standards Act of 1938 are included, this law had begun the process of bringing wage equity for the two sexes. But it did not eliminate the wage gap.

The gap exists primarily because so many women work in female-dominated employment—what many call the "pink collar ghetto"—with jobs in this sector being paid less, across the board, than male jobs requiring comparable—or even less—training. In the 1980s in Minnesota, for example, highly trained women stenographers earned nearly $400 a month less than unskilled male laborers.

Even though there has never been a national law calling for comparable pay, unions have been able to win important victories in several places. In 1981 in San Jose, California, for example, predominantly female city workers went on strike for comparable worth–based wages, and they won—owing at least in part to the presence of a 7–4 female majority on the San Jose City Council. The workers' claims were based on formulas that have been developed for weighing the wages of female-dominated jobs against those of male-dominated jobs.

Opponents of comparable worth argue that it is difficult, if not impossible, to work out precise formulas for determining which jobs held primarily by women should be compared to which jobs held primarily by men. States have massively resisted legislative remedies. Comparable worth is unlikely to disappear as an issue, however, because unions have been able to recruit women into their ranks on the strength of promising to pursue it.

SEE ALSO

Equal Pay Act (1963)

FURTHER READING

Albeda, Randy, Steven Shulman, and Robert Drago. *Unlevel Playing Fields: Understanding Wage Inequality and Discrimination.* New York: McGraw-Hill, 1997

Computers

Although people usually think of computer hackers as male, in fact, there are many women in the field of computer science, and thousands of women are employed as software designers and as engineers and marketing specialists in this thriving industry. Women are professors of computer science at prestigious universities.

No woman has made a greater contribution to computer science than Rear Admiral Grace Hopper. Born in 1906, she was raised in a household where her father was a civil engineer. As a child, she began taking things apart and putting them back together so as to learn how they worked. At Vassar College she majored in math and physics, going on to obtain a master's and a doctorate in math from Yale. She was teaching at Vassar when she decided to join the navy during World War II. While in the navy, she was introduced to the primitive computers then being used for processing military data.

After the war ended, Hopper went to be a researcher at Harvard, where she created the first operating programs for the Mark I computer, an early model of computer. Then she went into private industry, working for a firm that eventually merged with the Sperry Corporation, and helped develop the first commercially viable computer for business use. Other achievements include inventing automatic programming, aimed at making computing easier for non-mathematicians, and helping develop the COBOL computer language.

The navy recalled Hopper to active service to work on its computers in 1967, and she retired with the rank of rear admiral in 1986.

In June 1994 a group of women came together in Washington, D.C., in the "Grace Hopper Celebration of Women in Computing." Though the participants were a distinguished group of academic and industry leaders, not all the news they discussed was good news. In fact the trend among young women is going in the wrong direction for computers. In 1984, 37.4 percent of the bachelor's degrees in computer science and computer engineering went to women. Ten years later the percentage dropped to 16. The convener of that group, Dr. Anita Borg, speculates that in the intervening years the identification of computers with "nerds" became more complete, and that was off-putting to young women.

Confederate women

On both sides of the conflict during the Civil War (1861–65), women organized themselves to give aid to the soldiers. A few women actually put on male clothes and fought in battles. Women also nursed, spied, raised money for medical supplies, and collected food.

By the end of the Civil War, there was widespread privation on the home front in the South. Here a group of women tries to salvage old clothes, tinware, and other castoff items so that they can continue to maintain their households.

Northern and Southern women thus had much in common, but there were also profound differences in the war experience for the two regions. Only in the South did the men go off to battle leaving women to supervise a slave labor force whose loyalty was, for very good reason, suspect. Many more battles were fought on southern than on northern terrain—to say nothing of Union general William Tecumseh Sherman's destructive march through Georgia to the sea. As a result, a larger percentage of women in the South than in the North had to confront the devastation of war face to face. Finally, because of the proportionately much greater loss of life on the Confederate side, women's morale was severely undermined as the bloody war went on, the staggering loss of life continued, and the need for sacrifice seemed unending.

After the war ended, Southern women, many of whom had lost husbands, sons, and homes, were active in constructing the myth of the "lost cause," a romanticized Old South in which the slaves were happy in their bondage and problems appeared only when greedy Yankees interfered. The United Daughters of the Confederacy, a group founded in 1894, has as its primary purpose to encourage the preservation of records and sites important to the history of the South and the Confederate cause.

SEE ALSO

Civil War

FURTHER READING

Clinton, Catherine. *The Plantation Mistress: Woman's World in the Old South.* New York: Pantheon, 1982.

———. *Tara Revisited: Women, War, and the Plantation Legend.* New York: Abbeville Press, 1995.

Faust, Drew Gilpin. *Mothers of Invention.* Chapel Hill: University of North Carolina Press, 1996.

Congress, U.S.

The first woman elected to Congress, Jeannette Rankin (Republican–Montana), took her seat in 1917. Since that time nearly 200 women have served—and are serving—in the House of Representatives and in the Senate. Four—Margaret Chase Smith (Republican–Maine), Barbara Ann Mikulski (Democrat–Maryland), Olympia Jean Snowe (Republican–Maine), and Barbara Boxer (Democrat–California)—served both in the House and the Senate. The numbers of women have gone from a handful to a few dozen in the House and from one or two in the Senate to nine in 1998.

In both houses of Congress, however, women confronted institutions that had a remarkably "old boy" feel to them until the 1990s. Getting elected has been only the first part of the battle for women—the second is being taken seriously by their male colleagues. Women have chaired very few major committees in either house, and they have usually not been part of the leadership, either formally or informally.

For many years the surest way for a woman to enter Congress was via widow's succession, that is, replacing a dead husband. For example, the distinguished Republican Senator Margaret Chase Smith won a seat in the House that way. It still happens: in 1998 Mary Bono (Republican–California) was elected to succeed Sonny Bono, and Lois Capps (Democrat–California) was elected to replace Walter Capps.

Most congresswomen belong to the Congressional Caucus on Women's Issues, which deals with matters such as child care, women's health, and work-

Equal Rights

VOL. XVIII, No. 20
FIVE CENTS

SATURDAY
JUNE 18, 1932

A Woman Makes Senate History

Hattie W. Caraway, Senator from Arkansas, wrote a new chapter in Senate history when she presided over the sessions of that body May 9. She was the first woman ever to rule over the deliberations of the Senate, and is shown occupying the Vice-President's chair. She recently announced her candidacy in the forthcoming Senatorial election in her State.

Hattie Caraway, Democrat of Arkansas, was the first woman to have a career of any length in the U.S. Senate. Here she presides over the Senate in 1932—the first woman ever to do so.

place family leave policy. As the number of women holding office has increased, especially since the Year of the Woman in 1992 that followed public outcry over Anita Hill's treatment by the Senate Judiciary Committee in 1991, their ability to be advocates for other women has increased dramatically. For many years, when they were a tiny minority, it was impossible to be outspoken on such women's issues as breast cancer research and to be effective. Moreover, women tended to be low-profile on other issues as well. In 1998 a number of women in both Houses and from both parties played highly visible roles in the debate over the impeachment of Bill Clinton.

Not only are there now more women, there is a more diverse group of women in Congress. Elected in 1968, Shirley Chisholm (Democrat–New York) was the first black woman in the House. Carol Moseley-Braun (Democrat–Illinois) was the first black woman in the Senate after the 1992 election. That same year Lucille Roybal Allard (Democrat–California) became the first Mexican-American woman in the House and the second Latina; Ileana Ros-Lehtinen (Republican–Florida) was the first in 1989. First elected in 1964, Patsy Takemoto Mink (Democrat–Hawaii) was the first Asian-American woman in the House as well as the first woman of color. Another important first occurred in 1973 when Yvonne Brathwaite Burke (Democrat–California) became the first member of Congress to be granted a maternity leave.

Although the number of women in Congress continues to increase, the United States still lags behind most other industrial democracies in the percentage of the national legislature that is female.

SEE ALSO

Chisholm, Shirley; Mink, Patsy Takemoto; Politics; Rankin, Jeannette; Smith, Margaret Chase

FURTHER READING

Witt, Linda, Karen M. Paget, and Glenna Matthews. *Running as a Woman: Gender and Power in American Politics.* New York: Free Press, 1994.

Consciousness-raising

During the late 1960s and early 1970s, women gathered together for talkfests known as consciousness-raising sessions. In many parts of the country, but especially in cities or university communities, women talked about what was wrong—and sometimes right—with their lives.

The generation of women coming to maturity at that period had been trained to believe that, because women had received the vote in 1920, they had full access to the benefits of U.S. society. Yet the law still treated men and women very differently. Women were often denied access to jobs or education on the basis of gender. Women had a hard time getting credit in their own names. When women shared their experiences with each other, they began to see a pattern of common discrimination based on gender, rather than individual problems.

With their consciousness raised as a result of these discussions, women could then seek political solutions to the problems.

FURTHER READING

Evans, Sara M. *Personal Politics: The Roots of Women's Liberation in the Civil Rights Movement and the New Left.* New York: Knopf, 1979.

Constitution, U.S.

For all Americans, women and men alike, the U.S. Constitution contains the fundamental law of the land, sets up the form of government, and, in a number of key amendments, defines citizens' rights. Yet women were not mentioned at all in the original document. The male framers did not need to spell out their own legal supremacy over women; it suffused all the cultural presumptions of the day.

In the early days of the young nation, each state determined the citizenship status of its residents. Throughout the country, the law assumed that a married woman had no independent legal identity. The 14th Amendment to the Constitution, ratified in 1868, established the universality of U.S. citizenship for "all persons born or naturalized in the United States," but women would not be granted the right to vote until the 19th Amendment was passed in 1920. In the 1970s courts also began to make judicial decisions favorable to women—at long last—based on the 14th Amendment.

Even though the unamended Constitution had not specified any rights for women, it did contain language about "persons," rather than about "men," which has proven useful to women because "persons" could more readily be interpreted to include women. Moreover the 1st Amendment, which protects freedom of speech and assembly, has made possible the pursuit of greater rights for women, as for every other group of Americans.

SEE ALSO

Citizenship; 14th Amendment; 19th Amendment

Consumer culture

From the beginning of American history people have bought certain goods, such as milled flour, in addition to what they have grown or made themselves. But over time, the proportion of what people produce for themselves versus what they buy has shifted dramatically. Now people purchase almost everything they use.

In colonial times, most of the American population lived on farms rather than in towns or cities, and people did little buying and selling. A farm woman might have taken her butter and eggs to a local market, but she may

Frigidaire and other companies promoted the purchase of home appliances with images of glamorous and attractive women. Refrigerators, the ad proclaims, offered women the twin virtues of efficiency and gracious living.

well have swapped them for something rather than being paid in cash, since money was relatively scarce.

About the time the new nation came into being in the late 1700s, vast economic changes were taking place: in England the production of fabric was becoming mechanized, and soon many other goods would be machine- rather than handmade. The United States participated in these changes only slightly later than England. As the country became ever more industrial, it also became more urban, with more and more people living in cities. City dwellers were forced to buy things—particularly food and clothing—because they couldn't grow or make their own.

By the early 20th century, there was, in addition to a multitude of factories, an enormous network of railroads that could carry goods all over. At this point, it made economic sense for companies to produce national brands that could be nationally advertised: a manufacturer could now get the goods into the hands of nearly all consumers who might be able to afford them.

The 1920s saw the development of an advertising industry to promote the new brands such as General Foods, General Mills, Kellogg, and Post. This was the start of a true consumer culture, because Americans, especially women, devoted a relatively large portion of their time to shopping for, rather than to making, such items as soap and clothing. After World War II and the birth of television, these trends intensified because it was possible to advertise goods ever more compellingly. Women were distinguished from men as an audience for advertising, and increasingly products for the home, from washing machines and vacuum cleaners to foods, were targeted to the women who would buy them for their families.

In the period since World War II ended in 1945, consumer culture has grown apace. A sustained postwar economic boom placed more money in more people's hands that ever before. The 1920s had seen the innovation known as installment buying so that Americans could more readily buy appliances. In the postwar era banks introduced credit cards that made it even easier for people to purchase goods that they might not have been able to afford if they paid with cash. And as women moved from the home to the workplace, increasingly earning their own incomes, they became independent consumers of everything from clothing to cars to entertainment. In the 19th century the duty of every housewife was to be as careful and as frugal as possible, saving every scrap of soap, darning socks, remaking old clothes. As the consumer culture has taken hold, each American is now expected to spend to maintain prosperity.

FURTHER READING

Finnegan, Margaret Mary. *Selling Suffrage: Consumer Culture and Votes for Women.* New York: Columbia University Press, 1999.

Lury, Celia. *Consumer Culture.* New Brunswick, N.J.: Rutgers University Press, 1996.

Seiter, Ellen. *Sold Separately: Children and Parents in Consumer Culture.* New Brunswick, N.J.: Rutgers University Press, 1993.

Cooking

The preparation of food has been, and to a large extent still is, women's work. Though burdensome, it can also be enjoyable for those who have the time to devote to it. But because so many Americans live such busy lives, they increasingly rely on convenience foods, fast-food restaurants, and take-out delis for their meals—one government study, for example, found that away-from-home meals and snacks accounted for 47 percent of the country's expenditures on food in 1994, as compared with 34 percent in 1970. (Oddly, the cookbook publishing industry is booming at the same time that the average person does less cooking than ever—evidently people like to read recipes more than they like to cook.)

Meals are more than the occasion for people to take in nourishment: they are also an opportunity for household members to communicate with one another. They are rituals that define who is and who is not close enough to be worthy of breaking bread with the household. Sometimes, for holiday or birthday celebrations, meals help create religious meaning or give someone the chance to feel special because his or her favorite food is being featured.

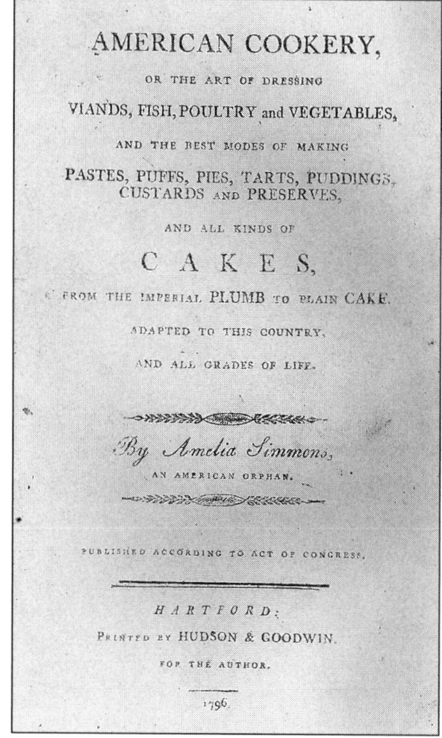

AMERICAN COOKERY,

OR THE ART OF DRESSING

VIANDS, FISH, POULTRY and VEGETABLES,

AND THE BEST MODES OF MAKING

PASTES, PUFFS, PIES, TARTS, PUDDINGS, CUSTARDS AND PRESERVES,

AND ALL KINDS OF

C A K E S,

FROM THE IMPERIAL PLUMB TO PLAIN CAKE.

ADAPTED TO THIS COUNTRY,

AND ALL GRADES OF LIFE.

By Amelia Simmons,

AN AMERICAN ORPHAN.

PUBLISHED ACCORDING TO ACT OF CONGRESS.

HARTFORD:

PRINTED BY HUDSON & GOODWIN.

FOR THE AUTHOR.

1796.

Amelia Simmon's 1796 cookbook was another small declaration of independence, as the first to register the uniquely American ingredients and dishes that housewives had evolved since landing in the New World. Her recipes were "adapted to this country, and all grades of life."

Although people do not often think in such elaborate terms about what they are cooking and what its larger significance might be, cooking is, in fact, one of the most important human activities. For much of human history, populations lived so close to the famine level and had so little choice about what their food might be that "cooking" as a skilled art was far from their minds. As a society enters into a phase in which food is abundant enough so that more than just the elite can look forward to variety and occasionally elaborate preparations at mealtime, then cooking becomes a learned skill.

After the American Revolution, the new United States was at just such a moment of transition, with many households prosperous enough to look forward to a varied cuisine. The first American cookbook, *American Cookery* by Amelia Simmons, was published in 1796, and it included recipes for such classics as roast turkey and pumpkin pie.

When millions of immigrants began to arrive in the United States in the late 19th century—bringing with them an immense variety of foods and ways to prepare them—many native-born Americans were concerned that the immigrants' diets might not conform to "correct" American standards of the day, which featured meals that strike us today as very heavy, involving a great deal of meat. Well-meaning home economists and visiting nurses tried to persuade, say, an Italian-American household to give up garlic-flavored pasta in favor of something more meaty and more bland. In general, however, immigrants clung to the old ways for many years. Indeed what seemed strange and possibly dangerous to reformers of 100 years ago—pizza, tacos, Chinese food—is now standard American fare.

One of the most interesting aspects of American cookery lies in the contributions of African-American women. Often cooks in other people's households—first as slaves and later as domestic servants—as well as in their own homes, they developed a tradition of skilled cookery and fine baking whose importance to our cuisine is only now being fully recognized. They brought knowledge based on African foods and techniques as well as becoming adept at the technical skills required to make light pie crust, for example.

Today women have the chance to become professional chefs owing to feminist-inspired struggles to conquer what had been an all-male bastion. For the first time—since the 1970s—members of the sex that has done most of the world's cooking can anticipate making a paid career of it.

SEE ALSO

Child, Julia McWilliams

FURTHER READING

Gabaccia, Donna. *We Are What We Eat.* Cambridge: Harvard University Press, 1998.

Cooper, Anna Julia Haywood

- *Born: Aug. 10, 1858, Raleigh, N.C.*
- *Education: Oberlin College, A.B., 1884, M.A., 1885; University of Paris (Sorbonne), Ph.D., 1925; author,* A Voice from the South *(1892);* L'Attitude de la France à l'Égard de l'Esclavage pendant la Révolution *(1925);* Le Pelerinage de Charlemagne *(1925);* Life and Writings of the Grimké Family *(1951)*
- *Died: Feb. 27, 1964, Washington, D.C.*

Anna Julia Cooper, daughter of a slave woman and her master, became one of the first African-American women in the country to complete a four-year course at an accredited college and then later one of the first African-American women to obtain a doctorate.

Cooper's mother, freed by emancipation, worked hard to give her advantages, and in 1877 the young woman married a promising clergyman—who died only two years later. Cooper managed to find her way to Oberlin College in Ohio and there obtained both an A.B. in 1884 and a master's in 1885. Then she began her life work of teaching.

Cooper spent most of her career in the nation's capital, serving for some years as the principal of the M Street High School, a prep school for African-American students. She wrote extensively in both English and French, publishing *Equality of Races and the Democratic Movement* in 1942. At the age of 66, she obtained a doctorate from the Sorbonne in Paris for her research on the French attitude toward slavery during the French Revolution. Not until the age of 84 did she retire from the classroom. Born when slavery was legal in the United States, she lived to witness Martin Luther King's crusade, dying at the age of 105.

FURTHER READING

Cooper, Anna Julia. *A Voice from the South.* New York: Oxford University Press, 1988.

Gabel, Leona C. *From Slavery to the Sorbonne and Beyond.* Northampton, Mass.: Smith College Department of History, 1982.

Courtship

The process by which men and women choose to marry one another has changed dramatically over the generations. Indeed, during the colonial period, a marriage was not so much a matter of choice for the prospective husband and wife as it was for their families, because most marriages were arranged. If parents were affectionate, they might have allowed either of the young people a veto, but this was as far as it went. If love appeared between a man and woman, this was a result of the marriage, rather than a cause of it. During an age of arranged marriages, courtship was more a matter of getting acquainted than of romance.

Scholars believe that this began to change in the mid-1700s, and that all family relationships then began to be more intense and emotional. Marital love began to be depicted in novels and poems as one of the supreme human experiences—and if this were the case, then a young person wanted more of a say-so. Courtship—in which a man visited and wooed a prospective wife, along with her varied responses of encouragement or discouragement—began to be an important cultural phenomenon.

The next stage in the history of courtship appeared in the 19th century, when young people began "walking together," or seeing one another under

Radcliffe College students and their male guests in the 1940s. College dorms were rigidly segregated by gender, so even if this had been a coeducational college instead of a women's college, the men would have been there as guests.

supervision. Only when an engagement was formal and a marriage was imminent was a couple allowed to be alone together. A woman who did not abide by these rules risked tainting her reputation—a mistake from which it might have been difficult to recover. Of course there were enormous variations based on class, race, religion, region, and ethnicity. New immigrants, for example, might well have attempted to duplicate the system from their homeland—arranged marriage, say—in the new environment. And in the working-class, as young women began to go to work in factories, the old, formal rules started to break down, because it was so much more difficult for girls' parents to chaperone them.

Dating is a 20th-century development. Having access to cars made a tremendous difference in courtship, because it gave young people greater freedom. No matter how much parents wanted close supervision, they were unlikely to be able to achieve it, and throughout the 20th century young people have seized more freedom over their own sexual conduct. Another change has been that dating, unlike earlier courtship practices, does not necessarily mean that the young people have marriage in mind. Rather, dating is a way for them to socialize with each other, and also to participate in the consumer culture by going to movie theaters, dance halls, and other entertainment venues.

The accelerating pace of the sexual revolution in the years since World War II, with improved access to birth control after the invention of the pill in 1960, has meant that the rules of courtship continue to change. The roles of men and women in courtship have grown less distinct. The man is no longer always expected to pick up the woman for a date—often they simply meet at an agreed location. And more and more women now propose marriage to men, contrary to tradition. Also, a significant number of men and women live together *before* marriage, a behavior that would have been unheard of except in the most freewheeling circles just a few decades ago. Between 1970 and 1994, the number of unmarried couples living together rose from about 500,000 to nearly 3.7 million, with some 35 percent of the latter households including children. It has been estimated that at least half of all couples who married after 1985 had first lived together.

SEE ALSO
Marriage

Coverture

SEE Citizenship

Crandall, Prudence

- *Born: Sept. 3, 1803, Hopkinton, R.I.*
- *Education: New England Friends' Boarding School, Providence, R.I.*
- *Accomplishments: Founder of a "school for young ladies and little misses of color," Canterbury, Conn. (1833)*
- *Died: Jan. 28, 1890, Elk Falls, Kans.*

Prudence Crandall, raised a Quaker, was a teacher and abolitionist who opened a school for girls in Canterbury, Connecticut. When she attempted to enroll an African-American girl, the other parents objected. In April 1833 Crandall announced that her school would close and then reopen as a school for the education of black girls. Harassed both in the courts and by a mob, she was forced to close the school in September 1834.

FURTHER READING

Foner, Philip S., and Josephine F. Pacheco. *Three Who Dared: Prudence Crandall, Margaret Douglass, Myrtilla Miner, Champions of Antebellum Black Education.* Westport, Conn.: Greenwood, 1984.

Strane, Susan. *A Whole-souled Woman: Prudence Crandall and the Education of Black Women.* New York: Norton, 1990.

Criminal justice system

Women commit far fewer crimes than do men, and they are arrested far less frequently. Of the crimes they *do* commit, a large percentage are nonviolent or victimless, such as drug abuse or white-collar economic crime. Not surprisingly, women constitute only a small percentage of those in jails and prisons, with about ten percent of jail inmates and about five percent of state and federal prisoners being female. Typically, women are incarcerated in separate women's prisons, a practice that began around 1836 and accelerated in the late 19th century.

Women have also been far less represented than men in law enforcement. Because of ingrained discrimination, police forces have strongly resisted hiring women, and as late as 1991 only 9 percent of public police officers were female. Women are much likelier to be involved in the criminal justice system as lawyers and as judges than as police officers. Indeed, a few women have been prosecutors in very high-profile criminal cases, such as Marcia Clark in the O. J. Simpson murder trial.

The first breakthroughs in hiring policewomen came in the late 19th century, when reformers succeeded in persuading cities to hire police matrons to deal with women under arrest. The first woman with the authority to make an arrest herself was Lola Baldwin, who was hired in Portland, Oregon, in 1905.

During the U.S. involvement in World War I (1917–18) women joined police forces in more than 200 cities, filling positions that had been created when men went off to war. These women were confined to sex-segregated duties, though, such as clerical work. In fact, women in law enforcement during these years often functioned more like social workers than like cops on the beat, and their pay and promotion opportunities reflected their second-class status.

More reform began to take place in the 1950s and 1960s, spurred on by the growth of the modern women's movement. Activists secured help from the U.S. Justice Department in forcing legal compliance with antidiscrimination measures in local police departments by withholding federal money from departments found to practice sex discrimination. The percentage of law enforcement officers who are female began a modest climb from 1.5 percent in 1972 to 3.38 percent in 1979 to 8.8 percent in 1986. But there is still much room

Affirmative action has changed the composition of prison guard forces. Formerly dominated by white males, the guard force at Stateville prison in Illinois was nearly one-quarter female and nearly one-half African-American and Hispanic by the early 1990s.

for improvement, not only in the numbers of women employed but also in changing a macho working environment that has often been uncomfortable for women.

SEE ALSO

Law; Prison reform

FURTHER READING

Miller, Susan L., ed. *Crime Control and Women: Feminist Implications of Criminal Justice Policy.* Thousand Oaks, Calif.: Sage, 1998.

Van Wormer, Katherine Stuart, and Clemens Bartollas. *Women and the Criminal Justice System.* Boston: Allyn and Bacon, 2000.

Croly, Jane Cunningham

- *Born: Dec. 19, 1829, Leicestershire, England*
- *Education: Schooled at home*
- *Accomplishments: Manager, New York* World *woman's department (1862–72); founder, Sorosis club for women (1868); founder,* Woman's Cycle *(1889); founder, General Federation of Women's Clubs (1890)*
- *Died: Dec. 23, 1901, New York, N.Y.*

Jane Cunningham Croly was a pioneer in two respects: as a journalist and as the founder of a women's club.

Her family moved to Poughkeepsie, New York, from their native England in 1841. Needing a way to support herself, Jane Cunningham first taught school and then moved to New York City to try her fortune as a writer. By 1857 her newspaper column "Parlor and Side-walk Gossip" had become probably the first syndicated feature by a woman in the country. In 1856 she married fellow journalist David Goodman Croly, and they later had four children.

Croly wrote under the name Jennie June; pen names were common for women journalists at the time because women were still shy about public exposure. Immensely popular and dedicated to improving the lives of women, she published in both newspapers and women's magazines.

In 1868, reacting to women journalists' exclusion from a New York Press Club reception for Charles Dickens, Croly founded a women's club called Sorosis, (a word that has the same root as *sorority* and means sisterhood). The club provided a forum for literary and civic discussion. In 1889 a national convention of Sorosis members led to the founding in 1890 of the General Federation of Women's Clubs, the largest group of organized women in the country.

SEE ALSO

General Federation of Women's Clubs (GFWC); Media

FURTHER READING

Blair, Karen. *The Clubwoman as Feminist.* New York: Holmes & Meier, 1980.

Croly, Jane Cunningham. *The History of the Woman's Club Movement in America.* New York, H. G. Allen, 1898.

Custody, child

When a marriage ends in divorce, one of the most important issues to resolve is who will gain custody of the children. Throughout most of American history, that issue was automatically settled in favor of the father, but by the early 20th century, that was no longer true.

The father was the custodial parent because the law treated his wife as a dependent being, not unlike the children themselves. In a sense, all of them had originally been his property. During the 19th century, women's rights advocates pressed for reform in custody law as one of their key issues, though divorce was rare at the time.

By the early 20th century, the activism of a generation of social welfare reformers and feminists had convinced judges to apply a new standard in making decisions about custody of the children: the children's own best interest. Usually, judges decided children were better off if they remained with their mothers. Fathers were to fulfill their parental obligations by making child-support payments to the mother.

Since the 1980s, fathers' rights groups have organized around the claim that the law has been unfair in granting custody so one-sidedly to mothers. As a result, child custody has become a very contentious part of divorce proceedings.

SEE ALSO

Divorce

FURTHER READING

Mason, Mary Ann. *From Father's Property to Children's Rights*. New York: Columbia University Press, 1994.

Dance

Dance is a part of every culture that makes up the United States—whether as part of worship or other sacred activities, for social and recreational purposes, or as a theatrical event.

Enslaved Africans brought along their dance traditions, for example, and it proved impossible for their masters to eradicate this heritage because it could be preserved in people's heads. Even in the 20th century, some dance forms embraced as part of American culture—such as the Charleston, which was wildly popular in the 1920s—reflect African influence. Another important portion of the American dance mosaic is the tradition among Native Americans, where dance remains a vital sacred ritual.

Dancing as theater began to be significant in the United States in the 19th century. European-trained dancers brought ballet to these shores, and it gradually attracted an audience. By the early 20th century, when the Russian star Anna Pavlova toured the United States, ballet had become established as one of the performing arts. "Ballet is woman," proclaimed the master choreographer George Balanchine, thinking, no doubt, of the many superb ballerinas for whom he crafted roles and of the way in which the male dancer supports dazzling turns and leaps by his female partner.

As in so many other endeavors, however, women have had less power in commanding resources in dance than have men, except for the handful of those who have founded companies (Lucia Chase of the American Ballet Theatre) or who have been respected choreographers (Agnes de Mille). Moreover, American ballerina Gelsey Kirkland wrote in her 1986 memoir that more than hard work may be required to make it as a ballerina: a woman may be under so much pressure to be thin, from ballet masters and choreographers who want their dancers to project the image of highly trained racehorses, that she may develop an eating disorder.

Of course, ballet in the United States has benefited from its glorious women dancers, such as Cynthia Gregory, Maria Tallchief, Judith Jamison, Suzanne Farrell, and Melissa Hayden. Their art has inspired countless girls to want to follow in their footsteps.

The 20th century has also seen the birth of the modern dance movement, a

Isadora Duncan revolutionized modern dance with her unconventional choreography and costumes. In the years after this photo was taken in 1899, she would scandalize critics and audiences by dancing barefoot.

genre in which women such as Isadora Duncan, Ruth St. Denis, and Martha Graham have been the pioneers. Modern dance has a more fluid and extensive range of movements than does the more rigid ballet, which is derived from the dance practices of the royal courts of Europe.

Isadora Duncan was one of the first to make a radical break with the prescriptions of ballet. She developed an improvisational, spontaneous style of natural movements, which she accentuated with flowing, draped gowns modeled after classical Greek clothing. Ruth St. Denis also opted for a rather exotic approach in her break with ballet, and many of her dances derived from Oriental sources. Martha Graham, who studied with Ruth St. Denis, developed a somewhat more austere, avant-garde style, and was the first to codify her type of movement into a coherent, completely new technique that is now considered central to many types of modern dance. All three of these seminal dance styles celebrated the earthy power of femininity, bringing the woman down from the rarified and idealized pedestal upon which ballet had placed her. Graham's technique in particular emphasizes gravity and the body's connection with the ground—dancers were now no longer airborne sylphs but earth goddesses.

Dancing as a popular pastime is derived from early folk dances, influenced by ethnic and regional variations as well as the stars of Hollywood, such as Ginger Rogers, who first danced with Fred Astaire in 1933 in the musical *Flying Down to Rio*. A progression of fads began with the Charleston in the 1920s, and proceeded to the jitterbug in the 30s and 40s, jive in the 50s, the twist in the 60s, and disco in the 70s. Since the 1970s popular dancing has grown more free-form, with few prescribed steps and little definition between men's and women's roles.

SEE ALSO

Duncan, Isadora; Tallchief, Maria

FURTHER READING

Ashley, Merrill, with Larry Kaplan. *Dancing for Balanchine*. New York: Dutton, 1984.

De Mille, Agnes. *Martha: The Life and Work of Martha Graham*. New York: Vintage, 1992.

Easton, Carol. *No Intermissions: The Life of Agnes de Mille*. Boston: Little, Brown, 1996.

Farrell, Suzanne. *Holding On to the Air: An Autobiography*. New York: Summit, 1990.

Kirkland, Gelsey. *Dancing on My Grave*. Garden City, N.Y.: Doubleday, 1986.

Terry, Walter. *The Dance in America*. Rev. ed. New York: Da Capo, 1981.

Darwinism

In the late 19th century, the English biologist Charles Darwin published two books, *On the Origin of Species* and *The Descent of Man*, that transformed the way we think about human origins.

Darwin argued that over the millennia humanity has evolved from more primitive life forms. He further contended that the male struggle for mates has fueled the evolutionary process, because it has led to "the survival of the fittest." That is, the male who was the strongest, smartest, or otherwise most fit was the one who won the female and who therefore got to pass his genes to his offspring.

Most biologists today agree that Darwin was right about evolution, but there is still debate about natural selection, the term that he used to describe the struggle that leads to "improving" a species by making it more fit. Indeed, feminist scientists have suggested that the quality of female nurture may play a more important role in the evolutionary process than Darwin allowed by fostering the survival of the young.

Darwin's ideas have been profoundly influential, and not just in terms of scientific theory. Certain social thinkers used Darwin's insights to argue for a view of society that was as brutal as the natural world Darwin described. If male struggle for mates, no matter how bloody, ultimately leads to betterment in nature, then perhaps human society would be better off if it allowed people to struggle without interference in the form of charity or aid. This argument is known as Social Darwinism, and it was immensely popular in the late nineteenth century because it seemed to justify the fierce economic competition then taking place.

Modern feminists have contended that both classic Darwinian theory and Social Darwinism had unfortunate results for women, because these theories glorified male traits and behaviors while dismissing as irrelevant to progress activities in which women tend to excel, such as nurture and language use.

FURTHER READING

Bowler, Peter J. *Darwinism*. New York: Twayne, 1993.

Stefoff, Rebecca. *Charles Darwin and the Evolution Revolution*. New York: Oxford University Press, 1996.

Daughters of Bilitis

Founded in San Francisco in 1955 by Del Martin and Phyllis Lyon, the Daughters of Bilitis was the first lesbian civil rights organization in the United States. The founders, themselves lovers, took inspiration from the recent formation of the Mattachine Society, also in San Francisco, an organization of gay men.

In 1955 to be lesbian was to encounter rejection and discrimination in many different ways. Lyon and Martin wanted to create a haven where lesbians could feel a sense of belonging. They began publishing a monthly newsletter, *The Ladder,* which provided a forum for discussing issues of concern to their community, including the rearing of children by lesbian couples and the problems of the still-married lesbian. In addition the newsletter contained poetry, fiction, and articles about history. Publication of the newsletter is one item in Martin and Lyon's long history of activism, which includes the co-founding of the Alice B. Toklas Memorial Democratic Club in 1972 to serve as an advocacy group for gay and lesbian issues.

The name *Bilitis* came from an 1898 publication by a Frenchman, Pierre Louÿs, entitled *Les Chansons de Bilitis* (Songs of Bilitis). The book claimed to offer translations from Greek about lesbians in the ancient world, and it became an important text to lesbians. Martin and Lyon believed that the name they chose would sound bland to most people but convey meaning to those they most wanted to reach. The only surviving chapter of the Daughters of Bilitis is active in Cambridge, Massachusetts.

SEE ALSO
Lesbians

Davis, Rebecca Harding

- *Born: June 24, 1831, Washington, Pa.*
- *Education: Washington (Pa.) Female Seminary, graduated 1848*
- *Accomplishmwnts: Author,* Margaret Howth *(1862);* Waiting for the Verdict *(1868);* Pro Aris et Focis—A Plea for Our Altars and Hearths *(1870);* John Andross *(1874);* A Law Unto Herself *(1878);* Natasqua *(1886);* Silhouettes of American Life *(1892);* Frances Waldeaux *(1896);* Bits of Gossip *(autobiography, 1904)*
- *Died: Sept. 29, 1910, Mount Kisco, N.Y.*

Rebecca Harding Davis, herself the daughter of a middle-class family, was one of the first American writers to explore the plight of working-class people in fiction. Her powerful story "Life in the Iron Mills" was rediscovered in the 1970s and widely discussed for its insight into the suffering of mill workers.

Born in Pennsylvania, Rebecca Harding spent the first five years of her life in plantation country in Alabama, then moved to Wheeling, Virginia (later West Virginia), with her family as a young child. There she had the opportunity to see firsthand the poverty and hopelessness that were the fate of people who worked in the iron mills. She left home to attend the Washington Female Seminary in Pennsylvania (a girls' high school), from which she graduated in 1848. Returning home, she helped her mother with her domestic duties but also began to write. "Life in the Iron Mills" was published in the *Atlantic Monthly* in 1861.

Continuing to write, Rebecca Harding married Lemuel Clarke Davis in 1863 and became the mother of three children. In 1869 she became a contributing editor of the *The New York Tribune*. In later life she became more conservative, approving of careers only for unmarried women, though she herself continued to write, publishing her last book, the autobiographical *Bits of Gossip,* in 1904.

FURTHER READING

Davis, Rebecca Harding. *Life in the Iron Mills.* Edited by Cecelia Tichi. Boston: Bedford, 1998.

Rose, Jane Atteridge. *Rebecca Harding Davis.* New York: Twayne, 1993.

Day, Dorothy

- *Born: Nov. 8, 1897, Brooklyn, N.Y.*
- *Education: University of Illinois, attended 1914–16*
- *Accomplishments: Co-founder,* Catholic Worker *monthly paper (1933)*
- *Died: Nov. 29, 1980, New York, N.Y.*

Dorothy Day was the voice and conscience of progressive Roman Catholics for much of her life, a beloved and revered figure in American public life. A professed anarchist, she devoted her energies to promoting causes such as pacifism and the establishment of houses of hospitality for the urban poor.

While attending the University of Illinois, Day became involved with the Socialist party and with certain affiliates of the Communist party. But then her life took a different turn when she converted to the Roman Catholic Church, to which she brought her humanitarian concerns, in 1927. In 1933 she co-founded a newspaper, the *Catholic Worker,* which became a passionate advocate for the poor. She also started a hospitality house for the homeless in New York City. In addition, Day worked on behalf of

A devout Catholic, Dorothy Day nevertheless advocated many causes unpopular with the Catholic Church, including nuclear disarmament, opposition to the Vietnam War, and support for migrant farm workers. According to Day, "The greatest challenge of the day is: how to bring about a revolution of the heart."

the labor movement, going to California as an old woman to picket on behalf of the United Farm Workers, for example, and for disarmament and peace.

FURTHER READING

Coles, Robert. *Dorothy Day: A Radical Devotion.* Reading, Mass.: Addison-Wesley, 1987.

Day, Dorothy. *The Long Loneliness.* 1952. San Francisco: Harper & Row, 1981.

———. *Dorothy Day, Selected Writings: By Little and by Little.* Edited by Robert Ellsberg. Maryknoll, N.Y.: Orbis, 1992.

Miller, William D. *Dorothy Day.* San Francisco: Harper & Row, 1982.

Declaration of Independence

In 1776, as the members of the Second Continental Congress increasingly despaired that they could resolve the colonies' differences with Great Britain, they turned to Thomas Jefferson to draft a document that would enumerate their grievances against King George III and the mother country and explain the large political and philosophical reasons that could justify a revolution. The declaration that Jefferson produced embodied the most advanced thinking of his day about human rights—and about the requirement that government protect those rights. Members of the congress approved the declaration on July 4, 1776.

Jefferson said nothing about women's rights in his declaration. In his day, the issue of women's rights was only barely beginning to be formulated by a few thinkers. But when he said that "we believe that all men are created equal," he provided language that could and did inspire many groups, such as women, to question their inferior status in American society. Suffragist Elizabeth Cady Stanton, for example, borrowed much of Jefferson's language for the Declaration of Sentiments that she produced for the Seneca Falls Convention in 1848, the first meeting devoted to women's rights in the United States.

SEE ALSO

American Revolution; Declaration of Sentiments; Seneca Falls Convention

Declaration of Sentiments

Written by Elizabeth Cady Stanton and presented to the Seneca Falls convention in 1848, the Declaration of Sentiments was the founding statement of American feminism. Stanton used much of the familiar language and style of the Declaration of Independence but added her own thoughts to make it a revolutionary document: "We believe that all men *and women* are created equal," she proclaimed.

The declaration contained the first public demand for woman suffrage in the United States, and this was its most controversial premise. But the document also dealt with many other forms of inequality between the sexes, such as women's relative lack of access to educational and employment opportunities and the sexual double standard whereby men had more freedom than women. It was a bold statement, one that ruffled feathers among some of the more conservative people in attendance at Seneca Falls but inspired many others then and since. It was signed by 68 women and 32 men, less than one half of those present.

SEE ALSO

Seneca Falls; Stanton, Elizabeth Cady

FURTHER READING

Goldberg, Michael. *Breaking New Ground: American Women 1800–1848.* New York: Oxford University Press, 1994.

Sigerman, Harriet. *An Unfinished Battle: American Women 1848–1865.* New York: Oxford University Press, 1994.

Democratic party

One of the two major political parties in the United States, the Democratic party was not as ready as the Republican party to take women voters seriously after the ratification of the 19th Amendment in 1920. That began to change during the 1930s, when Eleanor Roosevelt was First Lady. The wife of Democratic President Franklin Delano Roosevelt, she crusaded to get women appointed to office and involved in party affairs. Eleanor Roosevelt was aided in her efforts by a powerhouse named Molly Dewson, who headed the Women's Division of the Democratic party. Dewson organized tens of thousands of women Democrats to get out the female vote, and that caught the male party leaders' attention. In short, the groundwork for the current prominence of such women Democrats as Patricia Schroeder, Geraldine Ferraro, and Hillary Rodham Clinton was laid in the depression decade.

Since the 1960s, as the Republican party has been moving in a more conservative direction—beginning to oppose the Equal Rights Amendment in the 1980s, for example, after a long history of supporting it—the Democratic party has been the party of choice for the majority of women by up to 20 percentage points. Democrats have been in favor of reproductive rights as well as other issues of concern to women, such as child care and family leave.

President Bill Clinton has appointed an unprecedented number of women to high offices, and that has solidified the party's hold on women voters. So worried are some Republicans about attracting women voters, put off by the party's ties to the religious right, that in California in 1999 one Republican coined the phrase "It's the women, stupid," a paraphrase of the Clinton campaign's slogan in 1992, "It's the economy, stupid."

SEE ALSO

Politics; Republican party

FURTHER READING

Ware, Susan. *Partner and I: Molly Dewson, Feminism, and New Deal Politics.* New Haven: Yale University Press, 1987.

Depression, Great

During the 1930s the U.S. economy collapsed following the crash of the stock market in 1929, and then a round of wage cuts and firings. Millions of Americans were out of work, and millions lacked some of the basic necessities of life. President Franklin Delano Roosevelt introduced his New Deal legislation to help reduce the suffering by providing jobs and aid, but only World War II, which started in 1941, truly reversed the country's economic difficulties by spurring a vast amount of government spending to equip the armed forces.

The Great Depression was hard on families. Unemployed breadwinners,

This photograph taken by Dorothea Lange, which is known as "Migrant Mother," has become one of the best-known images of the suffering during the Great Depression. The woman and her family had gone to California to pick crops and had found much hardship.

Though most Americans suffered during the Great Depression of the 1930s, it was hardest for poor families. Here a Mexican-American woman works at home, no doubt for a low wage, to help her family keep going.

usually men at that time, often became depressed about their situation and hard for others to live with. Men and women postponed marriage or starting families, owing to unstable or absent employment. Thousands of young people hit the road looking for a chance at a future.

For women, there were paradoxical developments. Although they suffered with their families, women were less likely to lose their jobs than men because most worked in sex-segregated employment and earned low wages, both of which made them less vulnerable to being fired.

During the Great Depression, the American labor movement scored a number of important victories. Until this time, women had been largely outside of organized labor, mainly because of sexism on the part of labor leaders. With the labor militancy of the 1930s and with unions looking aggressively for new members, the situation began, slowly, to change, and at the end of the decade there were some 800,000 women in unions; there had been only 250,000 at the decade's start.

FURTHER READING

McElvaine, Robert. *The Depression and New Deal.* New York: Oxford University Press, 1999.

Watkins, Tom H. *The Great Depression: America in the 1930s.* Boston: Little, Brown, 1993.

Dickinson, Emily

- *Born: Dec. 10, 1830, Amherst, Mass.*
- *Education: Amherst Academy and Mount Holyoke Female Seminary (attended 1847–48)*
- *Accomplishments: Poet*
- *Died: May 15, 1886, Amherst, Mass.*

Emily Dickinson was a poet whose work remained mostly unpublished during her lifetime except for a tiny handful (out of many hundreds of poems) that appeared in local newspapers. She rarely left the house during much of her adult life, and her legend is so powerful and so strange that at times it has taken attention away from her achievements.

Born to a well-established Massachusetts family, Dickinson briefly attended Mount Holyoke Female Seminary. Her one year there was a terrible trial to her because of fierce pressure to convert to evangelical Christianity; however, and she withdrew. A few years later her father served one term in Congress, and young Emily joined the rest of the family in visiting him in the nation's capital. But there were very few subsequent trips

In her own lifetime, the poet Emily Dickinson was unknown outside of a small circle of family and friends. This daguerreotype is the only known adult likeness of the poet.

away from Amherst, and by the late 1860s, Dickinson found it difficult to leave her bedroom in her parents' home, let alone the house or the city. The solitary life she chose is reflected in her poetry:

I'm Nobody! Who are you?
Are you nobody too?
Then there's a pair of us.
Don't tell—they'd banish us, you know.

How dreary to be somebody.
How public—like a frog—
To tell your name the livelong June
To an admiring Bog.

All the while Dickinson was writing her passionate, deeply felt yet spare poetry. Scholars have concluded that the writing was stimulated in part by her devotion to the Reverend Charles Wadsworth, a married clergyman she encountered in Philadelphia on her way home from a trip to Washington, D.C. She was desolated to learn in 1863 that Wadsworth had decided to accept an appointment to a church in San Francisco.

The same month that Wadsworth departed for the West, Dickinson wrote to Thomas Wentworth Higginson, a distinguished member of Boston literary circles, because she wanted to make contact with someone from outside her home. Higginson visited her and befriended her, but was incapable of truly understanding her genius. Indeed, he wanted to revise her poems and make them more conventional. Another literary friend was Helen Hunt Jackson, the author of the popular novel *Ramona.*

When Dickinson died at the age of 55, she left behind an astonishing body of work, found in 40 hand-sewn volumes in a locked chest. Spare and unsentimental, her poems wrestled with the great questions of human life and death.

SEE ALSO

Literature

FURTHER READING

Benfey, Christopher E. G. *Emily Dickinson: Lives of a Poet.* New York: Braziller, 1986.

Dickinson, Emily. *The Letters of Emily Dickinson.* Edited by Thomas H. Johnson. Cambridge: Harvard University Press, 1986.

Olsen, Victoria. *Emily Dickinson.* New York: Chelsea House, 1990.

Disability

Millions of American women suffer from physical disabilities. And women have been at the forefront of the movement to organize the disabled and create political pressure for legislative change, such as the Architectural Barriers Act of 1968 that requires that most buildings constructed with federal funds be accessible to the disabled; the Education for All Children with Disabilities Act of 1975 that requires that states receiving federal financial assistance provide all children with disabilities a free and appropriate education in the least restrictive setting possible; and the 1990 Americans with Disabilities Act that prohibits discrimination against the disabled.

During the 1960s and 1970s, a time of widespread social ferment in the United States, the disabled movement began to win other important victories, too. In New York City, for example, Judith Heumann sued the board of education and won the right to teach in the city's schools while in a wheelchair. She subsequently founded an independent living center in Berkeley, California, that spawned similar centers around the country. In 1971 she planned and led a weeks-long sit-in of the Federal Building in San Francisco by disabled activists to dramatize the need for better policies.

In 1999 Heumann is an Assistant Secretary for Education, charged with protecting the rights of disabled youngsters to a fully equal education under current legislation.

Divorce

Laws governing marriage and divorce have changed dramatically during the course of American history, and so, too, has the frequency with which people enter into a divorce. English law had treated marriage as impossible to dissolve, and that was how it was treated for the most part in the colonies, though a few colonies, such as Pennsylvania, Connecticut, and Massachusetts, allowed divorce in certain cases. After the American Revolution and the emergence of a new nation in the 1780s, however, divorce law began to be less strict, although it would be many years before the stigma attached to a failed marriage began to diminish.

After the founding of the new nation, judges instituted a system to try to determine who was at fault in a breakup. If a wife were the innocent party, then she could expect to receive monetary compensation, or alimony, but if she were the guilty party, she got nothing. During the 19th century, this was the basic philosophy that governed court proceedings, and divorce began to be more frequent, especially toward the end of the century. Some scholars have suggested that the very idealism and high expectations invested in marriage during this period may have contributed to increasing the divorce rate: people expected to be happy, and if they were not, they were likelier than before to seek legal recourse.

During the 20th century, the judicial trend has been to eliminate the concept of "fault" and to try to achieve fairness in property settlements, rather than base property divisions on who was judged to be the "guilty" party. Courts must also decide who will have custody of children and how much child support will be paid. Because women still earn, on the average, much less than men, they are likelier than men to see their standard of living decrease after a divorce.

The divorce rate rose rapidly between the early 1960s and the late 1970s, as divorces became easier to obtain, as more women were gainfully employed and able to support themselves, and, some have suggested, as more husbands were threatened by their wives' ambitions. Currently about one in two marriages in the United States ends in divorce, the highest rate in the country's history—in 1994 there were 17.4 million divorced adults in the country, four times the 4.3 million in 1970. Several studies have concluded that the institution of no-fault divorce laws was a significant factor in the increased divorce rates.

SEE ALSO

Custody, child; Marriage

FURTHER READING

Gleick, Elizabeth. "Should This Marriage Be Saved?" *Time,* February 27, 1994.

Riley, Glenda. *Divorce.* New York: Oxford University Press, 1991.

Dix, Dorothea Lynde

- *Born: Apr. 4, 1802, Hampden, Maine*
- *Education: Some high school*
- *Accomplishments: Founder or main impetus for founding of 32 mental institutions in the United States; superintendent, Civil War (Union) army nurses (1861–65)*
- *Died: July 18, 1887, Trenton, N.J.*

A reformer in the 19th century, Dorothea Dix is best known for her work with the mentally ill and for being the superintendent of army nurses during the Civil War (1861–65).

Dix had become a schoolteacher and was living the rather austere life of a New England spinster—her one engagement was broken off for unknown reasons—when at the age of 39 she found her life's work. She taught a Sunday school class for women prisoners and while there encountered a group of mentally ill women who had been locked up along with the criminals. Henceforth Dix crusaded tirelessly to improve the treatment for such people. She helped found 32 mental hospitals in the United States and influenced the founding of many more both here and abroad.

Dix's Civil War work was less effective. By the time she offered to oversee the recruitment of nurses for the Union, she had become rather inflexible and often difficult. Even those who respected her reform contributions agreed that she was not a good administrator.

Dorothea Dix was a one-woman committee to improve the care of the mentally ill, and she also supervised the recruitment and training of military nurses for the North during the Civil War.

FURTHER READING

Gollaher, David. *Voice for the Mad: The Life of Dorothea Dix*. New York: Free Press, 1995.

Schlaifer, Charles, and Lucy Freeman. *Heart's Work: Civil War Heroine and Champion of the Mentally Ill, Dorothea Lynde Dix*. New York: Paragon House, 1991.

Domesticity

During the 19th century, home and motherhood began to enjoy an unprecedented respect in the United States. Historians refer to this glorification of the home as an "ideology of domesticity" or even "cult of domesticity."

The home was seen as a woman's chief responsibility before, during, and after the height of the domestic ideal. What had been considered, however, routine and humdrum work in the colonial period—and what women have often tried to escape in the 20th century—became suffused with the deepest cultural and Christian spiritual values between about 1830 and 1870, when domesticity was at its peak. Horace Bushnell, a leading Protestant theologian, described the home as vitally important to the process of salvation, for example, and male advice givers to other men described the home as "the empire of the mother," In consequence, women, as guardians of this sacred place, gained a moral authority they

In the 19th century, middle-class Americans venerated domestic bliss as they never have before or since. The sewing machine in this idealized depiction of home, however, hints at the many changes that would soon occur when the home itself began to be industrialized.

had not had earlier. Some women reformers began to use this authority to craft a distinctive female political culture, based not on voting but on uplift. During the Civil War of 1861–65, for example, generals listened to women bringing humanitarian relief when the latter claimed to be acting in the name of the soldiers' mothers.

The domestic ideal was tied to a particular moment in U.S. history when the country was still overwhelmingly Protestant (because large numbers of immigrants from non-Protestant countries had not yet arrived). It gave women cultural power—if they conformed to very strict roles as demure and proper housewives—but it also reinforced stereotypes that have kept women "in their place" in the home.

Today's domesticity is no longer tied to moral authority. Rather, it is linked to consumption patterns and to the media. To cite just one example, Martha Stewart has built an empire around people's yearnings for an upscale version of home, and she can be seen on television and in the pages of her magazine promoting that vision.

FURTHER READING

Matthews, Glenna. *"Just a Housewife": The Rise and Fall of Domesticity in America.* New York: Oxford University Press, 1987.

Domestic violence

Every year hundreds of thousands of women—some estimates say that the number is as high as 4 million—suffer physical abuse, including permanent injury or death, at the hands of their husbands or boyfriends. Since the 1970s, many communities have established shelters for battered women, and police departments have started training programs to sensitize their officers to deal more effectively with the problem by listening to victims more carefully and more respectfully.

The National Coalition Against Domestic Violence, established in 1978, has lobbied successfully for legal changes that give battered women the right to stay in the house while the batterer is evicted and the right to continue to receive child support. Nonetheless, domestic violence remains a problem.

When most people lived in villages or small towns and when many women lived close to their families, an abusive man might well have had to answer to a woman's relatives or neighbors for his actions. Now women are more likely to be isolated and, as a result, more vulnerable. Some abusive men are so dangerous that even when there is effective police intervention, a woman may have to move away—and even adopt a new identity—in order to protect herself.

Why do men—and a few women—become violent to those they supposedly love? Researchers suggest that a batterer was probably beaten himself as a child and suffers from a lack of self-esteem and that he more than likely abuses alcohol or other substances. Not having received love himself, he lashes out at those he sees as standing in the way of his gratifying his wishes. Studies also suggest that violence cuts across the lines of social class and that it affects gay and lesbian households as well as those of heterosexuals.

FURTHER READING

Gordon, Linda. *Heroes of Their Own Lives: The Politics and History of Family Violence, Boston, 1880–1960.* New York: Viking, 1988.

Kwuon, Im Jung. "Facing Down Abusers: Teaching Convicted Batterers How to Change Their Ways Is a Difficult, Dangerous Process." *Newsweek,* August 10, 1998.

Smolowe, Jill. "Behavior: When Violence Hits Home." *Time,* July 4, 1994.

Douglas, Helen Gahagan

- *Born: Nov. 25, 1900, Boonton, N.J.*
- *Education: Barnard College, attended 1920–22*
- *Accomplishments: Various Broadway appearances (1922–36); member, national advisory committee to the Works Progress Administration (1939); U.S. Representative (Democrat–Calif., 1945–51); delegate, United Nations General Assembly (1946); author,* The Eleanor Roosevelt We Remember *(1963)*
- *Died: June 28, 1980, New York, N.Y.*

A three-term congresswoman, Helen Gahagan Douglas is best known for losing to Richard Nixon in the 1950 California race for a U.S. Senate seat. That race was historic because Nixon employed dirty tactics against her. But to know her only for that reason distorts the legacy of a woman who was a groundbreaking figure in the history of women and politics, because she played so high-profile a role in Congress at a time when very few women served there. For example, in 1947 she carried a shopping basket into the House to dramatize a speech she made on behalf of housewives and their problems with high prices.

Born to a wealthy family, Helen Gahagan attended Barnard College in New York City. While still in college, she was "discovered" in a school play and cast in a Broadway production, for which she received glowing reviews. One critic wrote that she was not only one of the 10 most beautiful women in the country, but all 10 rolled into one. Her biographer believes that the confidence she derived from this early triumph served her well in her subsequent political career.

Many years later, after she had enjoyed a stage career and had married fellow actor Melvyn Douglas, Helen Douglas found herself living in Hollywood but

Helen Gahagan Douglas poses with supporters in front of a campaign sound truck during her 1950 Senate campaign. Much of the financial support for her campaign came from her Hollywood friends.

lacking acting jobs. This was during the Great Depression of the 1930s, when there was widespread suffering among the poor and unemployed. Douglas began to take an interest in the plight of the Dust Bowl refugees, people who had gone from the Midwest to California to find work only to meet with few opportunities and indifference. It soon came to the attention of President Franklin Roosevelt and First Lady Eleanor Roosevelt that a glamorous actress was making speeches about the poor. They recruited her to get involved in Democratic party politics. In 1944, Douglas ran for Congress.

Serving in the House of Representatives from 1945 to 1951, Douglas was a passionate advocate for the rights of African Americans, and she supported organized labor, granting federal money for cancer research, and other liberal causes. She was never part of the "insider" circles in Congress because of her sex, but she drew public attention to the issues she cared about.

Deciding to run for the Senate in 1950, Douglas had to face her opponent Richard Nixon's unsupported charges that she was a communist sympathizer. Though her career in electoral politics ended with this election, she continued to be active on behalf of her causes for the rest of her life.

SEE ALSO

Congress, U.S.; Democratic party; Politics

FURTHER READING

Scobie, Ingrid. *Center Stage.* New York: Oxford University Press, 1992.

Duncan, Isadora

- *Born: May 27, 1878, San Francisco, Calif.*
- *Education: Elementary school*
- *Accomplishments: Pioneer of modern dance; author,* My Life *(autobiography, 1927)*
- *Died: Sept. 14, 1927, Nice, France*

Isadora Duncan was an important and innovative modern dancer, but to her contemporaries in the early 1900s, she also seemed the very embodiment of the freer spirit of the new century. Insisting that she would dance only to the music of the greatest composers such as Beethoven and Wagner, she cast aside convention both in her life and in her art.

Born in San Francisco, Isadora was raised in Oakland by a freethinking mother who had divorced the child's father shortly after she was born. This unusual household anticipated the way of life and values of hippies living in the San Francisco Bay Area during the 1960s. Isadora began to study dance as a young girl, and by the time she was 10, she had dropped out of school and was herself giving dance lessons. From that time on, she acquired an education only by spending time at the Oakland Public Library.

A stunningly beautiful young woman, Isadora moved with her mother to New York in 1896 to dance. At the age of 21, she went to Europe, where she further developed her style of dance, which rejected the formal movements of ballet for improvised natural movements of her own devising. In her dances she dressed unconventionally in loose, flowing, and (for that time) rather revealing clothes. Captivating audiences in New York and in Europe with her spontaneous expressiveness, which began to integrate movements stylized from classical Greek sculpture, she became friendly with experimental artists working in several fields. Her revolutionary approach to dance paved the way for the later acceptance of modern dance forms developed by Martha Graham and others.

Duncan's life, which had many triumphs, on the stages of Europe especially, also had its share of tragedies. The mother of two children, she lost both in 1913 when the car they were riding in rolled into the Seine River in Paris. In 1922 she married for the first time, but her husband, a young Russian poet, was mentally unstable. Duncan never fully recovered from the death of her children, and in 1927 she herself died in a horrifying car accident caused by the long silk scarf that she was wearing. The scarf caught in the wheel of a sports car Duncan was entering, and when the car started off, the scarf twisted around the spokes of the wheel and broke her neck.

SEE ALSO

Dance

FURTHER READING

Blair, Fredrika. *Isadora: Portrait of the Artist as a Woman.* New York: Quill, 1986.

Daly, Ann. *Done into Dance: Isadora Duncan in America.* Bloomington: Indiana University Press, 1995.

Duncan, Isadora. *My Life.* New York: Award, 1966.

Kozodoy, Ruth. *Isadora Duncan.* New York: Chelsea House, 1988.

Duniway, Abigail Scott

- *Born: Oct. 22, 1834, Groveland, Ill.*
- *Education: Self-taught*
- *Accomplishments: Founder,* New Northwest *newspaper (Portland, Oreg., 1871); organizer, Oregon Equal Suffrage Association (1873); editor,* Pacific Empire *(1895–98)*
- *Died: Oct. 11, 1915, Portland, Oreg.*

Abigail Scott Duniway was a pioneer who traveled on the Oregon Trail with her family to the West Coast when she was 17, and she later became a suffragist leader.

The Scott family's trek to Oregon was marred by tragedy. Abigail's mother died of cholera during the journey, and when the family reached Oregon, the youngest member, a three-year-old boy, died also. Plunging immediately into the life of the new settlement nonetheless, young Abigail began teaching school, and a few months later she married Benjamin Duniway, a farmer. She soon had two children.

Duniway's difficult life became even more difficult when her husband was permanently disabled. Forced to be the family breadwinner, Duniway once again taught school and then opened a shop to sell hats and sewing notions.

During her shopkeeping days, Duniway talked to her customers about *their* difficulties, and she became convinced that only the ability to vote would make it possible for women to protect their interests. In 1871 she moved to Portland and began to publish a weekly women's rights newspaper. She then spearheaded the formation of the Oregon Equal Suffrage Association and became its first president. She did

Abigail Scott Duniway was the Northwest's best-known suffragist. After traveling to Oregon with her family in the mid-19th century, she lived almost long enough to vote in 1920.

not live to see the ratification in 1920 of the 19th Amendment, granting women the right to vote, but she did witness Oregon's granting suffrage to women in 1912. Duniway was given the honor of being the state's first registered woman voter.

SEE ALSO

Suffrage, woman

FURTHER READING

Moynihan, Ruth Barnes. *Rebel for Rights: Abigail Scott Duniway.* New Haven: Yale University Press, 1983.

Sigerman, Harriet. *Laborers for Liberty: American Women 1865–1890.* New York: Oxford University Press, 1994.

Dyer, Mary

- *Born: Date unknown, probably Somersetshire, England*
- *Education: Unknown*
- *Accomplishments: Religious martyr*
- *Died: June 1, 1660, Boston, Mass.*

Mary Dyer was a martyr to her Quaker beliefs—hanged because the colony of Massachusetts had banned Quakers on penalty of death, and she went there anyway.

Dyer and her husband moved to Massachusetts from England in the 1630s and were admitted to the Puritan church there, an important achievement because the Puritans maintained strict standards about who could join. But Mary Dyer soon got into trouble with the colony's leaders when she sided with a woman named Anne Hutchinson who criticized the Puritan church for not being adequately filled with the Holy Spirit. Hutchinson and her supporters were all banished from the colony.

During the next several years Mary and William Dyer settled in Rhode Island and began raising a family. In 1652 they returned to England for an extended stay. There, Mary Dyer met the founder of the Society of Friends, or Quakers, and became a convert. (Indeed, the Quakers' "Inner Light" of communion with the divine bore a resemblance to Anne Hutchinson's teachings about the significance of each individual's own revelations.)

Returning to New England, Mary Dyer was appalled to discover that Massachusetts, committed to upholding the Congregationalist faith, had passed a law banning Quakers from residing there. Out of the depths of her commitment to her Quaker beliefs, she insisted on challenging the law, repeatedly returning to Boston, from which she was repeatedly banished, resolving to "look the bloody laws in the face." In 1658, the city passed a law banishing Quakers on "pain of death." When Mary Dyer returned in 1660, she paid with her life.

In 1959 Massachusetts erected a statue of Mary Dyer that stands on the grounds of the State House.

SEE ALSO

Hutchinson, Anne; Quakers

Earhart, Amelia

- *Born: July 24, 1897, Atchison, Kans.*
- *Education: High school, graduated 1916*
- *Accomplishments: First woman to fly across the Atlantic (1928); first person to fly from Hawaii to California (1935)*
- *Died: Around July 2, 1937*

Aviator Amelia Earhart died at the height of her fame, lost under mysterious circumstances on an attempted flight

The legendary aviator Amelia Earhart captured the imagination of her fellow Americans from the start of her flying career. The fact that her plane was lost in the Pacific under still-mysterious circumstances only added to the legend.

around the world. Ever since, Americans have been intrigued by her story.

The daughter of a well-to-do family, Earhart became fascinated by planes as a young woman. She started taking flying lessons in her early 20s, and made her first solo flight in 1921. Soon thereafter, her parents divorced, the family inheritance vanished, and Earhart had to start supporting herself in more practical ways, first as a teacher and then as a social worker. She continued to be devoted to flying, though.

In 1927 Charles Lindbergh made his solo flight across the Atlantic, a feat that captivated the country as few exploits have in U.S. history. In 1928 Earhart was chosen by publisher George Palmer Putnam to be the only woman aboard another pioneering transatlantic flight. As it happened, she bore a striking resemblance to Lindbergh and thus she became known as "Lady Lindy." Not necessarily the most accomplished woman pilot of her time—others had more actual flying experience—she was the most celebrated because of this quirk of nature; though she was on the transatlantic flight, her role consisted of keeping the flight log.

During the next few years, Earhart had many achievements, such as writing a book about the flight and becoming vice president of Lusington Airlines, and married George Palmer Putnam. When she set off on her doomed flight in 1937 headed for an island in the mid-Pacific, she was flying in a plane specially fitted out for her by Purdue University, which had hoped to gain information valuable for aeronautical research. Earhart disappeared over the Pacific, and as yet no one knows exactly what happened to her.

In the late 1990s, researchers put together evidence that strongly suggests that she crash-landed on Gardner Island (about 1,000 miles north of Fiji) and died awaiting rescue. They found remains of American-made shoes there, and also turned up records from British work crews who, in 1939, found a skull and some bones along with a sextant box near the remains of a campfire. Though the bones themselves have yet to be located, their measurements were recorded, and these would suggest that the skeleton was that of a rather tall Caucasian woman like Earhart.

In the days when many professions were closed to women, the courageous Earhart was a role model for a generation of girls.

FURTHER READING

Morrissey, Muriel Earhart. *Amelia, My Courageous Sister.* Santa Clara, Calif.: Osborne, 1987.

Shore, Nancy. *Amelia Earhart.* New York: Chelsea House, 1987.

Rich, Doris. *Amelia Earhart: A Biography.* Washington, D.C.: Smithsonian Institution Press, 1989.

Ware, Susan. *Still Missing: Amelia Earhart and the Search for Modern Feminism.* New York: Norton, 1993.

Eating disorders

The two principal eating disorders in the United States in the 20th century are anorexia nervosa and bulimia. Someone suffering from anorexia refuses to eat enough food to maintain a healthy weight. She may also over-exercise as a way of whittling away at her body. In acute cases she may actually starve to death. Bulimia is a related disorder; a bulimic person artificially induces vomiting after an eating binge so as not to gain weight.

For reasons that are not yet fully understood, eating disorders afflict women far more than men, and young women more than those who are older. A girl may develop a disorder as the result of society's unrealistic expectations of thinness as a female goal—thinness that has become ever more desirable in the late 20th century—as well as because of tensions within her family, which may stem from sexual abuse, domestic violence, or overly high expectations her parents have for her. Medical professionals have learned that the cure for an eating disorder may involve changing how members of the family interact.

Food refusal by young women has been recorded for centuries and in many different cultures, as with some of the European women (such as Catherine of Siena) who were subsequently canonized as Catholic saints. Often associated with the onset of puberty, its causes are still inadequately understood. Since 1960 the incidence of eating disorders has risen (it is estimated that in the mid-1990s about 1 percent of adolescent girls suffered from anorexia, and that about 4 percent of college-age women had bulimia), most likely because the cultural images of desirable women have been so extraordinarily thin during this time. When girls see such women in movies, on TV, and in magazines, they often try to starve themselves into looking like these stars.

FURTHER READING

Apostolides, Marianne. *Inner Hunger: A Young Woman's Struggle Through Anorexia and Bulimia.* New York: Norton, 1998.
Brumberg, Joan Jacobs. *The Body Project.* New York: Random House, 1997.

Eddy, Mary Baker

- *Born: July 16, 1821, Bow, N.H.*
- *Education: Schooled at home*
- *Accomplishments: Founder, First Church of Christ, Scientist (1879); founder, Massachusetts Metaphysical College (1881); founder,* Christian Science Journal *(1883),* Christian Science Sentinel *(1898), and* The Christian Science Monitor *(1908); author,* Miscellaneous Writings *(1896);* Retrospection and Introspection *(1892);* Unity of Good *(1887);* Rudimental Divine Science *(1908)*
- *Died: Dec. 3, 1910, Chestnut Hill, Mass.*

The founder of the Church of Christ, Scientist, Mary Baker Eddy participated in a wave of religious innovation that swept her native New England during the 19th century.

Mary Baker was often ill as a child. A woman who would marry three times and spend years in quest of good health, she suffered from excessive nervousness for most of her life. In 1862 she consulted a healer named Phineas Quimby, whose methods brought her relief. Quimby emphasized the importance of the mind—disease was a false "belief"—

Mary Baker Eddy, the founder of Christian Science, as a mature woman. She had triumphed over a sickly childhood, and this accomplishment, in the view of some scholars, helped convince her that illness is an illusion.

to the healing process, and his teachings made a deep impression on Baker. Indeed, he had used the term "Christian Science," no doubt one of the reasons she would use it. In the years to come, she elaborated on Quimby's ideas and added some of her own about the power of mind in the healing process. She also began to develop a vision of leading a Christian Science church. In 1875 the first Christian Science services were held in Lynn, Massachusetts, and that same year she published the book that set forth her ideas about the spiritual dimensions of healing, *Science and Health.*

Mary Baker Eddy's long life was tempestuous—there were many controversies with former followers over the ownership of ideas—but the religion she founded spread throughout the United States and into many other countries.

SEE ALSO
Religion

FURTHER READING

Eddy, Mary Baker. *Science and Health: With Key to the Scriptures.* Boston: First Church of Christ, Scientist, 1994.

Gill, Gillian. *Mary Baker Eddy.* Reading, Mass.: Perseus, 1998.

Smith, Louise A. *Mary Baker Eddy.* New York: Chelsea House, 1991.

Education

Although women in the United States have benefited from a national commitment to schooling that gave them opportunities not enjoyed by women elsewhere, they have also had to fight to obtain access to higher education and to graduate and professional training. Despite the success of the schools for girls and very young women built from the 1790s on and the high literacy rate for women in the United States, women have had to struggle to be taken seriously in academia. And they gained unfettered access to graduate school only after the passage of Title IX of the Education Act Amendments in 1972.

The Founding Fathers considered an educated citizenry essential to the success of the American experiment in self-government, and the nation became committed to educating white girls. Although girls could not grow up to be citizens in the same way that boys could—that is, they could neither vote nor serve on juries—they would be the mothers of citizens. Because they would be training the next generation of voters, women would need to be literate and conversant with political topics. An educated citizenry also required an abundance of teachers, and early in the 1800s unmarried women began to be the favorite choice for this position because they could be paid less than men. These rationalizations for female education did not, of course, require that girls attend college or pursue true

Women students work in the chemistry lab at Florida State College for Women about 1910. Higher education for women, particularly in the sciences, was still relatively unusual at that time.

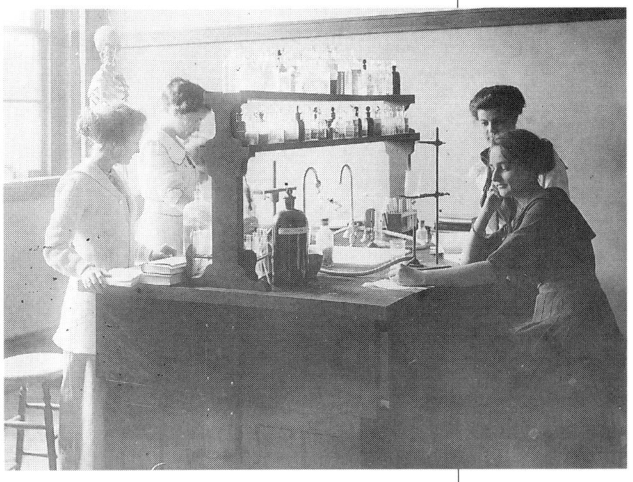

proficiency in a learned discipline.

Yet even though male and female education was born unequal in that no one thought that girls should be trained for careers or serious intellectual pursuits, the mere fact that so many girls began to receive systematic education laid the groundwork for profound social change. Then when public elementary schools began to be built between 1820 and 1850, girls and boys started sharing the same classrooms. Each generation of American women born in the 19th century had broader and better educational opportunities than the preceding one, with higher education beginning to be available by mid-century, and each generation pushed the demand for women's rights a little further. By the late 19th century, a number of women's colleges had been established, and they were providing a truly challenging curriculum to their students.

As for women of color, their struggle for education was even more difficult than that of whites. Slaves of both sexes were forbidden to read and write, and free blacks often had to use their own scarce resources to set up schools, because they were unwelcome in white public schools. Until the Supreme Court decision of *Brown* v. *Board of Education* in 1954, it was legal to segregate children of color. For Native American women, to receive an education from a white public school might well have meant being removed from their families and being forbidden to speak their native languages.

Today, although women and men do not yet have equality throughout the educational system—men still outnumber women as professors, for example—there has been immense progress. Women are college professors as well as elementary school teachers. They are principals and superintendents. They are college presidents. And they are students in law schools and medical schools, where less than 10 percent of the student body was female in the 1970s.

SEE ALSO

Education Act Amendments (1972); Teaching; Universities; Women's colleges

FURTHER READING

Harwarth, Irene. *Women's Colleges in the United States: History, Issues, and Challenges.* Washington, D.C.: National Institute on Postsecondary Education, 1997.

Horowitz, Helen L. *Alma Mater: Design and Experience in the Women's Colleges from Their Nineteenth-Century Beginnings to the 1930s.* Amherst: University of Massachusetts Press, 1993.

Education Act Amendments (1972)

Title IX of the Education Act Amendments of 1972 is one of the most important laws expanding the rights of women ever to have been passed by Congress. Before Title IX, colleges and universities routinely discriminated against women in athletics and in their admission policies to graduate and professional schools. This law changed that.

Bitterly opposed by the educational establishment, Title IX created a contractual arrangement between the federal government and every institution of higher education. Because their operating costs are often very high, most universities and colleges rely heavily on federal funds. If a university wanted federal dollars for research, it had to quit discriminating against women, thus creating a powerful financial incentive for change.

Women's participation in sports has grown tenfold since Title IX has been on the books because women can now, for example, compete for athletic scholarships, and women's team sports are now covered on television. The female enrollment in many high-powered professional programs, which had been disproportionately male, now approaches or exceeds 50 percent.

Environmental movement

An attempt to draw attention to environmental damage and work to preserve natural resources, the environmental movement has drawn strength from the participation of many women over the years. Indeed, it is estimated that women constitute some 60 to 80 percent of the membership of today's mainstream environmental organizations.

In the late 1800s and early 1900s, even before women could vote, they had started to agitate to preserve natural resources. Though none of the women from these years is as famous as, say, Sierra Club founder John Muir, their energy was indispensable in various campaigns to set aside land for state and national parks.

One early writer about the natural landscape was Mary Austin, author of *The Land of Little Rain,* published in 1903, which was a poetic evocation of California's Owens Valley. Somewhat later, in the late 1940s, activist-writer Marjory Stoneman Douglas played an important role in the creation of Everglades National Park in Florida by writing a book, *The Everglades: River of Grass,* about the ecological importance of this area of saltwater marsh and swampland.

The modern environmental movement began in the 1960s. One of the catalysts for it was the publication of Rachel Carson's *Silent Spring* in 1962. Her outcry against the environmental damage done by pesticides rallied public opinion and helped lead to the creation of the Environmental Protection Agency in 1970, the first comprehensive federal agency established to monitor and control pollution.

In the 1970s many new organizations were founded, the older ones such as the Sierra Club, founded in 1892 to

Following in a long tradition of activist women, these young women learn about California's complex water delivery system through field education with the Save the Bay group.

protect the environment, grew in membership, and Congress passed an unprecedented amount of environmental legislation such as the Clean Water Act and the Safe Drinking Water Act, aimed at cleaning up lakes and rivers and at setting federal standards for purity of water.

During this era of environmental awareness, women were also involved in many local, grassroots reforms. Throughout many parts of the country, women organized to protect the landscape and with great effect. In the San Francisco Bay Area, for example, a group of faculty wives at the University of California, Berkeley, started a group called Save the Bay. They fought so effectively to preserve the coastline that they succeeded in halting any further private development along the shore of the bay.

On the other side of the continent, in New York State, a blue-collar housewife named Lois Gibbs organized her neighbors into the Love Canal Homeowners' Association in 1978 to protest the degradation of their surroundings owing to the discharge of toxic industrial waste into the canal. The association succeeded in winning compensation from the state for homes whose property values were destroyed.

So integral has environmental activism been in many women's lives that one strand of feminism is known as ecofeminism, a visionary outlook that sees connections between women as mothers and women as stewards of the earth, and sees direct parallels between the progress of the ecology movement and that of the feminist movement.

SEE ALSO

Carson, Rachel

FURTHER READING

Keene, Ann. *Earthkeepers*. New York: Oxford University Press, 1994.

Seager, Joni. *Earth Follies*. New York: Routledge, 1993.

Equal Pay Act (1963)

The impetus for legislation to equalize the pay for men and women performing the same jobs came from more than one direction: male trade unionists wanted it so that employers could not save money by hiring women as cheap labor, and organized women's groups wanted it as a matter of equality.

Unions began campaigning for equal pay in the late 19th century, and then during World War II (1941–45), the National War Labor Board endorsed the principle of equal pay for the duration of the war. After the war ended, the U.S. Women's Bureau joined the campaign, a crusade that bore fruit during the administration of John F. Kennedy in the early 1960s.

As passed by Congress in 1963, the Equal Pay Act reaches a relatively narrow segment of the workforce, those covered by the Fair Labor Standards Act of 1938. Now many women's groups campaign for equal pay for jobs that are not exactly the same but have "comparable worth."

SEE ALSO

Comparable worth; Women's Bureau, U.S.

Equal Rights Amendment (ERA)

In 1972 Congress overwhelmingly passed a proposed amendment to the U.S. Constitution and sent it off to be ratified by the required number of

The League of Women Voters did a takeoff on the famous Grant Wood painting American Gothic *to promote passage of the ERA. The message: equal rights for women were as American as apple pie, straight from the heartland.*

states. The amendment said, "Equality of rights under the law shall not be denied or abridged by the United States or by any State on account of sex." Opinion polls showed that the amendment was popular, and most people believed that it would soon be ratified by the required 38 states. But it was not.

The Equal Rights Amendment (ERA) had had a curious history. Originally introduced into Congress in 1923 using very similar wording, it had been the brainchild of Alice Paul, leader of the feminist National Woman's Party. She and her group argued that women needed to be treated as individuals, with the exact same rights as men, no more and no less. But this approach refuted the movement to protect the rights of women workers as a special category (for example, rights to a maximum number of hours), a position that had been upheld in the U.S. Supreme Court decision in *Muller* v. *Oregon* in 1908, which asserted that women were in a class by themselves, and need special legislation for their protection from exploitation. Therefore both organized labor and most organized women's groups—which had crusaded to secure special protection for women workers—opposed the ERA, a stance that would not fully change until the birth of the modern women's movement.

Over the decades, the ERA gradually picked up support from more individuals and groups; the National Federation of Business and Professional Women endorsed it in 1937. By the time that John F. Kennedy entered the White House in 1961, he felt pressure from different portions of the electorate. Organized labor continued to oppose the ERA, but many women's groups were reexamining the issue. This controversy played a large role in leading him to convene the first Presidential Commission on the Status of Women early in his administration.

The Kennedy Commission plus the passage of important legislation—such as the Equal Pay Act of 1963, Title VII of the Civil Rights Act of 1964, which prohibited discrimination on the basis of sex in employment, and the founding of the National Organization for Women in 1966—helped create the climate of opinion that led Congress to pass the ERA in 1972.

What supporters had not reckoned on was the depth and strength of the opposition, most effectively organized by anti–women's liberation activist Phyllis Schlafly's STOP-ERA. Opponents of the ERA charged that the amendment would undermine the strength of the American family by taking away the legal rights of wives, that it would lead to unisex rest rooms, that it would require women to fight side by side with men in times of war.

In the end the ERA fell three states short of the number needed to ratify, with the opposition most concentrated in the South, where Christian fundamentalists and other conservatives are strongest. Under the constitution, the ERA had only a limited amount of time to garner support, and that time ran out in 1982, even after Congress had granted it one extension. It failed despite the fact that polls consistently showed that a majority of Americans supported it.

Political scientists suggest that the amendment failed not only because of the hard work of the opposition but because many feminist groups had not yet learned to be effective at the level of the state legislatures, where the ratification decisions were being made.

SEE ALSO

Commission on the Status of Women; *Muller* v. *Oregon* (1908); National Woman's Party; STOP-ERA

FURTHER READING

Mansbridge, Jane. *Why We Lost the ERA.* Chicago: University of Chicago Press, 1986.

Schlafly, Phyllis. *The Power of the Positive Woman.* New York: Jove Publications, 1977.

Evert, Chris

- *Born: Dec. 21, 1954, Fort Lauderdale, Fla.*
- *Education: High school, graduated 1973*
- *Accomplishments: Winner, 18 tennis Grand Slam singles titles (1975–86); president, Women's Tennis Association (1982–91); voted greatest woman athlete in the past 25 years by the Women's Sports Foundation (1985); founder, Chris Evert Charities (1989); Women's Tennis Association Award (1992); International Tennis Hall of Fame (inducted 1995)*

Chris Evert was one of the tennis champions of the modern era as well as one of the outstanding women athletes of the 20th century. When she was on a winning streak, she was almost unbeatable.

The daughter of a tennis-pro father, Evert showed her talent at an early age. As a teenage amateur, she had one winning streak of 46 consecutive matches. Later, as a pro, she had a winning streak of 56 matches. In 1981 she won one of tennis's biggest events, Wimbledon, without losing a set on her way to victory. Her game relied not so much on power as on steadiness and steely nerves.

Just as Evert rose to prominence, Billie Jean King, the reigning tennis champ, was mounting a crusade to secure more money for women tennis champions, a crusade from which Evert benefited. Her fame also brought her endorsements, and, in turn, those endorsements enhanced her visibility, making Evert one of the best-known women in the country at the height of her career. At the same time, Evert's rivalry with the slightly younger Martina Navratilova challenged each woman to play her best and brought many new fans to tennis.

Although they competed on the court, Evert and Navratilova admired and respected one another. They faced

Known for her coolness under pressure, Chris Evert won at least one Grand Slam singles championship every year from 1974 to 1986, a record. During her career, she won 157 professional singles titles, including six U.S. Open championships.

each other 14 times in Grand Slam events (the U.S. Open, Wimbledon, the French Open, and the Australian Open), with Navratilova winning on 10 occasions. Each woman, however, finished her career with the same number of Grand Slam singles victories—18.

Four times the Associated Press's woman athlete of the year, Evert is married to Andy Mills, a skier, whom she wed in 1988 after a brief first marriage to John Lloyd. When she retired from professional tennis in 1989, Evert founded Chris Evert Charities, which raises money to fight drug abuse and help neglected, drug-exposed, and abused children. She is also active as a tennis commentator on television.

SEE ALSO

King, Billie Jean Moffitt; Navratilova, Martina; Sports

FURTHER READING

Evert Lloyd, Chris. *Chrissie: My Own Story.* New York: Simon & Schuster, 1982.

Families

Whom do we count as part of our families and whom do we exclude? This might seem straightforward, but, in fact, cultures differ in the answers they give. Put another way, what matters most—blood ties or people's feelings about one another? American families have changed dramatically over the centuries in composition and in the way family members interact with one another.

One of the major reasons for so much change lies in the fact that there was a much higher infant mortality rate and a much lower life expectancy in the 18th and 19th centuries than in the 20th (as late as 1900, for example, life expectancy was just 47 years, whereas at the end of the 20th century, Americans could expect to live well into their 80s). As a result, parents often lost one or more children to death, and the children who survived could not count on getting to know their grandparents, as they are likely to now. The omnipresence of death shaped the character of family life.

In preindustrial America most European immigrants formed the kind of family that scholars call "traditional." This kind of family was organized around production, and most family members were expected to contribute to the household economy by doing their share of the workload on the farm or in the workshop. Households were usually large, owing to the presence of servants and possibly apprentices, but there were rarely three generations under one roof, usually because the grandparents had already died. The authority belonged to the father, with the mother as his second-in-command rather than his equal. Slave families differed from white families in that African Americans clung to earlier patterns from their homelands that played up the importance of the extended family of aunts, uncles, and cousins, and not just the immediate nuclear family.

In the early 19th century, industrialization began to usher in a new family form in which the father left the household to go to work in an office or factory, while his wife stayed home. The household was no longer the center of production. Rather, the mother's "job" was now concentrated on maintaining the emotional health of family members, and the children's "job" was to secure an education. The birthrate began to decline immediately, for complicated reasons including a lesser need for children's labor. Scholars also believe that this "modern" family was more democratic than its predecessor, with authority shared more evenly between husband and wife. As succeeding waves of immigrants arrived in this country, they, too, began to assimilate to American ways, including American family patterns. But the modern family in its classic form was a middle-class formation to which newcomers could only aspire at first.

The modern family is what most Americans think about when they talk about an "ideal" family, though in fact it was the creation of a specific historical period. Since the 1960s, with the rise in divorce, with the increase in the number of households composed of only a single individual, with millions of women entering the workforce, with explosive changes in gender roles, and with increasing acceptance of gay and lesbian parenting, scholars now refer to a new and more flexible family type—the postmodern family. In this new type of family, ties of marriage or kinship may be much less important than in the past. Now modern and postmodern families coexist, with immigrant continuing to arrive with their own family forms that will adapt to the United States over time.

SEE ALSO

Childhood; Custody, child; Divorce; Marriage

FURTHER READING

Coontz, Stephanie. *The Way We Never Were*. New York: Basic Books, 1992.
Degler, Carl. *At Odds: Women and the Family from the Revolution to the Present.* New York: Oxford University Press, 1980.

Fashion

The fashion in American women's clothing has always reflected a great number of influences—from the latest designs in Europe to the general level of prosperity—or lack thereof—in the United States. What a woman chooses to wear is also influenced by her own class position as well as her age. Thus a rich woman today might wear designer clothes, while a less affluent one may wear something from a discount store.

In the 18th century, such differences were written into the law of the Puritan colonies in New England. So-called sumptuary laws forbade poorer women from wearing clothes made of silk and from wearing certain styles that seemed overly ostentatious. These laws were often ignored, however, by women who wanted to wear the latest fashion.

Legislators tried to regulate fashions in part to maintain status differences, and in part because fabric itself was a rare and precious commodity in the days before the Industrial Revolution brought machine-made goods into American households. Beginning around 1800 domestic factories could produce more cloth, so fabric began to be more readily available, and the huge skirts over hooped petticoats that were fashionable in the mid-19th century reflected its abundance. No longer did lawmakers try to regulate what women wore.

Women's fashions also reflect the position of women in a society. American women's clothing, for example, used to be much more restrictive than it is now, with tight corseting and cumbersome skirts that permitted little freedom of movement. As women have won more freedom in the 20th century, their clothing has reflected that development. The flappers of the 1920s, for example, wore loose clothing and much shorter skirts than ever before. Women wearing pants began to appear during the 1940s. The 1950s, a conservative decade, saw a brief return to big, long skirts and waist-cinching Merry

Godey's Lady's Book *for February 1862 showed the lastest in women's and children's fashions. In later years, many other women's magazines would take over as arbiters of fashion and style.*

Widow bras, but then the 1960s brought miniskirts and more women and girls wearing pants in more places, including school.

In the 1970s, women in the workplace often echoed the styles of their male colleagues, particularly in corporate offices, where the motto was "Dress for success," but in the '90s those self-enforced rules began to loosen. The fact that women now wear so much athletic apparel reflects the fact that women now play more sports than ever before.

SEE ALSO

Bloomer, Amelia Jenks; Clothing; International Ladies' Garment Workers Union (ILGWU); Needlework

FURTHER READING

Banner, Lois. *American Beauty.* Chicago: University of Chicago Press, 1983.

Cunningham, Patricia A., and Susan Voso Lab, eds. *Dress in American Culture.* Bowling Green, Ohio: Bowling Green State University Popular Press, 1993.

Murray, Maggie Pexton. *Changing Styles in Fashion: Who, What, Why.* New York: Fairchild, 1989.

Oliver, Valerie Burnham. *Fashion and Costume in American Popular Culture: A Reference Guide.* Westport, Conn.: Greenwood, 1996.

Smith, Barbara Clark, and Kathy Peiss. *Men and Women: A History of Costume, Gender, and Power.* Washington, D.C.: Smithsonian Institution Press, 1989.

Feminism

There are many strands of American feminism, but they all recognize that women have been treated unequally in U.S. society, that that is wrong, and that something can and should be done about it by collective endeavor.

Women have often acted together to improve their situation, but they did not use the term *feminist* to describe themselves till the early 20th century, and it is therefore not entirely accurate to apply the term to any of the earlier women activists. The word itself came from French activists, and Anglo-American women began to use it in the 1910s.

The term *feminism,* however, usually refers to the women's movement that was born in the late 1960s and that drew strength and inspiration from many sources. Both white and black feminists saw role models in the African-American women leading grassroots efforts to demand their civil rights during this era. At the same time, young women who were active in the student protest movements of the 1960s came to understand that they, too, were oppressed; they felt that their male colleagues did not treat them with respect or grant them equal leadership opportunities because of their sex. Then there was the network of activists set in motion when President John Kennedy established the Commission on the Status of Women in 1961. This commission, and the state counterparts that were created in its wake, led to the creation of the National Organization for Women (NOW), the first true civil rights group for women of the modern era.

Within a few years, the feminist movement scored stunning triumphs. On August 26, 1970, for example, tens of thousands of American women demonstrated to celebrate the 50th anniversary of suffrage, the largest feminist gathering in U.S. history. Soon Congress began to pass historic legislation, such as Title IX of the Education Act Amendments that opened opportunities in sports and higher education, and the U.S. Supreme Court began to apply the 14th Amendment to gender-discrimination cases for the first time, meaning that women could bring suit on this basis.

In the late 1960s women began meeting in consciousness-raising groups, they began to challenge injustice on many fronts, and some began to question unsatisfying marriages. The slogan "the personal is political" that the movement generated helped women make the connection between their own problems and

Members of a women's liberation group display banners in front of the Statue of Liberty in 1970. On the box in the center is the biological symbol for females combined with a fist, an emblem that represents feminists' militancy and unity.

the larger arena of activism. Beginning around 1970 women began to form new groups such as the bipartisan National Women's Political Caucus, aimed at electing more women to office. Women also founded feminist law firms to pursue gender discrimination cases. A number of pioneer feminists—Betty Friedan, Gloria Steinem, Bella Abzug—became prominent orators and writers in the cause.

The feminist movement lost some of its power as the United States turned in a more conservative direction in the 1980s. Some veterans of the movement are still activists, but others are reaping the benefits of the revolution they launched. Many younger women find it difficult to understand how much things have changed in a generation. Their mothers and grandmothers, for example, remember a time when there were not only no athletic scholarships for women, but there were almost no organized teams, either.

Today feminist energy expresses itself in many ways. Even a very sketchy list of all the different varieties of feminism suggests how much energy the movement still has: there is lesbian feminism, liberal feminism, radical feminism, cultural feminism, ecofeminism, and feminism centered in many different racial/ethnic communities. In general, differences among feminists have to do with whether they believe that change can happen within the current system of government and family life (liberal feminism) or whether they think that more fundamental change will be required, either in the political system or in the family (radical feminism). Ecofeminism emphasizes women's role as mother and nurturer to call upon women to play a special part in saving the earth.

The 1980s and 1990s have seen a backlash against feminism—vividly described in Susan Faludi's 1992 book *Backlash*—but also many gains long sought by feminists, such as the legal remedies now being offered for sexual harassment. One of the most striking changes has been the growth in the number of women running for and getting elected to political office, especially since Anita Hill's testimony in 1991 about being sexually harassed by then–U.S. Supreme Court nominee Clarence Thomas (now a Supreme Court Justice). Sine the Thomas-Hill confrontation galvanized women around the country to get involved in electoral politics, the total number of women in Congress has risen from 31 to 65. As a direct result of the activism of women in Congress, there are now many more funds available to conduct research on women's health. Finally, in the 1990s, the United States has had a First Lady, Hillary Rodham Clinton, who has symbolized the new opportunities available to women.

What feminism did not adequately address—and what constitutes one of the most pressing problems in our country—is the plight of millions of poor women, many of them single mothers, who lack both jobs and the education to qualify for decent employment. The women's movement primarily, though not exclusively, has improved the opportunities available to middle-class women.

SEE ALSO

Abzug, Bella Savitsky; Civil rights movement; Commission on the Status of Women; Consciousness-raising; Friedan, Betty; National Organization for Women (NOW); Steinem, Gloria; Student movements

FURTHER READING

Chafe, William H. *The Road to Equality: American Women Since 1962*. New York: Oxford University Press, 1994.

Faludi, Susan. *Backlash: The Undeclared War against American Women*. New York: Anchor, 1992.

Freeman, Jo. *The Politics of Women's Liberation*. New York: McKay, 1975.

Klein, Ethel. *Gender Politics*. Cambridge, Mass.: Harvard University Press, 1984.

Wolf, Naomi. *The Beauty Myth: How Images of Beauty Are Used against Women*. New York: Morrow, 1991.

Ferraro, Geraldine

- *Born: Aug. 26, 1935, Newburgh, N.Y.*
- *Education: Marymount College, B.A., 1956; Fordham University Law School, J.D., 1960*
- *Accomplishments: U.S. Representative (Democrat–N.Y.) (1979–85); chair, Democratic platform committee (1984); Democratic candidate for Vice President (1984); permanent member, United Nations Commission on Human Rights (1993–)*

Geraldine Ferraro was the first woman to be nominated for the Vice Presidency by one of the major national political parties. This historic event in 1984, although it did not result in her election, inspired countless other women to run for office at lower levels of government.

Born to an Italian immigrant family, Ferraro graduated from Marymount

Geraldine Ferraro speaks at the New Jersey Chamber of Commerce in November 1999 on the subject of "Women in the Workplace." Since the beginning of her political career she has been a strong advocate of women's and human rights.

Manhattan College in 1956 and then obtained a law degree from Fordham University in 1960. That same year she wed John Zaccaro, a marriage that produced three children. In 1974 she became an assistant district attorney in Queens, New York, and that was the start of her public career. She ran successfully for the U.S. House of Representatives in 1978.

In Congress Ferraro had a career that was different from what most women had experienced there. Typically a woman, no matter how hardworking and smart, had been treated like an outsider. Not so with Ferraro. She became close to the most powerful man in the House, Democratic Speaker Thomas P. ("Tip") O'Neill. She allied herself with O'Neill partly because of her own impressive personality and partly because changing times and the emergence of the modern women's movement allowed women to be taken more seriously.

Her relationship with O'Neill, as well as her good standing with various groups of organized women, made her a good choice for Walter Mondale's running mate in 1984. By all accounts, Mondale knew that he had little chance to defeat the enormously popular President Ronald Reagan, so he wanted to make history by choosing to run with a woman. Moreover, beginning with the election of 1980 (when Reagan was elected for the first time), a "gender gap" emerged between male and female voters. Men have been more likely to vote Republican than women since 1980, and the Democrats hoped that if they had a woman on the ticket in 1984, they could attract an even larger number of female voters.

As it happened, this did not work in 1984—Ronald Reagan got a majority of both male and female votes—but Mondale did fulfill his goal of making history with Ferraro. Since 1984 Ferraro has twice run unsuccessfully for the U.S. Senate in New York, and she has also been a commentator on television.

SEE ALSO

Gender gap; Politics

FURTHER READING

Ferraro, Geraldine, with Linda Bird Francke. *Ferraro: My Story.* New York: Bantam, 1985.

Fleming, Peggy

- *Born: July 27, 1948, San Jose, Calif.*
- *Education: Attended Colorado College in 1966*
- *Accomplishments: World figure skating champion (1966–68); Olympic gold medal, figure skating (1968)*

Peggy Fleming won a gold medal in the 1968 Winter Olympics and has been a tireless advocate for the sport. With her dazzling grace and charm, she helped give women athletes a higher profile than they enjoyed in the past.

Like all champions, Fleming had to work hard herself. Like most, she was also fortunate enough to have a family that helped her realize her dreams. For example, her father, a newspaper press operator, took a job in Colorado so that she would be able to train there with the renowned coach Carlo Fassi. All the hard work of daily practice and sacrifice paid off when Fleming thrilled the world with her grace and athleticism at the 1968 Winter Olympics, where she won the only gold medal for the United States.

Though not as athletically proficient as today's skaters—she accomplished double jumps, and the best women now routinely perform triples—she captured the country's imagination as no woman skater had since the Norwegian Sonia Henie in the 1930s. The 1968 Olympics were the first broadcast live and in color, and Fleming's elegance and grace, products of her ballet training, were mesmerizing. In 1961, the entire United States figure skating team had been killed in a plane crash on the way to a world championship, and Fleming's television visibility and great energy were a major force in revitalizing the country's figure skating programs. All female skaters are in her debt for helping to popularize the sport.

FURTHER READING

Van Steenwyk, Elizabeth. *Peggy Fleming: Cameo of a Champion.* New York: McGraw-Hill, 1978.

Flynn, Elizabeth Gurley

- *Born: Aug. 7, 1890, Concord, N.H.*
- *Education: Some high school (left in 1907 to join Industrial Workers of the World)*
- *Accomplishments: Co-founder (1918) and secretary (1918–22), Workers' Liberty Defense Union; co-founder, American Civil Liberties Union (1920); author,* I Speak My Own Piece *(autobiography, 1955); chairman, national committee, U.S. Communist party (1961–64)*
- *Died: Sept. 5, 1964, Moscow, Soviet Union*

One of the best-known American radicals of the 20th century, Elizabeth Gurley Flynn began her career as an agitator and soapbox orator when she was only 16 by giving a speech on women and socialism. From that moment, she became known as the "rebel girl."

Coming from a long line of Irish rebels, she joined the anarchist-oriented Industrial Workers of the World, or Wobblies, in 1907. From then until her death in 1964, she threw herself into revolutionary politics aimed at bringing about a new political system in the United States.

Elizabeth Gurley Flynn addresses striking silk workers in Paterson, New Jersey, in June 1913. The "Rebel Girl," as she was known, was a very effective public speaker.

As a Wobbly, Flynn was involved in labor strikes and in giving public addresses that would test the limits of American free speech. Following the Russian Revolution in 1917, she began to turn toward communism as the means to achieve the change she hoped for, eventually joining the Communist party in 1936. She then wrote a regular column for the party newspaper, the *Daily Worker.* One of the best-known American communists, she was sent to prison for two years during the 1950s for violating the Smith Act, which prohibited anyone from joining the Communist party.

Flynn was always publicly loyal to the party and died on a trip to the Soviet Union, where she was given a heroine's funeral.

SEE ALSO

Anarchism; Communism; Industrial Workers of the World (IWW)

FURTHER READING

Camp, Helen C. *Iron in Her Soul.* Pullman: Washington State University Press, 1995.

Folk art

SEE Painting

Foreign policy

The conduct of foreign policy, including decisions about war and peace, has been one of the bastions of male dominance in U.S. government. Of course, the nation was founded on the belief that all of politics belonged to men's "sphere," and later, when women gained any influence at all in the political realm, it usually pertained to schools or human welfare issues—in short, to areas that seemed to be related to women's "sphere."

Despite the fact that military decisions seemed remote from women's expertise, women have sometimes exercised influence on war and peace decisions to a surprising extent. Before the Civil War (1861–65), for example, northern women spoke out about the moral antislavery dimensions of a possible conflict. In 1917 Jeanette Rankin, the first woman elected to the U.S. House of Representatives, was one of only 50 members of Congress to vote against declaring war on Germany (she also was the only legislator to vote against the declaration of war on Japan after the Pearl Harbor attack in 1941. After World War I American women agitated for a lasting peace and rallied support for the Kellogg-Briand Pact of 1928, a formal attempt to outlaw war which the United States joined.

Few women have held high positions inside the official, governmental foreign policy hierarchy until the 1980s. President Ronald Reagan made a significant break with tradition when he appointed Jeane Kirkpatrick to be his ambassador to the United Nations in 1981. Even more significant was President Bill Clinton's choice of Madeleine Albright to be his secretary of state (the cabinet position that runs U.S. foreign policy) in 1997.

Earlier in the century, a few women had paved the way with their assignments to high-level diplomatic posts. In the 1930s President Franklin Roosevelt appointed Ruth Bryan Owen to be his minister to Norway, the first woman of ministerial rank, and in the 1950s President Dwight Eisenhower appointed Clare Boothe Luce as ambassador to Italy, the first woman ambassador to a major country.

SEE ALSO

Albright, Madeleine Korbel; Civil War; Peace movements

FURTHER READING

Jeffrey-Jones, Rhodri. *Changing Differences: Women and the Shaping of American Foreign Policy, 1917–1994.* New Brunswick, N.J.: Rutgers University Press, 1995.

McGlen, Nancy E. *The Status of Women in Foreign Policy.* Ithaca, N.Y.: Foreign Policy Association, 1995.

Foster, Abigail Kelley

- *Born: Jan. 15, 1810, Pelham, Mass.*
- *Education: Quaker schools, Worcester, Mass.*
- *Accomplishments: Secretary, Lynn (Mass.) Female Anti-Slavery Society (1835–37); co-founder, New England Non-Resistant Society (1838)*
- *Died: Jan. 14, 1887, Worcester, Mass.*

Abigail Kelley Foster was a tireless and courageous advocate for the antislavery cause in the years before the Civil War (1861–65) as well as an outspoken lecturer on behalf of women's rights, including suffrage. Indeed, she had to defend women's rights in order to defend her own right to be a public lecturer.

Raised a Quaker, and therefore exposed to women preachers, Abby Kelley grew up to be a teacher. As a young woman, she read William Lloyd Garrison's abolitionist newspaper, *The Liberator,* and converted to the cause. She circulated petitions and raised money, and as Garrison became more radical in his views about what it would take to end slavery, Kelley joined him in advocating an immediate end to slavery.

Kelley made her first public speech to a mixed audience of men and women—then a daring thing to do—in 1838. So successful was her speech that others begged her to devote herself full-time to antislavery lecturing. Resigning her teaching job, she thought for months about what to do and then took to the road to speak.

Few women of her day endured the insults and the abuse Kelley did as she traveled for the cause. Even fewer stuck it out so resolutely. Ministers denounced her as "vile," and others implied that she was a prostitute because she was publicly outspoken in an era when good women were supposed to be silent in public. Nothing kept her from going on. In 1845 she acquired a companion on her travels—and in her life—when she married fellow reformer Stephen Symonds Foster. The two then had a daughter in 1847, their only child.

SEE ALSO

Abolitionism

FURTHER READING

Sterling, Dorothy. *Ahead of Her Time: Abby Kelley and the Politics of Anti-Slavery.* New York: W.W. Norton, 1991.

14th Amendment

Designed to establish the citizenship of African Americans in the wake of the Civil War of 1861–65, the 14th Amendment was ratified on July 28, 1868. It declared that no state could deny the right to vote to "any of the male inhabitants" of the state who were "twenty-one years of age and citizens of the United States." The 14th Amendment also specified male voters in the Constitution for the first time in discussing the basis for a state's representation in Congress. As a result, the amendment was bitterly opposed by one wing of the woman suffrage movement led by Susan B. Anthony and Elizabeth Cady Stanton.

The amendment's citizenship clause, however, stated that all people born in the United States are citizens, and this seemed to include women. It specifically guaranteed that no state shall "deprive any person of life, liberty, or property, without due process of law; nor deny to any person within its jurisdiction the equal protection of the laws."

As early as 1873, in the case of *Bradwell* v. *Illinois,* a lawyer made the attempt to argue for women's rights before the U.S. Supreme Court on the basis of this language—but he was unsuccessful in winning his client Myra Bradwell the right to be admitted to the Illinois State bar. It was not until the case of *Reed* v. *Reed* in 1971 that the Supreme Court applied the amendment to women's rights in a case about inheritance laws and about whether a father should automatically become a deceased child's executor rather than the mother.

SEE ALSO

Citizenship; *Bradwell* v. *Illinois* (1873); *Reed* v. *Reed* (1971); Supreme Court, U.S.

Freeman, Elizabeth

- *Born: Around 1744, place unknown*
- *Died: Around 1829, Mass.*

Elizabeth Freeman, also known as "Mumbet," was a party to a 1781 suit that was one of two suits ending slavery in Massachusetts. A slave in the household of Colonel and Mrs. John Ashley, Freeman overheard conversations about political rights in the days leading up to the American Revolution—at least according to legend. Folklore in western Massachusetts also holds that her hearing about these rights gave *her* the idea that she, too, had rights, and that it was inappropriate that she be held in bondage.

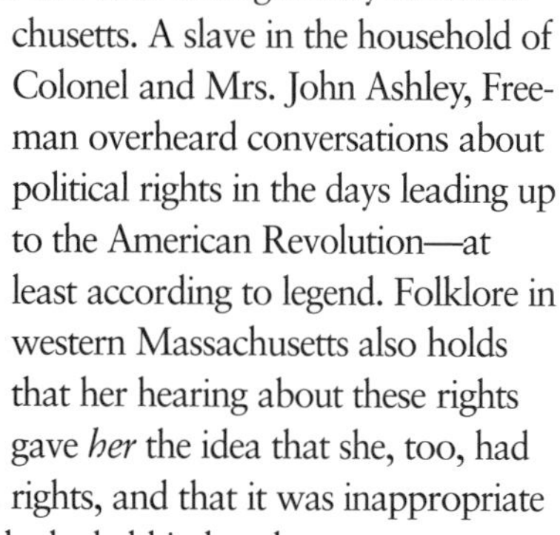

When Elizabeth Freeman (Mumbet) was an old woman and no longer a slave, Susan Sedgwick painted this watercolor portrait of the woman who was then a beloved family servant.

It is impossible for historians now to determine how much of the initiative in *Brom and Bett* v. *Ashley,* in fact, came from Freeman. What is clear is that in winning, Freeman helped overturn the legality of slavery in Massachusetts. Many years later the novelist Catharine Sedgwick wrote a memoir of Freeman—who had become a servant in the Sedgwick home after being freed—in which Sedgwick portrayed Mumbet as inspired by the ideas in the Declaration of Independence.

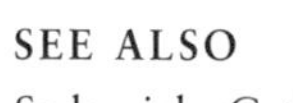

SEE ALSO

Sedgwick, Catharine Maria

FURTHER READING

Felton, Harold W. *Mumbet: The Story of Elizabeth Freeman.* New York: Dodd, Mead, 1970.

Freudian theory

One of the most important influences on modern American thought and culture has been the Viennese psychiatrist Sigmund Freud. In addition to seeing disturbed patients, Freud wrote extensively, and by the 1920s his ideas had begun to permeate American intellectual circles. They then percolated into other segments of society, and soon people who had not themselves read Freud knew about the Oedipus complex or "penis envy." The therapeutic method Freud developed is known as psychoanalysis, and it still has both practitioners and adherents.

Freud argued that boys are in competition with their fathers (the Oedipus complex) for the love of the woman who is mother of one and wife of the other, and that this conflict—and how it is or is not resolved—shapes all of a man's subsequent life. Seeing men and male experience as the human norm, Freud also argued that girls inevitably suffer from feeling inadequate when they encounter the male anatomy and realize that they are lacking the same equipment.

Scholars are still debating Freud's ideas today. Modern feminists have worked to define female identity differently from Freud and his followers so that women would not be taught to see themselves as incomplete men, forever pining after what they do not have.

FURTHER READING

Buhle, Mari Jo. *Feminism and Its Discontents.* Cambridge: Harvard University Press, 1998.

Muckenhoupt, Margaret. *Sigmund Freud: Explorer of the Unconscious.* New York: Oxford University Press, 1997.

Friedan, Betty

- *Born: Feb. 4, 1921, Peoria, Ill.*
- *Education: Smith College, B.A., 1942*
- *Accomplishments: Co-founder (1966) and president (1966–70), National Organization for Women; founding member, National Women's Political Caucus (1971); author,* The Feminine Mystique *(1963);* It Changed My Life: Writings on the Women's Movement *(1976);* The Second Stage *(1981);* The Fountain of Age *(1993)*

Betty Friedan meets with students at her alma mater, Smith College, after receiving an honorary degree in 1975. Looking back on her career in 1999, Friedan wrote, "The energy released by the move to women's equality was stronger than that released by the H-bomb."

Betty Friedan accomplished something that most writers dream about, but very few manage to pull off: she wrote a book that altered the course of history. Although change for women was in the air in 1963, the year she published *The Feminine Mystique,* it was her book that brought the national debate about the role of women into focus.

Born Betty Goldstein, she graduated from Smith College in 1942, spent one year studying psychology as a graduate student at the University of California, Berkeley, worked briefly as a journalist, and then wed Carl Friedan in 1947. They had three children and then the marriage ended in divorce in 1969.

As a housewife and mother, Friedan began to notice that many of her friends seemed dissatisfied with their lives, even if they lacked no material comforts. She decided to survey her classmates from Smith about their lives. Out of that effort came the book, in which she identified "the problem with no name," a feeling of emptiness many women described to her. When *The Feminine Mystique* appeared, thousands of women wrote to say that they recognized themselves on every page. Friedan's face was on the cover of national magazines, and her name did, literally, become a household word.

After attracting so much attention with her writing, Friedan went on to be the founding president of the National Organization for Women, serving from 1966 to 1970. She was also one of the conveners of the National Women's Political Caucus in 1971, the first-ever group to organize to get women elected to office.

Friedan has written several other books, but none with the impact of her first, which galvanized women to fight for the right to enter the public world beyond the home.

SEE ALSO

Feminism; National Organization for Women (NOW)

FURTHER READING

Blau, Justine. *Betty Friedan.* New York: Chelsea House, 1990.

Horowitz, Daniel. *Betty Friedan and the Making of The Feminine Mystique: The American Left, the Cold War, and Modern Feminism.* Amherst: University of Massachusetts Press, 1998.

Matthews, Glenna. *"Just a Housewife": The Rise and Fall of Domesticity in America.* New York: Oxford University Press, 1987.

Fuller, Margaret

- *Born: May 23, 1810, Cambridgeport, Mass.*
- *Education: Schooled at home*
- *Accomplishments: Published translation of* Eckermann's

Conversations with Goethe (1839); editor, The Dial (1840–42); author, Woman in the Nineteenth Century (1845); literary critic and foreign correspondent, New York Tribune (1844–50)

- *Died: July 19, 1850, at sea*

Margaret Fuller was one of the greatest American intellectuals of the 19th century, a woman of passionate intensity and dazzling intellect. From her youth, when she was known for being arrogant as well as brilliant, to her tragic death in a shipwreck, she kept her contemporaries talking about her.

The first child of a man who had wanted a son, young Margaret both benefited and suffered from her father's method of teaching her. He trained her as rigorously as he would have prepared a young man for Harvard. At seven years old, for example, she was reading classic writings in Latin. She later felt, however, that her father had undermined her health by forcing such an education on her. Because she was a woman, Fuller lacked the option of going to college and had to figure out another course.

Undaunted, Fuller began to conduct "conversations" among her female friends, a circle of other very bright women. She also began to develop her contacts with leading literary men such as Ralph Waldo Emerson, who became a lifelong friend. For a while she was the editor of a publication called the *Dial*, to which many of New England's brightest literary talents contributed. She then moved to New York and wrote for the *New York Tribune*. She used her *Tribune* articles to develop her book *Woman in the Nineteenth Century*, one of the earliest books about women's rights to be written by an American.

Restless, in part because she was never fully accepted as an equal by certain of her male peers, Fuller went off to Europe in 1846, armed with introductions to many prominent men and women in England and on the continent. She found herself in Italy shortly before a revolution broke out there in an unsuccessful attempt to rid Italy of rule by Austria. Fuller threw herself into the Italian cause and was crushed when it failed.

This photograph captures the intellectual qualities of Margaret Fuller, the brilliant Transcendentalist writer. What it does not adequately convey is the depth of her emotional life, emotions that fully flowered when she reached Italy in time for the Revolution of 1848.

Fuller was devoted to Italy, not least because she had discovered there the personal happiness that she had not found in the United States. She fell in love with a much younger Italian nobleman, Count Giovanni Angelo Ossoli, who loved her in return. It is still not known with certainty whether they were able to marry, but they did have a son together. After the defeat of the revolution, though, Italy was not a friendly place for those who had been its supporters. The couple decided to move to the United States.

In 1850 Fuller, Ossoli, and their son were sailing across the Atlantic to make a new life when their ship went down off the coast of New York City. All three drowned. Heartbroken, Emerson published a memoir of his friend. He was not the only one to be deeply affected by her death. In fact, many women in the late 19th century turned to Fuller for inspiration. She had lived a life of high adventure, a life that most women could only dream of.

FURTHER READING

Balducci, Carolyn Feleppa. *Margaret Fuller: A Life of Passion and Defiance.* New York: Bantam, 1991.

Capper, Charles. *Margaret Fuller.* New York: Oxford University Press, 1992.

Fuller, Margaret. *The Portable Margaret Fuller.* Edited by Mary Kelley. New York: Penguin, 1994.

Kornfeld, Eve. *Margaret Fuller: A Brief Biography with Documents.* Boston: Bedford, 1997.

Gage, Matilda Joslyn

- *Born: Mar. 25, 1826, Cicero, N.Y.*
- *Education: Received college-level schooling from her father*
- *Accomplishments: Founding member (1869–90) and president (1875–76), National Woman Suffrage Association; co-founder (1869) and president (1875–79), New York State Woman Suffrage Association; editor,* National Citizen and Ballot Box *(1878–81); founder, Woman's National Liberal Union (1890); author,* Woman, Church, and State *(1893)*
- *Died: Mar. 18, 1898, Chicago, Ill.*

Matilda Josyln Gage was a gifted writer and organizer who worked on behalf of woman suffrage for several decades in the late 19th century. Today she is best remembered for having coauthored with Susan B. Anthony and Elizabeth Cady Stanton the first three volumes of the *History of Woman Suffrage.*

At a time when it was difficult for a girl to get a good education, Matilda Joslyn was lucky to have a father who devoted himself to seeing that she was well taught (her mother had probably not had access to much education herself). Her abolitionist father taught her at home, instructing her in such subjects as Greek and mathematics, which few girls had the chance to learn. He also encouraged her to think for herself.

At 18, she married merchant Henry Gage and soon gave birth to five children. She waited until she no longer had a young family at home to join the suffrage battle. When she did get involved, she quickly rose to a leadership position, making a particular contribution as an editor and writer for the suffragist newspaper, *The Revolution.* So well-respected was she that Stanton and Anthony turned to her as a co-author.

After losing her husband in 1884, Gage spent her last years at the Chicago home of her daughter Maud, who had married L. Frank Baum, the author of the *The Wonderful Wizard of Oz* and other books.

SEE ALSO

Oz books; Suffrage, woman

Gender gap

The term *gender gap* refers to the difference in male and female voting behavior that first became apparent in 1980 with the election of Republican Ronald Reagan to the Presidency. Fifty-four percent of men voters chose Reagan, while only 46 percent of women voters did. This was the largest such gap since the Gallup poll had begun questioning voters in 1935, and political analysts have been studying it ever since. (Started by statistician George Gallup, this poll—now known officially as the American Institute of Public Opinion—was the first to apply to political issues the market research technique of getting information from a selected sample of the population and using it to predict the preferences of the population as a whole.)

Since Reagan's election, the gender gap has seemed to operate in favor of Democratic candidates. In 1996, for example, the victorious Bill Clinton won 54 percent of the female vote, while Bob Dole received only 38 percent. For the gender gap to work in the Democrats' favor, women have to go to the ballot box in numbers proportional to their percentage of the population, where they constitute a slight majority. When they do not, as in the 1994 congressional elections in which Republicans took control of both houses of Congress, the Republican party will benefit.

SEE ALSO

Politics

FURTHER READING

Witt, Linda, Karen Paget, and Glenna Matthews. *Running as a Woman: Gender and Power in American Politics.* New York: Free Press, 1994.

General Federation of Women's Clubs (GFWC)

In a speech to the delegates of the first conference, Ella Dietz Clymer said, "We look for unity, but unity in diversity. We hope that you will enrich us by your varied experiences . . . ," thus providing the motto for the General Federation of Women's Clubs. Today the organization boasts more than 1 million members in the United States and 20 other countries.

The General Federation of Women's Clubs (GFWC) was an umbrella organization of clubs formed in 1890. At its peak in 1955, it had a membership of 830,000 women.

When Jane Cunningham Croly formed a club called Sorosis in New York in 1868, she inspired many others, too. Following that, clubs appeared throughout the country, uniting mostly middle-class women around civic issues and literary interests. A convention of Sorosis members in 1889 led to the founding of the federation a year later. Though the group eventually became relatively apolitical, in its first years it brought women together for action on municipal reform to benefit women and children.

The organization's racial politics were troubled in the early 20th century. When black women wanted to participate, white southern clubwomen let it be known that they would not belong to an organization that included black women. As a result, the federation did not admit black women's clubs until the mid-20th century.

SEE ALSO

Clubs, women's; Croly, Jane Cunningham

FURTHER READING

Blair, Karen. *The Clubwoman as Feminist.* New York: Holmes & Meier, 1980.

Sigerman, Harriet. *Laborers for Liberty: American Women 1865-1890.* New York: Oxford University Press, 1994.

Gibson, Althea

- *Born: Aug. 25, 1927, Silver, S.C.*
- *Education: Florida Agricultural and Mechanical University, B.A., 1953*
- *Accomplishments: Winner, Wimbledon women's singles and doubles titles (1957–58); women's professional singles title (1960); author,* I Always Wanted to Be Somebody *(autobiography, 1958); elected to the National Lawn Tennis Hall of Fame (1971)*

Althea Gibson was the first African American to win a major tennis title.

Althea Gibson reaches for a high shot during the Wimbledon semifinals in 1957. She went on to win the tournament, becoming the first black tennis player to capture a Grand Slam title.

She inspired young girls all over the country to believe in their dreams of athletic greatness.

After graduating from Florida A&M University in 1953, Gibson soon began devoting most of her attention to tennis. In 1956 she won the French Open, followed by victories in the singles at the U.S. and British opens in 1957–58. During those years, she was the top-ranked American woman amateur. In 1958 she turned pro to be able to play for money. There was not a tour with big prize money for women pros at that time, however (and there would not be one until Billie Jean King spearheaded the formation of a tour in 1971). Gibson therefore did not have the same opportunities to make money that later women would enjoy.

In 1980 Althea Gibson was one of the first six athletes inducted into the Women's Hall of Fame. Besides her exploits on the tennis court, she also served as New Jersey's commissioner of athletics from 1975 to 1985.

SEE ALSO

King, Billie Jean Moffitt; Sports

FURTHER READING

Biracree, Tom. *Althea Gibson.* New York: Chelsea House, 1989.

Davidson, Sue. *Changing the Game: The Stories of Tennis Champions Alice Marble and Althea Gibson.* Seattle: Seal Press, 1997.

Gilman, Charlotte Perkins Stetson

- *Born: July 3, 1860, Hartford, Conn.*
- *Education: Rhode Island School of Design, brief attendance*
- *Accomplishments: Delegate, International Socialist and Labor Congress, London (1896); editor and publisher,* Forerunner *monthly (1909–16); co-founder, Woman's Peace Party (1915); author,* In This Our World *(1893);* Women and Economics *(1898);* Concerning Children *(1900);* The Home *(1903);* Human Work *(1904);* What Diantha Did *(1910);* The Man-Made World *(1911);* The Crux *(1911);* Moving the Mountain *(1911);* His Religion and Hers *(1923);* The Living of Charlotte Perkins Gilman: An Autobiography *(1935)*
- *Died: Aug. 17, 1935, Pasadena, Calif.*

Feminist Charlotte Perkins Gilman expounded her views in both non-fiction and fiction. Her 1892 story "The Yellow Wallpaper" became a feminist classic, and Herland, *a fantasy novel, portrayed an ideal society inhabited only by women.*

Charlotte Perkins Gilman was an early 20th-century thinker who analyzed the way that female economic dependence on men prevents women from achieving full equality. Most modern feminist scholars regard her work as fundamental to their own thought.

Gilman's personal life was difficult. Her father, Frederick Beecher Perkins, was a member of the famed intellectual family that included writers Catharine Beecher and Harriet Beecher Stowe. He left his wife, Mary Fitch Perkins, soon after Charlotte's birth, and the family then faced very difficult times without a male breadwinner.

Unable to achieve much education, starved for affection by a mother who wanted her to be tough enough to survive in a harsh world, Charlotte Perkins began to support herself with teaching jobs while in her teens. In 1884 she married Charles Stetson, an artist, and the next year she gave birth to a daughter.

But rather than being happy as a wife and mother, Charlotte Perkins Stetson plunged into a profound depression, from which she would suffer off and on for the rest of her life. Doctors advised her to take it easy, to withdraw from mental activity and stay in bed in order to get well. She eventually rejected this advice and forged a new life for herself, one that no longer included her husband—they divorced in 1894—and included her daughter only intermittently. The child lived mostly with her father and his second wife.

In the 1890s Charlotte Perkins Stetson then turned to writing and lecturing for an income. During the next years, she wrote a series of important books about women's issues, the best known of which is *Women and Economics,* which presents a powerful argument for the importance of being self-supporting. Gilman had seen her mother's struggles after her father left the family, and her personal experience no doubt added to the urgency of her argument.

Even as a very successful woman, however, she had to struggle for serenity: she was never able to take on domestic responsibilities without risking a return of her depression. Happily, she found a second husband who understood and respected her nature, George Gilman, whom she married in 1900. A friend moved in with them and performed the household chores. George Gilman died in 1934, and she committed suicide the following year because she knew she was fatally ill with breast cancer.

FURTHER READING

Lane, Ann J. *To Herland and Beyond: The Life and Work of Charlotte Perkins Gilman.* New York: Pantheon, 1990.

Ginsburg, Ruth Bader

- *Born: Mar. 15, 1933, Brooklyn, N.Y.*
- *Education: Cornell University, B.A., 1954; Harvard Law School, attended 1956–58; Columbia Law School, J.D., 1959*
- *Accomplishments: Professor, Rutgers University Law School (1963–72) and Columbia Law School (1972–80); founder and director, Women's Rights Project of the American Civil Liberties Union (1972–80); judge, U.S. Court of Appeals, District of Columbia Circuit (1980–1993); U.S. Supreme Court Justice (1993–)*

The second woman appointed to the U.S. Supreme Court, Ruth Bader Ginsburg had a legal background that included specific expertise in the law of sex discrimination. This was the first time in U.S. history that anyone had been appointed to the Court with that particular set of credentials.

Ruth Bader attended Cornell University and graduated in 1954, the same year that she wed lawyer Martin Ginsburg. After her marriage, she entered Harvard Law School, where she was elected to the Law Review. She left Harvard, however, to follow her husband to New York City, where she attended Columbia Law School. She graduated in 1959, tied for first place in her class. She failed to receive a single offer from a law firm, however, owing to the prevailing prejudice against women at the time.

Ginsburg was able to secure a position as a clerk for a U.S. district judge,

The second woman to sit on the U.S. Supreme Court, Ruth Bader Ginsburg rose to legal prominence because of her work in cases involving discrimination against women. She is known for being both tough-minded and brilliant.

and after that she taught at Rutgers University Law School and began to take up sex discrimination cases as a specialty. In 1972 she became the first tenured woman professor at Columbia Law School, a position she held until 1980. President Jimmy Carter nominated Ginsburg to the U.S. Court of Appeals that year.

After many years as a judge, Ginsburg in 1993 was the first person chosen by President Bill Clinton for a Supreme Court appointment. In 1999 she wrote the majority opinion in *NCAA* v. *Smith,* a case that turned on whether the National Collegiate Athletic Association, which receives dues from member universities that receive federal funding, must abide by the anti-sex-discrimination provisions of Title IX of the Education Act Amendments of 1972. The court held that receipt of dues from federally funded entities was not enough to make the organization subject to Title IX.

SEE ALSO

Law

FURTHER READING

Bredeson, Carmen. *Ruth Bader Ginsburg: Supreme Court Justice.* Springfield, N.J.: Enslow, 1995.

Girl Scouts of America

Since its founding in 1912, the Girl Scouts of America has enrolled some 40 million girls and young women as members. Girls can become Brownies (the designation of the youngest Scouts) in the second grade, and they can stay in the Girl Scouts until they graduate from high school.

Juliette Low of Savannah, Georgia, founded the Girl Scouts after having lived in Scotland during the birth of the British Boy Scouts movement launched by Lord Baden-Powell in 1908. Low went home to Georgia and started the first Girl Guides troop (as she called it the first year) on March 12, 1912, to teach girls and young women how to cooperate in group activities.

Scouting caught on quickly. Today there are about 3 million members, about one-sixth of whom are adult leaders and helpers, making the Girl Scouts of America the largest voluntary organization for girls in the world. Members learn rules of good citizenship—they pledge "On my honor I will try to do my duty to God and my country"—as they earn merit badges for crafts and for skills such as cooking and sewing. Scouting also provides the opportunity for members to go camping and enjoy other outdoor activities. Today's Girl Scouts also learn skills unthought-of in earlier generations, skills that might suggest careers as entrepreneurs or scientists, for example, to young women with greater opportunities than those open to their mothers and grandmothers.

Godey's Lady's Book

The most influential and popular women's magazine of the 19th century, *Godey's Lady's Book* offered its readers not only fiction but also thought-provoking editorials about the need for more educational opportunities for women, for example. It also provided scintillating color plates (hand-tinted by up to 150 women employed for the purpose) of the latest fashions, so that readers could keep up-to-date with fashion news and learn how to construct new dresses. From 1850 or so until the advent of sewing patterns in the 1870s, magazines published diagrams so that readers could construct the dresses pictured in their pages.

Louis Godey began publishing the magazine in 1830, and from 1837 to 1877, its content was shaped by its editor, Sarah Josepha Hale. She had an eye for writing talent, so many of the country's best writers, such as Harriet Beecher Stowe, Edgar Allan Poe, and Nathaniel Hawthorne, appeared in the pages of *Godey's*. What did not appear was coverage of the more divisive issues of the day, including the sectional strife that led up to the Civil War because Hale deemed it inappropriate for a women's magazine. The publication went downhill after she left, and ceased to appear in 1898.

SEE ALSO

Hale, Sarah Josepha Buell

FURTHER READING

Olian, JoAnne, ed. *80 Godey's Full-color Fashion Plates, 1838–1880*. Mineola, N.Y.: Dover, 1998.

Spaulding, Lily May, and John Spaulding. *Civil War Recipes: Receipts from the Pages of Godey's Lady's Book*. Lexington: University Press of Kentucky, 1999.

Goldman, Emma

- *Born: June 27, 1869, Kovno, Russia*
- *Education: Limited formal education*
- *Accomplishments: Founder and editor,* Mother Earth *(1906–17); author,* Anarchism and Other Essays *(1910) and* The Social Significance of the Modern Drama *(1914)*
- *Died: May 14, 1940, Toronto, Canada*

Emma Goldman, the child of Russian immigrants, deported from the United States as an adult, nevertheless had a profound impact on the United States because she wrote, spoke, and agitated tirelessly for her anarchist beliefs.

Born to a Jewish family in what is now Lithuania, Goldman saw injustice firsthand, directed against Jews in the larger society and against girls in her own family, where her father let her know that he was deeply disappointed that she was a girl. She began to take an interest in radical politics, and after immigrating to the United States in 1885 with her half-sister, Goldman's interest in political and social questions intensified.

In the United States, Goldman saw how working-class people suffered because of low pay, long hours, and working conditions that were unsanitary and unsafe. She herself worked in a clothing factory at first. In 1889 she became an anarchist, someone who believed that the existing government could not ensure justice for the poor. Anarchists looked to voluntary, cooperative associations as the solution. To achieve their goals of overthrowing the system, they were willing to use violence, a tactic that Goldman originally endorsed but ultimately thought was wrong.

In 1892 Goldman was convicted of stirring up a crowd to riot in New York City, and she was sent to prison for a year. While jailed, she was interviewed

Between 1906 and 1917 Emma Goldman and her fellow anarchists published the magazine Mother Earth. *The cover of the first issue reflects the idealism of the movement.*

by journalist Nellie Bly, who wrote a sympathetic article about "Red Emma." Goldman emerged from prison to find herself a famous woman.

Goldman then spent many years traveling around the United States giving speeches about her anarchist beliefs and about the need for women to be able to prevent unwanted pregnancies. She was one of the first women to openly discuss sexuality in public lectures and yet retain the ability to attract an audience. She was also an important advocate of birth control, "inner freedom," and free love. When the country entered World War I in 1917, Goldman publicly opposed the military draft and spent two years in prison as a result. In 1919 the federal government deported her to Russia as an undesirable alien.

Goldman's next years were difficult. She left Russia after a short period—the country was undergoing a revolution and she came to dislike the revolutionaries as too repressive themselves—and traveled extensively in Europe. In 1925 she married a British man to obtain British citizenship. (She had had a brief, unhappy marriage that had ended in divorce in the 1880s.) To the end of her life, she stood by her beliefs, inspiring devotion among her many friends and fear and dislike among her even more numerous enemies.

SEE ALSO

Anarchism; Seaman, Elizabeth Cochrane (Nellie Bly)

FURTHER READING

Falk, Candace. *Love, Anarchy, and Emma Goldman.* New York: Holt, Rinehart & Winston, 1984.
Goldman, Emma. *Living My Life.* 1931. Reprint, New York: New American Library, 1977.
Waldstreicher, David. *Emma Goldman.* New York: Chelsea House, 1990.
Wexler, Alice. *Emma Goldman in America.* Boston: Beacon, 1989.

Gone with the Wind

In one of the 20th century's best-selling and best-loved books, southern-born author Margaret Mitchell presented a southerner's view of the Civil War and its aftermath. That she also provided a compelling love story between Scarlett O'Hara and Rhett Butler ensured that she would have a multitude of readers for *Gone with the Wind.*

The book is an interesting blend of old and new. What is new is that Scarlett is far from a "magnolia blossom" type of southern heroine: she is shrewd, driven, and prepared to be unscrupulous. Mitchell presents a female character who is strong, if amoral, and who can be seen almost as a role model of how a woman can survive a difficult situation. The view of sectional strife is, however, a completely traditional and uncritical representation of the Confed-

Vivian Leigh sizes up Clark Gable in the 1939 film Gone with the Wind. *Leigh's portrayal of the strong-willed and independent Scarlett O'Hara won her an Oscar.*

erate point of view, complete with rascally Yankees and blacks who need oversight by their former masters.

Published in 1936, the book sold 50,000 copies in a single day, was translated into at least 25 languages, and made its author into a famous woman. It won the Pulitzer Prize in 1937. The film version, starring Vivien Leigh and Clark Gable, has proven to be one of the most successful movies of all time.

FURTHER READING

Harwell, Richard, ed. *Gone with the Wind as Book and Film.* Columbia: University of South Carolina Press, 1983.

Taylor, Helen. *Scarlett's Women: Gone with the Wind and its Female Fans.* New Brunswick, N.J.: Rutgers University Press, 1989.

Graham, Katharine Meyer

- *Born: June 16, 1917, New York, N.Y.*
- *Education: Vassar College, attended 1935–36; University of Chicago, B.A., 1938*
- *Accomplishments: President (1963–69), publisher (1969–79), and chairman and CEO (1973–91), Washington Post Company; Pulitzer Prize for* Personal History *(1998)*

Born to a wealthy family, Katharine Meyer Graham built on her inheritance to become one of the premier newspaper publishers of her generation, running the family-owned *Washington Post* for many years between 1963 and the 1980s. She also played a pioneering role as a female business executive—the first or the only woman to serve in many different leadership capacities in the publishing and the business worlds.

Graham's father, Eugene Meyer, made a fortune as a banker before purchasing the then-struggling *Post* in 1933. Her mother, Agnes Meyer, was unusually intellectual and activist for her time. One of their five children, Katharine graduated from the University of Chicago in 1938, having majored in history. She then began a journalistic career that seemed to be an apprenticeship for a role at the *Post.* But she placed her own career on hold when in 1942 she married a young lawyer named Phillip Graham, with whom she had four children.

In the early 1940s Eugene Meyer chose Phillip Graham to be his successor at the *Post,* an assignment Graham took up after serving in the military in World War II. He more than repaid his father-in-law's confidence, taking the *Post* to new heights and becoming a close friend of powerhouse politicians such as future President Lyndon Johnson. But there was a dark side to Phillip Graham: he suffered from manic depression, a disease then poorly understood and inadequately treated. In 1963 he killed himself.

His widow was suddenly thrust into a new leadership role as publisher at the *Post,* with little preparation and without the luxury of time to learn her new occupation. Under her guidance, the paper skyrocketed to national prominence, especially after it played a major role in publicizing President Richard Nixon's misdeeds during the Watergate scandal in the 1970s.

In 1980 Graham became the first woman to chair the American Newspaper Publishers Association, then an all-male organization, except for her. She was the first woman to serve on the Associated Press's board of directors. For many years she was the only woman to head a *Fortune* 500 company. In 1998 she capped her career by winning a Pulitzer Prize for her autobiography, *Personal History.* Her son Donald Graham has now succeeded her as publisher of the *Post.*

SEE ALSO

Business; Media

FURTHER READING

Felsenthal, Carol. *Power, Privilege, and the Post: the Katharine Graham Story.* New York: Putnam, 1993.

Graham, Katharine. *Personal History.* New York: Knopf, 1997.

Grasso, Ella

- *Born: May 10, 1919, Windsor Locks, Conn.*
- *Education: Mount Holyoke College, B.A., 1940, M.A., 1942*
- *Accomplishments: Connecticut Secretary of State (1958–70); U.S. Representative (Democrat–Conn.) (1971–74); Governor of Connecticut (1974–80)*
- *Died: Feb. 5, 1981, Hartford, Conn.*

Democrat Ella Grasso was the country's first woman to be elected governor of a state in her own right, that is, not as a successor to her husband.

Ella Tambussi obtained a master's degree in 1942 from Mount Holyoke College, and shortly thereafter married Thomas A. Grasso. A protégé of Connecticut's legendary Democratic leader John Bailey, in 1952 she ran successfully for the Connecticut state legislature—she never lost an election after that. She then served from 1958 to 1970 as the secretary of state, in which capacity she developed a reputation for being attentive to citizens' concerns.

Next she moved up to the U.S. House of Representatives, serving two terms between 1970 and 1974 and becoming one of the best-known politicians in the state. When she ran for governor in 1974, she won, and she was reelected in 1978. Voters respected the way she tackled difficult fiscal problems that the state was having at the time.

Cancer forced Grasso to resign in 1980, cutting short a distinguished career.

SEE ALSO

Politics

Great Awakening

In the early 1700s, the American colonies were overwhelmingly Protestant. Each colony had one denomination that was its chief religion, such as the Quakers in Pennsylvania, the Anglicans (now the Episcopalians) in Virginia, and the Congregationalists in Massachusetts. In many of the colonies, the chief denomination was even "established," or tax-supported. The Quakers were the only dominant denomination that allowed women to play a public role in their services. In short, it was an orderly and conservative religious landscape.

Beginning in the 1730s, however, much of the familiar landscape changed: a burst of religious revivalism swept up and down the eastern seaboard, creating much greater religious diversity. After a revivalist preacher had created dissatisfaction with the congregation and the minister they already had, people called New Lights founded new congregations. The revival was called the Great Awakening, and it lasted until 1760 or so. During this time, New Lights also founded institutions besides churches under the impetus of their renewed religious conviction. Princeton University in New Jersey, for example, owes its birth to New Lights.

One of the aspects of the Great Awakening that was the most horrifying to the conservative members of established denominations (Old Lights) was that it liberated women to play a more publicly visible role. Even if they were not speaking in public—and some women were—they were, for the first time in American history on so large a scale, making personal choices about their religious lives.

Scholars know from diaries, letters, and accounts of conversions that women were wrestling with their consciences in order to make a choice between Old and New Lights, a choice they believed would affect their immortal souls. This was at a time when women could not vote, could not choose to attend college, and likely could not choose whom to marry.

A few decades later, around 1800, the new nation would be swept by another revival known as the Second Great Awakening, which would also play a role in generating new roles for women.

SEE ALSO

Religion

Great Depression

SEE Depression, Great

Grimké, Angelina and Sarah

- *Born: Nov. 26, 1792, Charleston, S.C. (Sarah)*
- *Born: Feb. 20, 1805, Charleston, S.C. (Angelina)*
- *Education: No formal education*
- *Accomplishments: Authors,* An Appeal to the Christian Women of the South *(Angelina, 1836);* An Epistle to the Clergy of the Southern States *(Sarah, 1836);* Appeal to the Women of the Nominally Free States *(Angelina, 1837);* Letters on the Equality of the Sexes and the Condition of Women *(Sarah, 1838)*
- *Died: Dec. 23, 1873, Hyde Park, Mass. (Sarah)*
- *Died: Oct. 26, 1879, Hyde Park, Mass. (Angelina)*

The Grimké sisters from South Carolina were pioneers as antislavery lecturers and as women's rights activists. Moreover, born in the South to a privileged, slave-owning family, they were more outspoken than any of their fellow southerners not only about the evils of slavery but also about the evils of racism. Deeply devout, the sisters inspired many of their contemporaries with their courage.

Sarah was 13 years older than Angelina. Each received an education from the private tutors their well-to-do parents could afford. The sisters learned more than the tutors intended, though. As they were growing up, first one and then the other began to notice how brutally their enslaved fellow human beings were treated and to rebel against this. Sarah converted to the Quaker faith and moved to Philadelphia in 1821, where she was joined in 1829 by the recent Quaker convert Angelina.

In Philadelphia the two women were part of an antislavery Quaker circle. They lost that haven, however, when

Angelina (top) and Sarah Grimké were pioneers in women's rights and in the abolitionist movement. The fact that they were born and raised in South Carolina and were members of a slave-owning family makes their story all the more remarkable.

in 1835 Angelina wrote to the radical abolitionist William Lloyd Garrison to praise his newspaper *The Liberator* and to tell him that she had witnessed firsthand the evils he was denouncing. He published her letter. Garrison was too radical for the Quakers, and as a result the sisters became estranged from their Philadelphia friends.

Both sisters then became the first paid female agents of an abolitionist society, their well-known southern name attracting much attention to their pamphlets and lectures (Angelina was the more proficient public speaker). In the South their "treason" provoked fury, and postmasters destroyed their pamphlets rather than delivering them. In fact, the two women were never able to return to their native region and never saw their mother again. Even in the North, their public appearances sparked outrage and denunciation by conservative ministers, who thundered that no respectable woman would give a public speech.

During the next several years the sisters were at the center of a storm of controversy. In 1838 Sarah wrote an impassioned pamphlet, *Letters on Equality of the Sexes and the Condition of Woman,* in which she systematically defended their right to behave as they were doing and linked black and white oppression of women and enslavement of blacks. After Angelina married fellow abolitionist Theodore Dwight Weld in May 1838, however, the sisters retired from the front lines of action, their place in American history secure.

As older women, they had one more significant opportunity to live out their principles when they welcomed into the family the two sons of their late brother by his slave mistress. The aunts helped their nephews Archibald Grimké and Francis Grimké secure their educations at Harvard Law School and at Princeton Theological Seminary, respectively. In the late 19th century, these men were leaders of the African-American community in the nation's capital.

SEE ALSO

Abolitionism; Grimké, Charlotte Forten

FURTHER READING

Lerner, Gerda. *The Feminist Thought of Sarah Grimké.* New York: Oxford University Press, 1998.

———. *The Grimké Sisters from South Carolina: Pioneers for Woman's Rights and Abolition.* New York: Oxford University Press, 1967.

Grimké, Charlotte Forten

- *Born: Aug. 17, 1837, Philadelphia, Pa.*
- *Education: Higginson Grammar School (Salem, Mass.), graduated 1955*
- *Accomplishments: First black teacher of white students, Epes Grammar School, Salem, Mass. (1856–57); educator of free blacks, South Carolina, during the Civil War*
- *Died: July 23, 1914, Washington, D.C.*

Charlotte Forten Grimké, the daughter of a prominent free black family in Philadelphia, was a teacher and diarist whose most significant achievement was that she went South during the Civil War as part of a humanitarian effort to educate those who were being freed from slavery. One of more than 70 teachers, most of whom were white, she then wrote about this experience for a northern audience.

Charlotte Forten's early life was filled with tension because she was drawn to the "high" culture of white America but realized that she would never truly find full acceptance owing to the level of racism, even in the North. Moreover, she had little access to knowledge about her African heritage at that time, and there was little in the culture that might have affirmed its value.

Forten believed that teaching the freed people during the Civil War was an important task, because many thought that they were uneducable. She went South to the coastal island of Port Royal, off South Carolina, with high hopes, but found teaching to be a terrible strain for many reasons, including the racism of some of her "idealistic" white colleagues.

Charlotte Forten found personal happiness in her marriage in 1878 to Francis Grimké, a clergyman who was one of the leaders of the black community in Washington, D.C. Her journal was published 30 years after her death and remains a valuable source for understanding the Port Royal experiment, the ultimately successful effort to educate freed people in which she participated.

FURTHER READING

Billington, Ray A., ed. *The Journal of Charlotte Forten.* 1953. New York: Norton, 1981.

Stevenson, Brenda, ed. *The Journals of Charlotte Forten Grimké.* New York: Oxford University Press, 1988.

Griswold v. *Connecticut* (1965)

Griswold v. *Connecticut* was a landmark decision, a turning point in women's ability to prevent pregnancy. In *Griswold* the U.S Supreme Court, in essence, established a constitutional right to marital privacy that ensured access to birth-control information and devices for married women.

Starting in the mid- to late 19th century, states passed laws forbidding access to birth-control devices and to information about how to prevent pregnancy, even for married women. By 1960 most such laws were no longer on the books. Connecticut's law, however, still stood. In 1961 Estelle Griswold, the executive director of the Planned Parenthood League of Connecticut, was arrested for giving birth-control information to married people. She and the physician arrested with her were convicted, and the decision was upheld by two appeals courts.

By a majority of 7 to 2, however, the Supreme Court decided that the "due process" clause in the 14th Amendment, which says that no state shall "deprive any person of life, liberty, or prosperity without due process of law," can be interpreted to protect marital privacy, because it had already begun to be interpreted more broadly during this period. Justice William O. Douglas wrote the opinion. Because the Constitution does not specifically employ the word *privacy,* critics of the Court have argued that the justices went too far in the direction of reading rights into the Constitution in their decision.

SEE ALSO

14th Amendment; Planned Parenthood; Privacy

FURTHER READING

Wawrose, Susan. *Griswold v. Connecticut: Contraception and the Right of Privacy.* New York: Watts, 1996.

Hale, Sarah Josepha Buell

- *Born: Oct. 24, 1788, Newport, N.H.*
- *Education: Schooled at home by her mother and brother*
- *Accomplishments: Editor,* Ladies' Magazine *(*American Ladies' Magazine *from 1834) (1828–37); founder, Seaman's Aid Society (1833); editor,* Godey's Lady's Book *(1837–77); author,* The Genius of Oblivion *(poems, 1823);* Northwood, a Tale of New England *(1827);* Poems for Our Children *(1830);* Woman's Record, or Sketches of Distinguished Women *(36 volumes, 1853, 1869, 1876)*
- *Died: Apr. 30, 1879, Philadelphia, Pa.*

Throughout much of her long life, Sarah Josepha Hale was one of the country's most influential people: she edited the leading women's magazine, *Godey's Lady's Book,* for 40 years, finally giving up the editorship when she reached her 90th year.

It is difficult to categorize Hale's outlook. An opponent of suffrage, she nonetheless strongly believed in improving the education available to women and took a very expansive view of what might be considered appropriate employment for her sex. She thought that women and men belonged to "separate spheres" but spent many years crusading in print for reforms, such as laws ensuring a married woman's right to control her own property, that she thought male politicians should enact.

To achieve her goals, Hale wrote to and lobbied tirelessly with the country's main power brokers. When President Abraham Lincoln proclaimed Thanksgiving to be a national holiday in 1863, this was a personal triumph for Hale, because Thanksgiving was her pet project.

Educated primarily at home, young Sarah Buell benefited from her brother's guidance, training that he based on his own education at Dartmouth College. In 1813 she married lawyer David Hale and then gave birth to five children. Her happy life as a wife and mother ended in 1822 when her husband died of pneumonia, and Hale needed to support her family. At first she opened a hat shop but soon found her way to writing and then editing. She was one of the most accomplished and most thoroughly professional editors of her century, printing only original contributions at a time when editors were known to appropriate articles from other publications.

As the editor of Godey's Lady's Book *for several decades, Sarah Josepha Hale enjoyed an influence on American culture typical of few other women of the day. Though opposed to woman suffrage, she campaigned for other reforms such as better educational and occupational opportunities for women.*

SEE ALSO

Godey's Lady's Book

FURTHER READING

Okker, Patricia. *Our Sister Editors: Sarah J. Hale and the Tradition of Nineteenth-Century American Women Editors.* Athens: University of Georgia Press, 1995.

Rogers, Sherbrooke. *Sarah Josepha Hale: A New England Pioneer.* Grantham, N.H.: Tompson and Rutter, 1985.

Hamer, Fannie Lou Townsend

- *Born: Oct. 6, 1917, Ruleville, Miss.*
- *Education: Elementary school*
- *Accomplishments: Vice-chairperson, Mississippi Freedom Democratic Party (1964–68); author,* To Praise Our Bridges: An Autobiography *(1967); member, Democratic National Committee for Mississippi (1968–71); member, Policy Council, National Women's Political Caucus (1971–77)*
- *Died: Mar. 14, 1977, Mound Bayou, Miss.*

Born to a sharecropper family in Mississippi as the youngest of 20 children, Fannie Lou Hamer grew up to be one

Fannie Lou Hamer captured public attention at the 1964 Democratic National Convention when she explained on national television the injustices of segregation in the South.

of the leaders of the civil rights movement during the 1960s.

She and her husband, Perry Hamer, whom she married in the early 1940s, adopted two daughters. Like most African Americans in the rural South in those years, the family had to contend with discrimination in many forms. Despite the guarantees in the U.S. Constitution that people cannot be prohibited from voting because of race or sex, patterns of formal harassment and informal terrorist tactics had grown up in Mississippi to prevent African Americans from even trying to go to the ballot box.

In 1962 Hamer went to a civil rights meeting that ignited her enthusiasm for doing something about this situation. With steadfast determination, she attended workshops designed to equip activists to withstand the scorn and hatred they would undoubtedly face when they tried to change long-established patterns. She also endured beatings at the hands of whites who wanted to keep things as they were.

Hamer's greatest moment came in 1964 when she explained on national television why it was so important to challenge the regular Democratic party of Mississippi, a bastion of white supremacy that had been part of the old system of keeping blacks from voting. She and her colleagues had come to the Democratic National Convention in Atlantic City as delegates from the Mississippi Freedom Democratic Party (MFDP), which had garnered more votes in the Mississippi primary than the main Democratic party. Despite the MFDP's performance at the polls and Hamer's powerful speech, the party was not allowed official seats at the convention, partly because President Lyndon Johnson was afraid of losing his white support in the South.

Nevertheless, the eloquence of this relatively uneducated woman spoke volumes about the need to remedy injustice and make it possible for black people to vote. As she described to the convention a severe beating she had received after being arrested for civil rights activities, Hamer asked, "Is this America, the land of the free and the home of the brave, where we are threatened daily because we want to live as decent human beings?"

SEE ALSO

Civil rights movement

FURTHER READING

Lee, Chana Kai. *For Freedom's Sake: The Life of Fannie Lou Hamer.* Urbana: University of Illinois Press, 1999.

Mills, Kay. *This Little Light of Mine.* New York: Dutton, 1993.

Hamilton, Alice

- *Born: Feb. 27, 1969, Fort Wayne, Ind.*
- *Education: University of Michigan, M.D., 1893; postdoctoral studies at Johns Hopkins University*
- *Accomplishments: Professor of pathology, Northwestern University Women's Medical School (1897–1902); director, Occupational Disease*

Commission of Illinois (1910–11); first female faculty member, Harvard Medical School (1919–35); author, Industrial Poisons in the United States *(1925),* Industrial Tocixology *(1934, 4th ed. 1983),* Exploring the Dangerous Trades *(1943); president, National Consumers League (1944–49)*
- *Died: Sept. 22, 1970, Hadlyme, Conn.*

Alice Hamilton was a pioneer in two respects: as one of the developers of industrial medicine and as one of the first woman doctors to have a high-profile career.

Born to a family that placed great emphasis on education—her sister Edith became a well-known classicist—Alice earned an M.D. from the University of Michigan in 1893. She then pursued more medical studies at Johns Hopkins University and in Germany.

After returning to the United States, Hamilton studied the link between occupation and health for both the state of Illinois and the federal government, and she crusaded for owners to improve plant conditions. Her findings about the extent of work-related disease and injury underlaid the passage of workmen's compensation laws whereby an employee is able to hold an employer liable for job-related illness.

From 1919 to 1935 Hamilton was assistant professor of industrial medicine at Harvard Medical School. As such, she was the university's first woman professor. Even today, those who are trying to protect health and safety of workers turn to her memoir *Exploring the Dangerous Trades* for guidance and inspiration.

SEE ALSO
Medicine

FURTHER READING

Sicherman, Barbara. *Alice Hamilton, A Life in Letters.* Cambridge: Harvard University Press, 1984.

Hansberry, Lorraine

- *Born: May 19, 1930, Chicago, Ill.*
- *Education: University of Wisconsin, attended 1948–50*
- *Accomplishments: New York Drama Critics' Circle Award (1959) and Cannes Festival special award (1961) for* Raisin in the Sun*; Author (plays),* Raisin in the Sun *(1958);* The Sign in Sidney Brustein's Window *(1964); author,* To Be Young, Gifted, and Black *(posthumous selection of her writings, 1969)*
- *Died: Jan. 12, 1965, New York, N.Y.*

An African American whose award-winning first play was produced in New York in the 1950s, Lorraine Hansberry died soon after this triumph, at the age of 34.

Hansberry, whose father was a real estate broker and banker, was raised in Chicago. After studying drama at the University of Wisconsin, she moved to New York to try her fortune at writing for the stage. *Raisin in the Sun* was the result. Up to this point African Americans had usually been portrayed in plays written by whites—if portrayed at all—and in a stereotypical fashion. Hansberry's play was a sympathetic and insightful depiction of the struggles of a contemporary black family in Chicago and thus a stunning departure from what was usually seen on the New York stage.

Winning the New York Drama Critics Circle Award as the best play of 1959, *Raisin in the Sun* opened up new opportunities for blacks in the American theater. In 1969, four years after Hansberry's tragic early death from cancer, the play *To Be Young, Gifted, and Black*, based on her autobiographical writings, was produced off-Broadway. She was survived by her husband, Howard Nemiroff, a songwriter.

FURTHER READING

Cheney, Anne. *Lorraine Hansberry.* Boston: Twayne, 1984.
Keppel, Ben. *The Work of Democracy: Ralph Bunche, Kenneth B. Clark, Lorraine Hansberry, and the Cultural Politics of Race.* Cambridge: Harvard University Press, 1995.

Harlem Renaissance

During the Jazz Age of the 1920s and 1930s, there was an extraordinary outpouring of creativity from African-American men and women that centered in the Harlem neighborhood of New York City, the "Negro capital of the world" as many then called it.

After World War I (1914–1917), thousands of Southern blacks migrated to Harlem, drawn by job opportunities created in the post-war economic boom and by the relative tolerance of New York City. As the neighborhood filled with blacks from all walks of life, including many prosperous and educated professionals, the community developed an unprecedented vitality and cultural liveliness. This cultural ferment, centered in literature, music, and the performing arts, is known as the Harlem Renaissance; it constitutes the most substantial affirmation of African American worth until the "Black Pride" of the 1960s. Not only did it enrich American culture but it also laid the groundwork for effective political action by African Americans in the years after World War II.

Many of the brightest lights of the Harlem Renaissance were women. Jessie Fauset, for example, was the literary editor of the National Association for the Advancement of Colored People's monthly magazine *The Crisis*. She published the work of the poet Langston Hughes for the first time and encouraged many other important figures. She herself wrote four well-received novels.

Chorus girls at a Harlem club evoke the glamour that Harlem nightlife possessed during the Roaring '20s.

Another important Renaissance writer was Nella Larsen, author of two novels that deal with the difficulties of being a mixed-blood woman. And Zora Neale Hurston became known as an anthropologist, folklorist, novelist, and memoirist. Hurston's novel *Their Eyes Were Watching God* is now widely acknowledged as one of the most important works of 20th-century American fiction.

At the same time that jazz and other forms of black music were attracting national attention, female blues singers were gaining acclaim; Bessie Smith became the best known because of the raw power of her singing. Other women—such as the sexy and glamorous dancer Josephine Baker, who took Paris by storm in 1925—were creating heady new styles of singing and dancing characterized by jazz rhythms. By the time the Harlem Renaissance ended, African-American artists had embraced their heritage and become committed to exploring black identity through new styles, rather than following white models.

SEE ALSO

Hurston, Zora Neale; Smith, Bessie

FURTHER READING

Huggins, Nathan Irvin, ed. *Voices from the Harlem Renaissance.* New York: Oxford University Press, 1976.

Wall, Cheryl. *Women of the Harlem Renaissance.* Bloomington: Indiana University Press, 1995.

Watson, Steven. *The Harlem Renaissance: Hub of African-American Culture, 1920–1930.* New York: Pantheon, 1995.

Harper, Frances Ellen Watkins

- *Born: Sept. 24, 1825, Baltimore, Md.*
- *Education: Elementary school and self-educated*
- *Accomplishments: Touring lecturer for Anti-Slavery Society, through Maine (1854–56) and the East and Midwest (1856–60); director of black activities, National Woman's Christian Temperance Union (1883–90); director, American Association of Education of Colored Youth (1894–96); co-founder (1986) and vice-president (1897), National Association of Colored Women; author,* Forest Leaves *(1845);* Poems on Miscellaneous Subjects *(1854);* Sketches of Southern Life *(1872);* Iola Leroy; or, Shadows Uplifted *(1892)*
- *Died: Feb. 22, 1911, Philadelphia, Pa.*

Born to a free black family in Maryland at a time when slavery was still a legal institution there, Frances Ellen Watkins Harper became an outspoken antislavery lecturer—an activity that required courage from all women who undertook it but perhaps even more from an African-American woman, because she would have to contend with racism as well as sexism. In addition to being a reformer, Harper was also a poet and novelist.

Born free in Baltimore, a slave city, Frances Ellen Watkins Harper was raised by her abolitionist uncle and became an accomplished writer and lecturer. A longtime advocate for African Americans and women, she was a founding member of the National Association for the Advancement of Colored Women in 1896.

An orphan at the age of three, young Frances Watkins found a home with her uncle, a hardworking man who ran a school for free blacks. Under his care, the girl learned her lessons and also a work ethic she possessed for the rest of her life. As a young adult, she worked as a sewing teacher, but she also read widely. As early as 1845 she published a volume of her poetry and prose called *Forest Leaves.* In 1854 she began her antislavery lecturing, work that took her to many northern states. She married Fenton Harperin in 1860 and settled with him on his farm in Ohio. After his death in 1864, she resumed lecturing.

In the years following the Civil War (1861–65), Harper devoted herself to crusading against alcohol abuse as well as to fighting for women's rights and improving the situation of African Americans. Energetic into old age, she organized clubs and Sunday schools as well as kept up with her writing. In 1892 she published *Iola Leroy,* a novel historically significant because it was among the first novels by a black woman to reach a wide audience.

SEE ALSO
Literature

FURTHER READING

Boyd, Melba Joyce. *Discarded Legacy: Politics and Poetics in the Life of Frances E. W. Harper.* Detroit: Wayne State University Press, 1994.

Harper, Frances Ellen Watkins. *A Brighter Coming Day: A Frances Ellen Watkins Harper Reader.* Edited by Frances Smith Foster. New York: Feminist Press, 1990.

Hayes, Helen

- *Born: Oct. 10, 1900, Washington, D.C.*
- *Education: Sacred Heart Convent (Washington, D.C.)*
- *Accomplishments: Academy Award as best actress in* The Sin of Madelon Claudet *(1931) and as best supporting actress in* Airport *(1970); Tony Award as best actress in* Happy Birthday *(1947); Presidential Medal of Freedom (1986)*
- *Died: Mar. 17, 1993, Nyack, N.Y.*

Known as the First Lady of the American Theater for much of her long life, Helen Hayes was one of the most acclaimed actresses of the 20th century. Indeed, there is a Broadway theater named for her.

Hayes learned her craft young, making her stage debut at the age of five in vaudeville acts, the variety shows in the early 1900s that provided training for many performers who later appeared in movies or on Broadway.

Early in her career Hayes played young women on stage and in film, and as she aged, she kept expanding the range of roles she undertook—unlike some of her contemporaries, who got locked into being cast as girls. Film star Mary Pickford, for example, had a short career because once she outgrew young roles, audiences would not accept her as a mature woman. Hayes played classical roles, such as the women in Shakespeare's plays, in New York, and she also appeared in a number of movies in Hollywood, winning two Academy Awards: one for best actress in 1931 in *The Sin of Madelon Claudet*, and one for best supporting actress in 1970 in *Airport*. Perhaps her greatest stage triumph came as Queen Victoria in *Victoria Regina* on Broadway starting in 1935. She was married to the writer Charles MacArthur.

SEE ALSO
Theater

FURTHER READING

Hayes, Helen, with Katherine Hatch. *My Life in Three Acts.* San Diego: Harcourt Brace Jovanovich, 1990.

Murphy, Donn B. *Helen Hayes: A Bio-Bibliography.* Westport, Conn.: Greenwood, 1993.

Health, women's

One of the most successful elements of the modern women's movement has been the campaign to improve women's health and health care, which has resulted in more research being devoted to this area and also to women increasingly taking responsibility for getting screened and tested for serious disease such as breast cancer.

Women's health movements have come in various waves. One of the earliest, the Popular Health Movement of the 1830s and 1840s, advocated general education about health and disease prevention. It focused on women as primary caretakers in families, and emphasized such things as exercise and good diet, the elimination of corsets, and family size control through sexual abstinence. After the Civil War ended in 1865, the next wave of progress for women's health issues was spurred by the increased number of women attending medical schools. These women physicians challenged prevailing ideas about women's physical frailty and susceptibility to hysteria, and they were also active in creating women's hospitals to deal specifically with women's health. Around the turn of the century, women's health movements focused in particular on issues surrounding birth control and motherhood and prenatal care.

For much of the 20th century, the medical profession had been dominated by men; male doctors were the ultimate authority figures—over their female nurses as well as their female patients. Moreover the male body was seen as the human standard for medical research purposes. Researchers regarded the hormonal fluctuations in women's bodies as a nuisance, and an overwhelming percentage of medical research was conducted using men. The result is that until the 1980s much less was known about women's health problems than about men's. Now, women's health gets much more attention than formerly, and more resources have been allocated to it. Notably, the Harvard Nurses' Study has been tracking systematically the health of a large group of women over time.

Change and improvement have come about in several ways. In the first place, there are now thousands of women doctors as well as women nurses, and that has made women patients more comfortable with going to see a doctor. In the second place, women patients have organized a number of self-help groups so as to acquire more medical knowledge on their own and therefore be able to challenge a doctor's authority if they disagree with his or her conclusions. In 1976 the Boston Women's Health Collective published *Our Bodies, Ourselves,* which challenged women to take more responsibility for their own health and promoted the growth of a women's health movement.

Finally, as more women have been elected to Congress, they have made it a priority to redress the imbalance in

Every year the National Cancer Institute distributes booklets about breast cancer awareness. Although early detection results in higher cure rates, breast cancer remains the leading cause of cancer death of adult women under the age of 54.

funding for male and female health problems. Today, for example, breast cancer research is funded far more generously than at any other time in U.S. history (for example, in the 1990s Congress designated $737.5 million of the defense budget to be used for breast cancer research).

A good example of how women have organized for self-help is La Leche League (The Milk League) for nursing mothers. In the 1940s and 50s, a new mother who wanted to breast-feed her baby might well have been discouraged by hospital personnel—and left with no place to go for support. Doctors and nurses might also have told her that her milk supply was inadequate or that the bottle was easier, for reasons having to do with their own lack of training on the subject. In October 1956 a group of American women started La Leche League so that new mothers could help one another out by sharing their experiences in meetings. As of the late 1990s, there were 3,000 branches in 60 countries. A new mother can contact La Leche for specific, practical help with any number of difficulties.

Although there is much good news about women's health, many problems remain. For example, depression affects more women than men, for reasons that are still poorly understood. Also, we still know far too little about how to promote a sense of well-being in postmenopausal women. As of 1999, about 40 million American women were postmenopausal, but this figure is expected to increase to 60 million by 2025. With almost unrestricted access to medical and scientific studies for women, and with more women taking prominent roles in government—in addition to a greater general awareness by women of their own health—the gap between men's and women's health resources is expected to narrow still further.

SEE ALSO

Medicine; Nursing

FURTHER READING

Boston Women's Health Book Collective. *Our Bodies, Ourselves for the New Century.* New York: Simon & Schuster, 1998.

Hellman, Lillian

- *Born: June 20, 1905, New Orleans, La.*
- *Education: New York University, attended 1922–24, Columbia University, attended 1924*
- *Accomplishments: Member, American Academy of Arts and Letters; Gold Medal for Drama, National Institute of Arts and Letters (1964); MacDowell Medal (1976); author (plays),* The Children's Hour *(1934);* The Little Foxes *(1939);* Watch on the Rhine *(1941);* The Searching Wind *(1944);* Another Part of the Forest *(1946);* The Autumn Garden *(1951);* Toys in the Attic *(1960); author (memoirs),* An Unfinished Woman *(1969);* Pentimento *(1973);* Scoundrel Time *(1976);* Maybe: A Story *(1980)*
- *Died: June 30, 1984, Martha's Vineyard, Mass.*

Lillian Hellman was a highly succesful playwright as well as the author of three widely read volumes of memoirs.

Born to a Jewish family in New Orleans, Hellman went north for college, attending both New York University and Columbia University. Her first play, *The Children's Hour,* about a girls' school and a rumored lesbian relationship between two of the teachers, was produced on Broadway to excellent reviews in 1934. The author was only in her 20s, and many other successes followed. She also began a stormy relationship with the author Dashiell Hammett, and the two became involved with a number of radical political causes, including an uncritical admiration for the Soviet Union during the 1930s.

Later, during the very conservative 1950s, this earlier behavior created difficulties for Hellman (and for many other Americans), and she was summoned to testify before the House Un-American Activities Committee investigating the radical activities of the 1930s. She refused to testify, saying that she did not want to give the names of others she had known who were also involved. In her memoirs she wrote vividly both about her own radicalism and its problems—not without controversy, because she created some unflattering portraits of her contemporaries who had cooperated with the committee as she had not, and had provided the names of others to be investigated.

FURTHER READING

Towns, Saundra. *Lillian Hellman.* New York: Chelsea House, 1989.
Wright, William. *Lillian Hellman: The Image, the Woman.* New York: Simon & Schuster, 1986.

Hispanic Americans

SEE Latinas

Home economics

Home economics, also known as domestic science, is an academic discipline that developed in the late 19th century. Accomplished women scientists who could not find jobs in the male-dominated fields of chemistry, biology, or economics, especially the trained chemist Ellen Swallow Richards, began to study such subjects as the chemistry of home sanitation and of nutrition. Out of their efforts came a crusade to make the home more efficient and more sanitary. By the early 20th century, home economics courses were being taught in high schools, colleges, and universities throughout the country.

The courses taught generations of young women how to cook and sew, but the field has failed to deliver all of its initial promise of reform. This happened because prestigious universities have generally regarded it as relatively unimportant. For many decades women with advanced degrees in chemistry, economics, or even history were channeled into university home economics departments, a sort of female ghetto in the system, where they were taken less than seriously by their male colleagues despite their research and teaching accomplishments. After World War II ended in 1945, the home ec departments at most prestigious universities were dismantled as the universities sought to upgrade their reputations. Only at agricultural schools and in rural areas, where the mission is one of service to the community, has the discipline flourished in the 1980s and 1990s.

SEE ALSO

Richards, Ellen Swallow; Science

FURTHER READING

Stage, Sarah, and Virginia Vincenti, eds. *Rethinking Home Economics.* Ithaca, N.Y.: Cornell University Press, 1997.

Hosmer, Harriet Goodhue

- *Born: Oct. 9, 1830, Watertown, Mass.*
- *Education: High school and private training*
- *Accomplishments: Internationally celebrated sculptor*
- *Died: Feb. 21, 1908, Watertown, Mass.*

The first American woman to have an international reputation as a sculptor, Harriet Hosmer lived a remarkably independent and successful life. Though 20th-century art critics are relatively unimpressed by the quality of her work, it sold well in her lifetime.

Growing up as a tomboy in western Massachusetts, young Harriet was fortunate to become acquainted with some of the well-known women of her day through the school she attended, which attracted the support of many accomplished women. It was the actress Fanny Kemble who encouraged the girl to pursue the field of sculpture. Thanks to her father's financial support—he was a physician—Harriet Hosmer went to Rome to study sculpture seriously in 1852.

In subsequent years Hosmer was part of a Roman circle that included such cultural "stars" as the poets Robert and Elizabeth Barrett Browning. Her statues based on mythological figures and her busts of living people sold well in England and in the United States. As an old woman, she returned to her native Massachusetts, where she died at the age of 77.

FURTHER READING

Sherwood, Dolly. *Harriet Hosmer, American Sculptor.* Columbia: University of Missouri Press, 1991.

Household size

The number of people living in the average American household has changed dramatically over the years: in 1790 the average household contained 7 people, and in 1970 it contained 3.2.

In the colonial period a household might have consisted of a mother, father, seven or eight children, many of whom might have died before reaching adulthood, three or four servants, and possibly a few men who were apprenticed to the father and learning a trade.

Since then the number of children in a family has declined as the birthrate went down, the servants have dwindled in number, and apprentices have disappeared altogether. Indeed, a substantial percentage of American households now consist of only one person, something that would have been unheard of in earlier times. The decrease in household size has also meant that those living in a home are much likelier to have a room of their own than in earlier times and that they can also look forward to having more privacy.

TOTAL POPULATION AND HOUSEHOLD SIZE: 1790 TO 1970

Year	Total Population (Millions)	Households (Millions)	Inviduals per Household
1790	3.9	0.6	7.0
1800	5.3	—	—
1810	7.2	—	—
1820	9.6	—	—
1830	12.9	—	—
1840	17.1	—	—
1850	23.2	3.6	6.4
1860	31.4	5.2	6.0
1870	38.6	7.6	5.1
1880	50.2	9.9	5.0
1890	62.9	12.7	5.0
1900	76.0	16.0	4.8
1910	92	20.3	4.5
1920	105.7	24.4	4.3
1930	122.8	29.9	4.1
1940	131.7	34.9	3.8
1950	150.7	43.6	3.5
1960	179.3	52.8	3.4
1970	203.2	63.4	3.2

Source: U.S. Census

SEE ALSO

Privacy

Housework

Housework is the labor it takes to maintain a home. Now largely performed by the woman who lives there—with help from others, if she is lucky—it once included the efforts of servants or slaves, unless a woman were poor. Indeed, in the days before consumer goods were readily available, the housework for one home might have required the labor of several people.

Throughout the country during preindustrial times—and then on the frontier as the more settled parts of the country moved into the consumer age—the housewife was the coordinator of massive efforts to do all the housework. In order to the laundry, for example, soap first had to be manufactured using fat that was saved from cooking plus ashes that had been saved for their lye. Someone, perhaps an older son, chopped wood to build a fire to heat the water. Someone else had to draw and transport enough water from a well for both the soapy liquid and the rinsing. Then someone had to scrub the clothes by hand and someone had to hang them to dry. In short, doing laundry was a hard day's work for more than one person.

In the early 19th century, technological changes began to appear that would transform the nature of housework. At the dawn of the century, women were cooking over open hearths. By century's end most women had a wood-burning stove. Also, during the century the sewing machine was invented, there were improvements in refrigeration, and the work of laundry began to be lightened by store-bought soap and indoor plumbing. Moreover, at the Chicago World's Fair in 1893, an exhibition demonstrated what the home of the future would be like, because it showed the prototypes for many different electrical appliances such as electrified pans, washing machines, and irons.

Some scholars have suggested that all the new consumer goods and technological innovations have not helped women as much as one would think, because standards of cleanliness have risen so much over the generations. For example, laundry is still a lot of work because people now expect fresh clothes every day. Given the difference in the way laundry was done in the last century and the way it is done today, however, women have also clearly benefited from the change.

Washday was strenuous labor for a housewife in 1915. Women scrubbed the clothes in wooden washtubs before running them through a hand-cranked wringer. Few labor-saving machines were available for mass consumption before 1920.

SEE ALSO

Consumer culture; Servants

FURTHER READING

Cowan, Ruth Schwartz. *More Work for Mother.* New York: Basic, 1983.

Hoy, Suellen. *Chasing Dirt: The American Pursuit of Cleanliness.* New York: Oxford University Press, 1995.

Strasser, Susan. *Never Done.* New York: Pantheon, 1982.

Howe, Julia Ward

- *Born: May 27, 1819, New York, N.Y.*
- *Education: Privately educated*
- *Accomplishments: Author, "The Battle Hymn of the Republic" (1862); co-founder (1868) and president (1868–77, 1893–1910), New England Woman Suffrage Association; founder (1868) and president (1871), New England Women's Club; founder (1870) and editor (1870–90),* Woman's Journal; *first woman elected to the American Academy of Arts and Letters (1908); author,* Passion Flowers *(1854);* Words for the Hour *(1857);* Leonora, or the World's Own *(1857);* A Trip to Cuba *(1860)*
- *Died: Oct. 17, 1910, Newport, R.I.*

The northern men who fought in the Civil War (1861–65) marched off to battle singing Julia Ward Howe's "The Battle Hymn of the Republic," set to the music of "John Brown's Body." It was one of those rare songs that has perfectly captured the national mood at a crucial time in U.S. history. Howe's heartfelt lyrics helped endow the Union cause with sacred purpose.

> Mine eyes have seen the glory of the coming of the Lord
> He is trampling out the vintage where the grapes of wrath are stored,
> He has loosed the fateful lightening of
> His terrible swift sword
> His truth is marching on.

In consequence, as she aged, she was increasingly seen as a national treasure. This was an ironic ending for a woman whose earlier life had been filled with trouble.

Having received a better than average education for a girl of her day, Julia Ward married the reformer Samuel Gridley Howe in 1843. A man with a national reputation of his own for his humane treatment of the blind and deaf, he had stern views and believed it was inappropriate for a married woman to be involved in public life. In fact, he was a domestic tyrant who criticized his wife endlessly and refused to permit her to be involved with the burgeoning abolitionist and women's movements. She gave birth to six children, but the marriage tottered on the brink of divorce (a disgraceful outcome at the time) on more than one occasion.

Howe had published poetry before "Battle Hymn" but nothing that enjoyed major success. Following the Civil War, she refused to obey her husband and *did* become a public figure. Her activities included working for the suffrage movement and the women's club movement, writing about causes she believed in, and preaching in Unitarian and Universalist pulpits. Samuel Howe was much older than his wife, and lived until 1876. Toward the end of his life, the couple achieved a reconciliation.

Julia Ward Howe, who lived to be 91, was active almost to the end of her long life. In 1908 she became the first woman elected to the American Academy of Arts and Letters.

FURTHER READING

Clifford, Deborah Pickman. *Mine Eyes Have Seen the Glory.* Boston: Little, Brown, 1979.

Hurston, Zora Neale

- *Born: Jan. 7, 1891, Notasulga, Ala.*
- *Education: Howard University, attended 1921–24; Barnard College, B.A., 1928*
- *Accomplishments: First African-*

American woman to attend Barnard College; author, Jonah's Gourd Vine *(1934);* Mules and Men *(1935);* Their Eyes Were Watching God *(1937);* Tell My Horse *(1938);* Moses, Man of the Mountain *(1939);* Dust Tracks on a Road *(autobiography, 1942);* Seraph on the Suwanee *(1948)*
- *Died: Jan. 28, 1960, Fort Pierce, Fla.*

In 1935 Zora Neale Hurston published Mules and Men, *the first collection of African-American folklore by a black scholar. Hurston's work would later influence such writers as Ralph Ellison and Toni Morrison.*

The novelist Zora Neale Hurston contributed to the flowering of African-American culture in the 20th century and lived a life filled with achievement. Nonetheless, she spent her last years in poverty and obscurity. She was buried in an unmarked grave in 1960, but fellow novelist Alice Walker paid for a gravestone in 1973; Walker also crusaded to see to it that Hurston receive the recognition she deserved.

MULES AND MEN

Behold means to look and see.
Look at dis woman God done made,
But first thing, ah hah!
Ah wants you to gaze upon God's previous works.
Almighty and arisen God, hah!
Peace-giving and prayer-hearing God,
High-riding and strong armded God
Walking acrost his globe creation, hah!

Wid de blue elements for a helmet
And a wall of fire round his feet
He wakes de sun every morning from his fiery bed
Wid de breath of his smile
And commands de moon wid his eyes.
And Oh—
Wid de eye of Faith
I can see him
Standing out on de eaves of ether
Breathing clouds from out his nostrils,
Blowing storms from 'tween his lips

Hurston was raised in an all-black small town in Florida, a town she re-created in her fiction years later. She attended Howard University and later graduated from Barnard College with a bachelor's degree. Her scholarly interest was in folklore: the lore she heard while growing up, the culture of southern blacks. She pursued that interest as far as beginning graduate studies in anthropology at Columbia University, although she never completed her doctoral degree. She was sidetracked by other work, most notably her novel *Their Eyes Were Watching God,* about a young woman in a small town in Florida, published in 1937.

Hurston's intellectual maturity coincided with a burst of artistic development among American blacks known as the Harlem Renaissance. Her particular contribution to the Harlem Renaissance was to write vividly about the life of her small town, as in *Their Eyes Were Watching God,* to invest American literature with the sensibility of one who had grown up in such a place—as Mark Twain had done with the experience of growing up along the banks of the Mississippi.

Hurston's life took a tragic turn toward extreme poverty, in part because she had to contend with sexism in the African-American community as well as with racism in the larger community. Prominent black male intellectuals such as Richard Wright were dismissive of her work. In recent years her work has been rediscovered and reevaluated by scholars, and she has been read as she never was in her own lifetime.

SEE ALSO

Harlem Renaissance

FURTHER READING

Howare, Lillie P. *Zora Neale Hurston.* Boston: Twayne, 1980.

Lyons, Mary E. *Sorrow's Kitchen: The Life and Folklore of Zora Neale Hurston.* New York: Charles Scribner's Sons, 1990.

Hutchinson, Anne

- *Born: 1591, Alford, England*
- *Education: No formal education*
- *Accomplishments: Religious thinker*
- *Died: Around August 1643, New Netherland (now New York)*

Anne Hutchinson, a loving wife and the mother of a large family, seems at first glance to have been an unlikely person to have stirred up a crisis in Boston in the first decade of its settlement. But she did, in fact, create a profound crisis: she challenged the Puritan clergy by claiming that a person's own state of grace was more important in the salvation process than the ministers' teachings. Many prominent people agreed with her, and this made her a dangerous person because these beliefs threatened to destroy the structure of authority in the colony.

Hutchinson talked her merchant husband William into emigrating from England to Massachusetts in 1634 out of her devotion to Puritan religious beliefs. Once in Boston, he entered the cloth trade, and the family joined the best circles of society. Anne Hutchinson, who had given birth more than a dozen times, began to assist at the birthing beds of other women and while there to talk to them about their religious beliefs.

Hutchinson became convinced that most of the ministers were preaching an erroneous doctrine, that they were emphasizing a person's good deeds at the expense of emphasizing the importance of the individual's inner state. In effect, she pitted herself against most of the colony's religious authorities, and she also began to say these things to mixed audiences of men and women.

Before too much longer, the authorities took action against her and tried her for defaming the ministers. The fact that it was a woman speaking out in public made them all the angrier. In fact, Hutchinson *had* created a dangerously divisive situation in the new colony. She received two trials, one religious and one civil, both of which she lost.

In 1638 she, her family, and their supporters were banished. They eventually made their home in what is now New York City, where in 1643 Hutchinson and most of her younger children died at the hands of Indians. (William had died a year earlier.) For many generations in New England, Anne Hutchinson's name was a byword for a Jezebel, a woman who sought undue influence.

SEE ALSO

Religion

FURTHER READING

Dunlea, William. *Anne Hutchinson and the Puritans: An Early American Tragedy.* Pittsburgh, Pa.: Dorrance, 1993.

Hall, David D., ed. *The Antinomian Controversy.* Durham, N.C.: Duke University Press, 1990.

Williams, Selma R. *Divine Rebel.* New York: Holt, Rinehart & Winston, 1981.

Immigration

Most Americans are the descendants of immigrants—unwilling ones in the case of African Americans. Exceptions include those of Native-American or Hawaiian background, and those descended from the Mexicans who inhabited the Southwest.

Most immigrants to the United States faced some level of hardship and discrimination because they did not speak English or because of their religious affiliation or cultural preferences, and for many immigrant groups the male and female experiences were very different. Europeans, however, especially those from Western Europe, tended to receive better treatment in general than other groups. Most have enjoyed the artificial privilege that comes with being defined as "white," although for some immigrants that designation took decades to obtain. None have been enslaved. Few have encountered problems obtaining U.S. citizenship if they have entered this country legally.

Unlike many others, most Europeans were allowed to enter the United States as families. The government even allowed young women of select European groups, in particular the Irish and Scandinavians, to immigrate alone and to obtain employment as domestic servants. Some Europeans voluntarily sent their men alone as short-term "sojourners" (meaning that they intended to return home eventually) so that they could make enough money to restore the family fortunes in the homeland. A frequent pattern was for the man to secure employment, get settled, and then send for the rest of the family.

Options such as these were not available to Asians, who usually suffered the worst hardships in immigrating. In 1882 Congress had passed the Chinese Exclusion Act, a law that closed the door to all but a trickle of immigration from China. The few Asians who made it into the country were men who were not allowed to bring their families with them or even send for them later. Discriminatory U.S. policies required that Asian men come alone as a way of discouraging the formation of families.

Asian-American communities' gender ratios thus remained unbalanced until the 1940s—the Chinese Exclusion Act was not repealed until 1943. Not only did the U.S. government discourage female immigration for Asians, until 1952 it prohibited Asian immigrants from becoming naturalized citizens, although their children born in the United States *were* citizens. In 1965, for the first time ever, American law ceased to discriminate against those from Asia with the passage of the Immigration Act

Immigrant families in the early 20th century, such as these Polish migrant workers in the fields near Baltimore, often had little to start with when they arrived in America. As this Lewis Hine photograph shows, women and children often did hard field labor to help support the family.

of 1965, which ended quotas based on national origins.

This law also meant that certain European groups that had been discriminated against, such as those from Southern and Eastern Europe, no longer were singled out for unique treatment. All immigrants, male and female alike, suffered from hardship. For women, though, moving to the United States opened up the possibility of liberation from the patriarchal society of the homeland. Immigrating *could* provide opportunities for a woman that never would have existed in her native country, such as economic independence and a role in public life.

On the other hand, many immigrant women have toiled under unusually harsh conditions in sweatshops, performing poorly paid domestic work, and in general doing the country's dirtiest and least desirable work. This was true of women working in miserable tenements in big cities 100 years ago, and it is still true in the 1990s. In California's Silicon Valley, for example, which often receives media coverage for its high-tech success stories, immigrant women stuff circuit boards under conditions that frequently involve exposure to harsh chemicals.

One hundred years ago such conditions inspired middle-class women to found settlement houses in immigrant neighborhoods. Today there are advocacy group,s such as California's Asian Immigrant Women Advocates, that provide legal and moral support for those who are vulnerable.

SEE ALSO

Asian Americans; Muslims; Settlement-house movement

FURTHER READING

Glenn, Susan. *Daughters of the Shtetl.* Ithaca: Cornell University Press, 1990.

Jacobson, Matthew Frye. *Whiteness of a Different Color*. Cambridge: Harvard University Press, 1998.

Yung, Judy. *Unbound Feet: A Social History of Chinese Women in San Francisco.* Berkeley: University of California Press, 1995.

Indentured servants

Many people who chose to sail across the Atlantic to build lives in one of the American colonies came out of religious conviction. Many who were somewhat prosperous came because they wanted to increase their wealth. And even more came because they were desperately poor in the Old World and wanted a chance to improve their condition.

Tens of thousands of those who were poor arrived in America as indentured servants, bound to serve a master for a specified length of time, most often four to seven years. A man or woman received free passage to the New World after signing a contract of indenture; a woman was most often destined to be a domestic servant. Those who paid for the indentured servants' trip did so because they needed the workers. While under contract, the servants received no pay except room and board.

Once in America, the servant would have to accept harsh conditions until becoming free, and perhaps then would marry and start a better life. Masters were legally obligated to provide these servants with little besides their clothing upon their obtaining freedom, but an enterprising servant might well have contrived to put together a small amount of capital. Servants could own property and could have saved any gifts they had received. Because such servants were bound to obey their masters, there *was* opportunity for exploitation, including the sexual exploitation of women, although not as much opportunity as under the much harsher system of slavery.

Modern scholars have estimated that a very substantial proportion, one-half to two-thirds, of all European immigrants to the American colonies came as indentured servants: for example, a majority of those who emigrated from England in the 17th century belonged to this category. Estimates are that men from all countries outnumbered women by a factor of 3 to 1.

After the American Revolution, indentured servants began to disappear. They were replaced by hired help in the North and by slaves in the South.

FURTHER READING

Bailyn, Bernard. *The Peopling of North America.* New York: Knopf, 1986.

Industrialization

The Indusrial Revolution that began at the end of the 18th century transformed the lives of all women, as it did those of all men. It had a very different impact on the two sexes, however. Women's work in the home, while affected by industrialization, retained some of the qualities of preindustrial work much longer than did the work of the average man.

Before the Industrial Revolution, which began in England and arrived in the new United States in the 1790s, work was task-oriented rather than performed according to a rigid schedule. A farmer and his wife would rise with the sun and do the work of the day, according to the season, until that day's task was complete. When factories appeared, however, workers awakened to a factory bell, and then were required to report to work at a specified time and remain for a specified number of hours.

Though the Industrial Revolution created a greater abundance of goods for those in the middle class, it led to dreadful exploitation of workers, including children. A major goal of many women reformers in the early 20th century was the abolition of child labor.

Housework, on the other hand, continues to be task-oriented to this very day.

Although most factory workers were male until well into the 20th century, among the first groups of factory hands in the 1820s and 1830s were young women who worked in New England's textile mills. Known as the "Lowell mill girls" because the town of Lowell, Massachusetts, was one of the most important centers of textile manufacture, these young women were recruited from surrounding farms, attracted by a new opportunity for independence. They were white, Protestant, and accustomed to tight control by their parents. In consequence, mill owners had to promise parents that the girls would be strictly supervised before they were allowed to leave the farms. The overwhelming majority of them married after a few years of employment, able then to invest some of their earnings in setting up a household.

While working at the mills, the young women lived in chaperoned boardinghouses to which they retreated

This photograph of women at the machinery of a textile mill in New England was taken in 1850, well before legislation was implemented to ensure safety and proper working conditions for garment workers.

after extraordinarily long days of work. A 70-hour workweek at substandard wages (one to two dollars a week) was typical. In 1834 and 1836 they went on strike, much to the chagrin of mill owners, who had hired them in part because they were presumed to be docile. Though they won nothing as a result of the strikes, the young women's fighting spirit demonstrated that women workers could not be mistreated with impunity.

With the rise of mass immigration in the 1840s, the composition of the female factory workforce changed dramatically. The next generation of women workers were immigrants who were poor and likely to remain so throughout their lives. Over time, an increasing percentage of industrial labor was performed by women, most of European immigrant stock; indeed, in industries such as food processing, women constituted the majority of the production workers by the early 20th century. Not until World War II did African-American women secure this type of employment.

One of the most unfortunate consequences of industrialization lay in the potential to exploit children. In farm communities, even fairly young children had worked side by side with the rest of the family. This may have been hard on children, but at least they were being supervised by people who presumably loved them. When poor families sent their young children, girls and boys both, into factories, this was no longer the case. Children were deprived of education, cruelly overworked, and even forced to labor in hazardous environments such as mines and quarries.

One of the key reforms advocated by women activists in the early 20th century was the elimination, or at least control, of child labor, a goal that has been substantially achieved. The principal achievement in this area was the 1938 Fair Labor Standards Act (better known as the Federal Wage and Hour Law), which included a prohibition of labor by children under the age of 16, and allowed minors older than 16 to work only in non-hazardous jobs.

In the world of industrial work, women laborers have often not been taken seriously by male-controlled labor unions. A particularly tragic example of exploitation of women laborers occurred at the Triangle Shirtwaist Company in New York City on March 25, 1911. Women crowded into a sweatshop on the top floors of the Asch building near Washington Square Park had been locked in by their supervisors as a measure against theft, and when a fire broke out, 146 of them died—burning to death or jumping in desperation out of eighth-to-tenth-story windows.

As women have become an increasingly important component of the workforce, the attitude of officials and leaders has changed, to the mutual benefit of organized labor and women workers. Women have come to represent the best opportunity for the growth of the labor movement.

SEE ALSO

Labor movement

FURTHER READING

Dublin, Thomas. *Transforming Women's Work*. Ithaca, N.Y.: Cornell University Press, 1994.

Eisler, Benita, ed. *The Lowell Offering: Writings by New England Mill Women (1840–1845)*. Philadelphia: Lippincott, 1977.

Hellerstein, Erna Olafson, Leslie Parker Hume, and Karen M. Offen, eds. *Victorian Women: A Documentary Account of Women's Lives in Nineteenth-Century England, France and the United States*. Stanford, Calif.: Stanford University Press, 1981.

Industrial Workers of the World (IWW)

Among the most militant of American labor unions in the early 20th century was the group known as the Industrial Workers of the World, or Wobblies, founded in 1905. Dedicated Wobblies would try to recruit new members in the fields and mines, where other organizers disdained to put much effort because they believed that the workers were too lowly and vulnerable to make good union members. Moreover, far more than the mainstream labor movement, the IWW welcomed women, immigrants, and people of color into its ranks; the Wobblies believed in "one big union" for all workers.

Although much of its strength was in the West among male miners, farm laborers, and timber workers, the IWW did stage two strikes in the East that reached out to women textile workers. The strikes in Lawrence, Massachusetts, in 1912, and in Paterson, New Jersey, in 1913, were not successful other than in the short run—the employers granted strikers' demands and then reneged—but they were notable for the solidarity they built among women workers, for the help proffered by such well-known women radicals as Elizabeth Gurley Flynn and Margaret Sanger, and for the national attention they attracted.

Believing in "one big union," the Wobblies scorned any political involvement, including the support of woman suffrage. Opposed to U.S. entry into World War I in 1917, the Wobblies spoke out against it. In addition, some of them *may* have engaged in acts of sabotage against employers. Without ever proving that this had occurred, both federal and local authorities engaged in fierce repression of the group, and vigilante attacks were directed against it. By 1920, the IWW had diminished as a force in the American labor movement, though it was still in existence at the end of the 1990s, with active branches throughout the United States and the world.

FURTHER READING

Dubofsky, Melvyn. *We Shall Be All: A History of the Industrial Workers of the World.* Urbana: University of Illinois Press, 1988.

Salerno, Salvatore. *Red November, Black November: Culture and Community in the Industrial Workers of the World.* Albany: State University of New York Press, 1989.

International Ladies' Garment Workers Union (ILGWU)

The International Ladies' Garment Workers Union (ILGWU) was the first large union to consist primarily of women members—although the name itself refers to the makers of clothes for women, rather than to the gender of the workers themselves.

Initially organized by men in 1900, the ILGWU soon began to recruit the young immigrant women who were an increasingly significant part of the labor force in New York City, where the union was born. In 1909 female shirtwaist (blouse) makers began a massive strike, sustained heroically by Jewish and Italian immigrant women who picketed in freezing temperatures and withstood police brutality. At first these women were disregarded by the male-led mainstream labor movement, but they did receive significant support from the Women's Trade Union League, which had been organized in 1903 by a coalition of working-class and middle-class women.

As support for the strike grew among women in the trade, the ILGWU hired organizers to help recruit strikers. The best-known of these was Rose Schneiderman, who would become a confidante of Eleanor Roosevelt and a leader of American working women for half a century from 1904 through the 1950s.

The International Ladies Garment Workers' Union was one of the first successful unions to have a substantially female membership. This pamphlet from the 1930s evokes a sense of militant female power that would have appeared in few other images of the day.

As a consequence of the partially successful strike, the membership in the ILGWU soared. Although the leadership continued to be mostly male until the postwar era, by 1916, women made up 50 percent of its members.

SEE ALSO

Labor movement; Women's Trade Union League (WTUL)

FURTHER READING

Glenn, Susan. *Daughters of the Shtetl.* Ithaca, N.Y.: Cornell University Press, 1990.

Inventions

There have not been a great many women inventors in the United States. On the other hand, the fact that there have been any at all before the 20th century testifies to human creativity under adverse conditions. Not only have women not had a good chance of receiving a technical education until the 1970s, but men have been the ones responsible for maintaining equipment around the home or farm. If a farm wife in the mid-19th century had offered to have a look at a broken plow, for example, she would most likely have been seen as venturing outside her area of expertise.

Scholars estimate that women were responsible for about 1 percent of the patents in the 19th century, with a slight increase in the 20th century up to the birth of the modern women's movement in the 1960s, when women gained improved access to engineering school as a result of Title IX of the Education Act Amendments of 1972. In the 1970s, as a sign of the changing times, two different women were chosen as Inventor of the Year: Mary Olliden Weaver in 1977 as part of a team of agricultural scientists, and Barbara Askins in 1978 for a process to enhance X-ray images.

One of the best-known women inventors was the movie star Hedy Lamarr, who wanted to help the U.S. war effort during World War II. In the 1940s Lamarr worked on an antijamming device for radar that was ultimately used by the Navy, an invention that anticipated modern techniques for dealing with this problem.

SEE ALSO

Education Act Amendments (1972)

FURTHER READING

Casey, Susan. *Women Invent: Two Centuries of Discoveries that have Shaped our World.* Chicago: Chicago Review Press, 1997.

Macdonald, Anne L. *Feminine Ingenuity: Women and Invention in America.* New York: Ballantine, 1992.

Showell, Ellen Harvey. *From Indian Corn to Outer Space: Women Invent in America.* Peterborough, N.H.: Cobblestone, 1995.

Stanley, Autumn. *Mothers and Daughters of Invention.* Metuchen, N.J.: Scarecrow, 1993.

Vare, Ethlie Ann. *Mothers of Invention: From the Bra to the Bomb.* New York: Morrow, 1988.

Jackson, Helen Maria Fiske Hunt

- *Born: Oct. 15, 1830, Amherst, Mass.*
- *Education: Ipswich Female Seminary; Spingler Institute*
- *Accomplishments: Special Commissioner of Indian Affairs (1882); author,* Verses *(1870);* Mercy Philbrick's Choice *(1876);* A Century of Dishonor *(1881);* Ramona *(1884);* Sonnets and Lyrics *(1886)*
- *Died: Aug. 12, 1885, San Francisco, Calif.*

Helen Hunt Jackson wrote one of the best-selling books of the late 19th century, *Ramona* (1884), a novel that helped raise the awareness of the American public about the plight of Indians. Her achievement followed a devastating series of personal tragedies.

Before she was 20, Helen had lost both her mother and her father. After marrying Lieutenant Edward Bissell Hunt in 1852, she gave birth to two sons. By 1865, however, all three males in the family were dead, and friends feared for her mental stability.

At this low point in her life, Helen Hunt began to write, mostly poetry; she developed a literary reputation and was soon able to support herself writing both prose and verse. In 1875 she married William Sharpless Jackson, a Quaker banker. With his resources at

Helen Hunt Jackson's 1885 novel Ramona *was a bitter indictment of the U.S. government's treatment of Native Americans. A good friend of the reclusive poet Emily Dickinson, Jackson was an accomplished essayist, poet, and novelist.*

her disposal, she gained the opportunity to write what she most wanted to, rather than what would sell.

Jackson had never been especially interested in social reform, but in 1879 in Boston she heard a speech by the Ponca chief Standing Bear about tribal troubles. She dedicated the rest of her life to publicizing the wrongs done to the American Indians, such as their forcible removal from tribal lands, researching extensively and writing not only *Ramona* but also a work of nonfiction, *A Century of Dishonor,* published in 1881, which strongly criticized the federal government for its conduct of Indian affairs. But she reached a far greater audience with her novel *Ramona,* a story of doomed love and the misdeeds of greedy whites. *Ramona* enjoyed immense popularity, going into more than 300 printings.

Later critics have charged that *Ramona* did more to encourage the romanticizing of the Spanish past in California than to get people to do something about injustice against Indians. Yet Jackson deserves credit for trying to wake up her country about the subject.

FURTHER READING

Mathes, Valerie Sherer. *Helen Hunt Jackson and Her Indian Reform Legacy.* Austin: University of Texas Press, 1990.

May, Antoinette. *The Annotated Ramona.* San Carlos, Calif.: Wide World/Tetra, 1989.

Jacobi, Mary Putnam

- *Born: Aug. 31, 1842, London, England*
- *Education: New York College of Pharmacy, graduated 1863; Female (later Women's) Medical College of Pennsylvania, graduated 1864; École de Médecine, Paris, M.D., 1871*
- *Accomplishments: Professor, Woman's Medical College of the New York Infirmary for Women and Children (1871–89); organizer (1872) and president (1874–1903), Association for the Advancement of the Medical Education of Women (later the Women's Medical Association of New York City); lecturer on children's diseases, New York Post-Graduate Medical School (1882–85)*
- *Died: June 10, 1906, New York, N.Y.*

At the height of her career, Mary Putnam Jacobi was the leading woman physician in the United States. In addition to seeing patients and working to improve the medical education available to other women, she wrote more than 100 medical articles.

The daughter of the well-known American publisher George Palmer Putnam and his wife (temporarily living in London when Mary was born), Mary Putnam received a fine education when she was growing up in upstate New York. Twenty years younger than Elizabeth Blackwell, the first woman doctor in the United States, Putnam benefited from the establishment of the Female Medical College of Pennsylvania, from which she graduated in the early 1860s.

Dissatisfied with the quality of the medical education she had been able to obtain in the United States, however, Putnam went to France in 1866 to study further. There she became the first woman admitted to the École de Médecine. She won a bronze medal for her thesis in 1871.

Back in the United States, Jacobi combined highly regarded clinical skills with a remarkable output of papers on such topics as neurology, pathology, and pediatrics. She also dedicated herself to improving conditions for other women doctors. In 1872 she organized the Association for the Advancement of Medical Education for Women, where she served as president from 1874 to 1903.

In addition to her many other activities, Mary Putnam Jacobi was also active in the fight for woman suffrage. In 1873, Putnam married fellow physician Abraham Jacobi, and they became the parents of three children.

SEE ALSO

Blackwell, Elizabeth; Medicine

FURTHER READING

Morantz-Sanchez, Regina. *Sympathy and Science.* New York: Oxford University Press, 1985.

Jacobs, Harriet

- *Born: 1813, Edenton, N.C.*
- *Education: No formal education*
- *Accomplishments: Author,* Incidents in the Life of a Slave Girl *(1861)*
- *Died: Mar. 7, 1897, Washington, D.C.*

Under the pen name of Linda Brent, Harriet Jacobs wrote the most extensive slave narrative that we have from a woman author. Her extraordinary tale, published as *Incidents in the Life of a Slave Girl* in 1861, was long thought to be based more on imagination than on lived reality, but it has recently been reevaluated. After conducting additional research, scholars now believe that a substantial portion of the narrative is true.

Jacobs was the prey of a white man who wanted to have a sexual liaison with her. To avoid this man, whom she despised, she gave herself to a second man—without the ceremony of marriage. She believed the second man to be capable of protecting her from the first, and he did for a time. The narrative also details a long period of subsequent hiding in her grandmother's house, where Jacobs could protect herself from harm. She finally escaped from the clutches of the slavery system in 1842 and managed to bring her children north in later years.

Deciding that her story should be made public—and hoping to influence the slavery debate in the northern states—Jacobs at first approached the novelist Harriet Beecher Stowe for help selling her book to a publisher. Stowe, however, wanted to use Jacobs's narrative as the basis for her own fiction. Jacobs wanted to be in control of her own story, so she then turned to the writer Lydia Maria Child, who aided her in the finer points of writing and publishing. Both Child and Jacobs displayed impressive courage in this venture, because the book appeared at a time when public opinion judged harshly a woman who had strayed from conventional sexual morality, as Jacobs had when she lived with a man without the sanction of marriage.

SEE ALSO

Child, Lydia Maria; Slavery

Jewett, Sarah Orne

- *Born: Sept. 3, 1849, South Berwick, Maine*
- *Education: Berwick Academy, graduated 1865*
- *Accomplishments: Author,* Play Days *(1878);* A Country Doctor *(1884);* A Marsh Island *(1885);* Betty Leicester *(1889);* The Country of the Pointed Firs *(1896);* Betty Leicester's English Christmas *(1897);* The Tory Lover *(1901); many short stories*
- *Died: June 24, 1909, South Berwick, Maine*

The author of one of the important regional novels of American literature, *The Country of the Pointed Firs* (1896), about a declining Northeastern seaport and its people, Sarah Orne Jewett enjoyed great popular success in her day. She was born and died in the same small town in Maine, a region she knew, loved, and wrote about. In the intervening years, she did travel extensively, though, both in the United States and in Europe. A woman who never married, she had the gift of making enduring friendships with both men and women, and she included many other distinguished writers in her circle.

Late in her life, Jewett developed a close relationship with the young writer Willa Cather. Though the two women wrote about very different parts of the country—Cather's greatest work is set in Nebraska—they shared a common genius for capturing the spirit of place.

SEE ALSO

Cather, Willa Sibert

FURTHER READING

Blanchard, Paula. *Sarah Orne Jewett: Her World and Her Work*. Reading, Mass.: Addison-Wesley, 1994.

Silverthorne, Elizabeth. *Sarah Orne Jewett: A Writer's Life*. Woodstock, N.Y.: Overlook Press, 1993.

Jones, Mary Harris (Mother)

- *Born: May 1, 1830, Cork, Ireland*
- *Education: High school*
- *Accomplishments: Co-founder, Social Democratic Party (1898); co-founder, Industrial Workers of the World (1905); author,* Autobiography of Mother Jones *(1925)*
- *Died: Nov. 30, 1930, Silver Spring, Md.*

Mary Harris Jones was known as "Mother" to the miners whose cause she made her own. She lived to be 100 years old, and spent the last several decades of her life traveling from one labor trouble spot to another, lending her presence, helping to generate support for striking workers, and organizing both men and women to fight for their rights against business owners who used blacklists and violence to intimidate their employees.

Born in Ireland, Jones immigrated to the United States as a child and supported herself as a teacher and dressmaker until she married in 1861. She and her husband, an iron molder and a staunch supporter of the labor movement, had four children. In 1867 yellow fever took the lives of the whole family except for Mother Jones herself. She then worked at a variety of jobs over the next few years until she found her life's work in the labor movement.

With her personal life so devastated, Jones made striking workers her family, visiting mines and miners' homes throughout the country to encourage their militancy. The owners of the coal companies detested her, but nothing they did could discourage her. She was convicted of conspiracy charges in West Virginia in 1913 and later pardoned by the governor. A woman of unflinching courage, Jones became a living legend as she led demonstrations in so many parts of the country, and when she died, 50,000 miners attended a memorial service in her honor.

As outspoken as any woman of her day, Mother Jones was on a different path than that taken by the suffrage movement. Indeed, she opposed woman suffrage, because she thought it would mainly benefit middle-class women.

SEE ALSO

Labor movement

FURTHER READING

Atkinson, Linda. *Mother Jones, The Most Dangerous Woman in America*. New York: Crown, 1978.

Jones, Mary Harris. *The Autobiography of Mother Jones*. Chicago: Charles Kerr, 1972.

Jones, Mother. *The Speeches and Writings of Mother Jones.* Edited by Edward M. Steel. Pittsburgh: University of Pittsburgh Press, 1988.

Kraft, Betsey Harvey. *Mother Jones: One Woman's Fight for Labor.* New York: Clarion, 1995.

Joplin, Janis Lyn

- *Born: Jan. 19, 1943, Port Arthur, Tex.*
- *Education: University of Texas at Austin, attended 1962*
- *Accomplishments: First female rock star*
- *Died: Oct. 4, 1970, Los Angeles, Calif.*

The first woman to be a rock star, Janis Joplin sang with astonishing power and raw emotion. Although she did not live to see her 30th birthday, she left an indelible mark on the music of her generation.

Born to a middle-class family in Port Arthur, Texas, Janis was drawn to the music of the great African-American blues artist Bessie Smith when she was growing up. After Joplin completed high school, she traveled around the country for two years, including a stay in San Francisco's North Beach, then a haven of the budding counterculture.

After returning to Port Arthur, Joplin began to sing in coffeehouses and then enrolled at the University of Texas as an art student. A painful episode in which she was nominated as "the ugliest man on campus" led her to drop out of college. During this time, Joplin was also using increasing amounts of drugs.

Joplin moved back to San Francisco and soon embarked on the singing career that would bring her international celebrity. In 1966 she joined the group Big Brother and the Holding Company, with whom her successes began—such as her electrifying performance at the Monterey Jazz Festival in 1967. Deciding to go solo in 1968, Joplin developed her trademark style of uninhibited expressiveness. "Piece of My Heart" and "Me & Bobby McGee" were two of her best-known standards. After only a few years of fame, she died of a heroin overdose in 1970.

Janis Joplin's unique style of blues and funk vocals captured the spirit of the rebellious 1960s. Her death from a drug overdose at the age of 27 made her a legend—a symbol of the promise and tragedy of her generation.

FURTHER READING

Echols, Alice. *Scars of Sweet Paradise: The Life and Times of Janis Joplin.* New York: Metropolitan Books, 1999.

Friedman, Myra. *Buried Alive: The Biography of Janis Joplin.* New York: Harmony, 1992.

Journalism

SEE Media

Judaism

Although women have been active in Jewish life in many ways, they have played a distinct and secondary role in the practice of the Jewish religion until relatively recently, with rare exceptions.

For centuries, the highest religious achievement for a Jew was to live the life of the Talmudic scholar, one who studied an ancient compilation of Jewish law and theology (the Talmud) originally composed in Babylonia and supplemented with medieval texts and commentaries. This life was for men only, forbidden to women until the 20th century. For this reason, the religious commentaries contained in the Talmud do not reflect women's experiences and viewpoints, although they speak to the role of women from the viewpoint of men.

During the mid-19th century, observant Jews began to differ over a number of matters, such as whether men and women should sit together in the synagogue and whether music would be played. As a result, the religion split into three principal divisions: Orthodox, Conservative, and Reform. Orthodox Jews are the most traditional in their observance, including the role of women, who as a result are under more obligation to follow Jewish law. This includes, for example, the requirement that women sit apart and hidden from men during religious services, and that they keep their hair and arms and legs fully covered in the presence of men.

The goal of Conservative Judaism is to preserve the essential elements of the traditional religion while allowing for certain practices to be modernized. These allowances for modernization are less radical, however, than those made by Reform Judaism, which has changed or even abandoned many of the traditional laws and practices of Judaism in order to adapt more completely to the modern world.

One of Reform Judaism's first innovations in liberalizing gender roles was the abolition of separate seating for men and women in synagogues beginning in the late 19th century, a necessary step toward including women more fully in the service. Over the course of the 20th century, the bat mitzvah has evolved for non-Orthodox girls as a parallel ceremony to the bar mitzvah for boys.

A girl in California prepares for her bat mitzvah—a Jewish ceremony to celebrate a girl's 13th birthday—by learning to read the Torah. She uses a traditional silver pointer so that her finger will not mar the letters, which are always copied by hand in ink.

The first bat mitzvah in the United States took place in 1922. In both ceremonies the young person at age 13 is publicly called to read the sacred text of the Torah—the first five books of the Bible—in recognition of his or her adult religious responsibility. By the late 1960s the bat mitzvah ceremony was widespread in the United States among Reform and Conservative Jews.

The ordination of women as rabbis began in the 1970s, and more than 200 Reform and Conservative women rabbis and cantors, who direct chanting during services, have been ordained since then.

Many of the most important founding mothers of the modern women's movement have been Jewish—Congresswoman Bella Abzug, writer Betty Friedan, and editor Gloria Steinem, to name three—so it is not surprising that Jewish feminism has been so vital and that there has been so much change, so much challenge to tradition-based sexism, in the last decades.

There remain many women, however, particularly those in the Orthodox and ultra-Orthodox (Hasidic) sects, who celebrate the traditional roles that women have played in Judaism since ancient times. Women are instrumental in keeping a kosher household (free of items, actions, and food considered unlawful or unclean), and have certain domestic religious responsibilities, such as lighting the candles for the Sabbath. Women are also the essential link in the inheritance of Jewish identity—a child must have a Jewish mother in order to be born a Jew (the father's ethnicity is not relevant). The more traditional Jewish women emphasize the importance of these roles as central to Judaism.

American Jewish women have also been very active in organizing to promote various causes. One of the oldest such organizations is Hadassah, the Women's Zionist Organization of America, a volunteer organization founded in 1912 by scholar and activist Henrietta Szold. Its mission is to promote ties between the American and Israeli Jews and to provide continuity for Jewish life through education. The National Council of Jewish Women is also active in using education, research, and community service to work for better health and individual rights for women and children.

FURTHER READING

Greenberg, Blu. *On Women and Judaism: A View from Tradition.* Philadelphia: Jewish Publication Society, 1994.

Heschel, Susannah, ed. *On Being a Jewish Feminist.* New York, Schocken, 1983.

Hyman, Paula E., and Deborah Dash Moore, eds. *Jewish Women in America: An Historical Encyclopedia.* New York: Routledge, 1997.

Schreier, Barbara A. *Becoming American Women: Clothing and the Jewish Immigrant Experience 1880-1920.* Chicago: Chicago Historical Society, 1994.

Weinberg, Sydney Stahl. *The World of Our Mothers: The Lives of Jewish Immigrant Women.* New York: Schocken, 1988.

Kahn, Florence Prag

- *Born: Nov. 9, 1866, Salt Lake City, Utah*
- *Education: University of California at Berkeley, B.A., 1887*
- *Accomplishments: U.S. representative (R–Calif.) (1925–37)*
- *Died: Nov. 16, 1948, San Francisco, Calif.*

The first Jewish woman to serve in Congress, Florence Prag Kahn was also one of the first women to leave a substantial legislative legacy. Representing one of the two congressional districts in San Francisco, the Republican Kahn was the person that city leaders turned to when they wanted to get something done.

Kahn came from a well-established San Francisco family that had temporarily relocated to Salt Lake City at the time of her birth. Her mother, Mary Goldsmith Prag, was a respected high school teacher who, in fact, was appointed to the San Francisco school board later in life. Prag urged her daughter to attend the newly established University of California at Berkeley, from which the young woman graduated in 1887, one of only 7 women and 33 men to do so that year.

Florence Prag then became a teacher, too. In 1898 she married a rising young Republican politician named Julius Kahn. He was elected to the U.S. House of Representatives that year, and they moved to Washington, D.C. There, Florence Kahn gave birth to two sons and also served as her husband's secretary.

Thus when Julius died in 1924 (he had been in Congress for all but two years since their marriage), Florence was well prepared to take his place. At the time she was elected to the House, only a tiny handful of women had served there. Kahn quickly established herself as capable and trustworthy and in 1929 became the first woman to serve on the House Armed Services Committee. With this key appointment, she sponsored much important legislation for San Francisco and the Bay Area, such as the bill that secured federal approval to build the Bay Bridge linking San Francisco and Oakland.

The immense popularity of Democratic President Franklin Roosevelt contributed to Kahn's defeat in 1936, but not before she had carved out a name for herself as an effective representative. Indeed, one of her obituaries in 1948 referred to her "occasionally frightening talent for ramming through legislation."

SEE ALSO

Congress, U.S.; Politics

FURTHER READING

Matthews, Glenna. "'There Is No Sex in Citizenship': The Career of Congresswoman Florence Prag Kahn." In *We Have Come to Stay: American Women and Political Parties, 1880-1960*. Edited by Melanie Gustafson, Kristie Miller, and Elisabeth Perry. Albuquerque: University of New Mexico Press, 1999.

Kelley, Florence

- *Born: Sept. 12, 1859, Philadelphia, Pa.*
- *Education: Cornell University, B.A., 1882*
- *Accomplishments: Secretary, National Consumers League (1899–1932); co-founder, National Association for the Advancement of Colored People (1909); organizer, Women's International League for Peace and Freedom (1919)*
- *Died: Feb. 17, 1932, Philadelphia, Pa.*

Florence Kelley was one of the most significant reformers of the early 20th century, a woman who devoted herself to helping poor children and working women. Possessing formidable strength of personality, she inspired those who came to know her to attempt great things themselves. It was said that when Kelley came into a room, "everyone was brave."

Florence Kelley, long-time head of the National Consumers' League, was a woman with a remarkable education for the late 19th century. She was originally denied entry to the University of Pennsylvania, however, on the basis of her gender.

The daughter of a prominent Pennsylvania politician and his wife, Kelley graduated from Cornell University in 1882. Refused admittance to the University of Pennsylvania graduate school because she was a woman, she went to Europe with her brother and learned that she could attend the University of Zurich for graduate study in social science. While enrolled there, she became a convert to socialism, a political theory advocating government ownership of all or most of the important industries. Kelley began to correspond with leading European socialists, and she also married a fellow student, Lazare Wischnewetzky, who shared her beliefs.

The young couple moved to the United States in 1886. Though they eventually had three children, the marriage was troubled and eventually ended in divorce. As a single woman again, Kelley received legal permission to resume the use of her maiden name. She then threw herself into the settlement-house movement, in which middle-class women were moving into slum neighborhoods to provide aid and training for poor people. Indeed, she became a resident of Chicago's Hull House and a lifelong friend and colleague of Jane Addams. (While living at Hull House, she installed her children and her mother in a nearby apartment.)

Eventually, Kelley became an official factory inspector for Illinois, charged with looking for abusive treatment of women and children and reporting it so that the authorities could act against offenders.

In 1899 Kelley moved to New York and became the general secretary of a new group called the National Consumers League, which proposed to use the buying power of shoppers to pressure employers to treat employees in a more humane way. She held this position for the rest of her life, using it as a launching pad for tireless advocacy for such causes as ending child labor and securing minimum wage laws for women.

SEE ALSO

Addams, Jane; National Consumers League (NCL); Settlement-house movement

FURTHER READING

Sklar, Kathryn Kish. *Florence Kelley and the Nation's Work*. New Haven: Yale University Press, 1995.

King, Billie Jean Moffitt

- *Born: Nov. 22, 1943, Long Beach, Calif.*
- *Education: Los Angeles State College (now California State University at Los Angeles), 1961–66*
- *Accomplishments: Winner, five Wimbledon singles titles (1966–68, 1972–73); Outstanding Female Athlete of the World (1967); first woman to earn more than $100,000 in one season of sports competition (1971); first woman named* Sports Illustrated *Sportsperson of the Year (1972); founder (1973) and president (1973–75, 1980–81), Women's Tennis Association; founder, Women's Sports Foundation (1974)*

Billie Jean Moffitt King was a gifted tennis player, but she has also been a dedicated activist on behalf of women athletes. By founding a tour for women tennis players, she helped transform the payment system so that a woman athlete's paycheck more nearly approximates a male athlete's.

Billie Jean King, tireless in her crusade to equalize the pay for men and women athletes, became the fist president of the Women's Tennis Association. When Bobby Riggs challenged her to a battle-of-the-sexes tennis match in 1973, she defeated him in straight sets before millions of television viewers.

Interested in many sports as a young girl, King began to focus on tennis when she was 11. She was coached by the former champion Alice Marble, and when she was only 17 she won her first Wimbledon title teamed with Karen Hantze in the women's doubles. She went on to win a record 20 Wimbledon titles in all, including 6 singles titles. She also won 4 U.S. Open singles.

As impressive as her tennis victories were, King gained national attention with her outspoken advocacy on behalf of women athletes. When she became a champion, there was no tour for women tennis pros and thus no systematic means of earning money. Her leadership led to the founding of a tour in 1971. (A tennis tour is a set of cash-prize tournaments held in different parts of the world—each is played around the same time each year, and professional players move from one to the next.) She also founded a players' union in 1973 and served as its first president.

No doubt King's outspokenness and militancy made her more than one enemy, but most of them maintained a low profile, unlike former tennis champion Bobby Riggs. At 55 years old, Riggs claimed that he could defeat King easily and challenged her to a five-set match. On September 20, 1973, the two of them played before 30,472 spectators in the Astrodome in Houston, the largest crowd ever to watch a tennis match. King won easily. In conjunction with her other achievements on and off the courts this match made her one of the best-known women in the country. For many years she was married to fellow tennis player Larry King, whom she wed in 1965 and divorced in 1987. In 1981 a lesbian affair was publicly exposed by her former lover, thus ending her chances of lucrative endorsements.

SEE ALSO

Sports

FURTHER READING

King, Billie Jean. *Billie Jean.* New York: Harper & Row, 1974.

Kirkpatrick, Curry. "Sportsman and Sportswoman of the Year." *Sports Illustrated,* December 25, 1972

Kingston, Maxine Hong

- *Born: Oct. 27, 1940, Stockton, Calif.*
- *Education: University of California at Berkeley, B.A., 1962*
- *Accomplishments: Winner, National Book Critics' Circle Award for* Woman Warrior *(1976); winner, American Book Award for* China Men *(1980); author,* Woman Warrior: Memoirs of a Girlhood Among Ghosts *(1976);* China Men *(1980);* Hawaii One Summer *(1987);* Tripmaster Monkey: His Fake Book *(1989)*

The author of *The Woman Warrior* (1976), Maxine Hong Kingston has been a major force in transforming the subject matter of American literature to include the experiences of Chinese Americans. In her first book she also created a new literary form, part fiction and part autobiography.

The daughter of Chinese-born parents who owned a laundry in California's Central Valley, Kingston spoke only Chinese at home. When she started school, she found it so scary to speak English that she did not talk at all while in school for many years. Despite this unpromising start, she went on to attend the University of California at Berkeley—with the aid of 11 scholarships—and to become a teacher. She also dedicated herself to becoming a writer.

In 1976 *A Woman Warrior* appeared. In this book Kingston wove together Chinese folktales she had heard from her mother—called Brave Orchid in the book—and her own personal experiences of growing up Chinese. She has subsequently published two more books, *China Men* and *Tripmaster Monkey,* dealing with Chinese Americans in northern California as well as many poems. Since 1962 she has been married to fellow author Earl Kingston.

SEE ALSO

Asian Americans

FURTHER READING

Kingston, Maxine Hong. *Conversations with Maxine Hong Kingston.* Edited by Paul Skenazy and Tera Martin. Jackson: University Press of Mississippi, 1998.

Simmons, Diane. *Maxine Hong Kingston.* New York: Twayne, 1999.

Skandera-Trombley, Laura E. *Critical Essays on Maxine Hong Kingston.* New York: G. K. Hall, 1998.

Knights of Labor

The Knights of Labor, founded in 1869 and virtually nonexistent by 1900, was nonetheless important in the history of American women because it allowed—

even encouraged—women to join. It would be generations before organized labor would once again treat women so well.

Because the Knights sought to organize all those in the "producing classes"—as opposed to property owners or managers—into their ranks, they took a much broader view of who would make an appropriate member than most contemporary labor groups, which were interested in organizing skilled males only. In 1881 women shoe workers in Philadelphia created the first all-female local assembly of the Knights. (Although the union admitted women, it required them to join sex-segregated assemblies.) In 1886, just before the organization suffered its rapid decline, there were about 100,000 women in the Knights.

Ever since 1886, scholars and labor activists have debated the reason for the Knights' sudden collapse. For conservative unionists, the lesson was clear. Bringing women or less-skilled workers into the ranks creates a weak union, because they are thought to have less staying power and to be more vulnerable in a strike than men. Progressive activists have countered that poor leadership about *other* matters may have been more significant in the Knights' collapse.

SEE ALSO

Labor movement

FURTHER READING

Levine, Susan. *Labor's True Woman.* Philadelphia: Temple University Press, 1984.

Ku Klux Klan (KKK)

There have been at least four distinct periods in the history of the racially motivated terrorist group known as the Ku Klux Klan (KKK). In only one period were women significant as members, but in all periods issues of women's roles—how to maintain the "purity" of womanhood, for example—have powerfully figured in the group's beliefs and activities.

The first time the Klan appeared was right after the Civil War (1861–65). Federal troops were stationed in the defeated South to protect the newly freed slaves from injury. Charging that

The second phase of the Ku Klux Klan, in the 1920s, featured prejudicial behavior toward Catholics and immigrants as well as African Americans. During this phase the Klan had a substantial number of female members, such as these women gathering in New Castle, Indiana, in 1923.

white women were vulnerable to sexual attack from these freed slaves, who were allegedly being coddled by their federal protectors, gangs of night-riding, hooded men threatened and murdered African Africans whom they saw as too "uppity" or whom they believed were perpetrators of alleged crimes. By the 1870s the group had disappeared owing both to federal intervention and to internal dissension.

The KKK reappeared in 1915, and this time it was a rather different group. Responding to the recent wave of immigration, it opposed the "sinister" influence of Catholics and Jews as well as directing its energy against people of color. With this stance, it attracted members in the Midwest as well as in the South. And finally, many women, apparently concerned about being inundated by foreigners, now joined the Klan's crusade for white supremacy. Riding high in the 1920s, by 1930 its membership had dwindled into insignificance. Equally vicious in rhetoric, this version of the Klan was less violent than its predecessor.

During the last two periods of the Klan, from 1930 to 1980 and since 1980 (during which time it has allied with paramilitary groups), it has once more been mostly male and mostly based in the South. As in its first appearance, the KKK proclaims white supremacy and opposes racial equality. It is solidly opposed to the agenda of women's rights, though still claiming to be protecting the sanctity of womanhood.

FURTHER READING

Blee, Kathleen M. *Women of the Klan.* Berkeley: University of California Press, 1991.

MacLean, Nancy. *Behind the Mask of Chivalry: The Making of the Ku Klux Klan in a Georgia Town.* New York: Oxford University Press, 1994.

Labor movement

Women today constitute a vital part of the American labor movement. Female workers, in fact, are increasingly important in the workforce, and because organized labor is eager to increase its female membership, unions continue to try to attract nonunionized female workers. In the past, however, unions not only ignored women but excluded them from membership.

Though women working in the textile industry were the country's first factory workers—the "Lowell mill girls" of the 1820s—they were not the backbone of the labor movement when it developed during the later years of the 19th century. The women in Lowell, Massachusetts, had gone out on strike on more than one occasion, but male union leaders nonetheless often clung to stereotypical views about women—they were thought to be too meek and mild to be good union members and their place was in the home—to justify creating predominantly male organizations.

The short-lived Knights of Labor (founded in 1869) actively sought women members, but the American Federation of Labor (AFL), which replaced it in the mid-1880s as the main organization for working people, took much less interest.

In the early 1900s women in the settlement-house network of reformers began to take a kindly interest in working-class women, and that led to the creation of the Women's Trade Union League, a cross-class alliance to help working women. About the same time, the first large-scale organization of women workers, the International Ladies' Garment Workers Union (ILGWU), began to take shape in New York City.

Real progress for women workers began to occur during the Great Depres-

One of the most effective leaders of the International Ladies' Garment Workers Union in the 1930s was Rose Schniederman, later a good friend of Eleanor Roosevelt. At a time when the workplace could be dangerous and the work poorly paid, Schneiderman was passionate and vocal about protecting women workers.

sion of the 1930s. These were years of growth for the labor movement in general, and these were years of a labor-friendly administration in Washington, led by President Franklin Delano Roosevelt and seconded by First Lady Eleanor Roosevelt. In addition, a woman, Frances Perkins, served as secretary of labor during Roosevelt's administration. Prominent female labor leaders such as organizer Rose Schneiderman and Rose Pesotta (who rose to be a vice president of ILGWU) dedicated themselves to recruiting women members.

As a result of all this, the number of women in organized labor tripled, from 250,000 to nearly 800,000 during the 1930s—in part, too, because the AFL had competition for women members from a new and more inclusive group, the Congress of Industrial Organizations, or CIO. The AFL did not want the CIO to grow any bigger than could be helped, hence the older group began to recruit women to prevent them from joining the CIO.

During World War II (1941–45), with 12 million men in the armed forces and 6.5 million new women in the workforce to do the jobs the men left behind, the number of women belonging to unions swelled to several million. The leadership of unions, even those with preponderantly female membership, was still, however, almost invariably male, the exception being lower-level leadership positions held by women in a few unions. Male-led unions were much more eager to protect the interests of the men who had gone off to fight than to help their female replacements. Scholars have found, for example, that when unions fought for equal pay for a woman holding a previously male job, they were concerned to protect the salary level of the man who would hold the job again after the war.

With the birth of the modern women's movement around 1970, with additional millions of women employed outside the home, a new day dawned for women in organized labor. In 1974 the first woman joined the board of the AFL-CIO—the two had merged in the 1950s—Joyce Miller of the Coalition of Labor Union Women. Unions now take seriously many issues of concern to their female members, such as sexual harassment, comparable worth, and family leave.

The labor movement itself has had tough times in the 1980s and 90s owing to a hostile political climate and, perhaps, to its own mistakes—in selling short the involvement of women and new immigrants and in failing to commit massive resources to organizing. The percentage of American workers in unions, 14.1 percent in 1997, is the lowest it has been in decades. Many observers believe that if labor wants to bounce back, much of the growth will have to come in service industries, where so many women are employed.

SEE ALSO

AFL-CIO; Coalition of Labor Union Women (CLUW); Comparable worth; Congress, U.S.; Industrialization; International Ladies' Garment Workers Union (ILGWU); Perkins, Frances; Politics; Women's Trade Union League (WTUL)

FURTHER READING

Brody, David. *In Labor's Cause: Main Themes on the History of the American Worker.* New York: Oxford University Press, 1993.

Milkman, Ruth. *Women, Work, and Protest.* Boston: Routledge & Kegan Paul, 1985.

Weiner, Lynn. *From Working Girl to Working Mother: The Female Labor Force in the United States, 1820–1980.* Chapel Hill, University of North Carolina Press, 1985.

Lange, Dorothea

- *Born: May 26, 1895, Hoboken, N.J.*
- *Education: New York Training School for Teachers, 1914–17; Columbia University, 1915; apprenticeships to private photographers*
- *Accomplishments: Recipient, Simon Guggenheim Foundation Fellowship (1940); author,* An American Exodus: A Record of Human Erosion *(photograph collection, 1939)*
- *Died: Oct. 11, 1965, Marin County, Calif.*

Dorothea Lange was a photographer whose body of work is one of the most powerful set of documents in American history. Her photos depicting the victims of the Great Depression helped all Americans understand the suffering caused by the country's economic downturn in the 1930s.

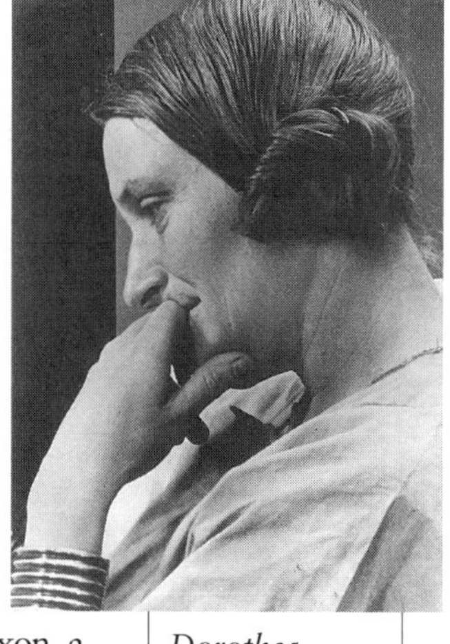

Dorothea Lange was a photographer with an especially compassionate eye for human suffering. In fact, she was no stranger to suffering herself, having been crippled by polio in her youth.

Trained by some of the country's best portrait photographers while living in the East, Lange went to California in 1918 and soon set up her own studio in San Francisco, where she took pictures of the well-to-do. In 1920 she married the artist Maynard Dixon, a union that produced two children.

The Great Depression changed Lange's life: she was drawn to portray the faces of those in need instead of the well-off. Then in 1935 she began a collaboration with Paul Taylor, a University of California economist who was studying the lives of rural migrants to California. He interviewed and she took pictures—many of which are now in museums. During the course of their collaboration they fell in love, left their respective spouses, and married one another.

Of all her pictures, the best-known is one of a care-worn woman with her children. Known as *Migrant Mother,* it joined John Steinbeck's novel *The Grapes of Wrath* in awakening the conscience of the country to the plight of the so-called "Okies," desperate refugees from rural poverty in the Southwest, and their problems of joblessness, poor housing, and inadequate food when they finally reached the Golden State of California.

FURTHER READING

Becker, Karin E. *Dorothea Lange and the Documentary Tradition.* Baton Rouge: Louisiana State University Press, 1980.

Heyman, Therese Thau, Sandra S. Phillips,

and John Szarkowski. *Dorothea Lange: American Photographs.* San Francisco: San Francisco Museum of Modern Art/Chronicle Books, 1994.
Lange, Dorothea, Robert Coles, and Therese Heyman. *Dorothea Lange: Photographs of a Lifetime.* New York: Aperture, 1998.
Meltzer, Milton. *Dorothea Lange: a Photographer's Life.* New York: Farrar Straus & Giroux, 1978.

Latinas

The term *Latina* includes women from Mexico, the Caribbean, Central America, and South America—parts of the world that were colonized centuries ago by people from Spain and Portugal. In the colonized countries, Europeans mixed with the indigenous peoples and with the Africans imported to be slaves. *Latina* also refers to women who have descended from some of the pioneer families of the American Southwest, where invading Spaniards and members of the native population often intermarried. Because of this history of racial mixing, Latinas, even those whose physical appearance might suggest a largely European ancestry, have typically been seen as women of color.

Although they have this history in common—and often the Spanish language as well—there is much economic and cultural diversity among Latinas based on when their families immigrated and to which region of the country. The first time that the United States had a substantial Latino/a population was after the annexation of Texas in 1845, followed soon thereafter by the acquisition of the rest of the Southwest in 1848. The entire region had been part of the Spanish empire and had subsequently belonged to Mexico after Mexican independence from Spain in 1821. The United States had then begun to cast a covetous eye on the Southwest,

Surrounded by members of the Workers Alliance, Emma Tenayuca raises her fist during a demonstration in San Antonio, Texas, in 1937. The Mexican labor movement of this period was characterized by increasing numbers of Mexicana workers. Tenayuca joined the labor movement when she was 16 years old.

to the dismay of Mexico. War erupted between the two countries in 1846. The United States won and was able to buy the Southwest (excluding Texas, which was already independent of Mexico and which the United States had already annexed) for a low price.

The United States and Mexico signed the Treaty of Guadalupe Hidalgo to end hostilities, and the United States promised that people living in the Southwest would have all the privileges of U.S. citizenship and that their property rights would be protected. Starting in 1849, however, the California gold rush brought hordes of invading settlers into the region, and they did not respect the rights of those already there. Within a generation, most of the land had gone from Latinos to whites, except in New Mexico, where the Latino population was large enough to protect its interests.

Like Native Americans, many Latinas and Latinos live on land that once belonged to their ancestors. Often feeling that they are being treated like second-class citizens, some Hispanics have assumed a militant stance and demanded, for example, better treatment for undocumented immigrants coming to this country to flee poverty in Mexico or Central America.

For Latinas, there have been many special challenges. They have had to keep their families together under circumstances of great hardship and poverty. In the early years of American conquest of the Southwest, many women were vulnerable to rape by the invaders. As large-scale immigration from South and Central America has increased since Congress passed a more liberal immigration law in 1965, women have often been relegated to the bottom of the occupational hierarchy, where they have toiled as domestic servants or child-care providers. Tens of thousands of women work in *maquiladoras*, plants owned by American companies that are located on the Mexican side of the U.S.-Mexican border, where they work long hours for low pay because the Mexican labor market offers low-skilled women very few opportunities.

The Latino population was the fastest growing minority in the United States by the year 1999, constituting 11.6 percent of all U.S. citizens, and its growth rate (53 percent between 1980 and 1990; it is estimated that in the first two decades of the 21st century Latinos will become the largest minority group in the country) indicates that Latino issues will be seen in the forefront of politics and society in the coming years. In the 1990s a powerful strain of Latina activism flourished. Some women have become involved in ethnically based organizations dealing with homelessnes, AIDS, or domestic violence within Latina feminism.

There has been, for many decades, a tradition of Latina leadership in trade unionism as with Luisa Moreno, an organizer for the CIO in the 1930s and 40s, and Dolores Huerta, vice president of the United Farm Workers from its founding in the 1960s. Popular culture is also recognizing the talents and preferences of Latinas, in the monthly magazine *Latina,* premiered in 1996, for example, and in the cross-cultural fame of such performers as Jennifer Lopez, Gloria Estefan, and Selena.

SEE ALSO

Moreno, Luisa; United Farm Workers (UFW)

FURTHER READING

De la Torre, Adela, and Beatriz M. Pesquera, eds. *Building with Our Hands: New Directions in Chicana Studies.* Berkeley: University of California Press, 1993.

Ruiz, Vicki. *From Out of the Shadows: Mexican American Women in Twentieth-Century America.* New York: Oxford University Press, 1999.

Law

The subject of women and the law can be divided into two parts: first there is the way women have been treated *by* the law and second there is the way women have—or have not—been able to *practice* law. Not surprisingly, the two are related.

Women have been treated unequally by the law since the dawn of U.S. history—although the situation has been improving during the past 100 years or so. Early colonists drew upon many of the basic tenets of English common law in setting up their legal codes, including the presumption of coverture, that is, that a married woman was "covered" by her husband and had no independent civic identity. Because of this doctrine, married women could not control property (with rare exceptions) until legal reforms began to take place in the mid-19th century. Women could not vote, serve on juries, or bear arms, all evidence of unequal legal treatment.

All of these prohibitions have subsequently been overturned as a result of generations of agitation by women and their male allies. Beginning with the case of *Bradwell* v. *Illinois* (1873), women began to file lawsuits to end gender discrimination, mostly employing arguments drawn from the Constitution's 14th Amendment, ratified in 1868, which defined citizenship for the first time and guaranteed equal protection of the law to all citizens. Interestingly enough, the pioneering *Bradwell* suit revolved around Myra Bradwell's attempt to practice law in Illinois. After being turned down by the state bar of Illinois, Bradwell appealed to the U.S. Supreme Court, which ruled against her.

The court would not be prepared to use the 14th Amendment to rule against gender discrimination until after the birth of the modern women's movement, around 1970. Even the ratification of the 19th Amendment in 1920, granting women the vote, did not change public opinion about women and citizenship enough to persuade the court to use the 14th Amendment to protect women's rights. Indeed, when the National Woman's Party decided to push for an Equal Rights Amendment beginning in 1923, it was specifically designed to battle gender discrimination in the courts.

Finally, in the *Reed* v. *Reed* decision of 1971 the Court used the 14th Amendment forcefully on behalf of women's rights, striking down an Idaho inheritance law as gender-biased. There have subsequently been so many significant decisions in the area of women and the law—cases such as *Roe* v. *Wade* (1973), which granted women the right to an abortion—that whole courses are now offered on the subject at the nation's law schools.

The fact that law schools currently deal with gender discrimination owes partly to the growth in such cases and partly to the sheer number of women students they now have, in some instances 50 percent or more. This, too, represents a dramatic departure from the past.

Before the late 19th century, a few women such as Maryland's Margaret Brent informally performed some of the functions typically handled by an attorney. The first woman to be admitted to a state bar after study and examination was Belle Mansfield in Iowa in 1869, shortly before Myra Bradwell's unsuccessful attempt in Illinois. Charlotte Ray was admitted to the District of Columbia bar in 1872, the country's first black woman lawyer. In 1879 Belva Lockwood became the first woman to be admitted to practice before the U.S. Supreme Court.

Despite these courageous pioneers, the rate of progress slowed down to a snail's pace as the country entered a more conservative period; women were 1 percent of all lawyers in 1910, 2 percent by 1930, and nearly 3 percent by 1960. Women were often treated unequally while at law school, such as the practice of Lady's Day at Harvard, the only day of the year on which women were allowed to speak in class.

Since the explosive social changes of the 1960s, including the birth of modern feminism, women have flocked to law schools. In 1992 Herma Hill Kay became the first woman to head a major law school when she took the post at Boalt Hall, the law school at the University of California at Berkeley (and Boalt had been the first to hire a woman law professor, Barbara Armstrong, in 1919). Women are now being elected and appointed to the judiciary, and they are prosecutors, often in highly visible cases, such as Marcia Clark in the O .J. Simpson trial. In 1993 President Bill Clinton appointed Janet Reno as his attorney general, the first woman to be the nation's "top cop." Moreover, two women sit on the U.S. Supreme Court.

Where women continue to lag far behind in the legal profession is in the partnerships of prestigious firms. How much of this owes to continuing gender discrimination in such firms and how much owes to women's own refusal to work the 80-hour weeks expected of junior partners (because women still bear a disproportionate share of family and domestic responsibility) is an open question.

SEE ALSO

Bradwell v. *Illinois* (1873); Brent, Margaret; Citizenship; 14th Amendment; Lockwood, Belva Ann Bennett; Married Women's Property Acts; Ray, Charlotte E.; *Reed* v. *Reed* (1971); *Roe* v. *Wade* (1973)

FURTHER READING

Drachman, Virginia G. *Sisters in Law: Women Lawyers in Modern American History.* Cambridge: Harvard University Press, 1998.

Morello, Karen Berger. *The Invisible Bar: the Woman Lawyer in America 1638 to the Present.* New York: Random House, 1986.

Wheaton, Elizabeth. *Myra Bradwell: First Woman Lawyer.* Greensboro, N.C.: Morgan Reynolds, 1997.

League of Women Voters

Founded in 1919 as the direct successor to the most important suffrage organization, the National American Woman Suffrage Association, the League of Women Voters had two main goals: to prepare women for their newly attained right to vote (granted by the 19th Amendment in 1920) and to continue working for the social-welfare legislation that suffragists had long advocated. More than 75 years after woman suffrage was granted, the league continues to be a widely respected organization.

Nonpartisan, the league takes stands on issues but not on candidates. League issues—which could be foreign policy, environmental protection, or better schools—receive support only after a long process of evaluation by membership at the local level. Because the group has built up so much trust with the American public by its voter education efforts, it is frequently selected to run candidates' forums, including some of the Presidential debates.

For many years—before women were made welcome by working politicians—women who wanted to be involved in politics found this group to be virtually their only congenial home.

SEE ALSO

National American Woman Suffrage Association (NAWSA)

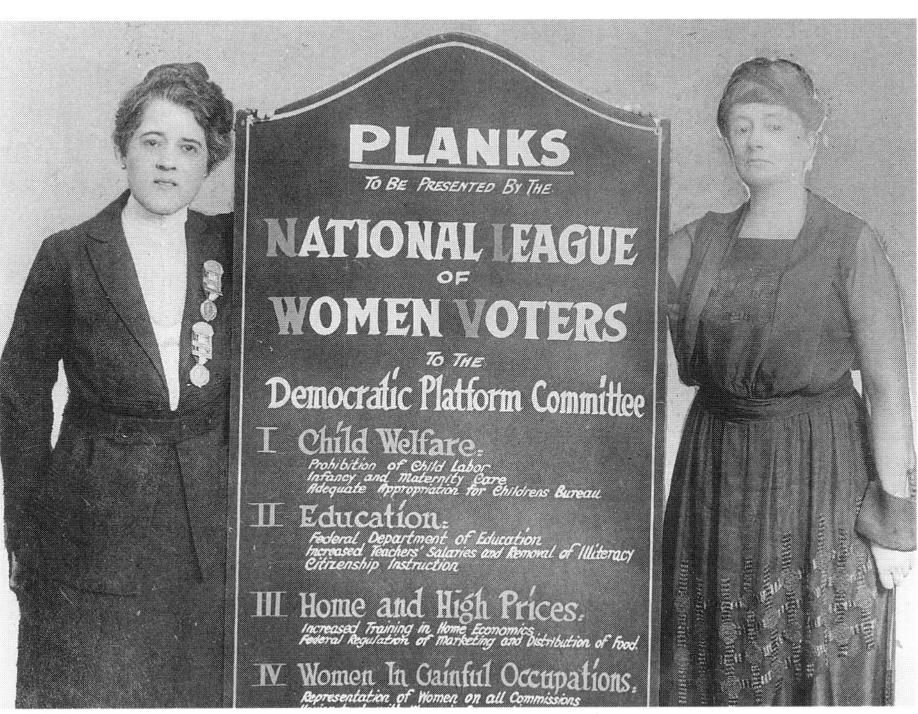

Before the ratification of the 19th Amendment, delegations from the newly formed League of Women Voters attended both the Republican and Democratic conventions of 1920. The Democrats accepted all of the planks, or demands, that the delegates presented.

Lee, Ann

- *Born: Feb. 29, 1736, Manchester, England*
- *Education: No formal education*
- *Accomplishments: Founder, Shaker movement in America (1770s)*
- *Died: Sept. 8, 1784, Niskeyuna, N.Y.*

Mother Ann Lee was the founder of a religious sect known as the Shakers (so called because of the dances they performed as part of their devotions). She also held what people in the modern United States would think of as eccentric ideas about the relationship between men and women.

Tragedy scarred Ann Lee's life when all of her four children died in infancy. While imprisoned in 1770 for her religious views, she had a vision that she was a second incarnation of Christ, and that sexual union is the chief source of human evil. She and a small group of followers left England for America in 1774 seeking religious freedom and the chance to convert others to her beliefs. Interestingly, her husband—a man whom she had married only reluctantly in 1762 and whose bed she had forsaken after her revelation about sexuality—was part of the group. They established themselves in upstate New York.

By the time of Ann Lee's death in 1784, the foundation had been laid for 11 communities based on her principles. Shaker communities prohibited physical love and kept the sexes separate in worship and work, but also established egalitarian relations between men and women. They lived simple but industrious and deeply religious lives under the motto "hands to work, hearts to God." By 1826, there were some 18 Shaker communities in various areas of the United States, but they eventually dwindled to mere vestiges. Scholars believe that Mother Ann's commitment to equal rights and responsibilities for both sexes anticipated the 19th-century women's movement.

SEE ALSO

Religion

FURTHER READING

Campion, Nardi Reeder. *Mother Ann Lee: Morning Star of the Shakers.* Hanover, N.H.: University Press of New England, 1990.

Garrett, Clarke. *Origins of the Shakers: from the Old World to the New World.* Baltimore: Johns Hopkins University Press, 1998.

Giles, Janice Holt. *The Believers.* Lexington: University Press of Kentucky, 1989.

Lesbians

Women who choose to share physical intimacy with other women are known as lesbians. The word itself derives from the Greek island of Lesbos, said to be populated by women loving women. Throughout history there have been ebbs and flows in the freedom society grants to homosexuals. In ancient Greece, for example, homosexuality was regarded as completely acceptable. At other times all forms of sexuality, including same-sex activities, have been relatively repressed.

In the United States in the late 19th century, many women lived in virtually all-female communities, either as reformers in settlement houses located in slum neighborhoods or among female-dominant faculties at women's colleges. Other women lived together as couples in what were known as "Boston marriages," so-called because the practice originated in New England. Although it is impossible to document which of these women shared physical intimacy, there was little social stigma attached to their lifestyles.

The 20th century introduced great change in the area of sexuality. In the first place, the advent of the consumer culture began suggesting to Americans that personal pleasure, including sexual pleasure, was their birthright. In the second place, many educated people read the Viennese psychiatrist Sigmund Freud, from whom they derived the message that it was "unhealthy" to repress their sexual desires. As women explored those impulses, some realized that their desires were directed toward members of their own sex. Yet at the same time, the culture was beginning to take a much harsher view of close bonds among women, let alone lesbian bonds, because they seemed potentially "abnormal."

In the 1950s and 1960s there was a niche audience for lesbian fiction, though most lesbians were still in the closet owing to ferocious discrimination against them.

Despite societal disapproval, communities of lesbians have existed in most large U.S. cities throughout the 20th century. But because they were subject to so much discrimination and punishment, such as the loss of employment, they mostly kept their sexual orientation "in the closet" to protect themselves from harmful consequences.

The explosive social changes since the end of World War II in 1945, above all the birth of the modern women's movement around 1970, have created a much more positive climate for lesbians in this country than in the past. One important milestone happened in 1955 when two San Francisco women founded the Daughters of Bilitis, the first civil rights organization for lesbians. There are now many organizations, publications, and support groups, and lesbians have proposed an ambitious agenda for the future that calls, among other things, for greater respect for their relationships and more acceptance of lesbian motherhood.

SEE ALSO

Boston marriage; Consumer culture; Daughters of Bilitis; Sexual orientation

FURTHER READING

McGarry, Molly, and Fred Wasserman. *Becoming Visible: An Illustrated History of Lesbian and Gay Life in 20th Century America.* New York: Penguin, 1998.

Penelope, Julia and Susan J. Wolfe, eds. *Lesbian Culture, an Anthology: The Lives, Work, Ideas, Art and Visions of Lesbians Past and Present.* Freedom, Calif.: Crossing Press, 1993.

Life expectancy

How long a person will live, on the average, has a lot to do with whether a person is born male or female. In the United States women live longer than men—for reasons that scientists still do not fully understand—but women's greater life expectancy is a modern phenomenon, one that requires good nutrition and safe childbirth to produce. In the 1770s, for example, the average life expectancy was only 35 years; this had increased to 47 by 1900. In 1998 the expectancy was 73 years for men and 80 years for women, but there are also differences along racial lines. For instance, in 1998 the life expectancy for black men was only 66 years, and 75 for black women.

In societies where there is not enough food to go around, the less powerful—usually, the women—get less of this precious resource, with the result that, on the average, their lives are shorter. Whatever "biological" superiority women may possess emerges only in a society with abundant food and good health care.

LIFE EXPECTANCY (IN YEARS) BY RACE AND SEX: 1900 TO 1970

Year	Entire Population	Men	Women	White	Non-White
1900	47.3	46.3	48.3	47.6	33.0
1910	50.0	48.4	51.8	50.3	35.6
1920	54.1	53.6	54.6	54.9	45.3
1930	59.7	58.1	61.6	61.4	48.1
1940	62.9	60.8	65.2	64.2	53.1
1950	68.2	65.6	71.1	69.1	60.8
1960	69.7	66.6	73.1	70.6	63.6
1970	70.9	67.1	74.8	71.7	65.3

Source: U.S. Census

Lincoln, Mary Todd

- *Born: Dec. 13, 1818, Lexington, Ky.*
- *Education: No formal education*
- *Accomplishments: First Lady, 1861–65*
- *Died: July 16, 1882, Springfield, Ill.*

The wife of Abraham Lincoln, Mary Todd Lincoln lived a life of searing personal tragedy that virtually destroyed her.

As an attractive young woman of 20, Mary Todd left her native Kentucky to live with a married sister in Illinois. There she met the up-and-coming young prairie lawyer whom she would marry. Though their courtship was troubled—Abraham battled depression, Mary was often bedeviled by personal insecurity, and her relatives opposed the marriage—the two wed in 1842. Abraham's career flourished, and the couple was generally happy, sharing a deep devotion to their four sons. The first blow came when their son Eddie died early in 1850.

As a girlhood companion remembered her, First Lady Mary Todd Lincoln was vivacious and impulsive, with an interesting personality—but "she now and then could not restrain a witty, sarcastic speech that cut deeper than she intended."

During the balance of the decade, the sectional strife that would result in the Civil War was intensifying. With strong antislavery views (shared by Mary despite her southern birth) and a gift for eloquent expression of them, Abraham became one of the well-known political leaders in the country. In November 1860 he was elected President, and in December 1860 South Carolina seceded from the Union. When the Lincolns moved to Washington, D.C., early in 1861 to take up their official duties, they both knew they were facing a time of crisis.

Although they must have known they would be tested, they had no way of knowing how severe the test would be. Mary was criticized for being a southerner and for her alleged monetary extravagance, among other reasons. Abraham had to direct a war whose toll would eventually reach more than 600,000 dead on the two sides. Together, the couple had to face the loss of another son, Willie, who died in 1862. When Abraham Lincoln was shot by John Wilkes Booth in April 1865, Mary Todd Lincoln was left a broken and desolate woman.

For the rest of her life she had to face difficult, and sometimes unbearably sad, problems. Her son Thomas (Tad) died in 1871. Abraham's former law partner published a book claiming that Abraham's real love had been another woman named Ann Rutledge. In the mid-1870s Mary was judged insane and briefly confined to an asylum. Throughout this period, she received relentlessly bad press. Only since the 1970s has she received sympathetic treatment from biographers and historians.

FURTHER READING

Baker, Jean H. *Mary Todd Lincoln.* New York: Norton, 1987.

Lincoln, Mary Todd. *Mary Todd Lincoln: Her Life and Letters.* Edited by Justin G. Turner and Linda Levitt Turner. New York: Fromm International, 1987.

Neely, Mark E. *The Insanity File: The Case of Mary Todd Lincoln.* Carbondale: Southern Illinois University Press, 1993.

Literacy

Women and men have not had the same access to education—and hence to literacy—for most of human history. In some Third World countries even today, twice as many men as women can read. Because access to knowledge provides power, the inability to read cripples women's capacity to advance their own interests.

The United States has been somewhat of an exception to the general pattern. Though boys and young men received a better education, on the average, than girls and young women until well into the 20th century, most white girls learned to read, even in the colonial period. Probably the major reason for this was the influence of Protestant Christianity, with its emphasis on each believer reading her or his Bible. Girls may not have been able to attend college in the early days, but they could read the Word of God—and that meant that they could also read novels and newspapers and learn much other information about their world.

By 1850, the first census year in which literacy information was gathered, there was very little difference in male and female rates of being able to read. The women who *could not* read in 1850 were enslaved African Americans. Throughout the South, laws forbade teaching slaves of either sex to read and write. In 1998 there remained little difference in the literacy rates of men and women in the United States: 97 percent of men and women at age 15 or over were able to read and write, although about 22 percent of these functioned at the lowest level of literacy.

Scholars now believe that female literacy correlates with much that is socially beneficial. Indeed, many believe that the single most important factor in the reduction of the American birthrate in the 19th century was women's access to literacy. An educated woman is far likelier to want a smaller family so as to give her children advantages and to make choices for her own life.

Literature

There is perhaps no area of artistic endeavor to which American women have made a greater contribution nor from which they have derived greater benefit than that of literature. A few women started writing in the early colonial period, such as Anne Bradstreet and Phillis Wheatley, and as the trickle became a flood over the ensuing decades, women writers such as Harriet Beecher Stowe, Emily Dickinson, Willa Cather, Edith Wharton, Zora Neale Hurston, Lillian Hellman, Flannery O'Connor, and Toni Morrison penned some of the classic poems, plays, novels, and short stories of American literature. Many female authors have written about the female experience, and some have dreamed of better lives for women, visions that their works have helped transform into reality.

In the 1830s white women began writing novels about domestic life that enjoyed immense popularity in the middle decades of the 19th century. A domestic novel typically featured an orphaned girl who needed an education and who also needed to be schooled in the skills of housewifery. These books were read by both men and women, although they were especially beloved by the female audience. Some of the novels celebrated the lives of ordinary women during the same decades that the women's rights movement was taking shape and imparted a message of female strength and solidarity. Harriet Beecher Stowe's *Uncle Tom's Cabin* was this sort of domestic novel but rose above the genre with its powerful story of injustice to slaves.

In 1859 there appeared the first novel written by an African-American woman, *Our Nig,* by Harriet Wilson. Though we know little about her, it seems that the circumstances of her life probably paralleled those of her heroine, Frado, a young black servant woman who is cruelly treated by her employer.

In the late 19th and 20th centuries, women novelists such as Sara Orne Jewett and Willa Cather wrote vividly about the regions they knew best, Maine and Nebraska, respectively, and Edith Wharton wrote about upper-class New York. Other women, most memorably Gertrude Stein, were pioneers of the avant-garde, experimental writing now known as modernism.

As more and more groups of women have acquired an education, literary works representing an ever-broader range of experience have been published. In the first quarter of the 20th century, for example, two young Jewish women published important books illuminating the lives of immigrants from eastern Europe: Mary Antin's *The Promised Land* (1912) and Anzia Yezierska's *Bread Givers* (1925). Many of the important black writers working during the Harlem Renaissance in the 1920s and 1930s were female, such as Nella Larsen and Zora Neale Hurston.

Eudora Welty was one of the many women writers to receive critical acclaim in the 1940s and 1950s. She hailed from a long line of literary-minded women, and one biographer noted that "books were so valued that once when the house caught fire, her mother threw out volumes of Dickens before getting herself to safety."

In the years since the end of World War II in 1945, women of color have come into their own as authors. Toni Morrison, author of powerful novels about the African-American past, won the Nobel Prize for literature in 1993. Louise Erdrich and others have written vividly about Native-American life. Sandra Cisneros, Ana Castillo, and Cherrie Moraga have done the same for the Latina experience. Maxine Hong Kingston and Amy Tan have introduced hundreds of thousands of readers to Chinese-American life and culture. In 1950, Jade Snow Wong published her book *Fifth Chinese Daughter,* one of the earliest by a Chinese-American woman to appear in the English language. *Fifth Chinese Daughter* describes the author's search for identity as a woman caught between two cultures as she grew up in San Francisco's Chinatown.

From Anne Bradstreet and Phillis Wheatley in the colonial period to Emily Dickinson in the 19th century to Edna St. Vincent Millay, Elizabeth Bishop, Marianne Moore, Sylvia Plath, Anne Sexton, Gwendolyn Brooks, and Adrienne Rich in the 20th century, women have also shaped American poetry. Though using domestic imagery more often than men, women poets have plumbed the range of human experience. In the late 19th century Dickinson wrote small, understated poems that almost explode off the page. In the mid-20th century, Plath and Sexton, among others, pushed confessional poetry about women's lives to a new level of intensity.

SEE ALSO

Bradstreet, Anne; Cather, Willa Sibert; Dickinson, Emily; Hellman, Lillian; Hurston, Zora Neale; Jewett, Sarah Orne; Kingston, Maxine Hong; McCarthy, Mary; Millay, Edna St. Vincent; Morrison, Toni; Plath, Sylvia; Rich, Adrienne; Stein, Gertrude; Stowe, Harriet Beecher; Tan, Amy; Wharton, Edith Newbold Jones; Wheatley, Phillis; Yezierska, Anzia

FURTHER READING

Davidson, Cathy N., and Linda Wagner-Martin, eds. *The Oxford Companion to Women's Writing in the United States.* New York: Oxford University Press, 1995.

Davis, Cynthia, and Kathryn West. *Women Writers in the United States: A Timeline of Literary, Cultural, and Social History.* New York: Oxford University Press, 1996.

Gilbert, Sandra M., and Susan Guber, eds. *The Norton Anthology of Literature by Women.* New York: Norton, 1996.

Knight, Denise D., ed. *Nineteenth-Century American Women Writers: A Bio-Bibliographical Critical Sourcebook.* Westport, Conn.: Greenwood, 1997.

Mainiero, Linda, ed. *American Women Writers: A Critical Reference Guide from Colonial Times to the Present.* New York: Ungar, 1979–82 (5 volumes).

Moers, Ellen. *Literary Women.* Garden City, N.Y.: Doubleday, 1976.

Perkins, Barbara, George Perkins, and Robyn Warhol, eds. *Women's Work: An Anthology of American Literature.* New York: McGraw-Hill, 1994.

Lockwood, Belva Ann Bennett

- *Born: Oct. 24, 1830, Royalton, N.Y.*
- *Education: Genesee College (now Syracuse University), B.A., 1857; National University Law School, J.D., 1873*
- *Accomplishments: First woman admitted to practice law before the U.S. Supreme Court (1879); delegate, International Congress of Charities, Correction, and Philanthropy, Geneva (1896)*
- *Died: May 19, 1917, Washington, D.C.*

In 1879 Belva Lockwood, a pioneer of women's rights and suffrage, became the first woman lawyer admitted to practice before the U.S. Supreme Court. To achieve this distinction—in fact, to become a lawyer at all—she had to overcome daunting obstacles.

An early marriage left young Belva McNall with a four-year-old daughter

"THE LIBERATOR AND ELEVATOR OF WOMEN." "THE TEACHER AND LOVER OF CHILDREN." "THE UNTIRING FRIEND OF THE SICK AND THE POOR." "THE ERUDITE SCHOLAR AND ACCOMPLISHED LADY."

THE DISTINGUISHED ORATOR AND QUEEN OF THE AMERICAN BAR,

BELVA

"The Champion of Equal Civil and Political Rights."

LOCKWOOD

SEE OTHER SIDE

WHO WAS NOMINATED FOR

PRESIDENT

OF THE UNITED STATES.

AT IRVING OPERA HOUSE,

WARSAW, N. Y.

Friday Evening, Nov. 26th, 1886.

ADMISSION, 35 & 50 CENTS.

Reserved Seats for sale at Whitlock & Pratt's.

HENRY L. SLAYTON, Manager, CENTRAL MUSIC HALL CHICAGO.

This handbill advertises a speech by Belva Lockwood, who ran for President in 1886. Her greatest contribution lay in her pioneering role as a lawyer at a time when few women had been admitted to state bar associations.

to support, after her husband died in an accident. She secured a B.S. from Genesee College in New York in 1857 and then taught until she was admitted to National University Law School, a new institution in the nation's capital. By this time she had remarried, to a much older man by the name of Ezekiel Lockwood.

Belva Lockwood had to fight to get into law school, repeatedly applying after rejections based on her sex, and later had to fight to practice before the U.S. Court of Claims. She won the battle after one of her cases reached that jurisdiction by successfully lobbying to practice before the Supreme Court, an achievement that conveyed the right to practice before lower federal courts. She reasoned that if women were allowed to practice law at all then they should be able to practice throughout the judicial system, and she eventually persuaded prosuffrage senators to introduce a bill to this effect, which passed Congress in 1879.

Not surprisingly, given all the struggle, Lockwood began to take an interest in the suffrage movement. In 1872 she initially supported the flamboyant Victoria Woodhull's bid for the Presidency of the United States. Lockwood herself ran on the National Equal Rights Party ticket in 1884 and 1888. In neither case did the women garner more than a handful of votes, but their candidacies helped attract attention to the cause of suffrage. The greatest part of Lockwood's legal practice consisted of pension claims against the federal government. When Oklahoma, New Mexico, and Arizona brought statehood bills before Congress, Lockwood wrote amendments to them that granted suffrage to women in the new states. She was also instrumental in the passing of laws giving women government employees equal pay for equal work and giving wives equal child custody opportunities in divorce proceedings.

SEE ALSO

Supreme Court, U.S.; Woodhull, Victoria Claflin

FURTHER READING:

Fox, Mary Virginia. *Lady for the Defense: A Biography of Belva Lockwood.* New York: Harcourt Brace Jovanovich, 1978.

Lowell, Josephine Shaw

- *Born: Dec. 16, 1843, West Roxbury, Mass.*
- *Education: Schooling in Paris; Miss Gibson's School, N.Y.*
- *Accomplishments: First woman appointed to the New York State Board of Charities (1876); founder, New York City Charity Organization Society (1882); vice president, Anti-Imperialist League of New York (1901–05)*
- *Died: Oct. 12, 1905, New York, N.Y.*

The daughter of one leading Boston family and the widow of a man who belonged to another, Josephine Shaw Lowell developed new ways of doing social work in the late 19th century, insisting that it must be efficient and well-managed as well as compassionate. In 1876 she became the first woman to be appointed to New York's State Board of Charities, the group officially charged with dispensing help to the poor and unfortunate.

Brought up in a family that was deeply committed to abolitionist principles, young Josephine Shaw met many prominent New Englanders and even foreign intellectuals as she was growing up. The Civil War started when she was 17, she married Colonel Charles Russell Lowell when she was 19, and she became a widow at 20 when her husband was killed in the fighting. She also lost her brother, Robert Gould Shaw, who died while commanding the heroic African-American regiment, the 54th Massachusetts.

After the war, Lowell had a powerful need to live up to the legacy left by her husband and brother. She filled that need first by working on behalf of the newly freed slaves and then by other charitable endeavors. In 1890 she was the moving spirit behind the founding of the Consumers' League of New York, a group that tried to pressure owners to improve conditions for their workers by the threat of a buyers' boycott. She also was one of the prominent Americans who opposed the United States' acquisition of the Philippines following the Spanish American War of 1898. A woman of immense intelligence and administrative ability, she left a lasting mark on her field.

FURTHER READING

Waugh, Joan. *Unsentimental Reformer: The Life of Josephine Shaw Lowell.* Cambridge: Harvard University Press, 1998.

Lynching

Lynching is the term given to mob violence that results in the death, usually by hanging, of one or more people. In the United States, lynching originated in frontier areas where vigilantes would bring accused criminals to mob "justice" without waiting for the legal system to proceed in an orderly fashion. Over the generations, however, lynching spread to other parts of the country. For example, in 1933 a mob in San Jose, California, lynched two confessed kidnappers.

Though lynchings have occurred in many places and have been directed against many different types of people, by far the largest number of lynchings has occurred in the South, where African-American men have been the victims. After the end of the Civil War, many southerners, determined to teach the newly freed slaves their "place," resorted to mob violence. Mobs lynched their victims on flimsy evidence and often charged a black man with rape or with insulting a white woman. Between 1882 and 1923 more than 500 black people, mostly men, were lynched in the state of Georgia alone.

Women played a very important role in combating lynching. One of the earliest and most outspoken crusaders against mob rule was the black journalist Ida Wells-Barnett, who published her denunciation of it in *The Red Record* in 1895. In the early 20th century, the National Association of Colored Women also joined the battle, lobbying unsuccessfully to get Congress to pass a bill that would turn lynching into a federal crime. After years of effort, black women finally succeeded in enlisting support from white southern women in the 1920s and 1930s. In 1930 Jessie Daniel Ames founded the Association of Southern Women for the Prevention of Lynching, a whites-only group. The crime itself did not truly end until the civil rights movement of the 1950s and 1960s brought more blacks into government in the South.

SEE ALSO

National Association of Colored Women (NACW); Wells-Barnett, Ida B.

FURTHER READING

Duster, Alfreda, ed. *Crusade for Justice.* Chicago: University of Chicago Press, 1972.

Hall, Jacquelyn Dowd. *The Revolt against Chivalry.* New York: Columbia University Press, 1979.

Lisandrelli, Elaine Slivinski. *Ida B. Wells-Barnett: Crusader Against Lynching.* Springfield, N.J.: Enslow, 1998.

Lyon, Mary

- *Born: Feb. 28, 1797, Buckland, Mass.*
- *Education: Buckland (Mass.) village school to age 13, then self-taught*
- *Accomplishments: Founder, Mount Holyoke Female Seminary, now Mount Holyoke College (1837)*
- *Died: Mar. 5, 1849, South Hadley, Mass.*

Mary Lyon founded Mount Holyoke Female Seminary (now Mount Holyoke College) in 1837 and in so doing gave a powerful boost to the caliber of education available to women. The Female Seminary would evolve into a true college, and scholars see the school and its founders as the source of the movement for women's colleges.

In the 1830s Oberlin College in Ohio was the only coeducational college in the country, and there were then no women's colleges, but Lyon saw to it that her students received a superb education, in some instances from professors who taught at nearby colleges for men. She raised money from the surrounding communities and also realized that the students could perform their own domestic work, thus eliminating the need for and expense of servants. Energetic and dedicated, she inspired her young women to high intellectual achievement, as she inspired many others to revise their opinions of the female capacity for achievement.

SEE ALSO

Education; Women's colleges

FURTHER READING

Horowitz, Helen. *Alma Mater.* New York: Knopf, 1984.

Porterfield, Amanda. *Mary Lyon and the Mount Holyoke Missionaries.* New York: Oxford University Press, 1997.

Rosen, Dorothy Schack. *A Fire in Her Bones: The Story of Mary Lyon.* Minneapolis: Carolrhoda, 1994.

Mary Lyon founded Mount Holyoke College, originally called Mount Holyoke Female Seminary, in 1834 with the intention of providing education equivalent to that at men's colleges.

Magazines, women's

In the years before women could gain election to political office or enjoy the privilege of controlling a newspaper or a publishing house, to edit a women's magazine was one of the surest ways to affect public opinion. The best example of this is the career of the mid-19th-century editor of *Godey's Lady's Book,* Sarah Josepha Hale. Editing her influential publication for 40 years, Hale's crusades included better educational opportunities for women and access to the medical profession for them. Another of her pet projects was to get the President to proclaim Thanksgiving as a national holiday, which happened in 1863 during the administration of Abraham Lincoln.

During Hale's heyday, women's magazines were aimed mainly at an elite audience. By the late 19th century, they began to be mass circulation and thus to be pitched to the larger group of middle-class white women. It was during this time period that three of the best-known were founded: *Ladies' Home Journal, McCall's,* and *Good Housekeeping,* all of which are still being published. In the early 1900s they and others which have subsequently disappeared began to campaign against contaminated drinking water and on behalf of pure food and drugs. Many important writers published fiction in their pages. Following the ratification of the 19th Amendment in 1920, women's magazines ran articles aimed at educating the new voters. In short, they were serious publications. Women could turn to them for recipes and ideas about fashion and decorating, but also for ideas about needed reforms.

Magazines such as this Ladies' Home Journal *from January 1908 offered advice to women on perfecting their housekeeping and nurturing skills, and advertised a range of consumer products for personal beauty and the home.*

Another genre of women's magazine lay in those devoted primarily to fashion. *Harper's Bazaar* first appeared in 1867 and *Vogue* in 1892. Each is still being published, and each has had, at various times in its history, an editor so influential on American fashion that she has become a legend, such as *Vogue*'s Diana Vreeland in the mid-20th century.

Over time, the serious content in women's magazines diminished as the priorities of advertisers desirous of avoiding controversy garnered ever more attention from editors and publishers. By the 1950s Betty Friedan could denounce women's magazines in *The Feminine Mystique* as staunch upholders of the status quo where women's roles were concerned.

In 1965 a new type of women's magazine emerged, aimed at sexually active young women. Helen Gurley Brown, who had just published *Sex and the Single Girl,* persuaded Hearst publications to let her take over *Cosmopolitan* and turn it in a new direction. The *Cosmo* woman was hip, and she knew how to have fun.

In the feminist 1970s a host of new women's magazines appeared, most especially *Ms.*, which began to be published in 1971. Gloria Steinem and other editors worked to turn *Ms.* into a forum for the exchange of feminist ideas, and they published outstanding fiction, too, such as the writing of Alice Walker and Erica Jong. In 1970 a magazine for black women who worked outside the home arrived on the scene, *Essence.*

Despite such positive changes as the fact that today women rather than men edit all the major women's magazines, many problems remain. So difficult is it to get advertisers to support serious editorial content, for example, that in 1989 *Ms.* gave up on relying on advertising for revenue, and it survives only on income from subscriptions. Moreover, the mainstream magazines reflect the celebrity-obsessed culture and feature articles about movie stars far more than the serious content of times past.

SEE ALSO

Godey's Lady's Book; Hale, Sarah Josepha Buell

FURTHER READING

Damon-Moore, Helen. *Magazines for the Millions: Gender and Commerce in the Ladies' Home Journal and the Saturday Evening Post, 1880–1910.* Albany: State University of New York Press, 1994.

Humphreys, Nancy K. *American Women's Magazines: An Annotated Historical Guide.* New York: Garland, 1989.

McCracken, Ellen. *Decoding Women's Magazines: From Mademoiselle to Ms.* New York: St. Martin's, 1993.

Zuckerman, Mary Ellen. *A History of Popular Women's Magazines in the United States, 1792–1995.* Westport, Conn.: Greenwood, 1998.

Mankiller, Wilma

- *Born: Nov. 18, 1945, Tahlequah, Okla.*
- *Education: San Francisco State College, 1973–75; Union for Experimenting Colleges and Universities, B.A., 1977; University of Arkansas, graduate coursework, 1979*
- *Accomplishments: Principal Chief, Cherokee Nation (1985–95); American Indian Woman of the Year (1986); John Gardner Leadership Award (1988); National Women's Hall of Fame (1993); Author,* Mankiller: A Chief and Her People *(1993)*

Former Cherokee chief Wilma Mankiller during a press conference in Tulsa, Oklahoma, in 1997. Mankiller spent her formative years in San Francisco, where she learned about the women's movement and organizing.

Wilma Mankiller was the first woman to be principal chief of the Cherokee Nation—or of any major American Indian tribe.

Born in Oklahoma, Mankiller moved to San Francisco with her family when she was 11 as part of the federal government's plan to relocate Indians to cities and thereby into the mainstream of American life. Adjusting to the culture shock, Mankiller went on to attend San Francisco State College, to marry, and to give birth to two children.

In 1969 a group of Indians occupied the former federal prison at Alcatraz in San Francisco Bay to call attention to the need for a better policy for their people. Mankiller's participation reawakened her interest in her Indian heritage, and from that time on, she has been a dedicated activist.

Mankiller moved back to Oklahoma in 1975—the same year her first marriage ended in divorce—and threw herself into full-time service to the Cherokee Nation. In 1983 she was elected to be deputy chief, and in 1985 she became principal chief. In 1986 she married fellow Cherokee Charlie Soap.

As chief, Mankiller made economic growth her most important goal, trying to find a way to promote rural development to break the cycle of poverty while remaining true to traditional values. In 1990 Yale University awarded her an honorary doctorate in recognition of her achievements. The Cherokees had a history of female leadership before the European invasion, and Mankiller has reinvigorated this proud tradition among her people.

SEE ALSO

Native Americans

FURTHER READING

Mankiller, Wilma. *Mankiller: A Chief and Her People.* New York: St. Martin's, 1993.

Marriage

Throughout American history the vast majority of women have married. Moreover, the proportion of those never marrying has been remarkably steady, hovering at around 10 percent from the time nationhood began in 1789 until the late 20th century. Although this figure has been a constant, many other aspects of marriage have changed dramatically over time—such as courtship practices, the laws governing a married woman's rights, the relationship between husband and wife, and the percentage of marriages ending in divorce.

In the colonial period the law of marriage throughout the colonies was based on English common law. Under English common law the wife was considered "civilly dead," which meant that the husband and wife were regarded as a single legal entity, with the husband as its public representative. A married woman's name from that period, for example, typically shows up in very few public records, because her husband transacted all the business. With the balance of legal power in his favor, the husband also was the authority figure in the household. Finally, for several generations, marriage was arranged by parents, rather than the result of choices made by young people.

This couple, in Florida in the 1940s, were wed in a traditional Christian marriage ceremony. For families in many different social and ethnic groups, the investment in a wedding may be exceeded only by that for a home or a college education.

Ideas about marriage began to change in the late 1700s and early 1800s. Marital love began to be depicted as one of the pinnacles of human experience. To choose one's own marriage partner seemed essential. Moreover, what scholars have called companionate marriage—one with more equality between husband and wife rather than one in which supreme authority rests with the man—began to be typical. At the same time, laws governing married women's property were undergoing reform.

As with the laws governing property, those governing divorce and child custody were also weighted decidedly in favor of the husband until reform began in the late 19th century. Earlier, a husband gained custody of the children more or less automatically. After the reforms, the mother was typically the custodial parent.

Today marriage is much more unstable than in the past, and many women are choosing to remain single. There has been a general decline in marriages since 1963, and even more recently, between 1990 and 1997, the marriage rate per 1,000 unmarried women age 15 and older steadily declined to below 50 percent. This trend may be the result of a number of influences on women's decision making, but particularly the so-called sexual revolution beginning in the 1960s, which gave women freedoms that have allowed more more of them to choose careers over families, and to make choices about their lives unrestricted by social taboos of earlier times.

SEE ALSO

Courtship; Custody, child; Divorce; Married Women's Property Acts

FURTHER READING

Cherlin, Andrew J. *Marriage, Divorce, Remarriage.* Cambridge: Harvard University Press, 1992.

Luchetti, Cathy. *"I Do!": Courtship, Love, and Marriage on the American Frontier: A Glimpse at America's Romantic Past through Photographs, Diaries, and Journals, 1715-1915.* New York: Villard, 1995.

May, Elaine Tyler. *Great Expectations: Marriage and Divorce in Post-Victorian America.* Chicago: University of Chicago Press, 1980.

Popenoe, David, Jean Bethke Elshtain, and David Blankenhorn, eds. *Promises to Keep: Decline and Renewal of Marriage in America.* Lanham, Md.: Rowman & Littlefield, 1996.

Married Women's Property Acts

Until the second quarter of the 19th century, married women in the United States could not control property in their own names. Even if they brought property into a marriage, even if their earnings had paid for the property, the husband was the one who controlled it. This legal practice derived from the English common law doctrine of coverture, whereby a husband "covered" his wife's identity and possessed the sole capacity to enter into contracts. This doctrine not only crippled women's capacity to be full citizens, but gave them an economic handicap.

Beginning in the late 1830s, states started to reform these laws. By 1860, 14 states had passed some form of a Married Women's Property Act, thereby granting women a greater measure of economic independence because they could now own property in their own names. Demand for such laws became one of the rallying cries of the 19th-century women's movement, although the earliest ones actually preceded the birth of the movement. Scholars believe that at first their passage owed a great deal to men wanting to protect their estates from greedy sons-in-law and pass them on to their daughters.

It has taken generations of struggle and many new laws as well as many key judicial decisions to erase the legacy of coverture, so that, for example, married women can now secure credit—the right to borrow money—in their own names.

SEE ALSO

Citizenship; Marriage

Matrilineal descent

The words *matrilineal* and *patrilineal* are used to characterize family systems in various cultures. A matrilineal system is one in which the family identity and

the inheritance pass through the mother's line. In a patrilineal system descent goes through the father's line. Sometimes—but not invariably—descent systems reveal something about the distribution of power in a culture. That is, a matrilineal system may confer more power on women than a neighboring patrilineal culture would. In the period before European conquest, many Native-American tribes were matrilineal.

McCarthy, Mary

- *Born: June 21, 1912, Seattle, Wash.*
- *Education: Vassar College, B.A., 1933*
- *Accomplishments: Author,* The Company She Keeps *(1942);* The Oasis *(1949);* The Groves of Academe *(1952);* Venice, Observed *(1956);* The Stones of Florence *(1959);* Memories of a Catholic Girlhood *(1957);* The Group *(1963);* Vietnam *(1967);* Hanoi *(1968);* Birds of America *(1971);* The Mask of State *(1974);* Cannibals and Missionaries *(1979);* How I Grew *(1987);* Intellectual Memoirs, New York, 1936–38 *(1992)*
- *Died: Aug. 25, 1989, New York, N.Y.*

Mary McCarthy was not only a distinguished novelist but also one of the country's leading intellectuals in the second half of the 20th century. In the pages of the influential *New York Review of Books,* she wrote memorably about public affairs such as the war in Vietnam in the 1960s and 1970s, as well as about literature.

Orphaned at a young age, McCarthy graduated from Vassar College and soon began writing book reviews for the *Partisan Review.* In 1942 she published her first novel, *The Company She Keeps,* a series of somewhat autobiographical stories about a society woman who goes through a divorce and psychoanalysis. Her best-known novel was *The Group* (1963), a fictionalized version of her own experiences at Vassar.

McCarthy was married four times, the second time to the writer Edmund Wilson. She wrote about her life in two volumes of memoirs, *Memories of a Catholic Girlhood* and *How I Grew.*

FURTHER READING

Brightman, Carol. *Writing Dangerously: Mary McCarthy and Her World.* New York: Clarkson Potter, 1992.

Gelderman, Carol. *Mary McCarthy: A Life.* New York: St. Martin's, 1988.

McClintock, Barbara

- *Born: June 16, 1902, Hartford, Conn.*
- *Education: Cornell University, B.S., 1923, M.A., 1935, Ph.D., 1927*
- *Accomplishments: Guggenheim Fellowship (1933); president, Genetics Society of America (1944); Nobel Prize in medicine/physiology (1983)*
- *Died: Sept. 2, 1992, Cold Spring Harbor, N.Y.*

Barbara McClintock was a biologist with an unconventional career capped by the triumph of winning a Nobel Prize in her 80s, as well as one of the MacArthur Foundation "genius" awards.

One of the 20th century's most creative scientists, biologist Barbara McClintock discovered "jumping genes" in corn. At the age of 81, she was awarded both a Nobel Prize and a MacArthur "genius" grant.

The daughter of a physician and his wife, McClintock was eager for a college education but had to overcome the resistance of her very conventional parents, who had their own ideas of what a woman should do with her life, to fulfill her dream. She graduated from Cornell University as a biology major and then went on to obtain both a master's degree and in 1927 a doctorate in botany from the same institution. McClintock had been researching the genetics of corn, work to which she would dedicate herself for the rest of her life.

When she was ready to go on the academic job market, however, she had few attractive options. Her alma mater did not hire a woman in a regular faculty position other than home economics until 1947, and that was typical of most research universities. McClintock managed to find a laboratory at Cold Spring Harbor, New York, however, out of which to conduct her research. There she kept going for many years, with the help of grants, until she became a faculty member at Cornell in the 1960s.

Put simply, McClintock's research revealed how changeable genes could be—the so-called "jumping genes," which moved on a chromosome and changed future generations of plants. That she could make her discoveries while working outside the usual academic framework is a testament to her determination. The Nobel Prize was awarded in recognition of the fact that her research changed our understanding of plant genetics.

SEE ALSO

Science

FURTHER READING

Fine, Edith Hope. *Barbara McClintock: Noble Prize Geneticist*. Springfield, N.J.: Enslow, 1998.

Keller, Evelyn Fox. *A Feeling for the Organism: The Life and Work of Barbara McClintock*. San Francisco: Freeman, 1983.

Kittredge, Mary. *Barbara McClintock*. New York: Chelsea House, 1991.

Mead, Margaret

- *Born: Dec. 16, 1901, Philadelphia, Pa.*
- *Education: Barnard College, B.A., 1923; Columbia University, M.A., 1924, Ph.D., 1929*
- *Accomplishments: Curator (at various levels), American Museum of Natural History (1926–78); president, American Association for the Advancement of Science (1974); Presidential Medal of Freedom (posthumous, 1979); author,* Coming of Age in Samoa *(1928);* Growing Up in New Guinea *(1930);* Sex and Temperament in Three Primitive Societies *(1935);* Balinese Character: A Photographic Analysis *(with Gregory Bateson, 1942);* Continuities in Cultural Evolution *(1964);* A Rap on Race *(with James Baldwin, 1971)*
- *Died: Nov. 15, 1978, New York, N.Y.*

Anthropologist Margaret Mead taught her fellow Americans to think about cultural differences in new ways: cultures could be flexible, and what the average American thought of as fixed human characteristics might not be manifest in another society, such as certain types of sexual behavior.

She wrote *Coming of Age in Samoa,* which was published in 1928,

Anthropologist Margaret Mead plays with a child in New Guinea in 1928 on her second field trip there. Her field research and books on human behavior brought her international attention.

while still a young woman. The book reached a broad audience of general readers with its vivid descriptions of puberty, courtship, and the family in the South Seas, which were based on Mead's own observations while living there. From the late 1920s until she died in 1978, Mead had the ability to command attention with her views about the family as an institution as well as with her ideas about other aspects of U.S. society, in particular her critiques of traditional stereotypes about men and women. She played an important role in challenging vestiges of Victorian attitudes about sexuality.

Mead graduated from Barnard College in 1923 and then earned a doctorate in anthropology from Columbia University in 1929. She spent the major part of her working years as the curator of ethnology (the study of races) at the American Museum of Natural History in New York rather than in a conventional academic position. Though she was one of the most famous anthropologists in the country—and continued to publish extensively—universities did not hire women except in departments of home economics when Mead was in her prime. She did teach at Fordham University later in her life.

Her marriage to fellow anthropologist Gregory Bateson produced one daughter, Catherine Bateson. In the last decade of her life, Mead published a memoir, *Blackberry Winter.* Since her death, many of her research findings about Samoa have been challenged on the grounds that she misunderstood or misreported fundamental characteristics of that South Seas society and that she relied too much on observation and not enough on other types of data.

Although she may have been incorrect in certain areas, few women have had the influence Mead enjoyed in her lifetime. Quirky, opinionated, and outspoken, she conceded motherhood might affect the division of cultural roles into male and female, but otherwise preached a gospel of the malleability of human nature.

FURTHER READING

Bateson, Mary Catherine. *With a Daughter's Eye: A Memoir of Margaret Mead and Gregory Bateson.* New York: Morrow, 1984.

Mark, Joan. *Margaret Mead: Coming of Age in America.* New York: Oxford University Press, 1999.

Mead, Margaret, and Nancy Lutkehaus. *Blackberry Winter: My Earlier Years.* Edited by Philip Turner. New York: Kodansha, 1995.

Media

Journalism was one of the earliest careers to which a woman could aspire, and some women enjoyed considerable success as writers or editors well before there were many professional women of any sort in the country. Sarah Josepha Hale, the editor of *Godey's Lady's Book* for many decades in the mid-1800s, is the best example. Under Hale's guidance, *Godey's* was widely read, by influential men as well as by women, and Hale successfully pursued many crusades, such as getting Abraham Lincoln to proclaim Thanksgiving a national holiday in 1863. On the other hand, women reporters for newspapers were almost invariably consigned to the women's pages, a kind of female ghetto where they could only write about society and fashion, until the 1970s. In other words, it was the rare woman journalist who had Sarah Josepha Hale's clout.

In the late 1800s, women reporters were breaking into journalism in increasing numbers during a period of

The daytime talk show The View *features a team of five dynamic women of different ages, experiences, and backgrounds, discussing compelling events of the day. The program has received critical acclaim since premiering in August 1997.*

great innovation in the field, which saw newspapers scrambling for new readers with sensational stories. There was a new possibility for women: they could be "stunt girls" or "sob sisters." These were intrepid women who disguised themselves and went undercover to get a sensational exposé, playing up the emotional angle for all it was worth. Nellie Bly was the best-known woman journalist working in this genre, and she traveled around the world on one stunt for Joseph Pulitzer's *World* in New York City.

Though some of this reporting may have been overblown or silly, it also resulted in greater public awareness of serious social problems, such as the harsh treatment of women factory workers. A few women, such as Ida Tarbell, who exposed the concentration of power in the oil industry, were, in fact, distinguished journalists. But then the public's appetite for exposés diminished, and the need for women doing this type of writing disappeared.

Throughout the succeeding decades leading up to the birth of the modern women's movement around 1970, it was the rare woman journalist who broke away from the women's pages. Indeed, one of the many favors that First Lady Eleanor Roosevelt performed for her fellow women was to permit only women journalists at her news conferences during her husband's administration in the 1930s and 1940s. Since she often made front-page news, this automatically promoted the reporters' stories to that section of the paper. During these years, journalist Dorothy Thompson was a commentator on politics and foreign policy on the radio, had a syndicated column, and wrote for the *Ladies' Home Journal*, the exception to the general pattern.

When the broadcast media became mainstream—radio in the 1920s and television in the 1940s and 1950s—there was no tradition of female journalistic excellence, other than in the women's pages. Not surprisingly, the first announcers and news broadcasters were male. (Dorothy Thompson was an exception here, too, with a regular broadcast on NBC radio in the 1930s.)

When modern feminism came into being around 1970, women journalists in both print and broadcasting launched struggles to be taken more seriously, to get opportunities to report a greater variety of news, to be able to write editorials and think pieces, and to be allowed on TV as anchors. Women employees even went so far as to sue the *New York Times* to improve their opportunities there, a change that has been slowly occurring. In the old days a newsroom often resembled a men's club with one or two women—who wrote for the society page—sprinkled in. That is no longer the case, although men still dominate the top positions.

Today, although women are far from full equality, they are represented at all levels of the communications industry. Television talk show hosts such as Oprah Winfrey and Rosie O'Donnell enjoy immense influence. Women news broadcasters are employed as anchors in many markets, and women such as Jane Pauley, Diane Sawyer, Barbara Walters, Connie Chung, and Cokie Roberts are respected commentators or host their own shows. Still, even with all the progress, it remains easier for middle-aged and older men to stay professionally active than for women, whose good looks may have provided the original professional entrée—at least in television.

Women write political commentary for the most prestigious newspapers and also work as editors and managers. Katharine Graham of the *Washington Post* enjoys a near legendary status as a courageous publisher, owing to the role her newspaper played in uncovering the Watergate scandal during Richard Nixon's presidency in the 1970s.

Linda Johnson Rice, president of the Johnson Publishing Company that puts out *Ebony* and *Jet,* the leading periodicals for the African-American community, is a good example of the high-powered women in this field. A 1980 graduate of the University of Southern California in journalism, she now oversees a vast family-owned business—with annual sales of $275 million in 1992—while also sitting on numerous corporate boards and serving as a trustee of USC. A generation ago she would have had few or no counterparts among either black or white women.

SEE ALSO

Graham, Katharine Meyer; Hale, Sarah Josepha Buell; Seaman, Elizabeth Cochrane (Nellie Bly); Television; Thompson, Dorothy

FURTHER READING

Greenwald, Marilyn S. *A Woman of the Times: Journalism, Feminism, and the Career of Charlotte Curtis.* Athens: Ohio University Press, 1999.

Ritchie, Donald A. *American Journalists: Getting the Story.* New York: Oxford University Press, 1998.

Stahl, Lesley. *Reporting Live.* New York: Simon & Schuster, 1999.

Thomas, Helen. *Front Row at the White House: My Life and Times.* New York: Scribner, 1999.

Medicine

Before there were many medical doctors or any medical schools as we now know them, there were women who acted informally as medical practitioners, especially for their families, for whom they might brew healing remedies passed down through generations. During childbirth, a woman typically called on the services of other women in the community and on a midwife, a woman who possessed special experience and knowledge in this area. As the profession of medicine took shape and grew in the 18th century, it developed into an all-male discipline, and no women were admitted for medical training in this country in the early years.

An all-female surgical staff performs an operation, witnessed by students at the Women's Medical College of Pennsylvania in the early 20th century.

The situation changed in 1849 when Elizabeth Blackwell became the first woman in the United States to receive a medical degree from Geneva College in New York. She later learned that her fellow students thought her application was a joke. She immediately began to write and organize to help women gain access to medical training. As a result of her work and the involvement of other dedicated women, a number of medical schools for women were founded, including the Woman's Medical College of Philadelphia, the Woman's Medical College of the New York Infirmary, and the Chicago Female Medical College.

In 1867 Rebecca Cole received her degree from the Woman's Medical College of Philadelphia and became a pioneering African-American woman physician. In 1871 the University of Michigan medical school opened its doors to women, and other schools gradually followed. By 1900 about 5 percent of the physicians in the country were female, a percentage that did not change much until the 1960s.

Although women constituted a small percentage of the overall medical profession in these years, they made many remarkable contributions. Alice Hamilton, for example, pioneered the specialty of industrial medicine, researching the occupational health of workers in hazardous jobs, and later finishing her career as a professor at Harvard. Helen Taussig developed the surgery to save the lives of babies born with congenital heart defects in the early 1940s. Virginia Apgar worked out a method for evaluating the viability of newborn babies, so that delivery room personnel could immediately determine which babies needed special attention in order to survive. Known as the Apgar Scale, it first came into use in 1952 and is still used today. Even today many women choose to specialize in obstetrics/pediatrics and public health services.

But despite the achievements of many women doctors, by the mid-20th century, the medical field remained a difficult one for young women to enter. As medicine became ever more dedicated to scientific objectivity and then became increasingly high-tech, it seemed a profession geared to males. Moreover, medical schools might admit women, but could, completely legally, restrict them to a very small quota. Girls with an interest in medicine were routinely counseled to become nurses, and it took courage to persevere in the ambition to practice medicine.

The modern feminist movement produced activism, struggle, and change in the field. Girls who are interested in medicine can now look forward to being either doctors or nurses. The passage of Title IX of the Education Act Amendments in 1972 discouraged universities from discriminating against women. Women began to critique the masculine arrogance they saw represented in the profession. Today about one-third of doctors are women, and about one-half of the population of medical students is female.

The new composition of the medical profession has also helped direct more attention to issues of women's health.

SEE ALSO

Blackwell, Elizabeth; Childbirth; Education Act Amendments (1972); Hamilton, Alice; Health, women's; Midwifery; Nursing

FURTHER READING

Abram, Ruth J., ed. *Send Us a Lady Physician: Women Doctors in America, 1835–1920.* New York: Norton, 1985.

Morantz, Regina Markell, Cynthia Stodola Pomerleau, and Carol Hansen Fenichel, eds. *In Her Own Words: Oral Histories of Women Physicians.* Westport, Conn.: Greenwood, 1982.

Morantz-Sanchez, Regina. *Sympathy and Science: Women Physicians in American Medicine.* New York: Oxford University Press, 1985.

Perone, Babbette, H. Henrietta Stockel, and Victoria Kruegel. *Medicine Women, Curanderas, and Women Doctors.* Norman: University of Oklahoma Press, 1993.

Menstruation

The onset of menstruation, whereby the uterus sheds its lining once a month unless the female has become pregnant, is the way that nature prepares girls at puberty for the biological task of giving birth. This biological fact has not changed over the centuries, but certain aspects of it have, such as the average age at which girls begin menstruating and the societal attitudes toward the menstruating woman.

The change in age is connected to diet. Girls and women need adequate nutrition or they cease to menstruate. This condition, known as amenorrhea, occurs in entire populations in a time of famine and in selected individuals in the case of eating disorders. As a rule, the better the nutrition and general level of health in a given population, the earlier the average age at which a girl starts her period. Over the generations of American history, increasing abundance has meant better diets for more girls, and the result has been a downward trend in average age of the start of puberty.

The attitudes toward a woman once she has begun menstruating have also changed over time in the United States. And attitudes vary among different ethnic groups. Some cultures, for example, Navajo Indians, celebrate the onset of puberty with coming-of-age rituals. On the other hand, some cultures in other parts of the world require a woman to live apart during the time that she is menstruating.

Americans believed until well into the 20th century that menstruation should prevent women from certain types of demanding activity—not housework or factory labor, but sports and even intellectual activity. One of the arguments against coeducation in higher education 100 years ago was that a young woman having her period would be unable to keep up with the young men in the same classroom.

Midwifery

A midwife is a woman who delivers babies. She may or may not have medical training, but if she lacks formal training, she is likely to have real-life experience. Before the 18th century, midwives attended at virtually all births. Now their presence is much rarer, although since the birth of modern feminism, around 1970, there has been a resurgence in midwifery.

Beginning in the late 18th century, male doctors increasingly took over as childbirth practitioners, especially among the white population. It seemed to women and their families that a doctor could offer more skill and safety than a midwife (which may or may not have been true, depending on the individuals involved). But among the African-American population—and others such as Mexican Americans where a folk medicine tradition flourished—midwives continued to be important until well into the 20th century.

With the modern resurgence in midwifery—spurred by the desire to have a woman control birth—there are two quite different approaches. In one, the midwife is part of a medical team that includes doctors and even hospitals if the birth seems likely to be complicated. In the other, the midwife and her patient reject the hospital altogether, the birth takes place at home, and every attempt is made to avoid calling on a physician. In the mid-1990s, some 200,000 births per year were assisted by certified nurse-midwives, mostly in hospitals, and the numbers have been rising from year to year.

SEE ALSO

Childbirth; Medicine

FURTHER READING

Leavitt, Judith. *Brought to Bed: Childbearing in America, 1750–1950.* New York: Oxford University Press, 1988.

Litoff, Judy Barrett. *American Midwives.* Westport, Conn.: Greenwood, 1978.

Ulrich, Laurel Thatcher. *A Midwife's Tale.* New York: Vintage, 1990.

Military

The story of women and the military is important not only for its own sake, but because political theory and popular thought have always linked citizenship with the right to bear arms. How can women be taken seriously as citizens, and even be considered for election to the Presidency, if women and men have different obligations in defending their country?

In some ways, the debate over what role women should play in the military is odd because a few women have fought in American wars going back to the Revolution, as in the case of Deborah Sampson, who fought with the Patriots while disguised as a man. But their arms bearing was informal, and

These combat-ready Marines of the all-female 4th Battalion demonstrate how far women have come in their integration into military units. In earlier years, military women served only as nurses and clerical workers.

when the fighting ended, they typically received little or no recognition.

A few white women were allowed to join in the military during World War I as army or navy nurses. But the systematic recruiting of women did not take place until World War II when the Women's Army Corps (WACS) and the navy unit called Women Accepted for Volunteer Emergency Service (WAVES) were created. Although both sexes served in the armed forces, men were forced to register for the draft, and if called, they had no choice about serving. Women, on the other hand, were volunteers. Moreover, women who did join the military saw no combat. Rather they worked as nurses or performed clerical duties. Also, there was a rigid limit on the percentage of the armed forces that could be female.

The early 1970s saw great change in the situation of military women. The earlier WACS, WAVES, and other women's units were disbanded. The military moved toward an all-volunteer army, because the Vietnam War, which the United States was then fighting, was so unpopular that thousands of men were refusing to comply with the draft. Hence the military leaders decided that the military forces would be most efficient if the people fighting wanted to do the job. Further, Congress lifted the ceiling on the number of women soldiers. The composition of the armed forces changed dramatically in response: more women in general and more people of color, including women, signed up.

The fighting that has taken place in the 1990s has seen women inching ever closer to a full combat role, and the United States has even produced, as during the Gulf War of 1991, female war heroes. Major Marie Rossi of the United States Army died in a helicopter crash, and Dr. Rhonda Cornum, another Army Major, wrote a book about her experiences as a prisoner of war. As of 1993, women constituted 11.8 percent of uniformed personnel. There have been and are now women generals and admirals. Women now fly military planes, including fighters. But the military is a long way from solving all of its difficulties about how to treat women.

The public has increasingly become aware of how vulnerable military women are to sexual harassment. Indeed, leaders of the various armed forces have, gingerly, acknowledged that this constitutes a major problem for women and for morale in general. Further, the question of how fully units should be integrated with respect to gender is far from being resolved. Still unknown is, if the United States were to be involved in fighting so heavy that the military would want to reinstitute a draft, whether women would be drafted the same as men.

Ever since World War II, certain women in Congress have singled out the treatment of military women as an issue of special concern to them. Those who have played the most prominent role have been the late Republican senator Margaret Chase Smith of Maine and former Democratic congresswoman Patricia Schroeder of Colorado, who called for better and more equal treatment.

SEE ALSO

Citizenship; Sampson, Deborah

FURTHER READING

Brewer, William B. *War and American Women.* Westport, Conn.: Praeger, 1997.

De Pauw, Linda. *Battle Cries and Lullabies: Women in War from Prehistory to the Present.* Norman: University of Oklahoma Press, 1998.

Herbert, Melissa S. *Camoflauge Isn't Only for Combat: Gender, Sexuality, and Women in the Military.* New York: New York University Press, 1998.

Sherrow, Victoria. *Women and the Military: An Encyclopedia.* Santa Barbara, Calif.: ABC-Clio, 1996.

Millay, Edna St. Vincent

- *Born: Feb. 22, 1892, Rockland, Maine*
- *Education: Vassar College, B.A., 1927*
- *Accomplishments: Pulitzer Prize for* Ballad of the Harp-Weaver, *1923; author,* Renascence and Other Poems *(1917);* A Few Figs from Thistles *(1920);* Second April *(1921);* Two Slatterns and a King *(1921);* The Lamp and the Bell *(1921);* Ballad of the Harp-Weaver *(1922);* The King's Henchman *(1927);* The Buck in the Snow *(1928);* Fatal Interview *(1931);* Wine from These Grapes *(1934)*
- *Died: Oct. 19, 1950, Austerlitz, N.Y.*

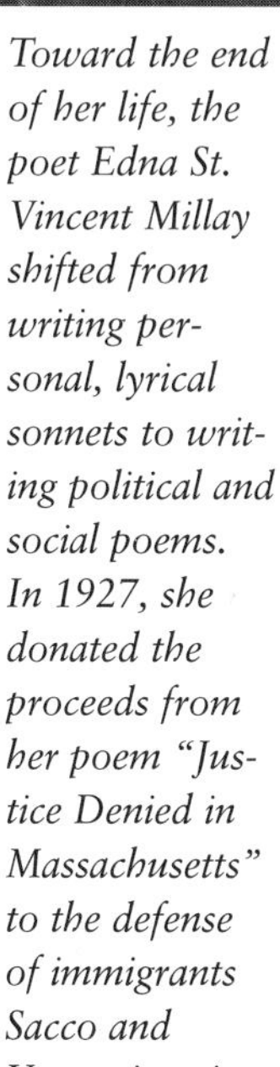

Toward the end of her life, the poet Edna St. Vincent Millay shifted from writing personal, lyrical sonnets to writing political and social poems. In 1927, she donated the proceeds from her poem "Justice Denied in Massachusetts" to the defense of immigrants Sacco and Vanzetti against murder charges.

Now seen as a relatively minor poet, Edna St. Vincent Millay seemed, at the height her fame, to be the female voice of her liberated generation. A Vassar graduate, Millay went from college to New York City's Greenwich Village, where many writers and artists lived. There she attracted much attention with her vibrant good looks and winning personality. She soon began to publish poems and magazine articles.

In 1923 Millay won the Pulitzer Prize for her volume of poetry *Ballad of the Harp-Weaver*—the first woman to achieve this. In the same year she wed the importer Eugen Boissevain. By the late 1920s her intense lyrics had made her a true literary star. But even in her lifetime, her work attracted increasingly unfavorable criticism as out of sync with the experimental writing that was coming into prominence. Today she is best known for the poem that begins: "My candle burns at both ends / It will not last the night." In this she celebrated the youth-oriented 1920s, of which she was a potent symbol.

FURTHER READING

Brittin, Norman A. *Edna St. Vincent Millay.* Rev. ed. Boston: Twayne, 1982.
Daffron, Carolyn. *Edna St. Vincent Millay.* New York: Chelsea House, 1989.

Mink, Patsy Takemoto

- *Born: Dec. 6, 1927, Paia, Hawaii*
- *Education: University of Hawaii, B.A., 1948; University of Chicago, J.D., 1964*
- *Accomplishments: U.S. Representative (D–Hawaii, 1965–77, 1990–)*

"It is easy enough to vote right and be consistently with the majority . . . but it is often more important to be ahead of the majority and this means being willing to cut the first furrow in the ground and stand alone for a while if necessary."
—Representative Patsy Mink, Honolulu Star-Bulletin, *October 8, 1973*

Patsy Takemoto Mink was the first woman of color as well as the first Asian-American woman to be elected to the U.S. Congress.

She was born and raised in Hawaii. With a B.A. from the University of Hawaii in 1948, she went on to obtain her law degree from the University of Chicago in 1951. She then served several terms in the Hawaiian state legislature before successfully running for the U.S. House of Representatives in 1964.

Mink arrived in Congress in 1965, just after the passage of the historic Civil Rights Act of 1964, which prohibited discrimination on the basis of sex as well as of race. In other words, she arrived at a time when women were being taken more seriously by legislators. Mink has made many contributions to the fight for women's rights. She was, for example, one of the cosponsors of Title IX of the Education Act Amendments in 1972, a key law to combat discrimination against women in higher education.

Mink first served in the House from 1965 to 1977. She has been in the House for a second time since 1990. In 1992 the American Bar Association gave her its Margaret Brent award, established to honor outstanding women attorneys.

SEE ALSO

Congress, U.S.; Education Act Amendments (1972); Law

FURTHER READING

Davidson, Sue. *A Heart in Politics: Jeannette Rankin and Patsy T. Mink.* Seattle: Seal Press, 1994.

Minor v. *Happersett* (1875)

In the late 19th century, following the ratification of the 14th Amendment to the U.S. Constitution in 1868—which forbade states from enforcing laws that restricted the "privileges or immunities of citizens of the United States"—women made more than one attempt to use the amendment to obtain rights. Virginia Minor, president of the Missouri Woman Suffrage Association, tried to use it to justify going to the polls to vote. None of these attempts was successful, but the fact that the attempts were made at all demonstrates how resourceful and how motivated the activists were.

One of 150 suffragists around the country who attempted to vote in 1872 (including Susan B. Anthony), Minor tried to register as a voter and was denied that opportunity by the registrar, Reese Happersett. Her attorney husband then filed suit, claiming that the "privileges and immunities" clause in the 14th Amendment means that all citizens—defined as those born in the United States and thus women as well as men—are entitled to the protection of their privileges and immunities. This, in turn, means that a state cannot make a law restricting suffrage to men only, Francis Minor argued. The case of *Minor* v. *Happersett* was appealed all the way to the U.S. Supreme Court, where the judges unanimously declined to accept the Minors' argument.

SEE ALSO

Citizenship; 14th Amendment

Mitchell, Maria

- *Born: Aug. 1, 1818, Nantucket, Mass.*
- *Education: High school*
- *Accomplishments: First female member of the American Academy of Arts and Sciences (1848); member, American Association for the Advancement of Science (1850); professor and director of the college observatory, Vassar College (1865–88); president, Association for the Advancement of Women (1974–76)*
- *Died: June 28, 1889, Lynn, Mass.*

Maria Mitchell was the first prominent woman scientist in the United States, an astronomer and also a gifted teacher at Vassar College. Remarkably, she became a college professor without ever having attended college herself.

Growing up on the island of Nantucket, a whaling port, Mitchell absorbed the local devotion to sky-watching. The men who went to sea needed to make close observations of the stars, and they needed help from people on land. Her father checked ships' chronometers (exacting ship clocks) using stellar observations, and his daughter became his assistant. Over time, their work attracted admiring attention, and the Nantucket lookout became a station of the U.S. Coast Survey, which was charged with observing the stars. Making thousands of observations, Maria Mitchell was fortunate (and hardworking) enough to discover a new comet on October 1, 1847.

The astronomer Maria Mitchell leads a class of Vassar College students in 1878. They are standing in front of the observatory the college built for Mitchell.

Mitchell's discovery sealed her fame. The king of Denmark awarded her a medal, and she began to be elected to previously all-male scientific societies. Therefore, it is not surprising that in 1865 when Matthew Vassar was recruiting faculty for the new women's college he was developing, he thought of Maria Mitchell. She hesitated, unsure whether it was appropriate for a relatively unschooled woman to teach in such an institution. To help entice her, Vassar promised to provide her with a 12-inch telescope, which would be the third largest in the country. She finally accepted, and she fulfilled all of his expectations by being an inspirational teacher while continuing her own research. She also became active on behalf of women's rights generally and women's right to a scientific education in particular.

SEE ALSO

Science

FURTHER READING

Gormley, Beatrice. *Maria Mitchell: The Soul of an Astronomer.* Grand Rapids, Mich.: Wm. B. Eerdmans, 1995.

Rossiter, Margaret. *Women Scientists in America: Struggles and Strategies to 1940.* Baltimore: Johns Hopkins University Press, 1982.

Monroe, Marilyn

- *Born: June 1, 1926, Los Angeles, Calif.*
- *Education: High school*
- *Accomplishments: Actress; cultural icon*
- *Died: Aug. 5, 1962, Los Angeles, Calif.*

In her brief life Marilyn Monroe defined what it meant to be a movie star, and after her death she became, if anything, even more famous as a symbol of glamour. But for all her success, she was always haunted by insecurity, and she eventually took her own life.

She was born Norma Jean Mortenson (later adopting Baker, her mother's name), the daughter of a woman with a history of mental problems, who was unmarried at the time of Norma Jean's birth. The girl who would grow up to be Marilyn Monroe had a loveless childhood. She married young, but the marriage did not last long. Soon she was getting modeling jobs and working toward a career in Hollywood. She appeared in her first movie in 1948, having been renamed by her studio, and by the early 1950s she was beginning to be a star. Her studio cast her primarily as a sex goddess.

Monroe wanted, however, to be taken seriously as an actress. With this goal in mind, she went to New York to study at the Actors Studio, known for training the performers in a naturalistic style known as "the method." But despite much box-office success, her behavior at work became increasingly difficult for her fellow actors to deal with. She was often late, for example, and did not always know her lines.

Marilyn Monroe pauses during the filming of Some Like it Hot *(1959) for a publicity photo with co-star Tony Curtis. "Hollywood is a place where they'll pay you a thousand dollars for a kiss," she once said, "and fifty cents for your soul."*

The problems in her personal life no doubt added to her unhappiness. In the 1950s she married two of the most famous men in the country: the former baseball star Joe DiMaggio and the playwright Arthur Miller. Neither of these marriages lasted very long.

Monroe died after taking an overdose of sleeping pills at her home in Los Angeles. She left behind a number of movies in which she had created memorable roles, such as Sugar Kane in *Some Like It Hot,* Lorelei Lee in *Gentlemen Prefer Blondes,* and Pola Debevoise in *How to Marry a Millionaire.*

SEE ALSO

Movies

FURTHER READING

Guiles, Fred Lawrence. *Legend: The Life and Death of Marilyn Monroe.* Lanham, Md.: Scarborough House, 1991.

Rollyson, Carl E., Jr. *Marilyn Monroe: A Life of the Actress.* 1986. Reprint, New York: Da Capo, 1993.

Moody, Helen Wills

- *Born: Oct. 6, 1905, Centerville, Calif.*
- *Education: University of California, Berkeley, B.A., 1927*
- *Accomplishments: U.S. Tennis champion (1923–25, 1927–29, 1931); Olympic gold medal (1924); Wimbledon singles champion (1928–30, 1932–33, 1935, 1938); author,* Tennis *(1928) and* Fifteen-Thirty: The Story of a Tennis Player *(1937); International Tennis Hall of Fame (1959)*
- *Died: Jan. 1, 1998, Carmel, Calif.*

One of the great athletes of the 20th century, Helen Wills Moody dominated women's tennis in the 1920s and 1930s. Until Martina Navratilova came along in the 1970s, no other woman was able to win eight singles championships at Wimbledon, where the English championships are held. Wills Moody also added many other titles to her string of victories.

In 1927 Wills graduated from the University of California at Berkeley, having already begun her incredible winning ways on the tennis court. After marrying Frederick Moody in 1929, she competed using her married name—although the marriage ended in divorce in 1937. She later married again.

Known for her power and grace while playing tennis, Wills Moody was also known for her fierce concentration—so much so that she acquired the nickname of "Little Miss Poker Face." She was a path-breaking figure in establishing women athletes as serious competitors. She was also, according to her obituary in the *New York Times,* "the first American-born woman to achieve international celebrity as an athlete."

SEE ALSO

Navratilova, Martina

FURTHER READING

Englemann, Larry. *The Goddess and the American Girl: The Story of Suzanne Lenglen and Helen Wills.* New York: Oxford University Press, 1988.

Lumpkin, Angela. *Women's Tennis: A Historical Documentary of the Players and Their Game.* Troy, N.Y.: Whitston, 1981.

Moreno, Luisa

- *Born: 1907?, Guatemala*
- *Education: High school*
- *Accomplishments: Organizer, first National Congress of Spanish-Speaking People (1938)*
- *Died: 1990?*

Luisa Moreno was a path-breaking figure in organizing workers of all ethnic backgrounds to join unions and also in organizing Latino immigrants to claim their civil rights as Americans.

Born in Guatemala to upper-class parents, she moved to Mexico, where she married, and then on to New York City in 1928. When the U.S. economy began to collapse in the early 1930s, Moreno began working in Spanish Harlem as a sewing machine operator. There she founded a Latina garment workers union, an achievement that brought her to the attention of the American Federation of Labor (AFL), the mainstream labor organization. The AFL hired her as a professional organizer, but she soon switched to the rival and more progressive Congress of Industrial Organizations (CIO), which was more to the liking of this increasingly radical woman.

In 1938 the CIO launched the United Cannery, Agricultural, Packing, and Allied Workers of America (UCAPAWA), and Moreno became one of the

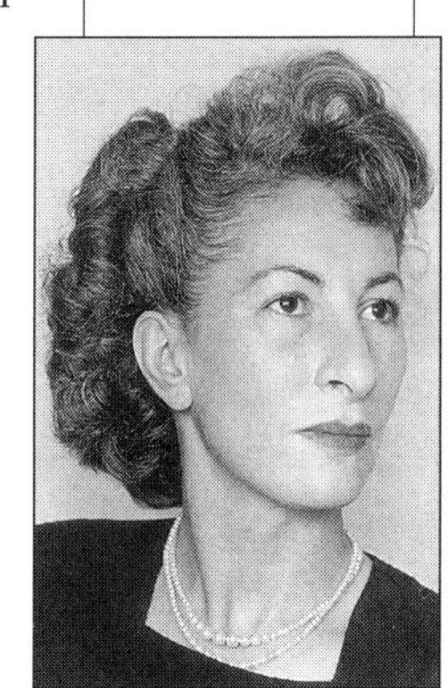

Luisa Moreno helped lead the pecan shellers' strike in Texas in 1930. Mexicana and Chicana workers who picketed were gassed, arrested, and jailed, but ultimately were victorious.

key organizers for it. In this capacity she brought thousands of Mexican food-processing workers in the Southwest, 75 percent of them women, into the ranks of organized labor. In 1939 she also organized El Congreso de Pueblos Que Hablan Español (Spanish-Speaking Peoples' Congress), the first Latino civil rights assembly.

After World War II the United States became much more conservative than it had been in the 1930s. UCAPAWA disintegrated, and Luisa Moreno was deported on the grounds that she had once belonged to the Communist party. Though the details of her life are sketchy, and much of what she worked to build did not survive, she remains a towering figure in American labor history because of her pioneering work.

SEE ALSO

Labor movement

FURTHER READING

Ruiz, Vicki. *Cannery Women, Cannery Lives.* Albuquerque: University of New Mexico Press, 1987.

Mormons

Women belonging to the Mormon church, officially known as the Church of Jesus Christ of Latter-day Saints, have had a history like no other group of American women. This is because in the early stages of the religion's growth and development, it permitted plural marriages, with one man able to marry several wives. Only when the federal government banned plural marriage in 1884, thus barring Utah (the home of most Mormons) from statehood, did the church rescind the policy.

Founded in 1830 by self-proclaimed prophet Joseph Smith during a time of widespread social ferment, the Mormon church endured much persecution owing to its ideas about the family before members found a safe home on the shores of the Great Salt Lake in Utah in the 1840s.

The "Benevolence Panel" on the Relief Society Centennial Memorial in Salt Lake City honors the work of women. It depicts a strong, mature woman giving encouragement to a young mother, a boy, and an aged grandmother.

Some of the Mormons' ideas about women reflected the egalitarian philosophy being propounded by progressive thinkers during the 1830s, and some of their beliefs supported traditional sex roles. Smith, for example, attributed great spiritual gifts to women, and his successor Brigham Young urged women to attend college. On the other hand, a housewife named Sonia Johnson was excommunicated in 1979 for publicly endorsing the Equal Rights Amendment. Today, Mormon women are more likely to attain a university education than are non-Mormons. Yet they are more conservative than the average American woman when it comes to support for large families and opposition to abortion.

One activity that has sent Mormon women out of the home has been their missionary work on behalf of the church, work that often has them living abroad for years in developing countries.

FURTHER READING

Bushman, Claudia L., ed. *Mormon Sisters: Women in Early Utah.* New ed. Logan: Utah State University Press, 1997.

Bushman, Richard, and Claudia L. Bushman. *Mormons in America.* New York: Oxford University Press, 1998.

Hurd, Jerrie W. *Our Sisters in the Latter-day Scriptures.* Salt Lake City: Deseret Book Co., 1987.

Morrison, Toni

- *Born: Feb. 18, 1931, Lorain, Ohio*
- *Education: Howard University, B.A., 1953; Cornell University, M.A., 1955*
- *Accomplishments: National Book Critics Circle Award and American Academy and Institute of Arts and Letters Award for* Song of Solomon *(1977); Pulitzer Prize for* Beloved *(1987); Nobel Prize in literature (1993); author,* The Bluest Eye *(1970);* Sula *(1973);* Song of Solomon *(1977);* Tar Baby *(1981);* Dreaming Emmett *(1986);* Beloved *(1987);* Jazz *(1992);* Paradise *(1999)*

Toni Morrison is widely recognized as one of the greatest American writers of the 20th century. Her searing novels have illuminated the African-American experience, making it integral to the unfolding of American history.

Born Chloe Anthony Wofford to a working-class black family in Ohio, the young woman graduated from Howard University in 1953 and subsequently obtained a master's degree in English from Cornell University. She then wed Harold Morrison, a marriage that produced two sons and ended in divorce in 1964. During this period of her life, she taught and then went to work for the publishing company Random House, where she rose to the position of senior editor. Morrison also wrote her own novels at the same time, including *Song of Solomon* and *The Bluest Eye.*

Toni Morrison, the first black woman to receive a Nobel Prize in Literature, has always taken her teaching as seriously as her writing. In 1987 she became the first black woman writer to hold a named chair at an Ivy League university, Princeton.

With the publication of *Beloved* in 1987, about the long-term evil consequences of slavery, Morrison established herself as part of the canon of American writers. The novel won the Pulitzer Prize and undoubtedly played a major role in her winning the Nobel Prize in 1993. In 1988 Morrison was appointed to an endowed chair at Princeton University, a pinnacle of academic success.

FURTHER READING

Century, Douglas. *Toni Morrison.* New York: Chelsea House, 1994.

Middleton, David L. *Toni Morrison's Fiction: Contemporary Criticism.* New York: Garland, 1997.

Taylor-Guthrie, Danille. *Conversations with Toni Morrison.* Jackson: University Press of Mississippi, 1994.

Moskowitz, Belle Lindner Israels

- *Born: Oct. 5, 1877, New York, N.Y.*
- *Education: Teachers College, Columbia University, attended 1894–95*
- *Accomplishments: Political advisor to N.Y. governor Al Smith; campaign manager for Al Smith's presidential campaign (1928)*
- *Died: Jan. 2, 1933, New York, N.Y.*

In the 1920s the most politically powerful woman in the United States was Belle Moskowitz, someone that most people had never even heard of. But if you were an insider in New York politics, you knew about Moskowitz, because she was the right-hand woman of Democratic governor Al Smith: with a superb grasp of technical aspects of governance, she advised him on nearly every major decision.

It is ironic but not surprising that a woman who never ran for office was more influential than the handful of female officeholders in the first decade after the achievement of woman suffrage. There was no tradition then of female authority (except in the home and in school), let alone one of powerful women in U.S. government. Moskowitz worked behind the scenes, took pains not to call attention to herself, and knew that she was valuable to the governor and to the state.

Born to a family of Jewish immigrants from Poland, Belle Lindner studied for one year at Columbia University before starting her work with a settlement house (where middle-class women set themselves up in a slum neighborhood in order to provide aid and training to the poor residents). After marrying Charles Israels in 1903, she became the mother of three children but continued to be very active in reform circles. New York granted women the right to vote in 1917, and Al Smith began looking for someone who could help him build bridges to the new voters. He was introduced to Moskowitz (by then remarried after having been widowed in 1911), and the two of them formed one of the most potent partnerships in U.S. political history. One of their most significant achievements was the modernization of the state's antiquated administrative structure.

SEE ALSO

Politics

FURTHER READING

Perry, Elisabeth Israels. *Belle Moskowitz.* New York: Oxford University Press, 1987.

Motherhood

Motherhood is both a biological part of life and a socially created condition, and the circumstances surrounding motherhood have changed over time. How safe will childbirth be? How many children will a woman have—and will she be able to control her own reproductive destiny? Who will rear the children? How much moral authority will a mother enjoy in the society? How much power will she have in the family? Will a woman have to sacrifice her personal ambition in order to be a parent (as a man does not)? What are the chances that either death or divorce will end her relationship with her child's father before the child is grown? Indeed, will she be married to the child's father? The answers to all of these questions have changed dramatically during the centuries of American history.

In the colonial period, family size was large, and so far as we now know, women did nothing to control their fertility until the Quakers began practicing family limitation in the 18th century. Childbirth could be quite dangerous for both the mother and her baby. Women had little choice in such concerns, however, since family decisions largely rested with the husband.

In the 19th century, Americans began to sentimentalize motherhood as never before and, as a consequence, began to regard women as morally superior to men. As a result, women who lacked many of the rights of citizenship were able to use the reverence for motherhood quite effectively to assert influence within the family and also in the larger society. During the Civil War, for example, women argued for their right to take humanitarian initiatives in the name of their motherhood.

The sentimentalization of motherhood also had its costs for women. The ideal mother was a Protestant, middle-class, white woman, and those who did not fit that mold might not have been able to benefit from the social respect that others enjoyed. Indeed, immigrants and women of color were often assumed to be less competent mothers than their white, middle-class counterparts and had to suffer the indignity of being preached to by middle-class reformers about their maternal duties.

In the 20th century, family size has shrunk, women now have ready access to birth control, children are increasingly being born to or reared by single women, and lesbian couples are slowly winning acceptance of their legal rights to co-mother children. All these developments demonstrate how much motherhood has changed over time. In the area of technology, too, there has been such vast change as to make the very term *mother* difficult to define. For example, when a woman acts as a surrogate mother for an infertile couple, is she considered the mother or is it the adoptive parent who will rear the child?

SEE ALSO

Birth control; Childbirth; Families

FURTHER READING

Blakely, Mary Kay. *American Mom: Motherhood, Politics, and Humble Pie.* Chapel Hill, N.C.: Algonquin, 1994.

Hays, Sharon. *The Culture Contradictions of Motherhood.* New Haven, Conn.: Yale University Press, 1996.

Spain, Daphne, and Suzanne M. Bianchi. *Balancing Act: Motherhood, Marriage, and Employment Among American Women.* New York: Russell Sage Foundation, 1996.

Mother's Day

On May 9, 1914, President Woodrow Wilson proclaimed the second Sunday of May as Mother's Day, a national holiday. This followed a short campaign launched by Philadelphian Anna Jarvis in 1907 after the death of her own mother.

Between 1907 and 1914, Jarvis wrote letters and sought support among the Protestant churches for her holiday. In fact, home and motherhood had been considered sacred throughout the 19th century, and others had suggested that such an observance might be appropriate before Jarvis began her campaign. In 1872, for example, Julia Ward Howe, author of "The Battle Hymn of the Republic," proposed setting aside June 2 as a day dedicated to peace and to honoring mothers. In 1907 Jarvis provided, in effect, the spark for a movement that was ready to catch fire.

Mott, Lucretia Coffin

- *Born: Jan. 3, 1793, Nantucket, Mass.*
- *Education: Private high school*
- *Accomplishments: Co-organizer, Anti-Slavery Convention of American Women (1837); co-organizer, Seneca Falls women's rights convention (1848); president, American Equal Rights Association (1866); co-organizer, Free Religious Association (1867)*
- *Died: Nov. 11, 1880, Roadside, Pa.*

One of the leaders of the 19th-century women's movement, Lucretia Mott was a Quaker preacher, an abolitionist, and a pioneer suffragist. She was also a devoted wife and mother, blessed with a husband who fully supported all of her causes for the 57 years of their marriage.

Raised in a Quaker household in which women's rights were taken very seriously, Lucretia Coffin married the teacher James Mott in 1811, after having briefly worked as a teacher herself. She gave birth to six children, but she also found time to

This 1841 portrait of abolitionist and feminist Lucretia Mott was used on her visiting card and is the earliest known likeness of her.

interest herself in reform and to become a minister, a type of training for public speaking that was then unavailable to women outside the Quaker faith. In 1837 she helped organize the Anti-Slavery Convention of American Women.

In 1840 she was chosen to attend the World's Anti-Slavery Convention in London. The London event was an important turning point. After traveling across the Atlantic Ocean, Mott and the other American women in attendance found that, because of their gender, they were denied recognition as delegates. Though many American men protested, there was no recourse.

Mott had not wasted her time by going to London, however, because there she met Elizabeth Cady Stanton. Eight years later the two women, recalling their exclusion at the London meeting, convened the first women's rights meeting in the United States, held in Seneca Falls, New York.

As she grew older, Mott continued to be a source of inspiration for younger women, owing to her ceaseless labors in the cause of human freedom. (The Mott home, for example, harbored runaway slaves in the years before the Civil War.) She was also influential in Quaker circles, moving her faith in more religiously liberal directions, such as the rejection of the doctrine of inborn human depravity.

SEE ALSO

Seneca Falls Convention; Stanton, Elizabeth Cady; Suffrage, woman

FURTHER READING

Bryant, Jennifer. *Lucretia Mott: A Guiding Light.* Grand Rapids, Mich.: Eerdmans, 1996.

Flexner, Eleanor, and Ellen Fitzpatrick. *Century of Struggle.* Cambridge: Harvard University Press, 1996.

Mott, Lucretia. *Lucretia Mott, Her Complete Speeches and Sermons.* Edited by Dana Greene. New York: E. Mellen, 1980.

Movies

Ever since movies became an important part of American popular culture in the early 1900s, the screen has been filled with glamorous women who could inspire fantasies. Women have been temptresses, mothers, or flirty girls. What they usually have not been is powerful—except in terms of their sexual allure. If female characters on-screen have been successful, they have also often been depicted as love-starved or frustrated. That most of the powerful positions in the movie industry, other than that of performer, have typically been filled by men has no doubt contributed to the distorted view of womankind seen on-screen.

Interestingly, women *did* play a significant role off-screen before the movies became a big business with the emergence of the studios in the 1920s. Women directed, wrote screenplays, and even produced. For example, 26 women directed movies in Hollywood between 1913 and 1927. The best-known movie star from the early years, Mary Pickford, even participated in the founding of a studio, United Artists. As the studios took over more and more of the movie production, however, the off-screen power of women diminished—though it never vanished completely.

A tremendously savvy businesswoman, the actress Mary Pickford controlled every facet of her career with a firm hand. Film historian Kevin Brownlow describes her as "one of the few great stars who was also a great producer."

Were someone to screen a few of the best-known films from each decade in the 20th century, she would gain some insight into the changing roles of American women. At first, movies were silent, and actors and actresses mimed their performances. The silent era produced some great stars, such as Mary Pickford, who was "America's Sweetheart" in girlish roles during the 1910s. The Roaring 20s introduced the fun-loving flapper, best personified by Clara Bow, with her short dark hair, short skirts, and fun-loving demeanor.

With the invention of sound in 1927, female roles continued to evolve. The 1930s saw a diverse array of big stars—from the platinum blonde Jean Harlow, who often played a spunky working-class woman, to the temptress Mae West, to the little girl star, Shirley Temple. Marlene Dietrich was another glamorous beauty. In 1932's *Shanghai Express,* she played a shady lady who befriended another woman, a Chinese national, a daring plot line for those unenlightened days of rampant on-screen racism.

Indeed, certain of the big women stars of the 1930s such as Dietrich, West, Harlow, Greta Garbo, Bette Davis, and Katharine Hepburn played strong women. But during these years—and well beyond—if a woman was depicted as having a career, this was seen as an indication that she was unfulfilled as a female. She usually gave up her job in the last scene, having found Mr. Right.

World War II (1941–45) and the postwar years brought immense changes in women's roles in society and a great deal of anxiety about the extent of the transformation. These were years in which movies portrayed very few strong women but many glamorous ones, above all, Marilyn Monroe.

The social change that exploded throughout the country during the 1960s and 1970s, a period in which both ideas about women's roles and racial attitudes were being transformed, not surprisingly brought new types of women to the screen. For example, in *Alice Doesn't Live Here Anymore,* (1975) Ellen Burstyn played a small-town wife and mother who, newly widowed, sets out with her son to find herself. In *Norma Rae* (1979) Sally Field played a textile worker who finds the courage to help organize a union. Both women won Academy Awards for best actress for their performances.

Sally Field in the title role of the 1979 film Norma Rae *protests conditions in the textile plant where she works, mirroring earlier events in women's history.*

Since the 1980s women have once again been filling many significant off-screen roles. In 1980 Sherry Lansing became the first woman of the modern era to head a studio, Twentieth-Century Fox. There are now many well-established women directors and producers, as well as many women editors and screenwriters. In 1996 actress Emma Thompson won an Academy Award for her screenplay of *Sense and Sensibility.*

Male stars, however, currently constitute the overwhelming majority of those who can "open" a movie, that is, draw an audience into a theater. As a genre, action films typically enjoy the most success at the box office, supported by young males who are avid moviegoers, and they often feature few or no women in important roles. As a consequence, male stars are typically command higher salaries than do females.

SEE ALSO

Monroe, Marilyn; Pickford, Mary; Black, Shirley Temple; West, Mae

FURTHER READING

Acker, Ally. *Reel Women: Pioneers of the Cinema, 1896 to the Present.* New York: Continuum, 1993.

Basinger, Jeanine. *A Woman's View: How Hollywood Spoke to Women, 1930–1960.* New York: Knopf, 1993.

Cook, Pam, and Philip Doo. *Women and Film: A Sight and Sound Reader.* Philadelphia: Temple University Press, 1993.

Haskell, Molly. *Holding My Own in No Man's Land: Women and Men, Film and Feminists.* New York: Oxford University Press, 1997.

Muller v. *Oregon* (1908)

Muller v. *Oregon* was a landmark Supreme Court decision, because for the first time the Court accepted sociological evidence in addition to arguments based on legal precedent in arriving at an opinion. The case upheld laws protecting working women and is important for both women's history *and* for constitutional history.

In the early 20th century, reformers—often led by settlement-house women living in slum neighborhoods—tried to find ways of improving working conditions for women in factories. Under their prodding, a state would pass a law setting up maximum hours for women, only to see conservative judges overturn the law (mostly on the basis that it violated freedom of contract).

Tired of such defeats, a young lawyer named Louis Brandeis decided to try a radically new approach to justify the protection of women workers. When there was a challenge to an Oregon law that had established maximum hours for women, Brandeis submitted a massive brief defending the law to the Supreme Court, a brief that included more than 100 pages of statistical information about the relationship between women's hours and their health and morals. The Court unanimously accepted Brandeis's argument and upheld the Oregon law. States could then pass laws on behalf of women's welfare secure in the knowledge that such legislation was likely to be upheld.

Modern feminists have debated whether the Brandeis brief may have cost women more than it benefited them, because it provided arguments for treating the two sexes differently—potential mothers had to be treated as more fragile than men—and may have hindered women from securing well-paid jobs. At the time, though, it was seen as an unqualified success.

SEE ALSO

Settlement-house movement

FURTHER READING

Woloch, Nancy. *Muller v. Oregon: A Brief History with Documents.* Boston: Bedford, 1996.

Murray, Judith Sargent

- *Born: May 1, 1751, Gloucester, Mass.*
- *Education: Extensive informal education*
- *Accomplishments: Poet and regular columnist ("The Gleaner" column) for the* Massachusetts Magazine *(1792–94); author,* The Medium, or A Happy Tea Party *(1795) and* The Traveller Returned *(1796)*
- *Died: July 6, 1820, Natchez, Miss.*

Born in the middle of the 18th century, Judith Sargent Murray was one of the very earliest Americans to write about women's rights. Using the pen name of Constantia in essays for various periodicals, she discussed such topics as improving the education available to girls or the need for young women to develop a healthy self-respect.

Young Judith Sargent, the eldest child of a wealthy shipowner and his wife, was fortunate enough to obtain a good education: her family allowed her to participate in her younger brother's preparations for Harvard. After marrying at 18, she became a widow while still a young woman and subsequently married her pastor, John Murray, with whom she had two children. John Murray was the founder of American Universalism, a Christian denomination that emphasized the human capacity for improvement rather than more traditional ideas about original sin.

With her unorthodox views on gender joined to her unorthodox ideas about religion, Judith Sargent Murray left a body of writing in which she explored themes that were very much ahead of her time. Indeed, her *On the Equality of the Sexes* was the first feminist tract to be published in the United States.

FURTHER READING

Skemp, Sheila A. *Judith Sargent Murray: A Brief Biography with Documents.* Boston: Bedford, 1998.

Murray, Pauli

- *Born: Nov. 20, 1910, Baltimore, Md.*
- *Education: Hunter College, B.A., 1933; Howard University, LL.D., 1944; Yale University, J.D., 1965; General Theological Seminary, ordained 1977*
- *Accomplishments: Co-founder, National Organization of Women (1966); first black woman Episcopal minister (ordained 1977); author,* Proud Shoes: The Story of an American Family *(1956),* Dark Testament and Other Poems *(1970), and* Song in a Weary Throat: An American Pilgrimage *(1987)*
- *Died: July 1, 1985, Pittsburgh, Pa.*

Black activist Pauli Murray distinguished herself in several different fields of endeavor: she was a lawyer, taught in the university, wrote poetry and nonfiction, and late in life, served as an Episcopal priest, the first African-American woman to be ordained in that denomination.

Born in Baltimore, Murray graduated from Hunter College in New York City in 1933. She then obtained a law degree from Howard University, where she was the only woman in her class, and soon thereafter became a deputy attorney general of California. She pursued further legal study at both the University of California at Berkeley and at Yale, from which she received the degree of Doctor of Juridical Science in 1965. Between 1968 and 1973 she was a professor of American Studies at Brandeis University. She next attended a theological seminary in New York and was ordained as a priest in 1977.

ELECT

PAULI MURRAY

for CITY COUNCIL

10th Senatorial District

FORMER DEPUTY ATTORNEY GENERAL

Citizen's Union says: A lawyer with an unusually keen intellect, broad social vision, and a wealth of experience in public affairs.

Education
Hunter College B.A., 1933
Brookwood Labor College, 1936-7
Howard University, L.L.B., *Cum Laude,* 1944
University of California, L.L.M., 1945

Background
Lawyer
Formerly staff member, Workers Defense League; American Jewish Congress; National Urban League
Deputy Attorney General, State of California

Member:
N. A. A. C. P.
National Council of Negro Women
Citizens Committee of Children
N. Y. County Lawyers Association
Liberal Party, Civil Liberties Committee

Indorsed by Americans for Democratic Action.

TENANTS — IF YOU HAVE LANDLORD TROUBLES CONSULT YOUR LOCAL LIBERAL PARTY CLUB FOR FREE SERVICE

Issued by the LIBERAL PARTY, Kings County
66 Court Street • TR. 5-8026

VOTE ROW D

A poster for one of Pauli Murray's first campaigns lists her "wealth of experience in public affairs." Murray was a distinguished fighter in the campaign for civil rights for African Americans as well as in the struggle for women's rights.

With a full professional life, Murray also found the time to be active on behalf of civil rights as well as the women's movement. Indeed she called upon African-American women to carry on both struggles simultaneously as she did. As a young woman she had helped organize sit-ins at two Washington, D.C., restaurants to desegregate them. Later in life, she was one of the founders of the National Organization for Women. In addition to poetry, she published an autobiography, *Song in a Weary Throat,* in 1987. The book opened with the following poem:

Hope is a crushed stalk
Between clenched fingers.
Hope is a bird's wing
Broken by a stone.
Hope is a word in a tuneless ditty
A word whispered with the wind,
A dream of forty acres and a mule,
A cabin of one's own and a moment
  to rest,
A name and a place for one's children
And children's children at last . . .
Hope is a song in a weary throat.

FURTHER READING

Murray, Pauli. *Pauli Murray: The Autobiography of a Black Activist, Feminist, Lawyer, Priest, and Poet.* Knoxville: University of Tennessee Press, 1989.

Music

Women have long received great acclaim in some areas of music—as singers and instrumental soloist—and have had great difficulty achieving access in others, such as composing, conducting, and performing as part of either a symphony orchestra or a band that plays popular music. Women won the right to perform in symphony orchestras, for example, only in the 1960s. Indeed, at the end of the 20th century, the famed Vienna Philharmonic in Austria is still all-male, because, it is claimed, women musicians would ruin the group's sound quality.

The reason for this odd split between what was and what was not acceptable for women owes to a musical version of the idea that a woman's place was in the home. In the 18th and 19th centuries, women's music was supposed to be amateur and domestic, while men performed the serious professional music in concert halls outside the home. To play the piano and sing well enough to entertain friends at home was one of the necessary accomplishments of a well-brought-up young lady, but this did not mean that music lessons were supposed to lead to high levels of artistic achievement.

Yet the 19th century also saw the beginnings of significant change. Two European sopranos, in particular, toured the United States to massive acclaim. Americans adored Jenny Lind, "the Swedish nightingale," and the Italian Adelina Patti (who actually grew up in New York City). Operas—with leading roles going to female performers—began to be immensely popular, and Americans began to accept the idea of women as professional musicians. In the 1880s all-women orchestras began to appear in certain cities.

One area in which women began to compose as well as participate was religious music. Some of the best-known and best-loved American Christian hymns, such as "Jesus Loves Me," were written by women in the 19th century.

Toward the latter part of the century appeared the first important American woman composer of classical music, Amy Beach, who insisted on being known as Mrs. H. H. A. Beach. Trained as a pianist, Beach composed her *Gaelic Symphony* and saw it performed by the Boston Symphony in 1896, a historic event because it was believed to be the first time a woman's symphony was publicly performed by a major orchestra. Some of Beach's religious music is still part of the Protestant repertory.

The 20th century has seen more composers as well as many female performers of classical music, both vocal and instrumental. Women conductors have also appeared, the best known of whom, Sarah Caldwell, founded her own company—the Opera Company of Boston—and in 1976 conducted at the Metropolitan Opera in New York, the

Amy Beach (seated) with members of the Tollefson chamber group, at the Neighborhood Music School in Brooklyn, New York, 1940. A child prodigy, she began composing music at age four and performing publicly at age seven. Beach wrote more than 150 numbered works ranging from chamber and orchestral works to church music and songs.

first time that a woman had been accorded that honor. Further, women have helped keep classical music alive through their involvement as patrons and volunteers. During the middle decades of the 20th century, their efforts sustained the Community Concerts series, which brought performers to small cities throughout the country. During this time women also formed all-woman orchestras, so as to be able to have the experience of performing classical music for orchestras themselves.

In popular music, too, women have had more success as vocalists than in other areas of the field. Some of the greatest blues and jazz artists have been female vocalists, such as Gertrude ("Ma") Rainey, Bessie Smith, Billie Holiday, Ella Fitzgerald, and Carmen McRae. A few women—Janis Joplin, Diana Ross, and Madonna, for example—have become stars in rock music. Soul singers Mahalia Jackson and Aretha Franklin have built bridges between the music of the black church and the world of pop music. Whitney Houston is one of the best-loved pop singers in the country.

Successful country vocalists include Kitty Wells, Patsy Cline, Loretta Lynn, Tammy Wynette, and Dolly Parton. Other women have built enormous followings as folk artists, women such as Joan Baez, Joni Mitchell, and Judy Collins. As for Barbra Streisand, she has acted in and directed movies in addition to the millions of albums she has sold as an immensely popular vocal performer.

Today's concertgoer will encounter a scene very different from anything seen just a few decades ago. At classical concerts men and women play side by side. In rock music, women performers, including instrumentalists, are beginning to gain more acceptance and even acclaim, as witnessed by the great popularity of the all-women-performers Lilith Fair tours organized by singer Sarah McLachlan in 1997, 1998, and 1999. The name of the event evokes the Hebrew folk tale about Lilith, Adam's first wife, who refused to subordinate herself to Adam and was banished from Eden to become a spirit associated with the seductive aspect of woman's nature.

SEE ALSO

Joplin, Janis; Rainey, Gertrude Pridgett ("Ma"); Smith, Bessie

Ella Fitzgerald in 1964. Of the magic her voice produced, the New York Times *drama critic Brooks Atkinson wrote, "She manages things that the human voice can't do."*

FURTHER READING

Ammer, Christine. *Unsung: A History of Women in American Music.* Westport, Conn.: Greenwood, 1980.

Neuls, Bates, Carol, ed. *Women in Music: An Anthology of Source Readings from the Middle Ages to the Present.* Rev. ed. Boston: Northeastern University Press, 1996.

Pendle, Karen, ed. *Women and Music: A History.* Bloomington: Indiana University Press, 1991.

Muslims

Many but not all Muslims in the United States come from the Middle East. The Islamic faith has believers in Indonesia, Malaysia, and certain African countries as well as in the Middle East. Moreover, thousands of African Americans, such as the Black Muslims, have been converts to Islam.

Since the founding of the state of Israel in 1948, there has been tension between Israel and the Arab world, and Palestinians seeking a homeland have committed acts of terrorism against Jews. Such terrorism and Jewish retaliation have sustained regional patterns of violence. This violence, as well as the rise of a fundamentalist, militant strain of Islam in several parts of the Middle East, has helped form the American public's negative perception of Muslims, especially those from the Middle East. The overwhelming majority of Middle Eastern and other Muslim immigrants, however, are law-abiding and hardworking people who have come to the United States for economic opportunities and to give their children a better life.

Muslim immigrants belong to several different strains of Islam. Among some, women must obey dress codes and follow rules about public demeanor so as not to seem sexually enticing to men. Because of perceived public prejudice against Muslims, women have been known to cling to their familiar roles from the homeland all the more tightly so as to make a statement of affirmation of their heritage in the face of public hostility.

FURTHER READING

Anway, Carol Anderson. *Daughters of Another Path: Experiences of American Women Choosing Islam.* Lee's Summit, Mo.: Yawna, 1996.

Haddad, Yvonne Yazbeck, ed. *The Muslims of America.* New York: Oxford University Press, 1991.

Haddad, Yvonne Yazbeck, and John L. Esposito, eds. *Islam, Gender & Social Change.* New York: Oxford University Press, 1998.

Naff, Alixa. *The Arab Americans.* New York: Chelsea House, 1988.

National American Woman Suffrage Association (NAWSA)

Founded in 1890 as the result of a merger between two rival suffrage organizations, the National American Woman Suffrage Association (NAWSA) was the major suffrage group in the United States when women won the right to vote in 1920.

Until the Reconstruction period following the Civil War, the woman suffrage movement was small, but it was united. In the late 1860s, however, serious disagreements arose over the question of the vote for African-American men. Some suffragists agreed with the abolitionist men that the time was right for getting the vote for freedmen and that to introduce the question of woman suffrage at the same time might fatally weaken the whole enterprise.

Other suffragists felt betrayed that

their interests were being set aside at the very moment when the whole nature of citizenship was being questioned and renegotiated.

The first group, led by Lucy Stone and Henry Ward Beecher, called itself the American Woman Suffrage Association. The other group, consisting of women only and led by Elizabeth Cady Stanton and Susan B. Anthony, called itself the National Woman Suffrage Association. After a generation of bad feelings, the two groups united in 1890 as NAWSA, with Stanton as the first president. They were able to reunite because time had elapsed and black men had already gotten the vote, so that was no longer a divisive issue.

SEE ALSO

Anthony, Susan Brownell; Reconstruction; Stanton, Elizabeth Cady; Stone, Lucy; Suffrage

FURTHER READING

DuBois, Ellen Carol. *Feminism and Suffrage.* Ithaca, N.Y.: Cornell University Press, 1978.

Graham, Sara Hunter. *Woman Suffrage and the New Democracy.* New Haven, Conn.: Yale University Press, 1996.

National Association for the Advancement of Colored People (NAACP)

The National Association for the Advancement of Colored People (NAACP) has been the major civil rights organization for African Americans throughout most of the 20th century. Women participated in the founding conference in 1909, and they have been important to the group ever since. Indeed, three have led it, including most recently Myrlie Evers Williams in the 1990s. Throughout its history, many of the civil rights cases the NAACP took up featured female leadership, such as the Montgomery Bus Boycott in 1955.

Following a terrible race riot in Springfield, Illinois, in 1908 in which whites wreaked violence on blacks, a group of 60 women and men gathered to figure out ways to combat racism.

Sidewalk recruiting stations for the NAACP, such as this one in New York City in 1961, helped increase participation in the organization. Starting with 60 charter members in 1909, the NAACP boasts more than 500,000 members today.

Two black women, Mary Church Terrell and Ida B. Wells-Barnett, signed a call for racial justice that the gathering issued, which became the founding statement of the NAACP. Many white women also signed the document, including Hull House founder Jane Addams. The organization then launched a program of lobbying and public speaking. During the 1920s a black woman named Jessie Fauset served as the literary editor of the group's monthly journal, *The Crisis*.

In the years after World War II, the NAACP brought many key lawsuits that helped undermine racial segregation, including the landmark case of *Brown* v. *Board of Education of Topeka, Kansas,* in which the U.S. Supreme Court declared school segregation unconstitutional. Once a renewed civil rights movement led by the charismatic preacher Dr. Martin Luther King, Jr., took shape in the 1950s and 1960s, the NAACP began to lose its preeminent position in the African-American community, because the new groups seemed to possess greater moral urgency.

SEE ALSO

Terrell, Mary Eliza Church; Wells-Barnett, Ida B.

FURTHER READING:

Finch, Minne. *The NAACP, Its Fight for Justice*. Metuchen, N.J.: Scarecrow, 1981.

Kellogg, Charles Flint. *NAACP: a History of the National Association for the Advancement of Colored People*. Baltimore: Johns Hopkins University Press, 1967.

Wedin, Carolyn. *Inheritors of the Spirit: Mary White Ovington and the Founding of the NAACP*. New York: Wiley, 1998.

Ovington, Mary White. *Black and White Sat Down Together: The Reminiscences of an NAACP Founder*. New York: Feminist Press, 1995.

National Association of Colored Women (NACW)

When the National Federation of Afro-American Women and the National League of Colored Women merged into the National Association of Colored Women (NACW) in 1896, the resulting organization became a powerful voice for justice and progress in the African-American community. Many of the most accomplished and educated women of the day—such as educators and activists Mary McLeod Bethune and Mary Church Terrell—threw their energy into their work with the NACW.

During its heyday in the early part of the 20th century, members of the group set up settlement houses in poor neighborhoods, established schools and hospitals, and worked for suffrage and civil rights. With the founding of the National Council of Negro Women in 1935, the influence of the NACW waned, but it is still an important force in the black community on behalf of mothers and children.

SEE ALSO

Bethune, Mary McLeod; Clubs, women's; Terrell, Mary Eliza Church

National Congress of Parents and Teachers

Founded as the National Congress of Mothers in 1897, the group became the National Congress of Parents and Teachers in 1924. Most Americans, however, know it by its informal name of PTA (Parent Teacher Association). Critics of the PTA point out that it has often reflected the middle-class bias of its founders by seeing white mothers as the desirable norm. On the other hand, for much of the 20th century, the PTA has been the major organization funneling the energy of parents into the public schools.

PTA parents have raised money for such things as band uniforms and field trips, they have cooperated to support school bond issues (by which voters approve or veto borrowing to finance school construction) and they have generally worked to build public support for school programs. Moreover, in the days before the women's movement gained power in the 1970s, the PTA also served as a valuable training ground for female leadership.

FURTHER READING

National Congress of Parents and Teachers. *The Parent-Teacher Organization, Its Origins and Development.* Chicago: National Congress of Parents and Teachers, 1944.

National Consumers League (NCL)

Founded in 1899, the National Consumers League (NCL) was an important cross-class alliance that united working-class women and middle-class reformers in the effort to improve the working conditions for laborers.

Recognizing that women make the majority of purchases for their families, NCL members hoped that middle-class women could be educated to buy products created by well-treated workers. Its leader for many years, Florence Kelley, traveled tirelessly throughout the country, speaking to women's clubs, labor unions, and legislative committees and trying to influence public opinion about consumption choices and about the need to improve working conditions. At its height in the early 20th century, the NCL had 60 branches around the country.

The National Consumers League (NCL) tried to educate women to buy products made by well-treated workers. NCL catalogs reminded shoppers that "Clothes sometimes make the woman, but more often women make the clothes—YOUR clothes."

The NCL is given much of the credit for getting states to adopt protective labor legislation for women workers. On the strength of the argument that as future mothers women should not be overtaxed, states, beginning in the early 20th century, regulated the length of the workday for women and mandated rest periods for them. Later, feminists contended that this approach was a mistake, because it provided an excuse to pay women poorly and give them less access to a full range of employment options. This criticism notwithstanding, Florence Kelley and the NCL did raise public awareness about the problems of women workers and lay groundwork for legislation affecting both men and women. The NCL's influence and energy sputtered out after Kelley's death in 1932.

SEE ALSO

Kelley, Florence

National Council of Negro Women

The National Council of Negro Women, the first all-encompassing coalition of black women's organizations, was founded in 1935 by the activist (and member of President Franklin Delano Roosevelt's New Deal administration) Mary McLeod Bethune.

Bethune had long been aware of the problem of sexism within the African-American community, and this was her response. The goal of unification has always been difficult to implement—black sororities, for example, have held aloof—but the NCNW has been a highly effective organization. The Council has worked with other national organizations, such as the Urban League and the National Women's Political Caucus, to implement educational programs. The NCNW has also developed an international division for outreach to African nations.

SEE ALSO

Bethune, Mary McLeod; Clubs, women's; National Association of Colored Women (NACW); National Women's Political Caucus (NWPC)

National Federation of Business and Professional Women (BPW)

The National Federation of Business and Professional Women (BPW), founded in 1919, currently has a membership of approximately 800,000. Over the decades, the BPW has been one of the most effective advocates for such legislative change as the Equal Pay Act of 1963 and the Equal Credit Opportunity Act of 1974. Dedicated to protecting the interests of working women, the club sponsors workshops for personal and professional development and also offers opportunities for networking.

SEE ALSO

Clubs, women's

National Organization for Women (NOW)

With the founding of the National Organization for Women (NOW) in 1966, a new type of post-suffrage civil rights organization for women appeared, one dedicated to using legal means to improve women's status and to fight gender discrimination—in the courts, if necessary.

The early 1960s had seen the passage of crucial legislation such as the Equal Pay Act of 1963 and Title VII of the Civil Rights Act of 1964, which included prohibitions against sex discrimination. After these laws were passed, however, they were not always enforced, especially the laws against sex discrimination. A group of feminists led by author Betty Friedan decided to organize and build support for better enforcement. Within a few years, the organization she helped to found had grown into a major force fighting to improve women's lives, with 365 chapters and some 15,000 members nationwide and with the resources to pay for legal expertise. In 1970 NOW created a separate, tax-exempt Legal Defense and Education Fund.

After initial successes in such areas as getting newspapers to eliminate sex-segregated want ads and securing better enforcement of laws against sex discrimination, the group encountered difficulties in the 1970s when it tackled the issue of lesbian rights—thereby antagonizing some members—and when it

Feminists from the National Organization for Women (NOW), wearing chains to represent women's unequal political status, protest outside the White House in 1969.

made an all-out attempt to secure ratification of the Equal Rights Amendment. Patricia Ireland, president of NOW in the 1990s, has been a forceful voice for feminist issues, given greater visibility by the fact that the organization she heads has more than 600 chapters, despite the loss of members owing to the controversies over lesbian rights and the ERA. At the end of the 1990s, the organization's big issues included promoting a woman-friendly workplace and electing more women to office.

SEE ALSO

Civil Rights Act (1964); Equal Pay Act (1963); Equal Rights Amendment (ERA)

National Woman's Party

In the days just before the ratification of the 19th Amendment giving women the right to vote in 1920, the National Woman's Party was known as the country's most militant suffrage group. After suffrage was won, the Woman's Party became the originator of and spark plug for the Equal Rights Amendment (ERA).

The driving force behind the Woman's Party was a young Quaker woman named Alice Paul. After going to England to study early in the 1900s, she returned to the United States full of admiration for the militancy of the British suffragists. Paul soon became critical of what she saw as the timidity of the mainstream U.S. suffrage group, the National American Woman Suffrage Association, then led by Anna Howard Shaw.

Before long, Paul and her colleagues had launched a series of actions, including parades and demonstrations, and even picketed the White House soon after Woodrow Wilson had taken occupancy in 1913. At first the group called itself the Congressional Union but changed to National Woman's Party in 1917. Composed primarily of young, white, middle- and upper-class women,

Alice Paul (second from left), the best-known leader of the National Woman's Party (NWP), joins other feminists in Geneva in 1932. The NWP's tactics were more militant than those employed by the National American Woman Suffrage Association.

the group garnered much publicity for the cause of woman suffrage.

In 1923 the Woman's Party secured the introduction of the ERA into Congress, a Constitutional amendment that was then unpopular with most of organized womanhood because it would have eliminated protective labor legislation for women workers. Over the decades the group stayed true to its goal, and eventually many others came to support the ERA, too.

The Woman's Party still survives, though not as an important force as it once was. Over the decades it attracted few younger women, the older stalwarts died off, and the group became more conservative as it dwindled in size.

SEE ALSO

Equal Rights Amendment (ERA); National American Woman Suffrage Association (NAWSA); Paul, Alice

FURTHER READING

Cott, Nancy. *The Grounding of Modern Feminism.* New Haven: Yale University Press, 1987.

Ford, Linda. *Iron-Jawed Angels: The Suffrage Militancy of the National Woman's Party, 1912–1920.* Lanham, Md.: University Press of America, 1991.

Lunardini, Christine A. *From Equal Suffrage to Equal Rights: Alice Paul and the National Woman's Party, 1910–1928.* New York: New York University Press, 1986.

National Women's Political Caucus (NWPC)

Founded in 1971, the National Women's Political Caucus (NWPC) was the first organization in U.S. history devoted to electing women to office. Bipartisan, the NWPC is dedicated to electing women who support a woman's right to have an abortion and who concur with the group's bottom-line issues such as support for the Equal Rights Amendment. With some 35,000 members in 45 states, the caucus recruits, trains, and nurtures potential women leaders.

SEE ALSO

Politics

Nation of Islam

The Nation of Islam is a black nationalist and Muslim organization that emphasizes racial pride, solidarity, and self-determination. Founded by Elijah Muhammad in the 1930s, the Nation of

Islam, also known as the Black Muslims, began to attract national attention in the 1950s. The fiery eloquence of Muhammad's leading spokesman Malcolm X galvanized African Americans throughout the country into a new racial pride.

The Black Muslims based their philosophy on the tenets of the Islamic faith such as the belief in Allah, but not exclusively so. As in most other Islamic groups, women were largely consigned to a subordinate and domestic role, and expected to wear special long dresses.

After Elijah Muhammad's death in 1975, the Nation of Islam split into two branches—one led by Louis Farrakhan and consisting of those loyal to Muhammad's ideas and the other led by Wallace Muhammad, one of Elijah's sons. The latter has merged with the worldwide Islamic movement and stresses more progressive roles for African-American women than does the Farrakhan-led branch.

FURTHER READING

Haddad, Yvonne Yazbeck, and John L. Esposito, eds. *Islam, Gender, and Social Change.* New York: Oxford University Press, 1997.

Lee, Martha F. *The Nation of Islam: An American Millenarian Movement.* Syracuse, N.Y.: Syracuse University Press, 1996.

Monroe, Sylvester. "The Mirage of Farrakhan." *Time,* October 30, 1995, p.18.

Raboteau, Albert J. *African-American Religion.* New York: Oxford University Press, 1999.

Native Americans

The subject of Native American women is vast and complex, because there are today in the United States more than 450 Indian nations, and each possesses its own distinct language and culture. Women's roles differ according to region, environment, and tribal history, but Native American women do share a number of similarities.

No Indian society possessed a belief system as male-centered as that of the Christianity of the invading Europeans. For Christians, God the father created the world, without the help of any mother. And in the story of human creation, God first created a man, Adam, and then created Eve out of Adam's rib. There are many different origin stories among Native Americans, but they always include females, and some sort of sexuality, as part of the creative process.

In addition, many tribes were matrilineal—that is, descent (and often inheritance of property) passed through the mothers rather than through the fathers, as among Europeans. Generally, matrilineal societies were those in which the women played a significant role in the tribe's survival. In such societies, women usually were the farmers, in addition to their child-rearing and food preparation tasks, and the male contribution lay in hunting.

In these societies where women's contributions were essential to survival, they also often had a say in decisions

Recognized as fine weavers since the 18th century, Navajo women in the late 19th century had turned from weaving blankets for their own use to weaving rugs for the retail trade. These early-20th-century women helped support their families with their craft while watching over their children.

about war and peace. Men were almost always the warriors, however, as among the Europeans.

Marriages among Native Americans were usually arranged by the families and based on economic considerations rather than emotions. Typically, the two sexes spent considerable time apart because the men were often away on hunts or other expeditions.

As American settlers moved across the country, they took over tribal lands and confined Indians to reservations. Tribal cultures and family systems were profoundly disrupted. Neither Indian men nor women were able to become U.S. citizens on the same basis as white people until 1924. They were aliens in their ancestral lands, and they still suffer from many social problems, such as poverty and alcoholism, that are a legacy of their treatment by the U.S. government and white society.

In the 1960s a new and more militant generation of Native Americans provided the leadership for cultural resurgence among many tribes. The Cherokees' Wilma Mankiller is the best known of many women who have been part of this movement.

SEE ALSO

Mankiller, Wilma

FURTHER READING

Crow Dog, Mary. *Lakota Woman.* New York: Harper, 1994.

Demos, John. *The Tried and the True: Native American Women Confronting Colonization.* New York: Oxford University Press, 1995.

Golston, Sydele E. *Changing Woman of the Apache: Women's Lives in Past and Present.* Danbury, Conn.: Watts, 1996.

Green, Rayna. *Women in American Indian Society.* New York: Chelsea House, 1992.

Niethammer, Carolyn. *Daughters of the Earth: The Lives and Legends of American Indian Women.* New York: Collier, 1977.

Navratilova, Martina

- *Born: Oct. 18, 1956, Prague, Czechoslovakia*
- *Education: High school*
- *Accomplishments: Winner, 167 tennis titles, the most of any player; Wimbledon champion (1978–79, 1982–87, 1990); Australian Open champion (1981, 1983, 1985); French Open champion (1982, 1984); U.S. Open champion (1983–84, 1986–87); author, (with George Vecsey)* Martina *(1985); (with Liz Nickles)* The Total Zone *(1994);* Breaking Point *(1996); and* Killer Instinct *(1997)*

The woman tennis player with the all-time record for victories, Martina Navratilova provided a model of how hard work and remarkable discipline can produce a champion. Her achievements include seven years of being ranked No. 1 in the world, a feat unequaled by any other woman.

Born in Czechoslovakia, Navratilova defected to the United States in 1975 and became a U.S. citizen in 1981.

With a game based on power, Navratilova developed her strong serve by endless working out and by extraordinary dedication to polishing her skills. She had a worthy rival in another woman player, Chris Evert, and they brought out the competitive fire in one another.

By the time she retired in 1994, Navratilova had won a total of 54 Grand Slam (the U.S. Open, the French Open, Wimbledon, and the Australian Open) events, including singles, doubles, and mixed doubles. She had also earned more than $20 million, the most prize money ever won by a woman tennis champion. Moreover, she gained fame—and notoriety—as one of the first well-known women to come out of the closet as a lesbian.

SEE ALSO

Evert, Chris; Sports

FURTHER READING

Zwerman, Gilda. *Martina Navratilova.* New York: Chelsea House, 1995.

Needlework

In the years before people bought ready-made clothes, probably the single activity shared by more women than any other was needlework. If a woman belonged to a well-to-do family, she had someone else to do the cooking and she might also have had someone else to do the daily, necessary sewing, but she would have done the fancy needlework herself. Indeed, to be able to stitch a fine seam or create beautiful embroidery was one of the prime accomplishments of a lady. Young girls created samplers as part of their initiation into the craft. In short, virtually all women used their needles, but some worked much harder at it than others.

Necessity required most women to sew all the clothes for their families, an unending task. Because fabric was often difficult to obtain and expensive, they learned to remake and recycle garments. There were no patterns available, so cutting and fitting required great skill—and sometimes women would purchase the help of an experienced needleworker for this part of the task.

As more ready-made goods became available in the early 19th century, more women began to be able to devote time to sewing as a form of recreation and aesthetic expression. Quilts helped people stay warm in their beds at night, but making them also furnished the opportunity for busy women to get together and socialize, and as women gained more time, they were able to make them beautiful as well as practical. Surviving quilts from the 19th century tell stories of women's political causes (abolitionist women stitched their convictions into quilts, for example), of their regional identification, and in some cases of their ethnic backgrounds. A tradition of quilting among African-American women, still carried on today, may reflect an influence from their African heritage, owing to their use of designs that resemble West African art.

This quilt, pieced by Kitty Jones and quilted by Atleaver Jones in the 1970s, comes out of the powerful—and improvisational—African-American quilt tradition. Some scholars have argued that there are affinities between this tradition and West and Central African textile motifs.

FURTHER READING:

Atkins, Jacqueline M. *Shared Threads: Quilting Together—Past and Present.* New York: Viking/Museum of American Folk Art, 1994.

Hedges, Elaine. *Hearts and Hands: Women, Quilts, and American Society.* Nashville, Tenn.: Rutledge Hill, 1996.

New Deal

During the years when Franklin Delano Roosevelt was President, from 1933 to 1945, more women held more influential government positions than ever before in U.S. history. Before World War II changed the nation's priorities, starting in

This panel entitled "Women in the WPA" was prepared for the Women's Exposition in St. Louis in 1939. New Deal programs created an unprecedented number of jobs for women.

1941, FDR's "New Deal" administration proposed and guided through Congress a whole host of reforms aimed at dealing with the distress caused by the Great Depression. Many of the reforms promoted by Roosevelt's New Deal legislation—such as unemployment insurance and aid to poor families with children—represented goals that had been developed by a women's network of reformers earlier in the 20th century. First Lady Eleanor Roosevelt also deserves much credit for pushing her husband to include women in his administration.

As a rising young Democratic politician, Roosevelt contracted polio in 1921 and had to withdraw from public life for many years. Eleanor Roosevelt filled in for him in cultivating New York State politicians and in being active in the state's Democratic party, and in so doing became an accomplished politician herself. She also developed close ties with a talented group of women reformers who were trying to improve working conditions and make the society more humane.

When Roosevelt recovered enough to reenter politics and to run successfully for governor of New York in 1928, his wife lobbied to get him to appoint some of these women to high office. He complied, and, as a consequence, when he became President in 1933, he had a record of having appointed women and having seen them do a superb job.

The best-known woman in Roosevelt's Presidential administration was Secretary of Labor Frances Perkins, the first woman to serve in the cabinet. She had been industrial commissioner of New York during his governorship. But there were many other women who were part of the New Deal at lower levels. Together these women fought for such changes as Social Security—there had been none before—and for reform in the laws governing labor unions so that workers would be guaranteed the right to organize if they so chose. Many of the New Deal's benefit programs helped women as well as men. For example, the Works Progress Administration (WPA) gave women pay equal to men's for the same work, and sponsored projects specifically to employ what were then viewed as women's skills: sewing, library work, clerical work, arts, and education.

SEE ALSO

Perkins, Frances; Roosevelt, Eleanor

FURTHER READING

Deutsch, Sarah Jane. *From Ballots to Breadlines: American Women 1920–1940.* New York: Oxford University Press, 1994.

Ware, Susan. *Beyond Suffrage: Women in the New Deal.* Cambridge: Harvard University Press, 1981.

19th Amendment

The 19th Amendment, proclaimed part of the Constitution on August 26, 1920, gave all American women the right to vote. Representing a tremendous victory for suffragists, it was the fruit of generations of effort by many thousands of women and their male allies. Their many years of untiring work culminated in the addition of this simple but powerful sentence to the Constitution: "The right of citizens of the United States to vote shall not be denied or abridged by the Unites States or by any State on account of sex."

Suffragists had waged their campaign to secure the vote along two lines. They had worked to obtain the vote at the level of individual states and had enjoyed many successes: by January 1919 the women of 30 states had the right to vote. But this was not yet total victory, and it had been very costly in human resources to wage 30 campaigns in 30 states.

In late 1916 and early 1917, the National American Woman Suffrage Association (NAWSA) began a renewed effort to obtain a constitutional amendment. NAWSA opened a new headquarters in Washington, D.C., and pledged to work toward helping the U.S. effort in World War I, which the country was just entering, as well as to work toward a suffrage amendment. The militant National Woman's Party led by Alice Paul also played a huge role in calling attention to the justice of the demand for woman suffrage.

In January 1918 the House of Representatives voted on the amendment, with 274 ayes to 136 noes, one vote more than the two-thirds necessary under the Constitution. But the Senate did not vote in favor of it that year, and it was not until the following year that both branches of Congress passed it. The amendment then had to be ratified by three-fourths of the states, or 36. The final state required to reach that number, Tennessee, ratified it on August 18, 1920, and on August 26, Secretary of State Bainbridge Colby proclaimed it to be officially part of the Constitution.

SEE ALSO
Suffrage, woman

FURTHER READING

Deutsch, Sarah Jane. *From Ballots to Breadlines: American Women 1920–1940.* New York: Oxford University Press, 1994.

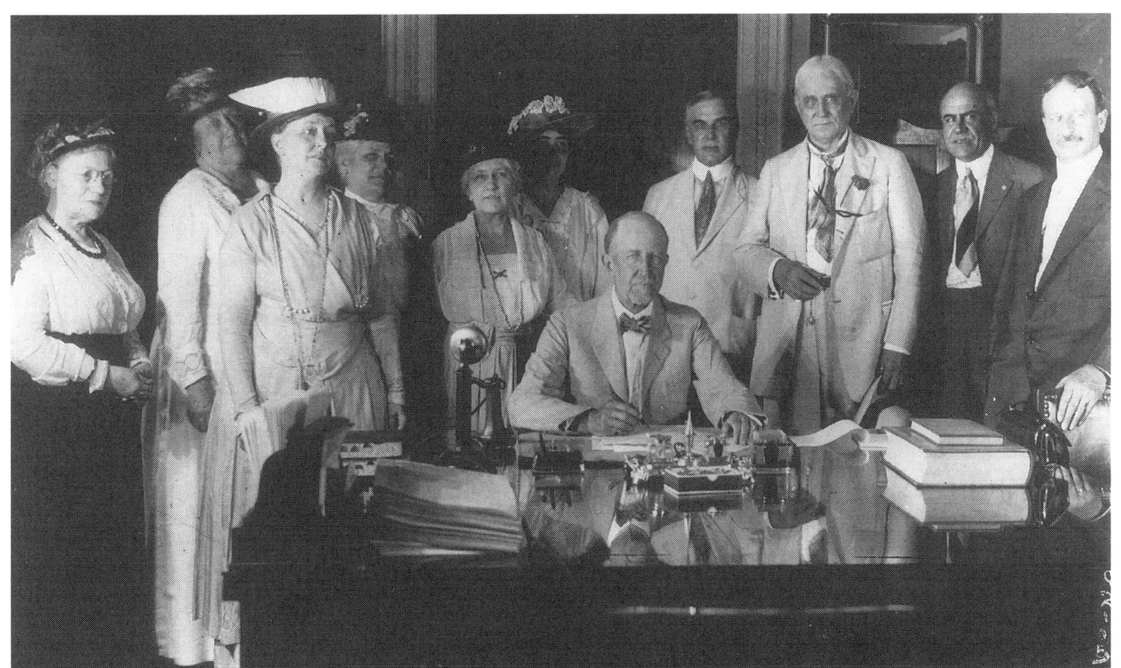

Speaker of the House Frederick H. Gillette (seated) signs the Federal (Woman) Suffrage Amendment in the House of Representatives in 1919.

Flexner, Eleanor, and Ellen Fitzpatrick. *Century of Struggle*. Cambridge, Mass: Harvard University Press, 1996.
Smith, Karen Manners. *New Paths to Power: American Women 1890–1920*. New York: Oxford University Press, 1994.

Nursing

Nursing is a profession that is predominantly but not exclusively female. Like many other occupations in the so-called "pink-collar ghetto"—work that is dominated by women—it has not always been financially rewarded as well as male jobs requiring comparable training. Nurses have, however, made tremendous strides in upgrading their standing within the medical profession as a whole. Thirty years ago, for example, nurses on duty in a hospital station were expected to rise as a sign of respect when a doctor first arrived on their floor. Now that is no longer the case.

The profession grew out of the nursing that women did during the Civil War (1861–65). Housewives had always been in charge of caring for the sick in their own families, and they had also been expected to help out in the community, but this was untrained work. During the war, women nurses proved that attention to the details of sanitation and nutrition could save lives, and this created the impetus for formal nurses' training. These were also years of growth and development for hospitals as institutions, and skilled nurses proved valuable additions to the hospital team.

In 1873, with the founding of the Connecticut Training School for Nurses and the Bellevue Hospital Training School in New York, nurses began to be trained in hospitals, where student nurses were poorly paid apprentices for two or three years before receiving a diploma. The oldest nursing school still in operation to be established on a university campus is the University of Minnesota's School of Nursing, which opened in 1909. By the early 1920s nursing leaders had created the American Nurses Association to help professionalize the occupation. Over time, the standards for education and receiving credentials have become more rigorous, and the pay has gone up, too.

Bertha Wright holds two of her young patients at the Children's Hospital in Oakland, California. Wright, along with other concerned women, founded the hospital in 1912.

For most of its history, the medical field relegated women to the lowly and poorly paid nursing jobs, but even within that category, there was discrimination. It was difficult for African-American women to gain access either to training or to a job. In some instances black communities, in desperate need of good nurses, set up their own alternative institutions to train them. After World War II (1941–45), African-American women began to have more opportunities in the nursing profession as a whole.

Despite the problems they have faced as women in a male-dominated profession, nurses have taken the lead in several areas. In the early 1900s, for example, they created the field of public health nursing, allied with the settlement-house work that was then going on, and visited poor people in their homes to give them better access to health care. Nurses were also instrumental in founding many hospitals around the country. And during times of war, there are still many opportunities for nurses in the military. About 10,000 women served as military nurses in Vietnam in the 1960s and 70s—a handful paid with their lives.

Today, nursing is in a period of rapid change. The medical field is becoming more filled with paperwork, and this can take away from the time that a nurse would like to spend with her patients. But she—or he in some cases—now has a vigorous professional organization defending her interests, better pay than in the past, and much more respect within the medical field.

SEE ALSO

Civil War; Medicine

FURTHER READING

Hine, Darlene Clark. *Black Women in White*. Bloomington: Indiana University Press, 1989.

Norman, Elizabeth M. *Women at War: the Story of Fifty Military Nurses who Served in Vietnam*. Philadelphia: University of Pennsylvania Press, 1990.

Reverby, Susan. *Ordered to Care: The Dilemma of American Nursing, 1850–1945*. New York: Cambridge University Press, 1987.

O'Connor, Sandra Day

- *Born: Mar. 26, 1930, El Paso, Tex.*
- *Education: Stanford University, B.A., 1950, LL.B, 1952*
- *Accomplishments: Assistant attorney general, Arizona (1965–69); Arizona state senator (1969–75); U.S. Supreme Court (1981–)*

When Sandra Day O'Connor graduated from Stanford Law School in 1952, she could hardly have anticipated that someday she would be appointed to the U.S. Supreme Court. In the early 1950s not only had there never been a woman in that position but it was difficult for a woman to secure any type of legal job, no matter how good her record at law school. President Ronald Reagan's choice of O'Connor for the high court in 1981 was a personal triumph for her and a victory for all American women.

After graduating from Stanford Law School, Sandra Day O'Connor initially had a hard time starting her legal career because of her gender. One prominent law firm offered her a job as a secretary. She went on to make history as the first woman to sit on the U.S. Supreme Court.

Sandra Day earned a B.A. and then a law degree from Stanford University and married law school classmate John O'Connor soon after graduation. John then served in the U.S. military in West Germany, and Sandra became a civilian attorney for the army. When the couple returned to the United States, they settled in Phoenix, Arizona.

Sandra Day O'Connor began to practice law in Arizona and then became involved in Republican politics after their youngest child had started school. From 1965 to 1969 she served as the state's assistant attorney general. In 1969 she was appointed to the state senate, winning reelection twice. In 1973 she was chosen as senate majority leader.

After resigning from the legislature, O'Connor was elected to be a superior court judge in Phoenix in 1974 and then chosen to be a judge on the Arizona court of appeals in 1979. After Reagan chose her as the first woman to sit on the U.S. Supreme Court, the U.S. Senate confirmed her nomination by a vote of 99 to 0. She is generally regarded as a conservative justice who is fair to all parties.

During her first decade on the Court, when it was evenly split between conservatives and liberals, her vote often determined the outcome. For example, she provided the fifth vote (in a five-to-four decision) to strike down a state-mandated moment of silence at the beginning of a school day. In 1989 Justice O'Connor wrote the majority opinion in an affirmative action case in which she upheld the legality of programs established to correct previous *government* discrimination, but not those aimed at rectifying prior discrimination by the society at large.

SEE ALSO

Law

FURTHER READING

Bentley, Judith. *Justice Sandra Day O'Connor.* New York: Messner, 1983.
Huber, Peter W. *Sandra Day O'Connor.* New York: Chelsea House, 1990.
Maveety, Nancy. *Justice Sandra Day O'Connor: Strategist on the Supreme Court.* Lanham, Md.: Rowman & Littlefield, 1996.

O'Keeffe, Georgia

- *Born: Nov. 15, 1887, Sun Prairie, Wis.*
- *Education: Art Institute of Chicago, attended 1904–05; Art Students League of New York, attended 1907–08*
- *Accomplishments: American Academy of Arts and Letters (elected 1962); solo retrospective exhibition of paintings, Whitney Museum of American Art (1970); author,* Georgia O'Keeffe *(autobiography, 1976)*
- *Died: Santa Fe, N. Mex., Mar. 6, 1986*

Living long enough to become a legend, painter Georgia O'Keeffe created such powerful images of the Southwest that many people automatically conjure up her work when they think of the region.

Born in Wisconsin, O'Keeffe studied at both the Art Institute of Chicago and the Art Students League of New York. She developed her style—deeply imbued with the light and colors of the West—when she taught art in Canyon, Texas, in the years between 1912 and 1918, her first encounter with the region she would later depict so memorably.

While she was teaching in Texas, a friend showed some of her drawings to the photographer Alfred Stieglitz, the founder of a modernist gallery in New York. He liked what he saw, became a sponsor of O'Keeffe's work, and the two fell in love, marrying in 1924. By this time she had returned to the East to pursue her career.

O'Keeffe's paintings of the 1920s often featured huge flowers, dazzling in their scale and coloring, as well as a brief period of painting skyscrapers, and her work began to attract favorable attention. In 1929 she spent the summer in New Mexico. She did not move to New Mexico permanently until after Stieglitz's death in 1946, but she was clearly entranced by the state's vivid light and dramatic landscapes.

In her later years O'Keeffe won many honors, such as her election to the American Academy of Arts and Letters in 1962, and much public acclaim. She died in 1986 at the age of 98.

SEE ALSO

Painting

FURTHER READING

Berry, Michael. *Georgia O'Keeffe.* New York: Chelsea House, 1989.
Castro, Jan Garden. *The Art and Life of Georgia O'Keeffe.* New York: Crown, 1995.
Eisler, Benita. *O'Keeffe and Stieglitz: An American Romance.* New York: Doubleday, 1991.
Hassrick, Peter H., ed. *The Georgia O'Keeffe Museum.* New York: Abrams/ Georgia O'Keeffe Museum, 1997.

Onassis, Jacqueline Bouvier Kennedy

- *Born: July 28, 1929, Southampton, N.Y.*
- *Education: George Washington University, B.A., 1951*
- *Accomplishments: First Lady (1961–63); editor, Viking Press (1975–77) and Doubleday (1978–94)*
- *Died: May 19, 1994, New York, N.Y.*

One of the most beloved First Ladies, Jacqueline Kennedy was the wife of President John F. Kennedy. From her first moments of national fame in the late

President John F. Kennedy and First Lady Jacqueline Kennedy in a Washington, D.C., motorcade in 1963. Few First Ladies have captured the public imagination as Mrs. Kennedy did.

1950s until her death in 1994, she captivated her fellow Americans with her sense of style and grace. Indeed, so intense was the public interest in her life that at times she considered it oppressive.

Jacqueline Bouvier was born to a wealthy and socially prominent family. She attended Vassar College and the Sorbonne in Paris and then graduated from George Washington University in Washington, D.C., in 1951. After graduation, she became the "inquiring photographer" for the *Washington Times-Herald,* and she met the handsome young senator John F. Kennedy while on assignment in 1952.

The couple wed in 1953, and after pausing for the honeymoon, Senator Kennedy—himself the son of wealth and privilege—returned to the task of furthering his political career. By all accounts, she was less interested in politics than he was, and the marriage suffered many rocky moments. Further, the American public has learned, since John Kennedy's death, that he engaged in extramarital affairs and that Jacqueline Kennedy had to share her husband not only with his male political cronies but also with a series of other women.

Despite the accommodations Jacqueline Kennedy had to make, the public saw a radiantly beautiful young woman at the side of John Kennedy when he ran for President in 1960. Once in the White House, she, her clothes, her sophisticated tastes, her knowledge of French—all of this made wonderful copy for press coverage. Jackie, as the press called her, seemed to be an American princess, with an intellect that matched her glamour. Whispers of her extravagant spending on clothes reached the public, but they did little to affect her popularity.

Jackie Kennedy had what seemed to be an idyllic existence as First Lady and as the mother of two children, Caroline and John, but her life began to take a tragic turn in mid-1963 when she lost their third child, Patrick, a few days after his birth. Later that year she was riding in the motorcade alongside her husband when he was assassinated in Dallas. If she had dazzled people earlier, she impressed them even more with her dignified demeanor during the terrible days of national mourning for the slain young president.

Kennedy then had to forge a life for herself and her children in what seemed to be a dangerous country. After she lost her husband in 1963, she saw her brother-in-law Robert Kennedy gunned down a few years later. The year of that death, 1968, she married one of the richest men in the world, Greek shipping tycoon Aristotle Onassis. Some speculated that she believed that he and his enormous wealth could protect her privacy and the lives and privacy of her children. Before his death in 1975, however, the relationship had become a marriage in name only.

Twice widowed, Jackie Onassis found a new professional calling as an editor in New York City, with Viking and then Doubleday. In the 1970s she started a campaign to save New York City's Grand Central Terminal and restore it to its original splendor. Her efforts culminated after her death with the rededication of the terminal in 1998. Still one of the best-known women in the world, she fought tenaciously for her privacy. Later in life, she received acclaim for the superb job she had done raising her children in the harsh glare of worldwide attention.

FURTHER READING

Andersen, Christopher P. *Jackie after Jack.* New York: William Morrow, 1998.
Baldrige, Letitia. *In the Kennedy Style: Magical Evenings in the Kennedy White House.* New York: Doubleday, 1998.

Oz books

This beloved series, originated by L. Frank Baum, created a fantasy world featuring brave and resolute girls. Dorothy courageously follows the Yellow Brick Road to the Emerald City in *The Wonderful Wizard of Oz* (1900)—subsequently made into one of the most popular movies of all time—and in later books the reader encounters the female ruler Ozma and an all-female army. There are male characters, but they are not nearly as interesting as the girls. Thirteen other Oz books by Baum followed *The Wonderful Wizard of Oz.*

That Baum imagined a world of strong women was no accident. He married Maud Gage, the daughter of Matilda Joslyn Gage, one of the most prominent women's rights activists of the 19th century, with whom he had a close relationship. Dorothy is as spunky as any character in American literature, and she has inspired generations of girls with an image of independence and pluckiness—much like Jo March of *Little Women*, a girl character who rebelled against societal norms of female submissiveness. After Baum's death, Ruth Plumly Thompson carried on the series, publishing more than a dozen additional Oz books.

SEE ALSO
Gage, Matilda Joslyn

Painting

Because the usual access to a career in painting has been through formal training—and as a result of someone being willing to invest in the talent of a young person—it has been difficult for women to establish themselves in this field until the mid-20th century. There have, nonetheless, been a number of American women painters whose work has been of a quality to find an audience and a place in museums. Not surprisingly, the early ones came from atypical families.

The first American woman painter to earn her living at it was Sarah Miriam Peale. She was born in 1800 to a distinguished family of artists whose patriarch was Charles Willson Peale. Born to Charles's younger brother and fellow artist James, and trained by her father and her male cousins, Sarah Peale traveled extensively and painted more than 100 commissioned portraits, many of which can be found today in museums throughout the country. In 1848 the Pennsylvania Academy of Fine Arts in her home state became the first arts institution to admit women, a development that made it more possible for them to aspire to an artistic career.

A generation after Peale came Lilly Martin Spencer, whose reform-minded father took her to study painting with professional artists when she was a girl. Marrying and becoming the mother of seven children, Spencer painted domestically inspired pictures that were the visual equivalent of the novels being written in the mid-19th century that celebrated the life of housewives. Spencer's husband devoted himself to helping her career and even to managing their household while she worked.

By the late 19th century, opportunity was beginning to open to women in a number of fields—women were starting to attend college, for example—so it was not quite as unusual for a girl to announce that she wanted to pursue an artistic career as it had been for earlier generations, though it was still far from easy. The outstanding woman painter of the period—and the only American painter of either sex accepted as a peer by the French impressionists—was Mary Cassatt. Coming from a wealthy family, Cassatt was able to study first at the Pennsylvania Academy of Fine Arts and then in Paris, where she eventually made her home. Cassatt is especially celebrated for her portraits of mothers and children.

The Bath *(1891), by Mary Cassatt, is one of the artist's most mature and widely reproduced works. It was Cassatt's early paintings, however, that brought her to the attention of Edgar Degas and into the Impressionists' artistic circle in 1877.*

In the 20th century women painters excelled in a variety of genres. Georgia O'Keeffe is best known for her evocative paintings of flowers, bones, and the New Mexico landscape. Alice Neel, whose career received an early boost from federal arts programs during Franklin Roosevelt's presidency in the 1930s, painted in a realistic, gritty style and recorded the lives of people from many different classes. Important women painters in the abstract mode include Helen Frankenthaler and Elaine de Kooning.

It has always been the case that far greater numbers of women were self-taught painters, creating work in the "folk art" mode, than the relatively small number of those fortunate enough to receive formal training. One of the best-known women folk artists is Anna Mary Robertson, "Grandma Moses," who began painting in her seventies; her works celebrate rural traditions and community life. Women of color have often had even less access to formal training because, in most cases, it would have been so difficult for their families to invest in their talent. Since the civil rights and women's movements of the 1960s and 1970s, all women have had better access to artistic training, a greater likelihood of seeing their work displayed in galleries and museums, and a better chance of selling it.

SEE ALSO

Cassatt, Mary; O'Keeffe, Georgia

FURTHER READING

Biracree, Tom, et al. *Grandma Moses.* New York: Chelsea House, 1989.

Cherry, Deborah. *Painting Women: Victorian Women Artists.* New York: Routledge, 1993.

Eldredge, Charles, C. *Georgia O'Keeffe.* New York: Harry N. Abrams, 1991.

Heller, Nancy G. *Women Artists: An Illustrated History.* New York: Abbeville, 1987.

Mancoff, Debra N. *Mary Cassatt: Reflections of Women's Lives.* New York: Stewart Tabori & Chang, 1998.

Puniello, Francoise S., and Halina R. Rusak. *Abstract Expressionist Women Painters: An Annotated Bibliography: Elaine De Kooning, Helen Frankenthaler, Grace Hartigan, Lee Krasner, Joan Mitchell.* Lanham, Md.: Scarecrow, 1995.

Parent-Teacher Association (PTA)

SEE National Congress of Parents and Teachers

Parks, Rosa McCauley

- *Born: Feb. 4, 1913, Tuskegee, Ala.*
- *Education: Alabama State Teachers College*
- *Accomplishments: Secretary, Montgomery (Ala.) chapter, NAACP (1943–56); Spingarn Medal (1979); founder, Rosa and Raymond Parks Institute for Self-Development (1987); Congressional Gold Medal (1999)*

On December 1, 1955, black seamstress Rosa Parks refused to surrender her seat on a bus to a white man, as the local ordinances of Montgomery, Alabama, dictated that she should. She was then arrested for this "crime." This episode, as much as any single event, triggered the birth of the modern civil rights movement.

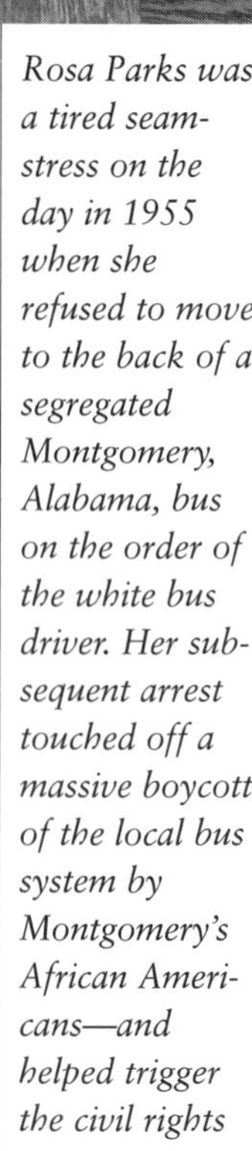

Rosa Parks was a tired seamstress on the day in 1955 when she refused to move to the back of a segregated Montgomery, Alabama, bus on the order of the white bus driver. Her subsequent arrest touched off a massive boycott of the local bus system by Montgomery's African Americans—and helped trigger the civil rights movement.

Born Rosa McCauley, the young woman attended Alabama State College in Montgomery and then married Raymond Parks in 1932. Both husband and wife were active in civic affairs. Earning her living as a seamstress, Rosa Parks served as the secretary of the Montgomery branch of the National Association for the Advancement of Colored People. In this capacity she received training in nonviolent methods of social activism and was therefore well prepared for her historic role.

On December 5, 1955, the civil rights leaders of Montgomery, including the Women's Political Council, called a one-day boycott of the local buses to protest Parks's arrest. When the white authorities responded with antagonism, the boycott lengthened to last a year, until the local bus system eventually changed its practices. As the boycott proceeded, the then-unknown Reverend Martin Luther King, Jr., assumed leadership. Only 25 years old, he proved to be an eloquent spokesman for justice.

Both Rosa Parks and her husband lost their jobs as a result of her role in precipitating the boycott. In 1957 the couple moved to Detroit, Michigan. After a period of financial struggle, Rosa obtained a job as an assistant to Democratic Congressman John Conyers of Detroit, a position she held from 1965 until she retired in 1988. Raymond Parks died in 1977. In old age, Rosa Parks has become a national icon, a heroine especially to young African Americans.

SEE ALSO

Civil rights movement

FURTHER READING

Hull, Mary. *Rosa Parks.* New York: Chelsea House, 1994.

Parks, Rosa, and James Haskins. *Rosa Parks: My Story.* New York, N.Y.: Puffin 1999.

Patriarchy

The word *patriarchy,* which is derived from the Latin word *pater* (father), is used to describe a clan, tribe, or larger society in which the father is dominant both formally in the legal system and informally because of social custom. The history of Western civilization has been characterized by patriarchy since ancient times, although in the 20th century the law has protected women's rights more than it did in times past. Nonetheless, it has proven difficult for feminist reformers to secure complete equality for women in a system that has considered men superior for thousands of years. No doubt the fact that both Judaism and Christianity see God as "the father" has reinforced the power of earthly fathers.

FURTHER READING

Lerner, Gerda. *The Creation of Patriarchy.* New York: Oxford University Press, 1986.

Paul, Alice

- *Born: Jan. 11, 1885, Moorestown, N.J.*
- *Education: Swarthmore College, B.A., 1905; University of Pennsylvania, M.A., 1907, Ph.D., 1912; Washington College of Law, LL.B., 1922; American University, M.A., 1927, Ph.D., 1928*
- *Accomplishments: Chairman, National American Woman Suffrage Association congressional committee (1912); founder, Congressional Union for Woman Suffrage (1913, became National Woman's Party, 1917); chairman, Woman's Research Foundation (1927–37); founder, World Party for Equal Rights for Women (1938); chairman, National Woman's Party (1942)*
- *Died: July 9, 1977, Moorestown, N.J.*

The force behind the National Woman's Party, Alice Paul played a key role in building support for the 19th Amendment, granting women the right to vote. After its ratification in 1920, she dedicated the rest of her life to the effort to secure ratification of the Equal Rights Amendment (ERA).

Raised a Quaker, Paul graduated from Swarthmore College in 1905. After a period of study in England, she went on to earn a master's degree and a doctorate in sociology from the University of Pennsylvania.

It was during Paul's stay in England that she became deeply involved in woman suffrage. At that time the British suffrage movement employed far more militant tactics than did its American

Alice Paul, leader of the National Woman's Party, celebrates in 1920 as the long battle for the vote drew to a victorious close. Her determined leadership played an important role in the victory.

counterpart. Alice Paul entered into the spirit of British suffrage and upon her return to the United States joined the reigning National American Woman Suffrage Association (NAWSA).

But NAWSA was too tame in its methods for Paul and the other women she organized into what would eventually become the National Woman's Party in 1917. At first calling themselves the Congressional Union, Paul and her colleagues began picketing the White House in 1913. Arrested for picketing, they then went on a hunger strike, the same tactics employed by British suffragists. The dedication and energy of Paul and her group were significant in helping to secure the eventual victory for woman suffrage.

In the 1920s Paul began what would be a lifetime commitment to the Equal Rights Amendment, which was originally proposed, under the sponsorship of the National Woman's Party, in 1923. For many decades Paul's home in Washington, D.C., was the center of ERA activism. Not until poor health forced her to slow down in 1972 did she slacken in her dedication to the cause.

SEE ALSO

Equal Rights Amendment (ERA); National Woman's Party; Suffrage, woman

FURTHER READING

Lunardini, Christine. *From Equal Suffrage to Equal Rights: Alice Paul and the National Woman's Party, 1910–1928.* New York: New York University Press, 1988.

Rupp, Leila J., and Verta Taylor. *Survival in the Doldrums: The American Women's Rights Movement, 1945 to the 1960s.* New York: Oxford University Press, 1987.

Peabody, Elizabeth Palmer

- *Born: May 16, 1804, Billerica, Mass.*
- *Education: Private tutors*
- *Accomplishments: Charter member, Transcendentalist Club (1837); publisher,* Aesthetic Papers *(journal, single number, 1849); founder, first formal kindergarten in the U.S. (1860); founder and editor,* Kindergarten Messenger *(1873–79); organizer and first president, American Froebel Union (1877); author,* First Steps to the Study of History *(1832);* Record of a School *(1835);* Moral Culture of Infancy, and Kindergarten Guide *(1863);* Kindergarten Culture *(1870);* The Kindergarten in Italy *(1872);* Letters to Kindergartners *(1886)*
- *Died: Jan. 3, 1894, Boston, Mass.*

In 1860 Elizabeth Peabody launched the first formally organized kindergarten in the United States in the city of Boston with the idea of encouraging the development of young children rather than imparting specific information, as was typical of the schools of the day. Had she done nothing else, she would have earned a minor place in the history books. But in fact she was also one of the truly significant intellectuals in 19th-century New England, a woman who participated in Margaret Fuller's conversation groups, who taught with the philosopher Bronson Alcott (the father of Louisa May Alcott), and who influenced many others. One of Peabody's sisters married the novelist Nathaniel Hawthorne and another the educational pioneer Horace Mann. Thus Elizabeth Peabody was a major participant in the most stimulating circles of her day.

Peabody was the oldest of seven children. Both parents influenced her in the direction of intellectual achievement: her father taught her Latin and inspired her to learn a total of 10 languages, and her mother taught her philosophy. It is not surprising that as she grew up, Peabody was attracted to such fellow New Englanders as Fuller, Alcott, and Ralph Waldo Emerson. When Emerson and other leading intellectuals founded the Transcendentalist Club in 1837, for discussions among like-minded people, Peabody and Fuller were the only two women to be charter members.

Peabody's most important contribution was her leadership, throughout her long life, in educational innovation: she believed in expecting the best from children. Though modern kindergartens have not followed her specific ideas, they share the underlying philosophy of trying, gently and carefully, to awaken a love of learning in young children.

SEE ALSO

Alcott, Louisa May; Fuller, Margaret

FURTHER READING

Boller, Paul F. *American Transcendentalism, 1830–1860: An Intellectual Inquiry.* New York: Putnam, 1974.

Ronda, Bruce A. *Elizabeth Palmer Peabody: A Reformer on Her Own Terms.* Cambridge: Harvard University Press, 1999.

Peace movements

There have been many peace movements in American history, and women have played a vital role in nearly all of them. In most cases, women have spoken out as mothers, saying, in effect, that because they bring life into the world, they have the right to oppose the taking of life. Women have also claimed that, as citizens, they have the right to a voice in the shaping of their country's foreign policy.

For most of the 19th century, peace movements, such as the one opposed to the Mexican War that broke out in 1844, were led by and composed primarily of white men. Toward the end of the century, female membership in peace movements increased and female leaders began to emerge. Many women's groups adopted peace advocacy as one of their causes.

The outbreak of World War I in 1914 transformed the role of women in peace advocacy. This bloody war engendered much opposition by both prominent men and women, including Hull House founder Jane Addams and activist Emma Goldman. Perhaps the most notable act of opposition to the war by a woman was Congresswoman Jeannette Rankin's vote against a declaration of war in the House of Representatives in April 1917. But the war, which ended in November 1918, divided opinion among suffragists, with some, such as Carrie Chapman Catt, supporting it because they believed that women had to prove their capacity to be good citizens.

When the ratification of the 19th Amendment, granting woman suffrage, looked imminent, many suffragists turned their attention to peace. Even

Mothers with baby carriages march for peace in Europe near the Woolworth building, New York City, in 1939. One sign reads, "We don't want to be war widows."

those who had supported the war now joined their opponents. A number of new groups emerged, including the Women's International League for Peace and Freedom, founded in 1919.

Throughout the 1920s women's groups carried on a campaign for peace. Their biggest single victory occurred when the Kellogg-Briand Pact, outlawing war, was signed in 1928.

During World War II (1941–45) and the cold war that followed it, most Americans supported policies to defend the United States and protect democracies around the world, and peace activism did not become a popular cause again until the 1960s. Women Strike for Peace, founded in 1961 to oppose the testing of nuclear weapons, would go on to oppose the Vietnam War.

In August 1964 Congress overwhelmingly passed the Gulf of Tonkin Resolution, which authorized a retaliation against the communist regime of

North Vietnam for an alleged aggression against U.S. ships, and was the only legal basis for the Vietnam War. At its height, hundreds of thousands of Americans were fighting in this undeclared war. A large number of women were involved in protesting the war, protests that stemmed from the war's questionable legality under the Constitution as well as from doubts about whether the South Vietnamese regime—known to be corrupt and unpopular—represented a worthy cause to fight and die for. By the late 1960s, hundreds of thousands of protestors would turn out for a single demonstration.

Women participated in all the major demonstrations, they campaigned tirelessly for peace, and certain groups devised especially effective strategies and slogans. The antiwar organization Another Mother for Peace coined the single best-known slogan of the era: "War is not healthy for children and other living things." Militant students taking part in some demonstrations may have disturbed undecided Americans, but it was difficult to dismiss antiwar mothers pushing baby strollers as radicals.

Many of those who participated in the unprecedented female activism of the Vietnam era moved from antiwar protest to feminism once the war was over because, among other reasons, they encountered monumental sexism among the young men of the anti-war movement.

Women's peace activism is now global in scope. In the 1980s, women peace activists camped out on the periphery of missile bases in the U.S. and Europe. In 1995 the late congresswoman Bella Abzug attended the Fourth World Congress of Women, in China, and called for 50–50 participation of women and men in all governmental bodies so as to further peace efforts. Networks of women working not only for peace but also for social justice can play a constructive role in challenging the bloody heritage of warfare.

SEE ALSO

Abzug, Bella Savitsky; Foreign policy; Rankin, Jeannette

FURTHER READING

Alonso, Harriet Hyman. *Peace As a Woman's Issue: A History of the U.S. Movement for World Peace and Women's Rights.* Syracuse, N.Y.: Syracuse University Press, 1993.

Hawlett, Charles F. *The American Peace Movement: References and Resources.* Thorndike, Maine: G.K. Hall, 1991.

Lynch, Cecelia. *Beyond Appeasement: Interpreting Interwar Peace Movements in World Politics.* Ithaca, N.Y.: Cornell University Press, 1999.

Perkins, Frances

- *Born: Apr. 10, 1880, Boston, Mass.*
- *Education: Mount Holyoke College, B.A., 1902; Columbia University, M.A., 1910*
- *Accomplishments: Executive secretary, New York Consumers' League (1910–12); executive secretary, New York Committee on Safety (1912–17); executive director, New York Council of Organization for War Service (1917–19); chairman, New York State Industrial Board (1926–29); New York state industrial commissioner (1929–33); U.S. secretary of labor (1933–45); author,* People at Work *(1934) and* The Roosevelt I Knew *(1946)*
- *Died: May 14, 1965, New York, N.Y.*

Frances Perkins, secretary of labor during President Franklin D. Roosevelt's administration of the 1930s, was the first woman to hold a cabinet position. As such, she was one of the most important woman politicians of the 20th century.

Perkins graduated from Mount Holyoke College in 1902 and obtained a master's degree from Columbia Uni-

The first woman to serve in the U.S. Cabinet, Secretary of Labor Frances Perkins, meets workers at the Carnegie Steel Company in Pittsburgh. Before her stint in Washington, she had been a social worker and a member of the settlement-house network.

versity in 1910. She married the wealthy Paul Wilson in 1913, and the couple had one child. Her husband lost much of his inheritance in 1918, and she switched from volunteer work to gainful employment. Belonging to the settlement-house network of women who served as advocates for working-class women and children, she became the executive secretary of the Consumers' League of New York. This group tried to influence middle-class people to choose their purchases based on how well companies treated their workers. Perkins then worked for Governor Al Smith before becoming industrial commissioner of New York overseeing the well-being of wage earners during the governorship of Franklin Roosevelt. Both Roosevelt and his wife, Eleanor, admired Perkins and considered her a logical choice for secretary of labor.

All her life Perkins had been preparing to head the Department of Labor. As executive secretary of the Consumers' League, for example, Perkins had come to know the need for protection of working people in times of economic distress, and she had also thought long and hard about the means by which government might be able to improve their lives. Roosevelt's New Deal program of legislation to aid the poor, unemployed, and elderly gave Perkins the chance to put her experience and her ideas to work at the highest level of government. She served until Roosevelt died in 1945. She then accepted a professorship in the School of Industrial and Labor Relations at Cornell University.

SEE ALSO
New Deal

FURTHER READING

Colman, Penny. *A Woman Unafraid: The Achievements of Frances Perkins.* New York: Atheneum, 1993.

Martin, George. *Madam Secretary, Frances Perkins.* Boston: Houghton Mifflin, 1976.

Pasachoff, Naomi E. *Frances Perkins: Champion of the New Deal.* New York: Oxford University Press, 1999.

Philanthropy

There is a long history of female philanthropy, that is, giving money to public or social causes. Despite their unequal access to employment and wealth, women have, since colonial times, endowed charities, founded educational institutions, and supported the arts when they have had control of enough money to make this possible. For example, Boston owes its magnificent Isabella Stewart Gardner Museum to the woman of the same name. Ima Hogg endowed many cultural endeavors in Houston. In the early 20th century, female philanthropy played a large role in underwriting the settlement houses in poor neighborhoods. Until the 1970s, however, women have typically given their largest contributions primarily to causes and institutions that disproportionately benefited men.

Two California women, Jane Stanford and Phoebe Hearst, exemplify the old and the new style of female philanthropy. Leland Stanford, Jane's husband, became immensely wealthy through investments in railroads in the years after the California gold rush. When the Stanfords' only son died, the couple decided to found a university in his honor. Leland himself died shortly thereafter, and it was up to his widow to oversee the founding years of what would become one of the world's great universities, and she deserves credit for devoted service to the school. She did not, however, consider the interests of women as a prime objective. The university was coeducational, but the number of women students was limited by Jane herself to only 500, a policy that was not changed until the 1930s.

Phoebe Hearst, on the other hand, made her first substantial gift to the University of California in the form of scholarships for women. The widow of another man who had become wealthy after the gold rush (and the mother of newspaper publisher William Randolph Hearst), she became the university's first female regent on the basis of her munificent gifts. Unlike Jane Stanford, Hearst often used her position to advance the interests of women, as in her sponsorship of designs by the architect Julia Morgan and her endowment of recreational facilities for women students.

Women of color have also been philanthropists when possible. Madame C. J. Walker, the African-American cosmetics company founder, for example, created scholarships for women students at Tuskegee Institute in Alabama in the 1910s.

Women have also been instrumental as patrons of the arts. Musician and composer Elizabeth Sprague Coolidge used her inheritance for music patronage, sponsoring the South Mountain (Berkshire) Chamber Music Festival (1918–24) and establishing a foundation in her name at the Library of Congress (1925) to fund festivals and sponsor composers and musicians. The foundation helped further the careers of composers such as Igor Stravinsky and Aaron Copland. In New York City, the socially prominent philanthropist Brook Astor oversaw the Vincent Astor Foundation for 30 years after the death of her third husband in 1959. Over the years the foundation gave $175 million to charities and cultural institutions such as the New York Public Library.

Today the whole landscape of female giving has changed. The modern women's movement and the legislative victories it has achieved have created a new world of female employment. Now women are executives as well as secretaries, doctors as well as nurses, and more of them can write bigger checks. And when they do write a check, it is likely to have the explicit goal of advancing women's interests.

FURTHER READING

McCarthy, Kathleen, ed. *Lady Bountiful Revisited.* New Brunswick, N.J.: Rutgers University Press, 1990.

Photography

Photography is younger than the other visual arts, and it has required less of an investment in expensive training than most. Because of this, women have had

The photographer Cindy Sherman examines traditional female roles in much of her work. Her "Film Stills" series, including this photograph taken in 1978, created a sensation in the contemporary art world.

access to this art from the beginning, and they have been among the greatest American photographers.

Photography grew out of the process of daguerreotyping, which had been developed in the 1830s. Within a very few years, women were taking pictures. Gertrude Kasebier was renowned in the late 19th century for her photographs in the "fine arts" style, often soft-focus pictures of women idealized as mothers. Alice Austen documented the circumstances of her friends' lives. Frances Benjamin Johnston took pictures of women factory workers.

After World War I (1914–18), women photographers began to branch out in new directions. Berenice Abbott was a realist who took architectural and scientific pictures. Louise Dahl-Wolfe was a leading fashion photographer for *Harper's Bazaar.* Imogen Cunningham took memorable portraits. The two giants of the mid-20th century were Dorothea Lange, whose portraits of the rural poor during the Great Depression of the 1930s stirred the conscience of the nation, and Margaret Bourke-White, a leading photographer for *Life* magazine who specialized in industrial pictures but who also covered World War II.

In the years after World War II ended in 1945, women became even more numerous in this field. One outstanding example is the African American Elaine Tomlin, who was the official photographer for the Southern Christian Leadership Conference, a leading civil rights organization in the 1960s.

Feminist photographers have made political statements with their pictures by trying to reclaim images of women from what they have seen as objectification in the work of male photographers and/or the mainstream media. Cindy Sherman explores the concept of identity in her work, disguising herself as another person, sometimes famous and sometimes anonymous, then taking a classical portrait of herself. She also addresses issues of objectification and body image in her photographs of dismantled mannikins, often disturbingly displaying blood or sexual organs. Barbara Kruger uses feminist irony by superimposing phrases such as "I shop therefore I am" over images taken by other photographers.

An exciting breakthrough for women photographers is the fact that, as of the 1980s, the number of women press photographers equaled the number of the men in the field. Thus, in both creative and press photography women have enjoyed opportunities and freedoms that were hard-won in other visual arts.

SEE ALSO

Bourke-White, Margaret; Lange, Dorothea

FURTHER READING

Frizot, Michael, ed. *A New History of Photography.* Köln, Germany: Könemann, 1998.

Newhall, Beaumont. *The History of Photography: From 1839 to the Present.* 5th ed. New York: New York Graphic Society/Little, Brown, 1982.

Rosenblum, Naomi. *A History of Women Photographers*. New York: Abbeville Press, 1994.

Pickford, Mary

- *Born: Apr. 8, 1893, Toronto, Canada*
- *Education: Unknown*
- *Accomplishments: Star of 194 films; co-founder, United Artist studio (1919); author,* Sunshine and Shadow *(autobiography, 1955)*
- *Died: May 29, 1979, Santa Monica, Calif.*

Known as "America's Sweetheart," Mary Pickford was one of the first major Hollywood stars to be a woman. In the movies, she was blonde, curly-haired, dimpled, and girlish. In reality she was a hardheaded business-woman—but the public refused to let her grow up.

Born Gladys Smith, she began to appear on stage at the age of five. As early as 1909 she began to star in silent films. Before too much longer Pickford was a popular favorite, going on to produce many of her own movies. In fact, she was one of the founders of the United Artists studio. Her "growing up" to the point where she was no longer believable as a young girl roughly coincided with the development of sound in films, so she never made a successful transition to talkies. But she left a lasting body of work in such silent films as *Poor Little Rich Girl* (1917) and *Rebecca of Sunnybrook Farm* (1917).

Married to the swashbuckling Douglas Fairbanks from 1920 to 1936, she subsequently married actor Buddy Rogers in 1937, a marriage that lasted until her death. After retiring from the movies, she wrote her memoirs and devoted energy to United Artists. In 1975 she received a special Academy Award for her contributions to film.

SEE ALSO

Movies

FURTHER READING

Eyman, Scott. *Mary Pickford, America's Sweetheart*. New York: D.I. Fine, 1990.

Whitfield, Eileen. *Pickford: The Woman Who Made Hollywood*. Lexington: University Press of Kentucky, 1997.

Pinckney, Eliza Lucas

- *Born: Dec. 28, 1722?, West Indies*
- *Education: Finishing school*
- *Accomplishments: Principal force behind expansion of the indigo industry in the southern U.S.*
- *Died: May 26, 1793, Philadelphia, Pa.*

A member of one of South Carolina's most distinguished families, Eliza Lucas Pinckney was the mother of two leaders of the revolutionary generation, Charles Cotesworth Pinckney—who represented South Carolina at the Constitutional Convention in Philadelphia in 1787—and Thomas Pinckney.

In addition to being a devoted wife and mother, she was also a woman of great learning and extraordinary competence in running her family's plantations. Indeed, she is given much of the credit for introducing the successful cultivation of indigo, a plant used to make blue dye, in South Carolina. That she began running a plantation when she was still a teenager makes her story all the more unusual.

Born in the West Indies, Eliza Lucas received an unusually good education, including schooling in England, owing to her family's wealth. When her father delegated her to run some of the family's holdings in South Carolina and urged her to experiment with various crops, she displayed an energy and resourcefulness that must have exceeded even his fondest hopes. She married

Charles Pinckney in 1744 and retired from active plantation management.

Left a widow in 1758, however, Pinckney resumed her supervisory activities. In the spirit of experimentation that saw such success in introducing indigo, she also imported cocoons and raised silkworms. She was widely respected in her lifetime for management skills and business sense, so much so that after she died on a trip to Philadelphia, George Washington asked to be one of the pallbearers at her funeral.

FURTHER READING

Williams, Francis Leigh. *Plantation Patriot; a Biography of Eliza Lucas Pinckney.* New York: Harcourt, 1967.

Planned Parenthood

This Planned Parenthood brochure advocates using birth control to prevent unwanted pregnancy. Founded in 1916, Planned Parenthood is the world's largest and oldest voluntary family planning organization.

Planned Parenthood is the major organization that runs family-planning clinics in the United States. It grew out of the efforts of Margaret Sanger and other courageous pioneers of the birth-control movement in the 1930s, and in 1942 its name was changed from the Birth Control Federation of America to Planned Parenthood. Ever since the organization has played a major role in expanding a woman's range of reproductive choices by advocacy at the national level and by making services available to women at the local level.

A woman who calls her local Planned Parenthood office will most likely be offered a range of services from birth-control information and devices to pregnancy testing to prenatal care to abortion. Since the 1970s pro-life groups have frequently picketed Planned Parenthood clinics because of their strong opposition to abortion, in some cases making it difficult for clients to enter. Court cases are being fought to determine if such picketing is legally protected free speech or if it interferes with the rights of others.

SEE ALSO

Birth control; Sanger, Margaret Higgins

FURTHER READING

Marshall, Robert B., and Charles A. Donovan. *Blessed Are The Barren: The Social Policy of Planned Parenthood.* San Francisco: Ignatius, 1991.

Mitchell, Carolyn B. *The Planned Parenthood Women's Encyclopedia.* New York: Crown, 1996.

Plath, Sylvia

- *Born: Oct. 27, 1932, Boston, Mass.*
- *Education: Smith College, B.A., 1955; Cambridge University, M.A., 1957*
- *Accomplishments: Pulitzer Prize for* Collected Poems *(posthumous, 1982); author,* The Colossus and Other Poems *(1960);* The Bell Jar *(1963);* Ariel *(1965);* Crossing the Water *(1971);* Winter Trees *(1971);* The Bed Book *(1976);* Johnny Panic and the Bible of Dreams *(1977);* Collected Poems *(1981)*
- *Died: Feb. 11, 1963, London, England*

A poet who committed suicide at the age of 30, Sylvia Plath is a major figure in 20th-century American literature. She has also been the subject of a personal legend so powerful that, even many years after her death, it is difficult to separate truth from myth, especially about her marriage. Was her suicide caused by her own psychic frailty or her husband's unfaithfulness?

Plath's father was a professor who died when his daughter was eight,

Sylvia Plath in 1955, the year she graduated from Smith College. She returned to Smith in 1957 to teach English, but left after only one year.

permanently scarring the girl. Her mother worked hard and kept the family afloat, and Plath entered Smith College in 1950, seemingly with a wonderful future before her. In the summer of 1953, she went to New York to be guest editor of *Mademoiselle* magazine, a glamorous assignment, after winning a competition. The job was stressful, however, and after the summer in New York, Plath went into a deep depression and nearly succeeded in killing herself with sleeping pills. But she did not die; she recovered, graduated in 1955, and won a Fulbright scholarship to attend graduate school at Cambridge University in England.

In England Plath met Ted Hughes, a fellow poet whom she married in 1956. She completed her Cambridge degree in English literature in 1957, and the young couple moved to the United States so that she could teach at Smith and he at the University of Massachusetts. During this period Plath began to hone her poetic talent, taking a seminar with the poet Robert Lowell, for example.

In 1959 Plath and Hughes returned to England, where her first book of poetry, *The Colossus,*came out to good reviews in 1960. Nonetheless, Hughes's success had been greater, and she began to type manuscripts for him as a dutiful wife. At the same time, she continued to write poetry and began work on her autobiographical novel *The Bell Jar,* which was largely based on Plath's 1953 suicide attempt and described a young woman's descent into depression, psychiatric treatment, and attempted suicide.

The couple's two children were born in 1960 and 1962, and then Plath discovered that Hughes had been having an affair with another woman. They separated, and she gained custody of the children. Plath continued to write poetry, but on a bleak February day in 1963, she put her head in a gas oven and succeeded—at last—in killing herself.

FURTHER READING

Alexander, Paul. *Rough Magic: A Biography of Sylvia Plath.* New York: Da Capo Press, 1999.

Bassnet, Susan. *Sylvia Plath.* New York: Barnes & Noble Books, 1987.

Malcolm, Janet. *The Silent Woman: Sylvia Plath and Ted Hughes.* New York: Knopf, 1994.

Strangeways, Al. *Sylvia Plath: The Shaping of Shadows.* Cranbury, N.J.: Farleigh Dickinson University Press, 1998.

Pocahontas

- *Born: 1595/96?, Virginia*
- *Died: Mar. 1617, London, England*

One of the earliest heroines in American history, Pocahontas, daughter of the Algonquin chief Powhatan, probably saved Captain John Smith from death when she was a little girl by rescuing him when he was on the verge of execution after being captured by Powhatan's brother. According to Smith's recounting of the incident, after Powhatan ordered his death, she intervened by flinging herself down to shield him from being clubbed. Because Smith himself wrote

This portrait of Pocahontas at the age of 20 is copied from a 1616 painting by William Sheppard. Pocahontas died two years later and was buried in England.

the account, historians are reasonably confident that the story is true, though not that his version was correct.

Pocahontas later married Captain John Rolfe, whom she met while held in captivity aboard a ship, and they had a son named Thomas. The family moved to England, where Pocahontas died when still quite a young woman. Other details of Pocahontas's life are unknown or shrouded in legend.

FURTHER READING

Abrams, Ann Uhry. *The Pilgrims and Pocahontas: Rival Myths of American Origin.* Boulder, Colo.: Westview, 1999.

Holler, Anne. *Pocahontas: Powhatan Peacemaker.* New York: Chelsea House, 1993.

Mossiker, Frances. *Pocahontas: The Life and Legend.* New York: Da Capo, 1996.

Political parties

The two major political parties—the Democrats and the Republicans—have been, for most of U.S. history, quite resistant to utilizing the abilities or accepting the influence of women.

In the 19th century, as the parties grew into an important feature of the American political landscape, meetings of members were all-male undertakings featuring drinking, smoking, and rough language. It was considered inappropriate for women to vote because a refined woman should want no part of such an environment. Even in this environment, though, a few women were beginning to chip away at the barriers, often because they wanted to be politically effective in order to ban alcohol.

In 1920 the 19th Amendment to the Constituion granted women the right to vote, however, and the parties knew that they had to find a way to secure the loyalty of the millions of new voters. The first response was to set up a Women's Division—each party had one—where the women would have their own domain and stay out of male business. But the male leaders granted no authority or substantive work to the Women's Divisions. A few women, such as California Republican congresswoman Florence Kahn, managed to penetrate into the inner circles of a party, but things did not really begin to change until the 1930s, under the influence of the Roosevelts and the New Deal—and then the change was glacially slow.

In this 1920 cartoon, a Democrat and Republican "Adam" each tries to take credit for the passage of the 19th Amendment. "Eve," sitting in the "Political Garden of Eden," holds a paper entitled "Woman Suffrage" while the men each claim "It was my rib, Eve."

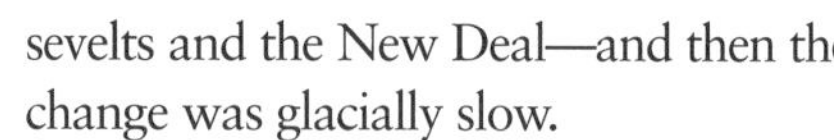

Only with the much more substantial political mobilization of women since the birth of modern feminism in the 1960s have the parties truly taken women seriously, because today women vote at the same rate as do men and—with new access to highly paid employment—they can write bigger checks than they could in the years before 1970. The 1990s have seen women voters mobilize so dramatically in certain elections, that both parties take them seriously, but the Democrats have been more responsive with respect to such issues as child care and reproductive rights.

SEE ALSO

Democratic party; Kahn, Florence Prag; New Deal; Populism; Republican party

FURTHER READING

Perry, Elisabeth, Melanie Gustafson, and Kristie Miller, eds. *We Have Come to Stay: American Women and Political Parties, 1880–1960.* Albuquerque: University of New Mexico Press, 1999.

Politics

In the late 20th century, women participate in U.S. electoral politics to an unprecedented extent—and to an extent that would have been unthinkable even a few years ago. Today numerous women sit on school boards, city councils, and county boards of supervisors. In California, for example, women constituted 3 percent of county board members in 1972, but that figure increased to 28 percent following the 1992 election.

Women now fill enough seats in state legislatures so that in most states they constitute a critical mass large enough to move women's issues into place for public policy decisions. A few women have been governors of large states—such as Ann Richards of Texas—although this position has been perhaps the most resistant to change other than the Presidency itself. Women serve in many other statewide capacities such as treasurer, controller, or lieutenant governor.

The number of women in Congress has increased dramatically since 1992, from 29 out of 435 to 56 in 1999. Though there were, in 1999, only nine women in the U.S. Senate, they were outspoken and high-profile. In the past, by contrast, Senator Hattie Caraway of Arkansas, who served from 1931 to 1945, was known as "Silent Hattie" owing to her reticence. Finally, two of the top positions in President Bill Clinton's cabinet are filled by women: the secretary of state is Madeleine Albright and the attorney general is Janet Reno.

Ann Richards was elected governor of Texas in 1991. Early in her political career, she managed the 1972 Texas House of Representatives campaign of Sarah Weddington, the lawyer who would go on to win the Roe v. Wade *case.*

For much of the period between 1920, when women got the vote, and 1970, when the modern women's movement began to pick up steam, women were marginal in the world of electoral politics. A few women served in Congress at any given time, and there might have been one or two women in a typical state legislature, but they had to present themselves as "honorary men," dressing in severe suits that would not call attention to their gender and avoiding any women's issues, rather than as advocates for other women.

One of the principal reasons that women politicians were not outspoken advocates for other women was the fact that until 1968 women voted, on the average, at a lower rate than men. Following the ratification of the 19th Amendment in 1920, women had to overcome centuries of believing that politics belonged to their husbands and fathers before they were likely to participate at the same rate as men.

As more women joined the workforce and entered public life, however, Americans found it easier to believe that women should have a role in politics, too. Moreover, women now hold a greater array of jobs with real authority in realms other than politics and that has smoothed the way for women officeholders. Since 1968 female voting has equaled or exceeded the male rate, and that trend has assisted the programs of women politicians, who can now hope to find support for their causes from their female colleagues.

Although the United States did not grant women the vote until 1920, women did, in fact, have an important role in political life during the 1800s. Based on the strength of public respect for home and motherhood, women reformers carved out a role of considerable influence. Women could not vote or, in most cases, plausibly run for office, but they could help call attention to problems in American society as advocates for slaves, for the poor, and for children. In a sense there were "separate spheres" of home and public life for women and men, and there were separate spheres of political influence, also.

Today, women are not only active in politics but they are active in ways similar to men while also able to be advocates for such women's issues as child care, breast cancer research, and reproductive choice. The bipartisan National Women's Political Caucus, organized in 1971, is devoted to helping secure the election of women to political offices. Women candidates are able, on the average, to raise money as readily as men. The political fund-raising group EMILY's List (an acronym for Early Money is Like Yeast, which "makes the dough rise") is a political action committee that raises money for pro-choice Democratic women candidates for elective office. Founded in 1985, it raised $6.2 million for its candidates in 1992 and played a significant role in increasing the number of women in Congress.

Though women candidates cannot necessarily rely on the votes of other women, in fact, they are often able to garner them, as seen in the voting patterns discovered for two Democratic senators from California, Dianne Feinstein and Barbara Boxer, both of whom (especially the latter) owed their victories to women voters. The League of Women Voters, a bipartisan organization, was founded in 1919 primarily for preparing women to exercise their new voting rights. Today it educates voters, championing a wide range of women's issues, rather than specific candidates.

SEE ALSO

Congress, U.S.; Political parties; League of Women Voters; National Women's Political Caucus (NWPC)

FURTHER READING

Whitney, Sharon, and Tom Raynor. *Women in Politics.* New York: Watts, 1986

Witt, Linda, Karen M. Paget, and Glenna Matthews. *Running as a Woman: Gender and Power in American Politics.* New York: Free Press, 1994.

Populism

The People's party, also known as the Populist party, was one of the most important third parties (a party other than the Democrats and the Republicans) in U.S. history. In the late 19th century, angry American farmers, unhappy about the unfair treatment they received from banks and railroad companies, formed a protest movement—populism—and also a political party, the People's party, to fight for their interests. Many women were active in the movement and even prominent in the People's party, virtually the first time that women played a significant role in partisan politics. Moreover, the Populists were far more sympathetic to woman suffrage than either the Democrats or the Republicans, as many third parties were.

In the late 1800s, more and more of the U.S. economy was being directed by large corporations rather than small businesses. Farmers felt themselves being squeezed by the high price of transporting their crops to market and by the difficulties they had borrowing money to pay for their expenses. In many parts of the country, but especially in the South and the Midwest, farmers began to organize to try to solve these problems. In some states Populists were elected to office, and the party ran Presidential candidates (unsuccessfully) in 1892 and 1896.

Annie Diggs and Mary Elizabeth Lease were the two best-known Populist women. As an adept politician serving on the Populist National Committee in 1896, for example, Diggs wrote, spoke, and organized very effectively behind the scenes. Lease was a fiery orator famed for advising farmers to "raise less corn and more hell." Though the movement and the party were both dead by 1900, many of the reforms they advocated, such as better regulation of banks and railroads, became law in the 20th century.

FURTHER READING

Kazin, Michael. *The Populist Persuasion: An American History.* Ithaca, N.Y.: Cornell University Press, 1998.

Pornography

The word *pornography* refers to sexually explicit material that is intended to cause sexual excitement. Men have typically been the audience for pornographic books, magazines, and films. Increasingly, in the past 20 years, there has been a market for pornography that goes beyond merely being explicit to depicting women in violent or degrading situations.

Women's movement activists have been deeply divided about this issue. The 1st Amendment to the Constitution protects free speech, which has been interpreted to include films, books, and videos. If society bans violent pornography, is this constitutional? How does one define what is too violent for distribution? One generation's art—such as James Joyce's book *Ulyssees*—may have been an earlier generation's pornography.

Some women have crusaded to have strict limits placed on sexually explicit material that depicts violence against women in the belief that this material increases sexual callousness toward women and may contribute to rape. The organization Feminists Against Pornography represents this set of beliefs. Others have argued that free speech is threatened by such bans, and they have accused antipornography crusaders of being puritanical in their approach to sexuality. The organization Citizens for Media Without Law has crusaded against media images of violence against women, but by pressuring corporations rather than calling for government regulation. The most recent battleground for these issues has been the Internet. That children and young people can readily access Web sites containing sexually explicit material has complicated the discussion.

FURTHER READING

Elmer-Dewitt, Philip. "On a Screen Near You: Cyberporn." *Time,* July 3, 1995.

Schlosser, Eric. "The Business of Pornography." *U.S. News & World Report,* Feb. 10, 1997.

Prison reform

Until the 19th century, prisons were simply places to lock people up. Further, the mentally ill were thrown in jail alongside criminals. The idea was to rid society of those who were a threat to others, with little thought given to reforming or curing them.

Women played a large role in changing this situation. In the mid-19th century, Dorothea Dix successfully crusaded to found mental institutions as separate facilities. Other women campaigned for the establishment of "reformatories" for women prisoners, places where they could learn how to fit into society as good wives and mothers. The reformatories were run by women and tended to be more humane in the physical treatment of inmates than prisons for men. They also tended to house only white women; women of color were sent to more purely custodial institutions that did not aim to "reform" the prisoners.

The legacy of early prison reformers, most especially Miriam Van Waters, who was superintendent of the Massachusetts Reformatory for Women from 1932 to 1957 and believed in rehabilitating rather than punishing people who had committed crimes, has survived in many ways. A domestic atmosphere is still seen as good for female inmates, for example. Prison reformers in the 1970s and 1980s crusaded to improve facilities so that mothers and children could have more interaction and to accommodate women's special health needs.

The goal of improving conditions for women prisoners, however, has bumped up against soaring prison populations and strained resources, resulting in budget cuts that have eliminated services. Currently women constitute about 10 percent of local jail inmates and about 5 percent of state and federal prisoners. As with male inmates, most of the prisoners are women of color rather than white.

Prisoners exercise during a recreation period at the Massachusetts Reformatory Prison for Women in 1920. The prison's setting was deliberately rural in an attempt to remove the inmates from corrupting urban influences.

SEE ALSO

Dix, Dorothea Lynde

FURTHER READING

Freedman, Estelle. *Maternal Justice: Miriam Van Waters and the Female Reform Tradition.* Chicago: University of Chicago Press, 1996.

Freedman, Estelle. *Their Sisters' Keepers.* Ann Arbor: University of Michigan Press, 1981.

Morris, Norval, and David J. Rothman, eds. *The Oxford History of the Prison: The Practice of Punishment in Western Society.* New York: Oxford University Press, 1995.

Privacy

The idea that privacy is a basic human right, something that people are entitled to, developed gradually over the past two centuries under the influence of market capitalism, smaller families creating more room in houses, and better access to education.

In a preindustrial village society, neighbors might have looked in one another's windows or keyholes if they thought that someone was up to no good and then later have testified quite unashamedly in court about what they had seen. People did not have rooms of their own, and they might not even have had beds of their own. Such lack of privacy might have had some advantages, however, such as offering protection from an abusive spouse, which is sometimes difficult to obtain from a police department today because the violence occurs in the home.

Over time the growth in respect for privacy and the growth in the power and respect enjoyed by women have coincided and reinforced one another because private life and the inner world of the home were the female sphere. In earlier times, the public world dominated by men was the focus of society's attention. Literature, for example, typically glorified male warriors rather than examining the private nature of love relationships, an area in which women are as important as men. In the 18th century, literature began to explore the realm of feelings much more systematically with the birth of the novel as a genre. Writers began to explore private life—courtship, for example—in new ways.

In general, respect for privacy has been good for women, and it has specifically provided justification for gains in reproductive rights. The U.S. Supreme Court in both *Griswold* v. *Connecticut* (1965) and *Roe* v. *Wade* (1973) used the right to privacy to decide that women should be able to control their own bodies; the government should not interfere, the Court ruled, if a woman wants to receive birth-control information or devices (*Griswold*) or if she wants to have an abortion (*Roe*).

Although the U.S. constitution does not specifically mention any right to privacy, the Court inferred such a right from other rights that *are* enumerated, for example, the 14th Amendment's explicit guarantee of individual liberty. As a result, the Court's doctrine remains controversial.

SEE ALSO

Griswold v. *Connecticut* (1965); *Roe* v. *Wade* (1973)

FURTHER READING

Alderman, Ellen, and Caroline Kennedy. *The Right to Privacy.* New York: Vintage Books, 1997.

Matthews, Glenna. *The Rise of Public Woman.* New York: Oxford University Press, 1992.

Prohibition

SEE Temperance

Prostitution

Prostitution is the sale of sex. For the most part, it involves male purchasers and female sellers—although not always.

Certain circumstances enhance the likelihood of commercialized sex. One is a disproportionately male population, as in California during the gold rush years in the mid-19th century. Another is an especially vulnerable population of girls and young women. In parts of the world with large-scale economic problems today, for example, desperately poor families have been selling their daughters as prostitutes. The practice flourishes as a result, and an international market in young women develops.

Prostitution started to be an issue in the United States around 1810 as cities began to grow rapidly, as young people flocked to cities from farms, and as low wages for women gave young women a reason to sell their bodies. Sex districts, also known as "red-light" districts, flourished in cities throughout the country. Local officials winked at the practice, often because they themselves received a cut of the profits.

The opposition to sex for profit grew, also in the 19th century. Reformers, including clergymen and women's groups, tried to shut down the red-light districts and to assist prostitutes in finding other ways of supporting themselves. By the 1920s municipal officials, under heavy public pressure, had begun to crack down on this subculture.

Throughout most of the United States today, prostitution is illegal, the exception being portions of Nevada (counties with less than 250,000 in the population). The laws reflect a sexual double standard, however, because typically it is the woman rather than her customer who is subject to arrest. In addition to the legal problems she is likely to encounter, a prostitute is at high risk for sexually transmitted diseases and for violence inflicted by a customer or by the man, known as a pimp, who typically manages her "business" and takes a share of the profits.

Late 19th-century prostitutes in front of "cribs," small rented rooms with a door facing the street. In western settlements where the population was disproportionately male, prostitution was a thriving business.

FURTHER READING

D'Emilio, John, and Estelle B. Freedman. *Intimate Matters: A History of Sexuality in America.* Chicago: University of Chicago Press, 1997.

Stange, Margit. *Personal Property: Wives, White Slaves, and the Market in Women.* Baltimore: Johns Hopkins University Press, 1998.

Protestants

When Martin Luther nailed his criticisms of the Roman Catholic Church to a church door in Germany in 1517, he had little thought of improving the status of women. But the Protestant Reformation that he launched had that effect.

The Reformation allowed Christians to find religious authority not in the pope and an all-male church hierarchy but in the Bible. Men dominated the institutional structures of the new faiths that were born as a result of the Reformation, but women now had a powerful incentive to learn to read and a license—limited at first, to be sure—to make up their own minds.

Most of the American colonies were settled by Protestants, among whom there began to be a number of distinct denominations, including Congregationalists, Episcopalians, Presbyterians, Methodists, Baptists, and Quakers. Very early in colonial history, in the 1630s, a woman named Anne Hutchinson took Protestant ideas to their logical conclusion and challenged the authority of the Boston clergy with her own ideas about the meaning of grace. She and her family were banished as a result.

Hutchinson was the first American Protestant female rebel, but many others followed. The more that an individual denomination encouraged a reliance on inner convictions—as with the Quakers—the more it fostered intellectual daring among its female members.

All Protestant women, black and white alike, received encouragement to learn to read and to think about theology. Moreover, starting as early as the 1790s they began to form religiously inspired voluntary organizations, which laid the foundation for much of the social activism of succeeding generations. Many Protestant women also took bold action by becoming missionaries beginning in the first half of the 19th century, both in this country and abroad, well before women routinely set off on such journeys for business or pleasure.

Protestant women, especially Quakers and Unitarians, formed the core of the 19th-century woman suffrage movement. They also crusaded throughout the century for a variety of other humanitarian reforms, such as the antislavery movement and the temperance movement (against the abuse of alcohol). On September 15, 1853, Antoinette Brown Blackwell was ordained as the minister of the First Congregational Church in Butler and Savannah, New York. Though her pastorate was short-lived, due to her religious views that were evolving toward Unitarianism, she nonetheless lives in history as the first ordained woman minister of a recognized denomination in the United States.

In the 20th century, Protestant women, black and white alike, have continued to form important organizations within their respective denominations. Among many liberal denominations women have won the right to be ordained, and their numbers have increased in the theological seminaries of Lutherans, Methodists, Episco-

Rev. Alice Winston and many other women preachers have played a large role in the history of African-American religion. "They shook up many men, white and black," said historian Rev. Frances Collier-Thomas. "They moved women closer to the seat of power."

palians, and Presbyterians. Fundamentalist Protestant denominations, on the other hand, not only have not permitted the ordination of women but also have constituted the most potent opponents of the Equal Rights Amendment and other feminist goals.

SEE ALSO

Blackwell, Antoinette Brown; Hutchinson, Anne; Quakers; Religion

FURTHER READING

Braude, Ann. *Women and American Religion.* New York: Oxford University Press, 1999.

Higginbotham, Evelyn Brooks. *Righteous Discontent: The Women's Movement in the Black Baptist Church.* Cambridge: Harvard University Press, 1993.

Reuther, Radford, and Rosemary Skinner Keller, eds. *Women and Religion in America.* San Francisco: Harper & Row, 1991.

Quakers

The Religious Society of Friends, commonly known as the Quakers because in England in 1650 one of its founders told a judge to tremble at the word of the Lord, has never been a large denomination—although its members did found the colony of Pennsylvania. Despite the group's small numbers, several women important to U.S. history, including the pioneer suffragists Lucretia Mott and Susan B. Anthony, were Quakers. The denomination encouraged women to participate in public life by permitting them to preach well before other denominations did and by establishing a system of governance that fostered female talent with its separate women's meetings run by women themselves.

The Society of Friends originated in England in the mid-1600s. George Fox, the founder, stressed the role of one's Inner Light, the revelation of Christ within, in bringing a person to salvation, and this Inner Light could visit women as well as men. From the earliest years, there were powerful Quaker women in the religion, and the Quakers also pioneered the idea of a marriage based on equality rather than a husband's authority.

Quaker women played a significant role in introducing their faith to the colonies. Some were traveling preachers who went far afield talking about the Inner Light. A few Quaker women, such as Mary Dyer, were executed when their beliefs led them to preach in colonies where their message was not welcome.

In the 19th century there were a number of divisions over theology, which served to sap some of the vitality from the group. These divisions notwithstanding, Quaker women were at the forefront of the woman suffrage movement, disproportionately represented relative to their small numbers in the larger society. In the mid- to late 20th century, there has been a coming together of various Quaker factions, and the Quakers have once again played a significant role in American society with the philanthropic relief provided for by the Friends Service Committee, which was founded in 1917.

SEE ALSO

Anthony, Susan Brownell; Dyer, Mary; Mott, Lucretia Coffin; Religion; Suffrage, woman

FURTHER READING

Bacon, Margaret Hope. *Mothers of Feminism: The Story of Quaker Women in America.* San Francisco: Harper & Row, 1986.

Baker, Hugh, and J. William Frost. *The Quakers.* Westport, Conn.: Greenwood, 1988.

Smith, Robert Houston. *The Passmores in America: A Quaker Family Through Six Generations.* Lewiston, N.Y.: Edwin Mullen Press, 1992.

Ma Rainey's Jazz Band, shown here in 1925, played vaudeville theaters in Chicago and the Midwest. Gertrude Rainey, known as "Ma," was not the first to record blues vocals, but nevertheless, she was acknowledged as "the mother of the blues."

Rainey, Gertrude Pridgett ("Ma")

- *Born: Apr. 26, 1886, Columbus, Ga.*
- *Education: Unknown*
- *Accomplishments: Blues Foundation Hall of Fame (1983); Rock and Roll Hall of Fame (1990)*
- *Died: Dec. 22, 1939, Columbus, Ga.*

Gertrude ("Ma") Rainey was one of a group of African-American musicians who popularized that most distinctive of American art forms, the blues.

When Gertrude Pridgett was growing up, a kind of variety show known as a minstrel show was a popular type of entertainment. Some minstrel performers were whites wearing blackface makeup, and others were themselves African Americans, but all were influenced by black culture and music. Gertrude Pridgett performed in these shows, and she married fellow entertainer Will ("Pa") Rainey in 1904. The two then did a song-and-dance act for the shows.

Ma Rainey pushed what was, in white hands, often a demeaning and stereotypical genre in new directions with her haunting songs of pain, loss, and survival—some of whose lyrics she wrote herself. In the 1920s she began to make records, leaving documentation of her contribution to the birth of the blues. She was immortalized in these recordings, as well as in the play *Ma Rainey's Black Bottom: A Play in Two Acts*, by August Wilson (1985), which is about musicians at an audition with Ma Rainey.

SEE ALSO

Music

FURTHER READING

Davis, Angela Y. *Blues Legacies and Black Feminism: Gertrude "Ma" Rainey, Bessie Smith, and Billie Holiday.* New York: Pantheon, 1998.

Lieb, Sandra R. *Mother of the Blues: A Study of Ma Rainey.* Amherst: University of Massachusetts Press, 1981.

Rankin, Jeannette

- *Born: June 11, 1880, Missoula, Mont.*
- *Education: University of Montana, B.A., 1902; New York School of*

Philanthropy (later Columbia School of Social Work), attended 1908–09
- *Accomplishments: Legislative secretary, National American Woman Suffrage Association (1914); first woman to serve in Congress, as U.S. Representative (R–Mont., 1917–19, 1941–43)*
- *Died: May 18, 1973, Carmel, Calif.*

The first woman to serve in the U.S. Congress, Republican Jeannette Rankin was also the first woman to be elected to a national legislature anywhere in the world. Her initial term, 1917–19, coincided with the U.S. entry into World War I, and Rankin, as a pacifist, was immediately thrust into the national limelight.

In 1916 Jeannette Rankin became the first woman elected to the U.S. Congress—and also the first woman to be elected to a national legislature anywhere in the world. She had been a suffrage leader in her home state of Montana.

Active in the suffrage movement in Montana, Rankin ran for the U.S. House of Representatives with the goal of focusing on issues of concern to women and children. As it happened, her first vote in the House would be cast on whether or not the United States should declare war on Germany, a looming choice she knew she would have to consider even before she took office because of Germany's increasingly hostile behavior. Suffragists were divided about what she should do. Should she stick to her peace-loving principles and vote against the war, or should she demonstrate that a woman in office would be just as patriotic as a man?

Rankin—and 49 congress*men*—voted against the war. Though she was not alone in her stance, she was the one the press focused upon. She had one other term in the House from 1941 to 1943, which coincided with the Japanese bombing of Pearl Harbor. On this occasion, too, Rankin voted against war, but this time she did stand alone.

SEE ALSO

Congress, U.S.; World War I

FURTHER READING

Josephson, Hannah. *Jeannette Rankin, First Lady in Congress.* Indianapolis: Bobbs-Merrill, 1994.

Rape

The traditional legal definition of rape has been "intercourse between a man and a woman not his wife, against the woman's will and without her consent." Though rape has been, in general, illegal, the enforcement of the laws in the United States has varied widely, depending on the race and the social position of both the victim and the alleged rapist.

In some cases women have been especially vulnerable. In the South during the time of slavery, for example, a white master could legally force a slave woman to have sex. After the Civil War, on the other hand, a black man who was merely rumored to have made improper advances to a white woman might well have died at the hands of a lynch mob.

Since the 1970s, feminists have worked to help rape victims obtain justice. Victims are now treated with greater sensitivity by the police, for example, and they are much less likely to be asked to testify in court about their own prior sexual history, information that defendants have often used to suggest that the rape was not their fault.

One area of growing concern is date rape, in which an acquaintance (rather than a stranger) forces sex on a woman. College women, in particular, face this risk. Some commentators have suggested that since the sexual revolution of the 1960s, it is more difficult for a woman to say "no" and be heard accurately.

Reliable statistics about rape are difficult to obtain. Some experts claim that for every reported rape, many more go unreported. Several researchers have found that one in five women on the campuses they were studying have reported being forced to have sex by an acquaintance. That figure is sometimes given for the larger incidence of rape, also.

FURTHER READING

Bode, Janet. *Voices of Rape*. Danbury, Conn.: Franklin Watts, Inc., 1999.

Ray, Charlotte E.

- *Born: Jan. 13, 1850, New York, N.Y.*
- *Education: Howard University, LL.B., 1872*
- *Accomplishments: First woman admitted to District of Columbia bar (1872); first black woman lawyer in the U.S.*
- *Died: Jan. 4, 1911, Woodside, N.Y.*

Charlotte Ray was the first African-American woman lawyer and also the first woman admitted to the bar in Washington, D.C.

The daughter of a New York family that had been active helping slaves escape via the Underground Railroad (safe houses positioned along potential escape routes), Ray dedicated herself to obtaining a good education. Around 1870 she began studying law at the newly formed Howard University in Washington. After graduating in 1872, she was admitted to the District of Columbia's bar, apparently without debate since the District of Columbia's legal code had recently been revised and "male" had been eliminated from the description of qualification for the bar. She was unable, however, to support herself as a lawyer because she had trouble finding clients who were willing to have their legal problems handled by a black woman. She then turned to a career in teaching. She also is known to have attended at least one woman suffrage convention.

SEE ALSO

Law

Reconstruction

The period after the Civil War (1861–65) is known as Reconstruction because the federal government took control of the governments in the former Confederate states (except for Tennessee) in order to "reconstruct" them enough to accept changes in the treatment of African Americans. Federal troops occupied the defeated states in order to ensure that whites did not deny ex-slaves their right to participate in society and government.

During Reconstruction, constitutional amendments protecting the rights of newly freed slaves were ratified, and black men were elected to high office in significant numbers for the first time, among other milestones in black history. The amendments were the 13th, ending slavery and ratified in 1865; the 14th, defining citizenship and guaranteeing citizens the right to due process and equal protection of the law and ratified in 1868; and the 15th, ratified in 1870, which contained the following language: "The right of citizens of the United States to vote shall not be denied or abridged by the United States or by any state on account of race, color, or previous condition of servitude."

Because the 15th Amendment was silent on the subject of sex, it enfranchised black men only. The whole question of citizenship was thus being

By the late 1800s, black teachers in many states were freedwomen. These women, however, often proved vulnerable targets for hostile whites who did not want ex-slaves to receive an education.

debated as vigorously as it had ever been in the nation's history, given the effort to guarantee the rights of citizenship to the freed people, and the issue soon involved women as well as blacks.

The woman suffrage movement divided into two camps based on whether members thought it was appropriate to enfranchise black men and leave women out of the picture. Elizabeth Cady Stanton and Susan B. Anthony led the wing known as the National Woman Suffrage Association and strongly attacked the Reconstruction amendments as being destructive of women's progress, because women were not specifically included in the amendments. The other wing, known as the American Woman Suffrage Association and led by Lucy Stone, accepted the amendments.

After the initial controversy over the amendments died down, certain suffragists began to examine closely the language of the 14th Amendment, which had aroused the ire of Stanton and Anthony because it had specified the rights of male voters in the Constitution for the first time. A husband and wife, the suffrage activists Francis and Virginia Minor, developed the theory that rather than denying women the vote, the 14th Amendment had actually enfranchised them because it also stated that all citizens had "privileges and immunities" (such as voting) that could not be abridged without due process of law. Virginia Minor attempted to vote in 1872, and they sued unsuccessfully in 1875 to gain her the vote on the basis of the 14th Amendment, in *Minor* v. *Happersett*.

This suffrage argument was known as the "New Departure," and it provided the basis for an innovative strategy whereby 150 women attempted to vote in the 1872 election (only 4 of whom succeeded). The New Departure did not bring lasting results, but it did demonstrate the resourcefulness of those in the woman suffrage movement.

SEE ALSO

Anthony, Susan Brownell; Citizenship; 14th Amendment; *Minor* v. *Happersett* (1875); Stanton, Elizabeth Cady; Stone, Lucy; Suffrage, woman

FURTHER READING

Foner, Eric. *A Short History of Reconstruction, 1863–1877.* New York: HarperCollins, 1990.

Sigerman, Harriet. *Laborers for Liberty: American Women 1865–1890.* Vol. 6 of *The Young Oxford History of Women in the United States.* New York: Oxford University Press, 1994.

Werstein, Irving. *This Wounded Land: The Era of Reconstruction, 1865–1877.* New York: Delacorte, 1968.

Reed v. *Reed* (1971)

In 1971 the U.S. Supreme Court fully applied the equal-protection clause of the 14th Amendment—"No state shall . . . deny to any person within its jurisdiction the equal protection of the laws"—to gender discrimination for the first time, and it struck down legislation, again for the first time, on the grounds that it discriminated on the basis of sex. With the case of *Reed* v. *Reed,* gender joined race in the "suspect" category, which means that cases involving discrimination on this basis now require strict scrutiny by the Court.

The case revolved around an Idaho man who had died without leaving a will. Richard Reed was survived by two adoptive parents, who, to complicate matters, had recently separated. The parents filed competing suits asking to be appointed to administer their son's estate, and the probate court, using Idaho statutes to guide the decision, awarded the preference to the father on the grounds that he was male. The mother then sued to overturn the probate court's decision.

In its unanimous verdict in her favor, the Supreme Court reflected the mood of the country at a time when women's rights were being discussed as never before. Chief Justice Warren Burger said in his opinion: "We have concluded that the arbitrary preference established in favor of males by . . . the Idaho Code cannot stand in the face of the Fourteenth Amendment's command that no state deny the equal protection of the laws to any person within its jurisdiction."

SEE ALSO

14th Amendment

FURTHER READING

Patrick, John J. *The Young Oxford Companion to the Supreme Court of the United States.* New York: Oxford University Press, 1998.

Religion

For women, religion has furnished not only the consolation and spiritual nourishment that it offers to all human beings but also the opportunity to assume leadership roles at times when otherwise they have had little power. At the same time, however, various religions have also provided rationales for the unequal treatment of women.

Throughout history, religion has offered certain brave women a chance to escape their traditional roles. The Roman Catholic saint Joan of Arc, who lived in France in the 1400s, heard voices that prompted her to take up arms to defend her country and go into battle to do God's will. She even personally led troops and died a martyr's death. Joan was perhaps the most famous but far from the only woman to hear voices urging her to do something outside the ordinary. Many other women mystics from both the Christian and the Jewish traditions have forged extraordinary roles for

Henrietta Szold lays the cornerstone of a hospital in Jerusalem, built in 1934 with funds raised by Hadassah, the Women's Zionist Organization of America. Szold was one of the founders of Hadassah, which is "dedicated to the ideals of Judaism, Zionism, American democracy, healing, teaching, and medical research."

themselves in this fashion; an inner voice authorizing bold behavior is a hard thing for others to dispute.

The first American woman to take issue with the established religious order was Boston's Anne Hutchinson; in the 1630s she led prayer meetings in which she challenged the authority of the clergy—for which she and her family were banished. But Hutchinson was not the last woman rebel, and many of her successors were far more successful than she. For example, in the late 1700s, at a time in which each state still had an official church, Mother Ann Lee founded a sect known as the Shakers, which led ultimately to the establishment of a number of religiously based Shaker communities in the Northeast.

The Judeo-Christian tradition that the European colonizers brought to America was patriarchal in many ways—it included an all-male clergy, God was considered the father (unlike the deities of Native American religions, which included males and females), and it supported a tradition that prohibited women from speaking in church or temple. As a result, women who wanted to challenge their traditional roles were often forced to challenge various religious doctrines as well.

Women reformers in the 1800s, for example, reacted to Saint Paul's declaration in the Bible that women need to keep silent in church. One reformer after another took issue with Paul—or claimed that he had been misinterpreted—because they knew how much power his prohibition had to carry over into the overwhelmingly Protestant mainstream culture. In the late 1800s Elizabeth Cady Stanton even took the controversial step of publishing *The Woman's Bible,* in which she offered commentary on parts of the Bible that seem demeaning to women, arguing that women were powerless not only because of laws and government, but because of the attitudes of predominant religions, whose "degrading ideas of women emanated from the brain of man." As Stanton had pointed out in a magazine article, "When those who are opposed to all reforms can find no other argument, their last resort is the Bible. It has been interpreted to favor intemperance, slavery, capital punishment, and the subjection of women."

Despite their difficulties with St. Paul and their lack of access to the ministry in most denominations, women began to forge a potent religious role in the 19th century. Both Catholic and Protestant women became missionaries, for example; Narcissa Whitman is perhaps the best known. Protestant women formed religious associations that in many cases led to their activism even outside the walls of a church. In the early 1800s Jarena Lee became a traveling preacher for the African Methodist Episcopal Church—after an inner voice prompted her to make an attempt. In 1853 Antoinette

Brown Blackwell was ordained in the Congregational denomination, the first woman in the country to be ordained by a mainstream Protestant church. Reform Jews began to dissent from Orthodox tenets about strict rules governing women's behavior. In the late 1800s Mary Baker Eddy founded the Christian Science Church. In short, the 19th century saw much progress for women in a variety of faiths.

By the late 1800s another important development lay in the role that black women were playing in various Protestant denominations, but especially among Southern Baptists. Though they had to struggle with male-dominated institutions—as were nearly all religious institutions at the time—they succeeded in organizing for self-help in the black community.

These black Baptist women were part of a pattern throughout U.S. history whereby female advocates of social change have also often been sustained by powerful religious faith. Black women in the civil rights movement of the 1950s and 1960s, for example, very often claimed that it was their strong Christian belief that enabled them to keep going in the face of violence—even murder—and multiple causes for discouragement.

Today there has been great change among many religious denominations, fueled by feminist revolts within them and the social transformations going on in the larger society. In many faiths women can now serve as clergy, for example, and even among many denominations that have resisted ordaining women—such as the Roman Catholic Church—female congregants serve as lay readers, thus participating in what was, until the last 20 years, an all-male domain. Feminist theology, challenging traditional views of women as weaker and more sinful than men, possesses great vitality, and its practitioners come from many different faith backgrounds, Christian and Jewish alike, and from many different ethnic groups.

On November 1, 1993, Mary Adelia McLeod became the first woman to serve as a diocesan bishop in the Episcopal Church. She was assisted at her consecration ceremony in Vermont by her son.

SEE ALSO

Catholicism; Eddy, Mary Baker; Hutchinson, Anne; Judaism; Lee, Ann; Mormons; Protestants; Quakers; Whitman, Narcissa Prentiss

FURTHER READING

Braude, Ann. *Women in American Religion.* New York: Oxford University Press, 1999.

Higginbotham, Evelyn B. *Righteous Discontent: The Women's Movement in the Black Baptist Church, 1880–1920.* Cambridge, Mass.: Harvard University Press, 1993.

Ruether, Rosemary Radford, and Rosemary Skinner Keller, eds. *Women and Religion in America.* 3 vols. San Francisco: Harper & Row, 1981.

Stanton, Elizabeth Cady. *The Woman's Bible.* Boston: Northeastern University Press, 1993.

Reproductive rights

For much of U.S. history, women did not think of themselves as having reproductive rights or the right to chose whether to have children and, if so, how many. Husbands and wives enjoyed the pleasures of the marital bed, God sent children, and women accepted them, often watching the little ones die in infancy or early childhood. Thomas Jefferson's much-loved wife, Martha, for example, underwent seven pregnancies in ten years, dying as a result of complications following the birth of the last child. The seven pregnancies produced only two daughters who survived to adulthood. In such circumstances, controlling one's fertility was less urgent than it would later become.

The first step toward what we now call reproductive rights lay in women's asserting their right to say "no" to their husbands. Nineteenth-century feminists thought of this refusal as "voluntary motherhood," and they were prepared to be advocates on its behalf—though with some delicacy. Only the most advanced thinkers discussed such issues in public, but in private, people in the 19th century began to act to limit family size by abstaining from sex, by male withdrawal during sex, or by women getting abortions. As a result, the birthrate declined from about 7 children per white married woman in 1800 to about 3.5 in 1900. (The data is incomplete for women of color.)

As awareness of the declining birthrate spread, some lawmakers became concerned about what they saw as evidence of a decline in morals: if people had sex while protecting themselves from the usual consequence of being at risk to have children, then sexuality might become much freer. In 1873 Congress passed the Comstock Act, named for the reformer Anthony Comstock, which made it illegal to send obscene material, including information about how to limit births, through the mail. State legislatures also began to pass laws to criminalize abortion for the first time.

Reproductive rights pioneers such as the anarchist Emma Goldman and Margaret Sanger, the person who did more than anyone else in the U.S. to change attitudes about birth control, began to speak out on behalf of contraceptive, or birth-control, devices in the early 20th century, and their activities spurred the birth-control movement. For their efforts, they faced prosecution under the Comstock Act and various state statutes. During the course of the 20th century, however, court decisions struck down laws prohibiting the distribution of birth-control information, thus laying the groundwork for the new notion of reproductive rights. The most definitive decision in this area was the Supreme Court decision of *Griswold* v. *Connecticut* in 1965, in which the Court struck down a state law forbidding doctors to prescribe contraceptives to married people.

In the late 1960s feminists began to be public advocates for a woman's right to terminate a pregnancy, and this marks the birth of a true reproductive rights movement. The birth-control pill had become available, U.S. Supreme Court decisions had eliminated barriers to obtaining contraception, and now feminists began to believe that a woman should be in complete control of her fertility. When the Supreme Court upheld the right to abortion in *Roe* v. *Wade* (1973), this was a tremendous victory for reproductive rights. But as those opposed to abortion have fought back, the issue of controlling one's fertility versus the rights of the unborn continues to be one of the most hotly contested in the country.

SEE ALSO

Abortion; Birth control; Goldman, Emma; *Griswold* v. *Connecticut* (1965); Planned Parenthood; *Roe* v. *Wade* (1973); Sanger, Margaret Higgins

FURTHER READING

Chesler, Ellen. *Woman of Valor: Margaret Sanger and the Birth Control Movement in America.* New York: Anchor Books, 1993.

Critchlow, Donald T. *Intended Consequences: Birth Control, Abortion, and the Federal Government in Modern America.* New York: Oxford University Press, 1999.

Gordon, Linda. *Woman's Body, Woman's Right: Birth Control in America.* New York: Grossman, 1976.

Muller, Jerry Z. "The Conservative Case for Abortion; Family Values vs. Family Planning." *The New Republic,* 213, nos. 8-9 (1995): 27–30.

Pacillo, Edith L. "Expanding the Feminist Imagination: An Analysis of Reproductive Rights." *American University Journal of Gender and the Law,* 6, no. 1 (1997): 113–138.

Petchesky, Rosalind. *Abortion and Woman's Choice: The State, Sexuality and Reproductive Freedom.* New York: Longman, 1984.

Republican party

The history of women and the Republican party, one of the two major political parties in the United States, is a curious one. Today, women voters tend to favor the Democratic party, evidently because of its support for reproductive rights, child care, family leave, and many other issues of concern to women. But until the 1960s the Republican party was more outspoken on women's rights.

The reason that the Democrats lagged behind the Republicans for decades lies in the complicated politics of the Equal Rights Amendment (ERA). First introduced in 1923, the ERA alienated many women activists, because it would have eliminated the protective labor legislation for women workers. Most women reformers and all of organized labor opposed the ERA. Organized labor was one of the Democrats' major constituencies, so the party backed away from endorsing this controversial measure for years. In 1940 the Republican party became the first to endorse the ERA, and in 1956 the party platform spoke out against sex discrimination.

As the Republican party has become more conservative since then, it has backed away from the women's rights agenda, reversing its position on the ERA in 1980, for example. It has also been much less friendly than the Democratic party to publicly supported child care or family leave laws.

Although the first generation of post-suffrage women officeholders tended to be Republican, now the reverse is true, and more women officeholders are Democratic than Republican. Nonetheless, there are still some female Republican officeholders serving with great distinction, for example, Maine's Senators Olympia Snowe and Susan Collins who follow in the footsteps of their illustrious predecessor, Maine's Republican Senator Margaret Chase Smith.

SEE ALSO

Democratic party; Equal Rights Amendment (ERA); Political parties

Rich, Adrienne

- *Born: May 16, 1929, Baltimore, Md.*
- *Education: Radcliffe College, A.B., 1951*
- *Accomplishments: Yale Younger Poet's Award (1951); National Book Award for* Diving into the Wreck *(1974);*

MacArthur Fellow (1994); author, The Will to Change; Poems 1968–1970 *(1971);* Diving into the Wreck: Poems 1971–1972 *(1973);* Pieces *(1977);* On Lies, Secrets, and Silence: Selected Prose, 1966–1978 *(1979);* A Wild Patience Has Taken Me This Far: Poems 1978–1981 *(1981);* Compulsory Heterosexuality and Lesbian Existence *(1981);* Sources *(1983);* The Fact of a Doorframe *(1984);* Of Woman Born *(1976);* Your Native Land, Your Life: Poems *(1986);* Time's Power: Poems 1985–1988 *(1989);* An Atlas of the Difficult World *(1991);* Collected Early Poems, 1950–1970 *(1993);* What Is Found There: Notebooks on Poetry and Politics *(1993);* Blood, Bread, and Poetry: Selected Prose 1979–1985 *(1994);* Dark Fields of the Republic *(1995);* Midnight Salvage: Poems 1995–1998 *(1999)*

Adrienne Rich is an award-winning poet as well as an important feminist thinker. In both her poetry and her nonfiction, she has exercised a profound influence on younger women. Rich has become a controversial figure because she has insisted on dealing with feminism and her lesbian sexual orientation in her writing. She has provoked some critics to rage—they charge that her work is more propaganda than literature—while inspiring others.

Rich attended Radcliffe College, and even before she graduated, the poet W. H. Auden had chosen her work for inclusion in the Yale series of young poets he was editing. The collection of her poetry appeared in 1951 under the title *A Change of World.* Later works include *Diving into the Wreck* (1973); her meditation on motherhood, *Of Woman Born* (1976); and her lesbian manifesto, *Compulsory Heterosexuality and Lesbian Existence* (1981).

In 1951 Rich married the economist Alfred Conrad; the couple subsequently had three sons. In 1966 they separated, and in 1970 Conrad killed himself, leaving Rich with three adolescent boys to care for. She was able to support herself and her family by teaching at a number of colleges and universities, starting with Swarthmore College in 1967. In 1999 she was living in Santa Cruz, California, with her partner and fellow writer, Michelle Cliff.

Her poetry is grounded in the daily realities of life. Yet she also announced in *Dark Fields of the Republic: Poems 1991–1995* that "the great dark birds of history screamed and plunged into our personal history," suggesting her engagement with the great events of her day.

FURTHER READING

Yorke, Liz. *Adrienne Rich: Passion, Politics and the Body.* London: Sage, 1997.

Richards, Ellen Swallow

- *Born: Dec. 3, 1842, Dunstable, Mass.*
- *Education: Vassar College, B.A., 1870; Massachusetts Institute of Technology, B.S., 1873; Vassar College, M.A., 1873*
- *Accomplishments: Founder, Women's Laboratory, MIT (1876); co-founder, Association of Collegiate Alumnae (1881; later the American Association of University Women)*
- *Died: Mar. 30, 1911, Boston, Mass.*

One of the founders of the field of home economics, Ellen Swallow Richards was also a chemist and a pioneer in environmental science and ecology. She used her scientific training to launch a new field widely seen as "appropriate for women" because it dealt with the home, a fact that reveals how few opportunities existed for educated women in traditionally male-dominated fields of study.

Ellen Swallow attended Vassar College, where she worked with the astronomer Maria Mitchell, and completed the four-year program in two years. After graduating in 1870, she decided to pursue graduate study in chemistry at the Massachusetts Institute of Technology, where she was admitted as a special non-paying student. She later learned that by refusing to charge her tuition, MIT was preserving its option of denying that she was enrolled. The first woman to be admitted there, she was treated as a second-class citizen, but she persevered, and in 1873 received a B.S. from MIT, and an M.A. in chemistry from Vassar by submitting a thesis in absentia. She continued to study at MIT but was never able to earn a doctorate because the school did not want to set a precedent of granting such degrees to women. In 1875 she married fellow scientist Robert Hallowell Richards.

The founder of home economics, Ellen Richards Swallow was the first woman admitted to the Massachusetts Institute of Technology (MIT). After becoming a professor there, she introduced biology to MIT's curriculum and founded its oceanographic institute.

Richards continued to pursue her scientific research at MIT, carving out a niche for herself in studying the chemistry of food and household articles. Initially her laboratory was financed by the Women's Education Association of Boston. When MIT set up her laboratory to study sanitation in 1884, she became an assistant instructor. In 1890, when MIT established a program in sanitary engineering (the first in any university) Richards taught the analysis of water, sewage, and air. Out of this movement to train young women in scientific principles came the impetus for home economics. It was understood that these young women would grow up to be housewives and with such an education have the benefit of the most up-to-date information.

In 1899 Richards provided the leadership for the founding conference of the field, held at Lake Placid, New York, and she held the position of president of the American Home Economics Association until shortly before her death in 1911. Richards also devoted herself to improving women's access to a scientific education, overseeing the admission of a small number of other women to MIT beginning in the late 1870s and working to improve secondary instruction in science for girls.

SEE ALSO

Home economics

FURTHER READING

Clarke, Robert. *Ellen Swallow: The Woman Who Founded Ecology.* Chicago: Follett, 1973.

Hunt, Caroline Louisa. *The Life of Ellen H. Richards, 1842–1911.* Washington, D.C.: American Home Economics Association, 1980.

Rossiter, Margaret. *Women Scientists in America: Struggles and Strategies to 1940.* Baltimore: Johns Hopkins University Press, 1982.

Ride, Sally

- *Born: May 26, 1951, Encino, Calif.*
- *Education: Stanford University, B.A. and B.S., 1973, Ph.D., 1977*
- *Accomplishments: First U.S. woman in space (1983)*

The first American woman in space, Sally Ride will always enjoy an honored place in the history books for that achievement. Her pioneering journey was, however, only one moment in a life devoted to scientific inquiry.

An excellent athlete, Ride was a nationally ranked tennis player while in college, but decided that she lacked the ability to be a pro. She graduated from Stanford University in 1973 with a double major in English literature and physics. She then applied for admission to the astronaut program—while also enrolled as a graduate student in astrophysics at Stanford. Shortly after finishing her doctorate, she reported to the Johnson Space Center in Texas to begin intensive training for her space mission.

In 1983 Sally Ride became the first American woman to orbit the earth. A Stanford-trained scientist, she was highly respected by her fellow astronauts.

She needed to learn, for example, how to fly a jet and how to communicate via radio under emergency conditions.

Ride's fearlessness, her discipline, and her seriousness of purpose made a highly favorable impression on others in the program. In June 1983 she flew aboard the *Challenger* as it made 96 orbits of the earth, the first American woman to do so and the first woman scientist to make a genuine contribution to a space mission by performing experiments, making observations, and recording data.

SEE ALSO

Science

FURTHER READING

Camp, Carol Ann. *Sally Ride, First American Woman in Space*. Springfield, N.J.: Enslow, 1997.

Chaikin, Andrew. "Sally Ride." *Working Woman*, Nov.-Dec. 1996, pp. 42–46.

Ride, Sally, with Susan Oakie. *To Space and Back*. New York: Lothrop, Lee & Shepard, 1986.

Right-to-life movement

Those who oppose a woman's right to choose an abortion call themselves the right-to-life movement; the life in question is that of the unborn baby, because these women and men believe that life begins at the moment of conception. (Those who are pro-choice, on the other hand, believe that abortion is not murder because the fetus is not viable as a human being on her/his own.)

Women who belong to the movement tend to be social conservatives. Many are strongly influenced by religious teachings, especially if they are Roman Catholics or fundamentalist Christians, denominations that hold that abortion is wrong. Sociologist Kristin Luker claims that women in the right-to-life movement tend to have less prestigious employment than women who are pro-choice. Hence, a typical right-to-life woman may not have had to make the same choice between motherhood and career that a typical pro-choice woman has had to face.

Though the vast majority of people in the movement are peaceful—demonstrating outside of family planning clinics is a frequent tactic, for example—a small handful has engaged in acts of violence, including murdering abortion providers. Because feelings are so strong on both sides of the issue, it has been very difficult for those who disagree to hold a civil conversation, let alone discuss compromises.

The most prominent right-to-life woman is Norma McCorvey. The Roe of *Roe* v. *Wade*—the landmark Supreme Court case in which she sued for the right to a legal abortion—McCorvey has recently changed her mind about the morality of abortion.

SEE ALSO

Reproductive rights; *Roe* v. *Wade* (1973)

FURTHER READING

Colker, Ruth. *Abortion & Dialogue: Pro-Choice, Pro-Life, and American Law.* Bloomington: Indiana University Press, 1992.

Luker, Kristin. *Abortion and the Politics of Motherhood.* Berkeley: University of California Press, 1984.

Martin, William. *With God on Our Side: The Rise of the Religious Right in America.* New York: Broadway, 1997.

Robins, Margaret Dreier

- *Born: Sept. 6, 1868, Brooklyn, N.Y.*
- *Education: Private primary education and independent study*
- *Accomplishments: President, Women's Trade Union League, Chicago branch (1907–13); president, National Women's Trade Union League (1907–22); executive boardmember of Chicago Federation of Labor (1908–17)*
- *Died: Feb. 21, 1945, Brooksville, Fla.*

Margaret Dreier Robins was the heart and soul of the Women's Trade Union League (WTUL), an early 20th-century organization, founded in 1903, that brought together middle-class women committed to social reform and working-class women who needed help in defending their interests. Under Robins' leadership the group crusaded for protective legislation for women workers and it organized support for women workers on strike.

Though she never attended college, Margaret Dreier gained exposure to the world of ideas because the values of her family included a commitment to civic responsibility and intellectual growth. As a young adult she began to be active in social-welfare groups, an interest that was solidified by her marriage to the Chicago reformer Raymond Robins in 1905. Through him Margaret Dreier Robins met the middle-class women involved in Hull House, a settlement house established by Jane Addams to offer help to the poor in a slum neighborhood.

Robins and her husband were each independently wealthy, and they made their home a gathering place for college professors, labor leaders, and interesting people in general. This network led to her being elected president of both the Chicago branch of the WTUL and the national organization in 1907. She held the Chicago office until 1913 and the national one for 15 years. Margaret Dreier Robins's particular strength was that she helped soothe tensions between the working women in the WTUL and their middle-class supporters. Late in life, she and her husband moved to their estate in Florida but continued their lifelong civic involvements with groups such as the Red Cross.

SEE ALSO

Addams, Jane; Women's Trade Union League (WTUL)

FURTHER READING

Dye, Nancy Schrom. *As Equals and as Sisters: Feminism, the Labor Movement, and the Women's Trade Union League of New York.* Columbia: University of Missouri Press, 1980.

Payne, Elizabeth Anne. *Reform, Labor, and Feminism: Margaret Dreier Robins and the Women's Trade Union League.* Urbana: University of Illinois Press, 1998.

Roe v. *Wade* (1973)

Few decisions by the U.S. Supreme Court have affected so many people and created so much controversy as has *Roe* v. *Wade,* in which the Court struck down a Texas statute restricting a woman's access to abortion. A generation after *Roe,* Americans continue to debate whether limitations should be placed on access to abortion; abortion clinics continue to attract hostile demonstrations; and certain religious denominations, most notably the Roman Catholic Church, continue to oppose abortion as morally wrong.

The Court's decision, written by Harry Blackmun, came at a time when women's rights were being debated in general, and women's access to abortion in particular, as never before in U.S. history. Feminist groups such as the National Organization for Women were calling for unrestricted access to abortion, and a few states were liberalizing their abortion laws.

"Roe" was Norma McCorvey, a Texas woman denied the right to an abortion. In the summer of 1969 McCorvey was a 21-year-old divorcée, whose five-year-old daughter was being cared for by grandparents. Out of work when she became pregnant, McCorvey unsuccessfully tried to locate someone to perform an illegal abortion. At this point she made contact with two young feminist attorneys, Linda Coffee and Sarah Weddington. They persuaded her to allow herself to be the test case in a suit against Texas's statute forbidding abortion, though the decision could not possibly be made in time for her to benefit personally. It was Sarah Weddington who eventually argued the case successfully before the U.S. Supreme Court.

Using arguments upholding marital privacy drawn from the *Griswold* v. *Connecticut* decision of 1965 and arguments upholding a single person's right to privacy used in the *Eisenstadt* v. *Baird* decision of 1972, the Court ruled that a state could impose virtually no restriction on abortions performed during the first three months of a pregnancy. The Court did allow states, however, to impose restrictions on abortions during later stages of a pregnancy.

As with so many of the key decisions regarding women's rights during these years, the Supreme Court relied on the 14th Amendment to the Constitution—guaranteeing that all citizens have "privileges and immunities" that cannot be abridged without due process of law—as the ultimate rationale for the decision.

SEE ALSO

14th Amendment; *Griswold* v. *Connecticut* (1965)

Roosevelt, Eleanor

- *Born: Oct. 11, 1884, New York, N.Y.*
- *Education: Finishing school (England)*
- *Accomplishments: First Lady (1933–45); author, "My Day" syndicated daily column (1935–45); U.S. delegate, first United Nations meeting (1945); chairperson, United Nations Commission on Human Rights (1945–52)*
- *Died: Nov. 7, 1962, New York, N.Y.*

Perhaps the most admired American woman of the 20th century, Eleanor Roosevelt was the First Lady for longer than anyone else in U.S. history because

Eleanor Roosevelt (center) with Fiorello LaGuardia, mayor of New York, and his wife. Mrs. Roosevelt was revered as "First Lady of the world" because of her broad compassion and diligent efforts for international peace.

her husband, Franklin Delano Roosevelt, was elected President an unprecedented four times. Americans got the chance to know her well, and though her passionate advocacy for sometimes unpopular causes made enemies, she won even more friends with the warmth of her personality and the strength of her convictions.

Born to a socially prominent New York family—she and her future husband Franklin were distant cousins—young Eleanor Roosevelt lost both parents during her childhood. Painfully shy, deprived of parental love, she was eventually sent to a school in England where she found the approval and encouragement she so desperately needed from the headmistress.

Family connections threw the young woman into contact with her dashing cousin Franklin soon after she finished school. Though they were dissimilar in many ways—he was pleasure-loving, handsome, and charismatic, and she was morally earnest—they fell in love. Historians have speculated that the ambitious young man recognized in his cousin the kind of personal strength that could help him achieve a significant career. Also, her uncle, Theodore Roosevelt, was President of the United States at the time the couple fell in love. They wed in 1904, and the marriage produced six children, one of whom died in infancy. Franklin Roosevelt became a lawyer, then a Democratic state legislator, then assistant secretary of the navy.

Eleanor Roosevelt had not attended college: in her day, socially prominent people thought that higher education was inappropriate for their daughters. In fact, her background handicapped her in many ways. In the circles in which she had been brought up, for example, it was acceptable to be prejudiced against African Americans, Irish Americans, and Jews. Women were not supposed to join clubs because that was considered too "common." And throughout most of her marriage, she had to combat a mother-in-law who espoused many of these values.

In 1918 Eleanor Roosevelt learned that her husband had been having an affair, and this profoundly unsettled their marriage. Then in 1921 he contracted polio and had to withdraw temporarily from public life. These two episodes helped propel Eleanor into new arenas of action. She threw herself into Democratic party politics in the 1920s and became a power in her own right. She had already developed a network of women friends among social activists and settlement-house workers. By the time that Franklin Roosevelt was elected governor of New York in 1928, his wife had a multitude of friends and commitments. He became President in 1933, and she became a new, much more activist First Lady. In the early White House years, her intense friendship with journalist Lorena Hickok sustained her emotionally as she forged her unprecedented role. She was eager to retain her own identity, hence during her entire time as First Lady she wrote, including a daily column called "My Day."

Though most Americans did not realize the extent of Franklin Roosevelt's disability at the time, he was severely limited physically and could not walk unaided. His wife became his eyes and ears, traveling throughout the country to investigate problems and report back to her husband. She descended into coal mines, she visited the rural poor, and she returned to Washington fired with the conviction that government could do something to help.

Though he did not always agree with her, Roosevelt usually listened, and his program of New Deal legislation reflected her influence, particularly in matters of social welfare, for example, the programs for young people. A favorite device was to seat an advocate of a cause she believed in next to the President at a White House meal so that he or she could gain access to the Presidential ear. Eleanor Roosevelt was the first prominent person to recruit other women to run for office on a systematic basis. She was also the first White House resident to reach out to African Americans in a significant way, attending meetings, inviting people to the White House, and corresponding tirelessly with black activists. In effect, she was the conscience of the New Deal.

When the country entered World War II in 1941, Eleanor Roosevelt's influence waned. Helping those in need might have been a woman's work, but fighting a massive war was not—at least in Franklin Roosevelt's eyes. After her husband's death in 1945, Eleanor Roosevelt continued to be an important figure in U.S. politics, serving as a member of the U.S. delegation to the United Nations for a time and also continuing to write as she had done throughout the White House years. By the time of Eleanor Roosevelt's death in 1962, many were referring to her as the "First Lady of the World."

SEE ALSO

New Deal; Settlement-house movement

FURTHER READING

Cook, Blanche Wiesen. *Eleanor Roosevelt.* 2 vols. New York: Viking, 1992, 1999.
Freedman, Russell. *Eleanor Roosevelt: A Life of Discovery.* New York: Clarion Books, 1997.
Goodwin, Doris Kearns. *No Ordinary Time.* New York, Simon & Schuster, 1994.
Lash, Joseph. *Eleanor and Franklin.* New York: Norton, 1971.

Rowlandson, Mary White

- *Born: Around 1635, South Petherton, England*
- *Education: Unknown*
- *Accomplishments: Published first widely read account of capture by Indians*
- *Died: After 1678*

Mary Rowlandson wrote an account of her capture by Indians, and her harrowing story has enthralled generations of readers.

Rowlandson's family had immigrated to Massachusetts from England when she was a child. At the time of her capture in the late 1670s, the colony was still a frontier. Rowlandson was in the difficult situation of being a wife and mother whose husband was

First published in 1682, Mary Rowlandson's narrative of her capture by the Narragansett Indians was so popular that it went through 22 printings by 1828.

A

NARRATIVE

OF THE

CAPTIVITY, SUFFERINGS AND REMOVES

OF

Mrs. *Mary Rowlandſon*,

Who was taken Priſoner by the INDIANS with ſeveral others, and treated in the moſt barbarous and cruel Manner by thoſe vile Savages: With many other remarkable Events during her TRAVELS.

Written by her own Hand, for her private Uſe, and now made public at the earneſt Deſire of ſome Friends, and for the Benefit of the afflicted.

BOSTON

Printed and Sold at JOHN BOYLE's Printing-Office, next Door to the *Three Doves* in Marlborough-Street. 1773.

away when Indians, engaged in an uprising known as King Philip's War, attacked the Rowlandson house, refuge for some three dozen villagers in all. In the attack 12 people were killed and 24 taken captive, including Rowlandson and her three children. Rowlandson would later call it "the dolefullest day that ever mine eyes saw."

She and two of the children survived the difficult ordeal, which lasted about three months. At the beginning of the captivity Rowlandson and her daughter Sarah—who died in her arms—were both suffering from bullet wounds. Over time the older woman's wounds healed, owing to the application of oak leaves. She suffered some abuse at the hands of the Indians, but ultimately her skill at sewing and knitting gained their favor, and the Indians showed some attachment for her when she left. The ordeal ended when Joseph Rowlandson paid a ransom for his wife, and the two children found their way to safety shortly thereafter.

In 1682 Rowlandson's written account of her experiences, including her encounters with her Indian captors and her reliance on her strong Christian faith, was published. Her narrative, titled "The Sovereignty and Goodness of God," was so popular that it has been called America's first international best-seller. Four editions were printed in the book's first year, and 23 editions had been printed by 1828.

FURTHER READING

Castiglia, Christopher. *Bound and Determined: Captivity, Culture Crossing, and White Womanhood from Mary Rowlandson to Patty Hearst.* Chicago: University of Chicago Press, 1996.

Demos, John. *The Tried and the True: Native American Women Confronting Colonization.* New York: Oxford University Press, 1995.

Lepore, Jill. *Encounters in the New World: A History in Documents.* New York: Oxford University Press, 2000.

Rowlandson, Mary White. *Sovereignty and Goodness of God: Being a Narrative of the Captivity and Restoration of Mrs. Mary Rowlandson and Related Documents.* Edited by Neal Salisbury. New York: Bedford, 1997.

Rowson, Susanna Haswell

- *Born: Around 1762, Portsmouth, England*
- *Education: Unknown*
- *Accomplishments: Theatre actor and writer (1792–97); founder and proprietor of Young Ladies Academy, Boston/Medford (1797–1822); author,* Victoria *(1786);* The Inquisitor, or, The Invisible Rambler *(1788);* Mentoria *(1791);* Charlotte Temple, A Tale of Truth *(1791);* Trials of the Human Heart *(1795);* Reuben and Rachel, or, Tales of Old Times *(1798);* Sarah, or, The Exemplary Wife *(1813)*
- *Died: Mar. 2, 1824, Boston, Mass.*

Susanna Rowson was one of the first women writers in the United States, the author of the immensely popular novel *Charlotte Temple,* published in London in 1791 and Philadelphia three years later, and the new country's first best-seller. (Since printed in more than 200 editions.)

Born in England, Susanna Haswell was a governess to the children of the duchess of Devonshire. She resigned to marry hardware merchant William Rowson in 1787. Having published her first novel while still employed by the duchess, she continued to write after her marriage, and she and her husband also took to the stage. It was their theatrical career that took them to the New World in the mid-1790s, and they eventually settled in Boston. After retiring from the stage, Rowson opened a girls' academy.

Today Rowson is known primarily for her best-selling novel. With a melodramatic plot focusing on the seduction of a schoolgirl, *Charlotte Temple* may strike a modern reader as overly sentimental. Nonetheless, feminist critics have noted its immense impact on readers, many of whom identified with the heroine. So intense was the devotion to the suffering Charlotte, a fictional character, that some anonymous person erected her tombstone in New York's Trinity Church yard and people placed flowers there.

SEE ALSO

Literature

FURTHER READING

Parker, Patricia L. *Susanna Rowson.* Boston: Twayne, 1986.

Rudolph, Wilma

- *Born: June 23, 1940, Clarksville, Tenn.*
- *Education: Tennessee State University, B.A., 1963*
- *Accomplishments: Olympic gold medalist in 100-meter dash, 200-meter dash, and 4x100-meter relay (1960); United Press and Associated Press Woman Athlete of the Year (1960); Sullivan Award (1961); Black Sports Hall of Fame (1980); U.S. Olympic Hall of Fame (1983); Women's Sports Foundation Award (1984)*
- *Died: Nov. 13, 1994, Nashville, Tenn.*

In 1960 track star Wilma Rudolph became the first American woman ever to win three gold medals in a single Olympics. Outstanding in many sports, Rudolph was all the more impressive because she had contracted polio at age 4 and wore leg braces until she was 12. The fact that she performed so well as an African American in the still-segregated South and as a woman before there were many resources available for female athletes proves her extraordinary drive as well as her sheer talent.

While still in high school in 1956, Rudolph won a bronze Olympic medal in the 4x100 meter relay, in which four people each run 100 meters. She was also selected to be on the all-state team in basketball. Attending Tennessee State University on a full track scholarship, Rudolph prepared for 1960. At the Rome Olympics that year, her gold medal events were the 100-meter dash, the 200-meter dash, and the 4x100-meter relay. When she retired from competition in 1962, she held the world's record in all three events (11.0 seconds for the 100-meter, 24.0 seconds for the 200-meter, and 44.5 seconds for the relay).

Rudolph married her high school sweetheart, Robert Eldridge, and the couple had four children. She devoted her life to working with and for young people by, among other things, coaching track and consulting on minority affairs at DePauw University. In 1984 she was selected as one of the five great-

Wilma Rudolph crosses the finish line during the 50-yard dash at a track meet in Madison Square Garden, 1961. Rudolph overcame considerable personal adversity to become a world-class athlete.

est American woman athletes. In 1994 she died of a brain tumor.

SEE ALSO

Sports

FURTHER READING

Dixon, Oscar. "Rudolph Hurdled Obstacles, Opened Doors for Women." *USA Today,* July 17, 1996, C12.

Rhoden, William C. "The End of a Winding Road." *New York Times Current Events Edition,* Nov. 19, 1994, A33.

Rudolph, Wilma. *Wilma.* New York: New American Library, 1977.

Sherrow, Victoria. *Wilma Rudolph.* New York: Chelsea House, 1995.

Ruffin, Josephine St. Pierre

- *Born: Aug. 31, 1842, Boston, Mass.*
- *Education: Finishing school*
- *Accomplishments: Founder and editor,* Woman's Era *magazine (1886–93); founder, Women's Era Club (1894); co-organizer, National Federation of Afro-American Women (1895); president, National Association of Colored Women (1896)*
- *Died: Mar. 13, 1924, Boston, Mass.*

Josephine St. Pierre Ruffin was an African-American civic leader and club organizer of immense energy and public-spiritedness.

When she married George Ruffin at the age of 16, young Josephine St. Pierre had not yet had the opportunity to secure much education. But she chose a mate with whom she could grow intellectually. After working as a barber, George Ruffin went to Harvard Law School, from which he graduated in 1869. Thereafter he became a state legislator, a city council member, and finally Boston's first African-American municipal judge. The couple had five children, one of whom died in infancy.

Given a social position in Boston by her husband's stature, Josephine Ruffin took advantage of this situation to make a powerful contribution of her own. Throughout her long life she devoted herself to civic purposes. In 1894, for example, she and her daughter organized the Woman's Era Club, a pioneering civic organization for black women, and she edited its monthly publication for several years. She also served on the board of Massachusetts Moral Education Association and the Massachusetts School Suffrage Association. In 1895, she called a conference of African-American women's clubs from all over the country, which resulted in the formation of the National Federation of Afro-American Women. The following year this group merged with the Colored Women's League of Washington, D.C., to form the National Association of Colored Women.

Ruffin also attempted to work with white clubwomen, but the General Federation of Women's Clubs refused to admit black women's clubs during these years out of deference to its white southern constituency.

SEE ALSO

Clubs, women's; General Federation of Women's Clubs (GFWC); National Association of Colored Women (NACW)

Sacajawea

- *Born: Around 1786, Idaho*
- *Education: No formal education*
- *Accomplishments: Instrumental in success of Lewis and Clark expedition (1805–06)*
- *Died: Dec. 20, 1812?, Dakota region*

Sacajawea, the Indian woman who served as an interpreter for the path-breaking expedition of Meriwether Lewis and William Clark, is a legendary figure in the history of the American West. After Lewis and Clark left St. Louis in 1805 to look for a route to the Pacific and to make observations about the plants, animals, and geography along the way, they encountered Sacajawea's French-born mate, Toussaint Charbonneau, in what is now North Dakota, and hired him as an interpreter and guide. She and their baby son went along, too. Sacajawea proved to be a valuable member of the expedition because she had knowledge of many Indian languages in addition to her native Shoshone, or Snake. Besides interpreting, she cooked, located edible wild foods, and served as a living symbol to various tribes that the Lewis and Clark expedition was not a war party.

There are two versions of Sacajawea's life after the Lewis and Clark expedition. One has her dying of a fever in 1812. An oral tradition among Indian peoples maintains that she settled with the Comanches and lived to be a very old woman.

FURTHER READING

Kessler, Donna J. *The Making of Sacagawea: A Euro-American Legend.* Tuscaloosa: University of Alabama Press, 1996.

Salvation Army

The Salvation Army is a Christian social-welfare organization with a quasi-military structure. In the more than 100 years of its existence, it has fed both the bodies and the souls of countless men and women in inner cities throughout the world.

The group began when the Methodist minister William Booth started preaching the gospel to the desperately poor in London's East End in 1865. Booth had the idea that one could not reach the soul of a hungry person without feeding his or her body first, an approach that proved popular with those in need. Many others came forward to volunteer, his ministry flourished, and in 1878 he named it the Salvation Army. In 1880 a group of activists brought the Salvation Army to the United States.

Booth had a gift for convincing others to participate in his crusade, and his wife and all eight of their children signed on. Starting as early as the 1860s Catherine Mumford Booth joined her husband in preaching, at the time a bold departure for a woman because most denominations, except the Quakers, thought that women were unsuitable for that duty. One of their daughters, Evangeline Booth, led the U.S. Salvation Army for 30 years, from 1904 to 1934.

Women's prominence in the organization received amused yet respectful attention in the play *Major Barbara* by George Bernard Shaw, written in 1905. In fact there were very few organizations at the time that gave women so much authority.

Between 1986 and 1993 the world leader of the Salvation Army (whose

A Salvation Army "lassie" hands out doughnuts. Once thought to be a marginal group of eccentrics, the Army evolved into the nation's largest charitable organization.

international headquarters is in London, England) was the Australian-born General Eva Burrows. The recipient of many honorary degrees, General Burrows led her organization back into Eastern Europe following the dissolution of the Soviet Union. During her first five years in office she personally visited 62 countries. She thus continued the example of strong female leadership set by Catherine Mumford Booth and her daughter Evangeline.

In the late 1990s the Salvation Army was at work in 103 countries. In the United States it has branches in all 50 states, with 36,000 employees and more than 45 million volunteers conducting its work.

FURTHER READING

Barnes, Cyril J. *God's Army.* Berkhamsted, U.K.: Lion, 1978

Winston, Diane. *Red-Hot and Righteous: The Urban Religion of the Salvation Army.* Cambridge: Harvard University Press, 1999.

Sampson, Deborah

- *Born: Dec. 17, 1760, Plympton, Mass.*
- *Education: Little formal education*
- *Accomplishments: Joined the army impersonating a man (1780–83)*
- *Died: Apr. 29, 1827, Sharon, Mass.*

Deborah Sampson dressed in male clothes and fought in the American Revolution, participating in several battles under the name of Robert Shurtleff before her true identity became known.

Young Deborah was a servant and a teacher. In 1780 the Baptist church she had joined in Middleborough, Massachusetts, expelled her for dressing in men's clothes and behaving like a soldier. Tall and strong, she then took on a false name and enlisted officially in the 4th Massachusetts regiment. In 1783 she was chosen by General John Patterson at West Point as an aide-de-camp. After having been wounded in a battle near Tarrytown, New York, she tended to her own wounds to avoid discovery, but her identity was discovered later that year when she became ill with a fever. She received an honorable discharge from on October 25, 1783.

After the war ended, Sampson married a Massachusetts farmer named Benjamin Gannett and gave birth to three children. In later years, she became locally famous for her wartime exploits, and she and her heirs received compensation from the federal government based on her military service.

SEE ALSO

American Revolution

FURTHER READING

Freeman, Lucy, and Alma Halbert Bond. *America's First Woman Warrior: The Courage of Deborah Sampson.* New York: Paragon House, 1992.

Sanger, Margaret Higgins

- *Born: Sept. 14, 1879, Corning, N.Y.*
- *Education: Attended Claverack College, Hudson River Institute, White Plains Hospital nursing program, and Manhattan Eye and Ear Clinic (1900)*
- *Accomplishments: Publisher,* Woman Rebel *monthly (1914); founder and publisher,* The Birth Control Review *(1917); founder, Brownsville Clinic, first birth control clinic in the U.S. (Brooklyn, N.Y., 1816); founder, American Birth Control League (1921); organizer, National Committee on Federal Legislation for Birth Control (1929)*
- *Died: Sept. 6, 1966, Tucson, Ariz.*

Margaret Sanger led the crusade to make safe contraception—devices or medication for the prevention of pregnancy—available to women. When she was born, it was illegal to distribute such devices or even information about them. By the time of her death, women had legal access to a number of means of contraception, including the birth-control pill, which began to be available about 1960.

Margaret Higgins was one of 11 children born to a mother who died at the age of 49. Seeing her mother's life cut short—at least partly due to multiple childbirths and the strain of raising 11 children—no doubt contributed to the passion she felt for her subsequent crusade. The young woman became a nurse and then in 1902 married William Sanger, an architect.

Having given birth to three children, Sanger became dissatisfied with her life as a housewife and became active in politics. With the radical Elizabeth Gurley Flynn, she worked on behalf of big labor strikes in Lawrence, Massachusetts, and Paterson, New Jersey. Relying on her combined expertise as a nurse and as a mother, Sanger also began to speak out on the need for sexual reform. Along with such other noted radical thinkers as the anarchist Emma Goldman, Sanger was becoming increasingly convinced that sexual liberation, freedom from the biological necessity of giving birth, should be an important goal for women, and that access to the means of preventing pregnancy would be essential in achieving that end.

Sanger began to focus on the need for good contraception, and in so doing ran afoul of the Comstock Law, a federal law passed in 1873 that forbade the mailing of obscene materials, which by the definition of the era included information about how to prevent pregnancy. In 1914 Sanger started publishing a newspaper called the *Woman Rebel,* in which she specifically announced her plans to discuss contraception. With this act of defiance, she ran into trouble with the U.S. Post Office, which accused her of mailing obscene material. She fled to Europe to avoid prosecution.

Despite Sanger's legal problems, these were years of growth and development for her. While in England, for example, she became acquainted with the psychologist Havelock Ellis who encouraged her in her crusading efforts. Upon her return to the United States, she was more determined than ever to pursue her cause of accessible contraception. Happily, the charges against her were dropped.

Several poor mothers brought their large families to court to support Margaret Sanger (center left, with buttons down her coat) during her 1916 trial on charges of distributing birth control information. Sanger was found guilty and served 30 days in jail.

These were also years of turmoil in Sanger's personal life. A daughter had died of pneumonia while Sanger was abroad, and her rocky marriage to William Sanger ended in divorce in 1920. But while she struggled with such crises she carried on with her mission. In 1916 she opened her first birth-control clinic in Brooklyn and provided contraceptive advice to 488 women before the clinic was closed by the police, because disseminating birth-control information remained illegal. Sanger was tried, convicted, and sentenced to 30 days in jail.

A legal ruling that came out of this case pointed the way to the eventual triumph for Sanger. The ruling established a physician's right to prescribe birth control in the service of a mother's health. Sanger began to refocus her efforts toward lobbying the medical profession, whose members had mostly had the same disapproving attitudes about birth control that had flourished elsewhere in American society. Finally, in 1937 the American Medical Association recognized contraception as a legitimate medical service. In 1965 in *Griswold* v. *Connecticut,* the U.S. Supreme Court established a married woman's legal right to obtain contraception. In 1972 in *Eisenstadt* v. *Baird,* the Court extended the same right to unmarried couples and individuals.

Sanger's critics have suggested that in shifting her attention toward the medical profession, she abandoned some of the more radical possibilities for sexual liberation that her crusade had once represented. In particular, she has been criticized for the eugenics arguments she used to justify birth control: that it could reduce the birthrate of "inferiors." Despite criticism, in 1921 she founded the American Birth Control League, which evolved into the Planned Parenthood organization.

In 1922 Sanger married the millionaire J. Noah Slee, the developer of 3-in-1 Oil, and although she was now wealthy, her commitment to the cause of birth control never slackened.

SEE ALSO

Birth control; *Griswold* v. *Connecticut* (1965)

FURTHER READING

Chesler, Ellen. *Woman of Valor: Margaret Sanger and the Birth Control Movement in America.* New York: Simon & Schuster, 1992.

Sanger, Margaret. *Margaret Sanger: An Autobiography.* New York: Dover, 1971.

Whitelaw, Nancy. *Margaret Sanger: "Every Child a Wanted Child".* New York: Dillon, 1994.

Schlafly, Phyllis Stewart

- *Born: Aug. 15, 1924, St. Louis, Mo.*
- *Education: Washington University, B.A., 1944; Harvard University, M.A., 1945; Washington University Law School, J.D., 1978*
- *Accomplishments: Founder, Eagle Forum (pro-family organization, 1972); author,* The Phyllis Schlafly Report *(monthly newsletter, 1966–);* A Choice Not an Echo *(1964);* Strike from Space: How the Russians May Destroy Us *(1965);* Kissinger on the Couch *(1975);* The Power of the Positive Woman *(1977);* Pornography's Victims; Who Will Rock the Cradle?: The Battle for Control of Child Care in America *(1989);* First Reader *(1994)*

One of the leading conservative writers and activists in the country, Phyllis Schlafly has dedicated her life to arguing against much of the social change ushered in by the modern women's movement. She believes that women, especially when they are mothers of young children, belong at home, and that they need male protection. She holds a B.A. and a law degree from Washington University, and is the mother of six children.

Schlafly first gained public attention with the campaign biography she published of Barry Goldwater, *A Choice Not an Echo*, when he was the Republican nominee for President in 1964. She then began to write a monthly newsletter for her conservative constituency, the *Phyllis Schlafly Report*, in which she focused principally on the dangers of communism, until she began to be alarmed about changes set in motion by the birth of modern feminism.

In addition to lecturing and to her many books and articles, Schlafly is best known for having organized STOP-ERA, in the wake of ERA's passing Congress in 1972, to oppose successfully the ratification of the Equal Rights Amendment.

In the 1990s Schlafly devoted her considerable energy to the Eagle Forum, a conservative "pro-family" organization, and to lecturing widely. She has used her legal training in preparing testimony before Congressional Committees and in sharpening the arguments she makes in lectures.

SEE ALSO

Equal Rights Amendment (ERA); STOP-ERA

FURTHER READING

Felsenthal, Carol. *The Sweetheart of the Silent Majority: The Biography of Phyllis Schlafly.* Garden City, N.Y.: Doubleday, 1981.

Science

Though a few American women have made remarkable discoveries in various scientific fields—Maria Mitchell in astronomy and Barbara McClintock in biology, to name two—there have been many barriers to women's success. Only in the last decades of the 20th century, in fact, have women begun to enjoy relatively equal access to scientific professions, because Title IX of the Education Act Amendments of 1972 has required universities to offer equal opportunities to men and women.

Before the late 19th century, science was most often the province of gentlemen amateurs—and occasionally their daughters. As universities developed doctoral programs in the late 1800s, however, those responsible for creating the various professions thought of them as "manly" and deliberately tried to distance themselves from women, whom they considered to be amateurs who would lower the professional standards if they were allowed to participate.

Women interested in science therefore first had to fight to get access to higher education at all. Then they had to fight to obtain graduate training. Even after they had completed the requirements for a doctorate, universities were often reluctant to grant the degree, so more battles were necessary. Degree in hand, a woman scientist was unlikely to be employable in a university, however, except in a department of home economics. Her best bet was to teach science in a women's college—where she would not have either the time or the facilities to conduct her own research that would have been available to a male colleague in a university.

A few women have excelled in spite of these difficulties. An outstanding example is the Nobel Prize–winning physicist, Rosalyn Yalow. Born Rosalyn Sussman in 1921 in a working-class area of New York City, the young woman graduated from Hunter College, a free city college for women, in 1941. Determined to become a scientist, she accepted a teaching assistant position in physics at the University of Illinois, Urbana. She married fellow physics student Aaron Yalow, received her doctorate in 1945, and moved with her new husband to New York City to

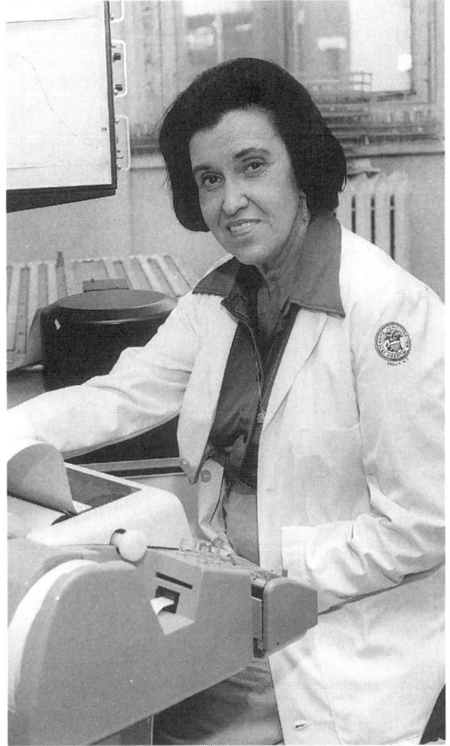

Rosalind Yalow, a medical physicist at the Bronx VA Medical Center in New York, won the 1977 Nobel Prize for medicine for her discovery of radioimmunoassay, a technique that enabled scientists to measure minute amounts of substances in body fluids. The technique has applications in treating diabetes, hepatitis, and many other diseases.

teach at Hunter College. In 1950 she took a permanent research position at the Bronx Veterans Administration Hospital, where she focused on the use of radioisotopes in the treatment of cancer. This research, conducted in conjunction with her colleague Solomon Berson, led to an explosion of uses for radioisotopes in medicine and to her Nobel Prize in 1977.

Since the 1970s feminist scientists have argued that the very structure of science has been hostile to women. Their goal has been to free this field as much as possible from stereotypical language and attitudes, such as in biological discussions of the "active" sperm and the "passive" egg. As women take advantage of better access to education and jobs, and as society becomes increasingly aware of the issues raised by feminists, such as gender-based stereotypes that can make women feel either inadequate or uncomfortable, it is likely that more women will become scientists in the future. Already their numbers are increasing: thirty-one percent of natural scientists were female in 1998, up from 20 percent in 1983.

SEE ALSO

Education Act Amendments (1972); McClintock, Barbara; Mitchell, Maria

FURTHER READING

Abir-Am, Pnina G., and Dorinda Outram. *Uneasy Careers and Intimate Lives: Women in Science, 1789–1979*. New Brunswick, N.J.: Rutgers University Press, 1987.

Haber, Louis. *Women Pioneers of Science*. New York: Harcourt Brace Jovanovich, 1979.

Rossiter, Margaret. *Women Scientists in America before Affirmative Action, 1940–1972*. Baltimore: Johns Hopkins University Press, 1995.

Sculpture

On the one hand, American women have been creating three-dimensional work from very early in our history, going back to the beautiful pottery and basketry made by Native American women even before the arrival of Europeans. On the other hand, up until the latter decades of the 20th century it has been much more difficult for women than for men to receive major commissions in this medium or to have their work displayed in galleries or museums.

The first American woman sculptor of historical record was Patience Wright, a Quaker widow who made wax portraits around the time of the American Revolution, which started in 1776. During the 19th century there was one quite famous woman sculptor, Harriet Hosmer, who was known internationally. Hosmer's work reflected her interest in literary or classical themes. Another outstanding woman sculptor of the period was Vinnie Ream, who created a marble sculpture of Abraham Lincoln for the U.S. Capitol.

Edmonia Lewis was a 19th-century sculptor whose work was little recognized until the final decades of the 20th century. Of African-American and Native-American descent, Lewis was educated with the encouragement and financial support of her older brother, and went on to attend Oberlin College and travel to Europe to further her artistic training career. In spite of prejudice and racial incidents directed at her, she persevered in creating neoclassical sculptures that related to the abolition of slavery and her racial heritage.

By the 20th century, increased opportunity for women was leading to an increased number of women in many different arts, including sculpture. Early in

Zenobia in Chains *(1859) was one of Harriet Hosmer's best-known works. Creating this monumental statue of a dignified queen in captivity gave Hosmer the opportunity to comment on the evil of human bondage just before the start of the Civil War.*

the century Abastenia Eberle was crafting bronze studies of poor immigrants. Alice Morgan Wright and Adelheid Roosevelt created experimental work that was clearly influenced by the European avant-garde. During the Harlem Renaissance of the 1920s, Augusta Savage drew upon themes from African-American culture for her work. The federal arts agencies of the 1930s commissioned the work of some women sculptors for public buildings such as post offices.

After World War II more women sculptors began gaining the fame that Harriet Hosmer had enjoyed in the 19th century. Louise Nevelson and Louise Bourgeois, for example, were celebrated for their innovative work. Judy Chicago and Miriam Schapiro developed new forms to explore themes of female sexuality and spirituality. Elizabeth Catlett—also a printmaker—created tributes to the African-American women in the civil rights movement. Moreover, women began to win major commissions for public sculpture. In the San Francisco Bay area, for instance, Ruth Asawa created fountains and bas reliefs for important buildings such as the federal building in San Jose.

The most famous and important sculpture created by an American woman is perhaps Maya Lin's Vietnam War Memorial of 1982. One of the most visited monuments in Washington, D.C., this memorial to the Americans who died in Vietnam, created by a young Asian-American woman, has a quiet power that moves many to tears.

Women are now creating public sculpture, but there is still relatively little public sculpture commemorating women, particularly individual, real women—as opposed to a goddess or an idealized "pioneer woman" or figure of motherhood. Recognizing the dearth of such images in the nation's capital, the Women in the Military foundation organized in the late 1980s to rectify the situation and to build a monument to the many women who have served in defense of the nation.

SEE ALSO

Hosmer, Harriet Goodhue

FURTHER READING

Heller, Nancy G. *Women Artists: An Illustrated History.* New York: Abbeville, 1987.

Rubinstein, Charlotte Streifer. *American Women Sculptors: A History of Women Working in Three Dimensions.* Boston: G. K. Hall, 1990.

Sherr, Lynn, and Jurate Kazickas. *Susan B. Anthony Slept Here.* New York: Random House, 1994.

Seaman, Elizabeth Cochrane (Nellie Bly)

- *Born: May 5, 1865?, Cochran's Mills, Pa.*
- *Education: Little formal education*
- *Accomplishments: Investigative reporter,* New York World *(1887–95)*
- *Died: Jan. 27, 1922, New York, N.Y.*

Under the pen name of Nellie Bly, Elizabeth Cochrane Seaman became one of the best-known journalists of the late 19th century, famous for going undercover to expose the sufferings of working women as well as for a celebrated trip around the world.

Not yet 20 and lacking much formal education, young Elizabeth Cochrane became indignant when she read a dismissive editorial, "What Girls Are Good For," in the *Pittsburgh Dispatch.* She wrote an angry reply that so impressed the editor that he gave her the chance to do more writing. Before long, she was a professional journalist, choosing the pen name Nellie Bly from a popular song. She quickly established

ON TIME!

Nellie Bly Arrived Yesterday at San Francisco and Is Speeding Home.

M. JULES VERNE OUTDONE.

A Rousing Welcome for "The World's" Globe-Girdler.

KIND GREETINGS EVERYWHLRE.

The Long Trip from Yokahoma Comes to an End and Miss Bly Starts in on the Homestretch—The Escort Corps Had a Perilous Time of it but Caught Her at Last—The Circumnavigator Sends a Despatch—Welcomes en Route.

Plucky Nellie Bly is flying homeward as

ALWAYS ON TIME!

Our Little Globe Girdler Is Welcomed Back to American Soil.

Nellie Bly arrived in San Francisco on January 22, 1890, having beaten Jules Verne's fictional hero of Around the World in Eighty Days *by several days. Her round-the-world trip thrilled her fellow Americans.*

her working method of subjecting herself to some terrible situation and then writing an exposé about it.

In 1887 Cochrane made her way to the big time and became a reporter for Joseph Pulitzer's *World* in New York City. There she wrote more sensational exposés about sweatshops where women workers were exploited, about the cruel treatment of the mentally ill, and about the plight of women prisoners, among other topics.

In 1889 Pulitzer sent Cochrane around the world to see if she could break the record of the fictional Phineas Fogg in Jules Verne's novel *Around the World in Eighty Days.* Sending dispatches home as she traveled, she completed the trip in 72 days and returned a famous woman. Her career was brief, however. She married the businessman Robert Seaman at the height of her fame and temporarily retired. After her husband's death in 1904, she ran his business until she was forced to declare bankruptcy in 1911. She then worked again as a journalist, but without regaining her earlier stardom.

SEE ALSO

Media

FURTHER READING

Ehrlich, Elizabeth. *Nellie Bly.* New York: Chelsea House, 1989.

Emerson, Kathy Lynn. *Making Headlines: A Biography of Nellie Bly.* Minneapolis, Minn.: Dillon Press, 1989.

Kroeger, Brooke. *Nellie Bly: Daredevil, Reporter, Feminist.* New York: Times Books, 1994.

Peck, Ira (ed.), Nellie Bly. *Nellie Bly's Book: Around the World in 72 Days.* Brookfield, Conn.: Twenty-First Century Books, 1998.

Ritchie, Donald A. *American Journalists: Getting the Story.* New York: Oxford University Press, 1997.

Sedgwick, Catharine Maria

- *Born: Dec. 28, 1789, Stockbridge, Mass.*
- *Education: Extensive education at home*
- *Accomplishments: Author,* A New England Tale *(1822);* Redwood *(1824);* Hope Leslie *(1827);* Clarence, a Tale of Our Own Times *(1830);* Home *(1835);* The Linwoods *(1835);* Morals of Manners *(1846);* Married or Single *(1857)*
- *Died: July 31, 1867, West Roxbury, Mass.*

Catharine Sedgwick was a popular novelist in the years before the Civil War (1861–65), and she was the country's best-known woman author until Harriet Beecher Stowe published *Uncle Tom's Cabin* in 1852.

The member of a distinguished Massachusetts family, young Catharine received an education, though chiefly at home, superior to what was available to most girls, owing to her father's interest in her reading. In 1822 she published her first book, *A New England Tale,* in which she provided descriptions of her native western Massachusetts. Many other novels and moral tracts followed.

Most critics believe that *Hope Leslie,* published in 1827, was Sedgwick's finest work. It tells the story of a 17th-century New England girl and is remarkably sensitive to and knowledgeable about the Mohawk Indians who then lived in western Massachusetts. The heroine rescues two different Indian women from jail because she believes they have been wrongly accused by the local magistrates.

Sedgwick's work is characterized by deep moral seriousness and vivid descriptions of western Massachusetts. Though the author belonged to many of the same circles as the leading reformers of her day, she believed that the abolitionists were too extreme and that the women's movement was attempting too much too soon. She did, however, join a group committed to prison reform.

SEE ALSO

Literature

FURTHER READING

Kelley, Mary. *Private Woman, Public Stage.* New York, Oxford University Press, 1984.

Seneca Falls Convention

In July 1848 a group of 200 women and 40 men met in Seneca Falls, New York, to discuss women's rights. This was the first time in U.S. history that such an event had taken place.

The pioneering activists Lucretia Mott and Elizabeth Cady Stanton called the meeting, giving prospective attendees a week's notice. The fact that 240 people responded to the call on such short notice owed something to the region and something to the era. Seneca Falls was in a part of the United States that has been called the "burnt-over district," because so many movements for social change swept through it. Also, 1848 was a year of revolution in France, Germany, and Italy, and change was in the air.

Stanton had drafted the document that formed the basis for discussion. Known as the Declaration of Sentiments, it called for much that was new and radical, such as the reform of married women's property laws and better access to education for women, and it included woman suffrage. Even Mott thought that the suffrage demand might be too extreme, but the great black abolitionist Frederick Douglass, who was in attendance, defended it. In the end, about 100 people signed the document.

In the period immediately following the Seneca Falls Convention, the local press made great sport of the meeting. Nonetheless, it was a historic event because it introduced women's rights as a reform issue of national concern. Today there is a national park commemorating these events in Seneca Falls.

SEE ALSO

Declaration of Sentiments; Mott, Lucretia Coffin; Stanton, Elizabeth Cady; Suffrage, woman

FURTHER READING

Dubois, Ellen Carol (ed.), Gerda Lerner. *The Elizabeth Cady Stanton-Susan B. Anthony Reader: Correspondence, Writings, Speeches.* Boston: Northeastern University Press, 1992.

Dubois, Ellen Carol. *Feminism and Suffrage: The Emergence of an Independent Women's Movement in America 1848–1869.* Ithaca, NY: Cornell University Press, 1980.

Flexner, Eleanor, and Ellen Fitzpatrick. *Century of Struggle.* Cambridge: Harvard University Press, 1996.

Sigerman, Harriet. *An Unfinished Battle: American Women 1848–1865.* New York: Oxford University Press, 1994.

Separate spheres

When people in the past talked about separate spheres for men and women, they meant both real places—the home for women, the world of paid work and politics for men—as well as broader concerns that, ideally, should be the province of one sex or the other.

In the preindustrial United States, both men's and women's work centered around the farm home. It is true that men had a wider "sphere," because they could attend a university, serve in the military, or go to sea, all options that were unavailable to women. Nonetheless, men's and women's spheres of activity substantially overlapped in an agricultural society.

As the country became more urban and industrial during the course of the 19th century, men's work moved to the office or the factory, while women continued to be responsible for the home and for child care. As this transition took place, ideas about "separate spheres" as an ideal became more rigid. Those who opposed woman suffrage, for example, used the argument that voting would take women out of their divinely appointed sphere by involving them with public issues, thus breaking down the division in terms of physical space—women would be leaving their homes to vote—and in terms of the allocation of responsibilities traditionally assigned to the two sexes.

As increasing numbers of women have come to work outside the home, run for public office, and speak out on public issues over the course of the 20th century—as well as achieving the vote in 1920—the idea of separate spheres for the two sexes has become ever more of an anachronism.

FURTHER READING

Davidson, Cathy. *No More Separate Spheres!* Durham, N.C.: Duke University Press, 1998.

Rosenberg, Rosalind. *Beyond Separate Spheres.* New Haven, Conn.: Yale University Press, 1986.

Sigerman, Harriet. *Laborers for Liberty: American Women 1865–1890.* New York: Oxford University Press, 1994.

Servants

Until the mid-20th century, the largest single occupation for women was domestic service. As other types of employment for educated women have opened up, women of color, new immigrants, undocumented aliens, and others who have lacked access to education have continued to be engaged as servants. Though it is difficult to find precise numbers because so many domestic helpers, such as housekeepers and nannies, are undocumented—paid "off the books"—estimates are that there were approximately 795,000 paid household workers in the U.S. as of 1997.

In earlier times households had two types of unpaid domestics—indentured servants (those who worked under contract for a limited time without pay) and slaves. By 1865, both of these institutions were gone, but people still needed servants. So demanding was the work to maintain a home that it often took the labor of many to do the laundry, sew, bake, cook, and clean. In the late 19th century, mass immigration from Europe and African Americans moving north provided a supply of women to perform this domestic labor.

By the 20th century, technological improvements had decreased the amount of housework and the need for servants began to decline. Convenience foods, clothes that do not need to be

DOMESTIC SERVANTS: 1800 TO 1970

Year	Households (Millions)	Domestic Servants (Hundreds of Thousands)*	Servants per Ten Households
1800	—	0.4	—
1810	—	0.7	—
1820	—	1.1	—
1830	—	1.6	—
1840	—	2.4	—
1850	3.6	3.5	1.0
1860	5.2	6.0	1.2
1870	7.6	10.0	1.3
1880	9.9	11.3	1.1
1890	12.7	15.8	1.2
1900	16.0	18.0	1.1
1910	20.3	20.9	1.0
1920	24.4	16.6	0.7
1930	29.9	22.7	0.8
1940	34.9	23.0	0.7
1950	43.6	20.0	0.5
1960	52.8	24.9	0.5
1970	63.4	—	—

Source: U.S. Census
*Ten or more years old.

ironed, and inexpensive ready-made apparel—to say nothing of washers and dryers—have all lessened the workload.

For much of human history home has been a place where servants have been exploited—either poorly paid or not paid at all—so that others could enjoy "the comforts of home." Although the extent of housework has diminished significantly, the achievements of many a highly paid professional woman still rest on the contributions of another woman in a job as housekeeper or nanny near the bottom of the occupational hierarchy.

SEE ALSO

Housework; Indentured servants; Slavery

FURTHER READING

Dudden, Faye. *Serving Women.* Middletown, Conn.: Wesleyan University Press, 1983.

Hunter, Tera. *To 'Joy My Freedom: Southern Black Women's Lives and Labors after the Civil War.* Cambridge: Harvard University Press, 1997.

Katzman, David. *Seven Days a Week.* New York: Oxford University Press, 1978.

Seton, Elizabeth Ann Bayley

- *Born: Aug. 28, 1774, probably New York, N.Y.*
- *Education: Educated at home*
- *Accomplishments: Founder, Sisters of Charity of St. Joseph Catholic order (1808); first American-born Catholic saint (canonized 1975)*
- *Died: Jan. 2, 1821, Emmitsburg, Md.*

Elizabeth Ann Seton, better known as Mother Seton, was the first American-born Roman Catholic saint, canonized in 1975 after a lengthy examination by the Church. A convert to the faith, she founded the first American religious order of nuns, the Sisters of Charity.

Born into a large family, Elizabeth Bayley married the merchant William Seton in 1794, and the couple became the parents of five children. In 1803 William and Elizabeth Seton traveled to Italy for William's health, leaving their four youngest children at home. William died in Italy, and his widow drew comfort from Catholic friends there as well as from priests. When she returned to the United States, she wrestled some months with her religious allegiance, converting to the Roman Catholic Church from the Episcopal faith in 1805. Many of her Protestant friends turned hostile, but Mother Seton, as she would become known, forged ahead with her new life.

In her remaining years Mother Seton impressed many of her contemporaries with her devotion, her virtue, and the depth of her spirituality. In 1808, in

Maryland, she founded the community that would become the Sisters of Charity and in 1809 took the vows to become a nun. The Sisters of Charity dedicated themselves to caring for the poor and educating children; the order's teaching activities are often considered to be the roots of the parochial school system in the United States. Mother Seton also remained a devoted mother to her children. By the late 19th century, her virtues were beginning to be seen as heroic, and in 1907 the church began an ecclesiastical court of investigation, the first step in the canonization process, a process which was finally completed in 1975.

SEE ALSO

Catholics

FURTHER READING

Dirvin, Joseph I. *The Soul of Elizabeth Seton.* San Francisco: Ignatius Press, 1990.

Melville, Annabelle M. *Elizabeth Bayley Seton.* New York: Scribner, 1960.

Power-Waters, and Alma Shelley. *Mother Seton and the Sisters of Charity.* New York: Vision Books, 1957.

Settlement-house movement

The settlement-house movement, whereby middle-class people, mostly women, moved into immigrant neighborhoods to lead urban reform, developed in response to the mass immigration and rapid industrialization of the late 19th century and, above all, to the festering, overcrowded slums in U.S. cities. During the movement's height, between the 1880s and the 1930s, reformers moved into slums and tried to help the newcomers adjust to life in this country.

Settlement-house workers—such as Jane Addams of Chicago's Hull House—conceived an ambitious program of uplift, education, and advocacy for slum dwellers. In essence, the settlement-house residents functioned as social workers, although the profession of social work had not yet been created when the first settlements were opened. Over time, the settlement houses became laboratories of social experimentation—generating creative ideas for helping the poor such as protective labor legislation for women workers—with close ties to urban universities, city governments, and religious institutions. Settlement-house workers strove for housing reform, for an end to child labor, and for better parks and playgrounds.

How good a job did the settlement houses do? Some historians praise these institutions for mobilizing an immense amount of energy and imagination on behalf of the urban poor. Moreover, Jane Addams and others tried to show appreciation for the culture of the immigrants' homeland by sponsoring festivals honoring the immigrants' cultural heritage, for example. Other scholars point out that settlement-house workers frequently showed prejudice based on religion or race, assuming that the American middle-class way was the best in child-rearing or housekeeping. Some even attempted to get immigrants to give up their own foods for American meat and potatoes.

Not all the women involved in the settlement-house movement were white Protestants, however. The African American Lugenia Burns Hope, for example, spent time with Hull House residents and then went to Atlanta, where she started a highly successful settlement house to serve the black community there. There were also Catholic and Jewish settlement houses and settlement-house workers.

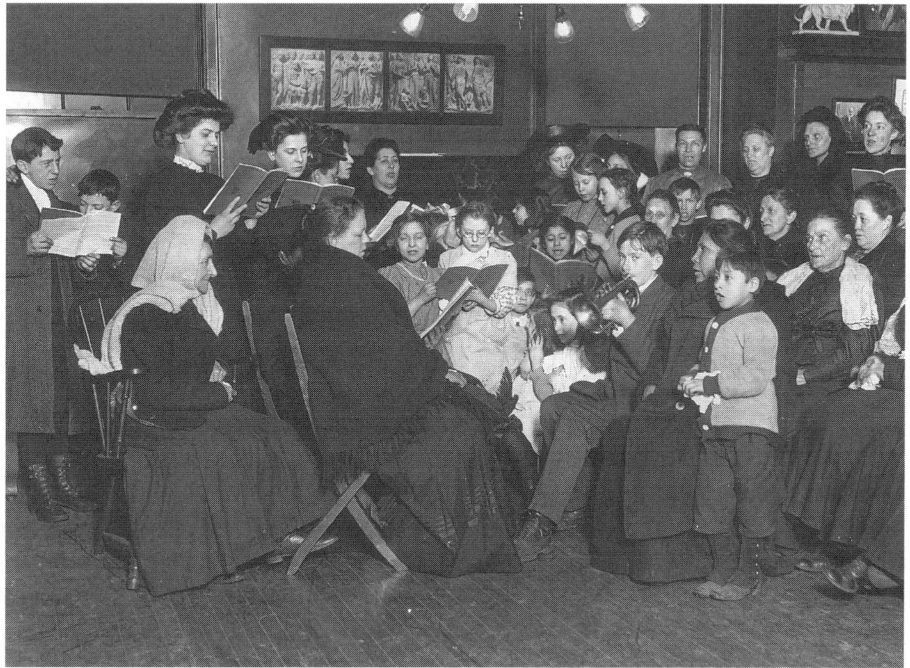

A singing class at Hull House in 1910, photographed by Lewis Hine. This famed Chicago settlement house, founded by Jane Addams, sponsored a wide variety of educational and recreational activities for the community.

In addition, the settlements created an unusual community for talented women. Residents lived together and ate together, sometimes for many years, and as a result they formed close bonds and nurtured one another emotionally. That so many of the early 20th century's important ideas for social reform came from women in the settlement-house network was no coincidence. These women spurred one another on to generate good ideas and to try to solve urban problems.

SEE ALSO

Addams, Jane; Industrialization

FURTHER READING

Carson, Mina. *Settlement Folk*. Chicago: University of Chicago Press, 1990.

Crocker, Ruth Hutchinson. *Social Work and Social Order: The Settlement Movement in Two Industrial Cities, 1889-1930*. Champaign, Ill.: University of Illinois Press, 1992.

Rouse, Jacqueline Anne. *Lugenia Burns Hope*. Athens: University of Georgia Press, 1989.

Wald, Lillian D. *The House on Henry Street (Philanthropy and Society)*. New Brunswick, N.J.: Transaction, 1991.

Sewing

Today some women sew as a hobby and some sew to save money, but most Americans buy their clothes. By contrast, in earlier times every stitch of clothing represented intensive hand labor. Not only did colonial women have to sew for their families, but they also had to spin the thread. Weaving the cloth, on the other hand, was usually not done in the individual home, but by the local weaver, because looms were a large investment. As a consequence of all this hard work, it was necessary to take as good care as possible of every garment; replacing it was no light undertaking.

In their diaries, 19th-century women who traveled out west describe how they had to keep up with their mending while riding in a wagon or sailing on a ship. Women also describe how they would endlessly recycle clothing, so that one daughter's cape could

A quilting party not only had practical results—warm quilts to survive winter on the plains—but also provided a sense of community for these late-19th-century Dakota women. The quilt pattern they are working on is a double Irish chain.

be transformed into a younger daughter's coat. On occasion, a woman might employ a skilled seamstress to help construct complicated clothing, but this did not permit the housewife to escape routine chores with her needle. So vast a quantity of work helped inspire the saying, "A woman's work is never done." And many a women's rights activist began her rebellion over the issue of needlework.

The process of clothing a family began to change as industrialization proceeded during the 19th century. First there were machine-made textiles and thread, beginning in the early 1800s. Then boys' and men's clothing began to be ready-made. At mid-century Elias Howe invented the sewing machine, which further lightened the housewife's load (if, of course, she could afford to purchase one). Not until the early 20th century did girls and women begin to wear ready-made clothing as a matter of course.

SEE ALSO

Fashion; Industrialization; Needlework

FURTHER READING

Gamber, Wendy. *The Female Economy: The Millinery and Dressmaking Trades.* Urbana: University of Illinois Press, 1997.

Sexism

The word *sexism* was coined in the 1960s to characterize prejudicial attitudes toward women and unequal treatment of women and men. Modern feminist scholars emphasize that sexism began with the creation of patriarchy—the rule of a family by the father—in antiquity, and that it has permeated most spheres of life, from education to occupational opportunities to intimate family relations. Attitudes of male superiority have been so deeply ingrained in

U.S. culture as to seem "natural"—until the birth of the modern women's movement challenged that assumption.

An early influential use of the term was in a manifesto written in 1969 by female civil rights workers. Entitled "Freedom for Movement Girls Now," it drew parallels between "sexism" and "racism." The term is now in general usage.

Sexual harassment

The term *sexual harassment* means unwanted sexual overtures with an implied threat of consequences if a woman does not comply, or repeated use of sexual innuendo in a school or work environment, so that a girl or woman is made uncomfortable or unwelcome. It was not invented until the 1970s—nor were there legal remedies for it until then—but the problem itself is much older. In fact, generations of women at work or at school have been vulnerable to men who have preyed on them for sexual favors or who "bantered" with them in unacceptable ways.

The courts are still deciding exactly how and when behavior crosses the line from being annoying or insulting to being illegal. There are certain general principles, however. If a man asks for sexual favors and threatens harm unless he is accepted, these acts are usually considered illegal—especially if the threat is fulfilled. A second type of harassment occurs when a man creates a hostile work environment by subjecting a woman to repeated offensive jokes or comments that, she makes clear, are unwelcome.

In almost all cases of reported sexual harassment, the harasser is male and victim is female. A few cases have, however, involved a woman boss and a male employee or a woman boss and a woman victim. But so rare have these cases been that the law is even murkier in these areas.

FURTHER READING

Lavelle, Marianne. "The New Rules of Sexual Harassment: The Supreme Court Defines What Harassment Is and Who Can Be Held Responsible." *U.S. News and World Report,* July 6, 1998.

LeMoncheck, Linda, and Mane Hajdin. *Sexual Harassment: A Debate.* Lanham: Rowman & Littlefield, 1997.

McGowan, Keith. *Sexual Harassment.* San Diego, Calif.: Lucent Books, 1999.

Sexuality

Sexuality is the exercise of sexual functions or appetites. The way that Americans have incorporated sexuality into their lives has changed greatly over the generations. During the colonial period, sex was intended for reproduction, and it occurred largely within marriage. During the 19th century it was romanticized in new ways as a supreme human experience to be shared with one's wife or husband. At the same time, however, prostitution also started to flourish, as cities grew and as so many disproportionately male settlements were being created in frontier areas.

The 19th century also saw the increasing use of various means to reduce family size, ranging from male withdrawal to primitive (by modern standards) types of contraception to abortion, which was not criminalized until the middle of the same century. All of this meant the beginning of the separation of sexuality from the original goal of sex: procreation.

In the consumer society of the 20th century, marriage and sexuality overlap far less than at any time in U.S. history: for many Americans sex is now for personal pleasure as well as for reproduction. As these large-scale cultural shifts have taken place and women have gained ever more control of their own fertility, girls and women have gained choices about their sexuality, including open lesbianism, that would have been unthinkable to generations before the 1960s. It was the decade of the 60s that saw the so-called sexual revolution take place. The birth-control pill came on the market early in the decade, followed in 1973 by the U.S. Supreme Court decision in *Roe v. Wade,* which gave women much more access to abortion. As a consequence of these and other developments, there was an increase in premarital sex, and a relaxing of the old "double standard," under which a man was granted much more freedom to be sexually active outside of marriage than a woman.

SEE ALSO

Abortion; Birth control; Marriage; Reproductive rights

FURTHER READING

D'Emilio, John, and Estelle B. Freedman. *Intimate Matters.* New York: Harper & Row, 1988.

Harmatz, Morton G., and Melinda A. Novak. *Human Sexuality.* New York: Harper & Row, 1983.

Gallagher, Catherine, and Thomas Laqueur, eds. *The Making of the Modern Body: Sexuality and Society in the Nineteenth Century.* Berkeley: University of California Press, 1987.

Sexual orientation

A person's sexual orientation is defined as heterosexual ("straight"), homosexual ("gay" or "lesbian"), or bisexual. Scientists are currently debating how much of one's sexual orientation is the result of personal choice and how much is the result of biological programming, childhood development, or social factors. It has proven difficult to gather reliable statistics about how many Americans are lesbian, gay, or bisexual because the fear of reprisal—discrimination in employment or housing—leads many to stay "in the closet." Currently estimates range from 5 to 10 percent of the population.

SEE ALSO

Lesbians

FURTHER READING

Hetter, Katia. "The New Civil Rights Battle: The Supreme Court Hands Gays a Win in the Struggle between Tolerance and Tradition." *U.S. News and World Report,* June 3, 1996.

Lacayo, Richard. "The New Gay Struggle." *Time,* Oct. 26, 1998.

Shaw, Anna Howard

- *Born: Feb. 14, 1847, Newcastle-on-Tyne, England*
- *Education: Albion College, attended 1873–76; Boston University, D.D., 1878, M.D., 1885*
- *Accomplishments: President, National American Woman Suffrage Association (1904–15); author,* The Story of a Pioneer *(autobiography, 1915); chairman, Women's Committee of the Council of National Defense (1917–19)*
- *Died: July 2, 1919, Moylan, Pa.*

One of the most remarkable women of her generation, Anna Howard Shaw was a minister, a physician, and a suffrage leader. More able as an orator than an organizer, she headed the National American Woman Suffrage Association (NAWSA) between 1904 and 1915, when Carrie Chapman Catt replaced her and led the final struggle for victory that culminated in the ratifi-

Anna Howard Shaw organized and lectured throughout the world for the causes of temperance, women's suffrage, and peace. Shaw was the first ordained woman to preach in Amsterdam, Berlin, Copenhagen, and London, and the first woman to deliver a sermon in the State Church of Sweden.

cation of the 19th Amendment in 1920.

Inspired to become a minister at a time when few denominations permitted women to be ordained, Shaw battled tirelessly to achieve her goal, a goal which required her to live on a pittance while in school because a woman did not have access to the financial support enjoyed by male ministerial students. In 1880 she became the first woman to be ordained by the Methodists and served in New England for seven years. But she came to believe that medicine would offer her more opportunity for service than ministry, so in 1883 she enrolled in the medical school of Boston University.

When she graduated in 1886, she had already decided that the most fundamental problem faced by women was the lack of the right to vote. She then became a paid lecturer for the Massachusetts Woman Suffrage Association. Before too much longer, she had become the protégée of suffrage leader Susan B. Anthony. She served as president of NAWSA at a time when it needed flexible leadership, which she was unable to provide. Hence her time in office is generally viewed as a failure.

After retiring from the presidency of NAWSA, Shaw devoted the last years of her life to coordinating women's contributions to World War I on behalf of the U.S. Council of National Defense.

SEE ALSO

Catt, Carrie Chapman; National American Woman Suffrage Association (NAWSA)

FURTHER READING

Linkugel, Wil A., Martha Solomon. *Anna Howard Shaw.* Westport, Conn.: Greenwood, 1991.

Shaw, Anna Howard, Barbara Brown Zikmund, eds., Leontine Kelly. *Anna Howard Shaw: The Story of a Pioneer.* Cleveland, Ohio: The Pilgrim Press, 1994.

Sheppard-Towner Act (1921)

The passage of the Sheppard-Towner Maternity and Infancy Act in 1921 represented a high-water mark of female influence on public policy in the immediate aftermath of suffrage. Women reformers had made improved maternal and child health a top priority as soon as they had achieved ratification of the 19th Amendment, giving women the right to vote, in 1920. When Congress passed the Sheppard-Towner Maternity and Infancy Act in 1921, women's groups could congratulate themselves: not only had they achieved the legislation they had worked hard for, but this act was the first federally funded social-welfare measure in the United States.

The law had been drafted by the Children's Bureau chief, Julia Lathrop, and it was originally introduced into an earlier Congress by Jeannette Rankin, the first woman member of the House of Representatives.

Bitterly opposed by the American Medical Association as "socialistic," the law mandated federal matching grants to help states set up prenatal and child health clinics, to distribute information on nutrition and hygiene, and to provide midwife training and visiting nurses for pregnant women and new mothers. The U.S. Children's Bureau, with the assistance of volunteers from women's clubs, administered the programs, which appeared to be successful in bringing down the infant mortality rate.

When women proved to be voting at a lower rate than men, however, politicians began to be less responsive to them and opponents forced the law's repeal in 1929.

SEE ALSO

Children's Bureau, U.S.

FURTHER READING

Muncy, Robyn. *Creating a Female Dominion.* New York: Oxford University Press, 1991.

Slavery

For the first 250 years of U.S. history, slavery was a legal institution in the South, and for the first 200 years it was also legal in the North. (After the American Revolution, slavery began to decline in the northern states, where it was less important to the local economies.)

Actually, when the first Africans landed in colonial Virginia in 1619, the first time there were Africans in what would become the United States, they were not yet lifetime slaves. Rather, they were indentured servants, bound by a contract to serve a master for a certain period of years. Both blacks and whites were indentured servants in the 17th century, but during the course of the century, the law began to treat the two races differently for reasons scholars still debate. Around 1680, the status of lifelong slave emerged for African Americans and their offspring after a decades-long deterioration that can be traced in legal cases. The most important component of lifetime and hereditary slavery was the fact that a slave mother could not produce a free child, which perpetuated the institution.

Slaves could not enter into contracts and therefore could not legally marry—although men and women did form committed, informal marriages within the limits of what was possible. Slave owners were under no obligation to respect slave families: husband, wife, and children could be sold away from one another. Slave families, as a result, adapted to these stresses by relying on traditional African forms of family life that encompassed a whole range of relatives and not just the nuclear family of husband, wife, and children.

A slave woman was also vulnerable to the sexual appetite of her master: she was his property. Neither a slave husband nor a white wife could do much to intervene. No doubt some unions between a slave woman and her master came about because of genuine love, but whether they occurred out of love or lust, a disproportionate share of power resided with the master.

Enslaved women worked both in the master's house doing domestic work and in the fields, where they most often toiled in single-sex work gangs. After working for the master or the mistress, they then had to cook and perform other domestic chores for their own families. Older women frequently provided child care for other slave women, but childhood was not the period of careful protection that it has become in the 20th century. Slave children were put to work as young as five or six in some instances.

The female community, as well as the extended family, sustained women in the midst of harsh circumstances. Slave women attended at childbirth for one another and helped one another with folk remedies for illness, and in this way built powerful bonds. Some slave women found an opportunity to fight slavery. Harriet Tubman escaped slavery in Maryland, helped many others escape to the North through the Underground Railroad, and worked as

Though many African-American female slaves worked indoors as domestics or taking care of their masters' children, many also toiled in the fields. Even after slavery ended, economic circumstances often forced black women to pick cotton.

a Northern spy after the Civil War broke out in 1861. Sojourner Truth gained her freedom in New York State before the Civil War, and despite her lack of formal education, became a noted abolitionist speaker.

At the beginning of the Civil War, not quite four million people were slaves in the southern United States. President Abraham Lincoln resisted ending slavery for many months in order to keep the border states (where slavery was legal, too) loyal to the Union. Pressured by abolitionists, especially women, Lincoln issued the Emancipation Proclamation on January 1, 1863, which declared the slaves in the rebellious Confederate states to be free but did not free the slaves in the border states. After the war ended, in 1865 Congress passed, and the states ratified, the 13th Amendment, making the end of slavery official throughout the nation.

SEE ALSO

Indentured servants; Truth, Sojourner; Tubman, Harriet

FURTHER READING

Stevenson, Brenda. *Life in Black and White.* New York: Oxford University Press, 1996.

White, Deborah Gray. *Ar'n't I a Woman?: Female Slaves in the Plantation South.* New York: Norton, 1999.

Smith, Bessie

- *Born: Apr. 15, 1894, Chattanooga, Tenn.*
- *Education: No formal education*
- *Accomplishments: Blues Foundation Hall of Fame (posthumous, 1980); Rock and Roll Hall of Fame (posthumous, 1989)*
- *Died: Sept. 26, 1937, Clarksdale, Miss.*

One of the most talented and innovative blues singers—indeed, one of the most influential women—in American musical history, Bessie Smith exerted a profound influence on such other musicians as the trumpeter Louis Armstrong (the trumpet player on nine of her records) and many female blues singers, who were inspired by her sharp phras-

A protegée of Ma Rainey, Bessie Smith was known as the "Empress of the Blues." Her biographer, Chris Albertson, says of her, "Bessie had a wonderful way of turning adversity into triumph, and many of her songs are the tales of liberated women."

ing and full, self-assured delivery. In essence, she blended African and Western music in a new synthesis. Many subsequent singers such as Billie Holiday, Dinah Washington, and Mahalia Jackson saw her as a mentor.

Born in the South to a family suffering from extreme poverty—and at a time of discrimination against African Americans—the self-trained Smith began performing on the streets of Chattanooga, Tennessee, while still a child. Early on, the blues artist Ma Rainey heard her sing and taught her the style of country blues. Bessie Smith then began to tour the South, performing in everything from carnivals and tent shows to bars to variety shows. Her singing, in a rich contralto voice, expressed the deep frustration of the blues, but also a joy in living.

Smith enjoyed her greatest success in the 1920s, when she performed in many parts of the country and recorded on the Columbia label for which her records sold well. She was billed as the "Empress of the Blues." In 1923 she married Philadelphia policeman Jack Gee, from whom she separated in 1930. The Great Depression reduced the size of her audience, though she still found popularity in the South, and years of heavy drinking took their toll. In 1937 she died after an automobile accident.

SEE ALSO

Rainey, Gertrude Pridgett ("Ma")

FURTHER READING

Davis, Angela Y. *Blues Legacies and Black Feminism: Gertrude 'Ma' Rainey, Bessie Smith, and Billie Holiday.* New York: Pantheon, 1998.

Smith, Margaret Chase

- *Born: Dec. 14, 1897, Skowhegan, Maine*
- *Education: High school*
- *Accomplishments: U.S. Representative (R–Maine, 1940–48); U.S. Senator (R–Maine, 1948–72); Presidential Medal of Freedom (1989)*
- *Died: May 29, 1995, Skowhegan, Maine*

Margaret Chase Smith was not the first woman to serve in the U.S. Senate—a few had preceded her—but she was the first to play a high-profile role there.

Margaret Chase, raised in a small town in Maine, went to work right after graduation from high school as a newspaperwoman. She married Republican politician Clyde Smith in 1930 but continued to be professionally active herself, working for the telephone company. She was also a leader in the Maine Business and Professional Women's Club. When Clyde Smith died in the midst of his 1940 campaign for the U.S. House of Representatives, his wife had the background to be a credible replacement for him.

Margaret Chase Smith served four terms in the House of Representatives before running successfully for the Senate in 1948. She then went on to serve four terms in the Senate before suffering defeat in 1972.

In her "Declaration of Conscience," delivered to the Senate in 1950, Senator Margaret Chase Smith spoke out boldly against Senator McCarthy's reckless accusations. She defended as basic principles of American life "the right to criticize; the right to hold unpopular beliefs; the right to protest; the right of independent thought."

A conservative woman about many economic and social issues, Smith was also deeply principled, and those principles gave her the courage to speak out against a senator of her own party. Indeed, she was the first senator of either party publicly to criticize Republican senator Joseph McCarthy for his irresponsible charges about communists in government in the 1950s. As far as advocacy for women is concerned, her pet cause was improving conditions for women in the military. Before she left the Senate, she had become the ranking Republican on the Senate Armed Services Committee.

SEE ALSO

Congress, U.S.; Politics

FURTHER READING

Gould, Alberta. *First Lady of the Senate: A Life of Margaret Chase Smith.* Mount Desert, Maine: Windswept House, 1989.

Schmidt, Patricia L. *Margaret Chase Smith: Beyond Convention.* Orono: University of Maine Press, 1996.

Smith, Margaret Chase. *Declaration of Conscience.* New York: Doubleday, 1972.

Vallin, Martin Boyd. *Margaret Chase Smith.* Westport, Conn.: Greenwood, 1998.

Socialism

Socialism is a theory of social organization that calls for government or collective ownership of large-scale enterprises. Various socialist philosophies over the centuries have attracted modest interest before becoming matters of purely intellectual concern. During the process of industrialization in the 19th century, however—at a time when workers were laboring long hours at hard factory jobs while business owners were making more money than ever before—some socialists dedicated themselves to bringing about a new society based on the ideas of German thinker Karl Marx.

European immigrants introduced modern socialism to the United States in the 1870s. The movement did not stay confined to immigrant circles for long, however. It attracted, among others, women in the Woman's Christian Temperance Union (WCTU). The WCTU's leader, Frances Willard, was herself a socialist who had become convinced that alcohol was a symptom rather than the cause of urban poverty. She was joined by many of her fellow members in believing that replacing American capitalist society with a socialist one would also eliminate the chief cause of alcohol abuse.

At its height in the late 19th and early 20th centuries, the Socialist party drew support from tens of thousands of Americans, including many women. Although the party was not as outspoken on women's issues as some of its female members wanted, it did address social justice issues such as the need for programs to improve public health, that attracted support from both sexes. Moreover, some of the outstanding Socialist leaders were women, in particular Kate Richards O'Hare, who crisscrossed Oklahoma urging farmers to defend their rights. Some of the earliest women elected to public office were socialists, such as Estelle Lindsay, elected to the Los Angeles City Council in 1915, she bacame the first American woman to serve on the city council of a

Women were very active in the Socialist party in the early 20th century. Here a group of striking New York garment workers sells The Call, *a socialist newspaper, in 1909.*

major metropolis. After the Russian Revolution and the founding of the Communist party, the Socialist party lost its vitality.

SEE ALSO

Communist party; Willard, Frances

FURTHER READING

Buhle, Mari-Jo. *Women and American Socialism.* Urbana: University of Illinois Press, 1981.

Dombrowski, James. *The Early Days of Christian Socialism in America.* New York: Octagon Books, 1966.

Sororities

Sororities are private, most often secret clubs for college women. Those that are honor societies or professional groups are not secret. The name can actually refer to any sisterhood but it generally refers to those on college campuses. Today there are sororities on a large number of campuses nationwide, although they no longer enjoy the power that they did at their height.

Typically, women live at the sorority house and form lasting friendships with their sorority sisters during the course of their college careers. The sorority chapters on individual campuses are branches of a national umbrella organization. In addition to the goal of encouraging good study habits among members, sororities typically undertake charitable projects in the larger community.

Greek-letter societies for men—fraternities—date from the early 19th century, with the Greek letters commonly referring to a motto that is secret to all but members. As higher education began to be available for women in the mid to late 19th century, sororities were founded, too, such as Kappa Alpha Theta in 1870 and Gamma Phi Beta, the first "fraternity" for women to call itself a sorority, in 1882. One of the largest was Chi Omega, founded in 1895, which had chapters on 87 campuses in the 1950s and 168 chapters in 1985.

Whatever their original sisterly purposes may have been, sororities had an almost frightening power when they were at their height in mid-20th century. Young women would be "rushed" or invited to a social event as part of a process that allowed the sorority to look them over for possible membership. In most cases, a single negative vote was enough to keep a prospective member out. Those who did not make the sorority of their dreams—or perhaps any sorority at all—were crushed by their rejection. Fraternity men, for example, might date only sorority women. In other words, young women saw membership in a sorority as crucial to their social success.

At first the Greek societies were for white Protestants. Over time members of other groups founded their own and established Jewish sororities and black sororities on many campuses. The first three black sororities, Alpha Kappa Alpha, Delta Sigma Theta, and Zeta Phi Beta, were founded at Howard University in Washington, D.C., between 1908 and 1920.

The more radical political currents of the 1960s and 1970s, above all the student protest movements of those years, undermined the popularity and influence of Greek societies on most campuses because they and their social priorities seemed dated. Since the 1980s they have enjoyed a comeback but have not won back the dominant position they once had. Today, sororities are much more ethnically diverse than in the past.

FURTHER READING

Scott, William A. *Values and Organizations: A Study of Fraternities and Sororities.* Chicago: Rand McNally, 1965.

Whipple, Edward G., ed. *New Challenges for Greek Letter Organizations: Transforming Fraternities and Sororities into Learning Communities.* San Francisco: Jossey-Bass, 1998.

Sports

Today a girl who is a good athlete can play organized sports. She can aspire to win an athletic scholarship to college, and she can dream of becoming a professional tennis player, golfer, figure skater, or even basketball player. Although the opportunities still are not equal to what is available for boys and men, they are much better than in the past.

In the last decades of the 19th century, the first substantial generation of young women to attend college had something to prove beyond just getting good grades. So widespread was the belief that they would undermine their health by engaging in vigorous exercise—especially during their menstrual periods—that playing a sport was virtually a revolutionary act.

In the early 20th century, Young Women's Christian Associations (YWCAs), ethnic clubs, and municipal leagues provided young working women with opportunities to play sports, such as basketball. As the century wore on, high schools and colleges began to require physical education classes for both sexes. In short, the idea that girls and sports were a dangerous mix had disappeared.

Nonetheless, girls were still treated differently. As late as the 1960s, for example, girls played basketball by a different set of rules than boys: they either played offense or defense, but they could not run up and down the full distance of the court until 1971. As Little League baseball developed, it was restricted to boys only, and there was no comparable activity for girls until the birth of modern feminism around 1970, which led women and men to crusade on behalf of their daughters.

The inequities were perhaps the greatest in college sports. During the course of the century, college sports for men became increasingly important, and men's programs—above all, football—consumed a huge percentage of an institution's athletic budget, including the allocation for scholarships. Women's sports were not a priority and received little funding. For example, at the University of California at Berkeley, around 1970, men's programs were a multi-million dollar budget item; however, before Title IX of the Education Act Amendments of 1972, the total women's athletic budget was only $50,000.

In 1971 the Association for Intercollegiate Athletics for Women (AIAW) was formed to certify national championships for women as the National Collegiate Athletics Association (NCAA) does for men. In 1982 the NCAA sanctioned its first national championships for women, and so in 1985 the AIAW ceased to operate. In 1991 Judith Sweet, of the University of California, San Diego, became the first woman to head the NCAA.

Particular individuals—such as tennis player Billie Jean King—and a reinvigorated women's movement pressured the American public to take women's sports seriously. In the early 1970s King fought to start a women's tennis tour and to increase the prize money available to women.

About the same time that King was agitating on behalf of women tennis players, Congress passed Title IX of the Education Act Amendments of 1972, which completely transformed the funding for women's sports at the college level, because it prohibited discrimination based on sex at any educational institution receiving federal funds. As a result of this law, the number of women in intercollegiate sports rose from 16,000 in the early 1970s to more than 160,000 in the late 1980s.

Despite the barriers, there is a wonderful tradition of American women athletes, featuring the exploits of tennis star Helen Wills Moody in the 1930s, of Mildred "Babe" Didrikson Zaharias (who won basketball and golf championships, and set world records in various track and field events) in the 1930s and 40s—Zaharias crusaded for professional women golfers to get decent prize money—and a plethora of talented Olympics stars. One recurring problem for the woman athlete has had to do with gender stereotypes regarding "tomboys." If a woman was good at something men excel at—that is, sports—did this mean that she might also be a lesbian? If she was, did it matter? This is another area in which there has been considerable change. Earlier, lesbian athletes stayed "in the closet." Now someone like tennis player Martina Navratilova can reveal herself to be a lesbian and still go on to be one of the most-respected and best-paid women athletes in the world.

As in so many other areas of American life, women of color have not had equal advantages in sports. Until Wilma Rudolph's gold medals in track at the 1960 Olympics and Althea Gibson's exploit of being the first black person to win a single's championship at Wimbledon in 1957 in tennis, there were few well-known women of color in the world of sports. Today, however, many of the best-known women athletes are women of color, such as basketball player Lisa Leslie, figure skaters Kristi Yamaguchi and Michelle Kwan, track stars Florence Griffith Joyner and Jackie Joyner-Kersee, and tennis players Venus and Serena Williams.

A particularly exciting development in the late 1990s has been the founding of the Women's National Basketball

Since Congress passed Title IX in 1972, there have been increased funding and better programming for women's sports at all levels. A peak moment came in July 1999 when the U.S. women defeated China to win the World's Cup in soccer—with a crowd of 90,000 on hand to witness the victory.

Association in 1997. And in 1999, in a highly publicized triumph for women's sports, 90,000 people watched in person and millions more on television as the U.S. women defeated China in the Women's World Cup of Soccer.

SEE ALSO

Education Act Amendments (1972); Evert, Chris; Gibson, Althea; King, Billie Jean Moffitt; Moody, Helen Wills; Navratilova, Martina; Rudoph, Wilma; Zaharias, Mildred Didrikson ("Babe")

FURTHER READING

Cahn, Susan. *Coming on Strong: Gender and Individuality in Twentieth-Century Women's Sports.* New York: Free Press, 1994.

Macy, Sue. *Winning ways: A Photohistory of American Women in Sports.* New York: Henry Holt, 1996.

McComb, David G. *Sports: An Illustrated History.* New York: Oxford University Press, 1998.

Oglesby, Carole A., ed. Doreen L. Greenberg, Karen Hill, ed. *Encyclopedia of Women and Sports in America.* Phoenix, Ariz.: Oryx, 1998.

Strudwick, Leslie. *Athletes.* (Women in Profile). New York: Crabtree, 1999.

Stanton, Elizabeth Cady

- *Born: Nov. 12, 1815, Johnstown, N.Y.*
- *Education: Troy (N.Y.) Female Seminary, graduated 1832*
- *Accomplishments: Author, Seneca Falls "Declaration of Sentiments" (1948); publisher,* Revolution, *women's rights newspaper (1868); co-author, with Susan B. Anthony,* History of Woman Suffrage *(3 vols., 1881–86); president, National Woman Suffrage Association (1869–92); author,* The Woman's Bible *(1895)*
- *Died: Oct. 26, 1902, New York, N.Y.*

Suffrage leader Elizabeth Cady Stanton was a woman of deep intellect and wide-ranging interests whose writings, even today, seem fresh and exciting—and even bold. Arguing for women's rights in 1892, at 77 years of age, she wrote,

> No matter how much women prefer to lean, to be protected and supported, nor how much men desire to have them do so, they must make the voyage of life alone, and for safety in an emergency, they must know something of the laws of navigation. . . . It matters not whether the solitary voyager is man or woman; nature, having endowed them equally, leaves them to their own skill and judgment in the hour of danger, and, if not equal to the occasion, alike they perish.

Young Elizabeth Cady received a splendid education. In her home she read widely under the tutelage of her Presbyterian minister. She also attended the

Elizabeth Cady Stanton, holding her controversial book The Women's Bible, *and Susan B. Anthony, with horn, flank George Washington in this cartoon. Entitled "The Apotheosis of Liberty," it mocks the efforts of the National American Woman Suffrage Association.*

Troy Female Seminary in New York, graduating in 1832. Few girls of her generation studied Greek, Latin, and mathematics (standard fare for a boy destined for college) as she did.

As an adult, Elizabeth Cady was attracted to reform causes, and in these circles she met the man who would become her husband, Henry Stanton. The two married in 1840 and went immediately to the World's Anti-Slavery Convention in London, where Stanton met fellow reformer Lucretia Mott. After being required to watch the convention's proceedings from the sidelines because of their sex, the women vowed someday to hold a woman's rights convention.

That opportunity came in 1848 when Stanton, her husband, and their children (there would eventually be seven) were living in Seneca Falls, New York. Mott was visiting nearby, and the two women decided to issue a call for a women's rights convention to be held a week later. Stanton authored the Declaration of Sentiments presented for deliberation at the meeting—and considered too radical by many because it made the first public call for woman suffrage.

A few years later Stanton met Susan B. Anthony, and they formed a powerful collaboration. Stanton was the more original thinker, and the unmarried Anthony (who had fewer domestic responsibilities) was the more energetic organizer and campaigner.

One of their early collaborations occurred during the Civil War when they formed the Women's National Loyal League to gather signatures on a petition pressuring President Abraham Lincoln to proclaim the end of slavery. Before they were through, the organization had secured several hundred thousand signatures.

After the Civil War, Stanton and Anthony parted company with many of their former abolitionist colleagues over the issue of suffrage for black men. The two women did not want to campaign to get the vote for black men at the expense of woman suffrage. In the end Congress passed and the states ratified both the 14th Amendment, which clearly defined citizenship for the first time but also used the phrase "male citizens" in a clause about representation, and the 15th Amendment, enfranchising black men. Both amendments were opposed by Stanton and Anthony in sometimes racist terms. Their stance created a split in the women's movement that was not healed until 1890.

As she aged, Stanton became not one bit less radical. One of her last projects was *The Woman's Bible,* an attack on what she saw as the sexism of traditional Christianity. Brilliant, sometimes outrageous, and always interesting, Elizabeth Cady Stanton was the mother of modern feminism.

SEE ALSO

Anthony, Susan Brownell; Mott, Lucretia Coffin; Seneca Falls Convention; Suffrage, woman

FURTHER READING

Banner, Lois W. *Elizabeth Cady Stanton: A Radical for Women's Rights.* New York: Addison Wesley Longman, 1998.

Flexner, Eleanor, and Ellen Fitzpatrick. *Century of Struggle.* Cambridge: Harvard University Press, 1996.

Griffith, Elizabeth. *In Her Own Right: The Life of Elizabeth Cady Stanton.* New York: Oxford University Press, 1985.

Stein, Gertrude

- *Born: Feb. 3, 1874, Allegheny, Pa.*
- *Education: Radcliffe College, A.B., 1898*
- *Accomplishments: Author,* Q. E. D. *(completed 1903, published as* Things as They Are, *1950);* Three Lives *(1909);* Tender Buttons *(1914);* The Making of Americans *(1925);* Useful Knowledge *(1928);* Before the Flowers of Friendship Faded Friendship Faded *(1931);* The Autobiography of Alice B. Toklas *(1933);* Portraits and Prayers *(1934);* Everybody's Autobiography *(1937);* Picasso *(1938);* Paris, France *(1940);* Wars I have Seen *(1944);* Brewsie and Willie *(1946)*
- *Died: July 27, 1946, Neuilly-sur-Seine, France*

Gertrude Stein was an avant-garde writer who spent much of her life in France, where she traveled in artistic circles that included such celebrated figures as Pablo Picasso and Ernest Hemingway, among many others.

Gertrude Stein was one of the architects of the literary movement known as Modernism. Except for her best-selling autobiography, her prose was experimental and abstract. Though she lived much of her life as an expatriate in Paris, photographer Carl Van Vechten made this portrait against the backdrop of an American flag.

Born in Pennsylvania to a prosperous Jewish family, Stein spent most of her girlhood in California. For college she went east, attending the Harvard Annex, which would soon become Radcliffe College. There she studied with the philosopher William James; he and other professors considered her a gifted student.

After graduating magna cum laude from Radcliffe in 1898, Stein attended Johns Hopkins University Medical School for three years before losing interest. She and her brother Leo then spent time in several European countries before settling in Paris in 1903. The Steins recognized Picasso's genius early on, bought his work, and became important patrons of the arts.

Gertrude Stein began to host a salon and entertain regularly at her home, to which many of the important artists, musicians, and writers of the day sought invitations. Her own writings began to appear, published by small presses because they were too obscure and experimental to enjoy commercial success—her literary style was fractured and contained slightly altered repetitions, paralleling the style of cubism in art. Nonetheless, her writing influenced the work of those in her circle, including Ernest Hemingway.

For many years Stein had a devoted relationship with Alice B. Toklas, her companion, typist, and lover. In 1933 Stein published *The Autobiography of Alice B. Toklas,* in which Stein uses the character of Toklas to describe life with Stein. Written in accessible language, this was Stein's first commercial success. Though not so popular as *The Autobi-*

ography, her later books also found an audience. Stein died of cancer in 1946 and is buried in Paris.

FURTHER READING

Bowers, Jane Palitini. *Gertrude Stein.* Women Writers. New York: St. Martin's Press, 1993.

La Farge, Ann. *Gertrude Stein.* New York: Chelsea House, 1988.

Mellow, James R. *Charmed Circle: Gertrude Stein & Company.* 1974. Reprint, Boston: Houghton Mifflin, 1991.

Steinem, Gloria

- *Born: Mar. 25, 1934, Toledo, Ohio*
- *Education: Smith College, B.A., 1956; University of Delhi and University of Calcutta, India, graduate study, 1957–58*
- *Accomplishments: Co-founder,* New York *magazine (1968) and* Ms. *magazine (1971); co-organizer, National Women's Political Caucus (1971); author,* Outrageous Acts and Everyday Rebellions *(1983),* Revolutions from Within: A Book of Self-Esteem *(1992), and* Moving Beyond Words *(1994); National Women's Hall of Fame (1993)*

For many Americans the name of Gloria Steinem is almost synonymous with modern feminism. She has been active in so many arenas for so many years that she is practically an institution.

Raised in the Midwest, Steinem graduated from Smith College and then began a career in journalism. In 1971 she was principally responsible for launching *Ms.* magazine, a publication that aimed to appeal to a broad readership with slick graphics and professional editing—but offered a more explicitly political content than any previous mainstream periodical for women.

Besides publishing articles about the lives of many different types of women, political issues, and women's health, *Ms.* invited its readers to send in their personal stories, many of which drew upon an earlier essay in the magazine by writer Jane O'Reilly, in which she had talked about the "click" of recognition, the moment when she understood the extent of her oppression as a woman. Readers wrote in describing their own personal "click" moments, thus turning the magazine into an important forum for exchange of feminist ideas. Steinem served as editor-in-chief from the founding until 1987.

At the 1983 observance of International Women's Day at U.N. headquarters, feminist writer and activist Gloria Steinem (center) moderated a discussion on "The Exploited Half: Women, the World's Poorest."

In addition to her magazine work, Steinem was a cofounder of the National Women's Political Caucus, and she has written a number of books, including the memoir *Outrageous Acts and Everyday Rebellions* in 1983 and the book-length essay on self esteem, *Revolution from Within* in 1992. She has also lectured tirelessly to promote feminist causes such as reproductive rights.

SEE ALSO

Feminism; National Women's Political Caucus (NWPC)

FURTHER READING

Daffron, Carolyn. *Gloria Steinem.* New York: Chelsea House, 1988.

Heilbrun, Carolyn. *The Education of a Woman: A Life of Gloria Steinem.* New York: Dial, 1995.

Stewart, Maria W. Miller

- *Born: 1803, Hartford, Conn.*
- *Education: No formal education*
- *Accomplishments: First American-born woman to give a public political speech*
- *Died: Dec. 17, 1879, Washington, D.C.*

The first American-born woman to give a public political speech, Maria Stewart belonged to the African-American community of Boston when she delivered her historic first address in 1832.

Maria Miller's parents were both dead by the time she was 5 years old. She was then "bound out" as an indentured servant until she was 15. With no formal education, she managed to acquire a certain level of knowledge from her employer's library. Married in 1826 to James Stewart of Boston, she was left a widow in 1829. Her husband left her a small estate, but his executors seemingly defrauded her of it.

Stewart fought back publicly. Inspired by the dawning abolitionist movement in Boston in those years, she gave four public addresses in 1832 and 1833 that were devoted to the situation of free blacks, urging them to secure an education so as to be able to defend their interests. The radical abolitionist William Lloyd Garrison also published some of her writings in his periodical, *The Liberator.*

As with so many of the women, white and black alike, who pioneered public speaking, Stewart had to contend with a hostile reaction, even from other African Americans. As a result, her speaking career was brief. In subsequent years she acquired more education, taught, and then worked with the freed people during the Civil War (1861–65). She was a woman of deep religious convictions, and her Christian faith shaped many of the decisions she made during her life.

FURTHER READING

Stewart, Maria W. *Maria Stewart, America's First Black Woman Political Writer: Essays and Speeches.* Edited by Marilyn Richardson. Bloomington: Indiana University Press, 1987.

Stone, Lucy

- *Born: Aug. 13, 1818, West Brookfield, Mass.*
- *Education: Oberlin College, B.A., 1847*
- *Accomplishments: Organizer, first national women's rights convention (1850); co-organizer, Woman's National Loyal League (1863); co-organizer, American Woman Suffrage Association (1869); editor,* Woman's Journal *(1872–93)*
- *Died: Oct. 18, 1893, Dorchester, Mass.*

A dedicated abolitionist in the years before the Civil War, Lucy Stone was also outraged by women's inferior status in American life: "I expect to plead not for the slave only, but for suffering humanity everywhere. Especially do I mean to labor for the elevation of my sex."

One of the most important suffragists of the 19th century, Lucy Stone was a pioneer in many respects. It was she, for example, who made a public issue of keeping her maiden name after marriage, and for the rest of the century a woman who chose to do so was known as a "Lucy Stoner."

Young Lucy devoted herself to securing an education, despite a lack of support from her father. Like many other women, she alternated periods of teaching (which did not require the credentials that it does today) with periods of education. In 1843, at the age of 25, she entered Oberlin College in Ohio, the first coeducational college in the country. There she met a woman who would be her lifelong friend and eventually her sister-in-law, Antoinette Brown (later Blackwell). Graduating in 1847, Stone was the first Massachusetts woman to earn a college education.

After college Lucy Stone became a paid abolitionist lecturer. She also devoted some of her talks to women's rights. When Henry Blackwell fell in love with her and sought to marry her, she agreed only on the condition that the marriage would not limit her. At the 1855 wedding the bride and groom read a protest against the injustice of the then current marriage laws. They had one child, the suffragist Alice Stone Blackwell.

After the Civil War, Lucy Stone was the most outspoken suffragist to advocate accepting the vote for black men without including women in the same measure. Based on the belief that the country was readier to accept black male voters than women voters, Stone's stance put her at odds with fellow suffragists Elizabeth Cady Stanton and Susan B. Anthony. As a result, for more than 20 years there were two different suffrage organizations working in the United States. The Stone group was known as the American Woman Suffrage Association, while Stanton and Anthony's was the National Woman Suffrage Association. The two merged in 1890.

In 1872 Stone became editor of an important periodical devoted to advancing suffrage, the *Woman's Journal.* After her death, Henry Blackwell carried on the work, and after his death their daughter, Alice, stepped in, keeping the periodical under unbroken family control for 47 years.

SEE ALSO

Blackwell, Alice Stone; Blackwell, Antoinette Brown; Suffrage, woman

FURTHER READING

Flexner, Eleanor, and Ellen Fitzpatrick. *Century of Struggle.* Cambridge: Harvard University Press, 1996.

Kerr, Andrea Moore. *Lucy Stone: Speaking Out for Equality.* New Brunswick, N.J.: Rutgers University Press, 1992.

STOP-ERA

The major organization created to oppose the Equal Rights Amendment (ERA) was STOP-ERA, led by Phyllis Schlafly. When Congress passed the amendment in 1972 by a huge margin and sent it off to the states to be ratified, most people assumed that the process would take place quickly. The amendment said, "Equality of rights under the law shall not be denied or abridged by the United States or by any State on account of sex," and polls showed that most Americans supported it. Yet it fell 3 states short of the 38 required for ratification.

No one outside of Schlafly's own circle anticipated what a determined and effective opposition she and her group could mount. They deluged state legislators with letters and visits—and got the politicians' attention in states with a substantial constituency of religious conservatives, who were apprehensive about the threat to the family that they saw feminists as constituting, particularly in regard to the issue of abortion. The typical STOP-ERA member was a middle-aged white housewife, religiously devout and married to a working-class man. STOP-ERA charged that the ERA would undermine the necessity for husbands to support their wives and families, lead to unisex restrooms, and allow women to be drafted for military service, all arguments that carried weight with state legislators serving rural or southern districts.

SEE ALSO

Equal Rights Amendment (ERA); Schlafly, Phyllis Stewart

FURTHER READING

Mathews, Donald G., and Jane Sherron De Hart. *Sex, Gender, and the Politics of ERA.* New York: Oxford University Press, 1990.

Stowe, Harriet Beecher

- *Born: June 14, 1811, Litchfield, Conn.*
- *Education: Hartford (Conn.) Female Seminary, graduated 1829*
- *Accomplishments: Author,* Uncle Tom's Cabin *(1852),* Dred; A Tale of the Great Dismal Swamp *(1956);* The Minister's Wooing *(1859);* House and Home Papers *(under pseudonym of Christopher Crowfield, 1865);* The Chimney-Corner *(1868);* Betty's Bright Idea *(1875),* Footsteps of the Master *(1877);* Our Famous Women *(1883),* Agnes of Sorrento (1890); Oldtown Folks and Sam Lawson's Oldtown Fireside Stories *(1896)*
- Died: July 1, 1896, Hartford, Conn.

Harriet Beecher Stowe was the author of the passionate, influential antislavery novel *Uncle Tom's Cabin.* Although Stowe's depiction of African Americans now seems dated, it roused Americans to the abolitionist cause when it was published in 1852. When President Abraham Lincoln met Stowe during the Civil War, he is said to have remarked, "So this is the little woman who started this great war."

Stowe came from a prominent religious and intellectual family. Her father, Lyman Beecher, was one of the best-known clergymen of the day, and her brothers all became clergymen, too; Henry Ward Beecher was the most famous Protestant clergyman of the late 19th century. Older sister Catharine was a spokeswoman for improved female education, among other accomplishments.

Having lost her mother at the age of four, young Harriet benefited from the attention of her scholarly older sister and later attended the same female seminary as Catharine in Hartford, Connecticut. Harriet married the clergyman Calvin Stowe in 1836, after the Beecher family had moved to Cincinnati. As a young wife and mother, she began to publish short sketches so as to supplement the household income.

In 1849 Stowe endured a loss that altered her life. An infant son died (she

Uncle Tom's Cabin *was the best-selling American novel of the 19th century. Stage and musical versions of the story were also popular; this sheet music cover depicts slave mother Eliza (looking curiously fair-skinned) fleeing to save her little boy from being sold away from her.*

eventually had seven children in all), and Stowe was devastated. When Congress passed a new and harsher fugitive slave law the following year, she felt she understood the pain of a slave mother who might be separated from her child, as Stowe herself had been separated from her baby. Her family respected her writing talents, and a sister-in-law urged her to write something about the evils of slavery in response to the law. Her sister Catharine, who never married, went to stay with the Stowe family to give Harriet more chance to write. The result was *Uncle Tom's Cabin,* which was serialized in *The National Era* daily newspaper in 1851 and published as a book in 1852. An astonishing international success, it became the best-selling novel of the 19th century.

Stowe's novel reflects her own piety—which helped it strike a chord in the overwhelmingly Protestant American society of her day. She creates a Christ-like character in the slave Uncle Tom and depicts many less-saintly characters as they struggle for redemption. The Christian home, overseen by a loving and competent housewife, is depicted as key to combating the greed that would separate family members to make a profit.

There had been antislavery non-fiction, but hers was the first novel to deal with the subject, to put a human face on the slaves' suffering. Needless to say, it was bitterly unpopular in the slave South.

Stowe now became a public figure. She corresponded with leading antislavery politicians, and she urged other women to enter the fray by, for example, renting halls for antislavery meetings. Moreover, she continued to publish. None of her later work had the impact of *Uncle Tom's Cabin,* but many of the later novels are still worth reading because of her loving depiction of early New England.

In later years Stowe had to endure more family tragedy in her life. Another son drowned while at college, and a third, who had fought in the Civil War, became an alcoholic.

SEE ALSO

Abolitionism; Beecher, Catharine Esther

FURTHER READING

Hedrick, Joan. *Harriet Beecher Stowe.* New York: Oxford University Press, 1994.
Jakoubek, Robert E. *Harriet Beecher Stowe.* New York: Chelsea House, 1989.
Tompkins, Jane. *Sensational Designs.* New York: Oxford University Press, 1985.

Student movements

Students have organized formally several times in U.S. history—during the 1930s, for example, they formed peace groups—but during the 1960s, and spilling over into the 1970s, students on American college campuses organized on a scale never before seen. Moreover, when young men in the movement failed to take their female counterparts seriously, they helped spur the birth of modern feminism.

Although the unpopular war in Vietnam played a huge role in mobilizing students to protest, the movement began before very many Americans were fighting in Southeast Asia. Starting in the early 1960s, the civil rights movement by and for African Americans sparked enthusiastic participation on campuses around the country. Later, when President Lyndon B. Johnson began sending thousands of U.S. troops abroad in the mid-1960s, a student infrastructure already existed on many campuses and could respond quickly to the escalation.

At the height of the movement, hundreds of thousands of students participated in demonstrations, teach-ins, nonviolent actions—and in a few cases, violent activities—aimed at stopping the fighting in Vietnam. Students were especially concerned about the war because young men were subject to an involuntary draft into the armed forces; if they were called into the military, they would then be forced to put their lives on the line for a cause they did not support. Opposition to the draft sparked passionate protest.

Even before the protests against the U.S. involvement in Vietnam heated up, two major student organizations (as well as many smaller local and regional ones) had taken shape. The Student Nonviolent Coordinating Committee, or SNCC (pronounced "snick"), the brainchild of civil rights leader Ella Baker, mobilized African Americans in the South with the help of idealistic young people from many parts of the country. At first biracial, it evolved into being a Black Power group in which whites felt uncomfortable. Because it operated at the local level, SNCC utilized the talents of many women. The top leadership was, however, male. By 1970 the group had dissolved—but not until it had created immense change in many communities by encouraging blacks to register to vote.

The other major group was Students for a Democratic Society, or SDS, the most important white, radical, "New Left" organization of the 1960s, as opposed to those who had joined or been influenced by the Communist party, the "Old Left," in an earlier period. Starting the decade as a small, primarily male movement, SDS grew to encompass chapters throughout the country. As young people became increasingly frustrated with the Vietnam War, SDS splintered into many groups, a few of which took a violent turn. By 1970, SDS, too, was dead.

During the Vietnam War era, students on large campuses and small were active in the antiwar movement. At Smith College, a women's school in Massachusetts, 74 percent of the student body participated in a 1968 fast for peace.

The sexism in both SNCC and SDS was legendary. Women were expected to perform secretarial functions while the men wrote position papers and planned for the new America. More than once, a young man let it be known that a movement woman's "duties" might involve sexual favors as well as making coffee. In fact, when SDS leader Tom Hayden drew up an indictment in 1962 of all that he thought was wrong with the country (a document called the Port Huron Statement), he never mentioned gender in any way—at a time when women faced discrimination at work, at school, and in society in general.

As young women in the movement began to realize the obstacles they faced both within the movement and in the larger society, they formed consciousness-raising groups, they protested, and they acted. By the time the student movement died down, a new generation of young American women had already learned how to mobilize for social change.

SEE ALSO

Baker, Ella; Civil rights movement; Consciousness-raising

FURTHER READING

Bloom, Alexander, and Wini Breines. *"Takin' It to the Streets": A Sixties Reader.* New York: Oxford University Press, 1995.

Cohen, Robert. *When the Old Left Was Young: Student Radicals and America's First Mass Student Movement, 1929–1941.* New York: Oxford University Press, 1993.

Evans, Sara. *Personal Politics.* New York: Knopf, 1979.

Suburbs

Very early in the history of the new nation, Americans began choosing an informal cottage type of housing whose small size and peaked-roof design evoked rural values, even though such houses were usually built just outside a town or city. Such cottages began to be immensely popular in the 1830s, thus creating housing patterns that would be recognized today as "suburban," although these early styles little resembled the archetypal ranch-style suburban home of the years following World War II.

In the late 19th century, improved transportation in the form of railroads, cable cars, or horse-drawn streetcars made it possible for large numbers of well-to-do families to move outside the city where a husband worked. As a result, "streetcar suburbs" began to appear on a widespread scale. Sometimes these suburbs had their own local government and were independent of the cities upon which their residents depended for a livelihood, and sometimes—as in the case of Los Angeles—they were all part of one giant city.

But it was in the years following World War II, the late 1940s and the 1950s, that suburbs truly came to define the American landscape. By this time an overwhelming percentage of Americans owned cars. Federal and state resources were being directed toward highway construction as never before in U.S. history. Both factors made it easier for men to commute to city jobs, and suburbs became an increasingly attractive place to live. Further, many people believed that their children would receive a better education in suburban schools. Finally, the federal government encouraged low-cost home loans for veterans, and the Federal Housing Authority's loan policies favored lending for single-family homes in "desirable areas," meaning where white people lived (at that time). For all of these reasons, the postwar years saw an explosion of growth in suburbs, along with the appearance of shopping malls, to serve the needs of suburbanites. Some suburban developments, such as Levittown in New Jersey and Lakewood in southern California, were on a scale that dwarfed any prewar suburbs.

Critics of suburbanization point to a number of problems they believe it created. For a housewife in the 1950s, a suburb was frequently lonely and isolating in those years before women went out to work in large numbers. Moreover, Federal Housing Authority policies discriminated against single women and people of color as home owners. Also a move to the suburbs has allowed people to cut themselves off from the problems of those who remain in the inner city. Finally, jobs tended to follow people into the suburbs, leaving those in the inner city even worse off because it was more difficult to secure desirable employment.

Still, in 1999 roughly half of the American population lived in a suburban environment, and suburban populations are growing more than twice as fast as urban ones: from 1980 to 1996, population growth in cities was 10.8 percent, while suburbs grew by 25.4 percent during the same years. In 1992, for the first time in American history, a majority of ballots in a Presidential election were cast by suburbanites. Americans like the space for lawns, gardens, and children's play areas that a suburb typically bestows on its residents, and they appreciate its relative safety.

FURTHER READING

Marsh, Margaret S. *Suburban Lives*. New Brunswick, N.J.: Rutgers University Press, 1990.

May, Elaine Tyler. *Pushing the Limits: American Women, 1940–1961*. New York: Oxford University Press, 1994.

Padgett, Tim. "Saving Suburbia: Families That Seek a Sense of Community Are Moving to New Suburbs Designed to Resemble Small Towns." *Time,* Aug. 16, 1999.

Suffrage, woman

One of the great movements for equality in U.S. history, the drive for woman suffrage consumed three quarters of a century before the 19th Amendment was ratified in 1920. When Elizabeth Cady Stanton drafted the Declaration of Sentiments, calling for votes for women, and presented it to the Seneca Falls Convention in 1848, she little knew how long it would take and how many separate battles would need to be waged before the war was won.

At first woman suffrage was the goal of only a small number of female and male reformers. After the end of the Civil War (1861–65), woman suffrage began to attract more attention as Americans discussed the nature of citizenship and the right to vote for ex-slaves. But as Congress and the nation debated whether and how newly freed male slaves might receive the vote, the woman suffrage community fell into bitter conflict. Some believed that this was "the Negro's hour" and that votes for black men should take precedence over votes for women. Others, led by Stanton and Susan B. Anthony, disagreed violently and believed that women should demand their right to vote at the same time. Those in the former camp formed the American Woman Suffrage Association, and those in the latter formed the National Woman Suffrage

Women suffragists march in front of the capitol on Pennsylvania Avenue, March 3, 1913. Five thousand women gathered for the event, stealing the spotlight from President Woodrow Wilson, whose inauguration was that day.

Association; the groups later reunited as the National American Woman Suffrage Association (NAWSA) in 1890.

By the time of the merger, woman suffrage had begun to attract some potent support, above all from the Woman's Christian Temperance Union (WCTU), led by Frances Willard. The WCTU, formed in the 1870s to combat alcohol abuse, was then the largest organized group of women in the country, so when Willard led her colleagues to endorse suffrage as necessary for women to be able to protect the sanctity of their homes, this was a huge victory.

By this time, too, women were beginning to receive a limited vote in certain states—in school board elections, for example. In 1890 Wyoming entered the union as the first full suffrage state. In 1893 the male voters of Colorado voted for a full suffrage provision for women. That same decade saw New Zealand give women the vote—in 1893—and become the first country in the world to do so. An international movement was beginning to gain momentum.

But the final triumph for woman suffrage in the United States was neither easy nor automatic. It took more decades of organizing, it took street demonstrations by Alice Paul's National Woman's Party, and it took the patriotic efforts of women during World War I to achieve victory.

Carrie Chapman Catt, leader of NAWSA at the moment of victory, later summarized the effort required and claimed that the fight for women's right to vote required 52 years of campaigning, 56 campaigns of referenda to male voters, 480 campaigns to urge legislatures to submit suffrage amendments to voters, 47 campaigns to induce state constitutional conventions to write woman suffrage into state constitutions, 277 campaigns at state party conventions, 30 campaigns at Presidential conventions, and 19 campaigns with 19 successive Congresses.

SEE ALSO

Anthony, Susan Brownell; Catt, Carrie Chapman; Citizenship; Declaration of Sentiments; National American Woman Suffrage Association (NAWSA); Paul, Alice; Seneca Falls Convention; Stanton, Elizabeth Cady

FURTHER READING

Dubois, Ellen Carol. *Feminism and Suffrage: The Emergence of an Independent Women's Movement in America.* Ithaca, N.Y.: Cornell University Press, 1980.

Flexner, Eleanor, and Ellen Fitzpatrick. *Century of Struggle.* Cambridge: Harvard University Press, 1996.

Kraditor, Aileen S. *The Ideas of the Women Suffrage Movement, 1890–1920.* New York: W. W. Norton, 1981.

Smith, Karen Manners. *New Paths to Power: American Women, 1890–1920.* New York: Oxford University Press, 1994.

Weatherford, Doris. *A History of the American Suffragist Movement.* Santa Barbara, Calif.: ABC-CLIO, 1998.

Supreme Court, U.S.

Until the 1970s, the U.S. Supreme Court was a bastion of male domination. No woman served on the Court until Ronald Reagan appointed Sandra Day O'Connor in 1981. Moreover, the Court did not consider discrimination against women as something that should be legally discouraged until the 1971 case of *Reed* v. *Reed*, in which it struck down an Idaho statute governing inheritance on the grounds that it discriminated against women.

Earlier, many Supreme Court decisions had upheld the idea that women belong in the home and that they, as a result, have different citizenship obligations than men. In *Bradwell* v. *Illinois,* for example, the Court upheld the judgment of an Illinois Court that Myra Bradwell not be admitted to the bar on the grounds that as a married woman she could not enter into a binding contract with her clients. In *Hoyt* v. *Florida* of 1961, the Court upheld a murder conviction in which a Florida woman, convicted of this crime, sued on the basis that she had been found guilty by an all-male jury. Juries in Florida were weighted toward men in the process of constituting a jury pool. The majority decision held that women's domestic duties were sufficiently onerous to justify their differential treatment in the process of jury selection.

The modern women's movement has scored one of its most significant victories in ensuring that the Court consider women's rights as well as in preparing the American public to accept women justices. At the end of the 1990s, two women sat on the Court: O'Connor, who is widely respected for her judicial independence, and Ruth Bader Ginsburg, who came to the Court after establishing herself as one of the leading legal experts in the country on the law of sex discrimination. As for clerking on the Supreme Court, the first woman to do so was hired by Justice William O. Douglas in 1944. In 1998, about one-quarter of the clerks hired by the current justices during their entire tenure were female.

In a speech in 1997, Ginsburg disclosed that she is conscious of the legacy she and O'Connor are jointly constructing. In 1996, for example, Ginsburg wrote the decision striking down the all-male admissions policy at Virginia Military Institute. In 1999 O'Connor added to the legacy by writing the majority opinion in a case, *Davis* v. *Monroe County Board of Education*, holding school districts accountable for one student's flagrant sexual harassment of another.

SEE ALSO

Bradwell v. *Illinois* (1873); O'Connor, Sandra Day; *Reed* v. *Reed* (1971)

FURTHER READING

Lindop, Edmund. *The Changing Supreme Court.* New York: F. Watts, 1995.

Patrick, John J. *The Young Oxford Companion to the Supreme Court of the United States.* New York: Oxford University Press, 1994.

Tallchief, Maria

- *Born: Jan. 24, 1925, Fairfax, Okla.*
- *Education: High school*
- *Accomplishments: First American-born prima ballerina; first prima ballerina, New York City Ballet (1948–60); founder (1981) and artistic director (1981–87), Chicago City Ballet; Kennedy Center honoree (1996)*

Born in rural Oklahoma, Maria Tallchief went on to become one of the most respected ballerinas of the 20th century and the toast of New York City and the ballet world while in her prime.

Tallchief was from a family of Osage Indians who had literally struck it rich from the oil deposits on their land. She began studying ballet when she was only four years old, and by the age of eight she had outgrown her Oklahoma teachers. Her family moved to Beverly Hills, California, where she was able to study with the best teachers then available, such as Bronislava Nijinska, the sister and artistic comrade of Russian ballet dancer Vaslav Nijinsky.

At 15, Tallchief danced a solo at the Hollywood Bowl. Soon thereafter she met George Balanchine, the choreographer who would become her husband and who would create stunning ballet roles for her in *Symphonie Concertante, Night Shadow,* and her signature role in *The Firebird.* In 1946 they married.

After moving to New York with Balanchine, Tallchief became the ranking soloist for the company that was then evolving into the New York City

Ballet. Her splendid technique, musicality, and striking appearance made her a popular favorite with audiences. In 1952 she and Balanchine divorced. Tallchief eventually moved to Chicago, where she allied herself with the Chicago Lyric Opera Ballet and founded the Chicago City Ballet.

SEE ALSO

Dance

FURTHER READING

Lang, Paul. *Maria Tallchief: Native American Ballerina.* Springfield, N.J.: Enslow, 1997.

Myers, Elizabeth P. *Maria Tallchief: America's Prima Ballerina.* New York: Henry Holt, 1997.

Tan, Amy

- *Born: Feb. 19, 1952, Oakland, Calif.*
- *Education: San Jose State University, B.A., 1973, M.A., 1974*
- *Accomplishments: National Book Award and* Los Angeles Times *Book Award for* The Joy Luck Club *(1989); author,* The Joy Luck Club *(1989);* The Kitchen God's Wife *(1991);* The Moon Lady *(1992);* The Chinese Siamese Cat *(1994);* The Hundred Secret Senses *(1995)*

Along with Maxine Hong Kingston, Amy Tan has changed the scope of American literature, opening it up to reflect the experiences of those growing up Chinese American. Tan's best-selling first novel, *The Joy Luck Club,* (1989) is about her relationship with her Chinese-born mother, but it is also about conflicts familiar to most loving American mothers and daughters.

Born in California as the middle child of a Baptist minister and his wife, Tan learned when she was 12 that her mother had had an earlier family in China: a husband killed during the communist revolution in the late 1940s and three daughters she had been forced to abandon when the Japanese invaded her home city of Shanghai some years earlier. This dramatic story forms the heart of Tan's first novel.

When she was 15, both Tan's father and her older brother died of brain tumors. After so terrible a tragedy, her mother moved the surviving family to Switzerland. But Tan soon returned to northern California and graduated from San Jose State University in 1973. In 1974 she married Lou DeMattei, a tax attorney.

Having earned a master's degree in linguistics from San Jose State, Tan then worked at a number of jobs, including business writing. In the mid-1980s she began to fulfill her childhood dream of writing fiction. The enormous success of *The Joy Luck Club* has propelled her into the front ranks of contemporary American authors.

SEE ALSO

Kingston, Maxine Hong

FURTHER READING

Kakatuni, Michiko. "Sisters Looking for Ghosts in China." *New York Times,* Nov. 17, 1995.

Lyall, Sarah. "In the Country of the Spirits." *New York Times,* Dec. 28, 1995.

Kramer, Barbara. *Amy Tan, Author of The Joy Luck Club.* Springfield, N. J.: Enslow, 1996.

Teaching

Teaching was for many years one of the few professions to which women could realistically aspire. Because women have been thought to be the "natural" instructors of the young, teaching was considered an appropriate occupation before there was any widespread approval of employment for women.

Early in the 19th century unmarried women began to outnumber men as teachers. In those early days—and last-

Well-dressed women teach the children of immigrants at a Boston kindergarten in the late 19th century. Many such women saw teaching as a moral mission and a way of achieving social reforms.

ing well into the 20th century in some locales—a prospective teacher did not need any special credentials, a college education, or even a high school diploma. Beginning in the 1830s, however, reformers began to push for more rigorous standards. A few teacher training programs were set up, a development that accelerated toward the end of the 19th century. By the 1920s most northern and western states required that a teacher have at least a high school diploma, and some began to require education beyond high school. Today a college degree is essential, and individual states often demand classroom training, a master's degree in education, or other specific credentials before allowing a person to teach in a public school.

Young women could aspire to be teachers and they could seek out teacher training programs, but it was difficult for a woman to think of teaching as a lifelong vocation, because until World War II (1941–45), school districts routinely required women teachers to be single. In the early 20th century, women began to challenge these laws, which did not completely disappear until severe teacher shortages occurred during World War II, a period of widespread labor shortages.

The pay and the working conditions for teachers improved after they founded unions to defend their interests. Starting as early as the 1890s, teachers organized, and today—in certain areas and in certain levels of education—teachers' unions are powerful and well funded. Where the unions have been able to engage in collective bargaining, they have succeeded in improving benefits packages for their members. In the late 1990s they turned to the issue of on-line instruction, fearful that this could be used to undermine employment opportunities or pay. Offering stable employment and benefits, teaching has been a means of achieving middle-class status for many women, including countless daughters of immigrant families.

Although teaching provided a way into the middle class for generations of white women, women of color generally lacked such opportunities. Black women could teach in all-black schools in the segregated South, but it was not until the labor shortages created by World War II that they were hired routinely in racially integrated districts in northern states. In another instance, Asian women had difficulty securing teaching positions in the San Francisco schools until World War II.

By the end of the 20th century, women constituted about 70 percent of the elementary and secondary teachers in the United States—a figure similar to that in the late 19th century. Women today, however, have a far better chance of being principals and administrators than they did before the modern women's movement began to press for change in the 1970s. They have also made slow but steady inroads in higher education, long an exclusively male arena: in 1991, 32 percent of college faculty were women.

SEE ALSO

Work, paid

FURTHER READING

Grumet, Madeleine R. *Bitter Milk: Women and Teaching.* Amherst: University of Massachusetts Press, 1988.

Kaufman, Polly Welts. *Women Teachers on the Frontier.* New Haven: Yale University Press, 1984.

Warren, Donald, ed. *American Teachers.* New York: Macmillan, 1989.

Technology

Until the 1970s, women had virtually no access to engineering programs in colleges and universities: they would have received no encouragement to study such subjects as undergraduates, and they would have been unlikely to be admitted for graduate work.

In the days before universities offered engineering programs, young men received their training by apprenticing to a master engineer, a process that also ruled out women as prospective engineers.

Despite these earlier formidable barriers, a few women made distinguished contributions before the 1970s, especially Emily Roebling, who oversaw the building of the Brooklyn Bridge between Brooklyn and Manhattan in the late 1870s and early 1880s. Roebling's husband was the chief engineer for the project, but he became disabled by the bends after descending into the East River to check on the underwater construction.

Though her husband and father-in-law were the engineers of record for the Brooklyn Bridge, Emily Warren Roebling was in charge of day-to-day construction after they both became disabled. She had to learn engineering and higher mathematics on the job.

With her husband unable to leave their apartment or to coordinate work with many of the assistants, Roebling dedicated herself to regular visits to the construction site, to correspondence, and to interviewing contractors. After the bridge was completed in 1883, Washington Roebling said that his wife's greatest contribution lay in her role as peacemaker among frequently warring participants.

Emily Roebling also had a natural gift for mathematics. As she devoted herself to the project—an early suspension bridge with no mid-river moorings that was then one of the technological wonders of the world—she became very conversant with the technical details. She also won the admiration of the assistant engineers. Today a plaque commemorating her role has been placed on each of the bridge's towers.

Since the birth of the modern women's movement and then the passage of Title IX of the Education Act Amendments in 1972, women have broad access to the field for the first time in U.S. history. The numbers of women graduating with degrees in engineering document the extent of change: in 1972, 44,190 people graduated in this field in the United States, of whom 525 were women, and in 1988 there were 63,262, of whom 11,796 were women. In percentage terms the change was from 1.19 to 18.65 percent.

SEE ALSO

Education Act Amendments (1972)

FURTHER READING

Cutcliffe, Stephen H., and Terry S. Reynolds, eds. *Technology & American History: A Historical Anthology from Technology & Culture*. Chicago: University of Chicago Press, 1997.

McCullough, David. *The Great Bridge*. New York: Simon & Schuster, 1972.

Television

In the late 1940s, with only a few thousand television sets in American homes, networks began broadcasting. Radio was already a well-established part of national life—families would gather around to listen to their favorite programs—but no one foresaw just how popular the new medium would be. Fifty years later, few forces had affected entertainment, education, communications, family life, and leisure as much as television. For example, in the early decades of television, families gathered around a common set to watch their favorite shows, many of which appealed to almost everyone except babies and toddlers. In the late 1990s, the trend was increasingly to tailor programming to specific age groups, and the number of shows families can watch together has dwindled.

Popular male stars appeared on TV in the early days, but the first megastar of either sex was Lucille Ball in *I Love Lucy.* Because her show was so beloved, she gained industry clout that was rare for a woman in any field in the 1950s. The character of Lucy on TV was a lovable if sometimes silly housewife, but behind the scenes Lucille Ball was a powerhouse who eventually ran Desilu Productions by herself.

From the pioneering days of television broadcasting in the early 1950s, there have been daytime soap operas, many of the first being carryovers from radio shows. The earliest opportunities for women in television were as creators of and writers for the soaps.

The first generation of female TV stars played housewives, most of

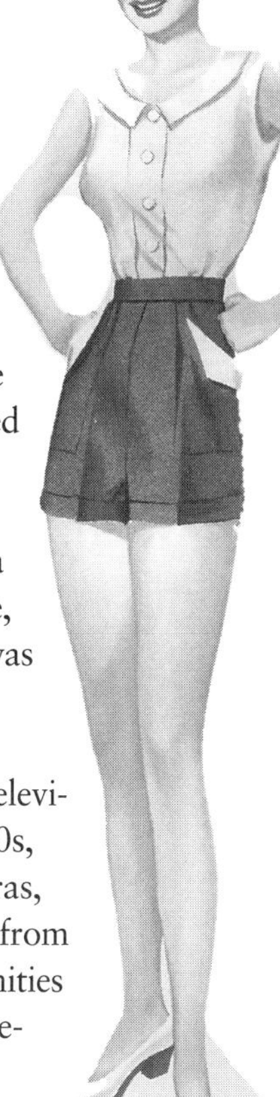

Lucille Ball and her husband, Desi Arnaz, created one of the first and most successful shows in television history: I Love Lucy *debuted in October 1951 and ran through 1960. Lucy starred in several subsequent shows, all of them popular favorites.*

whom smiled sweetly while yielding to the superior wisdom of their husbands. When Marlo Thomas played a young working woman on *That Girl* in the mid-1960s, it was a big departure from the usual female image. In the late 1960s Diahann Carroll played a nurse in the sitcom *Julia;* her starring role was a breakthrough for an African-American woman.

The first women to be shown as truly powerful on popular shows were not professional women with careers but women with supernatural powers: Elizabeth Montgomery was a witch on *Bewitched* and Barbara Eden played a genie on *I Dream of Jeannie.*

Beginning around 1970, with the birth of the modern women's movement, television roles for women began to reflect a much broader range of female experience. Women were cops, lawyers, doctors, television producers, political activists, and much more. A wife and mother, such as the one played by Phylicia Rashad on the immensely popular *Cosby* show in the 1980s, might also be a career woman, unlike a generation earlier. Also in the 1970s, women starred in their own variety shows—Carol Burnett and Cher being the best known—and debuted on the popular *Saturday Night Live.* Gilda Radner, Laraine Newman, and Jane Curtin of *SNL* represented a new style of hip female humor that was not seen on television up to that time.

In the late 1990s, in a momentous and controversial episode, the character played by actress Ellen DeGeneres came out of the closet as a lesbian on *Ellen* (as did DeGeneres herself). Despite a huge audience for that episode, the show was eventually canceled a year later, in early 1998, after its ratings sagged.

Many shows portraying high-powered career women, such as *Murphy Brown,* have gone off the air, making way for younger talent, as the teen audience has become ever more important to advertisers. A notable exception is *Ally McBeal.* Calista Flockhart, who plays a single lawyer trying to deal with the problems of love and work in Boston, has been one of television's most popular stars since the show's 1997 debut. Though she is a career woman, Ally has some of the same sublime silliness as her illustrious predecessor, Lucy.

That television images play a vital part in our culture was confirmed by Vice President Dan Quayle's attack on the character Murphy Brown during the presidential campaign of 1992. The character had just given birth to a child as a single mother and Quayle attacked this, and the program generally, for undermining "family values." Indeed, from the time of its first introduction, television has raised worries about its social impact. The very nature of television-watching, particularly as networks court specific audiences rather than the family as a whole, is thought to decrease communication among family members. It has also been feared that television could become a replacement for other forms of culture.

As television has grown away from whole-family entertainment, there has also been an increase in sex and violence in shows meant for adults that children and young adults also watch. This has led to controversial ratings systems, and the creation of blocking devices that deny unsupervised children access to shows deemed too adult by their parents.

On the other hand, the introduction of cable has increased the number of educational channels available, and also many television personalities have made themselves positive role models for young watchers. In the late 20th century, one of the most influential women on television—and in the country—is talk show host Oprah Winfrey. As one example of her clout, when she started her book club, millions of watchers picked up books recommended on her show, which had the side-effect of conveying best-selling status on authors who might otherwise have remained obscure.

SEE ALSO

Ball, Lucille; Media

FURTHER READING

Douglas, Susan J. *Where the Girls Are: Growing Up Female with the Mass Media.* New York: Times Books, 1994.
Krohn, Katherine E. *Lucille Ball: Pioneer of Comedy.* Minneapolis: Lerner, 1992.
Stahl, Lesley. *Reporting Live.* New York: Simon & Schuster, 1999.
Watson, Mary Ann. *Defining Visions: Television and the American Experience Since 1945.* Fort Worth, Tex.: Harcourt Brace, 1998.

Temperance

The crusade to end the use and abuse of alcohol in the United States occupied the better part of 100 years, from the early 19th century to the early 20th century. At its height, this crusade mobilized American women throughout the country as few causes have. Moreover, women joined the temperance movement to combat alcohol but often stayed long enough to become deeply involved in many other reforms, including woman suffrage.

Before the Civil War (1861–65), men led the temperance movement, and both sexes belonged to the same organizations. In the 1870s, however, a new, much more militant, all-female temperance movement took shape, led by the Woman's Christian Temperance Union (WCTU). These were the same years in which a much more militant suffrage association, the National Woman Suffrage Association, led by Elizabeth Cady Stanton and Susan B. Anthony, was taking shape. The WCTU was born when bands of praying women in the Midwest visited saloons and confronted the patrons and the owners of these establishments, asking them to give up alcohol in the name of having a pure Christian home. A permanent organization soon developed and attracted hundreds of thousands of women into its ranks.

Children aid the cause of the Woman's Christian Temperance Union (WCTU) at a temperance parade in Florida around 1910. WCTU women called for maternal values to shape public behavior, in order to protect innocent children from the evils of alcohol.

The WCTU's second president and most extraordinary leader was Frances Willard. She crusaded to have the group extend its goals to include suffrage, arguing that women could better defend the sanctity of the home against the intrusion of alcohol abuse if they had the right to vote. After her death in 1898, the WCTU was never again as vital an organization as it had been under her leadership.

The ratification of the 18th Amendment, outlawing the sale of alcohol, in 1919 (it was repealed in 1933) was a victory for the temperance crusade. By the early 20th century, however, a male-led Anti-Saloon League had nudged the movement in the direction of constitutional change as the solution to the problem of alcohol abuse. The short-lived 18th Amendment did not fulfill the WCTU's dreams of bringing about a new regime of harmonious and alcohol-free homes, because the law was widely flouted.

SEE ALSO

Anthony, Susan B.; Stanton, Elizabeth Cady; Willard, Frances

FURTHER READING

Bordin, Ruth. *Women and Temperance.* Philadelphia: Temple University Press, 1981.

Sigerman, Harriet. *Laborers for Liberty: American Women 1865–1890.* New York: Oxford University Press, 1994.

Temple, Shirley

SEE Black, Shirley Temple

Terrell, Mary Eliza Church

- *Born: Sept. 23, 1863, Memphis, Tenn.*
- *Education: Oberlin College, B.A., 1884*
- *Accomplishments: First black woman on District of Columbia Board of Education (1895–1906); first president, National Association of Colored Women (1896–1901); co-founder, National Association for the Advancement of Colored People (1909); author,* A Colored Woman in a White World
- *Died: July 24, 1954, Annapolis, Md.*

One of the leaders of the African-American community in the 20th century, Mary Church Terrell was a tireless advocate for women's rights as well as for civil rights for blacks. Indeed, at the age of 89, she was still picketing for her causes.

Born to a former slave mother and a free black father just as the institution of slavery was ending, young Mary Church Terrell had an unusual childhood: her businessman father became one of the first black millionaires from his real estate investments. No doubt this helped his daughter obtain a good education, and she graduated from Oberlin College in 1884. She then taught at Wilberforce College and in the public schools of Washington, D.C. Marriage to lawyer Robert Terrell, one of the first black graduates from Harvard, ended her teaching career, because school boards often required teachers to be single in those years.

Mary Church Terrell organized clubs in the African-American community and inspired countless other women to activism. Born into a wealthy family, she decided against living in Europe, where she might have encountered less bigotry, and returned to the United States to "promote the welfare of my race."

A brief sketch of her subsequent public career reveals a woman of extraordinary energy and dedication. For 11 years she served on the D.C. board of education, the first black woman so to do. In 1896 she became the first president of the National Association of Colored Women (NACW). After she had served three terms, NACW made her honorary president for life. In 1898 she addressed a national suffrage convention on "The Progress of Colored Women." She was a charter member of the National Association for the Advancement of Colored People. During Woodrow Wilson's Presidency, she picketed the White House on behalf of woman suffrage. She did not slow down until she was 90.

A devoted mother, Terrell lost her first three children in infancy, and she blamed their deaths on the segregated hospital system in Washington, D.C., which provided inferior care to blacks, she believed. She then traveled to New York City for the birth of her fourth child, a daughter who survived.

FURTHER READING

Jones, Beverly Washington. *Quest for Equality: The Life and Writings of Mary Eliza Church Terrell, 1863–1954.* Brooklyn, N.Y.: Carlson, 1990.

Sterling, Dorothy, and Benjamin Quarles. *Lift Every Voice: the Lives of Booker T. Washington, W.E.B. Du Bois, Mary Church Terrell, and James Weldon Johnson.* Garden City, N.Y.: Doubleday, 1965.

Theater

Despite the competition from movies and television, live theater remains an important aspect of American culture. Although women today perform, direct, produce shows, work backstage, design sets and costumes, and publicize events, they did not always have such opportunities.

In fact, women's parts were played by men until the late 1700s. When women did get the chance to perform in the United States, actresses were often seen as "fallen" or disgraced women because respectable women were not supposed to engage in public activity. Even so, women began to build a tradition of performing excellence, and a few women, such as Mercy Otis Warren and Susannah Rowson also wrote for the theater in the late 18th century.

The first big female star of the American stage was Charlotte Cushman, in the second quarter of the 19th century. Interestingly, one of Cushman's most stellar roles was as Shakespeare's Romeo, dressed in male clothes. By mid-century women were not only performing but also writing very popular plays—Anna Mowatt's *Fashion* of 1845 was the best known—and occasionally serving as actress-managers. The English-born Laura Keene was the most famous of the actress-managers; she was appearing in *Our American Cousin* at the Ford Theater the night Lincoln was assassinated in 1865. In combining business skills with performance, Keene and her sister actress-managers helped to reclaim the profession of actress from its disreputable reputation. In this period women were typically performers or they were servants of performers, but they had no positions of authority backstage or as directors.

Keene had a well-known successor as an actress-manager, Minnie Maddern Fiske. Fiske was at the height of her career in the early 20th century, at which time her particular contribution lay in staging plays by the Norwegian playwright Henrik Ibsen. That Ibsen was famed for his sympathetic and insightful portraits of women makes Fiske's role all the more noteworthy.

Minnie Maddern Fiske in a 1914 New York production of Henrik Ibsen's Hedda Gabler. *An Ibsen specialist, she was instrumental in ensuring the popularity of his plays in the United States.*

Later in the 20th century, women began to come into their own in the American theater—but not without the ongoing struggle against the old view of the theater as frivolous and sinful and actresses as "tainted" women. Actresses such as Ethel Barrymore, Katharine Cornell, Lynn Fontanne, Helen Hayes, and Jessica Tandy thrilled audiences with their artistry. The collective impact of their stirring performances as writers, queens, madwomen, and career women was a legacy of actresses being seen as fully respectable (of course, American mores were changing in many ways at mid-century, and the category of "fallen women" no longer carried the same power as in the past).

Women playwrights not only had their plays produced on Broadway but also occasionally won major awards such as Tony Awards or Pulitzer Prizes. Particularly well-known playwrights have been Lillian Hellman, for *The Children's Hour* and *Little Foxes*; Marsha Norman, for *'Night Mother*; Wendy Wasserstein, for the *Heidi Chronicles*; and Lorraine Hansberry, for *Raisin in the Sun,* the first African-American woman to have a play produced on Broadway.

Women can now aspire to a much broader range of occupational choices in the theater, rather than being relegated to the most menial, such as servants to the stars, as in an earlier period. In 1998, for the first time in history, two women directors won Tony Awards, one for a musical—Julie Taymor, for *The Lion King*—and one for a play—Garry Hynes, for *The Beauty Queen of Leenane.*

Until the modern civil rights era in the 1950s and 1960s, the only performing roles offered to women of color in mainstream productions—except for musicals, which were an exception because black women were becoming known as vocalists and dancers—would have been such stereotypical parts as maids. Although opportunities on Broadway are still limited, roles are opening up in regional theater, especially theater for racial and ethnic communities.

SEE ALSO

Hansberry, Lorraine; Hayes, Helen; Hellman, Lillian

FURTHER READING

Brown, Jared. *The Fabulous Lunts: A Biography of Alfred Lunt and Lynn Fontanne.* New York: Atheneum, 1986.

Johnson, Claudia D. *American Actress: Perspective on the Nineteenth Century.* Chicago: Nelson-Hall, 1984.

Leach, Joseph. *Bright Particular Star: The Life and Times of Charlotte Cushman.* New Haven, Conn.: Yale University Press, 1970.

Mogel, Ted. *Leading Lady: The World and Theater of Katharine Cornell.* Boston: Little, Brown, 1978.

Thomas, Martha Carey

- *Born: Jan. 2, 1857, Baltimore, Md.*
- *Education: Cornell University, B.A., 1877; University of Zurich, Ph.D., 1882*
- *Accomplishments: Dean (1885–94) and president (1894–1922), Bryn Mawr College; president, National College Equal Suffrage League (1908–17)*
- *Died: Dec. 2, 1935, Philadelphia, Pa.*

M. Carey Thomas is best known for her contribution to improving the quality of higher education available to women, a cause she served devotedly as president of Bryn Mawr College, near Philadelphia, from 1894 to 1922.

Raised as a Quaker, Thomas graduated from Cornell University in 1877 and then went to Europe to study for a Ph.D. In 1882 the University of Zurich granted her a doctorate with highest honors for her dissertation on an old English epic. She was both the first foreigner and the first woman to be awarded this degree by the university.

Returning home to the United States, Thomas learned that a new Quaker college for women, Bryn Mawr, was being launched and that her father was to be a trustee. She became a professor of English and a dean when the college opened in 1885, and then president in 1894.

Exposed to the most rigorous methods of a European education, and with resources to put her ideas into action, M. Carey Thomas insisted that Bryn Mawr always embody the highest possible standards for women. Very soon, the college became known for its brilliant faculty and high-achieving students. Unfortunately, Thomas was also responsible for a less admirable legacy: in her day Jewish instructors were discriminated against at Bryn Mawr, and black students were not admitted.

SEE ALSO

Education; Women's colleges

FURTHER READING

Horowitz, Helen. *The Power and Passion of M. Carey Thomas.* New York: Knopf, 1994.

Thompson, Dorothy

- *Born: July 9, 1893, Lancaster, N.Y.*
- *Education: Syracuse University, B.A., 1914*
- *Accomplishments: Foreign correspondent,* Philadelphia Public Ledger *(1921–28); Berlin bureau chief,* New York Evening Post *and* Philadelphia Public Ledger *(1925–28); syndicated columnist (1936–58); radio news commentator (1937–50s); author,* The New Russia *(1928);* I Saw Hitler! *(1932);* Refugees: Anarchy or Organization? *(1938);* Dorothy Thompson's Political Guide *(1938);* Once on Christmas *(1939);* Let the Record Speak *(1939);* Listen, Hans! *(1942); and* The Courage to Be Happy *(1957)*
- *Died: Jan. 30, 1961, Lisbon, Portugal*

Dorothy Thompson was one of the premier journalists of her generation and was especially known for being among the earliest to sound the alarm against Adolf Hitler.

The daughter of a Methodist clergyman and his wife, Thompson graduated from Syracuse University in 1914 and soon thereafter became active in the suffrage cause. In the early 1920s she began to work toward a journalistic career. By 1924 she was Berlin bureau chief for the *Philadelphia Public Ledger* and the *New York Evening Post.* This assignment afforded her the opportunity to become well acquainted with the politics of that part of the world.

Dorothy Thompson, the real-life model for Katherine Hepburn's character in Woman of the Year, *was a forceful and opinionated journalist. One critic compared her writing style to "someone bellowing in your ear."*

Thompson also began to cultivate a personal legend as an intrepid "girl reporter." A brief marriage to the Hungarian writer Josef Bard ended in 1927, and in 1928 she married one of the best-known American writers, Sinclair Lewis, with whom she had a son. She also embarked on a series of intense erotic relationships with women.

Throughout much of the 1930s Thompson's was one of the most powerful voices raised against Hitler. Moreover, as a radio commentator for NBC, she had a national forum for airing her opinions. She also wrote a regular women's interest column for the *Ladies' Home Journal,* an assignment that continued until her death, and her voice was heard in the many books she wrote on issues of her day.

Having separated from Lewis in 1937, Thompson divorced him in 1942 and the following year wed Austrian-born painter and sculptor Maxim Kopf, a marriage that lasted until his death in 1958. Other than First Lady Eleanor Roosevelt, perhaps no other woman of the time had such an impact on American public opinion.

SEE ALSO

Media

FURTHER READING

Kurth, Peter. *American Cassandra: The Life of Dorothy Thompson.* Boston: Little, Brown, 1990.

Ritchie, Donald A. *American Journalists: Getting the Story.* New York: Oxford University Press, 1997.

Title VII

SEE Civil Rights Act (1964)

Title IX

SEE Education Act Amendments (1972)

Triangle Shirtwaist fire (1911)

On March 25, 1911, 146 young women workers died in a fire in the Triangle Shirtwaist factory in New York City. As the public learned the facts about the tragedy, there was widespread outrage. The building did not have fire escapes, and the exits had been locked, so the workers had had the choice of either jumping to their death or perishing inside.

At the time of the fire, New York—and most other states—lacked effective legislation protecting the occupational health and safety of workers. Young women, the poorest paid and most vulnerable component of the workforce, often faced hazardous conditions. After the fire, public opinion demanded reform and the city and the state legislature complied with tougher municipal building codes—requiring fire escapes, for example—and a better system of factory inspections.

This photograph documents the horror of the Triangle Shirtwaist fire in 1911. Trapped in a burning building, many young women jumped to their deaths; the police could do nothing but wait for more jumpers.

SEE ALSO

Labor movement

Truth, Sojourner

- *Born: Around 1797, Hurley, N.Y.*
- *Education: No formal education*
- *Accomplishments: Author,* Narrative of Sojourner Truth *(with Olive Gilbert, 1850); traveling lecturer for blacks' and women's rights (1840s–70s)*
- *Died: Nov. 26, 1883, Battle Creek, Mich.*

Sojourner Truth, born a slave in New York State, became one of the best-known women of her day because of the abolitionist lectures she gave in the years before the Civil War (1861–65). Tall and impressive, she possessed a rich speaking voice and a gift for expression that more than outweighed her lack of a formal education.

Because Sojourner Truth was unlettered and left no written documents in her own hand, it has been difficult for scholars to piece together an exact account of her life. We know that she was originally named Isabella and that her first language was Dutch. She gave birth to at least five children by a fellow slave named Thomas and had to fight for her children's freedom, despite New York's having instituted laws that called for the gradual freeing of slaves. Around 1829, using the name of Isabella Van Wagener, she arrived in New York City. There she became attached to an intense, somewhat cultish, religious community, and when it broke up, lived quietly working as a servant for some years.

Having had her share of trials, she became extraordinarily devout and in the 1840s took to the road to preach, renaming herself Sojourner Truth. In speaking out against slavery, she attracted the attention of abolitionists and her fame grew. It is widely believed that in 1851, at the Women's Rights Convention in Akron, Ohio, she delivered a speech that became famous as "Ain't I a Woman?." However, her biographer, Nell Painter, argues that the speech is a myth.

When abolitionist Sojourner Truth became an itinerant preacher, she took a new name: "The Lord gave me Sojourner because I was to travel up and down the land showin' the people their sins. The Lord gave me Truth because I was to declare truth unto people."

During the Civil War she worked on behalf of the freed people, as a special counselor in the ways of freedom, and she also had the opportunity to visit President Abraham Lincoln in the White House in 1864.

After the war ended, Truth continued to lecture on behalf of women's rights and the rights of African Americans. To secure an income, she sold copies of her autobiography, as dictated to Olive Gilbert, and photographs of herself.

FURTHER READING

Krass, Peter, and Nathan I. Huggins, eds. *Sojourner Truth.* New York: Chelsea House, 1988.

Ortiz, Victoria. *Sojourner Truth: A Self-Made Woman.* Philadelphia: Lippincott, 1974.

Painter, Nell. *Sojourner Truth: A Life, a Symbol.* New York: Norton, 1996.

Tubman, Harriet

- *Born: 1820?, Dorchester County, Md.*
- *Education: No formal education*
- *Accomplishments: Rescued up to 300 people from slavery through the Underground Railroad (1850s)*
- *Died: Mar. 10, 1913, Auburn, N.Y.*

The most famous and most effective of those who rescued slaves in the years before the Civil War (1861–65), in the

Harriet Tubman (far left) with a group of former slaves whom she had led to freedom. Tubman was the best-known "conductor" on the Underground Railroad that led slaves out of bondage.

effort known as the Underground Railroad, Harriet Tubman was a woman of rare courage and decisiveness.

Born into slavery, Tubman decided to escape in 1849 after hearing rumors that she might be sold out of the state of Maryland. After making her own way to freedom, she rescued her sister and two children the following year. In 1851 she brought out her brother and his family. In all, it is estimated that she made 19 rescue missions, involving somewhere between 60 and 300 people. As her work became known, she was invited to address abolitionist conventions, which added to her fame. By the time the Civil War broke out, slaveholders in Maryland had posted a $40,000 reward for her capture.

After the Civil War began, Tubman continued to perform daring work: she went south and served as a spy and a scout on behalf of the Union forces for three years. She was able to secure military intelligence from African-American informants behind the Confederate lines.

A deeply religious woman, Tubman was sustained in her work by her Christian faith. Late in life, she received a pension from the U.S. government in recognition of her important contributions to the Union cause.

FURTHER READING

Buckmaster, Henrietta, and John G. Sproat, eds. *Let My People Go: The Story of the Underground Railroad and the Growth of the Abolition Movement.* Columbia: University of South Carolina Press, 1992.

Clinton, Catherine, and Nina Silber, eds. *Divided Houses: Gender and the Civil War.* New York: Oxford University Press, 1992.

Taylor, Marian. *Harriet Tubman.* New York: Chelsea House, 1991.

United Farm Workers (UFW)

The United Farm Workers (UFW), a California labor union founded by César Chávez in 1962 with substantial help from Dolores Huerta, who became the vice president and chief negotiator, was unique in the American labor movement at that time because Huerta and other women played leadership roles in running union offices and in stirring up support among liberals. Other unions, even if they had many women members, had preponderantly male leaders.

California has always had a different type of agriculture than the Midwest, where hired hands typically have worked side by side with family members. In California the field work has been performed by recent immigrants, by workers allowed to come over the Mexican border on a temporary pass, or by those who have entered the United States illegally to find work. In short, these farm workers have been among the most vulnerable members of society, and, due to poverty and deportation, union leaders have found it very difficult to organize them. Moreover, until 1974 farm workers were excluded from laws protecting workers passed during the 1930s. The farm workers were excluded from the protection of the National Labor Relations Act and the NLRB to appease the Southern Democrats.

Chávez, Huerta, and others devised ways around these problems, however, chiefly by instituting consumer boycotts of such products as grapes and lettuce, crops whose cultivation involved particularly harsh, underpaid working conditions and dangerous aspects such as pervasive use of pesticides that poisoned the workers who applied them. The UFW decided to pressure growers by cutting back on sales, because it was so difficult to win a strike in the field—there were too many desperately poor who were willing to work for any price. UFW members and their supporters would stand outside a supermarket and urge shoppers not to buy these products. As a consequence of decreased sales, the union obtained a number of contracts with growers that gave benefits and better wages , and in 1974 the state of California passed a law giving farm workers the protections they were denied under federal law. The law set up the Agricultural Labor Relations Board to supervise elections.

*Women picket on behalf of the United Farm Workers, calling for a strike (*huelga*) to protest unfair conditions. This union mobilized thousands of women—and afforded them leadership opportunities well before the mainstream labor movement did.*

After the initial successes of the 1970s, however, the union began to lose strength, partly because California governors have been hostile to it and partly because—according to critics—the union itself has made mistakes, such as withdrawing from rank-and-file involvement. Chávez died in 1993, but others, including Dolores Huerta, carry on his work, and women are still vital to the union's operation, an area in which men and women work side by side.

SEE ALSO

Labor movement

FURTHER READING

Baer, Barbara, and Glenna Matthews. "Women of the Boycott." *The Nation,* Feb. 23, 1974, 232–238.

Mooney, Patrick H., and Theo J. Majka. *Farmers' and Farm Workers' Movements: Social Protest in American Agriculture.* New York: Twayne, 1995.

Universities

For most of American history, universities have been dominated by men. For most of this time, too—indeed until the birth of modern feminism in the late 1960s and early 1970s—many prestigious institutions, such as Harvard, Yale, and Princeton, were for male undergraduates only.

No colleges or universities (the latter are designed for research as well as teaching) admitted women until Oberlin College did so in 1837. The early women there were enrolled in a special Female Department, and they were obliged to perform domestic chores for their male colleagues! Following that historic innovation, a trickle of other institutions of higher learning joined Oberlin—Antioch College in Ohio in 1852, and then a few western universities—but at a very slow pace. By 1870, only about one-third had become coeducational. Women undergraduates at coed universities in the late nineteenth century often felt that it was up to them to prove that men and women *could* be educated in the same institution of higher learning.

Even though many universities eventually changed their policies and admitted women as undergraduates in the late 1800s, women still had to struggle to be taken seriously as graduate students until well into the 20th century. And it was virtually impossible for women to secure teaching positions in universities, except in departments of home economics. To many women, the very culture of the university often seemed like that of a men's club, and the rare woman graduate student of earlier generations was frequently made to feel unwelcome.

Over the course of the twentieth century, leading up to the student movements of the 1960s and the birth of modern feminism around 1970, women established themselves as a vital presence as undergraduates. When universities then became hotbeds of student activism on behalf of civil rights for African Americans and against American involvement in Vietnam, women were in a position to play significant roles in these movements because by this time they were so significant a component of various student bodies.

Things began to change even more with the birth of the modern women's movement. In 1972 Congress passed Title IX of the Education Act Amendments, which required that all educational institutions receiving federal funds (that is, research universities) refrain from discriminating against women, athletic scholarships, academic programs, admissions, and hiring. Since that time, women have joined faculties in larger numbers—but they still hold less than half of these jobs, even though women constitute 50 percent of the general population. Women do, however, constitute at least 50 percent of the undergraduate population in many universities. Women generally experience little or no discrimination in securing entrance to graduate school. Finally, very few, if any, universities remain all-male, though there are still all-female colleges. Some of these all-women institutions, such as Smith College and Wellesley College, have developed very prestigious reputations. Indeed some now wonder whether women themselves do not, perhaps, flourish more in an all-female environment, because girls are socialized to defer to male opinion where both sexes are present.

SEE ALSO

Education; Education Act Amendments (1972); Home economics; Women's colleges

FURTHER READING

Solomon, Barbara. *In the Company of Educated Women.* New Haven: Yale University Press, 1985.

Wage Gap

SEE Comparable worth

Wald, Lillian

- *Born: Mar. 10, 1867, Cincinnati, Ohio*
- *Education: New York Hospital Training School for Nurses, graduated 1891*
- *Accomplishments: Founder, Henry Street Nurses Settlement (New York City, 1893); cofounder, National Child Labor Committee (1904); co-organizer and first president, National Organization of Public Health Nursing (1912); gold medal, National Institute of Social Sciences (1912); author,* The House on Henry Street *(1915); American Nurses Association Hall of Fame (1976)*
- *Died: Sept. 1, 1940, Westport, Conn.*

Founder of the Henry Street Settlement House in New York City, Lillian Wald provided home medical care for members of the community and taught newly arrived immigrant women the basics of home nursing, child care, cooking, and sewing. Her Henry Street Visiting Nurse Service survives today as the Visiting Nurse Service of New York.

Lillian Wald was a dedicated reformer whose most important contribution lay in combining public-health nursing with settlement-house work on behalf of the urban poor. Descended from a long line of rabbis and merchants in Poland and Germany, Wald grew up in a cultivated and prosperous home. As a young woman, she decided to obtain a medical education but switched career goals after encountering the desperate conditions in late-19th-century New York slums: she was called from a classroom to attend a sick woman living in poverty, and the experience changed her life.

Henceforth Wald devoted herself to public-health nursing among the poor, providing the leadership to establish a home for visiting nurses located in a slum neighborhood, the Henry Street settlement.

Though Henry Street originated as a medical facility, it soon evolved into being a full-scale settlement with civic and philanthropic work ongoing. By 1913 it encompassed seven houses on Henry Street. Wald devoted herself to campaigns for better parks and playgrounds, as well as public health issues such as the crusade against tuberculosis.

SEE ALSO

Settlement-house movement

FURTHER READING

Coss, Clare, ed. *Lillian D. Wald: Progressive Activist.* New York: Feminist Press, 1989.

Siegel, Beatrice. *Lillian Wald of Henry Street.* New York: Macmillan, 1983.

Walker, Alice

- *Born: Feb. 8, 1944, Eatonton, Ga.*
- *Education: Spelman College, attended 1961–63; Sarah Lawrence College, B.A., 1965*
- *Accomplishments: Pulitzer Prize for* The Color Purple, *1983; author,* Once *(1968);* The Third Life of Grange Copeland *(1970);* In Love and Trouble: Stories of Black Women *(1973);* Revolutionary Petunias and Other Poems *(1973);* Meridian *(1976);* You Can't Keep a Good Woman Down *(1981);* The Color Purple *(1982);* Horses Make a Landscape Look More Beautiful *(1984);* To Hell with Dying *(1988);* The Temple of My Familiar *(1989);* Possessing the Secret Joy *(1992);* The Same River Twice: Honoring the Difficult *(1996)*

An African-American daughter of the rural South, Alice Walker has written poems, novels, and essays that have shed light on many aspects of the American experience. Her first book of poetry, for example, dealt with abortion, her novel *Meridian* (1976) with the civil rights movement, her Pulitzer Prize–winning

Alice Walker is responsible for the rediscovery of the works of Zora Neale Hurston and other African-American women writers. "I am committed to exploring the oppressions, the loyalties, and the triumphs of black women . . . For me, black women are the most fascinating creations in the world."

book *The Color Purple* (1982) concentrated on domestic violence, and her novel *Possessing the Secret Joy* (1992) discussed female genital mutilation.

Though her parents were poor, Walker's mother encouraged her to write and bought her a typewriter when she was in high school. Blinded in the right eye as a child, Walker went on to win a scholarship for the handicapped to Spelman College in Atlanta, but she later transferred to Sarah Lawrence College in Bronxville, N.Y. When she traveled to Africa after her junior year, Walker found the experience so rewarding that she began writing poetry inspired by the trip. Activism in the civil rights movement and a marriage to a Jewish civil rights attorney that lasted 10 years and produced a daughter were intertwined with her growing success as an author.

In 1983 her third novel *The Color Purple* won the Pulitzer Prize for fiction and established her as a major American writer. Warner Brothers paid her $350,000 for the movie rights to the story of Celie, a black sharecropper who finds love in the midst of hardship, and when the film appeared a few years later, she became even better known. Walker lives in northern California and continues both to write and to be engaged with her feminist political causes though she herself prefers the term "womanist," which she coined.

SEE ALSO

Literature

FURTHER READING

Dieke, Ikenna, ed. *Critical Essays on Alice Walker.* Westport, Conn.: Greenwood, 1999.

Gentry, Tony. *Alice Walker.* New York: Chelsea House, 1993.

Warren, Mercy Otis

- *Born: Sept. 14, 1728, Barnstable, Mass.*
- *Education: No formal education*
- *Accomplishments: Author, satiric anti-Tory plays including* The Adulateur, A Tragedy *(1773) and* The Group *(1775); poetry,* Poems Dramatic and Miscellaneous *(1790); and historical study,* A History of the Rise, Progress, and Termination of the American Revolution. Interspersed with Biographical, Political and Moral Observations *(1805)*
- *Died: Oct. 19, 1814, Plymouth, Mass.*

Mercy Otis Warren, dedicated American patriot, was the United States's first woman historian. She was also a poet, playwright, and pamphlet writer, in addition to being a wife and mother.

Born to one of the most prominent families in colonial Massachusetts, Mercy Otis married into another when she wed merchant James Warren in 1754. The marriage produced five sons, to whom she was devoted. As the conflict with England heated up in the years before the outbreak of the American Revolution in 1776, Warren developed strong feelings about British tyranny—and a new career: she began to write political satire, poking fun at the British for their high-handed treatment of the colonies. She also corresponded with a number of outstanding Patriot leaders, many of whom were personal friends.

After the country achieved its independence, Warren continued to observe and comment on politics—though as a woman she could not vote. Passionately democratic in her sympathies, she even opposed the U.S. Constitution, because she thought that it would take away from the people's liberties.

These strong feelings led Warren to write an early history of the period, *History of the Rise, Progress, and Termination of the American Revolution,* published in 1805. Her three-volume history reflects her deep belief in the people's ability to govern themselves, and it led to a lengthy rupture with her old friends John and Abigail Adams, because she criticized John in her work. Having frequently bumped up against the limitations placed on women, Warren was an outspoken advocate of better educational opportunities for women.

SEE ALSO

American Revolution

FURTHER READING

Zagarri, Rosemarie. *A Woman's Dilemma: Mercy Warren Otis and the American Revolution.* Wheeling, Ill.: Harlan Davidson, 1995.

Waters, Alice

- *Born: Apr. 28, 1944, Chatham, N.J.*
- *Education: University of California at Berkeley, B.A., 1967*
- *Accomplishments: James Beard Special Achievement Award (1985); Le Tour du monde en 80 Toques, Metziner & Varaut (1991); Best Chef in America and Best Restaurant in America, James Beard Foundation (1992); author,* The Chez Panisse Menu Cookbook *(1982),* Chez Panisse Vegetables *(1996); founder, Edible Schoolyard program, Martin Luther King Junior High School (Berkeley, Calif., 1996)*

Alice Waters, who founded the restaurant Chez Panisse in Berkeley, California, in 1971, is internationally known as the originator of California cuisine, which stresses the use of fresh, seasonal ingredients and unfussy preparations. With cookbook author and television personality Julia Child, she has changed the way most Americans eat. In the late 1990s, for example, many supermarkets sell an array of fresh greens in addition to the old standby, iceberg lettuce. In the first years of Chez Panisse, a restaurant-goer might have been served a salad that, the waiter or waitress explained, featured greens grown in Waters's own backyard so as to ensure freshness.

It is especially noteworthy that two women have had such an impact, because the realm of gourmet cooking had been completely dominated by men. Women cooked at home and wrote homely cookbooks, but men cooked in fancy restaurants and wrote about fashionable food. Waters's success has helped open the world of cooking in expensive restaurants to women, especially on the West Coast.

Waters went to France in the early 1960s and fell in love with the food. She returned to California, where she had been a student, determined to start a restaurant that would take advantage of the fresh produce that abounds in the San Francisco Bay Area—while taking inspiration from French techniques. She has said, "Chez Panisse began with our doing the very best we could do with French recipes and California ingredients, and has evolved into what I like to think of as a celebration of the very finest of our regional food products." In so doing, she created a critically acclaimed restaurant and helped propel many of her fellow Americans into taking food more seriously.

She also believes in supporting small farmers and organic growers and makes a point of buying her restaurant produce from such sources, and she has started programs in schools and jails to involve people in growing (organically) and cooking their own food to develop responsibility and respect for the earth and each other. She is married to the wine merchant Stephen Singer, and they have one daughter.

SEE ALSO

Child, Julia McWilliams; Cooking

FURTHER READING

Reardon, Joan. *M.F.K. Fisher, Julia Child, and Alice Waters: Celebrating the Pleasures of the Table.* New York: Harmony Books, 1994.

Welfare state

In the 20th-century United States, local, state, and federal governments have made more provisions for people's basic welfare than in the past, adopting such measures as unemployment insurance, safety inspections of the workplace, minimum-wage laws, and Social Security. Many of these laws have treated men and women differently; mothers, for example, have received more benefits than fathers because of the assumption that poor children would most likely be under the care of their mothers. When a government takes such responsibility for the well-being of its citizens, it is called a welfare state.

Women played an important role in creating the welfare state. Even before the ratification of the 19th Amendment granted all American women the right to vote, activists were lobbying and agitating to persuade legislators to adopt new and more humane laws, such as those prohibiting child labor. One of their early successes occurred when states enacted "mothers' pensions," which set up the framework for giving aid to families with dependent children.

Settlement houses—which housed middle-class women who had moved into slum neighborhoods to provide help and advice to the poor—were seedbeds for the new approach to governing. Many of the ideas enacted into law during Franklin Roosevelt's New Deal of the 1930s—ideas that established the basic characteristics of the American welfare state—had originally been conceived by women in the settlement-house network. In the 1970s the welfare state became much more gender-neutral. Single mothers are, however, disproportionately raising children (relative to single men) and this often places them at risk to fall into poverty, because often they cannot command salaries adequate to pay for child-care *and* support their families. In the late 1990s, some of the basic assumptions of the welfare state were called into question. In 1996 Congress enacted and President Bill Clinton signed into law a massive overhead of public assistance whereby even mothers with young children receive help for a finite time—with consequences still to be fully understood.

SEE ALSO

New Deal; Settlement-house movement

FURTHER READING

Gordon, Linda. *Pitied but not Entitled: Single Mothers and the History of Welfare, 1890–1935.* New York: Maxwell Macmillan, 1994.
Muncy, Robyn. *Creating a Female Dominion in American Reform, 1890–1935.* New York: Oxford University Press, 1991.

Wells-Barnett, Ida B.

- *Born: July 16, 1862, Holly Springs, Miss.*
- *Education: Fisk University, teaching credential, 1884*
- *Accomplishments: Editor and co-owner,* Memphis Free Speech and Headlight *newspaper (1889–92); co-founder, National Association for the Advancement of Colored People (1909); author,* A Red Record *(1895) and* Crusade for Justice *(autobiography, 1970)*
- *Died: Mar. 25, 1931, Chicago, Ill.*

Ida B. Wells-Barnett was born to slave parents in the waning days of the Confederacy. Despite this difficult start in life, she went on to become one of the outstanding women of her generation, known both for her crusade against lynching and for her organizational work among African-American women.

As editor of the Memphis Free Speech and Headlight *at a time when lynching was rampant in the South, Ida B. Wells spoke out against this crime. "Where are our 'leaders' when the race is being burnt, shot and hanged?" she asked the then-silent government officials.*

Orphaned at the age of 16, Ida Wells accepted the responsibility for her younger brothers and sisters. She supported herself and them as a schoolteacher and then as a newspaper editor, having moved to Memphis, Tennessee, to pursue her career. In March 1892 a Memphis mob lynched three young black men whom she knew and admired. Horrified, Wells launched her crusade against mob violence—although she had to leave the South to be able to do this safely. Indeed, a mob destroyed her printing press after her paper published an antilynching editorial she had written. Wells herself was traveling in the North at the time.

Even in the North, however, Wells encountered resistance. What she had to say about race relations in the South was so controversial that she had to go to Britain, lecture, and establish a reputation there before she could command audiences in the United States. Her daring message was that Southerners were murdering black men for alleged rape of white women when, in fact, the sexual contact might have been consensual. This charge created rage in the South, and many southern newspapers attacked Wells as a woman of unsound morals.

Wells eventually settled in Chicago, where she married lawyer Ferdinand Barnett in 1895. That same year she published *A Red Record,* her account of the lynchings in the South during a three-year period. Taking a brief time away from political activities for the birth of her three children, Wells-Barnett soon returned to the fray. She founded the country's first African-American women's suffrage club in the early 20th century. In 1930 she ran unsuccessfully for the Illinois State Senate. Her crusade against lynching increased public awareness of the matter.

SEE ALSO

Lynching

FURTHER READING

McMurry, Linda O. *To Keep the Waters Troubled: The Life of Ida B. Wells.* New York: Oxford University Press, 1999.

Van Steenwyk, Elizabeth. *Ida B. Wells-Barnett: Woman of Courage.* New York: Franklin Watts, 1992.

West, Mae

- *Born: Aug. 17, 1892, Brooklyn, N.Y.*
- *Education: Little formal education*
- *Accomplishments: Star and screenwriter of many films, including* She Done Him Wrong *(1933),* I'm No Angel *(1933),* Belle of the Nineties *(1934),* Go West, Young Man *(1936),* My Little Chickadee *(1940)*
- *Died: Nov. 22, 1980, Los Angeles, Calif.*

Most Hollywood blondes have been glamorous but also vulnerable. Not Mae

Mae West plays the sexy saloon singer Lady Lou in her first star vehicle, She Done Him Wrong *(1933), which was based on her own Broadway play* Diamond Lil.

West. More than almost any other female movie star, she projected an aura of being in charge. In fact, she wrote her own lines for her movies of the 1930s and usually collaborated on the rest of the script. In 1935 she was the highest-paid woman in the United States.

Before Hollywood beckoned, West had appeared in vaudeville shows—she began her performing career at the age of five—and on the Broadway stage. In 1926 a play that she wrote, produced, directed, and starred in—called simply *Sex*—created both a sensation and a set of legal problems for West. She was arrested for obscenity and spent 10 days in jail.

Known for her naughty sense of humor, West created sayings that have become part of American folklore, such as, "It's not the men in my life that count; it's the life in my men." As an old woman she created a nightclub act and she also appeared in the movie *Myra Breckinridge* in 1975.

SEE ALSO

Movies

FURTHER READING

Leider, Emily Wortis. *Becoming Mae West.* New York: Farrar, Straus & Giroux, 1997.

Westward movement

From the first settlements by Europeans in the early 1600s until the conquest of the last resisting Indians in the late 1800s, the United States engaged in a ceaseless expansion into the west. The westward movement displaced Native Americans and disrupted their ways of life, and many did not survive. It also required immense effort and sacrifice from the European Americans—although it brought prosperity to some of them. For the men and women of both groups, the experience was very different.

In Native-American tribes, men and women often had more equal roles than they did among the invaders. Cherokee women, for example, had a share of what Europeans would call political power and they helped decide when the tribe would go to war and make peace, for example. The Europeans were often horrified by this balance of power, so one way tribes could prove they were "civilized" was to strip women of much of their customary influence. (In what is now Oklahoma there were the Five Civilized Tribes, whose members tried to live according to European-American customs.)

A letter from one Cherokee woman to Benjamin Franklin in 1787 illustrates the feelings of many women upon being stripped of their traditional power: "I am in hopes that if you Rightly consider that woman is the mother of All, and the Woman does not pull children out of Trees or Stumps nor out of old Logs, but out of their Bodies, so that they ought to mind what a woman says." There were also

Thousands of women found themselves trying to create a home-like atmosphere under difficult circumstances when their families moved west. A covered wagon was a poor substitute for a real kitchen, but women made do.

instances, as in the virtually all-male post–gold rush California of the 1850s, when Indian women were subjected to widespread rape by the invading Europeans.

The 19th century saw the greatest expansion into the West, because the United States obtained the Louisiana Purchase from France in 1803 and the Southwest from Mexico in 1848, following the Mexican War. In some cases, such as during the gold rush, with its focus on mining, the European Americans moving into the West were disproportionately male. In settlement areas dedicated to farming, however, family groups made up the bulk of the newcomers.

When a settlement was predominantly male, it usually experienced a great deal of turbulence and even violence. Men fought over mining claims, they fought when they had consumed too much alcohol, and they fought over the few women who were available, most often prostitutes. In these places men were usually eager to have "respectable" women arrive, because such women had the responsibility of taming a raw, new settlement by getting the men to stay home rather than drinking and brawling. The new western states with mostly male inhabitants were so eager to attract women that they led the way in granting women the right to vote; Wyoming Territory was the first, in 1869, and then the state of Wyoming did the same in 1890.

When whole families traveled together, such as on the Oregon Trail, it was usually the men who had pressed for the move so as to better themselves financially. The women then had to undergo the wrenching experiences of leaving behind their loved ones, of trying to maintain a family in a wagon train (sometimes even giving birth on the trail), and then of trying to keep house in a primitive, frontier setting when they finally reached their destination. They might also have had to confront hostile Native Americans who were unhappy about being displaced. Sometimes women bore arms to defend themselves and their families.

In the late 19th century, the U.S. Army maintained forts in thinly settled areas of the West in order to bring the resisting Indians under military discipline. Often the officers' wives lived at the fort, too, in circumstances that were very different from the usual life of a middle-class woman, because the women lived in nearly all-male enclaves. One woman who wrote, with mixed feelings, about the sense of adventure this required was Elizabeth Custer, the widow of General George Custer: "When a woman has come out of danger, she is too utterly a coward by nature not to dread enduring the same thing again; but it is something to know that she is equal to it."

In a few instances, women traveled west on their own—perhaps as prostitutes or as schoolteachers. Some women staked out their own land claims, and some even wore male clothing to achieve their ambitions. For many European-American men, the West represented a dream of freedom, and that was true for a certain number of women, too. One who was grateful for western opportunities was the performer Lotta Crabtree, the toast of San Francisco in the years after the gold rush. Many years later she gave the city a fountain, which still stands on Market Street.

SEE ALSO

Native Americans

FURTHER READING

Faragher, John Mack. *Women and Men on the Overland Trail.* New Haven: Yale University Press, 1979.

Leckie, Shirley. *Elizabeth Bacon Custer.* Norman: University of Oklahoma Press, 1993.

Jameson, Elizabeth, and Susan Armitage, eds. *Writing the Range: Race, Class, and Culture in the Women's West.* Norman: University of Oklahoma Press, 1997.

Jensen, Joan M. *One Foot on the Rockies: Women and Creativity in the Modern American West.* Albuquerque: University of New Mexico Press, 1995.

Wharton, Edith Newbold Jones

- *Born: Jan. 24, 1862, New York, N.Y.*
- *Education: Educated at home*
- *Accomplishments: Chevalier of the Legion of Honor (France, 1916); Pulitzer Prize for* The Age of Innocence *(1921); author,* The Decoration of Houses *(with Ogden Codman, 1897);* The House of Mirth *(1905);* Ethan Frome *(1911);* The Custom of the Country *(1913);* The Age of Innocence *(1920);* A Backward Glance *(autobiography, 1934)*
- *Died: Aug. 11, 1937, Saint-Brice-sous-Forêt, France*

Novelist Edith Wharton wrote primarily about what she knew best, the upper-class world she was born into in New York City. But in her best work, she was able to transcend the limits of her privileged background and touch upon universal human themes.

Novelist Edith Wharton as a young woman of 19. Wharton came from an upper-class family in New York, and she wrote vividly about this milieu.

Nothing in her girlhood would have pointed Wharton toward a writing career. She received only a token education, and, in fact, people in her class looked down upon artists and writers. As a young woman of 23, she married a banker 13 years her senior, Edward Wharton, and the childless couple began to devote themselves to the many amusements they could so readily afford.

But this life palled for Wharton. Following a yacht trip in 1888, she began to write (as she had done in her girlhood), and soon she was publishing stories in leading magazines. In 1905 her first major novel, *The House of Mirth,* was published; it was a withering look at the empty values of her money-hungry society and at their destructive effect on women. From that time on, she averaged a book a year for the rest of her life.

In addition to her writing vocation, Wharton had a serious interest in interior decoration and published *The Decoration of Houses* in 1897. Her own house, The Mount in Lenox, Massachusetts, displays the results of many of her ideas, which were, in essence, a revolt against the fussy Victorian interiors so popular in her youth.

As a mature woman and successful author, Wharton lived a remarkably independent life. After divorcing Teddy Wharton in 1913, she spent a major portion of time in France, where her circle included many of the best-known intellectuals of the day, such as the novelist Henry James.

SEE ALSO

Literature

FURTHER READING

Leach, William. *Edith Wharton.* New York: Chelsea House, 1987.

Lewis, R. W. B. *Edith Wharton: A Biography.* New York: Harper & Row, 1975.

Wheatley, Phillis

- *Born: Around 1753, Africa*
- *Education: Educated at home*
- *Accomplishments: First published African-American poet (1767); author,* Poems on Various Subjects, Religious and Moral *(1773)*
- *Died: Dec. 5, 1784, Boston, Mass.*

Phillis Wheatley, the first African-American poet, was also a child prodigy. Purchased off a slave ship in Boston Harbor in 1761, she was soon fluent in English and studying Latin.

Her owners were the deeply religious Susanna and John Wheatley of Boston. Recognizing their slave's unusual precociousness, they lightened her duties and provided access to the world of books. By the time that Phillis Wheatley was in her early teens, she was writing poetry in the style of her favorite English poet, Alexander Pope. Her mistress subsequently invested considerable effort in seeing that her poetry be published.

The young woman enjoyed many triumphs, including a trip to England and a meeting with General George Washington. But after both Wheatleys died and she was freed from bondage, the vulnerability of her position became clear. Cast out into the world, she married a free black man named John Peters, who was not always a reliable husband owing to his financial difficulties. Two of their three children died very young. The third died on the same day as Wheatley in December 1784.

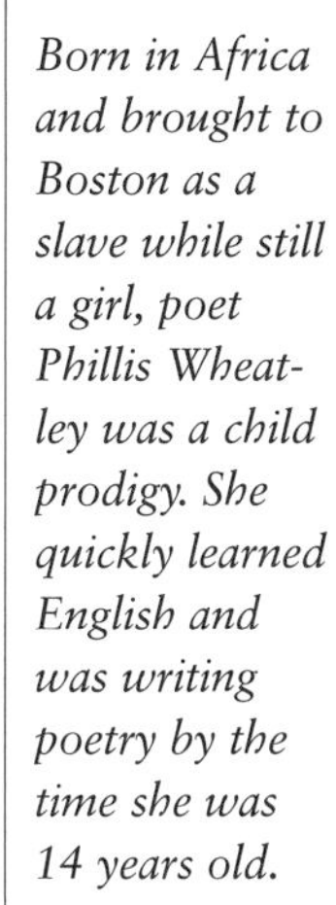

Born in Africa and brought to Boston as a slave while still a girl, poet Phillis Wheatley was a child prodigy. She quickly learned English and was writing poetry by the time she was 14 years old.

Even writing within the confines of the poetic conventions in her day, Wheatley pioneered the written expression of the black experience in the United States. Her poems were frequently devoted to either religious or patriotic themes.

Wheatley addressed this patriotic poem to "His Majesty's Principal Secretary of State for North America," that is the man who advised King George III:

Should you, my lord, while you peruse my song,
Wonder from whence my love of freedom sprung,
Whence plow these wishes for the common good,
By feeling hearts alone best understood
I, young in life, by seeming cruel fate,
Was snatched from Africa's fancied happy seat:
What pangs excruciating must molest,
What sorrows labour in my parents' breast?

Steeled was that soul and by no misery
moved
That from a father seized his babe
beloved:
Such, such my case. And can I then but
pray
Others may never feel tyrannic sway?

SEE ALSO

Literature

FURTHER READING

Kamensky, Jane. *The Colonial Mosaic: American Women 1600–1760.* New York: Oxford University Press, 1995.

Richmond, M. A. *Phillis Wheatley.* New York: Chelsea House, 1992.

Wheatley, Phillis. *The Collected Works of Phillis Wheatley.* Edited by John C. Shields. New York: Oxford University Press, 1989.

Whitman, Narcissa Prentiss

- *Born: Mar. 14, 1808, Prattsburg, N.Y.*
- *Education: Franklin Academy, N.Y. (entered 1827); possibly attended Troy Female Seminary, N.Y.*
- *Accomplishments: One of first two white women to travel the Oregon Trail (1836)*
- *Died: Nov. 29, 1847, Waiilatpu, Wash.*

Narcissa Whitman, a Presbyterian missionary to the Indians of the Northwest, was in 1836 one of the first two white women to cross the Continental Divide. Her life story features high adventure, displays of courage, errors in judgment, and terrible tragedy.

Like other young women of the day, Narcissa Prentiss dreamed of becoming a missionary. Marriage to Marcus Whitman, a physician pledged to missionary service in the West, helped her reach her goal, because the Presbyterian Church would never have sent an unmarried woman off on her own. The couple wed in February 1836 and soon set off on their long journey across the continent from her native New York.

The trip itself was a troubled one. The Whitmans were traveling with Henry and Eliza Spalding; Henry had been rejected as a potential husband by Narcissa several years earlier. Despite the friction caused by this situation, the Whitmans reached Fort Walla Walla on September 1, 1836, and decided to establish their mission nearby at a place called Waiilatpu, located in the tribal lands of the Cayuse Indians.

The Whitmans worked as a team: Marcus led services and provided medical care, and Narcissa taught. At first things went well. Then their only child, a two-year-old daughter, drowned, an event that plunged Narcissa into deep despondency. She began to display an ever haughtier demeanor toward the native peoples they were trying to convert, treating people who overwhelmingly outnumbered the whites with repugnance. Moreover, the Cayuse were concerned about the increasing numbers of white immigrants and about the devastation wrought among their tribe by white-introduced diseases—despite Marcus Whitman's medical attention. In November 1847 a small band of Cayuse warriors killed 14 whites at Waiilatpu, including both Whitmans, and took 47 prisoners.

FURTHER READING

Jeffrey, Julie Roy. *Converting the West: A Biography of Narcissa Whitman.* Norman: University of Oklahoma Press, 1991.

Whitman, Narcissa Prentiss. *My Journal, 1836.* ed. Lawrence Dodd. Fairfield, Wash.: Ye Galleon, 1982.

Whitman, Narcissa Prentiss, and Eliza Spalding. *Where Wagons Could Go.* ed. Clifford Merrill Drury. Lincoln: University of Nebraska Press, 1997.

Willard, Emma Hart

- *Born: Feb. 23, 1787, Berlin, Conn.*
- *Education: Mostly self-educated*
- *Accomplishments: Author,* Plan for Improving Female Education *(1818) and* The Fulfillment of a Promise *(poetry, 1831); founder, Troy Female Seminary (New York, 1821)*
- *Died: Apr. 15, 1870, Troy, N.Y.*

In 1821 Emma Willard opened the Troy Female Seminary in Troy, New York, a school attended by some of the greatest women of the 19th century, such as Elizabeth Cady Stanton. Troy Seminary was unparalleled in its day for the breadth of learning it made available to young women. Indeed, in some subjects, such as science, Troy's high school age students may have enjoyed more advanced courses than what was then available at nearby men's *colleges.*

The 16th child in a family of 17 and living in a rural backwater, young Emma Hart might seem to have been an unlikely candidate for the life of the mind. Her father was, however, both politically liberal and a dedicated reader, and he encouraged her to use her brain, even going so far as to discuss philosophy with her. She managed to secure enough formal education to become a teacher. In fact, she went far beyond the usual training then available for women teachers, acquiring knowledge in subjects such as mathematics and science then thought to be the province of men, in part on her own and in part by attending classes.

In 1809 Emma Hart married a physician, John Willard, and the couple had one child. Pursuing her educational career, she opened a school in their home in Middlebury, Vermont, in 1814 before deciding that there were greater opportunities in the neighboring state of New York. She failed in her attempt to secure financial help from the state for a women's school, but she did receive support from the Troy city council, so she located her school there. Passionate in her dedication to educating young women, she inspired many of them to high achievement. Her school, whose name was changed in 1895 to Emma Willard School, continues today to provide young women with an exceptional high-school education.

SEE ALSO

Education

FURTHER READING

Lutz, Alma. *Emma Willard, Pioneer Educator of American Women.* Boston: Beacon Press, 1964.

Solomon, Barbara Miller. *In the Company of Educated Women: A History of Women and Higher Education in America.* New Haven: Yale University Press, 1986.

Willard, Frances

- *Born: Sept. 28, 1839, Churchville, N.Y.*
- *Education: North Western Female College, Ill., graduated 1859*
- *Accomplishments: Dean, Woman's College of Northwestern University (1873–74); author,* Women and Temperance *(1883); president, Chicago Women's Christian Temperance Union (1874); president, National Women's Christian Temperance Union (1879–83); organizer and president, World Women's Christian Temperance Union (1883)*
- *Died: Feb. 17, 1898, New York, N.Y.*

At the height of her fame, the anti-alcohol crusader Frances Willard was among the best-known and best-loved women in the country. As head of the Woman's Christian Temperance Union (WCTU), she inspired her contemporaries with her energy and vision.

With little formal education, Willard nonetheless became a teacher. The opportunity to travel abroad with a wealthy young woman friend helped complete her education, and she eventually became dean of women at Northwestern University in Evanston, Illinois. Unhappy with Northwestern's president, Willard resigned in 1874 and soon thereafter became active in the temperance movement, which was then spreading, with the enthusiasm of a true crusade throughout the Midwest. That several members of Willard's extended family had experienced alcohol-related personal tragedy no doubt contributed to her enthusiasm for the cause. In an era in which few women worked outside the home, marriage to a drunkard could mean ruin for a woman and her children. The WCTU was an organization filled with women who wanted to improve their own and their children's lives, and its members became increasingly willing to advocate far-reaching reforms under Willard's prompting. After becoming president in 1879—a position she held until her death in 1898—she pushed the WCTU in the direction of endorsing such reforms as woman suffrage. "Do everything" was Willard's motto.

Eventually Willard moved from seeing alcohol as the principal cause of social problems to seeing its abuse as a symptom caused by inhumane conditions in the society, and in her last years she became a socialist, convinced that prison reform and public health advocacy required her energy. Slums were not filthy because the inhabitants were too drunk to care, rather filthy slums drove their inhabitants to drown their sorrows.

This statue of the leader of the Woman's Christian Temperance Union, Frances Willard, stands in the U.S. Capitol, evidence of the high esteem Willard enjoyed in her day.

SEE ALSO

Temperance

FURTHER READING

Bordin, Ruth. *Women and Temperance.* Philadelphia: Temple University Press, 1981.

Bordin, Ruth. *Frances Willard: A Biography.* Chapel Hill: University of North Carolina Press, 1986.

Leeman, Richard W. *"Do Everything" Reform: The Oratory of Frances E. Willard.* New York: Greenwood, 1992.

Winnemucca, Sarah

- *Born: Around 1844, Nevada*
- *Education: Some convent school education*
- *Accomplishments: Author,* Life Among the Piutes: Their Wrongs and Claims *(1883)*
- *Died: Oct. 16, 1891, Monida, Mont.*

In the late 19th century, Sarah Winnemucca was a well-known and effective spokeswoman for her people, the Paiute Indians of Nevada. The daughter

An activist for Native-American rights, Sarah Winnemucca first gained public attention as a translator for the U.S. Army. One of her most significant contributions was the establishment a school for American Indian children in Nevada.

of a Paiute chief, she spent enough time with Europeans to learn both Spanish and English. Converting to Christianity, she became Sarah rather than using her Paiute name, which is translated as "Shell-flower." Yet she also maintained her belief in the Spirit Father of the Paiutes, as she acted as a mediator between cultures.

Having learned to distrust the greed and dishonesty of the typical white Indian agent, as she saw her people being exploited, Winnemucca traveled to Washington in 1880 to plead the case for better treatment of her people before Secretary of the Interior Carl Schurz and President Rutherford B. Hayes. Shortly thereafter, she went east again on a lecture tour, during which she was especially well received in Boston by reformers such as Elizabeth Peabody. In 1883 she published *Life among the Piutes,* a memoir that was based on her lectures. Although Winnemucca did not succeed in persuading the federal government to respond to her pleas, she fought her battles with determination.

Winnemucca seems to have had two brief and unsatisfactory marriages early in life. In 1881 she was married again, this time to Lieutenant L. H. Hopkins, whom she had met while teaching Indian children in a barracks school. He accompanied her on the lecture tour, and his death in 1886 was a sore loss. Winnemucca herself died a few years later in 1891.

FURTHER READING

Canfield, Gae Whitney. *Sarah Winnemucca of the Northern Paiutes.* Norman: University of Oklahoma Press, 1988.

Scordato, Ellen. *Sarah Winnemucca: Northern Paiute Writer and Diplomat.* New York: Chelsea House, 1992.

Witches, persecution of

During the first century of European settlement in North America, about 300 women were accused of being witches; approximately half of these accusations took place in one 10-month period in 1692 in and around Salem, Massachusetts. The frenzy and frequent misguidedness of those Salem accusations contributed the phrase "on a witch hunt" to our language.

A group of girls and young women began to suffer from hysterical fits that year, and they accused various women of bewitching them. A witch was someone who had supposedly made a pact with the devil and had then been

A 19th-century artist created this highly romanticized rendering of a dramatic moment in the Salem witchcraft trial: while one woman testifies, another writhes on the floor in a fit.

granted strange powers. Soon a contagion of accusations and even confessions spread through Salem. A special court was convened, and before the witchcraft trials ended, 16 women and 3 men had been executed, and 50 had confessed to being witches.

Ever since, historians have puzzled over why "witches" were persecuted in Salem and why so many were women. Scholars have argued that the typical woman at risk of being accused of witchcraft was single, without male relatives, no longer young, and trying to protect her property interests in a world where males generally controlled property. The theory is that women who were forced by circumstances to stand up for themselves in a male-dominated society took the chance of being defined as in league with the devil.

Moreover, many of the accused had devoted themselves to healing, and if their patients died, surviving family members might accuse a "doctor woman" of being a witch—especially if she had engaged in any strange practices such as tossing herbs into the hearth fire during the attempted healing. Scholars are clear, however, on one outcome of the Salem outbreak: it served to weaken the authority of the Puritan clergy, most members of which had supported the various witch trials. As the population lost its belief in witches, people also lost some of their veneration for their ministers.

FURTHER READING

Boyer, Paul, and Stephen Nissenbaum, eds. *Salem-Village Witchcraft: A Documentary Record of Local Conflict in Colonial New England.* Boston: Northeastern University Press, 1997.

Demos, John Putnam. *Entertaining Satan: Witchcraft and the Culture of Early New England.* New York: Oxford University Press, 1982.

Karlsen, Carol. *The Devil in the Shape of a Woman.* New York: Norton, 1987.

Reis, Elizabeth. *Damned Women: Sinners and Witches in Puritan New England.* Ithaca: Cornell University Press, 1997.

Woman suffrage

SEE Suffrage, woman

Women's Bureau, U.S.

The Women's Bureau, created on a temporary basis during World War I in response to pressure from groups such as the National Consumers' League and the Women's Trade Union League, was made into a permanent government agency in 1920. Located within the Department of Labor, the Women's Bureau is the only agency specially charged with protecting the interests of women workers, and in the early years it staunchly defended the protective labor legislation on behalf of women workers that had been the mainstay of so much of organized womanhood in the first decades of the 20th century.

For much of its existence, the bureau remained on the margins of the federal government, lacking real clout. Then during the administration of President John F. Kennedy, the bureau came into its own. Under the able leadership of trade union activist Esther Peterson, the bureau persuaded Kennedy to convene the first President's Commission on the Status of Women, which proved to be a catalyst for immense change of benefit to women primarily because it led to the creation of state commissions and to a network of women activists throughout the century.

The bureau was also instrumental in convincing Congress to pass the Equal Pay Act of 1963. The Women's Bureau has remained an important voice for working women, conducting research on women and work, and acting as an advocate within the government for women's rights in the workplace.

SEE ALSO

Commission on the Status of Women; Equal Pay Act (1963)

FURTHER READING

Peterson, Esther, with Winifred Conkling. *Restless: the Memoirs of Labor and Consumer Activist Esther Peterson.* Washington, D.C.: Caring, 1995.

Weber, Gustavus A. *The Women's Bureau; Its History, Activities, and Organization.* 1923. Reprint, New York: AMS Press, 1974.

Women's colleges

Women's colleges have played an extraordinarily important role in educating women in general and in educating women leaders in particular. In the mid-20th century, when the most prestigious male universities began admitting women, and some women's colleges, such as Vassar, became coeducational, the numbers of women's colleges began to decline—from 233 in 1960 to 90 in 1986 to 59 in 1999. They continue, however, to be a significant presence in higher education.

Women had to struggle for generations to gain access to higher education, whether in single-sex institutions or coeducational ones. Oberlin College in Ohio opened its doors to women and became coed in 1837, but few other colleges and universities followed this example right away. As a result, those who believed in higher education for women often founded a single-sex college.

The first two women's colleges were in the South—Georgia Female College in 1839 and Mary Sharp College in Tennessee in 1851. Then came the founding of the Seven Sisters (Vassar, Smith, Wellesley, Bryn Mawr, Radcliffe, Barnard, and Mount Holyoke), starting with Vassar in the 1860s. (Mount Holyoke was founded earlier by Mary Lyon as Mount Holyoke Female Semi-

Students from Wellesley, Radcliffe, and other women's colleges march proudly in a New York City suffrage parade around 1910.

nary.) Catholic orders also began to found women's colleges (19 between 1900 and 1930) and so did Protestant churches. White women missionaries founded Atlanta's Spelman Seminary for African-American women in 1881, and it became a college in 1923.

Women's colleges have played an important role not only because they frequently provided a rigorous education for their students but also because, for generations, they were the most realistic occupational destination for a would-be woman college professor. She could teach home economics in a coeducational university where professorships in other disciplines were reserved for men or she could teach her specialty in a women's college.

Social science research indicates that alumnae of women's colleges include a disproportionate share of high achievers. Such success may be the result of the close mentoring students received or because they could aspire to be student body president as well as secretary. First Lady Hillary Rodham Clinton, who graduated from Wellesley College in 1969, provides a good example of the leadership skills that can be nurtured in a women's college.

Critics have maintained that women's colleges do not reflect the reality of the world outside the college. Yet, although their numbers have dwindled, they seem unlikely to disappear, given the fierce loyalty they often inspire in their graduates.

SEE ALSO

Education; Home economics; Lyon, Mary; Universities

FURTHER READING

Horowitz, Helen. *Alma Mater: Design and Experience in the Women's Colleges from Their Nineteenth-Century Beginnings to the 1930s.* New York: Knopf, 1984.

Kendall, Elaine. *"Peculiar Institutions": An Informal History of the Seven Sister Colleges.* New York: Putnam, 1976.

Solomon, Barbara Miller. *In the Company of Educated Women: A History of Women and Higher Education in America.* New Haven: Yale University Press, 1986.

Women's Trade Union League (WTUL)

The Women's Trade Union League (WTUL) was the only major organization to bring together women from both the middle class and the working class so as to mobilize both groups for improving the lives of women workers.

When the WTUL was founded in 1903, the male-led trade union movement was devoting few resources to potential women members. Most women workers were poorly paid and vulnerable to exploitation, and they needed all the help they could get—which they received from the WTUL. Members of the group raised money for funds to sustain strikers, for example. They also cooperated in lobbying for protective labor legislation for women workers.

The emblem of the Women's Trade Union League reflects its goal of protecting workers so they could support their families. The WTUL, composed of both working-class and middle-class women, proved to be one of the most effective defenders of the interests of working women.

Strongest in New York and Chicago, the WTUL benefited from having able leaders. Typifying the cross-class nature of the group, the first president was Margaret Dreier Robins from 1903 to 1926, daughter of a wealthy family, and the second was Rose Schneiderman, daughter of an immigrant family and a former factory worker, from 1926 to 1950 when the organization disbanded.

SEE ALSO

Robins, Margaret Dreier

FURTHER READING

Dye, Nancy Schrom. *As Equals and as Sisters.* Columbia: University of Missouri Press, 1980.

Woodhull, Victoria Claflin

- *Born: Sept. 23, 1838, Homer, Ohio*
- *Education: No formal education*
- *Accomplishments: Co-founder, Woodhull, Claflin and Company, first women-run brokerage firm (1870); co-founder,* Woodhull and Claflin's Weekly *(1870–76); candidate for U.S. Presidency, Equal Rights Party (1972)*
- *Died: June 10, 1927, Tewkesbury, England*

Victoria Claflin Woodhull is one of the most colorful characters in American history, a flamboyant adventuress but also a courageous exponent of new theories to legitimate woman suffrage.

As a young girl, Victoria participated with her family in a traveling medicine show. After marrying Canning Woodhull when she was 15, she gave birth to two children. Full of energy and married to a rather listless man, she drifted out of the marriage, rejoining the Claflin family and forming an especially close bond with her sister Tennessee. So-called propriety meant little to either sister, and they engaged in several love affairs at a time when women were expected to be chaste if unmarried and faithful if wed. They also became devotees of spiritualism, the belief that it is possible to contact the dead. Indeed, Woodhull claimed to be inspired by spirits.

The entire Claflin/Woodhull clan arrived in New York City in the late 1860s, where Tennessee attracted the attention of the newly widowed railroad baron Cornelius Vanderbilt. It was he, evidently, who financed the sisters' career as the country's first female stockbrokers. With his help, the "bewitching brokers," as they became known, pursued their ambition. Their firm, Woodhull, Claflin and Company, thrived.

Thomas Nast's 1872 cartoon "Get thee behind me, (Mrs.) Satan!" ridicules the free love philosophy of Victoria Woodhull. A wife burdened by children and a drunken husband tells Mrs. Satan (Woodhull), "I'd rather travel the hardest path of matrimony than follow your footsteps."

Having braved the financial world, Woodhull next decided to try her hand at politics, declaring herself a candidate for President of the United States in 1870, and being nominated by the Equal Rights Party in 1872. She and her sister began editing *Woodhull & Claflin's Weekly* so as to advance Woodhull's views on a number of subjects, including sexual freedom, a belief that distanced her from the "respectable" opinion of her day. So unconventional were the sisters' views that the complete text of Karl Marx's *Communist Manifesto* appeared in English for the first time in the *Weekly.*

In 1871 Woodhull testified before Congress, arguing that the 14th Amendment to the Constitution had, unintentionally, given women the vote. Her appearance on behalf of woman suffrage brought her the support of well-known suffragists, including Elizabeth Cady Stanton and Susan B. Anthony—who decided to ally themselves with the notorious Woodhull, despite her "tainted" reputation.

But Woodhull eventually spun out of control. In her paper, she accused Henry Ward Beecher, the best-known clergyman of the day, of sexual scandal. Although he was probably guilty, there was widespread public outrage at *her.* The two sisters were indicted on obscenity charges and spent time in jail before being acquitted. They then departed for London to escape the unpleasantness, but the whiff of scandal surrounding those who had supported Woodhull clung for years.

FURTHER READING

Gabriel, Mary. *Notorious Victoria: The Life of Victoria Woodhull, Uncensored.* Chapel Hill, N.C.: Algonquin Books, 1998.

Goldsmith, Barbara. *Other Powers: The Age of Suffrage, Spiritualism, and the Scandalous Victoria Woodhull.* New York: Knopf, 1998.

Work, paid

American women have always worked, but until the 20th century, the vast majority were not paid for it. Rather, they toiled in their own households, labored as slaves, or worked as unpaid indentured servants. The Industrial Revolution that began in the late 1700s changed this situation.

The first substantial group of factory workers at the dawn of American industrialization were the so-called "Lowell mill girls," who worked in textile factories in New England, beginning in the 1820s. But as industrialization proceeded, more men than women worked in the factories—with increasing levels of employment for women as the 20th century progressed.

When large-scale employment for women *did* begin to open up in the 19th century, it tended to be in the "pink-collar ghetto"—occupations whose jobs are exclusively or preponderantly held by women. Teaching was an early possibility for women, for example, and one that offered the chance for many daughters of working-class families to move into the middle class.

After the Civil War (1861–65) two new occupations began to be open to women—department store clerks and secretaries. The latter, in particular, became one of the predominantly female occupations and one to which large numbers of women gravitated, although paid domestic service continued to be the largest single female occupation until the mid-20th century. In this period young women might work until they married, but usually not afterward—unless they were African American. It was much more common for a black married woman to be employed than a white one because the poor jobs available to black men forced their wives to go to work.

In 1870, 97.5 percent of the clerical workforce was male, and the jobs were often apprenticeships to a full-fledged business career. With the invention of the typewriter and a growing need for office workers to keep up with the explosive growth in the American economy after 1870, employers began to turn to young women, at the same time redefining the job to be a dead-end one with relatively poor pay because they could not conceive of women holding business positions of real authority. Being a clerk would no longer be the first step on the ladder of business success—except for the unusually energetic and resourceful few. Though the job offered little in the way of growth potential, it was clean and respectable work—and virtually impossible for women of color to obtain until after World War II.

In the late 19th century, there also arose a few professional jobs for women besides teaching, such as nurs-

WOMEN IN THE CIVILIAN LABOR FORCE (MILLIONS): 1890 TO 1970

Year	Total	Single	Married	Widowed or Divorced
1890	3.71	2.53	0.52	0.67
1900	5.00	3.31	0.77	0.92
1910[a]	7.64	4.60	1.89	1.15
1920	8.35	6.43[b]	1.92	—
1930	10.63	5.74	3.07	1.83
1940	13.01	6.38	4.68	1.96
1950	16.55	5.27	8.64	2.64
1960	22.41	5.28	13.61	3.52
1970	30.76	6.94	19.18	4.64

[a] 1910 data not comparable with earlier or later censuses due to difference in basis of enumeration

[b] Includes widowed or divorced

Source: U.S. Census

WOMEN IN THE CIVILIAN LABOR FORCE (PERCENT OF FEMALE POPULATION): 1890 TO 1970

Year	Total	Single	Married	Widowed or Divorced
1890	18.9	40.5	4.6	29.9
1900	20.6	43.5	5.6	32.5
1910[a]	25.4	51.1	10.7	34.1
1920	23.7	46.4[b]	9.0	—
1930	24.8	50.5	11.7	34.4
1940	25.8	45.5	15.6	30.2
1950	29.0	46.3	23.0	32.7
1960	34.5	42.9	31.7	36.1
1970	41.6	50.9	40.2	36.8

[a] 1910 data not comparable with earlier or later censuses due to difference in basis of enumeration

[b] Includes widowed or divorced

Source: U.S. Census

ing, social work, and librarianship. The more prestigious and highly paid professional employment in the fields of law, medicine, or college teaching generally excluded women.

By the 1930s tens of thousands of white women were working in factories (with women of color still largely consigned to domestic service). In this decade of the Great Depression and of unprecedented labor militancy, women were finally welcomed into the ranks of organized labor, a development that would greatly benefit working-class women in most parts of the country. Even with this breakthrough, there was still widespread public disapproval of married women working outside the home, though, especially given the problem of joblessness for men in this time of economic distress

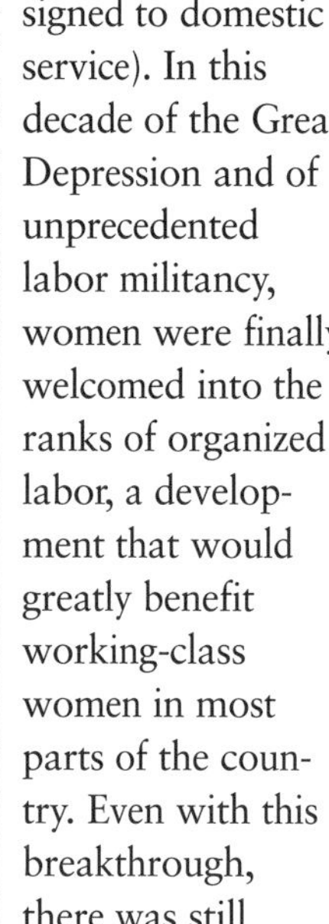

"Enfranchisement means the sky's the limit in woman's sphere." This cartoon shows the progress of women's access to employment and positions of influence. At the top of the ladder, after "equal suffrage," women had an opportunity for "wage equality," "political appointments," and even the "Presidency."

In the following decade the United States entered World War II, and public attitudes about employed women were transformed as increasing numbers of women took jobs. To win the war, the country needed all the workers it could get. Millions of women left their homes for factories, aircraft plants, and shipyards. The number of women belonging to unions quadrupled. All of a sudden black women could get jobs other than as maids. Although many women lost their jobs when the war ended, they did not lose the taste for a paycheck. In consequence the number of women working outside the home began a steady climb.

Owing to the birth of modern feminism in the 1970s and a spate of legislation opening up opportunities in higher education and in the workplace, such as Title VII of the 1964 Civil Rights Act and Title IX of the Education Act of 1972, young women today can aspire to a broader range of employment than at any previous time in U.S. history. As of 1997, women constituted about 46 percent of the total paid workforce. Still, millions of women continue to toil at jobs in the pink-collar ghetto, jobs that are typically poorly paid relative to comparable male work. In many cases, these jobs constitute the second household income. In 1997, 68 percent of married couples with children under 18 were both working.

SEE ALSO

Industrialization; Labor movement; Law; Medicine; Nursing; Servants; Teaching; Title VII, IX; World War II

FURTHER READING

Fletcher, Joyce K. *Disappearing Acts: Gender, Power, and Relational Practice at Work.* Cambridge: MIT Press, 1999.

Kessler-Harris, Alice. *Out to Work: A History of Wage-Earning Women in the United States.* New York: Oxford University Press, 1982.

World War I

The first great overseas war in which the United States was involved, World War I (1917–18) brought massive mobilization and large-scale social change, though neither on the scale of what would happen during World War II. As they would in greater numbers in the 1940s, women held jobs ordinarily filled by men who had gone off to battle.

But some American experiences during the two wars, especially the experiences of American women, were pro-

"Farmerettes" drive tractors on the home front during World War I. With the men away at war, many women worked at non-traditional jobs.

foundly different. Although World War II was fought by a united people, World War I was not and many Americans opposed U.S. entry into the war—usually because they thought that Europeans should fight their battles themselves or because they had a philosophical objection to war in general. And although women could vote in the 1940s, they could not—except in certain states—during World War I. Together, these circumstances created a dilemma for many women. Should they follow their consciences and oppose the war or should they take the path of expediency and support it to prove that they were loyal citizens and deserved the vote? Jeannette Rankin, the first woman to be elected to Congress, chose the former path, but most other suffragists opted to support the war.

For President Woodrow Wilson the contributions made by women during the war made a big difference. He had opposed suffrage when he had first entered the White House in 1913. Seeing how much women were doing on behalf of the war effort helped change his mind. As the 19th Amendment, granting women the vote, came up for debate in the U.S. Senate in 1918, Wilson made a rare personal appearance and pled for a favorable vote, using the role played by women on behalf of the war as the reason. The Senate eventually passed the amendment the following year, and by August 26, 1920, it had been ratified by enough states to become part of the Constitution.

SEE ALSO

Rankin, Jeannette; Suffrage, woman

FURTHER READING

Clarke, Ida Clyde Gallagher. *American Women and the World War.* New York, London: D. Appleton, 1918.

Greenwald, Maurine Weiner. *Women, War, and Work: The Impact of World War I on Women Workers in the United States.* Westport, Conn.: Greenwood, 1980.

Smith, Karen Manners. *New Paths to Power: American Women 1890–1920.* New York: Oxford University Press, 1994.

Terriberry, Gladys. *Diary of Gladys Terriberry: American Army Nurse, France, 1918.* Edited by David J. Riley. New Brunswick, N.J.: David Joseph Riley, 1998.

World War II

World War II (1941–45) was one of the most important events in U.S. history: So many men fought to defeat Nazi Germany and imperial Japan. So many women and men worked at new jobs. So many women entered the paid workforce, some for the first time. So many Americans moved to new cities to obtain war work. After the war so many things changed, especially attitudes about women's roles and race relations. To a certain extent, postwar change represented the fulfillment of long-term trends rather than simply being the results of war itself. But the war was a powerful catalyst for change.

In December 1941 the United States entered a conflict that had already started in Europe in 1939. The American declaration of war followed the Japanese bombing of Pearl Harbor in Hawaii. President Franklin Delano Roosevelt had been trying to prepare the country for war, given the aggressive behavior of Adolf Hitler, dictator of Germany, and of the Japanese. Nonetheless, when the war came, it required a massive mobilization of American resources, financial strength, and people power.

Twelve million men served in the armed forces during the war, leaving an enormous gap in the workforce. To meet the need, some 6.5 million women went to work, 3 million of whom were married. Until this point there had been a strong taboo against the employment of married women.

Moreover, the women who already had jobs were often able to move up to better jobs owing to the demand for more workers. This was especially beneficial for black women, many of whom had been employable only as maids. During the war they could move into factory jobs. Other women of color, too, experienced new opportunity. For example, in San Francisco, Chinese-American women who had had great difficulty securing jobs outside of Chinatown were able to get jobs in the shipbuilding industry.

Women war workers like this 20-year-old aircraft mechanic were nicknamed "Rosie the Riveter." For the first time (on a large scale) women riveted, welded, and made repairs on machinery.

Women from tight-knit ethnic communities who took jobs were able to gain new freedom from family control. This happened, for example, in Los Angeles's Mexican-American community, where daughters had had a history of being very closely chaperoned but now enjoyed the independence and mobility that came with a job.

Millions of women were employed outside of the home, and for the first time in U.S. history on this scale, tens of thousands joined the military: there were 140,000 in the Women's Army Corps (WAC), 100,000 in the navy unit called WAVES (Women Accepted for Volunteer Emergency Service), and 23,000 in the Marine Corps Women's Reserve. Military women worked as nurses and performed clerical work, as well as assorted other noncombat duties. For this, they received many veterans' benefits but no allotments for their dependents.

The war cost tens of thousands of American lives, required enormous sacrifice—and also created new opportunities. Yet even the opportunity came at a cost. Working mothers had terrible difficulties securing adequate child care. Food was rationed, making it harder for all housewives, whether employed or not, to feed their families. Many schools were overcrowded and overburdened, owing to an influx of war workers and their children. Housing for war workers was often inadequate. Civilian needs usually trailed behind the overwhelming priority of winning the war.

Once the war ended in August 1945, the returning male veterans had the option of reclaiming their former jobs. This meant that tens of thousands of women lost their good jobs. Despite this, there was no going back to the prewar situation. Too many people had experienced too much economic mobility and heightened freedom for that to be a possibility.

SEE ALSO

Work, paid

FURTHER READING

Anderson, Karen. *Wartime Women: Sex Roles, Family Relations, and the Status of Women During World War II*. Westport, Conn.: Greenwood, 1981.

Chafe, William. *The American Woman; Her Changing Social, Economic, and Political Roles, 1920–1970*. New York: Oxford University Press, 1972.

Wright, Frances

- *Born: Sept. 6, 1795, Dundee, Scotland*
- *Education: Self-educated*
- *Accomplishments: Author,* Views of Society and Manners in America *(1821); founder, Nashoba slave-emancipation commune (1825)*
- *Died: Dec. 13, 1852, Cincinnati, Ohio*

On July 4, 1828, Frances Wright gave a political address at New Harmony, Indiana in which she attacked what she saw as the undue influence of clergymen in American society. In so doing she became the first woman in American history to give such a talk to an audience composed of both men and women. No woman had done so before Wright because convention held that a respectable woman should be silent in public.

Born in Scotland in 1795 to an upper-middle-class family, Wright was orphaned at an early age. She came to maturity possessing financial independence—which also meant freedom. Even as a very young woman she made bold choices, traveling to the United States with her younger sister in 1818, for example. Over the next few years she wrote about the new American democracy and formed an acquaintance with some of the leading men of the day, including the Marquis de Lafayette, the Frenchman who had helped America win the Revolution. Through Lafayette she met prominent American politicians such as Thomas Jefferson and James Madison.

Deeply political, Wright was eager to see the new democracy live up to its ideals. With this goal in mind she set up a short-lived communal experiment in Nashoba, Tennessee, aimed at giving slaves a chance to purchase their freedom.

The speech Wright gave at New Harmony and the others that followed were part of a pattern of her commitment to social justice and democratic ideals. But Wright did not confine herself to abstract discussions of a better world. She also advocated "free love" (sexual freedom), the rights of workers, and other topics that were highly controversial. At first she attracted large crowds, but over time she became a social outcast. Indeed, *Fanny Wrightism* became a synonym for extremism.

Her personal life was unconventional, too, by the standards of the day. In 1831 she married the French reformer Guillaume d'Arusmont shortly after the birth of their first child. The marriage ended in divorce in 1850.

Ahead of her time in many ways, Wright helped set a reform agenda for the next several generations. She opposed slavery, supported labor unions, and believed in the need to improve the status of women in such areas as better education and the right to control family size, a radical stance in her day.

FURTHER READING

Morris, Celia. *Fanny Wright: Rebel in America.* Urbana: University of Illinois Press, 1992.

Yezierska, Anzia

- *Born: Around 1880–85, Poland*
- *Education: Teachers College, Columbia University, New York, 1900–04*
- *Accomplishments: Author,* Hungry Hearts *(1920);* Salome of the Tenements *(1923);* Bread Givers *(1925);* Arrogant Beggar *(1927);* All I Could Never Be *(1932);* Red Ribbon on a White Horse *(autobiography, 1950)*
- *Died: Nov. 21, 1970, Ontario, Calif.*

Anzia Yezierska wrote fiction that illuminates the experience of growing up in a family of Polish Jews. Born in the old world, she and her family came to the United States when she was a child.

In Yezierska's best-known work, *Bread Givers,* published in 1925, she tells the story of young Sara Smolinsky. One of four daughters, Sara is the only one to rebel against the fate her father seemingly has in store for her. He is a scholar of the Talmud (ancient Jewish texts), a role to which only men could aspire at that time. The women of the family are supposed to be the practical ones. Sara goes to work as an ironer, but she attends night school to prepare herself for college. Once she has obtained her treasured education, she can forgive her father and come to appreciate what is positive in her religious and ethnic heritage, such as the spiritual insight and scriptual wisdom.

In the 1920s Yezierska had a stint in Hollywood, writing for silent movies. She found the atmosphere stultifying, however, and returned to New York.

The great love of her life was the philosopher John Dewey at Columbia University, with whom she fell in love when he was 58 and she in her mid-30s. Because he was a married man, the relationship was of a brief duration. Her book *All I Could Never Be* is a fictionalization of her experience working with Dewey as a translator on a project with Philadelphia Poles.

Beginning in the 1950s Yezierska's fortune declined. She wrote several book reviews for the *New York Times* and essays in small journals. Toward the end of her life she wrote about Puerto Rican immigrants to New York City, and then in her last decade, about the plight of the aging. Her work was rediscovered in the 1970s, after her death.

FURTHER READING

Henriksen, Louise Levitas, and Jo Ann Boydston. *Anzia Yezierska: A Writer's Life.* New Brunswick, N.J.: Rutgers University Press, 1988.

Schoen, Carol B. *Anzia Yezierska.* Boston: Twayne, 1982.

Young Women's Christian Association (YWCA)

The Young Women's Christian Association, or YWCA, was first founded in London in 1855 but soon had its first American branch in New York City in 1858. Originally composed only of Christians, the Y is now open to women of all faiths. Moreover, there are currently YWCA groups in more than 70 nations.

The Y drew much of its early membership from those involved with the Social Gospel, a movement in the early 20th century of progressive mainstream Protestant denominations to apply Christian principles to social problems. With this determination to help the less fortunate, Y members were eager to reach out to working-class women in ways similar to the work then being done by settlement-house residents—helping working-class women join unions and lobbying for protective labor legislation for them. The Y also set up athletic facilities for women that were of particular benefit to working-class women. Now, Y facilities benefit a wide array of women outside the working class as well.

With a record of helping poor women, the YWCA began gradually moving in the direction of more enlightened policies about race in the 1920s and 1930s. Encompassing a substantial percentage of women of color among its membership, the Y pledged itself to racial integration in 1946. The group has continued to be an advocate for justice for women, endorsing the Equal Rights Amendment in 1973, for example, and lobbying for improved child-care facilities.

SEE ALSO

Settlement-house movement

FURTHER READING

Mjagkij, Nina and Margaret Spratt, eds. *Men and Women Adrift: The YMCA and the YWCA in the City.* New York: New York University Press, 1997.

Wilson, Elizabeth. *Fifty Years of Association Work among Young Women, 1866–1916.* New York: Garland, 1987.

Zaharias, Mildred ("Babe") Didrikson

- *Born: June 26, 1911, Port Arthur, Tex.*
- *Education: High school*
- *Accomplishments: All-American women's basketball player (1930–32); six gold medals and 4 world records in one afternoon, track and field (July 16, 1932); Olympic gold medals and world records, javelin and hurdles (1932); U.S. Women's Amateur golf champion (1946); British Women's Amateur golf champion (1947); U.S. Women's Open golf champion (1948, 1950, 1954); Associated Press Female Athlete of the Year (1932, 1945, 1946, 1947, 1950, 1954) and of the Half Century (1950); author, with Harry Paxton,* This Life I've Led; My Autobiography *(1955)*
- *Died: Sept. 27, 1956, Galveston, Tex.*

One of the outstanding American athletes of the 20th century, Babe Didrikson Zaharias enjoyed much success during her lifetime. She did not, however, enjoy the access or profit she would have had she been born several decades later, when the opportunities for women in sports had vastly improved. Her struggle helped transform the public's attitude toward women athletes.

Zaharias was so remarkable even as a schoolgirl that she received the nickname of "Babe" from her admirers, who thought she had the same kind of talent as baseball great Babe Ruth. She grew up playing basketball and sandlot baseball and then moved on to track and field. By 1932 she had set American, Olympic, or world's records in the 80-meter hurdles, javelin, high jump, long jump, and baseball throw. Limited to competing in only three events in the Olympics that year, she won gold medals in the javelin and in the hurdles. She then opted to turn pro.

Once she made this decision, however, Babe Didrikson had to face an almost total lack of opportunity for a professional woman athlete. She decided to focus on golf and eventually had great success in this area, too, winning an impressive number of matches. She cooperated with other women to found the Ladies Professional Golf Association in 1948. The Wilson Company, a sports equipment manufacturer, put up prize money for nine tournaments that year.

Marriage to the promoter George Zaharias in 1938 had brought Didrikson help with the business aspects of her career. The marriage also made it easier for the public to accept the boyish athlete. *Life* magazine proclaimed, "Babe Is a Lady Now." Fiercely competitive, she had succeeded in earning 1 million dollars before cancer ended her life in 1956. In 1950 the Associated Press chose her as the woman athlete of the half century.

SEE ALSO

Sports

Some people consider Babe Zaharias the greatest American athlete of the 20th century because she excelled at so many different sports. Golf proved to be the one that offered her the best chance of making money for her superb skills.

FURTHER READING

Cahn, Susan K. *Coming on Strong: Gender and Sexuality in Twentieth-Century Women's Sport.* New York: Free Press, 1994.

Cayleff, Susan E. *Babe: The Life and Legend of Babe Didrikson Zaharias.* Urbana: University of Illinois Press, 1995.

Lynn, Elizabeth. *Babe Didrikson Zaharias: Champion Athlete.* New York: Chelsea House, 1989.

APPENDIX 1

IMPORTANT DATES IN AMERICAN WOMEN'S HISTORY

1587
Virginia Dare is born on Roanoke Island, the first English child to be born in the New World

1607
Jamestown founded in what will become Virginia, the first English colony to survive; Pocahontas defends John Smith

1619
The first Africans land at Jamestown; not yet lifetime slaves, they are indentured servants

1620
The Pilgrims land at Plymouth Rock in what will become Massachusetts

1637–38
The trials and banishment of Anne Hutchinson for the "crime" of holding public prayer meetings at which the male clergy of Boston are criticized

1650
The publication of the first volume of poems by an American colonist, Anne Bradstreet's *The Tenth Muse Lately Sprung Up in America*

1660
Execution of Quaker Mary Dyer in the Congregationalist colony of Massachusetts

1765–1776
Patriotic women support the consumer boycott against British goods

1770
Publication begins of poems by Phillis Wheatley, the first African-American woman poet

1804
Sacajawea joins the Lewis and Clark expedition

1805
Publication of the history of the American Revolution by Mercy Otis Warren, the first American woman historian

1828
Frances Wright delivers the first public political speech by a woman in the United States at New Harmony, Indiana

1832
African American Maria Stewart delivers the first public political speech by an American-born woman

1834
Lowell mill "girls" strike for higher wages

1835
Angelina Grimké writes a letter to *The Liberator,* an abolitionist newspaper, that launches her career as an antislavery activist

1838
Oberlin College in Ohio admits its first women students, giving women access to higher education for the first time

1848
The first women's rights conference is held at Seneca Falls, New York

1851
Publication (serialized in *The National Era*) of Harriet Beecher Stowe's *Uncle Tom's Cabin,* the best-selling novel of the 19th century

1859
Publication of Harriet Wilson's *Our Nig,* the first novel by an African-American woman

1861–65
The American Civil War, during which women on both sides nurse and fund-raise for humanitarian purposes

1861
The founding of Vassar College, the first women's college to offer students an education parallel to that of a men's college; it opens after the Civil War

1868
The ratification of the 14th Amendment, designed to establish citizenship for African Americans, places the term "male voters" in the U.S. Constitution for the first time

1869
The founding of both the American Woman Suffrage Association and the National Woman Suffrage Association; they differed over whether to accept the 14th Amendment, with the latter (led by Elizabeth Cady Stanton and Susan B. Anthony) opposing it

The founding of the Knights of Labor, which would begin actively enrolling female members in 1879

The territory of Wyoming grants women the vote, the first jurisdiction to grant full suffrage

1872
Susan B. Anthony attempts to vote in Rochester, New York, and is arrested

1873–74
The founding of the Woman's Christian Temperance Union (WCTU), which will become the largest women's organization of the 19th century

1884
The pioneering woman lawyer Belva Lockwood runs for the Presidency

1887
Jane Addams founds Hull House in Chicago, the country's first settlement house

1890
The two rival suffrage organizations merge in the National American Woman Suffrage Association (NAWSA)

1896
The founding of the National Association of Colored Women (NACW)

1909
Thousands of women garment workers go on strike in New York

1911
A fire in the Triangle Shirtwaist Factory takes the lives of 146 young women workers

1912
Congress establishes the Children's Bureau as a direct result of lobbying by women

1913
The founding of a new, militant suffrage organization, the Congressional Union; it begins picketing the White House

1916
Jeannette Rankin is elected to Congress, the first woman elected to a national legislature anywhere in the world

1920
The ratification of the 19th Amendment, granting women the right to vote

1923
The Equal Rights Amendment is proposed by the National Woman's Party (which had evolved from the Congressional Union)

1933
Democrat Franklin Roosevelt takes office as President; Eleanor Roosevelt will become the most active First Lady in American history up to that time

1933
Roosevelt appoints Frances Perkins to Secretary of Labor; she is the first woman to serve in the Presidential cabinet

1938
Pearl Buck wins the Nobel Prize for Literature, the first American woman laureate

1939
Luisa Moreno provides the spark for organizing El Congreso de Pueblos Que Hablan Espanol (Congress of Spanish-Speaking Peoples), the first Latino civil rights group

1939
The great African-American opera singer Marian Anderson is denied the use of Constitution Hall in Washington, D.C., for a concert, because of her race; Eleanor Roosevelt helps arrange for a concert in front of the Lincoln Memorial instead

1941–1945
Millions of American women join the paid work force during World War II, permanently transforming the patterns of female employment

1950
Republican Senator Margaret Chase Smith becomes the first member of the U.S. Senate to publicly criticize Senator Joseph McCarthy for his tactics

1951
I Love Lucy goes on television, and Lucille Ball becomes one of the best-known women in the world as well as, in time, a media executive

1955
Rosa Parks refuses to surrender her seat on a Montgomery, Alabama, bus to a white person, and this act sparks the Montgomery bus boycott and the development of the civil rights movement

1961
Democratic President John F. Kennedy establishes the first Presidential Commission on the Status of Women, which becomes an important catalyst for change

1963
Congress passes the Equal Pay Act, which begins to bring salary equity to women workers

1964
Congress passes the Civil Rights Act, including Title VII forbidding discrimination based on sex as well as race; the Equal Employment Opportunities Commission is set up as a result of the new law

1964
Patsy Takemoto Mink, Democrat from Hawaii, is elected to Congress, the first woman of color to serve in the House of Representatives

1966
The founding of the National Organization for Women (NOW), the first post-suffrage civil rights organization for women

1970
Thousands of women around the country demonstrate for equality on the 50th anniversary of the ratification of the 19th Amendment

1971
The founding of the bi-partisan National Women's Political Caucus, the first organization devoted to electing women to office

In *Reed* v. *Reed,* the U.S. Supreme Court uses the 14th Amendment for the first time in a gender discrimination case

1972
Shirley Chisholm, the first African-American woman to be elected to Congress (in 1968), runs for the Presidency

Congress passes the Equal Rights Amendment (ERA) and sends it to the states for ratification

Congress passes Title IX, which gives women a weapon to use against gender discrimination in education; this transforms access to graduate and professional school for women and also their access to athletic opportunities

1973
In the *Roe* v. *Wade* decision, the U.S. Supreme Court upholds a woman's right to obtain an abortion, subject to certain limitations

1974
The founding of the Coalition of Labor Union women; its leader joins the executive board of the AFL-CIO, the first woman to serve in this capacity

1981
President Ronald Reagan appoints Sandra Day O'Connor to be the first woman to sit on the U.S. Supreme Court

1982
Time runs out on the ratification process for the Equal Rights Amendment; it falls three states short of the number required by the Constitution

1983
Astronaut Sally Ride becomes the first American woman to orbit the earth

1985
Wilma Mankiller becomes principal chief of the Cherokee Nation, the first woman to serve in this capacity

1984
Geraldine Ferraro is nominated on the Democratic ticket for Vice President, along with Walter Mondale for President; they lose to Ronald Reagan and George Bush

1992
This election cycle, known as "the Year of the Woman," sees an unprecedented number of women elected to high office, including Carol Moseley Braun, the first woman of color to be elected to the U.S. Senate

1993
President Bill Clinton appoints Janet Reno to be the first female Attorney General of the United States

1997
President Bill Clinton appoints Madeleine Albright to be the first woman Secretary of State, the highest-ranking Cabinet officer

APPENDIX 2

MUSEUMS AND HISTORIC SITES

Alabama

Helen Keller Birthplace and Shrine
300 West North Common
Tuscumbia, AL 35674
256-383-4066

California

Hearst Castle
Hearst San Simeon State Historical Monument
750 Hearst Castle Road
San Simeon, CA 93452
805-927-2020
www.hearstcastle.org
Items related to Phoebe Hearst, clubwoman and philanthropist; Julia Morgan, architect; and Marion Davies, movie actress.

Oakland Museum of California
1000 Oak Street
Oakland, CA 94607
510-238-2200
www.museumca.org
Costume and textile collections, plus large holdings on women in the West.

Colorado

Mother Cabrini Shrine
20189 Cabrini Boulevard
Golden, CO 80401
303-526-0758
Roman Catholic shrine honoring St. Frances Xavier Cabrini (1850–1917), first U.S. citizen to be canonized (1946).

Women of the West Museum
4001 Discovery Drive
Boulder, CO 80303-7816
303-541-1000
www.wowmuseum.org

Connecticut

Museum of Connecticut History
231 Capitol Avenue
Hartford, CT 06106
860-566-3056
Home to a large woman suffrage collection.

Prudence Crandall Museum
P.O. Box 58
Canterbury, CT 06331
860-546-9916

Harriet Beecher Stowe Center
77 Forest Street
Hartford, CT 06105
860-522-9258

Delaware

Winterthur Museum, Garden, and Library
Route 52
Winterthur, DE 19735
302-888-4600/800-448-3883
Collections and exhibitions on the domestic life of women, from the colonial era through the 19th century.

District of Columbia

Mary McLeod Bethune Council House National Historic Site
1318 Vermont Avenue, N.W.
Washington, D.C. 20005
202-673-2402
www.nps.gov/mamc
Exhibits on the life of Mary McLeod Bethune and on the role of African-American women in the history of the United States.

National Museum of American History Smithsonian Institution
14th Street and Constitution Avenue, N.W.
Washington, D.C. 20560
202-357-2700
http://americanhistory.si.edu
Includes extensive collections about women's history.

National Museum of Women in the Arts
1250 New York Avenue, N.W.
Washington, D.C. 20005
202-783-5000
www.nmwa.org

Sewall-Belmont House
144 Constitution Avenue, N.E.
Washington, D.C. 20002
202-546-1210
Material about Alice Paul, the National Woman's Party, the struggle for woman suffrage, and the Equal Rights Amendment.

Textile Museum
2320 S Street, N.W.
Washington, D.C. 20008
202-667-0441

Vietnam Women's Memorial
West Potomac Park
Washington, D.C. 20008

Florida

Bethune-Cookman College
640 Dr. Mary McLeod Bethune Boulevard
Daytona Beach, FL 32114
904-255-1401
College established by Mary McLeod Bethune.

Georgia

Juliette Gordon Low Birthplace
10 East Oglethorpe Avenue
Savannah, GA 31401
912-233-4501
Includes history and artifacts of Low, who founded the Girl Scouts of America in 1912, and her family.

Tubman African-American Museum
340 Walnut Street
Macon, GA 31201
912-743-8544

Illinois

Jane Addams Hull House Museum
800 West Halsted Street
Chicago, IL 60607
312-413-5353
Restored settlement house; includes material about Addams and the immigrant population she served.

Chicago Historical Society
1601 North Clark Street
Chicago, IL 60614
312-642-4600
www.chicagohistory.org
Includes displays of costumes, household technology, furniture, and decorative arts.

Frances E. Willard House
1730 Chicago Avenue
Evanston, IL 60201
847-864-1397
Residence of Willard (1839–98), the most important president of the Woman's Christian Temperance Union, serving from 1879 to her death in 1898. Includes furnishings and memorabilia.

Monument to Women Statuary Gardens
Nauvoo, IL 62354
Thirteen life-size sculptures in this restored Mormon community depict women in traditional activities.

Indiana

Historic New Harmony
The Atheneum Visitors Center
North and Arthur
New Harmony, IN 47631
812-682-4474
Site of two 19th-century experimental communities; offers material on prominent women, including Frances Wright.

Madame Walker Theatre Center
617 Indiana Avenue
Indianapolis, IN 46202
317-236-2099
Restored former headquarters of Walker's cosmetics company. Walker (1867–1919) was the first self-made African-American female millionaire in the United States.

Quilters Hall of Fame
P. O. Box 681
Marion, IN 46952
765-664-9333
www.west.net/~rperry/qhf.html
To be housed in the Marie Webster House, the only site designated as a national historic landmark that honors a quiltmaker.

Iowa

Mamie Doud Eisenhower Birthplace
709 Carroll Street
Boone, IA 50036
515-432-1896
Birthplace of Mamie Doud (1896–1979), wife of President Dwight D. Eisenhower.

Kansas

Carry A. Nation Home
211 West Fowler Avenue
Medicine Lodge, KS 67104
316-886-3553

Kentucky

Mary Todd Lincoln House
578 West Main Street
Lexington, KY 40507
606-233-9999
Restored home of Mary Todd from 1832 until her marriage to Abraham Lincoln in 1849.

Louisiana

Melrose Historic Home
Highway 119
Melrose, LA 71452
318-379-0055
A freed slave named Marie Therese Coincoin and her sons established Melrose Plantation in 1796.

Maine

Sarah Orne Jewett House
5 Portland Street
South Berwick, ME 03908
207-384-2454
www.spnea.org

Margaret Chase Smith Library
54 Norridgewock Avenue
Skowhegan, ME 04976
207-474-7133

Cordelia Stanwood Homestead Museum and Birdsacre Sanctuary
State Route 3, Outer High Street
Ellsworth, ME 04605
207-667-8460
Home of a pioneering ornithologist in the early 20th century. More than 100 species of birds make their home in the adjacent 130-acre wildlife preserve.

Maryland

Clara Barton National Historic Site
5801 Oxford Road
Glen Echo, MD 20812
301-492-6245
Home (1891–1912) of the founder of the American Red Cross.

Barbara Fritchie House
154 West Patrick Street
Frederick, MD 21701
301-698-0630
Reconstructed home of a legendary supporter of the Union during the Civil War.

National Shrine of St. Elizabeth Ann Seton
333 South Seton Avenue
Emmitsburg, MD 21727
301-447-6606
www.setonshrine.org
Includes a museum containing Seton's personal effects and the chapel where she is buried.

Massachusetts

Abigail Adams Birthplace
180 North Street
Weymouth, MA 02188
781-335-4205

Clara Barton Birthplace Museum
68 Clara Barton Road
P.O. Box 356
North Oxford, MA 01537
508-987-5375

Dickinson Homestead
280 Main Street
Amherst, MA 01002
413-542-8161
www.amherst.edu/~edhouse
Restored lifetime residence of Emily Dickinson, 19th-century poet.

Mary Baker Eddy Historic House
277 Main Street
Amesbury, MA 01913
978-388-1361/800-277-8943
www.tfccs.com/GV/MBE/MBEMain.html
There are three other Eddy homes in Massachusetts and one in New Hampshire.

Jewish Women's Archive
68 Harvard Street
Brookline, MA 02445
617-232-2258
www.jwa.org

Lowell National Historical Park
67 Kirk Street
Lowell, MA 01852
978-459-1000
Commemorates women workers in Lowell textile mills.

Maria Mitchell Birthplace House
1 Vestal Street
Nantucket Island, MA 02554
508-228-2896
Restored birthplace and home of the astronomer Mitchell; includes furnishings, personal items, and an observatory.

Edith Wharton Restoration
2 Plunkett Street
Lenox, MA 01240
413-637-1899
www.edithwharton.org
Partially restored mansion and gardens designed by the novelist; known as "The Mount."

Rebecca Nurse Homestead
149 Pine Street
Danvers, MA 01923
978-774-8799
Nurse was hanged as a witch in 1692 during the Salem witch trials. Restored cottage includes 17th- and 18th-century furnishings and artifacts.

Orchard House
399 Lexington Road
Concord, MA 01742
978-369-4118
www.louisamayalcott.org
Home of novelist Louisa May Alcott.

Plimoth Plantation and Mayflower II
137 Warren Avenue
Plymouth, MA 02360
508-746-1622
www.plimoth.org
A living history of the Plymouth Colony, founded in 1620, includes women's work in the settlement as of 1627.

Michigan

Henry Ford Museum & Greenfield Village
20900 Oakwood Boulevard
Dearborn, MI 48124
313-271-1620
www.hfmgv.org
Extensive collection of artifacts and information on women's work

Michigan Women's Historical Center and Hall of Fame
213 West Main Street
Lansing, MI 48933
517-484-1880
leslie.k12.mi.us/~mwhfame

Minnesota

Upper Midwest Women's History Center
749 Simpson Street
St. Paul, MN 55104
www.hamline.edu/~umwhc

Mississippi

Kate Freeman Clark Art Gallery
300 East College
Holly Springs, MS 38635
662-252-4211
More than 1,000 paintings by the early-20th-century artist (1876–1957); considered the world's largest collection of work by a single artist.

Missouri

Laura Ingalls Wilder–Rose Wilder Lane Historic Home and Museum
3068 Highway A
Mansfield, MO 65704
417-924-3626
Home of Wilder and her family from 1894 onward. Wilder wrote the Little House series here beginning in the 1930s.

Nebraska

Willa Cather Pioneer Memorial and Educational Foundation
326 N. Webster Street
Red Cloud, NE 68970
402-746-3285
www.willacather.org
Exhibits on the life of novelist Cather; also houses an archive of related documents and offers tours of her nearby childhood home.

New York

Susan B. Anthony House
17 Madison Street
Rochester, NY 14608
716-235-6124

National Baseball Hall of Fame and Museum
25 Main Street
Cooperstown, NY 13326
607-547-7200
www.baseballhalloffame.org
Permanent exhibition on the women's baseball leagues of the 1940s and 1950s.

Jane Colden Native Plant Sanctuary
Knox Headquarters State Historic Site
State Route 94 and Forge Hill Road
Vails Gate, NY 12584
914-561-5498
Garden named in honor of Colden (1724–66), the first woman botanist in America.

Fashion Institute of Technology
7th Avenue at 27th Street
New York, NY 10001
212-217-7999
www.fitnyc.suny.edu
History of fashion history and technology and women in advertising.

Lower East Side Tenement Museum
97 Orchard Street
New York, NY 10002
212-431-0233
Presentations of the immigrant experience in America.

National Shrine of Blessed Kateri Tekakwitha
State Route 5
Fonda, NY 12068
518-853-3646
Honors a 17th-century Mohawk Indian who has been beatified by the Roman Catholic Church. She was baptized at the site and made her home there.

National Women's Hall of Fame
76 Fall Street
Seneca Falls, NY 13148
315-568-2936

Narcissa Prentiss House
Prattsburgh Community Historical Society
7275 Mill Pond Road
Prattsburgh, NY 14873
607-522-4537
Birthplace of Narcissa Prentiss, early-19th-century missionary to the Indians with her husband, Dr. Marcus Whitman.

Eleanor Roosevelt National Historic Site
Route 9G
Hyde Park, NY 12538
914-229-9115
Val-Kill, Roosevelt's home from 1945 until her death in 1962.

Franklin D. Roosevelt Library and Museum
511 Albany Post Road
Hyde Park, NY 12538
914-229-8114
Home of Franklin and Eleanor Roosevelt. Includes Eleanor Roosevelt's papers and photos.

Elizabeth Cady Stanton Home
136 Fall Street
Seneca Falls, NY 13148
315-568-2991

Harriet Tubman Home
180 South Street
Auburn, NY 13021
315-252-2081

Women's Rights National Historical Park
136 Fall Street
Seneca Falls, NY 13148
315-568-2991
www.nps.gov/wori
Commemorates site of first women's rights convention in 1848.

North Carolina

Virginia Dare Memorial
Fort Raleigh National Historic Site
Route 1
Box 675
Manteo, NC 27954
252-473-5772
Honors the first English child born in the New World (1587). Fort Raleigh, on Roanoke Island, is the site of the first English colony.

Ohio

International Women's Air and Space Museum
Burke Lakefront Airport
1501 North Marginal Road
Cleveland, OH 44114
216-623-1111
www.iwasm.org

Oklahoma

Pioneer Woman Museum
701 Monument Road
Ponca City, OK 74604
580-765-6108

Oregon

Pioneer Mothers' Memorial Cabin Museum
8035 Champoeg Road, N.E.
St. Paul, OR 97137
503-633-2237

Pennsylvania

Pearl S. Buck International
520 Dublin Road
Perkasie, PA 18944
215-249-0100

Rachel Carson Homestead
613 Marion Avenue
Springdale, PA 15144
724-274-5459
Childhood home of naturalist Carson.

Betsy Ross House
239 Arch Street
Philadelphia, PA 19106
215-627-5343
www.libertynet.org/iha/betsy

South Dakota

Surveyors' House and Ingalls Home
Laura Ingalls Wilder Memorial Society
105 Olivet Avenue
De Smet, SD 57231
605-854-3383
Surveyors' House was the first South Dakota home (1870s) of Laura Ingalls Wilder. Later the Ingalls family moved into a new house nearby, built by Laura's father.

Tennessee

National Civil Rights Museum
450 Mulberry Street
Memphis, TN 38103-4214
901-521-9699

Country Music Hall of Fame and Museum
4 Music Square East
Nashville, TN 37203
615-256-1639

Texas

Lyndon Baines Johnson Library and Museum
2313 Red River Street
Austin, TX 78705
512-916-5136
www.lbjlib.utexas.edu
Houses manuscripts of Lady Bird Johnson as First Lady, including her extensive work on behalf on environmental awareness and wildflower preservation.

National Cowgirl Museum & Hall of Fame
111 West 4th Street #300
Fort Worth, TX 76102
817-336-4475
www.cowgirl.net
Honors rodeo performers and other women of the American West.

Babe Didrikson Zaharias Museum
1750 East I-10
Beaumont, TX 77703
409-833-4622/800-392-4401
www.beaumontcvb.com

Utah

Daughters of Utah Pioneers Museum
300 North Main Street
Salt Lake City, UT 84103
801-538-1050
History of pioneers in Utah, 1847–1900. Similar museums maintained around the state.

Vermont

Shelburne Museum
5555 Shelburne Road
Shelburne, VT 05482
802-985-3346
www.shelburnemuseum.org
The Shelburne Museum includes Webb's collections of American art and artifacts. The Webb Memorial houses major European paintings as well as works by American artist Mary Cassatt.

Virginia

Belle Boyd Cottage
101 Chester Street
Front Royal, VA 22630
540-636-1446
Mid-19th-century home of Boyd, a Confederate spy.

National Museum of Women's History
303 West Glendale Avenue
Alexandria, VA 22301
703-299-0552
www.NMWH.org

Mount Vernon Estate and Gardens
George Washington Parkway South
Mount Vernon, VA 22121
703-780-2000
www.mountvernon.org
Home of George and Martha Washington.

Washington

Sacajawea Interpretive Center
Sacajawea State Park
2503 Sacajawea Park Road
Pasco, WA 99301
509-545-2361
Honors the Native American woman who guided Lewis and Clark on their western expedition.

Whitman Mission National Historic Site
Route 2, Box 247
Walla Walla, WA 99362
509-522-6360; 509-529-2761
Memorial to Narcissa Prentiss Whitman and her husband; site includes a museum.

West Virginia

Pearl S. Buck Birthplace
Box 126
Hillsboro, WV 24946
304-653-4430
Buck's manuscripts are housed nearby at West Virginia Wesleyan College.

A Note on Resources for the Study of Women's History

State and local historical societies throughout the country are excellent sources for materials on women's history. A more extensive listing of women's historical sites may be found in: Sherr, Lynn, and Jurate Kazickas. *Susan B. Anthony Slept Here.* New York: Times Books, 1994.

DOING RESEARCH ON AMERICAN WOMEN'S HISTORY: FURTHER READING AND WEBSITES

Further Reading

Anderson, Karen. *Changing Woman: A History of Racial Ethnic Women in Modern America*. New York: Oxford University Press, 1996.

Archer, Jules. *Breaking Barriers: The Feminist Movement from Susan B. Anthony to Margaret Sanger to Betty Friedan*. New York: Viking, 1991.

Arnold, Eleanor. *Voices of American Homemakers*. Bloomington: Indiana University Press, 1992.

Barrett, Jacqueline K., and Jane A. Malonis, eds. *Encyclopedia of Women's Associations Worldwide: A Guide to Over 3,400 National and Multinational Nonprofit Women's and Women-Related Organizations*. London: Gale Research, 1993.

Beckwith, Karen. *American Women and Political Participation: The Impacts of Work, Generation, and Feminism*. New York: Greenwood, 1986.

Cahill, Susan, ed. *Writing Women's Lives: An Anthology of Autobiographical Narratives by Twentieth Century American Women Writers*. New York: Harper Perennial, 1994.

Cantarow, Ellen. *Moving the Mountain: Women Working for Social Change*. New York: McGraw-Hill, 1980.

Conway, Jill Ker, ed. *Written by Herself: Autobiographies of American Women: An Anthology*. New York: Vintage, 1992–1996.

Cott, Nancy F. *Root of Bitterness: Documents of the Social History of American Women*. 2nd ed. Boston: Northeastern University Press, 1996.

Cott, Nancy F., ed. *The Young Oxford History of Women in the United States*, 11 vols. New York: Oxford University Press, 1994–1995.

Cowan, Ruth Schwartz. *More Work for Mother: The Ironies of Household Technology from the Open Hearth to the Microwave*. New York: Basic, 1983.

Davis, Angela. *Women, Race and Class*. New York: Vintage, 1981.

Davis, Flora. *Moving the Mountain: The Women's Movement in America Since 1960*. Urbana: University of Illinois Press, 1999.

Degler, Carl N. *At Odds: Women and the Family from the Revolution to the Present*. New York: Oxford University Press, 1980.

D'Emilio, John, and Estelle Freedman. *Intimate Matters: A History of Sexuality in America*. New York: Harper & Row, 1988.

Ehrenreich, Barbara, and Deirdre English. *Witches, Midwives, and Nurses; A History of Women Healers*. Detroit: Black & Red, 1973.

Evans, Sara M. *Born for Liberty: A History of Women in America*. New York: Free Press, 1989.

Fenton, Jill Rubinson, et al. *Women Writers: From Page to Screen*. New York: Garland, 1990.

García, Alma M., ed. *Chicana Feminist Thought: The Basic Historical Writings*. New York: Routledge, 1997.

Garland, Anne Witte. *Women Activists: Challenging the Abuse of Power*. New York: Feminist Press, 1988.

Giddings, Paula. *Where and When I Enter: The Impact of Black Women on Race and Sex in America*. New York: Morrow, 1984.

Hedges, Elaine, and Ingrid Wendt, eds. *In Her Own Image, Women Working in the Arts*. New York: McGraw-Hill, 1980.

Hine, Darlene Clark, Elsa Barkley Brown, and Rosalyn Terborg-Penn, eds. *Black Women in America: An Historical Encyclopedia*. Bloomington: Indiana University Press, 1994.

Hoffman, Nancy. *Woman's "True" Profession: Voices from the History of Teaching*. New York: McGraw-Hill, 1981.

Huston, Perdita. *Motherhood by Choice: Pioneers in Women's Health and Family Planning*. New York: Feminist Press, 1992.

Hyman, Paula E., and Deborah Dash Moore, eds. *Jewish Women in America: An Historical Encyclopedia*. New York: Routledge, 1997.

James, Edward T., and Janet Wilson James, eds. *Notable American Women, 1607–1950: A Biographical Dictionary*. Cambridge, Mass.: Belknap Press of Harvard University Press, 1971.

Jensen, Joan M. *With These Hands: Women Working on the Land*. New York: McGraw-Hill, 1981.

Jones, Jacqueline. *Labor of Love, Labor of Sorrow: Black Women, Work and the Family from Slavery to the Present*. New York: Basic, 1985.

Kaufman, Polly Welts. *Women Teachers on the Frontier*. New Haven: Yale University Press, 1984.

Kerber, Linda K. *No Constitutional Right to Be Ladies: Women and the Obligations of Citizenship*. New York: Hill and Wang, 1998.

Kerber, Linda K., and Jane Sherron De Hart, eds. *Women's America: Refocusing the Past*. 5th ed. New York: Oxford University Press, 2000.

Kessler-Harris, Alice. *Out to Work: A History of Wage-Earning Women in the United States*. New York: Oxford University Press, 1982.

Markel, Robert, ed. *The Women's Sports Encyclopedia*. New York: H. Holt, 1997.

Matthews, Glenna.*The Rise of Public Woman: Woman's Power and Woman's Place in the United States, 1630–1970*. New York: Oxford University Press, 1992.

Morgan, Robin, ed. *Sisterhood is Global: The International Women's Movement Anthology*. Rev. ed. New York: Feminist Press, 1996.

Nicholas, Susan Cary, Alice M. Price, and Rachael Rubin. *Rights and Wrongs: Women's Struggle for Legal Equality.* 2nd ed. New York: Feminist Press, 1986.

Placksin, Sally. *American Women in Jazz: 1900 to the Present: Their Words, Lives, and Music*. New York: Seaview Books, 1982.

Rossiter, Margaret W. *Women Scientists in America: Before Affirmative Action, 1940–1972*. Baltimore: Johns Hopkins University Press, 1995.

———. *Women Scientists in America: Struggles and Strategies to 1940*. Baltimore: Johns Hopkins University Press, 1982.

Ruiz, Vicki. *From Out of the Shadows: Mexican Women in Twentieth-Century America*. New York: Oxford University Press, 1998.

Schultz, Jeffrey D., and Laura van Assendelft, eds. *Encyclopedia of Women in American Politics*. Phoenix, Ariz.: Oryx, 1999.

Showalter, Elaine, ed. *These Modern Women: Autobiographical Essays from the Twenties*. Rev. ed. New York: Feminist Press, 1989.

Sicherman, Barbara, and Carol Hurd Green, eds. *Notable American Women: The Modern Period: A Biographical Dictionary.* Cambridge, Mass.: Belknap Press of Harvard University Press, 1980.

Sonneborn, Liz. *A to Z of Native American Women*. New York: Facts on File, 1998.

Tierney, Helen, ed. *Women's Studies Encyclopedia*. Rev. ed. Westport, Conn.: Greenwood, 1999.

Tinling, Marion, ed. *With Women's Eyes: Visitors to the New World, 1775–1918*. North Haven, Conn.: Archon, 1993.

Ware, Susan. *Holding Their Own: American Women in the 30s*. Boston: Twayne, 1982.

Willard, Frances E., and Mary A. Livermore. *American Women: Fifteen Hundred Biographies with over 1,400 Portraits; A Comprehensive Encyclopedia of the Lives and Achievements of American Women during the Nineteenth Century.* 1897. Reprint, Detroit: Gale Research, 1973.

Websites

General / Overview

American Women's Diaries
A multicultural collection by 18th-, 19th-, and early-20th-century women.
www.newsbank.com/readex/scholarly/wdiar1.html

American Women's History: A Research Guide
frank.mtsu.edu/~kmiddlet/history/women/wom-mm.html

Gifts of Speech
The text of speeches made by influential contemporary women.
gos.sbc.edu

National Women's Hall of Fame
www.greatwomen.org

National Women's History Project
This nonprofit educational organization promotes women's rights through education about the past.
www.nwhp.org

University of Wisconsin System Women's Studies Librarian's Office Home Page
Contains links to a variety of resources, lists of books on women's studies, and selections from *Feminist Collections: A Quarterly of Women's Studies Resources*.
www.library.wisc.edu/libraries/WomensStudies/

Women in America 1820–1842
Selections from writers from abroad dealing with the role of women in America between 1820 and 1842.
xroads.virginia.edu/~HYPER/DETOC/FEM/home.htm

Women's History Magazine Vol. 2
Focused on women and work, includes articles and biographies.
www.thehistorynet.com/WomensHistory

Aviation

International Women's Air and Space Museum
www.iwasm.org/

Women's Achievements in Aviation and Space
www.hq.nasa.gov/office/pao/women gallery/sitemap.htm

Arts

A Celebration of Women Writers
Provides biographies and lists of works.
www.cs.cmu.edu/People/mmbt/women/ generate/USA.html

***Godey's Lady's Book* Online**
Contains text and illustrations of several issues of *Godey's Lady's Book* and the history of the publication.
www.history.rochester.edu/godeys/

Historical Women Composers
music.acu.edu/www/iawm/historical/ historical.html

International Archive of Women in Architecture
Includes biographies, bibliographies, and newsletter articles.
spec.lib.vt.edu/spec/iawa/iawa.htm

National Museum of Women in the Arts
Includes images from the collection, a video tour, and artists' profiles.
www.nmwa.org

Quilts and Quiltmaking in America
Interviews with quiltmakers and images from the American Folklife Center.
memory.loc.gov/ammem/qlthtml/ qlthome.html

Women Artists of the American West
Thousands of images, plus statements from the artists, biographical sketches, essays, and bibliographies.
www.sla.purdue.edu/waaw/

Government

The First Ladies of the United States of America
Biographical sketches of every First Lady.
www.whitehouse.gov/WH/glimpse/first-ladies/html/firstladies.html

Women in Congress
Biographies of U.S. Congresswomen.
clerkweb.house.gov/womenbio/alpha/alpha .htm

The Women's Legal History Biography Project
Includes detailed biographies of more than 100 early women lawyers and judges.
www.stanford.edu/group/WLHP/

Identities

African-American Women
The writings of several African-American women detail the slave experience in the United States at the personal level.
scriptorium.lib.duke.edu/collections/african -american-women.html

Jewish Women's Archive
Provides educational programs and information about historical resources. Rebecca Gratz, Molly Picon, and Lillian Wald are featured with photographs, speeches, film clips, letters, and more.
www.JWA.org

Lesbian History Project
Links to archives and oral history collections featuring lesbian history.
www-lib.usc.edu/~retter/main.html

Math and Science

The Ada Project
Biographies and photos of pioneering women in computer and math sciences, including a gallery of women and their amazing machines.
tap.mills.edu

American Nurses Association Hall of Fame
www.ana.org/hof/alphalst.htm

Archives of Women in Science and Engineering
Documents the history of women in these fields, individually and collectively, with excellent links to related sites.
www.lib.iastate.edu/spcl/wise/wise.html

Contributions of 20th Century Women to Physics
Includes biographies of women physicists and their contributions, publications, photos, and archival materials.
www.physics.ucla.edu/~cwp/

4,000 Years of Women in Science
Features more than 125 women distinguished in the field of science.
www.astra.ua.edu/4000WS/4000WS.html

Women in Math Project
Women mathematicians' biographies and links to their professional associations.
darkwing.uoregon.edu/~wmnmath/

Women Nobel Laureates
Includes extensive biographies, reading lists, and links.
www.almaz.com/nobel/women.html

Peace and War

Civil War Women
Includes photos, diaries, letters, and personal papers of women during the Civil War; a timeline of important events; and links to other relevant pages.
scriptorium.lib.duke.edu/scriptorium/civil-war-women.html

Minerva
Award-winning clearinghouse for information about women in military history.
www.minervacenter.com

Swarthmore College Peace Collection
Half of this site concerns women's role in peace work and other social justice movements. Includes personal papers of major peace figures, records of organizations, photographs, and ephemera.
www.swarthmore.edu/Library/peace

Women Airforce Service Pilots of World War II
Information about the first women to ever fly American military aircraft.
www.wasp-WWII.org

Women Come to the Front: Journalists, Photographers, and Broadcasters During World War II
From the Library of Congress exhibit of the same name.
lcweb.loc.gov/exhibits/wcf/

Women Veterans
Selected women from all of America's wars are profiled.
userpages.aug.com/captbarb/

State-Specific

A Guide to Uncovering Women's History in Archival Collections
A state-by-state listing of links to archives, libraries, and other repositories that have materials by or about women.
lib.utsa.edu/Archives/links.htm

State and Regional Resources
An on-line research guide to state and regional women's history resources.
frank.mtsu.edu/~kmiddlet/history/women/wh-state.html

Women's Rights Movements

Documents from the Women's Liberation Movement
Archive of articles, pamphlets, flyers, and booklets published from 1969 to 1974.
scriptorium.lib.duke.edu/wlm/

Living the Legacy: The Women's Rights Movement 1848–1998
Extensive chronology, historical essays, and resources.
www.legacy98.org

National Museum of Women's History
This exhibit examines the culture and imagery that evolved to promote woman suffrage in the U.S.
www.nmwh.org/exhibits/exhibit_frames.html

Suffragists Oral History Project
Oral histories of leaders and participants in the woman suffrage movement.
library.berkeley.edu/BANC/ROHO/ohonline/suffragists.html

Votes for Women
The most comprehensive site about women's suffrage campaign, including photos, biographies, essays, speeches, and extensive links.
www.huntington.org/vfw/main.html

Votes for Women
Contains selections from the National American Women Suffrage Association (NAWSA) Collection, 1848–1921: history of the suffrage movement, information on NAWSA and its president, Carrie Chapman Catt, and excerpts from the writings of several important suffragists.
lcweb2.loc.gov/ammem/rbnawsahtml/

INDEX

References to illustrations are indicated by page numbers in *italics*. References to main article entries are indicated by page numbers in **boldface.**

• INDEX •

PICTURE CREDITS

Copyright © 1999 ABC, Inc./Steve Fenn., 191; Alaska State Library, Historical Collections/P.E. Larss, photographer (PCA 41-54): 248; Carl Albert Center Congressional Archives, University of Oklahoma: 101; American Academy and Institute of Arts and Letters, New York City: 330; American Antiquarian Society: 99 (right); Amherst College Library: 96 (right); Archives and Special Collections on Women in Medicine, MCP Hahnemann University: 193; Archives of the Episcopal Church U.S.A.: 256; Articulate Art: San Francisco: cover (bottom); Art Institute of Chicago: 229; Ballentine Books, Inc.: 176; Billy Graham Center Museum: 249; Boston Athenaeum: 135, 141; Brown Brothers: 99 (left), 119, 127 (right), 147, 169, 236, 318: California State Library: 55; Chicago Historical Society: 301; Julia Child: 62; Coalition of Labor Union Women: 74; Cornell University/Kheel Center, Catherwood Library: 292; Lloyd DeGrane: 88; Copyright the Dorothea Lange Collection, The Oakland Museum of California, City of Oakland. Gift of Paul S. Taylor: 170; Geraldine Ferraro: 118; Michael Fitzpatrick: 71; Florida State Archives: 107 (bottom), 186, 313; Friends Historical Library of Swarthmore College: 205; George Eastman House: 154; Tom Gilbert/Tulsa World: 185; Hake's Americana & Collectibles: 65; Hadassah, 256; The Harvard Crimson: 203; Hearst San Simeon State Historical Monument: 29; Jane Hoffer/Sarah Lawrence College: 324; International Institute of Social History: 131; Evans Johnson/Impact Visuals: 162; John Fitzgerald Kennedy Library: 77, 227; Labor Archives and Research Center, San Francisco State University: 201; Photo © Elliott Landy/LandyVision.com: 161; Bettye Lane/National Women's History Project: 9; Eli Leon, photograph by Sharon Risedorph: 221; Kansas State Historical Society, Topeka, Kansas: 329; Library of Congress: cover (top left), 11, 22, 27, 31, 33, 34, 36, 39, 41, 51, 54, 56, 63, 73, 83, 95, 103, 107 (top), 111, 115, 127 (left), 137, 138, 149, 157, 177, 184, 189, 198, 211 (bottom), 213, 219, 232, 234, 240, 242, 254, 269, 273, 287, 290, 291, 296, 297, 305, 309, 311, 314, 315, 334, 336, 339, 340; Marquette University Libraries: 93; Massachusetts Historical Society, Boston: 122; Glenna Matthews: 224; Metro Pictures Photography: 238; Milne Special Collections and Archives Department, University of New Hampshire Library, Durham: 211 (top): Mount Holyoke College Library/Archives: 183; "Benevolence" by Avard Fairbanks/© by Intellectual Reserve, Inc./Museum of Church History and Art/Used by Permission: 202; Museum of City of NY/Jacob Riis Collection: 153; Museum of Modern Art, Film Stills Division: 207; National Archives: 18, 25, 45, 96 (left), 105, 262, 289, 343, 344; National Cancer Institute, Bethesda, MD: 143; National Japanese American Historical Society: 30; National Library of Medicine: 42, 188; National Museum of American Jewish History, Philadelphia: 323; N.C. Division of Archives and History: 69; Nevada Historical Society: 335; New Deal Network: 222; New York Historical Society: 23; New York Public Library/Geneology Division: 151, 283; New York Public Library Picture Collection: cover (top right), 21; New York Public Library Rare Books Division, 267; New York Public Library, Special Collections Office, 91; 246, 278; Oberlin College Archives, Oberlin Ohio: 299; Oxford University Press: 84; Patti Ramos Photography: 58; Photofest: 132, 200, 206, 328; Primedia Special Interest Publications, Harrisburg, PA: 79; Rachel Carson History Project: 52; Office of Ann Richards: 243; Rocky Mountain News: 342; FDR Library: 265; Salvation Army National Archives: 271; Save the Bay: 109; Schlesinger Library, Radcliffe Institute, Harvard University: 13, 86, 124, 164, 175, 179 (photograph by Judith Sedwick), 209, 215, 218, 276, 338; Schomburg Center, New York Public Library: 230, 251, 327, 331; Muriel Siebert: 49; Seneca Falls Historical Society: U.S. Senate/Historical Office: 252; 44; Smith College Archives, Smith College: 37, 123 (photo by Gordon Daniels), 241, 303; Smithsonian Institution: 81, 126, 181, 223; Sophia Smith Collection, Smith College: 28, 320; Special Collections and University Archives/Archibald S. Alexander Library/Rutgers, the State University of NJ: 310; State Archives of Michigan: 319; State Historical Society of North Dakota: 284; Supreme Court Historical Society: 129, 225 (Richard Strauss, Smithsonian Institution); Syracuse University Library: 317; Ira Toff: 60; Trustees of the Boston Public Library: 46: UC-Berkeley/Bancroft Library: 295; UN/DPI: 19; UN Photo/Milton Grant: 298; University of Pittsburgh, Archives Service Center: 156; UPI/Corbis-Bettman: 116, 140, 217;Urban League of Pittsburgh, Archives Service Center, University of Pittsburgh: 17; U.S. Department of Defense: 196; U.S. Department of Justice: 67; Copyright USGA. All rights reserved: 348; USTA/Russ Adams: 112; 165; The UT Institute of Texas Cultures at San Antonio: 171; VA Hospital, Bronx: 275; Vassar College Library: 197, 199, 261; Virginia Historical Society: frontis; Walter P. Reuther Library, Wayne State University: 5, 321; W. A. Swift Photograph Collection, Archives and Special Collections, Ball State University: 167; Jay R. West: 75; The White House: 72

Glenna Matthews is a historian with a special interest in the history of American women and in the history of California. Her first book was *"Just a Housewife": The Rise and Fall of Domesticity.* She then wrote two books on women and politics, *The Rise of Public Woman* and the co-authored *Running as a Woman.* She is completing *Silicon Valley Women and the California Dream,* for which she won a National Endowment for the Humanities Fellowship. She is currently a visiting scholar at the Institute of Urban and Regional Development at the University of California, Berkeley.

William H. Chafe is Alice Mary Baldwin Distinguished Professor of History and Dean of the Faculty of Arts and Sciences at Duke University. His numerous publications include *Civilities and Civil Rights: Greensboro, North Carolina and the Black Struggle for Freedom* (winner of the Robert F. Kennedy Book Award); *A History of Our Time: Readings in Postwar America* (edited with Harvard Sitkoff); *The Unfinished Journey: America Since World War II*; *The Paradox of Change: American Women in the Twentieth Century*; *Never Stop Running: Allard Lowenstein and the Struggle to Save American Liberalism* (winner of the Sidney Hillman Book Award); and *The Road to Equality: American Women Since 1962.* Professor Chafe is currently the president of the Organization of American Historians.

ACKNOWLEDGMENTS

Many people assisted in the preparation of this book, including Rachel Canon, Jenny Dichter, Elizabeth Ginno, Francisca Goldsmith, Elizabeth Hartmann, Lyn Reese, Rachel Sandy, Donna Schuele, and Kay Trimberger. Special thanks to my Oxford editor, Nancy Toff. My biggest debt, however, is owed to my mother, Alberta Ingles. At the age of 91, she worked with me so closely on this project as to be my virtual collaborator. Circumstances permitted me to be living with her during the writing. In consequence, I read each entry out loud for her critical comments—which proved very valuable. What's more, she served as my research assistant, calling the Woodland Hills (California) Public Library for dates as needed. And while I'm at it, thanks, too, to all the helpful librarians along the way.